Image
Interpretation
in
Geology

JOIN US ON THE INTERNET VIA WWW, GOPHER, FTP OR EMAIL:

WWW: http://www.thomson.com
GOPHER: gopher.thomson.com
FTP: ftp.thomson.com
EMAIL: findit@kiosk.thomson.com

A service of I(T)P

To Duncan and Alison

Image Interpretation in Geology

Second edition

S.A. DRURY

The Open University
Milton Keynes
UK

CHAPMAN & HALL
London · New York · Tokyo · Melbourne · Madras

Published by Chapman & Hall, 2–6 Boundary Row, London SE1 8HN

Chapman & Hall, 2–6 Boundary Row, London SE1 8HN, UK

Chapman & Hall Inc., 29 West 35th Street, New York NY10001, USA

Chapman & Hall Japan, Thomson Publishing Japan, Hirakawacho Nemoto Building, 6F, 1–7–11 Hirakawa-cho, Chiyoda-ku, Tokyo 102, Japan

Chapman & Hall Australia, Thomas Nelson Australia, 102 Dodds Street, South Melbourne, Victoria 3205, Australia

Chapman & Hall India, R. Seshadri, 32 Second Main Road, CIT East, Madras 600 035, India

First edition published by Allen & Unwin, 1987
Second edition 1993

Reprinted 1997

©1987, 1993 S.A. Drury

Typeset in 10/12 Times by EXPO Holdings, Malaysia
Printed in China by L. Rex Printing Co. Ltd.

ISBN 0 412 48880 9

A catalogue record for this book is available from the British Library

Library of Congress Cataloging-in-Publication data available

CONTENTS

CONTENTS

PREFACE

The first edition of *Image Interpretation in Geology* won a wide readership among undergraduate and professional geologists over its 5-year life. But, like any work based on an evolving technology and ever-widening application, parts of it became outdated. Moreover, its omissions and deficiencies grew obvious. This edition incorporates a thorough updating of the technology and has a new chapter covering application strategies within the general field of geosciences. Chapters 3, 5 and 8 have been completely restructured and extensively rewritten. A good proportion of the images, particularly the plates, have been replaced by more instructive ones, and the further reading has been brought up to date.

The topic is centred on remote sensing, by which is implied means of mimicking human sensory perception from a distance. Vision is far and away the most powerful and flexible of our senses. Remote sensing in the strict sense therefore focuses on the capture of information about the Earth's properties in the nearly continuous, two-dimensional fashion that is characteristic of images. This is only possible for those properties that control how Earth materials interact with electromagnetic radiation, including not only visible light but a spectrum that extends from gamma-rays to microwave radiation. Other attributes relating to variations in density, magnetic and electrical properties can be detected, but only in a discontinuous fashion. The same holds for variations in chemistry and geometric structure of rocks, both at and beneath the surface, plus a host of other kinds of geological information. Although some of these attributes can be measured from a distance, the immediate results are not images, hence their exclusion from proper remote sensing. They are not excluded from the book, however, because there are means of recasting numbers distributed irregularly in two cartographic dimensions into the form of images. Visual perception is unsurpassed in extracting nuances from any kind of image, whatever its means of derivation. So, there is an overlap between remote sensing and more familiar means of gathering geoscience information. Part of it is through images, and part through data analysis itself. One of the most important new tools in the latter is using computers to find patterns and correlations among far more layers of information than the human intellect can grasp. We deal as a matter of routine with spatial and to a lesser extent time dimensions, but a geological problem often involves tens of different dimensions. The vast bulk of the information is distributed in terms of geographic coordinates – it can be registered to maps. An extension from remote sensing is a sort of multidimensional aid to geological skills, within geographic information systems. Such systems naturally fall within the book's ambit.

Chapter 1 sets out to explain in relatively simple terms how matter and electromagnetic radiation interact. It is these interactions that laid the foundation for designing remote-sensing instruments, planning their use and interpreting the images that they generate. Though computers play an ever-increasing role in geoscience, they will never replace the geologist. At the end of the day it is the eye and a mental kitbag of skills, experience and intuition that generate ideas from perception of the real world. Chapter 2 makes a few important points about the functioning of our visual system, and its power and limitations, from a physiological standpoint and considers psychological aspects. This might seem strange in a geological text, but it is the key to matching the information contained within images to the make-up of the interpreter. The necessary background is completed in Chapter 3, in which many of the instruments involved in generating images are described. This chapter also reviews the most important sources of images, and links to information in Appendix C about how to get them.

Although remote sensing spans a large chunk of the electromagnetic spectrum, before 1970 the only easy source of images was aerial photography. The geological use of aerial photographs since the 1930s has left a priceless heritage of interpretive methods, on which remote sensing builds. Chapter 4 is the core of the book and concentrates on photogeological interpretation. Most of the images there are panchromatic photographs, often combined in stereopairs that can be viewed using a standard lens stereoscope. Some are images derived from digital remote-sensing systems, but are used for their content of information on geologically relevant landforms rather than their spectral features. Part of photogeology has traditionally been oriented to the extraction of geometric information and transfer of interpretations to maps, in other words, to photogrammetry. Lack of space prevented a proper treatment of this subject, other than aspects of photogrammetry that need to be carried out in the laboratory or the field, which are covered in Appendix A. There has been little advance in photogrammetry for geologists since the 1960s, and I have no hesitation in referring readers to older and more comprehensive texts on the subject, rather than presume to improve on our forebears.

Remote sensing entered the geological scene dramatically with the launch of sensors aboard continuously orbiting, unmanned satellites in the 1970s. The technology had been available for 10 or more years, but confined to the military intelligence community. Some of the first civilian systems emerging with declassification were oriented to a broad and coarse view of meteorology and the oceans. The most revolutionary aimed at visible and near-visible infrared parts of the spectrum, where vegetation is readily distinguished, for small segments of the surface, or scenes, with a resolution less than 100 m. The Landsat series, first launched in 1972, aimed at providing strategic economic information on the global cereal crop. This never materialized fully, but as well as many vegetation-oriented users, geologists seized on the new, wide and detailed view of landscape. The potential for complete, near-global cover in a standard form revitalized the ambition to extend geological mapping at scales better than 1:250 000 from 25% of the continents to the remainder, by using Landsat images as super-synoptic aerial photographs. But they are more than just that.

Because the vehicles that carried them were unmanned and in quite high orbits, transmission of images had to be in electronic form. Rather than using ordinary television methods, at an early stage the decision was taken to use digital means of data retrieval. What digital data comprises is covered in the early chapters. In Chapter 5 the reader will find the enormous opportunities for both tuning images to human vision and extracting from them hidden information that the digital mode provides. It focuses on the more easily understood spectral properties of materials in that part of the spectrum that derives from the Sun and is reflected by the Earth's surface. It is complemented in Appendix B by a brief account of digital methods of removing the inevitable blemishes and distortions that can plague many kinds of electronically captured data.

Conceptually more difficult to interpret are images that depend on the emission of thermal energy by the surface, and the strange interactions of artificial microwaves used in radar remote sensing. These form the topics of Chapters 6 and 7. Perhaps more so than systems operating at the familiar end of the spectrum, thermal and radar studies are attuned to geological phenomena, but there are relatively few geoscientists who are well versed in their intricacies, partly because images from them derive from experimental airborne systems. The 1990s promise to open new vistas with the deployment of such systems on satellites, and an early grasp of the possibilities will allow readers to take advantage of novel opportunities.

All manner of information is gathered by geoscientists, relating to natural force fields, environmental geochemistry and exploration records, as well as lithological and structural data. A gravity determination, an analysis of soil, a borehole log or even a measurement of dip and strike at an outcrop cost money, often an inordinate amount. Quite frequently, such data are gathered for a single purpose, perhaps an exploration programme, then set aside. The simple graphical expression of these variables in the past rarely exploited their full content, and often treated them in isolation. Transforming spatially distributed data into image form, applying digital enhancement methods, registering many types of data to a common geographic base and then applying multivariate analysis techniques opens new vistas. Not only can the data be revitalized in later programmes, but geographic information systems techniques permit a kind of information fusion where many lines of evidence come together in solving problems or generating new ideas. Full and often unsuspected value can be squeezed from the records. Moreover, the fusion also helps bring the combined experience and different skills of several people to bear on problems; not any easy task otherwise, as many a manager will verify. This new and growing approach to information forms the topic of Chapter 8.

A glaring omission from the first edition was any explicit guide to applications of image interpretation. Naturally, the best would be to use a battery of actual case histories, but the problem is to precis the best while extracting useful generalizations within set page limits. In Chapter 9, I have chosen to let the experts speak fully for themselves by referring to important case studies, and concentrate on some general principles of strategy and tactics. Several topics are covered: landform studies, geological mapping, hydrocarbon, metal and water exploration, engineering applications and studies of natural hazards. They are set in the framework of conventional approaches, but show how remote sensing can provide vital clues at critical stages.

Remote sensing aided by digital image processing is aesthetically pleasing, because all of us like colourful pictures. If we did not, then it would be a pretty sterile exercise, for it is stimulation of the visual cortex that draws us to find information and then interpret it. However, such sentiments cut little ice with exploration managers and referees of funding proposals. The key to their hearts is cost-effectiveness. A few figures can work wonders. Field mapping in remote areas costs between US$100 and 1000 per square kilometre, with an efficiency of between 1 and 10 square kilometres per day, depending on the level of detail. Preparing geological maps at the reconnaissance level using remote sensing costs from US$0.7 to 5 per square kilometre, and can run at efficiencies between 50 and 10 000 square kilometres per day, depending on whether airborne or satellite imagery is employed and on the information content of the images. While it has to be emphasized that remote sensing is no substitute for hitting rocks with hammers, the synoptic view and the access to invisible and rich spectral attributes of surface materials help orient field work to the most critical areas. They also permit confident extrapolation from visited areas to those no longer needing direct attention. Information fusion through geographic information system methods brings every conceivable lever to bear on the resolution of problems and opportunities when the data have been assembled.

S.A. Drury
Brampton, Cumbria

Note

Colour images (printed in separate sections) are referred to in the text by *italic* figure numbers. **Bold** printing in the text marks the first appearance of terms and concepts defined in the Glossary.

ACKNOWLEDGEMENTS

Like many geologists, I stumbled into remote sensing out of necessity, in my case by a need in 1977 for an idea of the regional structure of the Precambrian craton of South India. I had no access to aerial photographs or large-scale maps of the region. Without Landsat-2 any ambitious research programme on crustal evolution would have foundered. At about that time Dave Rothery and Mike Baker had begun postgraduate research involving Landsat data in the Oman and the Andes, but had to use image-processing facilities in a then secure military establishment. The late Ian Gass, then Chairman of Earth Sciences at the Open University, saw our plight and, typically, much wider opportunities. His fight for and winning of funds for image-processing facilities, together with long discussions, exchanges of ideas and differences of opinion, first with Dave and Mike and later with Gavin Hunt, Barros Silva and Beto da Souza, laid the groundwork from which this book emerged.

A book on image interpretation depends as much on its pictures as on its text. A fair proportion stem from my work, but the majority, including some of the most pleasing colour images I have ever seen, were provided by the effort and generosity of many colleagues around the world. As well as those people credited in captions a special mention is needed for a few willing providers. Henry Fuhrmann of the Jet Propulsion Laboratory, Pasadena, USA, fed me with images from that extremely open-handed source for over a year. Kerry O'Sullivan introduced me to the black arts of making silk purses out of the sow's ears of geophysical and other kinds of data. Peter Francis at the Open University and Brian Amos of the British Geological Survey helped me assemble many aerial photographs of fascinating areas from their collections. In this edition, many of the new images owe a lot to Beto's resourceful use of image processing at the Open University. Staff in the Open University photographic and print workshops printed many of the half-tones from negatives, and Andrew Lloyd and John Taylor of Earth Sciences drew several of the line figures.

There are undoubtedly errors of fact, oversights and gross oversimplifications remaining in this edition; they are hard to avoid in condensing a broad topic to manageable limits. That there are not more is thanks to Bob McConnell of Mary Washington College, Fredericksburg, USA, David Williams, now of BNSC, UK, Don Levandowski of Purdue University, USA, Pat Chavez of the US Geological Survey, Flagstaff, USA, and Ron Blom of JPL, Pasadena, USA, who read and constructively criticized chapters during production of the first edition. Ron Lyon of Stanford University refereed the proposal for this edition and gave the thumbs up. A veil needs to be drawn over the reason for an early appearance of a second edition, suffice it to say that the first became caught in the cogwheels of commercial publishing. That it re-emerged is thanks to Ruth Cripwell of Chapman & Hall, my commissioning editor. A satisfying format is due to Helen Heyes and Andy Finch of Chapman & Hall.

ACKNOWLEDGEMENTS

We are grateful to the following individuals and organizations who have given permission for the reproduction of copyright material (figure numbers are in parentheses):

Figure 1.5a reproduced from S. Valley, *Handbook of Geophysics and Space Environments*, 1965, McGraw-Hill Book Company; John Wiley & Sons Inc. (1.6, 1.8, 1.12, 1.13, 2.9e, 3.11, 3.15b and c, 3.23b, 3.27, 5.39, 6.1–, 8.4); Gordon and Breach Science Publishers (1.7); Economic Geology Publishing Co., University of Texas (1.9, 1.10, 1.16, 1.17, 3.24); G. Bell and Sons Ltd. (2.3, 2.16); Figure 2.9d reproduced with permission from *Photogrammetric Engineering and Remote Sensing*, **49**, 3, Daily, p. 352 ©1983, by the American Society for Photogrammetry and Sensing; Aerofilms Ltd (3.3, 3.5, 3.13); W.H. Freeman & Co. ©1978 (3.8); J.P. Ford, Jet Propulsion Laboratory, California Institute of Technology, Pasadena (3.21, 3.29, 4.19, 7.20); H.C. MacDonald, the University of Arkansas (3.23); Stuart Marsh, Sun Oil, Houston (3.24); Ronald Blom, Jet Propulsion Laboratory, California Institute of Technology, Pasadena (3.29, 7.17, 7.20); NOAA NESDIS, Washington DC (3.31); Jet Propulsion Laboratory, California Institute of Technology, Pasadena (3.36); European Space Agency (3.37a); National Space Development Agency of Japan (3.37b); The Principal Investigator, Dr Charles Elachi, and the National Space Science Data Center/World Data Center A for Rockets and Satellites, NASA (7.4); Figure 4.1 reproduced from V.C. Miller, *Photogeology*, 1961, McGraw-Hill Book Company; US Department of Agriculture, Agricultural and Conservation Service (ASCS) (4.2, 4.42, 4.48a, 4.50, 4.51b, 4.54); Figures 4.6, 4.17c, 4.47, 4.52, 4.55 and 4.56 reproduced with permission of the Department of Energy, Mines and Resources, Canada (EMERC), Copyright Her Majesty the Queen in Right of Canada; Clyde Surveys Ltd. (4.7a, 4.12b, 4.13b, 4.33, 4.38a, 4.49a, 4.55b, 9.5, 9.6); National Cartographic Information Center, US Geological Survey (NCIC), Kansas (4.7b, 4.8b); USGS (4.8a, 4.9, 4.11a, 4.15a, 4.19, 4.29); Figure 4.11b reproduced by permission of the Director of Planning, Department of Planning, West Yorkshire Metropolitan County Council; NCIC, Arizona (4.12a, 4.28, 4.37c, 4.42a); Figures 4.13a and 4.27a reproduced by courtesy of Amoco Inc.; Federal Ministry of Works, Nigeria (4.15b); Department of National Development and Energy, Australia (DNDE) (4.15c); I.G. Gass, Open University (4.16); University of Illinois Aerial Photography and Remote Sensing committee (4.21); Michael Smallwood, Optronix Inc. (4.22); NCIC Utah (4.28); Dave Rothery, Open University (4.31a, 4.45b, 5.40); P.W. Francis, Open University (4.33b); National Oceanic and Atmospheric Administration, Washington (4.33c); Institut Géographique National, Paris (4.37a); IGN Maroc (4.37b); NCIC, Texas (4.37c); Figures 4.40, 4.42b, 4.44, 4.45 and 4.46 reproduced by permission of the Dirección General de Fabricaciones Militares of Instituto Geografico Militar, Chile; NCIC Hawaii (4.42a); NCIC Los Angeles (4.49b); NCIC North Dakota (4.51a); NCIC New York (4.53); Pat Chavez, USGS (5.20, 5.22); Gary Raines, USGS (5.33); Ken Watson, USGS, Denver (6.6); Anne B. Kahle, Jet Propulsion Laboratory, California Institute of Technology, Pasadena (6.7, 6.11, 6.12, 6.14); Melvin Podwysocki, USGS (6.13); Figure 6.18 reproduced from Kahle & Rowan, *Geology* **8**, 1980 Figure 1, 234–9 by permission of The Geological Society of America; Harold Land, Jet Propulsion Laboratory, California Institute of Technology, Pasadena (6.20); Intera Technologies Ltd, Calgary (7.5, 7.23); Earl Hajic, University of California, Santa Barbara, and Goodyear Aerospace Corporation (7.22); Gerald Schaber, USGS, Arizona (7.24); Tom Farr, Jet Propulsion Laboratory, California Institute of Technology, Pasadena (7.26); Ronald Blom and Michael Daily, Jet Propulsion Laboratory, California Institute of Technology, Pasadena (7.27); American Association of Petroleum Geologists (7.28); Ronald Blom and Bill Stromberg, Jet Propulsion Laboratory, California Institute of Technology, Pasadena (7.29); Earth and Planetary Remote-Sensing Laboratory, Washington University, St Louis (8.15b); Charles Trautwein, EROS Data Center (8.13, 8.21); Stanley Aronoff (8.2, 8.6); Oxford University Press (8.3, 8.4, 8.5, 8.23); IEEE (9.7).

CHAPTER ONE

Electromagnetic radiation and materials

The key to designing remote-sensing systems, orienting their use and interpreting the results they produce is understanding the way in which electromagnetic radiation is generated, propagated and modified. The physical inseparability of this radiation from matter and other forms of energy inevitably means that when matter and electromagnetic radiation interact both are modified in some way. A complete treatment involves complex mathematics with which most readers will not be familiar. For this reason this chapter takes a simplified look at the phenomena involved. For those readers with the background and inclination, some of the texts in the Further Reading at the end of the chapter open the door to a deeper penetration into the theories involved.

1.1 The nature of electromagnetic radiation

In order to interpret remotely sensed data it is not necessary to know a great deal about the physics of generation and propagation of electromagnetic radiation (EMR). Light and all forms of EMR behave both as waves and as particles. They may be regarded as pure energy, in the form of linked electric and magnetic force fields, transmitted in packets known as **quanta** or **photons**, which have zero mass at rest. In the same sense, a particle of matter, such as an electron, displays wave behaviour under certain conditions. Pure energy and pure matter are totally abstract concepts. Mass and energy are inseparable and can be converted into one another through Einstein's famous relationship:

$$E = mc^2$$

where E is energy, m is mass and c is the velocity of EMR in a vacuum. This fundamental relationship has been demonstrated in practice by the net loss of mass in nuclear fission and fusion, and by the transformation of energy into sub-atomic particles in high-energy particle accelerators.

Most waves, such as sound or ripples on water, are propagated by the motion of particles of matter. Those associated with EMR are transverse waves, and involve vibrations at right angles to their direction of travel. However, EMR can travel through a vacuum, and although it can affect particles in a physical medium by changing their electronic, vibrational and rotational properties, it must propagate itself in the absence of matter. Each quantum has associated electric and magnetic fields at right angles to each other and to the direction of propagation (Fig. 1.1). These fields oscillate in a regular fashion that can be described by a sine wave. In such a wave the distance between wave crests is the **wavelength** (λ), and the number of vibrations passing a point in one second is the **frequency** (ν). Knowing one enables the other to be calculated from the equation:

$$\lambda\nu = c \qquad (1.1)$$

The electric and magnetic vibrations associated with a quantum can be in any orientation at right angles to the direction of propagation. However, if the fields for all quanta are lined up in one direction by some means, the radiation becomes plane-**polarized** – a familiar concept for

ELECTROMAGNETIC RADIATION AND MATERIALS

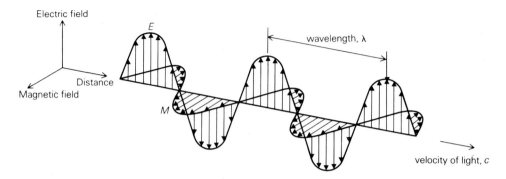

Figure 1.1 Electromagnetic radiation (EMR) comprises waves in electrical and magnetic fields. These fields are at right angles to each other and to the direction of propagation of the waves. The waves represent regular fluctuations in the fields and are described by sine functions. The distance occupied by a complete cycle from peak to peak is the wavelength (λ), and the number of cycles passing a fixed point in a second is the frequency of the radiation (ν). Since EMR has a constant velocity in a vacuum (c) it is easy to visualize the relationship between λ, ν and c shown in Equation 1.1.

any geologist who has used a polarizing microscope for petrography.

The frequency or wavelength of EMR is a function of the energy of the quanta. Max Planck formulated this relationship (**Planck's law**) as:

$$E = \nu h = ch/\lambda \qquad (1.2)$$

where h is Planck's constant ($6.62 \times 10^{-34}\,\text{J\,s}$). The shorter the wavelength or the higher the frequency of EMR, the greater the energy of each quantum.

The final basic property of EMR is its intensity, equivalent to the brightness of visible light. This may be regarded as either the number of quanta or the amplitudes of the electric and magnetic fields. The more quanta at a particular wavelength, the greater the energy which is transmitted. The energy of a single long-wavelength quantum is less than that of one at short wavelength. Consequently, more long-wavelength quanta must fall on a detector to produce a measurable response compared with the number of shorter wavelength quanta which produce the same response. In general therefore, systems aimed at long-wavelength EMR need to collect radiation either from a larger target area or over a longer time than those used for shorter wavelengths. This has important consequences for the resolution of remote-sensing systems and their ability to discriminate real objects from systematic noise.

1.2 The generation of electromagnetic radiation

This is a convenient point at which to introduce some of the terminology that is used when speaking of EMR. Electromagnetic radiation is a form of **energy**, and so the amount of EMR measured per unit time has the dimensions of $\text{J\,s}^{-1}$ (joules per second) or W (watts), which are units of **power**. The power incident on or emanating from a body is known as the **radiant flux**, but it is usually more useful to consider the amount of EMR measured per unit area – the **radiant flux density** ($\text{W\,m}^{-2}$). The radiant flux density falling on a given area of surface is known as the **ir-radiance**, whereas that leaving a surface is called the **emittance** (sometimes called the **exitance**).

Limitations to the size of measuring devices mean we can rarely measure directly all the EMR leaving a surface. Instead, what is measured is the amount of EMR intercepted by a small detector, which collects EMR travelling through a given solid angle. This gives the radiant flux per unit solid angle, which is called **radiance**. The units of radiance are $\text{W\,m}^{-2}\,\text{sr}^{-1}$ (watts per square metre per steradian, where steradian is the unit of solid angle).

Sometimes it is useful to consider the quantity of EMR measured at a specific wavelength only. For example, the **spectral radiant flux** is the power received or radiated by a body per unit area per unit wavelength. For convenience, this is often quoted in $\text{W\,m}^{-2}\,\mu\text{m}^{-1}$. Similarly, **spectral radiance** is measured in $\text{W\,m}^{-2}\,\text{sr}^{-1}\,\mu\text{m}^{-1}$.

Although it is more correct to quote the amount of EMR coming from a surface as radiance or spectral radiance, when writing or speaking informally or non-numerically the more familiar term **brightness** is often used instead. This term can refer either to the amount of EMR coming from the surface or to the appearance of a region within an image. For example, if a particular area in an image is said to be brighter than another area, it is clear what we mean, even though we may not be able to quantify the difference in terms of radiance units.

The generation of EMR is essentially a simple process. It is produced whenever the size or direction of an electric or magnetic field fluctuates with time. Radio waves can be produced by the flow of rapidly alternating currents in a conducting body or antenna. The alternation is, in effect, the repeated acceleration and deceleration of electric charges. At the shortest wavelengths, gamma-rays result from disruption of atomic nuclei during nuclear fission or fusion reactions. X-rays, ultraviolet and visible radiation are generated by electrons jumping from one stable orbiting shell around an atom to another. When an electron moves from a higher orbit to a lower one, the energy which it loses is converted into a photon of a specific wavelength. Infrared and microwave radiation is produced by vibration and rotation of molecules. Microwaves are also generated by fluctuations in electric and magnetic fields.

Electromagnetic radiation spans wavelengths of many orders of magnitude, from shorter than 10^{-13} m for the most energetic gamma-rays to longer than 100 km for very long radio waves. It is convenient to divide this vast range into several arbitrary regions, each with its own name. This spectrum of wavelengths and the conventional terminology are shown in Figure 1.2. A further subdivision of the near-infrared (NIR) is shown in Figure 1.5b.

In nature all these processes are in one way or another related to the temperature of the body emitting radiation. All matter in the Universe, even that in the near-perfect vacuum between the galaxies, is above absolute zero (−273.15°C) and emits some form of radiation. Just how much is emitted and the range of its wavelengths is a complex function of both temperature and the nature of the body itself. Matter capable of absorbing and re-emitting all electromagnetic energy that it receives is known as a **black-body**. The total energy emitted by a blackbody – its emittance (H) in $W m^{-2}$ – is proportional to the fourth power of its **absolute temperature** (T). This is the **Stefan–Boltzmann law**:

$$H = \sigma T^4 \qquad (1.3)$$

where σ is the **Stefan–Boltzmann constant** ($5.7 \times 10^{-8} W m^{-2} K^{-4}$).

At any particular temperature, a blackbody emits EMR with a range of wavelengths. However, its absolute temperature determines which wavelength transmits the maximum amount of energy. This dominant wavelength (λ_m in μm) is given by **Wien's displacement law**:

$$\lambda_m = 2898/T \qquad (1.4)$$

So, as temperature increases, total energy emitted rises very rapidly and the wavelength carrying most energy becomes shorter. The shape of the curve relating emittance to wavelength is important (Fig. 1.3). For any temperature there is a minimum wavelength of radiation, a nearby wavelength of maximum emittance and a long tail towards longer wavelengths. Thus a blackbody at 6000 K – the Sun's surface temperature – does not emit radiation with wavelengths shorter than 0.1 μm, has an energy peak at 0.5 μm, but emits all wavelengths beyond that up to about 100 μm. The total energy emitted is given by the areas beneath the curves in Figure 1.3.

GENERATION OF ELECTROMAGNETIC RADIATION

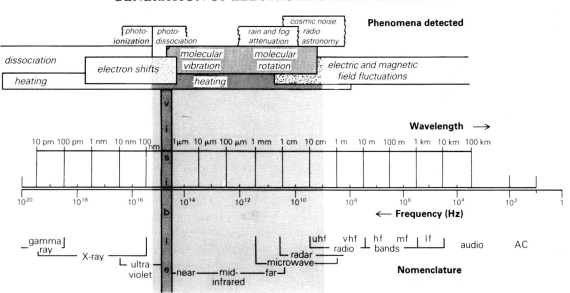

Figure 1.2 This summary of that part of the EM spectrum which is routinely detected by scientists shows the relationship between wavelength and frequency, the phenomena which are involved in generation and interaction of EMR, and the nomenclature for different parts of the spectrum (see Fig. 1.5b). Those portions covered by this book are highlighted, together with the processes relevant to geological remote sensing. The narrow visible band is useful as a reference. The wavelength and frequency scales are logarithmic.

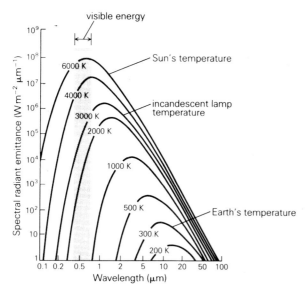

Figure 1.3 This family of curves on logarithmic axes expresses how energy emitted by a square metre of a blackbody at different temperatures varies with wavelength, and how the wavelength of maximum emittance and the range of wavelengths emitted change with absolute temperature. The area under each curve represents the total energy emitted at each temperature. Both the Stefan–Boltzmann and Wien laws control the shapes.

Of course, natural objects are not perfect blackbodies. In the case of the Sun – the source of most radiation exploited in remote sensing – many processes other than simple heating are involved. Consequently, the solar irradiation curve (Fig. 1.5) is a little different from the ideal case. As well as radiation in the 0.1–100 µm range, the Sun emits gamma-rays as a result of thermonuclear processes and long-wavelength radiation owing to fluctuations in its prodigious magnetic and electric fields.

Remote sensing is concerned with two categories of radiation from the Earth's surface – that which falls on it and is absorbed or reflected and that which is emitted by the surface itself. Reflected radiation derives in the main from the Sun, and systems detecting it are termed **passive** since no artificially induced energy is required. An **active** system involves artificial 'illumination', as in flash photography. In remote sensing the most widely used active systems employ **radar** (*r*adio *d*etection *a*nd *r*anging) transmissions and detection of the radar energy reflected back to a sensor by the Earth's surface. Experiments have demonstrated that other active systems employing artificial radiation, usually in the form of ultraviolet lasers, can produce data for limited ranges of applications.

Because the Earth's ambient temperature is about 300 K, Wien's displacement law implies that it has a maximum emittance at 9.7 µm, in the **mid-infrared (MIR)**. The energy involved in producing this emitted radiation derives from three sources: the flow of radiogenic heat from the Earth's interior, the heating of the surface by solar

radiation, and human activities. Long-wavelength infrared is not the only radiation emitted by the Earth. All rocks and materials derived from them contain variable proportions of the unstable isotopes ^{40}K, ^{232}Th, ^{235}U and ^{238}U, which emit gamma-rays when they decay. These too can be detected remotely, and add to the range of true remote-sensing techniques.

1.3 Matter and electromagnetic radiation

The key to understanding how remotely sensed data can be used to recognize different materials at the Earth's surface lies in the way EMR interacts with matter. To discuss this properly means examining the interactions at the molecular or atomic level. Only a very simplified version is given here.

For a single chemical element there are several possible states in which it can exist, each of which has a characteristic energy level. The range of states and the associated energy levels are unique for every element. An atom may jump from one state to another if it is excited by just the right frequency of EMR. A simple example is **fluorescence**, when EMR of one frequency causes a transition and the transition itself emits lower frequency EMR. There are three types of transition – **electronic**, **vibrational** and **rotational**. When an element is bonded with others in molecules, things become more complicated. The transitions are conditioned by such features as the types of bonds (covalent or ionic), the coordination state of atoms within the molecule, the valency of the atoms and much more besides.

Electronic transitions involve shifts of electrons from one quantum shell to another. They are the reverse of one means of generating EMR discussed in Section 1.2. A photon of a specific wavelength may induce an electron to move from a lower orbit to a higher one, thereby allowing the EMR energy to be absorbed. The wavelengths that can cause electronic transitions are determined by the principal quantum numbers, angular momentum and spin associated with quantum shells within a particular element. Electronic transitions occur in solids, liquids and gases, but are particularly important for elements like iron and chromium, which have several possible valence states, positions in molecular structures and coordinations in natural materials. These differences account for subtle changes in the wavelengths of electronic transitions depending on the host for the element. Since electronic transitions require high excitation energies, they are most common at short wavelengths – ultraviolet and visible light.

Vibrational transitions result in changes in the relative disposition of the component atoms of molecules. The easiest to visualize are distortions of bonds, either **stretching** or **bending** from one equilibrium state to another. As for sound, as well as a **fundamental** wavelength or 'note' associated with a transition, there are mathematically related **harmonics** or **overtones**. All these discrete wavelengths superimposed together comprise a **band** within which transitions are induced. Like electronic transitions, those associated with molecular vibrations and bonds characterize solids, liquids and gases. However, they require lower energies and so occur with longer wavelength EMR – in the infrared and beyond.

Transitions may also occur in the rotational properties of molecules, but they are restricted to gases. They relate to changes in the moment of inertia of the rotating molecules of gas. Rotational transitions are of most importance, together with vibrational transitions, in the interaction between EMR and the atmospheric gases through which the Earth's surface must be viewed by all remote-sensing systems (Section 1.3.1).

The energy detected by remote-sensing systems over the spectrum of EMR is therefore a function of how energy is partitioned between its source and the materials with which it interacts on its way to the detector. The energy of any particular wavelength of radiation may be **transmitted** through the material, **absorbed** within it, **reflected** by its surface, **scattered** by its constituent particles or **reradiated** at another wavelength after absorption. In nature, all possibilities combine together to one degree or another.

Three kinds of spectra can be measured for any material – **absorption** (and its inverse, **transmission**), **reflection** and **emission** spectra. An absorption/transmission spectrum is produced when the material is interposed between source and sensor. A reflection spectrum is measured when both source and sensor are on the same side of the material. For an emission spectrum the material itself is the source. A prism or diffraction grating spreads the composite radiation out into its component wavelengths, when intensities at discrete wavelengths may be related to specific emission or absorption processes. This is the technique used by astronomers to detect and measure element abundances in stars from atomic absorption bands in stellar spectra. The remote sensor, however, is more concerned with continuous spectra, which show the variation in energy/intensity over a range of wavelengths. They are more or less smooth curves in which

peaks and troughs indicate maxima and minima around wavelengths which correspond to some characteristic transition. Many macroscopic and microscopic factors conspire together to determine the width, strength and abruptness of these features, some of which are discussed later in this section and in other chapters.

The principle of conservation of energy determines that for any EMR–matter interaction, the incident radiant flux at one wavelength $(E_I)_\lambda$ is distributed between reflection $(E_R)_\lambda$, absorption $(E_A)_\lambda$ and transmission $(E_T)_\lambda$:

$$(E_I)_\lambda = (E_R)_\lambda + (E_A)_\lambda + (E_T)_\lambda \qquad (1.5)$$

Dividing throughout Equation 1.5 by $(E_I)_\lambda$ produces an expression allowing the macroscopic properties of the material to be defined in terms of the ratios $(E_R/E_I)_\lambda$, $(E_A/E_I)_\lambda$ and $(E_T/E_I)_\lambda$, which are the **spectral reflectance** (ρ_λ), **absorptance** (α_λ) and **transmittance** (τ_λ) respectively, so that:

$$(E_R/E_I)_\lambda + (E_A/E_I)_\lambda + (E_T/E_I)_\lambda = 1 \qquad (1.6)$$

i.e.
$$\rho_\lambda + \alpha_\lambda + \tau_\lambda = 1 \qquad (1.7)$$

The vast bulk of geological materials are opaque and transmittance is zero, so that Equation 1.7 reduces to:

$$\rho_\lambda + \alpha_\lambda = 1 \qquad (1.8)$$

which means in effect that reflectance and absorptance are interchangeable. Reflectance spectra are nearly always used.

Reflectance, defined as the ratio of the total radiant flux reflected by a surface to the total radiant flux incident on it, is sometimes known as the **albedo** of the surface.

The value of reflectance for a surface specifies the proportion of the incident energy which is reflected, but not the direction in which the reflected energy travels. This depends on whether the surface produces **specular reflection**, like a mirror, or **diffuse reflection** like a sheet of matte paper. In specular reflection, all the reflected energy is directed away at an angle equal and opposite to the angle of incidence. In diffuse reflection, the reflected energy is directed nearly equally in all directions, irrespective of the angle of incidence (Fig. 1.4). A perfect diffuse reflector is

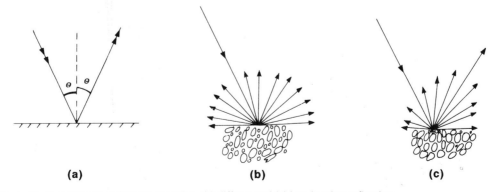

Figure 1.4 Schematic diagrams showing (a) specular, (b) diffuse and (c) Lambertian reflection.

often called a **Lambertian reflector**. Many surfaces combine specular and Lambertian properties, in that they reflect *some* energy in all directions, but reflect a larger proportion in the specular direction.

A surface behaves as a specular reflector if it is smooth, and as a diffuse reflector if it is rough. Smoothness and roughness depend on the wavelength of EMR. Generally, a surface behaves as rough if its texture is on a scale similar to, or greater than, that of the wavelength of the EMR, and in a smooth fashion if its texture is on a finer scale than the wavelength. Most surfaces, such as rock, soil or grass, are diffuse reflectors in the visible spectrum – they look equally bright in whatever direction they are viewed, even though tiny parts of a surface (individual mineral crystals, for example) behave specularly.

1.3.1 The effect of the atmosphere

Remote sensing of bodies such as the Jovian moon Io or the planet Mars is a geologist's delight. Both have very thin, almost transparent, atmospheres, except when volcanic eruptions in the case of Io or sand storms on Mars take place. Virtually the whole of the EMR spectrum is available for surveillance, given a suitable range of sensors. For the Earth however, all radiation must pass through a dense atmosphere. Before reception by a satellite-mounted sensor, solar radiation must pass down through the atmosphere and then back again to the sensor. For a sensor measuring radiation emitted by the Earth the path is single, but there is some effect nevertheless.

As well as oxygen and nitrogen, the atmosphere contains significant amounts of water vapour, ozone (O_3) and carbon dioxide. All interact with EMR by vibrational and rotational transitions, whose net effect is absorption of energy in specific wavebands (Fig. 1.5a). Incidentally, it is this absorption of short-wave solar radiation that heats the atmosphere. The growth in CO_2, water vapour and industrially emitted gases in the atmosphere as a result of human activities is the source of the so-called 'greenhouse effect'. At short wavelengths these bands are narrow, but increase in width in the infrared and microwave regions. Figure 1.5b shows that about 50% of the EMR spectrum is unusable for remote sensing of the Earth's surface, simply because none of the corresponding energy can penetrate the atmosphere. In the case of emitted gamma-rays, only by flying dangerously close to the ground can some energy be detected. It is possible to record absorbed wavelengths relating to gases, but this is for atmospheric studies that are beyond the scope of this book.

Another irritation to the remote sensor is blue sky. It is caused by one of a number of phenomena resulting from the diffusion of radiation by matter, commonly called **scattering**. The type of scattering changes with the size of the particles responsible. Where EMR interacts with particles

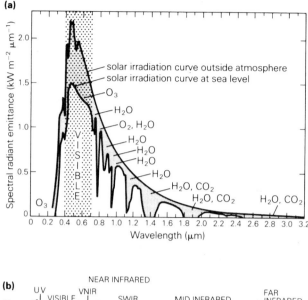

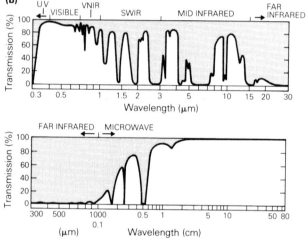

Figure 1.5 Various gases in the atmosphere absorb solar energy in different wavebands by vibrational and rotational transitions. As a result, the solar irradiation curves measured in outer space – upper curve in (a) – and at the surface – lower curve in (a) – are very different. The energy available for interactions with matter at the surface is divided into discrete atmospheric windows separated by bands dominated by atmospheric absorption (grey). In (b) the main atmospheric windows throughout the whole of the useful part of the EM spectrum are shown on a logarithmic scale, in terms of the percentage transmitted through the atmosphere. These two graphs, together with the spectral properties of natural materials, form the basis for designing remote-sensing systems.

smaller than the wavelength, such as molecules of oxygen and nitrogen, the degree of scattering is inversely proportional to the fourth power of the wavelength. This is known as **Rayleigh scattering** after its discoverer, Lord Rayleigh. The relationship means that the effects of Rayleigh scattering increase dramatically at short wavelengths – hence blue sky and distant blue mountains. The effect is to swamp the real reflected blue and ultraviolet radiation with a high scattered component, and to reduce the contrast.

Where atmospheric particles are similar in size to the wavelength of incoming radiation, as is the case for the giant molecules of water and for dust, **Mie scattering** results. This affects wavelengths longer than that of blue light, and is a problem in clear but humid or dusty atmospheric conditions. Red sunsets are attributed to the Mie scattering effect of very fine dust blown up from deserts or microscopic ash particles and acidic water droplets injected into the atmosphere by volcanic eruptions. Worse still, aerosol droplets in cloud or fog, which are much larger than most EMR wavelengths of interest in remote sensing, scatter all wavelengths in the visible and infrared spectrum. Aerosols are impenetrable, except by radiation beyond $100\,\mu m$ wavelength – microwave and radar. Even at such long wavelengths, heavy rain or snowfall can cause **non-selective scattering** of this kind, and as a result can be detected and even measured. The overall decrease in the spectral radiant emission at the surface compared with that in outer space is due to the combined effects of different types of scattering, one result of which is the return of a component of incoming solar radiation to space.

On a clear night stars appear to shift and wink, as do distant objects on a hot day. These distortions are produced by temperature variations in the air, which produce fluctuations in its refractive index, and a range of optical anomalies. Exactly the same effects are present when the Earth is viewed from above. Such **atmospheric shimmer** forms an important constraint on just how small an object remote sensing can detect, irrespective of the theoretical resolving power of each system. It is possible to overcome shimmer to some extent using sophisticated image-processing techniques.

All this implies that remotely sensed images of the Earth are unavoidably degraded in various ways by the atmosphere. It also means that only some wavebands are available for surveillance (Fig. 1.5b). Those wavebands that pass relatively undiminished through the atmosphere are referred to as **atmospheric windows**. They determine the framework wherein different methods of remote sensing can be devised. This is an appropriate point at which to introduce a broad division of the spectrum according to the source of the measured radiation in remote sensing. Figure 1.5a shows that radiant energy from the Sun falls to very low values beyond about $2.5\,\mu m$. In fact many of its longer wavelengths are strongly absorbed by Earth materials. Of that in the $0.4–2.5\,\mu m$ region a good proportion is reflected from the surface, depending on the material, so allowing remote sensing of the properties of the reflected radiation. This is the **reflected region**. The two windows between 3 and $5\,\mu m$ and 8 and $14\,\mu m$ are dominated by radiant energy that is emitted by the surface, as a result of its having been heated mainly by the Sun. This is the **emitted region**. The more or less transparent region beyond 1 mm is

the **microwave region**. Quite different technologies are needed to acquire remotely sensed data in these regions, as outlined in Chapter 3.

The other natural constraint on system design is the interaction between EMR and those solids and liquids that comprise the Earth's surface. There are only three important components: water, vegetation and the inorganic solids making up rock and soil. For the geologist, the interactions between EMR and rocks and soils are most important. However, since they can contain water or have vegetation growing on them, these materials must be considered too. The next three sections introduce some of these surface interactions, and they are expanded upon in later chapters.

1.3.2 Interaction of electromagnetic radiation with rocks and minerals

In this section only the most general features are covered, interactions specific to particular rock and soil types being dealt with in later chapters. Here the effects of common rock- and soil-forming minerals have primary importance. They are considered for three major ranges of EMR wavelength, $0.4–2.5\,\mu m$ [visible, **very near-infrared (VNIR)** and **short-wave infrared (SWIR)**], $8–14\,\mu m$ (emitted or **thermal MIR**) and 1 mm to 30 cm (**microwaves**). Radar interactions in the microwave region are discussed separately in Chapter 7, since they are fundamentally different from those of shorter wavelengths. The most important processes involved are electronic and vibrational transitions (Section 1.3), rotational transitions being restricted to gases.

Rocks are assemblages of minerals, and so their spectra are composites of those for each of their constituents. Minerals in turn comprise various proportions of different elements, held together as molecules by different kinds of bonds. Electronic transitions within atoms themselves require more energy than vibrational transitions within molecules, so the former characterize the short wavelength, ultraviolet to visible, range, whereas the latter dominate the longer wavelength SWIR. There is, however, some overlap between the ranges of these two fundamental processes.

The most common ingredients of rocks and the minerals of which they consist are oxygen, silicon and aluminium, together with varying proportions of iron, magnesium, calcium, sodium and potassium, and smaller amounts of the other elements. Oxygen, silicon and aluminium atoms have electron shells whose energy levels are such that transitions between them have little or no effect on the visible to near-infrared range. There, the spectra of minerals are dominated by the effects of less common ions and the molecular structures in which they are bonded. The characteristic energy levels of isolated elements are changed when they are combined in minerals because of the valence states of their ions, the type of bonding and their relationships to other ions: their coordination. Because they can exist as ions with several different valencies, the transition metals iron, copper, nickel, chromium, cobalt, manganese, vanadium, titanium and scandium exhibit a great range of possibilities. Since iron is by far the most abundant of these metals, its effects are the most common and most marked.

On Figure 1.6 are shown reflectance spectra of several iron-bearing minerals, which display features due to electronic transitions in ferrous (Fe^{2+}) ions. The different wavelengths of the features relate to the symmetry, degree of lattice distortion and coordination of ferrous ions in the different minerals. The features are troughs, indicating that absorption of energy takes place over the band of wavelengths involved, in order to cause the electronic transitions. All these features are due to transitions in discrete ions and result from **crystal-field effects**. Although there seems to be a wide range of possibilities for distinguishing the iron minerals in Figure 1.6, in reality they are only useful in a laboratory setting using fresh minerals. In the field minerals are assembled in different proportions as rocks, so that their spectra interfere. More important, they

are rarely fresh but covered with thin veneers of weathering products. Since visible and NIR radiation interacts only with the outer few micrometres of the surface, spectra of fresh minerals rarely affect the reflected radiation used in much remote sensing.

Another type of electronic transition results from the presence in metal ions of electrons that have sufficient energy that they are not strongly attached to any particular ion and may transfer from one ion to another. This is the property that imparts high electrical conductivity to metals. In a mineral, a similar transition, called a **charge-transfer**, can occur. It too is induced by energy in narrow wavebands of EMR, giving rise to absorption features. The most common charge-transfer is involved in the migration of electrons from iron to oxygen, and results in a broad absorption band at wavelengths shorter than about 0.55 μm. It is common to all iron-bearing minerals and is responsible for a steep decline in reflectance towards the blue end of the spectrum. The most noticeable effect is with iron oxides and hydroxides (Fig. 1.7), and is the reason why these minerals and rocks containing them are coloured yellow, orange and red. Such minerals form the main colorants in weathered rocks. They too display crystal-field absorptions, the most prominent being around 0.8–0.9 μm. As shown in Figure 1.7, the location and shapes of these bands vary subtly from mineral to mineral and, as discussed in Chapter 5, form a means for discriminating between these important minerals.

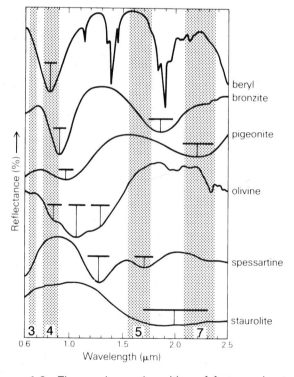

Figure 1.6 The number and position of features due to electronic transitions in iron minerals – T-shaped symbols – depend on the coordination of Fe^{2+} ions in the molecular structures of the minerals concerned. The spectra are offset vertically for clarity. In this figure and in Figures 1.7–1.10 and 1.15–1.17 the vertical bands indicate the widths of spectral bands sensed by the Landsat Thematic Mapper (Ch. 3), the most widely used orbiting remote-sensing system.

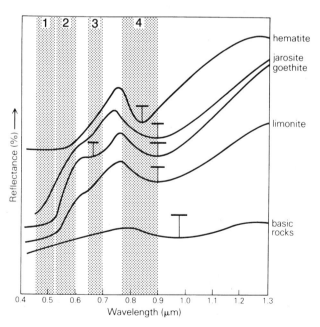

Figure 1.7 Iron oxides and hydroxides display absorption features due to Fe–O charge transfer and crystal-field effects in their reflectance spectra – T-shaped symbols. Substitution of iron in clay minerals superimposes similar features on clay spectra. The spectra are offset for clarity.

In the visible to SWIR part of the spectrum the most important vibrational transitions in minerals are those associated with the presence of OH⁻ ions or water molecules bound in the structure or present in fluid inclusions. The water molecule has three fundamental vibration transitions as a result of stretching of the H–O–H bond at 3.11 and 2.90 μm and bending at 6.08 μm. Owing to overtones and their combination, these result in absorption features at 1.9, 1.4, 1.14 and 0.94 μm, which are diagnostic of the presence of molecular water in minerals (Fig. 1.8). However, these features are completely swamped by the effects of water vapour in the atmosphere, and are only useful in a laboratory setting.

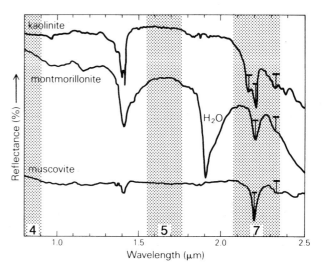

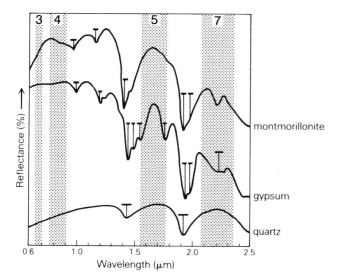

Figure 1.8 Minerals containing chemically bound water have particularly distinctive absorption features close to the theoretical overtone wavelengths for the H–O–H bond-stretching transitions – T-shaped symbols. None of the features for sulphates, such as gypsum, relate to SO₄²⁻ ions. The spectra are offset for clarity.

Many silicates and alteration minerals contain hydroxyl (OH⁻) ions, for which there is only one fundamental **bond-stretching transition** of the O–H bond at 2.7 μm. This may form overtones in combination with other transitions, the most important of which are **bond-bending transitions**, for the metal-hydroxyl bonds Mg–OH and Al–OH to produce absorption features near 2.3 and 2.2 μm respectively. Such features are prominent in aluminous micas and clay minerals (Fig. 1.9) and form signatures for other hydroxylated minerals containing magnesium, such as chlorites and serpentines. Provided the absorption features can be resolved, these spectral characteristics form a powerful tool in discriminating chemically different rock types. However, the wavebands highlighted in Figures 1.6 to 1.10, from the Landsat Thematic Mapper (Chapter 3), are too broad to enable more than simply detecting the presence of hydroxylated minerals.

Figure 1.9 The bending of Al–OH and Mg–OH bonds in clay minerals and micas produce distinctive absorption features in their reflectance spectra – T-shaped symbols. Together with other features of the spectra, they form a potentially powerful means of discriminating these minerals, which are important products of hydrothermal and sedimentary processes. The spectra are offset for clarity.

Similar vibrational transitions and overtones characterize carbonate minerals. They derive from stretching and bending of the C–O bond in the CO₃²⁻ ion. They give rise to a number of absorption features in the SWIR, of which that around 2.3 μm is most prominent (Fig. 1.10). That at 2.55 μm lies outside the atmospheric window.

Although the reflected part of the spectrum has limited potential for rock discrimination, sufficient diagnostic features are present that great effort has been put into devising

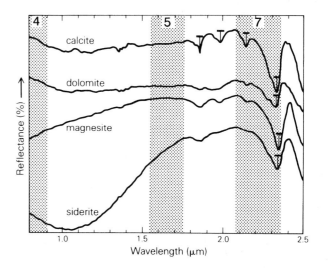

Figure 1.10 Vibrational transitions related to C–O bonds produce absorption features in the reflectance spectra of carbonates – T-shaped symbols. The most distinctive is that near 2.35 μm, which can potentially distinguish between carbonates and clays. The spectra are offset for clarity.

methods of capturing data with sufficient spectral resolution to separate the different features. This is discussed in Chapter 3.

In that part of the spectrum where the Earth's EMR emission reaches a peak, an atmospheric window between 8 and 14 μm allows radiation to be sensed remotely. An ideal emitter of EMR is a blackbody, when the total energy emitted and its distribution between different wavelengths are governed by the Stefan–Boltzmann and Wien laws (Section 1.2). A curve describing this distribution has a distinct shape (Fig. 1.3) but no distinct spectral features. A measure of a natural material's deviation from the ideal is its emissivity (e_λ): the ratio between its radiant emittance for a particular wavelength (λ) at a given temperature and that of a blackbody. A greybody has a constant emissivity less than 1.0 for all wavelengths. However, most natural materials have emissivities which vary with wavelength. They are selective radiators because vibrational transitions of bonds in their molecular structure impede emission at characteristic wavelengths. Quartz is a good example, as Figure 1.11 shows. It radiates as a nearly ideal blackbody up to 6 μm, but deviates from the ideal at longer wavelengths.

Because good emitters are also good absorbers of radiation their emissivities are equal to their absorptivities. The latter is difficult to measure and this relationship, known as Kirchoff's law after its initiator, can be transformed using Equation 1.8 to:

$$e_\lambda = 1 - \rho_\lambda \qquad (1.9)$$

The trough in the emittance curve for quartz between 8 and 9 μm is due to Si–O bond-stretching vibrations. This and related spectral structures are best shown by transmission spectra, and they occur in both silicates (Fig. 1.12) and

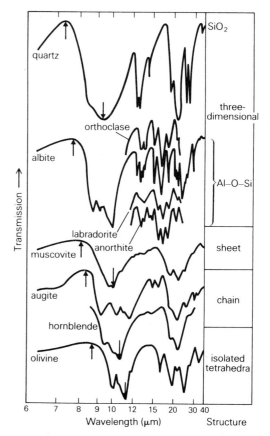

Figure 1.12 Because of differences in the structure of silicates, the positions of both the Si–O bond-stretching trough and its 'shoulder' at shorter wavelengths (arrows) occur at slightly different positions in the mid-infrared spectra of different silicate minerals. The spectra result from experiments using transmitted energy, but would appear very similar for emission. The spectra are offset for clarity.

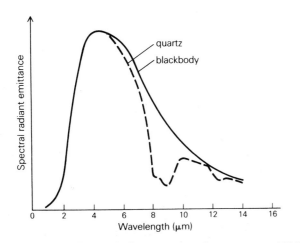

Figure 1.11 The emission spectrum for quartz, at 600 K, deviates from that for a true blackbody because of a strong feature induced by Si–O bond stretching. Quartz is therefore a selective radiator and not a greybody.

non-silicates (Fig. 1.13). This is because most minerals have chemical bonds whose energies of vibration fall in the thermal infrared region, and emission is hindered at the energy which coincides with each bond vibration. The most important feature in the silicate family of spectra (Fig. 1.12) is that the minimum of the main absorption trough shifts according to the type of silicate structure involved. So too does the peak at the short-wavelength edge of the absorption trough. A partial explanation for this is that in different silicates the SiO₄ tetrahedra share oxygens in different ways. The advantage for the geologist is that the progressive shift of the short-wavelength peak and the main trough towards longer wavelengths corresponds to a transition from felsic to increasingly mafic minerals (Ch. 6).

In this region of the spectrum, various vibrational transitions in non-silicates produce spectral features that are different from those of silicates (Fig. 1.13). The most important are those associated with carbonates and iron oxides, which are so distinct that even small amounts of

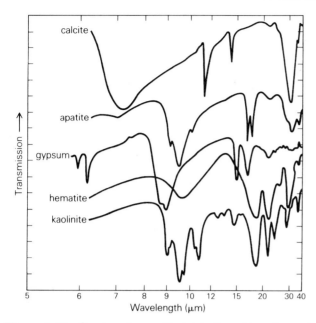

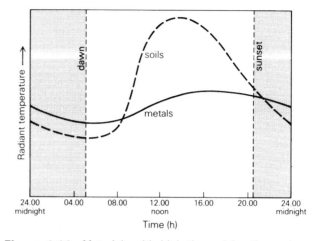

Figure 1.14 Materials with high thermal inertia, such as metals, show little range in diurnal temperature since they heat and cool slowly. Those like soils with low thermal inertia are prone to rapid heating and cooling, and so they reach high daytime and low night-time temperatures.

Figure 1.13 Spectra of non-silicates in the mid- or thermal-infrared part of the spectrum show completely different patterns of absorption features from silicates. They are also very different from one another, suggesting great potential for lithological discrimination by remote sensing of emitted thermal radiation. The spectra are offset for clarity.

these non-silicates in dominantly silicate rocks drastically alter their spectra. Indeed, limestones and ironstones should be easily distinguished from each other as well as from silicate rocks in this part of the spectrum.

The total energy emitted by rocks in the thermal infrared region is related to their temperature. By assuming the Stefan–Boltzmann law it is possible to calculate the **radiant temperature** of a surface from its total radiant emittance (Ch. 6). The temperature of a rock is contributed to by two sources of energy: the Earth's internal heat flow and solar energy absorbed during daytime. During a 24-hour cycle the temperature of the surface varies, heating to a maximum at the hottest part of the day and cooling by radiation to a minimum just before dawn (Fig. 1.14). The extremes and rates of this variation depend on a material's absorptance, transmittance and thermal capacity. These variables can be expressed empirically by thermal inertia, a measure of the time-dependent response of the material to temperature changes (Ch. 6). A rock with a high **thermal inertia** heats up and cools slowly, so showing a low range of diurnal temperatures. Those with low thermal inertia display large fluctuations during the 24-hour cycle.

At 300 K the Earth's surface emits radiation at wavelengths in the microwave region as well as infrared, albeit at intensities which decrease to very low levels as wavelength increases. Of this energy, that in the range 14 μm to 1 mm is mainly absorbed by the atmosphere. However, in the microwave region, to which the atmosphere is transparent, inten-

sities are still high enough to be measured by passive remote-sensing systems. A signal detected above the surface will include components emitted by the surface, emitted by the atmosphere and transmitted from below the surface. This last component is possible because rocks and soils have much larger transmittances at these wavelengths than they have in the visible and infrared parts of the spectrum. Thus passive microwave remote sensing is capable of providing information about buried materials as well as surface materials. Its potential use in geology is expanded in Chapter 7.

Rock spectra are composites of those of their constituent minerals. Depending on the structure and composition of these minerals, they may be detected if they are sufficiently abundant and their spectral features are strong enough. Discussion of rock spectra, their interpretation and uses is continued in later chapters.

1.3.3 Interaction of electromagnetic radiation with vegetation

Depending on the climate and whether soils are derived directly from underlying bedrock or have been transported, vegetation may show variations that relate to geology. Plants use solar energy to convert water and carbon dioxide to carbohydrate and oxygen through the process of photosynthesis. How they do this has a strong influence on their interaction with EMR. Being living organisms, their metabolism is strongly dependent on water-based vascular systems and cell structures. The abundance of water in their structure therefore controls these interactions too.

The catalyst for photosynthesis is the pigment chlorophyll, a complex of organic compounds containing iron. The function of chlorophyll is to absorb solar radiation and thereby fuel photosynthesis. This is achieved by absorption bands near 0.45 and 0.68 µm – in the blue and red parts of the visible spectrum (Fig. 1.15). That is why healthy leaves appear green. In addition to its absorption features, chlorophyll can be made to emit light, or **fluoresce**, in two narrow bands near 0.69 and 0.74 µm if illuminated with a strong beam of light, such as a laser. This is the basis of special laser remote-sensing techniques used to assess chlorophyll content of leaves or plankton. Chlorophyll, however, is unstable above certain temperatures. To protect it from thermal breakdown plants have evolved means of balancing energy. This is achieved by strong reflection of near-infrared radiation (Fig. 1.15), partly by shiny coatings to leaves, but mainly by the internal cells themselves. The structure of plant cells is such that up to 50% of incident, near-infrared radiation is reflected internally. The remainder is transmitted directly through the leaves. Water in the cells does absorb some energy at its characteristic overtones around 1.4 and 1.9 µm (Fig. 1.15), the absorptance depending on the proportion of cell water. Beyond about 2.0 µm leaves absorb near-infrared radiation.

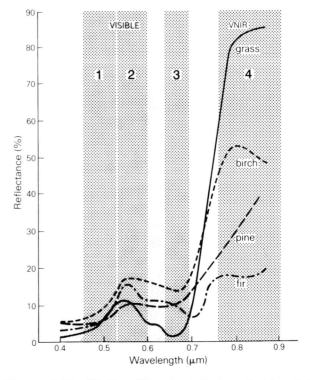

Figure 1.16 All the different attributes of chlorophyll content, leaf shape, area and number, together with overall plant structure, contribute to the spectral reflectance properties of a plant species. Whereas all four plants shown have rather similar properties in the visible spectrum, they are clearly distinguished by their near-infrared reflectance.

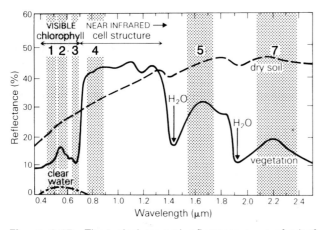

Figure 1.15 The typical spectral reflectance curve of a leaf shows the strong effect of absorption by chlorophyll in the visible part of the spectrum, the efficiency of reflection of near-infrared by its cells and the distinctive absorption features of water contained in its structure. Shown for comparison are spectra typical of soil and clear standing water.

The different cell structures, proportions of chlorophyll and other pigments, water content and surface morphology of different plants have a marked effect on their spectral properties in the visible to near-infrared spectrum. The spectral reflectance of vegetation increases very steeply with increasing wavelength between about 0.7 and 0.75 µm. This sharp change in spectral reflectance is sometimes known as the **red edge**. Figure 1.16 illustrates this effect for vegetation of different types. It is clear that not only does the height of the VNIR plateau depend on the species of plant responsible, but the exact position of the red edge

may vary according to plant type as well. These two factors can also vary within an individual plant species if the plants are under stress owing to deprivation of water or nutrients or poisoning by an excess of a toxic trace element such as chromium. Moreover, plants are assemblages of leaves, spaces, twigs and sometimes branches, with different leaf shapes and sizes and so on. All the individual interactions in such compound structure can interfere and further broaden the range of responses. This eases discrimination between species, and between healthy and stunted members of the same species.

Since organisms have life cycles of various durations, their spectral properties are not fixed. As a deciduous leaf matures before falling, its chlorophyll content decays away, removing the strong red absorption (Fig. 1.17). Consequently it changes colour from green through yellow to red. As cells shrink and dry they become less efficient at reflecting near-infrared. As leaves fall, progressively less of the plant intercepts solar radiation and the reflectance becomes dominated by the soil and leaf litter beneath it. When new leaves appear, near-infrared reflectance is well developed coupled with high yellow reflectance. As chlorophyll begins to be metabolized the blue and red absorption bands develop, until visible reflectance reaches a

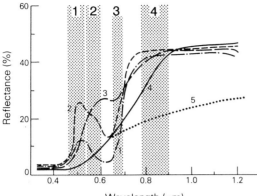

Figure 1.17 Spectra 1–5 show the progressive stages of colour change in beech leaves preceding autumn leaf fall, from dark green (1) through light yellow-green (2), orange-red (3), brown (4) and dead, dry leaves (5).

minimum at the height of the growing season. Coniferous trees do not shed their leaves during one season, and always display high chlorophyll abundances. However, since their leaves are small, less solar radiation is intercepted and so reflectance of the whole plant is lower than in deciduous trees in full leaf.

The response of vegetation in the thermal infrared is complex. Most of the energy absorbed at shorter wavelengths is re-emitted to maintain the energy balance. The radiant temperature of a plant can be as much as 10–15°C above air temperature during the daytime, and up to 5°C below at night. Plants also control their temperature by transpiration – the exhalation of moisture from pores on their leaves. Many factors play a role in determining the rate of **transpiration**: actual temperature, humidity, water supply to roots and light (which controls the opening and closing of pores). The use of emitted thermal infrared can therefore provide clues to many of these processes.

1.3.4 Interaction of electromagnetic radiation with water

Bodies of water have a rather different response to EMR than water bound up in the molecules of minerals. They do not exhibit the discrete vibrational transition bands so characteristic of molecular water. Instead, the spectral response curves show broad features (Fig. 1.15). In the visible range, the interactions depend on a variety of factors. Just considering reflectance properties, the amount of visible light reflected from a water surface depends on the illumination angle and the presence and nature of waves. In general, less than 5% of incident visible radiation is reflected by water.

Water has a high transmittance for all visible wavelengths, but it increases as wavelength decreases. As a result, in deep water only blue light penetrates beyond a certain depth, longer wavelengths having been absorbed at shallower levels. In clear water therefore, it is possible to estimate the depth from the intensity of visible radiation, particularly blue light, reflected from the bottom (*Fig. 1.18**). However, for depths greater than about 40 m, all visible radiation is absorbed and water bodies appear dark.

There is also a certain amount of scattering of light within water, which is responsible for the blue colour of clear water even when it is too deep to see to the bottom. There are two factors contributing to this effect: Rayleigh scattering ensures that short wavelengths are scattered more than longer ones, and the decrease in transmittance with increasing wavelength ensures that scattered blue light is unlikely to be absorbed before it escapes at the surface.

Suspended sediment, plankton and natural dyes, such as tannin from bogs, all increase the reflectance of visible light from water. Given the depth, it is thus possible to estimate the amount of suspended material in water from remotely sensed data.

In the near-infrared water acts almost like a perfect blackbody, and absorbs virtually all incident energy. It is the only natural material with this property, and so water bodies can easily be distinguished from other surface features in this part of the EMR spectrum, even if they are shallow or contain much suspended material.

Being a good approximation of a blackbody, water is a nearly perfect emitter of infrared radiation, as well as being a good absorber (Fig. 1.19). This means that measurements

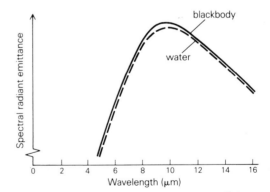

Figure 1.19 Experimental measurements of the spectral radiant emission of water reveal that it is a near-perfect blackbody. This ought to mean that measurements of energy emitted in the mid-infrared by water should give a true surface temperature. In practice, however, there are complications resulting from the chilling or warming effects of air on the surface film, so that only approximate, relative temperature measurements are possible.

*See note on page ix

of emitted infrared in the 8–14 µm region can be used to calculate the surface temperatures of water bodies very accurately.

The interaction of radiant energy with water held in the pore spaces of soils and rocks is controlled by a combination of the properties of water in bulk and those of molecular water. Pore water increases the absorptance of rock and soil, and so decreases their reflectance. Moist rocks and soils therefore appear darker than when they are dry. In the infrared, wet soil or rock displays in a muted fashion the reflectance troughs produced by vibrational transitions which are so distinct for minerals containing molecular water and for vegetation (Figures 1.8 and 1.15). In the thermal infrared region, the response of wet soil and rock is complicated by various environmental factors, such as wind cooling and humidity, in a fashion analogous to the effects of transpiration in plants.

Fresh *snow* is one of the most reflective natural surfaces at visible wavelengths, but in the near-infrared its reflectance decreases with the presence of some of the broad water vibrational features. As snow ages, it recrystallizes, forming larger crystals, and the effect of this is to reduce the reflectance, especially in the infrared. *Ice* has a similar spectral response, except that its visible reflectance is below 70%, but if it contains impurities (as in many glaciers) visible reflectance can be below 20%. Changes such as these in the spectral response of snow and ice as they recrystallize with age and incorporate impurities can be readily observed by remote sensing, and are useful in hydrological studies as well as in glaciology.

Further reading

The lists of recommended reading are not intended to be exhaustive bibliographies, but attempt to guide readers towards the most useful and up-to-date literature on a chapter-by-chapter basis. Each paper or book contains its own list of references, through which a more in-depth literature survey can be attempted. Examples have been taken from as many different parts of the world and as diverse a range of geological environments as possible. The bias towards those publications that highlight the role which remote sensing can play in geology and the exploration for and evaluation of the Earth's physical resources results from lack of space. Venturing into other applications areas, particularly those concerned with vegetation and geomorphology, can often reveal useful new approaches and unsuspected links. Remote sensing is not just a tool that happens to be useful to geologists, but increasingly plays a coordinating role in multidisciplinary studies that unify all aspects of the Earth's natural systems.

These references are the most important for expanding knowledge about the physics of remote sensing, in particular the spectral characteristics of Earth materials.

Bartholomew, M.J, A.B. Kahle and G. Hoover 1989. Infrared spectroscopy (2.3–20 µm) for the geological interpretation of remotely-sensed multispectral thermal infrared data. *Int. J. Remote Sens.* **10**, 529–544.

Hunt, G.R. 1977. Spectral signatures of particulate minerals in the visible and near-infrared. *Geophysics* **42**, 501–513.

Hunt, G.R. 1979. Near-infrared (1.3–2.4 µm) spectra of alteration minerals: potential for use in remote sensing. *Geophysics* **44**, 1974–1986.

Hunt, G.R. 1980. Electromagnetic radiation: the communication link in remote sensing. Chapter 2 in *Remote sensing in geology*, Siegal, B.S. and A.R. Gillespie (eds), pp. 91–115. New York: Wiley.

Hunt, G.R. and J.W. Salisbury, 1970. Visible and near-infrared spectra of minerals and rocks. I. Silicate minerals. *Modern Geology* **1**, 283–300.

Hunt, G.R. and J.W. Salisbury, 1971. Visible and near-infrared spectra of minerals and rocks. II. Carbonates. *Modern Geology* **2**, 23–30.

Hunt, G.R. and J.W. Salisbury, 1970. Visible and near-infrared spectra of minerals and rocks. III. Oxides and hydroxides. *Modern Geology* **2**, 195–205.

Lyon, R.J.P. 1965. Analysis of rocks by spectral infrared emission (18–25 microns). *Econ. Geol.* **60**, 715–736.

Lyon, R.J.P. 1972. Infrared spectral emittance in geologic mapping: airborne spectrometry data from Pisgah crater, CA. *Science* **175**, 985–985.

Milton, N.M. 1983. Use of reflectance spectra of native plant species for interpreting multispectral scanner data in the East Tintic Mountains, Utah. *Econ. Geol.* **78**, 761–769.

Milton, N.M., C.M. Ager, W. Collins and S.H. Chang 1989. Arsenic- and selenium-induced changes in spectral reflectance and morphology of soybean plants. *Remote Sens. Environ.* **30**, 263–269.

Smith, J.A. 1983. Matter–energy interaction in the optical region. Chapter 3 in *Manual of remote sensing*, 2nd edn, Colwell, R.N. (ed.), pp. 61–113. Falls Church, Virginia: American Society of Photogrammetry.

Suits, G.H. 1983. The nature of electromagnetic radiation. Chapter 2 in *Manual of remote sensing*, 2nd edn, Colwell, R.N. (ed.), pp. 37–60. Falls Church, Virginia: American Society of Photogrammetry.

Vincent, R.K., L.C. Rowan, R.E. Gillespie and C. Knapp 1975. Thermal infrared spectra and chemical analysis of twenty-six igneous rock samples. *Remote Sens. Environ.* **4**, 199–209.

| # *Human vision*

In the field or in the laboratory, geologists rarely use senses other than their sight. Even the surface texture of a rock or mineral is better defined by looking rather than by feeling. With the exception of distinguishing between silt and clay by the palatability test, preliminary classification of rocks and minerals is based on their appearance, either to the naked eye or with the aid of a petrological microscope. To delve much deeper needs purely artificial means – at the simplest by tests of hardness and at the extreme by using a mass spectrometer. Because of this, geologists have had to devise their own highly specialized jargon to organize the visible attributes of rocks. Given an understanding of how natural materials and EMR interact, it is no great hardship for geologists to use their well-practised visual capabilities in interpreting images. However, things are that much easier and more efficient if images are produced in a form which is attuned to the characteristics of human vision.

Of all the higher functions of animals, sight is the one with the longest evolutionary history. Although this is not the place to venture deeply into the processes of natural selection that have been involved in the development of vision, the survival advantages of being able to detect and estimate motion, distance and size, and to recognize shapes, patterns and colours, are fairly obvious. A curious thing about human vision is that, although the eye is physiologically capable of superb perception, it has remarkably little innate ability. From the immediate post-natal state of being able to recognize only crude face-shaped patterns, the diversity of human vision, its coordination with other functions and the intellectual capacity to analyse and describe the results are learned entirely through experience (Fig. 2.1). This means that thoroughly unfamiliar ways of displaying something, like the view vertically downwards from an aircraft or a representation of the way thermal infrared is emitted by an object, can only be interpreted through tuition, practice and the experience of success. It also means that tonal, textural and shape-related attributes of images, which in the normal course of life would be disregarded, can eventually be extracted efficiently from images, given motivation. In this chapter some of the functions of the human visual system are described in the context of remote sensing.

2.1 The eye and visual cortex

There are few fundamental differences between the optics of an eye and those of a camera. Both use a **lens** to form an inverted image on a light-sensitive surface. In the eye this surface – the **retina** – is a nearly spherical curved surface instead of a plane. The lens in an eye serves merely to adjust focus for objects at different distances and the main refraction is at the **cornea** (Fig. 2.2).

The diameter of the retina is about the same as the 24 mm width of 35-mm film, so the eye can be compared meaningfully with a 35-mm camera. The normal lens in that case has a focal length (f) of 50 mm. That of the eye is about 17 mm, producing a field of view of 180° compared with one of 50° for the camera. The curvature of the retina on which the image is focused compensates for the fish-eye

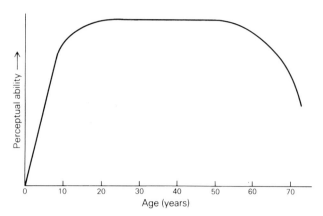

Figure 2.1 This schematic graph shows the relationship between perceptual ability and age. Most rapid development happens between birth and the age of eight. The ability of adults can be significantly changed by training and new experience.

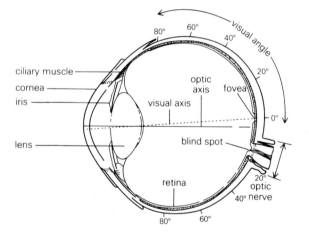

Figure 2.2 A cross-section of a human eye shows the main elements involved in the focusing of an image on the retina. The chambers in front of and behind the lens contain fluids with different refractive index. They perform most of the refraction in the eye. Muscles which change the shape and focal length of the lens are not shown.

distortion inherent in such wide-angle lenses. The range of distances in focus using a lens – the **depth of field** – varies inversely with the square of focal length, so the human eye has about nine times the depth of field of a normal camera at the same relative aperture. Rather than the eye elongating and contracting to focus objects at different distances, as happens with a camera, muscles attached to the lens change its thickness and therefore the overall focal length of the eye.

The amount of light gathered by the eye is controlled by the same mechanism as in a camera. The pupil diameter is changed by muscles in the iris over the range 2–8 mm. This corresponds to camera apertures of $f/8$ to $f/2$. This is a very limited range compared with a sophisticated camera. Pupil diameter also affects depth of field in much the same way as the aperture in a camera, and helps overcome optical aberrations, so improving image definition. However, not

only the intensity of light governs pupil size, but interest and mood too. The optimum for image interpretation is about 4 mm ($f/4$). The reader will be encouraged through some of the less stimulating aspects of image interpretation by the knowledge that this optimum can be achieved by occasional visual and, better still, physical contact with an attractive partner.

The retina is the eye's image-recording device, and again it has a photographic analogue. The grains of silver salts or photosensitive dyes in a film emulsion are represented by some 130 million light-sensitive **receptors** in the retina (Fig. 2.3). They are not immediately at the surface of the retina. To reach them light has to pass through several layers. The first is formed of optic nerve fibres, which gather to a bundle at the optic nerve (Fig. 2.2). The second is a network of blood vessels and **neural cells**, which perform some information processing. The receptors themselves are not distributed randomly, nor are they of one single type.

All receptors function through bleaching of a pigment when light is intercepted. This triggers a nerve signal and a simultaneous regeneration of the pigment. There are two kinds of receptor. Those equivalent to panchromatic film are known as **rods** because of their shape. They cover the whole retina, except for the point directly on the visual axis known as the **fovea**. Rods are most densely packed at about

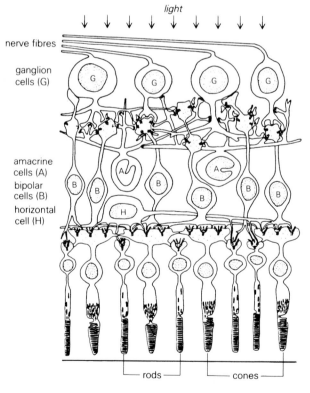

Figure 2.3 This simplified cross-section of the retina shows the two different types of receptor and a few of the complex neural connections between them.

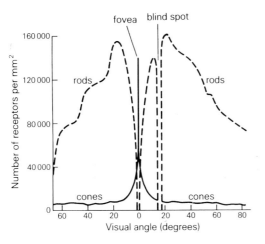

Figure 2.4 A plot of the density of receptors in the retina shows their uneven distribution, from a maximum around the fovea to a minimum at the periphery of vision.

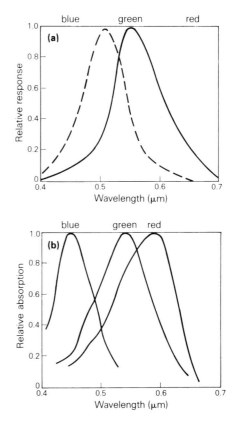

Figure 2.5 (a) The overall sensitivity of the eye peaks at different wavelengths for scotopic (dashed) and photopic vision. (b) The spectral absorption curves for the three different kinds of cone, normalized for comparison, show that two peak at blue and green but that normally associated with red light peaks at orange.

20° away from the fovea, and gradually fall off in number towards the edge of the retina. **Cones** contain three different kinds of pigment sensitive to red, green and blue light. They number only about 7 million, but are concentrated at and immediately around the fovea (Fig. 2.4), although there are some even in the outer area of the retina. At the point where the optic nerve leaves the eye there are neither rods nor cones (Fig. 2.4). This is known as the **blind spot**. It is rarely noticeable since the brain compensates for the discontinuity.

Rods cannot distinguish colours, and respond only to lightness. The peak of their sensitivity occurs in the blue part of the spectrum (Fig. 2.5), which happens to correspond with the wavelength of maximum atmospheric scattering. Rods are therefore sensitive to the component of surface illumination derived from the sky itself. They are more efficient than cones under conditions of low illumination, when their wavelength sensitivity comes into its own – at dusk and at night illumination is dominated by sky light. This **scotopic** or night vision only gives images of brightness which contain no colour. Blue objects are seen more clearly than red. Definition is also sacrificed in the same way as it is in a fast film. Vision under brighter conditions is described as **photopic**, and involves both rods and cones. The peak of sensitivity of cones and rods acting together in photopic vision is in the green part of the spectrum and corresponds to the maximum energy region in the solar spectrum (Fig. 1.5). The sensitivity curves for the three main types of cone are shown in Figure 2.5. Red and green are distinguished by cones only around the fovea, together with blue. Towards the periphery of vision only blue and yellow contribute to colour vision.

Motion or changes in lightness detected by rods on the periphery of vision signal the viewer to direct the foveal part of the retina towards the source of the change. It can then be examined in colour, with better resolution and with an element of information processing. The neurons, or nerve cells, in the retina can transmit impulses directly from the receptors to the visual cortex of the brain, and are in fact an integral part of the brain. Information processing begins on the retina itself. Neurons can inhibit or enhance the signals and also ignore them. In Figure 2.3 one kind of neuron (H) links many receptors, thus resulting in high sensitivity but low discrimination in the spatial domain or **acuity**. The same receptors are also connected through more specific neurons (B) for high acuity. Which of the alternative circuits is used by way of a switching mechanism depends on the stimulus itself and return signals from the visual cortex. Some of the connecting neurons respond only to specific shapes, orientations or directions of movement, based on assemblies of receptors forming a **receptive field**. When they are triggered they cause a specific cortical cell to fire.

The links between receptors, retinal neurons and cortical neural cells are grouped in circuits as **cell assemblies**. Every new visual experience excites a common core of neurons and in a sense imprints them with the experience. Exposure to a similar experience more easily re-excites the grouping and adds new neurons to broaden the experience. These imprinted neurons are sometimes unconnected with the visual cortex. For instance, exposure to a waterfall in real life imprints an assembly in the cortex based on neurons associated with visual, auditory and even tactile stimuli. Looking at an image of a waterfall later not only reactivates the visual neurons but can bring back the experience of the sounds and feel of falling water. There is nothing mystical in the feeling induced by a photograph or painting which so closely represents a waterfall that the observer can almost hear the roar and feel the spray. Producing such a response is an art, but has a base in natural phenomena in the brain as well as in the artist's ability to 'catch' the triggering mechanisms. In turn this is based on the artist's own experiences. In the same way experience of remotely sensed images is built up and art is employed in displaying them for best effect and easiest interpretation.

The memory involved is not sited in the brain alone. For simple shapes that build up alphanumeric characters, the basic features of a friend's face or familiar structures in rocks, the neurons on the retina have a memory capacity. Immediate recognition stems from this memory, but more complex analysis is performed in the visual cortex. A complex visual experience is built up in the visual cortex by the response of cortical neurons to particular stimulus patterns on the retina. Different cells respond to different categories of stimulus and each has its own receptive field on the retina. There are three types of receptive field and associated cortical cells. In the simple case a cell responds to a moving stimulus or a spot of light anywhere within the field, but is more responsive to a line or boundary parallel to the particular orientation of the cell's receptive field. **Simple cortical cells** are line or boundary detectors. **Complex cells** have larger receptive fields and can code directions of lines, boundaries and movements. **Hypercomplex cells** act as feature detectors for shapes made up of several lines or boundaries, such as the angle between two lines and the angular separation of two lines. They provide the information required in stereoscopic vision (Section 2.4). Acting together, the simple, complex and hypercomplex cells and their receptive fields provide all the information necessary for subconscious and conscious pattern recognition, so important in image interpretation. By the same token they also provide the conditions for optical illusions (Section 2.6), which can have an effect on image interpretation.

2.2 Spatial resolving power

The natural world is a continuum of matter in motion and cannot be broken into its constituent parts in isolation, except by abstract thought. This is expressed by the particle-wave duality of EMR, Heisenberg's principle of uncertainty and several other fundamental relationships. The human visual system produces an imperfect representation of the real world for a whole variety of reasons. Foremost amongst these is the way an image of reality is subdivided into small elements in terms of the spatial and tonal attributes of the natural continuum. Since the retina contains a mosaic of rods and cones, a continuous image falling onto it is recorded in the form of this mosaic. It is **dissected** into discrete packages. The unconscious scanning action of the eye and the aggregating function of the visual cortex smoothes out the discontinuities, so that the impression is of a smooth whole.

Every kind of artificial image is dissected too. It may be made up from brush strokes in a painting, of random grains of metallic silver in a photograph or the line raster of a television picture. Examining every half-tone and colour image in this book reveals them to be made up of assemblages of ink dots and spaces on the paper. As will be discussed in later chapters, dissection in a regular format is essential for the transmission and computer processing of many kinds of remotely sensed image. **Image dissection** by the visual system has an important bearing on what the human visual system can and cannot see.

Interpreting the spatial attributes of an image relies on a very complex series of interactions involving shapes, patterns, assemblages of tones and colours as different textures, the scale of the image and its context. This function is the most important in image interpretation. In many cases however, an image contains far more spatial information than the eye really needs in order to make a decision. A newspaper photograph of a pop star or a widely disliked politician contains between 250 000 and 1 million dots that are sufficient not only for instantaneous recognition but even to make the subject reasonably attractive. On the other hand, a skilled cartoonist or a mimic can reproduce instant recognition by a few sketched lines or suitably exaggerated grimaces. The newspaper image contains much **redundant** spatial information for the purpose of recognition. However, for the purpose of definite identification – the politician may easily have been substituted by a dummy – the image may not contain enough information. The question 'Is this the real Adolf Hitler or a rubber doll?' can only be resolved by more information about small physical characteristics, such as the presence of a mole or the precise geometry of a moustache.

For the sake of economy or convenience, many images have reduced spatial redundancy and attenuated tonal or colour redundancy (Section 2.3). For some interpretive purposes this makes little difference to the observer. Figure 2.6 shows an image taken from an aircraft that has been dissected to give different degrees of spatial redundancy. Some parts of the scene are recognizable on all images, others only appear in the least dissected image. Most observers will notice a jump in quality about halfway in the sequence, above which there is no clear improvement and

Figure 2.6 This series of images shows the appearance of the same data after dissection to component picture elements which increase in size on the ground from 10 m (a) through 20 (b), 30 (c), 40 (d) and 60 (e) to 80 m (f).

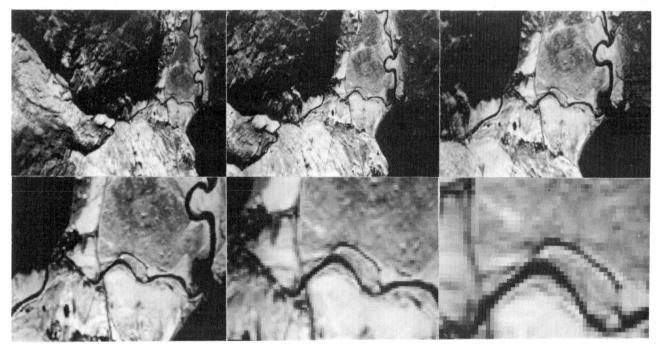

Figure 2.7 This series of images of the same data at progressively larger magnifications shows the breakdown in perceptual quality associated with the appearance of image dissection.

below which there is little apparent degradation. Viewing the images from increasing distances seems to cause the position of the transition to change, until all the images appear much the same. On the other hand, increasing the

magnification of a segmented image eventually results in the component parts interfering with the impression of the whole (Fig. 2.7). Below this magnification the elements are mentally fused into a coherent whole.

The chain of processes involved in visual interpretation of the spatial features of an image begins with **detection**. This is the near-threshold perception that something of interest exists in the image. Being able to define the position of this 'thing' is **localization**. **Recognition** that it is a particular category of 'thing', an automobile for example, and **identification** of its unique attributes – a 1969 VW Beetle with rusted fenders, driven by a friend – depends on observing increasingly intricate features of the object. This may not be possible if the scale of view is too small for the eye to resolve the component parts of the object on the retinal image. At too large a scale the image structure may dominate the view and destroy the visual form of the object. A view of only a few parts of the object in an unfamiliar context may also hinder recognition and identification.

The elements of image interpretation depend on the acuity of the visual system, mental fusion, the degree of dissection of the image, its scale, and on a combination of all these factors, which is expressed as resolution. Another, less well-defined, factor is the **context** of objects within the image.

The acuity of human vision is a measure of ability to distinguish spatial detail. It depends partly on factors inherent in the visual system and partly on purely external factors.

(a) Results from experiments depend to some extent on what the subject is called upon to do. Acuity is different for detecting the presence of a test object compared with discerning whether there is one object or two. Likewise, different results occur for localizing the position of the object, and for recognizing what it is.

(b) The polarity of the target also has an effect. Bright objects on a dark background are more easily detected than dark on light because scattering in the fluids within the eye broadens a bright stimulus.

(c) Contrast is important: a black object on a white ground is more easily detected than dark grey on light grey.

(d) If the pupil is dilated beyond the optimum of 4 mm, spherical and chromatic aberration in the eye degrades the retinal image. Constriction of the pupil results in degradation by diffraction.

(e) The eye takes time to adjust to changed illumination conditions, so there is a time-dependent effect on acuity.

(f) The illumination or overall brightness of an image has an effect depending on whether or not photopic vision is possible. Retinal rods have poor acuity compared with cones, and below a certain brightness they take over and scotopic vision is used. Very bright images degrade the acuity of cones as a result of glare.

(g) Under normal illumination conditions the colours in an image help determine acuity. It is higher for greens and yellows than for reds and blues. This is because of the increase in chromatic aberration in the eye at the two extremes of the visible spectrum.

Contrast is defined as the ratio of the difference between the brightness of an object and that of its surroundings to the sum of the two brightnesses, and is expressed as a percentage. The higher the contrast of an object, the more easily it is perceived. Moreover, there is a lower limit of contrast that the eye can deal with, around 0.5%. The effect of contrast is illustrated by Figure 2.8a, which illustrates the response of the eye to a point source of energy, such as a star. Although the real boundary between the point source and its background is sharp, the eye's response gradually changes with distance away from the point source, giving a bell-shaped curve termed the **point-spread function (PSF)**. The steeper the gradients involved in this curve, the more likely that the point will be perceived. The higher the contrast, the steeper are these gradients and vice versa, as shown respectively by the full and broken lines on Figure 2.8a. When the PSF is so smooth that variations are less than the lower limit of contrast perception, the point becomes invisible.

Detecting the presence of an object is one thing, but being able to distinguish between several is more important

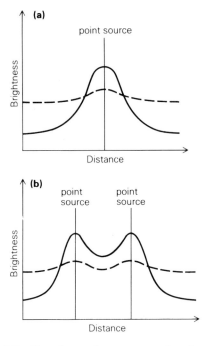

Figure 2.8 The change in response of an imaging system across a point source of energy produces a variation of image brightness with distance away from the point (a). This is known as the point-spread function or PSF. The more rapid the change away from the point to the level of the background, the better the resolution of the system. The rate of change with distance also depends on the ratio between the energy emitted by the point and by its surroundings. This ratio is the contrast. Low contrast and small brightness gradients (dashed lines) result in poorer resolution than high contrast with high gradients of brightness (solid lines). The two point sources in (b) can be resolved when contrast is high, but are barely distinguishable with low contrast.

for gathering detailed information. Figure 2.9c shows the response of the eye to two point sources. Where each has a high contrast, the response curve (full line) has a distinct saddle between the points, but for low contrast the saddle becomes much less marked (broken line). As the two points become closer the saddle becomes less marked, even at high contrast. The two points become inseparable when the contrast across the saddle falls below the lower limit of perception. So, the eye's PSF and the contrast control our ability to resolve separate objects.

An interesting series of experiments that are of direct relevance to image interpretation measured the response of the human visual system to targets on which simple spatial variations of brightness were shown. These consisted of regularly spaced spots and lines with different sizes and spacings. Some of the experiments were based on sharply bounded spots and lines, but the most informative approach involved objects whose brightness rose and fell in a sinusoidal fashion (Fig. 2.9a and b). A complete description of the target and the resulting image involves the direction, the wavelength or spatial frequency (the number of waves or

cycles per unit distance) and the amplitude (half the difference between the brightnesses at the peak and the trough of a wave). A measure of the accuracy of the detector, in this case the human eye, is the **modulation transfer function (MTF)**.

Modulation is the ratio of the amplitude of the response in the detector to that of the stimulus in the target. The MTF is a graph of modulation against spatial frequency. For a perfect detector the MTF is a horizontal straight line (Fig. 2.9c). A photograph records lower frequencies more faithfully than higher frequencies (Fig. 2.9c), the actual frequencies depending on the grain size of the film or paper. The MTF of the eye is different for coloured or chromatic images than for black and white or achromatic images (Fig. 2.9d). For frequencies lower than 2 cycles per degree at the retina (spacings in the image greater than about 0.2 mm) the **chromatic MTF** shows that the eye discriminates colour changes in space very well. This colour acuity drops rapidly for more closely spaced objects. However, the **achromatic MTF** shows a clear maximum of fidelity at around 7 cycles per degree (spacings in the image between 0.03 and

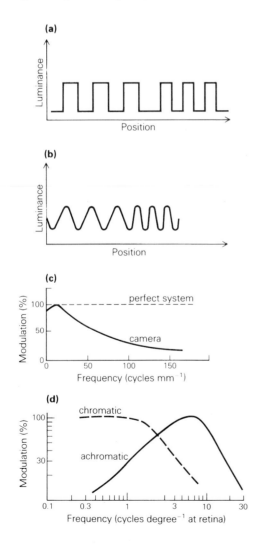

Figure 2.9 (a) The luminance across a bar target changes in abrupt steps. (b) A sine-wave target used in measuring modulation produces a gradual change in luminance with position. (c) The modulation transfer function of an optically perfect system (dashed line) correctly represents the amplitude of the target at all spatial frequencies. The MTF of a camera (solid line) only has high fidelity at low frequencies. (d) The chromatic and achromatic MTFs of the human visual system show different spatial frequency responses. The significance of the achromatic MTF can be checked with the test target (e) where frequency increases from left to right and contrast increases upwards.

0.06 mm). A black and white image is obviously better for analysing spatial detail. At higher spatial frequencies the modulation falls because of the physical size and distribution of receptors, and as a result of the blurring effect of unconscious eye movements. The fall at lower frequencies is explained below. In a sense therefore, when looking at black and white scenes, the eye performs as a **spatial frequency filter** (Ch. 5) and enhances frequencies around seven cycles per degree at the expense of others. It sorts the trees from the wood, but is unconcerned with the leaves.

Any image or natural scene can be regarded as, and indeed reconstructed from, a 'spectrum' of sine waves with different directions, wavelengths and amplitudes. Such a reconstruction is known as a **Fourier synthesis**, and the disassembly of an image into a family of sine waves is a **Fourier analysis** (Ch. 5). The spots, lines and bars which form the targets for tests of acuity, and form images too, are themselves made up of sine waves. Small dots and closely spaced lines are dominated by high amplitudes at high frequency. This is why they are difficult to discern. As size increases, high-frequency components become lower in amplitude and those in the frequency range to which the eye is attuned increase. Perception and distinction become easier. Beyond this, however, very low-frequency components increase in amplitude, effectively degrading perception and distinction.

The eye's MTF is of great importance in understanding what can be recognized in an image. It also demonstrates the potential power of artificially enhancing the spatial frequency distribution of brightness in an image (Ch. 5). Another instructive aspect is that, irrespective of the resolving power of an image-gathering device, the **scale** at which the image is presented is a crucial factor in interpretation. The retinal frequency (f cycles deg^{-1}) of features on an image is a function of image scale (1:S) and viewing distance (X m). The following equation relates these to spatial wavelength on the surface (λ m):

$$\lambda = SX\tan(1/f) \qquad (2.1)$$

The relationship in Equation 2.1, together with the effect of varying contrast, is of crucial importance in designing objective methods of image interpretation of different terrains. Even the best available image will have little effect on the limitations posed by the human MTF. To improve significantly the detail in an interpretation requires a dramatic increase in the scale. To examine very large features means an equally dramatic decrease in scale. As an example, for a black and white remotely sensed image at a scale of 1:500 000 being viewed from a distance of 1 m, features with dimensions of about 1.25 km on the ground will have most visual impact. Those with dimensions less than 0.5 km and more than 3.5 km will excite less than half the response in the human visual system. Therefore, for these purely physiological reasons, image interpretation is best achieved by combining images obtained from different

altitudes, whose degree of dissection need only be sufficient to avoid the obvious appearance of segmentation at the scale used (Figs. 2.6 and 2.7). Using a single image at different scales and viewing distances also helps extract more of the spatial information.

In practice, resolution combines the acuity of the eye with the resolving power of the imaging system, the means of reproduction, the scale of the image and the conditions under which it is viewed. It is defined as the ability to discriminate individuals in a set of small similar items. It is not really measurable in practice, being a threshold between can and cannot. Discrimination of objects is easier using a black and white image than with a colour image at the same scale.

There are some other interesting and useful features of the eye's performance in the spatial domain. First, lines can be separated more easily than points with the same width and spacing. This is because receptors are linked in arrays aimed at line detection. Second, it is easier to detect offsets in lines than to separate lines with a spacing equal to the offset. The absolute limits are 2 seconds of arc subtended at the eye for offsets and about a minute of arc for lines. The area on the retina with the greatest power for spatial resolution is near the fovea, where receptors are most densely packed. Optimum interpretation is, as a result, achieved by flicking direct attention from one part of an image to another.

2.3 Seeing brightness

The eye has a remarkable capacity for detecting light. In a darkened room a flash of light corresponding to 10 quanta absorbed by an area of retina containing about 500 rods can just be detected. This suggests that a single quantum has a realistic probability of exciting a single rod. However, a rod by itself cannot produce a sensible signal to the brain, but needs the simultaneous response of about 10 other rods. Curiously, this phenomenal detecting ability by no means enables the visual system to distinguish brightness variations in a continuous, quantum by quantum, fashion.

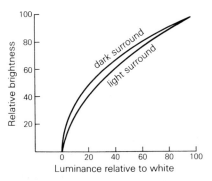

Figure 2.10 The relationship between the perceived brightness of a lamp and its luminance shows that the difference-detecting ability of the eye is non-linear.

Experiments on human light detection are based on the noticeability to an observer of changes in the **luminance** of a lamp or in those of sheets of exposed photographic paper with different grey tones. The term luminance is used to distinguish the objective measurement of the amount of light involved from the perceived brightness of a lamp and the lightness of a reflecting surface. One set of experiments shows that the difference-detecting capacity of the eye is non-linear (Fig. 2.10). The perceived brightness or lightness increases rapidly at low luminance and more slowly at higher luminances.

Another set of experiments focuses on the contrast-detecting powers of the eye. Contrast can have positive or negative values: dark object and light surround, and vice versa. For objects and surroundings with a large **visual angle** (the ratio between the dimensions of an object and its distance from the eye, expressed in radians) and high luminance, the minimum detectable contrast is 0.5%. This suggests that about 200 steps of contrast can be discriminated in a grey scale made up of sharply bounded luminances. This is very interesting. Although it is a phenomenal detector of light, the eye is not a good discriminator in terms of perceived brightness or lightness. In fact, as the visual angles of objects decrease to those most commonly found in images, the range of discernible contrast differences decreases to about 20–30 steps.

Returning for the moment to objects with large visual angles, it is interesting to note that contrast detection falls off towards lower luminances of object and surrounding. As a result the lightness perceived as the mid-tone of a sequence from black to high luminance in a grey scale is darker than the real mid-tone (Fig. 2.11). The perception of a grey tone also depends on whether the contrast is positive or negative. A grey patch on a black background appears lighter than an identical patch on a white background (Fig. 2.12a). The eye is thus capable of limited contrast enhancement. The reverse effect is produced when fine elements of black or white are introduced into a grey object (Fig. 2.12b). The poor performance of the eye with contrast differences is improved to some extent by a peculiar phenomenon associated with tonal boundaries. On Figure 2.11 narrow bands are seen immediately adjacent to the tone boundaries – light bands in the paler blocks and dark bands in the darker. Covering the adjacent blocks reveals that these **Mach bands** are illusory. Their effect is to enhance and sharpen tonal boundaries. When the boundary is covered it is difficult to distinguish the two adjacent grey tones.

Black and white photographs or television pictures can contain hundreds or thousands of discrete grey tones. The vast majority are redundant as far as an observer is concerned. If they are progressively reduced, little difference is noticed until the number falls below about 16 (Fig. 2.13). The obvious implication is that the tonal range of a black and white image can be severely truncated, without loss of interpretable information. This is in fact inevitable when high-quality photographs are screened before printing, and when limits have to be imposed on the tonal range of data gathered by digital remote-sensing systems for the sake of convenience and computing economy. However, the eye's limitations in the domain of grey tones is amply compensated for by its extraordinary efficiency in the colour domain.

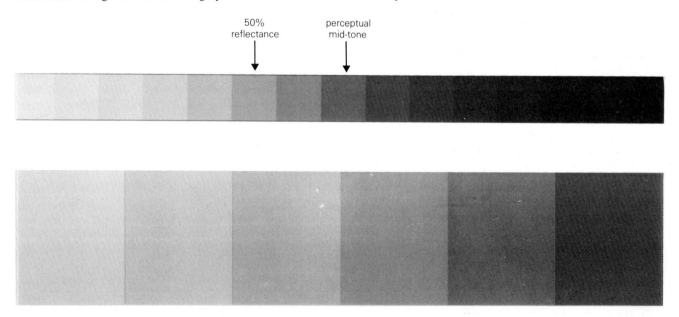

Figure 2.11 The observed midtone between black and white on a photographic grey scale (top) is in fact darker than a grey tone representing 50% reflectance. Another interesting optical enhancement is revealed by the apparent dark and bright lines slightly to each side of a boundary between grey tones (bottom). These Mach bands disappear when the boundary is covered and it is barely possible to separate the two adjacent grey tones.

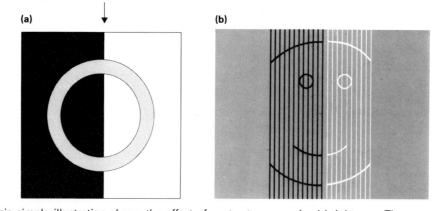

Figure 2.12 (a) This simple illustration shows the effect of contrast on perceived brightness. The grey circle appears darker against the white background. The effect is more pronounced if the vertical divide is masked with a pencil. (b) A uniform grey background appears lighter when partly filled with black lines and lighter when white lines are present.

Figure 2.13 In this series of photographs the same image is shown with 128, 64, 32, 16, 8 and 4 grey levels (from top left to bottom right) to show the futility of trying to perceive more than 20–30 grey tones distributed as small picture elements.

2.4 Producing, seeing and representing colour

Although visual perception is limited in practice to about 20–30 grey tones, the eye can easily distinguish a huge range of different colours. The limit is thought to be about 7 million. Colour dominates human vision. For this reason there is a long history of research into how colour is produced and perceived, enormous difficulty in truly cataloguing colours, and bitter controversy about the contribution of colour to aesthetics.

Thomas Young (1773–1829) – of Young's modulus and the wave theory of light – discovered that by projecting light through red, green and blue filters to produce overlapping circles several remarkable effects are produced.

First, where all three overlap – where the effects of all three add together – white light is produced. Since the spectrum of white light contains a continuum of colours, this was unexpected. Second, where two colours overlap, other colours are produced. For a red and blue mixture the resulting reddish-blue or magenta is predictable. So too is the production of cyan by an equal mixture of green and blue. The result of adding red and green is yellow, which has no red or green attributes at all. This is completely unexpected. By varying the relative luminosities of red, green and blue in the overlapping zone, Young was able to produce all the other spectral colours and many others too, such as brown and pastel shades. These phenomena are illustrated in *Figure 2.14*. Another of Young's observations

24

was that red, green or blue cannot be produced by mixtures of the other two. The three colours are so distributed in the visible spectrum as to be separate visual entities, and they are termed **additive primary colours**, because their effects result from addition. Other combinations of spectral colours also act as additive primaries, but only red, green and blue can produce the full range of colour sensations.

A complementary effect can be produced by subtracting red, green and blue components from white light, using filters. Subtraction of red produces cyan, white minus green gives magenta, and the result of subtracting blue is yellow. All three filters together transmit no light. Magenta plus yellow produces red, blue results from equally combined cyan and magenta, whereas yellow plus cyan transmits only green. Mixed combinations of all three **subtractive primary colours** with different luminances result in the whole gamut of colour sensations.

Additive primary colours are used in colour television screens coated with spots of red, green and blue phosphors. The subtractive primaries are used in colouring paints, in lithographic printing and in reversal colour film. However, the important point about primary colours, is not their usefulness or the physics involved, for the same effects are produced by broad spectral bands in filters as well as by truly monochromatic light. Colour is a product of cone receptors in the retina and the brain. Young did not know this, but he did realize that there must be a connection between his discovery and the way the eye works. He postulated a **tri-stimulus colour theory**, relating the three additive primaries to three different kinds of optical 'nerves'.

That cones have three ranges of sensitivity, peaking in red, green and blue (Fig. 2.15), was not demonstrated until 1964. But this does not explain all the oddities in full. When green is perceived through one eye at the same time as red is seen by the other, the sensation is yellow. This cannot be caused by the cones alone. For this reason, and several others, refinement of Young's hypothesis led to the assumption in the nineteenth century of three pairs of processes involving white–black, blue–yellow and red–green, in the **opponents colour theory**. This too has been confirmed by experiments, which suggest that signals from the cones to the brain take the form of one set encoding brightness signals from all three sets of cone and the rods, together with two sets relating to colour difference. The first of these weights the responses of red and blue cones and encodes their relative strengths. The other is a yellow versus blue signal carrying information from the blue cones and deriving yellow information from the red and green cones. The present consensus is that both the tristimulus and opponents processes are involved. Independent research on the transmission of colour television signals showed that the most convenient method involves a luminance signal and red–green and blue–yellow signals. These are converted in the television to red, green and blue

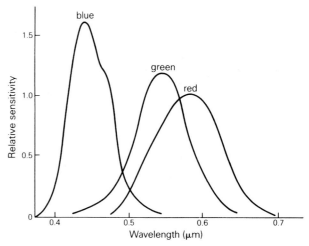

Figure 2.15 The three types of cone show different spectral sensitivity curves. Although the overall sensitivity for photopic vision peaks in the green, blue cones are most sensitive. This compensates for the smaller number of blue-sensitive cones in the retina.

controls of the electron streams emitted by guns focused on the three sets of different phosphors on the screen.

As if this were not sufficiently complex, the visual response to colour has many other peculiarities, some of which are significant to the interpretation of colour images. Some are physiological, others are entirely psychological.

Figure 2.12 showed that perception of brightness is altered by the contrast between an object and its surroundings. Very similar effects occur when identical colour patches are placed on light or dark backgrounds, or on differently coloured backgrounds. Not only are the apparent brightnesses different, the perceived colours are different too. This effect is physiological. A psychological effect also governs how colours are remembered. In general, light colours are remembered as lighter and dark colours as darker. Impure colours, such as brown, reddish-yellow and bluish-green, are remembered as being more strongly tinted by the dominant primary, and are interpreted as more red, yellow or green respectively. Memories of colour images are more vivid and simpler than reality.

Learning by experience and with guidance provides an association of colours with familiar objects, any perceived deviations from this being disturbing. Pale-blue skin, purple bananas and green meat are not attractive. The influence of learned associations is so strong that with lists of names of colours printed in the 'wrong' colours it is almost impossible to identify the colours used without some confusion. Remote sensing covers a wide spectral range in which the reflectance or emittance characteristics of familiar materials deviate from those in the visible range (Section 1.3). Images produced by assigning data from non-visible bands to red, green and blue give a totally 'false' impression. A common example is where near-infrared data are assigned to red, red data to green and green to blue. The appearance of vegetation in various shades of red is aesthetically disturbing. However, from an objective standpoint it is much more useful than a pleasing natural colour image, because of the great variation of infrared reflectance among plants (Section 1.3.3). If the information contained in EMR outside the visible range is to be exploited, this **visual dissonance** must be overcome by practice.

Psychophysiology may be the main control over the interpretation of and information extraction from colour images, but it is conditioned by the individual's sense of aesthetics. As a general rule, the most pleasing image is often the most suitable to work with. Human aesthetics is exceedingly curious. Our home planet Earth is regarded as a beautiful and stimulating environment, for the most part at least. The human visual system evolved in this environment. Considered objectively though, it is not particularly colourful. A vast proportion comprises shades of blues, greens, greys and browns. The full capacity of colour vision is reserved for only a tiny volume of flowers, fruits and animals in the natural world. In human society, development of aesthetics out of natural experience exercizes colour vision much further through art, clothing, furnishings and cosmetics. A few guidelines can be abstracted from this controversial area:

(a) Many people label some colours as 'warm' and others as 'cool', associated with fire or sunlight, and foliage and water respectively. There is a general preference for 'warm' colours.

(b) Given a choice of six spectral colours, experiments show that there is a clear order of preference from most liked to least liked of blue, red, green, violet, orange and yellow.

(c) For any given colour there seems to be a preference for a lightness that corresponds with the relative lightness of the colour in the spectrum – light yellow is preferred to dark yellow, but dark reds and blues seem more pleasing than light shades.

(d) How colours are arranged relative to one another in the spectrum appears to govern perceptual harmony. If they are arranged in a circle, adjacent colours, like yellow and green, or violet and red, harmonize well. So too do diametrically opposite colours, such as yellow and blue. Greatest clash is between combinations of red and yellow–green, for instance, that are about 90° apart.

(e) Different colours harmonize best when they are equally light and dark, or have the same saturation with a spectral colour.

It cannot be overemphasized that the pleasingness of a colour image varies widely from person to person. However, these general rules of thumb, governed by personal foibles, can be used to arrive at the most stimulating and most easily interpreted images of remotely sensed data. Although a certain amount of 'matching' to personality and

mood can be achieved during photographic processing, the ultimate depends on the control possible with image-processing computers (Ch. 5).

The enormous range of humanly sensible colours poses an immediate problem of nomenclature, measurement and cataloguing. Means of satisfying these requirements are necessary for many practical reasons as well as for teaching and research. The major step in systematizing colour was made by Albert Munsell in 1905, when he tried to produce a colour atlas. The system he devised (the **Munsell system**) is based on subjective comparison, but contains the elements of all subsequent objective systems.

Any coloured surface appears to have an attribute related to one of the spectral colours or to non-spectral purple. Munsell designated this the **hue** of the surface. His system has five principal hues – blue, green, yellow, red and purple or B, G, Y, R and P – and five intermediate hues, BG, GY, YR, RP and PB. These 10 hues are arranged in a colour circle so that the apparent differences in hue between adjacent surfaces are constant. The 10 segments are divided into 10 subdivisions, to give a useful range of 100 hues. A hue coded as 10GY is five steps from green–yellow (5GY) towards pure green (5G) (Fig. 2.16).

Any coloured surface has a luminosity equivalent to a shade of grey between black and white. This is referred to as its **Munsell value**, and ranges from 1 (black) to 10 (white). Colours also appear to be a mixture of a grey and a pure hue. A hue that contains no grey component is said to be **saturated**, and it possesses a high **chroma**. One with a high grey component has a low chroma. The chroma scale in the Munsell system ranges from 0 for achromatic greys to 16 or 17 for the highest conceivable saturation. As Munsell value decreases, so the number of discernible chromas decreases. The Munsell system is therefore three-dimensional, as shown in Figure 2.16, but occupies an irregular solid. This is because it is based on human perception of colour, which is

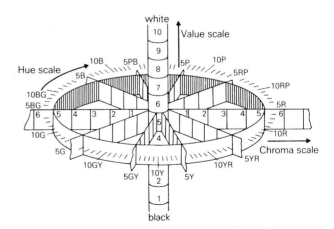

Figure 2.16 A schematic representation of the axes used by Munsell in devising his *Book of colour* shows the divisions that he used for hue, chroma and value. The value axis is a grey scale.

not regular. However imperfect it might be, it is still the only internationally accepted standard for visual comparison. It is used by soil scientists, textile and paint manufacturers, and many other groups.

In 1931 the Commission Internationale de l'Éclairage (CIE) produced the nearest approach yet to an objective means of describing and measuring colour. The **CIE colour coordinate system** is based on a tristimulus set of co-ordinates, in which the three primary colours are imaginary, yet produce a colour space which contains all perceptible colours. The CIE primaries stem from the real primaries red, green and blue. In the same way as all spectral colours can be made from different proportions of monochromatic red, green and blue light, it is possible to express the CIE tristimulus values involved in producing any monochromatic colour by three interfering curves shown in Figure 2.17a. For light with equal luminance at any visible wavelength the contributing tristimulus values can be read from the graph. These are divided by their sum to give three **chromaticity coordinates**, x, y and z. These coordinates sum to 1.0, so any colour can be specified by two coordinates and a value for the luminance. Coordinates x and y are plotted, all perceivable colours being contained within the curved line shown on Figure 2.17b. The numbered section of the line refers to saturated monochromatic light from violet (0.38 μm) to red (0.65 μm). The straight base of the enclosed area represents non-spectral purples.

There are two difficulties with the CIE chromaticity diagram. First, equally perceived differences in colour are not represented linearly. Second, it represents idealized conditions. How the chromaticity coordinates of samples are measured to classify materials in this system are beyond the scope of the book.

Various attempts have been made to simplify the Munsell and CIE systems, as aids to expressing remotely sensed data in the most visually stimulating way possible, with the least expenditure of computing time. One method has received particular attention. This simplifies the Munsell system to three measures of colour – **hue**, **saturation** and **intensity**. These approximate Munsell's hue, chroma and value in a conical colour space derived mathematically from red–green–blue colour space, which is amenable to very interesting means of enhancing colour and combining unrelated types of data. It is discussed further in Chapter 5.

2.5 Perception of depth

After colour vision, the most important aspect of the human visual system is based on the fact that it is binocular. A visible object subtends a perceptible angle at the retina of one eye which depends on the physical size of the object and its distance from the eye. Knowing the size of a familiar object allows the brain to estimate roughly how far away it is. For normally sighted people the fact that an image is focused on the retinae of both eyes enables them to receive a more exact impression of the position of the object in three dimensions. The fundamental reason for this is the 6–7 cm horizontal separation of the eyes, known as the **eye base**.

Rays extending from a point on an object to the eyes are separated by an angle which decreases as the distance of the object increases (Fig. 2.18). The angle in radians is approximated by the ratio between the eye base and the

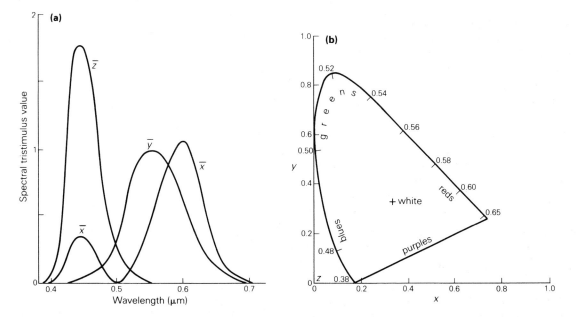

Figure 2.17 (a) These curves represent the variation with wavelength of tristimulus values for the imaginary primaries used in constructing the CIE chromaticity diagram. (b) The CIE chromaticity diagram is based on plots of the tristimulus values x and y in (a) for any given luminosity.

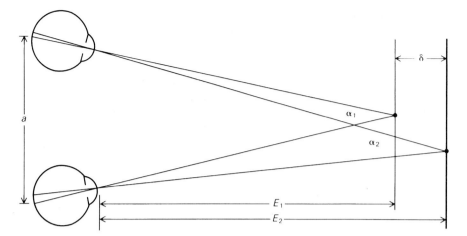

Figure 2.18 Points on two objects at different distances have different absolute parallaxes – a_1 and a_2 – measured in radians as a/E. The relative parallax is the difference between the two angles.

distance to the object. It is called the **absolute parallax** and is the angle at which the eyes must be converged to focus the point at or near the fovea. The two images are mentally fused, the outcome being a **stereomodel** of the location of the object in three dimensions. Because the retina can only resolve angular separations greater than about 1 minute of arc, there is a limit to **stereoptic vision**.

If a pencil is held at about 30 cm away, in front of a more distant object, alternate winking of each eye gives the familiar impression that the pencil moves relative to the distant object. Holding the pencil at arm's length reduces the apparent displacement. Alternately focusing on the pencil and the distant object with both eyes gives the stereoptic impression that the two objects are indeed separate distances away. With one of the objects stereoptically fused, the points of focus of each object are displaced on the retina. This is why two images of the distant object are observed when the pencil is in focus at the fovea. Figure 2.18 shows that the image of the more distant object falls further from the fovea in the right eye than it does in the left eye. To focus the distant object at the fovea requires a change in the angle of convergence. The difference between the two angles of convergence is the **relative parallax** of the two objects. It is this difference in parallax which is the most important stimulus for depth perception in the nearby environment. As

in the case of estimation of distance, it can only function for angles greater than 1 minute of arc. Binocular **stereopsis** is the basis for three-dimensional viewing of pairs of remotely sensed images in which large relative parallaxes are produced by the method of capturing images. This is explained in Appendix A, and used extensively throughout the rest of the book.

Because of the limited angular resolving power of the eye, beyond about 400 m objects are not seen stereoptically. Distance is estimated from various factors, such as the expected sizes of familiar objects, perspective effects and the decrease in luminosity caused by increasing absorption and scattering in the atmosphere. (As an aside, the absence of this last factor is responsible for the 'unreal' appearance of photographs taken on the Moon, where there is no decrease in luminosity of objects with distance.) Since most remotely sensed images represent a view from vertically above the Earth's surface, many inherent means of depth perception are of little use. One that is important is the interpretation of shadows – or misinterpretation of naturally dark surfaces – according to psychological rules that have evolved in the human visual system.

Shadows only result when illumination is from the side of an object. Much of the texture in a view of the Earth's surface results from shadows cast by hills into valleys.

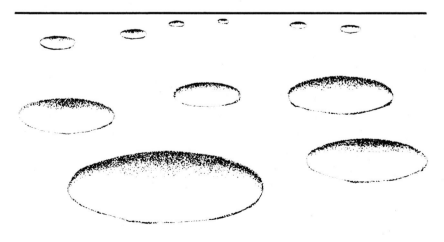

Figure 2.19 Adding crescentic shading to ellipses can create the impression of depth. Viewed this way up the ellipses appear as craters. Viewed from the top of the page they seem to be rounded hills. Viewed along the page they appear confusing because of the added effect of perspective employed in the drawing.

Shadows give a very real impression of depth, but unless the direction of illumination is known the impression is ambiguous. Figure 2.19 contains perspective clues suggesting an oblique view of a landscape with circular features. Most observers will interpret the features as craters in the surface. Inverting the figure gives the opposite impression. Staring at the figure rotated through 90° for a while enables both alternatives to seem possible, although for most of the time no depth is seen. Two interesting observations can be made. In the last experiment the perspective effect, the shading and the strange orientation of the 'horizon' cause visual dissonance. The first two experiments, however, suggest that there is a subconscious assumption that illumination is from the top of the figure. Strangely, an even more convincing illusion of depth results from oblique shading. Cartographers have long exploited this by shading contoured topographic maps as if they were illuminated from the top left, or NW. Remotely sensed images usually show no perspective, and shadows allow a moderately good impression of topographic relief. However, many of the examples in later chapters can show both 'positive' and 'negative' topographies, depending on how they are viewed. In images from satellites, such as Landsat or SPOT (Ch. 3), the time of capture is mid-morning with illumination from the SE in the northern hemisphere. This invariably gives the illusion of inverted relief in correctly oriented images.

2.6 Dangerous illusions

As well as the pseudostereoscopic tricks that shadowed images can play on the observer, certain aspects of the visual system's handling of spatial information can cause problems in image interpretation. There are hundreds of more or less well-known optical illusions and artistic tricks, which are discussed in most textbooks on human vision. Most are based on fairly simple, sharply outlined geometric figures. Remotely sensed images are infinitely more complex, but the peculiarities of vision involved in illusion may still play a role. As described in Section 2.1, simple, complex and hypercomplex receptive fields in the visual cortex perform the useful tasks of detecting lines, orientations and angles. They help link together disparate parts of an image, thereby enabling its component objects to be interpreted. Artists have known for millennia that human vision has a predilection for triangles and slanted lines, and incorporate them in paintings to add dynamism. For the world of the familiar this is fine. However, the eye can invent lines. It can also link separate points in smooth curves, and is prone to sensing the unfamiliar hidden in a familiar background – as children, we have all stared at complicated wallpaper and seen dreadful beasts lurking therein. Similar phantasms lie in wait for the unwary image interpreter.

Remotely sensed images are, by and large, less familiar than images of immediate surroundings. They contain information relating to the unknown, or at least the partly known. The positions from which they are acquired are totally outside normal human experience. Many of them relate to invisible parts of the spectrum. All contain a huge variety of detail, with both organized and random elements, and there lies the main source of illusions. The human visual system can assist in abstracting meaningful spatial information, but it can also overestimate the importance of those kinds of features – lines in particular – to which it is attuned. Moreover, there are suspicions that any interpreter perceives regular geometric patterns in objectively homogeneous images. Little research has been done in this area. That which has been published seems to indicate that the same image excites different responses in the spatial domain for different interpreters. Real features may be there, but some of those identified by the different subjects are probably spurious. All these factors must be borne in mind during photogeological interpretation of images (Ch. 4).

Further reading

References to the psychophysiology of vision, so important in presenting data as images for visual interpretation, are replete within the fields of psychology. Many are difficult to understand or contain only small sections of direct relevance here. The references that follow are useful guides.

Buchanan, M.D. 1979. Effective utilization of colour in multidimensional data presentation. *Proc. Soc. Photo. Opt. Instrument Eng.* **199**, 9–19.

Burns, K.L. and G.H. Brown 1978. The human perception of geological lineaments and other discrete features in remote sensing imagery: signal strength, noise levels and quality. *Remote Sens. Environ.* **7**, 163–167.

Burns, K.L., J. Sheperd and M. Berman 1976. Reproducibility of geological lineaments and other discrete features interpreted from imagery: measurement by a coefficient of association. *Remote Sens. Environ.* **5**, 267–301.

Cañas, A. A.D. and M.E. Barnett 1985. The generation and interpretation of false-colour principal component images. *Int. J. Remote Sens.* **6**, 867–881.

Cornsweet, T.N. 1970. *Visual perception.* New York: Academic Press.

Padgham, C.A. and J.E. Saunders 1975. *The perception of light and colour.* London: G. Bell & Sons.

Siegal, B.S. 1977. Significance of operator variation and the angle of illumination in lineament analysis on synoptic images. *Modern Geology* **6**, 75–85.

Stroebel, L., H. Todd and R. Zakia 1980. *Visual concepts for photographers.* London: Focal Press.

Wise, D.U. 1982. Linesmanship and the practice of linear geo-art. *Geol. Soc. Am. Bull.* **93**, 886–888.

CHAPTER THREE

How data are collected

Until relatively recently, most remotely sensed images used by geologists were acquired by photographic techniques. New data-gathering methods have developed rapidly for two main reasons. First, the increased emphasis on planetary monitoring by unmanned satellites and probes meant that it was impossible to retrieve film, except by costly return and re-entry manoeuvres. This demanded systems which would transmit data by microwave telemetry. Second, ventures into that part of the EMR spectrum where film will not respond required the development of new kinds of instruments based on electronic systems. Some of them, like television cameras, collect and transmit images which correspond to a 'snap shot'. They consist of representations of the intensity variations in a scene in the form of modulated radio signals. The signals are continuous and produce pictures which are described as analogue images. Photographs are one form of analogue image.

Other systems gather data as a sequence of small parcels of a scene. The sequence of data is reconstructed later to form a picture. For obvious reasons, the parcels are known as picture elements, or **pixels**. The intensities for each individual pixel are first expressed in analogue form as electrical potentials produced in a radiation detector by photons. However, precise analogue measurements, like 1.763 mV, are cumbersome to transmit back to the user. It is more efficient to rescale these numbers and transmit them as integers, or **digital numbers (DN)**. Transmission is easiest when numbers are in **binary** form. In binary arithmetic, any digital number can be expressed as a string of zeroes and ones, or 'offs' and 'ons'. The most commonly used range has eight binary **bits** (a binary bit is a single 'on' or 'off' – 1 or 0 – in a binary number) or one **byte**, representing a range of intensities by digital numbers from 0 (00000000 in binary) to 255 (01111111). As well as being simple to transmit, data in binary form are the numbers which computers were designed to manipulate. They are therefore ready for digital image processing, giving potentially enormous interpretive power to the user (Ch. 5).

All these recent developments do not imply that aerial or satellite photography has been completely superseded. There are vast archives of systematically gathered photographs, and they will continue to grow since photographs are easily and cheaply taken and are simple to use. Moreover, they represent fine spatial detail better than any existing or planned digital system. Interpretation of aerial photography forms the basis for geological analysis of all other forms of imagery. Chapter 4 focuses on photogeology as an introduction to the interpretation of other kinds of image.

In this chapter, Sections 3.1 to 3.9 outline the principles and techniques for each major method of data gathering used in remote sensing. Section 3.10 gives information about the different platforms from which images have been acquired and the characteristics of the images themselves.

3.1 Photography

The earliest means of remote sensing, photography, is also the most enduring and still plays the most important role in

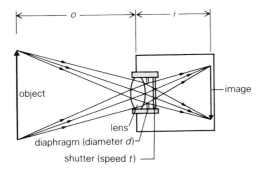

Figure 3.1 Refraction by the glass in a lens enables rays from an object to be focused on film through a much larger aperture than would be possible with a primitive pin-hole camera. More energy is available to sensitize the film and so exposure time can be much shorter. Moreover, the aperture and exposure time can be varied using an iris diaphragm and a timed shutter. These further refine the flexibility of a lens camera, as does the provision of films with different speeds or sensitivities to light.

geological applications. Of all methods of gathering data from a distance it is by far the simplest. All that is required is a lightproof box, a lens and shutter system, and film coated with an emulsion sensitive to EMR.

In a camera, radiation emanating from an object is refracted by the lens to form an inverted image on the film (Fig. 3.1). The most important attributes of the lens are its **focal length** and its diameter or **aperture**. The aperture may be varied using a diaphragm, and controls the radiation-gathering capacity of the lens. How much radiation falls on the film is also governed by the **speed** of the shutter – the length of time the film is exposed. All cameras have shutter speeds in a conventional sequence of fractions of a second, decreasing by factors of two – 1/2, 1/4, 1/8...1/250, 1/500, 1/1000. The energy E falling on the film during exposure is given by:

$$E = sd^2t/4f^2 \qquad (3.1)$$

where s is the radiant energy of the scene in $W\,mm^{-1}\,s^{-1}$, d the aperture in mm, t the exposure time in seconds and f the focal length of the lens in mm. Only t and d may be varied on the camera. The aperture is expressed conventionally as the ratio between focal length and aperture diameter, known as **f-stop**. It is arranged in a sequence of fixed settings that complement the shutter speed, so that a range of combinations of speed and aperture giving identical exposure of the film to radiant energy can be chosen. Since the energy is inversely proportional to the square of the f-stop, to achieve this a halving of exposure time must be matched by an increase in f-stop of $\sqrt{2}$, or 1.4 times. F-stops are then in the order $\sqrt{2}$, 2, $2\sqrt{2}$, 2^2 or $f/1.4$, $f/2$, $f/2.8$, $f/4$, familiar to all photographers.

In a normal camera, objects at different distances o must be focused on the film by changing the distance from lens to film i, governed by the relationship:

$$1/\text{focal length} = 1/o + 1/i \qquad (3.2)$$

In remote sensing, o is of course such a large distance that focusing is unnecessary, the film being located at the focal plane of a fixed lens system.

In all remote-sensing systems, two attributes are paramount: the minimum energy and the smallest object that can be detected on an image. The two are interrelated. The minimum separation between two objects at which they can be distinguished – usually after enlargement – is the **spatial resolution**. It is often described by the largest number of lines per millimetre that can be seen in the image, which can be related to dimensions on the ground using the optical geometry of the system. The faster the film, the coarser the resolution, and commonly used film ranges from ISO 8 to 640, with resolutions from 250 to 25 lines mm^{-1}, which correspond to ground resolutions of 6–60 cm at an image scale of 1:15 000. In practice spatial resolution is rated using test charts with high-contrast dark and light lines at different spacings. A better measure is the system's response to a point source of energy, like a star. This will be blurred and spread out to a greater or lesser extent, forming a pattern known as the point-spread function (Section 2.2, Fig. 2.8).

In photographs limits on resolution are posed by the quality and size of the lens, and are affected by defects such as spherical and chromatic aberration. Both affect the sharpness of focusing. Chromatic aberration results from the variation of refractive index and therefore focal length of lenses according to the wavelength of radiation. It produces different focusing of the component radiation on the film, so giving blurring. The film itself is coated with grains of photosensitive chemicals in an emulsion, the size of the grains varying with the speed of the film. A fast film has coarser grains and lower resolving power than fine-grained, slow film, but is able to record lower energies at a particular shutter speed and f-stop. Because fast film is more sensitive, there must be a trade-off between resolving power and detecting power.

Details of film design and processing technology can be found in the Further Reading for this chapter. Only the bare bones are given here, relating to spectral sensitivity of film and the properties of filters.

Black and white film depends on the photosensitivity of silver salts. When a photon strikes a grain in the film an electron is freed from the silver salt lattice. It migrates until it lodges at a defect in the lattice, where it converts a silver ion into a metallic silver atom. This triggers a chain reaction converting all silver ions in the grain into metal. The larger the grain, the greater the chance of an encounter with a photon, hence the reason fast films have coarser grain than slow films. Developing dissolves away the unconverted silver salt leaving a negative image of black silver grains, whose density represents the energy distribution falling on the film. Printing is the reverse of this process.

There are two main types of black and white film used in remote sensing, those sensitive to EMR with wavelengths

31

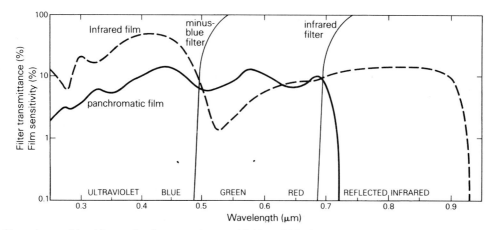

Figure 3.2 There is considerable overlap between the sensitivities of black and white panchromatic films and those sensitive to reflected infrared. To remove the swamping effect of scattering in the blue part of the spectrum, panchromatic film used in remote sensing is generally exposed through a yellow, or 'minus-blue' filter. This only transmits wavelengths to the right of its transmittance curve. To remove the effects of reflected visible radiation, infrared film is exposed through a dark-red filter.

up to 0.7 µm, covering the whole visible part of the spectrum – **panchromatic** – and those whose sensitivity extends to about 0.9 µm, including part of the near-infrared (Fig. 3.2). **Infrared-sensitive film** was originally devised as a means of distinguishing between vegetation, which strongly reflects VNIR radiation (Section 1.3.3), and green camouflage netting or paint, which does not.

As explained in Section 1.3.1, the blue end of the spectrum is dominated by atmospheric scattering and haze. To improve the contrast of panchromatic photographs they are normally exposed through a yellow, blue-absorbing filter, and are known as **minus-blue photographs**. Similarly, to reduce the effects of visible light, infrared film is usually exposed through a dark-red filter (Fig. 3.2), which absorbs blue and green light. Examples of both types of image are shown in Figure 3.3.

Whereas the human eye and colour television operate with additive primary colours – red, green and blue – colour film employs subtractive colour, for which the primaries are magenta, yellow and cyan (Section 2.4). Each results from subtracting one of the additive primaries from white light. A yellow filter subtracts blue, magenta subtracts green and cyan subtracts red. In colour positive film there are three layers of emulsion which are sensitive to blue, green and red light (Fig. 3.4a). When developed these emulsions retain yellow, magenta and cyan dyes respectively, in inverse proportion to the amounts of blue, green and red light to which they have been exposed. White light passing through the developed film has its primary additive colours filtered by the dye layers to produce a positive colour image. As an example, developing a film which has been exposed to blue light bleaches the yellow layer completely but does not affect the magenta and cyan layers. These layers filter out green and red from white light

transmitted through the film, leaving only the blue component.

Colour infrared film also includes yellow, magenta and cyan dye layers, but each has a different sensitivity compared with normal colour film (Fig. 3.4b). In this case all the layers are sensitive to blue light, as well as to green, red and near-infrared respectively. To remove the swamping effect of blue, a blue-absorbing yellow filter is placed in front of the lens.

The appearance of natural colour photographs needs no amplification here, except to mention that their fidelity may vary with different proprietary materials and developing processes. Colour infrared photographs however, express infrared, red and green radiation as red, green and blue respectively, and so have an unusual appearance (*Fig. 3.5*). They are examples of what are termed **false-colour images**. In their case, vegetation which reflects VNIR strongly and absorbs a high proportion of visible light appears as various shades of red and magenta. Red materials, such as hematite-stained sand, reflect infrared strongly too. The combination of weak blue, intense green and intense red in the false colour image imparts a yellow or orange tint (Section 2.4). Since water absorbs infrared totally, damp soil frequently appears in blue or cyan hues (*Fig. 3.5*).

The interpretation of panchromatic, infrared, natural colour and false colour photographs forms an important topic in later chapters. Here it must be emphasized that they are limited to that part of the spectrum with wavelengths shorter than 0.9 µm. Investigation of longer wavelengths requires electronic image-gathering devices. However, before discussing these it is necessary to introduce some of the geometrical attributes of photographs.

Photographs of the Earth's surface may be taken from any angle, but the most useful are those taken looking

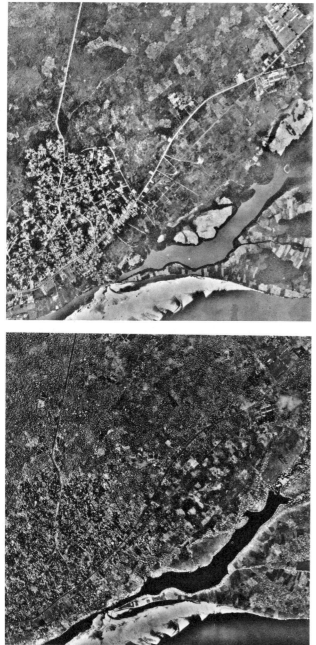

(a)

(b)

Figure 3.3 This pair of 1:40 000 minus-blue panchromatic (a) and infrared (b) aerial photographs are of the same area on the coast of West Africa. They were taken under heavy cloud cover and are dimly lit as a result. The panchromatic image shows most of the details of the township, roads and the coastal sand spit, but contains very little information relating to vegetation. The infrared image has higher contrast, and is an excellent means of discriminating vegetation, though the cultural features are poorly displayed. The silt-laden waters of the lagoon show in black, since water strongly absorbs near-infrared. This makes the water courses more clearly visible on the infrared image. Vegetation is a strong reflector of near-infrared radiation, and most of the variation in the fields is due to crops at different stages of growth. Individual trees, especially the mangroves near to the lagoon, show up as bright speckles. The panchromatic image in vegetated areas shows bare soil as light tones and crops and trees as a monotonous dark grey. Copyright Aerofilms Ltd.

vertically downwards to give a map-like view. Oblique photographs are sometimes taken, and they have one single advantage – they show perspective, which allows the brain to estimate distance and scale. However, the rapid changes in scale in oblique photographs renders them unsuitable for transferring information to maps.

Vertical photographs are normally taken one frame at a time by a mapping or **metric** camera employing a single lens. They are designed to take photographs on which accurate measurements of the surface can be made. They are built to high precision and use very high-quality lenses. Since they are most widely used to produce systematic, overlapping coverage of the surface, metric cameras expose film at a rate which is matched to that of their platform, either an aircraft or a satellite. To avoid motion blur, at each exposure the film is drawn across the focal plane at a rate which compensates for the ground speed of the platform. Within the optical system fiducial marks are placed precisely at the centre points of each side of the image, so that their appearance on the photograph can be used as a frame of reference for measurements. To check on the flying height and attitude, time and position in sequence, an image of an altimeter, a spirit level, a clock and a counter is also produced on the photograph.

A vertical photograph gives a view of the Earth that is rarely experienced, so at first sight it has an unusual appearance. Over a familiar subject, such as the centre of a city (Fig. 3.6), one cause of this unfamiliarity is evident at once. Tall buildings appear to lean outwards from the centre or **principal point** of the photograph. This **radial-relief displacement** is easily explained by the optical geometry involved (Fig. 3.7). When rays are traced through the lens system to the focal plane from the tops and bases of tall buildings, the angle subtended by the building at the focal plane changes from zero when the building is at the principal point to a maximum at the edge of the image. As a result, away from the principal point the top projects further from it than the base. Since the lens is circular, the same effect occurs everywhere and the amount of relative displacement of the top increases radially outwards from the principal point. The wider the field of view of the lens and the lower the camera height, the more pronounced the effect. From the geometry of Figure 3.7a and the principle of similar triangles it can be shown that the height of a building h is related to its distance from the principal point r, the radial displacement of its top relative to its base d and flying height H by:

$$h = Hd/r \qquad (3.3)$$

This means that accurate measurements of elevation can be made from vertical photographs, provided that h/H is significantly greater than zero, i.e. when flying height is not of the order of tens or hundreds of kilometres, when the displacement is very small.

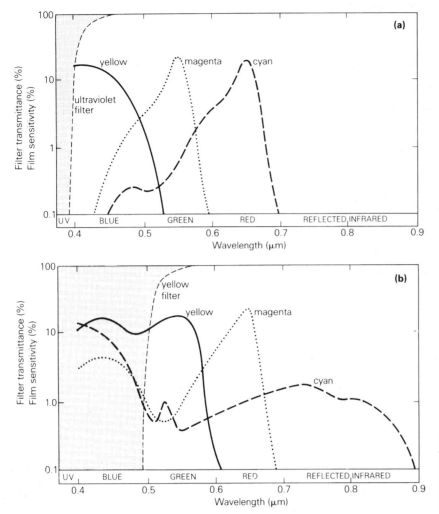

Figure 3.4 The ranges of sensitivity of the yellow, magenta and cyan dye layers in natural colour (a) and colour-infrared (b) positive films are different as are the ranges of transmittance of the filters used with them.

Another effect of varying height of surface features that can be seen on Figures 3.6 and 3.7 is that they cause variations in scale on the image. The separation of the tops of buildings A and B on Figure 3.7 is considerably greater than that of their bases, whereas both tops and bases are equidistant. Other distortions result from variable attitude of the platform on which the camera is mounted (Fig. 3.8), giving rise to slightly oblique photographs, the scale of which changes across the image. Scale may also change from one photograph to another in a sequence because of variations in flying height. Distortions of these kinds are unavoidable and can only be corrected by computer (Appendix B).

Another defect of photographs that is systematically related to their geometry is a radial decrease in overall brightness called **vignetting**. This is caused by radially increasing angle between camera lens and surface, and corresponding decrease in the apparent aperture or light-gathering capacity of the lens. The effect is generally compensated for by filters whose density increases towards their centre.

Vertical photographs are usually taken in sequence along flight lines. The interval between exposures is arranged to allow for sufficient overlap between images that every point on the ground appears on at least two separate photographs. This imparts parallax to objects with different heights. As a result, adjacent overlapping photographs can represent the views by left and right eyes, only with the eye separation increased to hundreds of metres or even several kilometres. When viewed with appropriate binocular lens or mirror systems, overlapping photographs can be used to simulate stereoscopic vision, giving an exaggerated three-dimensional view of the ground and enabling elevation measurements to be made (Appendix A).

3.2 Vidicon cameras

Television images can be produced by an image-producing element in a camera known as a **vidicon**. As in a photographic camera, radiation is gathered by a lens system, passed through various filters and focused on a flat target.

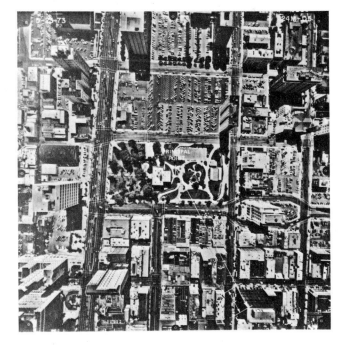

Figure 3.6 Vertical aerial photographs of urban areas dominated by high-rise buildings show clearly the effects of radial relief displacement, and of the increase in scale with increased elevation of the surface.

Instead of a photosensitive emulsion, a vidicon target is coated with a transparent photoconductive material. The electrical conductivity of the target increases with the intensity of the illuminating radiation.

An image is built up by scanning the target with an electron beam, which methodically sweeps the area of the target as a series of lines. This enables the variation in conductivity and hence the illumination intensity of the target to be mapped as an analogue electrical signal during a short period of time. The time involved is of the same order as when a photograph is taken, so the signal is effectively a snapshot. An image is produced simply by

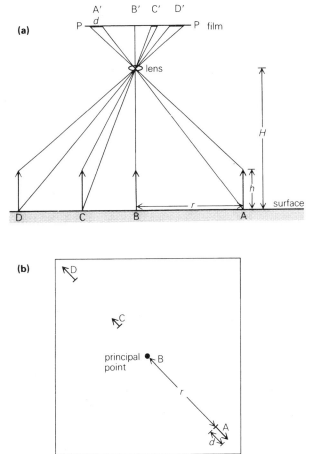

Figure 3.7 Tracing the ray paths from the tops and bases of equally tall buildings through the lens of a camera to the film (a) shows how radial relief displacement is produced in a vertical photograph. The further the building is from the point directly below the lens – the nadir which is imaged as the principal point of the photograph – the larger the angle it subtends at the film. On the film (b) the top of a building is imaged further from the principal point than its base, and both base and top are joined by a radial line to the principal point. The building therefore appears to lean away from the centre of the image (Fig. 3.6). Moreover, the scale at the level of the bases of the buildings is smaller than the level at their tops.

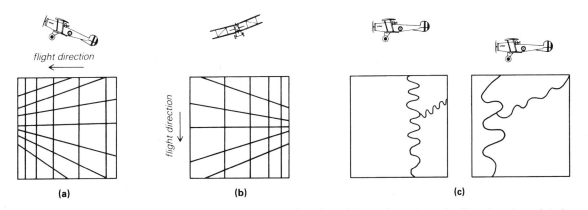

Figure 3.8 Apart from the distortions in scale due to varying elevation of the surface, the main distortions in aerial photographs are due to tilting of the aircraft (a and b) so that the view is slightly oblique. A perspective effect of changing scale is introduced. Convection cells in the atmosphere may cause the aircraft to change altitude so that adjacent images have different scales (c).

using the signal to modulate an electron beam sweeping across a phosphorescent screen. The light emission of the screen is proportional to the signal and therefore to the original illumination of the vidicon.

Vidicons produce only one signal, which can be rendered only in black and white. A colour imaging system involves three vidicons with different filters. Separate electron beams, each of which is focused on phosphor grains giving red, green or blue response, make up the final image on a colour video monitor. Like film emulsions, the materials used in vidicons are sensitive only to visible and near-infrared radiation. This, together with the physical limitations on resolution imparted by the size of the vidicon target and by the accuracy of the scanning electron beam, restricts the usefulness of vidicon cameras. To a large extent vidicons have been superseded in video cameras by charge-coupled devices (Section 3.4) mounted in arrays, but the principle was used in the early Landsat series (Section 3.8.3) and interplanetary missions.

3.3 Line-scanning systems

A video picture is built by a series of lines, or a **raster**, from the linear scanning of a vidicon plate. A similar effect can be produced by substituting a sequence of electrical responses of a photosensitive detector cell triggered by radiation emanating from a series of strips of the Earth's surface. One means of achieving this is by using a **line scanner**. The forward motion of the platform allows successive strips of the terrain to be monitored. Instead of radiation being collected by a lens and directed onto a film, a mirror is used together with photoelectronic detectors. A motor rotates the mirror, either through 360° or in a repeated cycle of small angles back and forth. For a completely rotating mirror the system only records data for a small part of the sweep. In most systems the sweep is perpendicular to the motion of the platform, and gathers data from immediately below and to either side of the flight path. A line-scan image is built up from straight lines or swaths oriented across the flight line. To ensure complete cover the frequency of sweeps is matched to the ground speed of the platform.

The radiation collected by the mirror is directed onto banks of detectors, usually after it has been split into a series of wavebands using diffraction gratings. The detectors sense all the chosen wavebands simultaneously (Fig. 3.9). Because of this arrangement the response of each detector corresponds exactly to the same portion of terrain as all the others at precisely the same instant. The data then consist of strings of signals, swath by swath, for each waveband that can be registered exactly. For the sake of improved resolution, a single sweep of the mirror generally directs radiation to several detectors for each waveband. The ground swath is then represented by several strings of signals, each of which represents a fraction of the scanned area, corresponding to a line of finite width on the ground.

Line scanners were originally devised to escape the spectral limitations of photographic and vidicon methods – limited to between 0.4 and 1.1 μm. Detectors have been

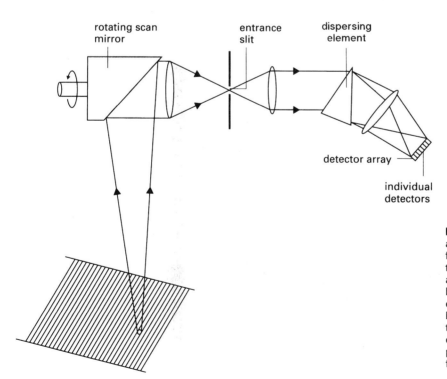

rotating scan mirror

entrance slit

dispersing element

detector array

individual detectors

Figure 3.9 Radiation gathered by a scan mirror in a line scanner is focused by an optical system through a dispersion system, either a prism or a diffraction grating, onto banks of detectors. There is at least one detector for each spectral band being sensed, and in most cases there are several so that one sweep of the mirror across the surface produces a number of lines of data for each band.

produced that can be used from the ultraviolet through to the region where energy emitted by the Earth reaches a peak. As Figure 3.10 shows, no single detector covers the whole range of the useful spectrum. Photomultipliers and silicon photodiodes are used for all visible wavelengths and part of the near-infrared. However, to cover all near-infrared wavelengths a lead sulphide detector must be used too. In the mid- or emitted infrared, detectors such as mercury–cadmium–telluride must be used. Many of these detectors only give measurable responses if they are cooled, either by liquid nitrogen or by exposure to the very low temperatures of outer space.

The resolution of a line scanner is similar to that of a photographic camera, but is a function only of the geometry of the optical system and the sensitivity of the detectors. At any instant the area on the ground from which radiation is focused on a detector depends on the focal length of the optics and the flying height. This is the **instantaneous field of view (IFOV)** and is another measure of resolution. It is defined as a solid angle at the apex of a cone, within which all radiation is intercepted by the detection system, but is generally expressed in terms of dimensions on the ground, given by:

$$d = h/I \qquad (3.4)$$

where d is the diameter of the area on the ground, h is the flying height and I is the cone angle or IFOV. This ground area, the time that energy from it is focused on the detectors and the size of the scanning mirror determine the total energy at all wavelengths that is available for detection. The system's ability to discriminate different energy levels is controlled by the sensitivity of the detectors. Whereas it may be technically feasible to have a very small IFOV, the detectors may only show the very broadest variations in

reflectance or emittance of the surface. The image would be of poor quality. The broader the range of wavelengths directed onto a detector the more energy is available for it to detect. So for a small IFOV, the broader the waveband, the better is the discrimination of different signals from the surface. With a large IFOV, a narrower waveband can be monitored and still discriminate different signals from the ground.

Any detector is subject to random fluctuations caused by electronic or structural defects in its design or power supply. To a greater or lesser degree all produce a response because of this noise in the absence of any incident energy. This generally appears as speckles on an image of an otherwise uniform surface. In practice the performance of a detector is assessed by its **signal-to-noise ratio (S/N)**. Noise is generally constant and so there is a minimum signal below which distinction is not possible. The signal-to-noise ratio at a particular wavelength $(S/N)_\lambda$ is affected by many variables:

(1) Quality of the detector at that wavelength (Q_λ).
(2) IFOV (I).
(3) Width of the waveband being detected ($\Delta\lambda$).
(4) Spectral radiant flux of the surface (E_λ).
(5) Time taken to sweep the portion of surface corresponding to a pixel (t).

The variables can be related empirically by:

$$(S/N)_\lambda = Q_\lambda \times I^2 \times \Delta\lambda \times E_\lambda \times t \qquad (3.5)$$

It is possible to use this empirical relationship to investigate the strategy of designing line scanners.

Several options are available for improving (increasing) the signal-to-noise ratio, without having to develop a better quality detector. These are: increasing the IFOV (coarsening the spatial resolution), widening the waveband, or increasing the time over which energy is collected for each pixel (slowing the scan speed of the mirror and the velocity of the platform).

Narrowing the waveband to detect small spectral features can only be achieved by increasing the IFOV, or by increasing the time taken to sweep each pixel. This is an important consideration, because many of the spectral features of interest shown in Chapter 2 are extremely narrow, and a small $\Delta\lambda$ is needed to resolve them.

Clearly there are trade-offs in trying to improve spatial and spectral resolution while keeping an acceptable S/N. The most important limiting factor is the time dwelt on each pixel, since this involves the velocity of the platform and the need to cover all parts of the surface. For spacecraft this velocity is fixed according to the orbit altitude, and has a lower limit for aircraft too. Moreover, the performance of the detectors is not constant with wavelength. The spatial and spectral resolutions and quality of data from operational line scanners have to be optimized.

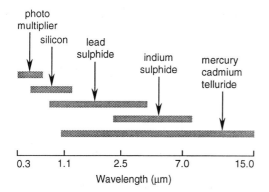

Figure 3.10 To cover the whole of the useful range of visible and infrared wavelengths a choice must be made from various commercially available detectors. Each has an optimum response over a relatively broad range. To produce data from narrow wavebands they must be used in conjunction with filters or be placed precisely in a spectrum produced by a diffraction grating. Except for photomultipliers or silicon diodes, most detectors need to be cooled.

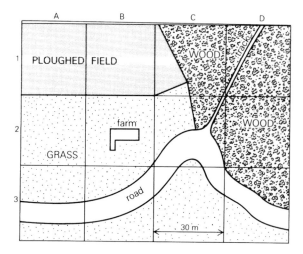

Figure 3.11 A series of 30-m pixels superimposed on the ground surface shows that most pixels include several objects and surface categories. Only pixels A1, B1 and D2 are 'pure'. The rest are mixed pixels. If the farm had a sufficiently high contrast with grass its effects on pixel B2 could be high enough that the pixel had a different brightness from those surrounding it. The farm might be detectable, but it could not be recognized as a farm. Similarly, the road could affect pixels A3, B3, C2, C3 and D3, and probably others beyond the map. Because road-containing pixels would be linked, however, the crude shape and orientation of the road could be seen. The track may be too narrow to have a noticeable effect. Pure luck has resulted in the boundary between the ploughed field and grass falling along a boundary separating four pixels. On the image it would be clear and represented accurately. All the other boundaries fall within pixels. Although they would contribute to the brightness of these pixels, on the image the boundaries would become steps in the brightness between pixels dominated by large classes. Their position and orientation would become 'blurred' by the rectangular raster.

There are two methods of recording line-scan data, in analogue or digital form, either on magnetic tape aboard the platform or after telemetry down to a ground receiving station. In the analogue case the signal can be used to modulate a light source which moves in lines across a photographic film, building up an analogue image in the form of a strip. More usually the recording is in digital format. The first step in achieving this is to divide the continuous signal from the detector into discrete blocks, either mechanically using a rotating shutter blade or electronically using a timer. In either case the blocks of signals correspond to finite lengths of recording time and thus to distances along the scanned swath. The signals in each block are averaged, rescaled and converted to a digital number, which is recorded. Each digital number represents the radiant energy in a particular waveband associated with a rectangular block or pixel on the ground. An image recorded in digital format therefore comprises a geo-metrically precise array of pixels in lines which is identical in structure for each waveband, so that they can be registered exactly. This orderly array of pixels is termed a **raster**, which lends itself not only to computer manipula-

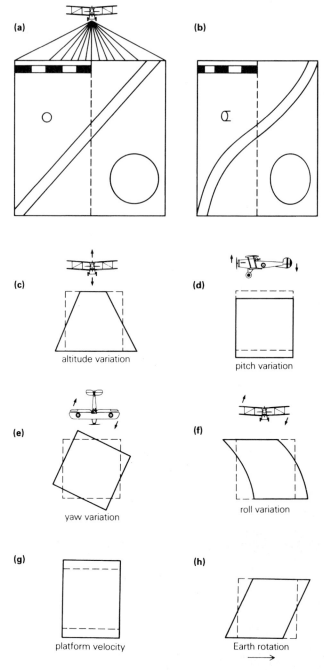

Figure 3.12 Because the distance on the ground covered by the same angle subtended at the scanning mirror increases away from the platform (a), all line-scan images decrease in scale away from the groundtrack of the platform (b). The scale along the groundtrack does not change, so straight linear features running diagonally across the surface are distorted in a characteristic sinusoidal fashion on the image (b). Tall objects appear to lean away from the groundtrack and the shapes of objects become distorted. As well as this effect, distortions resulting from instability of the platform result in the rectangular format of an image (dashed outlines) representing more or less irregular or displaced areas of the surface (c–g). In the case of satellites, the Earth rotates beneath the platform as it passes over. As a result the area imaged as a series of lines scanned during a period of time represents a parallelogram on the surface (h).

tion but also to display on a video monitor. The signals from a vidicon, which in raw form consist of analogue signals from electron-beam scan lines, can also be expressed as digital numbers as a raster-format image.

The IFOV is defined as a solid angle, and the size of each pixel is a function of IFOV and flying height. Although the resolution of the system is defined as the finest spacing of objects on the ground that can be discriminated in an image, it is the pixel size that is most commonly quoted as 'resolution'. Whether an object is detectable or not depends on its size, its contrast with its surroundings and its shape and orientation with respect to the raster pattern. Figure 3.11 shows that pixels often overlap several objects or ground classes. The response for each of these **mixed pixels** has a contribution from each enclosed object or part of an object, depending on the size and contrast of the object compared with its surroundings. An object smaller than a pixel may be detectable if it has a high contrast. However, this does not mean that it can be recognized, for recognition depends on shape, and shape is masked by that of the pixel itself.

Like vertical photographs, line-scan images suffer from a variety of distortions, resulting from both the optical system and the motion of the platform. Whereas optical distortions on photographs increase radially outwards from the nadir or principal point, those on a line-scan image increase outwards from the groundtrack along each line. This is because the mirror changes the viewing angle of the ground continuously during each sweep. Both scale and geometry

change away from the groundtrack, so that tall objects lean in parallel away from the mid-line of the image, and scale decreases in the same fashion. Because of varying lateral scale, the apparent direction of ground features changes across the image. Straight lines not parallel to scan lines or the groundtrack take on a sigmoidal shape as a result (Fig. 3.12a). As the separation between sensor and ground increases along the scan line, so the resolution becomes coarser towards the image edge. The higher the platform and the smaller the sweep angle, the smaller these distortions become, until with some satellite systems they are barely noticeable.

Distortions due to the motion of the platform are present in all line-scan images to a much greater degree than in photographs, which are near-instantaneous images whereas the former are built up over a relatively long period of time. Platforms may vary in altitude and flight direction. They can also roll, pitch, yaw and heave. In the case of satellites, the Earth rotates beneath them while the image is being scanned, so that a rectangular image is really a parallelogram on the ground (Fig. 3.12). Analogue images (Fig. 3.13) can rarely be corrected for such distortions, except by gyroscopic compensation in flight. Digital images, though, can easily be rectified to the local cartographic projection using computer techniques (Appendix B).

A final point about defects in line-scan images stems from their structure as a raster of lines and pixels. Any fluctuation in the response of an individual detector or miscalibration between detectors in an array for one wave-

Figure 3.13 This line-scan image of thermally emitted infrared over a power station in Nottinghamshire, UK, shows distortions of the type featured in Figure 3.12b. They are particularly noticeable for the road and the array of cooling towers. The light specks at lower left and lower centre are cattle. Copyright Aerofilms Ltd.

band results in striping parallel to the scan lines. Sometimes, a detector may fail temporarily, or its response may go out of phase with the others in an array. These failures produce, respectively, lines with no data and pixels displaced relative to those either side. Random electrical discharges in the system may also introduce spurious data into an image, which show up as bright pixels having no corresponding feature on the ground. These various defects and their removal are covered in Appendix B.

3.4 Pushbroom systems

Line scanners contain mechanical components that are subject to failure, have a poor signal-to-noise ratio and cannot have both high spatial and high spectral resolution, since the time dwelt on any pixel during a sweep of the mirror is very short. One way around this problem is provided by tiny (<10 μm across) radiation-sensitive cells, called **charge-coupled devices (CCDs)**. CCDs have been devised using the same materials as in Figure 3.10, which operate at wavelengths up to about 2.4 μm, so the full visible and NIR range in which so many spectral features of interest occur can be monitored. However, the thermally emitted infrared is not yet accessible to this technology. The CCDs are charged in proportion to the incident radiation and discharged very quickly to produce either an analogue or digital signal. In effect, they are light-sensitive **capacitors**. If they are arranged in thousands along a linear array onto which radiation from the ground is directed by an optical system, no moving parts are required to build up an image. Each array simply and directly measures radiation from pixels along a ground swath as the array is swept over it. For this reason such a device is known as a **pushbroom** system – it works in an fashion analogous to the sweeping of a wide brush or broom across the floor. This simple motion builds up an image of successive lines perpendicular to the flight path, each column of pixels corresponding to the response of each CCD in the array (Fig. 3.14).

Aside from their obvious advantages of simplicity and direct measurement from geometrically exact pixels, pushbroom systems are reliable and require little power. The SPOT pointable pushbroom, which can image areas to either side of its groundtrack by using a variably oriented mirror, is described in Section 3.12.3. The spatial resolution of a pushbroom system is a function of the size of each CCD, the optics and the flying height. The spectral resolution, like those of a line-scanning system, depends on the time each CCD is allowed to gather radiant energy.

Comparing two imaging systems, one based on a line scanner, the other a pushbroom, each producing images with pixels that are 30 m² arranged in lines 3000 pixels long, it is instructive to compare the times that each system dwells on a pixel. One sweep of the line-scanner's mirror takes a time t, so the time dwelt on each pixel is $t/3000$. For the same platform velocity, a 3000-pixel line is captured by a pushbroom also in time t, this being the time for which each CCD is exposed to radiation from each pixel. So a pushbroom allows radiation to be gathered for 3000 times longer than in a line scanner. This has three

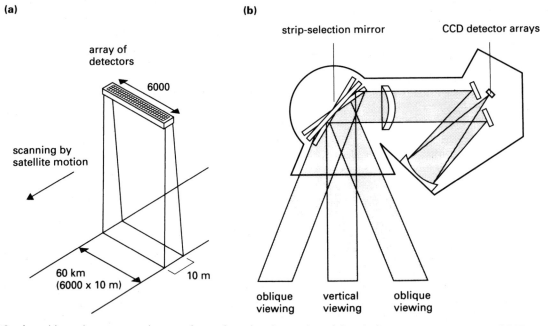

Figure 3.14 A pushbroom system produces an image by using the motion of the platform to sweep an array of CCDs across the surface (a). Radiation is directed onto the array by a mirror (b), whose angle can be changed to allow imaging ahead of the platform or to one side. This enables stereoscopic images to be acquired and, in the case of sideways direction, allows the same area to be imaged on several separate occasions without direct overpass.

implications. First, the signal-to-noise ratio is much better and lower radiation levels can be monitored. Second, the pixel size could be reduced considerably, by increasing the number of CCDs in the pushbroom and reducing the time of data collection for each line, thereby making it narrower on the ground. Thirdly, the term $\Delta\lambda$ in Equation 3.5 can be reduced, in other words the spectral resolution can be improved to match the narrowness of important spectral features. This last option is exploited in designing imaging spectrometers (Section 3.6).

3.5 Microwave imaging systems

The longest wavelengths used in remote sensing are more than a thousand times longer (1–25 cm) than those accessible to line-scan systems (<15 µm). This is the microwave region of the EMR spectrum. All materials above absolute zero emit microwaves, but for the ambient temperature of the Earth's surface (300 K) the energy curve (Fig. 1.3) shows that energies in this region are very low. However, microwaves are hardly attenuated at all by gases and clouds, and can pass through several metres of solids. Detection of natural microwaves from the Earth follows the same general principles as most other techniques, in that it is a passive method. Microwaves can also be generated electronically using klystron tubes, when coherent radiation of a single wavelength is produced. The detection and analysis of this artificial radiation when scattered back to a detector by the surface is therefore an active method, originally termed *r*adio *d*etection *a*nd *r*anging, or **radar** for short.

In passive microwave remote sensing the data are collected by an antenna, very like a radio-telescope, rather than by some kind of solid-state detector. Most surveys until recently have been profiles of microwave emittance along lines, rather than images. Images can be acquired, in the familiar form of line scans, where the antenna is swept from side to side beneath the platform. They can be in analogue form as film exposed to a light source modulated by the antenna response, or in digital form as a raster of pixels. These scanned images suffer from the same distortions as those of line-scan systems operating in the visible and near-infrared.

The IFOV of a passive microwave system is expressed as a solid angle (I), and is given by:

$$I = 1.2.\lambda/D \qquad (3.6)$$

where λ is wavelength and D is the diameter of the antenna. For microwave wavelengths and fine resolution D is much larger than feasible for a portable antenna, and except for very low flying heights the spatial resolution is coarser than with other imaging systems. Very few experiments in geological applications have been conducted using passive microwave technology for this reason. Its main use to date has been directed at climatology and oceanography.

Table 3.1 Coding of divisions in the microwave region employed by radar systems.

Band code	Wavelength (cm)
K_a	0.8–1.1
K	1.1–1.7
K_u	1.7–2.4
X	2.4–3.8
C	3.8–7.5
S	7.5–15
L	15–30
P	30–100

When radar was being developed during World War II different wavebands within the microwave part of the spectrum were given letter codes for security reasons (Table 3.1). Those most commonly used are Ka-band (0.86 cm), X-band (3.0 and 3.2 cm) and L-band (23.4 and 25 cm).

The operation of active microwave or radar imaging systems is fundamentally different from that of all other systems. Microwave radiation generated by an antenna is used to 'illuminate' the surface. In the majority of cases the **look direction** is downwards but to the side of the platform. Consequently, the technique is often referred to as **sideways-looking radar**. In imaging mode, instead of allowing the antenna to sweep a ground area, which would limit the size of the antenna and thus the resolution, the antenna is fixed and a long, narrow strip perpendicular to the flight direction of the platform is illuminated (Fig. 3.15a). For military purposes, resolution is usually not as important as detection of objects in real time, and so sweeping antennae are used, looking in any chosen direction.

To avoid interference between the emitted radiation and returns from the surface, illumination is made in discrete pulses of the order of microseconds. Since all the returns from the surface must be received before another pulse is transmitted, the timing of the pulses is crucial. It depends on the maximum distance to the side, or the **range** from which returns are expected. The frequency of the pulses is inversely proportional to the range, because the further the range, the longer returns take to reach the antenna.

The response of the antenna for each pulse comprises both a measure of the returning energy and the time elapsed since the pulse. This time (t) is obviously a measure of distance to the surface from which energy was returned. The distance is twice that from the platform to the object, which itself is known as the **slant range**. Since radar waves travel at the speed of light (c), the slant range is $ct/2$. As Figure 3.15a shows, the distance on the ground or **ground range** (r) is slant range multiplied by the cosine of the **depression angle** (α) for the radar beam at that point:

$$r = (ct \cos \alpha)/2 \qquad (3.7)$$

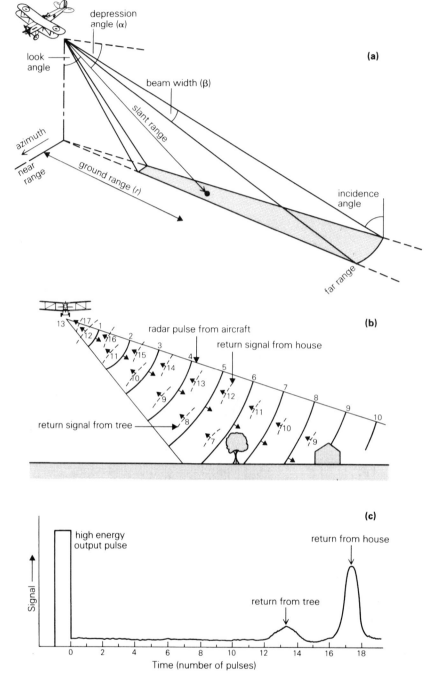

Figure 3.15 (a) The geometry involved in sideways-looking radar governs many of the intrinsic properties of radar images. The depression angle (α) is the angle between horizontal and a radar raypath. The look angle, sometimes quoted instead, is simply the angle between vertical and a raypath (90°– α). The incidence angle is the angle between an incident radar ray and a line at right angles to the surface. For a horizontal surface it is the same as the look angle, but varies with the slope of the surface. The beam width (angle β) determines how the illumination of the surface spreads out from near to far range. The slant range is the direct distance from the antenna to object, and is related to the true or ground range by the depression angle (Eqn 3.7). (b) The solid curves on this cartoon are spherical radar wavefronts emitted by the antenna, and their numbers indicate the time since they were emitted. The dashed curves are radar wavefronts backscattered from the house and tree. They have the same number convention indicating time. The wavefront from the house which has just been received at the antenna has travelled for 17 time units, that from the tree for 13. The graph (c) shows how radar energy returned from the house and tree is recorded at the antenna.

The depression angle decreases as range increases.

A line on the image is therefore a plot of energy with time, resulting from the outward propagation of a single pulse and its return from objects on the ground (Fig. 3.15b). When the next pulse is emitted the platform has moved forwards and another line of data is acquired. At its simplest the image is built up by the energy–time signal modulating the intensity of a single line cathode-ray tube. A film is exposed to this at a rate proportional to the platform speed, so building up a strip image of individual lines. The data can also be recorded digitally for later reproduction and manipulation.

Resolution on a radar image depends on two parameters: pulse length and beam width. The length of each pulse (time τ, distance $c\tau$) controls the resolution in the range direction. For two objects on the ground to be distinguishable, the returned signals from each object for the whole pulse must reach the antenna at different times. Any overlap between the two sets of signals means that the objects merge into one on the image. As Figure 3.16 shows,

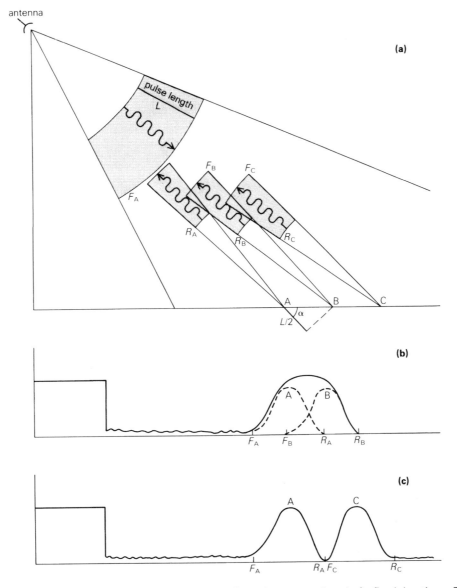

Figure 3.16 In (a), the surface is illuminated by pulses of radar from the antenna (grey) of a fixed duration τ. The pulse length L is equal to $c\tau$. The fronts of backscattered returns of a pulse from objects at A and B are at F_A and F_B, and the rears at R_A and R_B. The signals which these returned pulses generate at the antenna (b) overlap so that they are just indistinguishable, and form a single broad peak. Pulses returned from objects with a closer spacing than A and B would overlap even more. However, at spacings greater than AB, return signals are separate (c) and the two objects, such as A and C, can be distinguished. The limiting slant range, corresponding to the separation between A and B, is half the pulse length L. This is the slant-range resolution. In the ground range this resolution becomes $L/2\cos\alpha$.

the minimum separation between the objects along the slant range must be half the pulse length, or $c\tau/2$. This limiting distance, the **slant-range resolution**, is independent of distance from the platform. However the corresponding distance on the ground, the ground-range resolution (R_r), varies with the depression angle (α), so that:

$$R_r = (c\tau \cos \alpha)/2 \qquad (3.8)$$

and it increases away from the platform. However, it is theoretically independent of the altitude of the platform.

The width of the radar beam is expressed by an angle (β)

(Fig. 3.15a) and is directly proportional to the radar wavelength (λ) and inversely proportional to the length of the antenna (L). The width of the line on the ground illuminated by each pulse depends on the distance from the platform. As distance increases, so the beam fans out. The resolution parallel to the groundtrack of the platform, the **azimuth resolution** (R_a), is the width illuminated by each pulse. Azimuth resolution deteriorates in direct proportion to the ground range (r):

$$R_a = r\beta = (\lambda/L)(c\tau \cos \alpha)/2 \qquad (3.9)$$

43

Each line on an image therefore represents data which become increasingly degraded away from the platform. The azimuth resolution also deteriorates as the altitude of the platform becomes greater. So a satellite radar system based on sensors developed for aircraft would have equally good range resolution, provided the power was high enough, but very poor azimuth resolution. There are, however, ingenious ways of avoiding this limitation.

The most obvious way to decrease the beam width is to extend the antenna. From an altitude of 100 km an azimuth resolution of 100 m requires a beam width of 1 μrad. For 25 cm wavelength radar, substituting in Equation 3.9 shows that an antenna 250 m long will be required. Clearly, there are physical limits using this solution. Radars whose beam width is controlled by the length of their antennae are known as **real-aperture** systems. They have simple designs and recording systems, as outlined earlier, but they are only useful when mounted in aircraft. More complex systems use the coherent nature of artificial microwave radiation to simulate an extremely long antenna. They are called **synthetic-aperture radar (SAR)** systems, and are the only useful means for high altitude and satellite radar remote sensing.

Within the ground area illuminated by the pulsed radar beam (Fig. 3.17), parts of the surface are ahead of the platform, parts behind, and only a narrow strip, just as wide as the antenna itself, is in line at any instant. The returns from the areas ahead and behind are subject to a **Doppler shift**, just as sound would be. Imagine a train with its horn sounding. Sound echoed from ahead would have a higher pitch to an observer on the train than would that echoed from behind. Only echoes from the side would sound the same as the horn. The Doppler effect has altered the wavelength of the echoed sound. Exactly the same thing happens to EMR, including radar, although the shift is very small unless the platform travels at speeds close to that of light. Because radar is coherent these small differences can be detected electronically.

In a SAR system the time, the energy and the frequency of radar returns from the surface are recorded, different frequencies signalling the position of the object responsible relative to the motion of the platform. The frequency is measured by allowing the returns to interfere with a reference signal whose frequency is the same as that of the radar pulse itself. Those frequencies affected by Doppler shift produce interference patterns. A constructive interference produces a high signal, a destructive interference gives a low signal. These can be recorded optically as bright and dark spots arranged in lines parallel to flight direction, or digitally for computer processing. Each object on the ground, defined by the time of the response for successive radar pulses, is represented by several spots, from when it was ahead, in line and behind the moving platform. Because of the beam spread, the further an object is from the platform the more times it is 'looked at'. The net result is that the moving real antenna is transformed into a much longer, synthetic antenna, thereby improving the azimuth resolution. Because far-range objects are

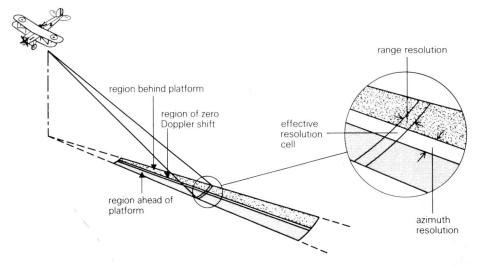

Figure 3.17 In a synthetic-aperture radar system interference occurs between a reference signal and the increased or decreased frequencies of radar waves returning from illuminated areas ahead of and behind the platform. Waves returning from a narrow strip at right angles to the flight path do not suffer a Doppler shift, and no interference occurs. This allows returns at any instant from the in-line strip to be discriminated from those from the rest of the illuminated surface during signal processing. This makes possible a much finer resolution in the azimuth direction than could be achieved with the same antenna used in a brute-force system. The further downrange an object is, the more times it can backscatter successive radar pulses as the platform flies by. Thus the discrimination of ahead, in-line and behind positions relative to the moving platform is independent of range. Azimuth resolution is theoretically constant in SAR images. In practice it is degraded with increasing range because the radar energy becomes weaker with distance as a result of the beam spread. Eventually, energy backscattered from the furthest range becomes too weak to be detected.

(a)

(b)

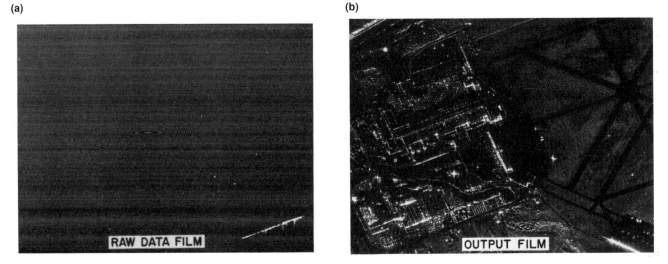

Figure 3.18 The raw data from a synthetic-aperture radar system is expressed on film as a hologram (a), which cannot be interpreted until it has been optically correlated. The patterns on the film represent interference between the Doppler-shifted frequencies of backscattered radar waves and a reference frequency generated by the system. Projection of a laser through a SAR hologram using a complex lens system optically correlates the interference patterns on the hologram to produce an image of the surface (b). Courtesy of Eric Kasischke, Environmental Research Institute of Michigan.

illuminated for longer in the spread beam than those at near range, the azimuth resolution is independent of range.

The record of the signals on film amounts to a one-dimensional interference, and is a radar **hologram** (Fig. 3.18a). By itself it is meaningless, but when illuminated by a laser it is **optically correlated** to produce a radar image (Fig. 3.18b). The digital records of the SAR signals can be unpacked by very powerful software to produce a digital image in raster format, which suffers none of the degradation inherent in optical correlation.

Because they are produced artificially, radar pulses can be transmitted in different modes of polarization, with vibrations restricted to a single vertical or horizontal plane. Likewise, the returns can be received in either a horizontal or vertical plane, enabling the rotations induced by reflections from different types of surface materials to be analysed. This and the other surface-dependent features of radar images are examined in Chapter 7. Here, some of the image peculiarities and distortions that result from radar systems themselves are outlined.

Because radar looks sideways, and because radar images represent energy and time, it produces some extraordinary geometric features as well as those resulting from platform instability and Earth rotation. Because the times recorded in a radar image represent direct or slant distances of objects from the platform, and each surface object subtends a different angle to the platform, uncorrected radar images vary in scale along range. The image is compressed at near range and only approaches true scale at far range, the opposite to line-scan images. This is explained by Figure 3.19, and results from the different **incidence angles** of radar wavefronts at different ranges. Such raw data are **slant-range images**. They can be converted to a nearly uniform scale by a hyperbolic transformation of the data down range to equate the scale to that which the surface would have if it were flat, thereby producing a **ground-range image**.

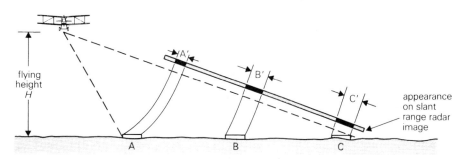

Figure 3.19 In a slant-range image the scale downrange increases because the depression angles of spherical wavefronts which meet the surface decrease away from the antenna. The apparent distances between objects and between parts of the same object are measured in time. The time taken to illuminate A is shorter than for B and C. Likewise, it takes longer for a wave to move from B to C than from A to B. The equal distances on the ground increase away from the platform on the slant-range image.

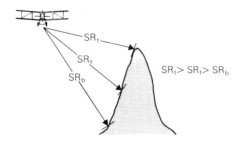

Figure 3.20 Because the whole of its slope which faces the platform is at a steeper angle than a radar wavefront, the top of the mountain is illuminated by the wavefront before its flank and base. This is translated into slant ranges – SR_t, SR_f, SR_b – which produce an image where the top is nearer to the platform than the base or flank. The mountain appears on the image to lean towards the platform.

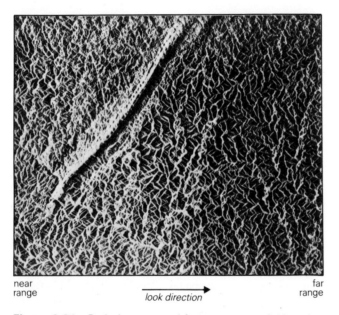

near range   far range

look direction

Figure 3.21 Both the near- and far-range parts of this radar image of a mountainous area in the NE USA are dominated by layover. It takes the form of arrays of triangular features which look like flatirons, not to be confused with the real flatirons which are so characteristic of eroded dipping strata on aerial photographs and other images in the visible and infrared. Courtesy of J.P. Ford, Jet Propulsion Laboratory, Pasadena.

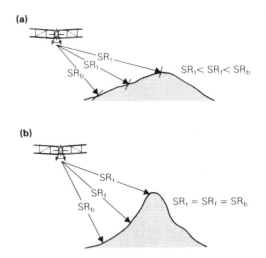

Figure 3.22 Where the surface slope is at a lower angle than radar wavefronts (a), the slant ranges of top, flank and base of a mountain are less than their true ranges on the ground. The result is that the slope facing the platform is compressed or foreshortened. Sometimes the surface has approximately the same angle as a wavefront (b). In this case the slant ranges for all parts of the surface are the same and the whole slope is compressed to a single line.

If the surface has high relief a strange effect is produced. Because the top of a mountain may be nearer to the platform than its base, and because radar images are time images, the top can be reproduced on an image closer to the platform than the base (Fig. 3.20). The mountain 'leans' towards the platform to give a phenomenon termed **layover**. Many radar images of mountainous terrain show arrays of layover phenomena, which bear a strong resemblance to the **flatirons** normally associated with dipping strata (Fig. 3.21). They have no relationship to dip and are purely artificial. The layover effect depends partly on the relief, but mainly on the depression angle. For high depression angles – for surfaces more nearly below the

platform – the effect is worst, whereas with a shallow depression angle the effect is only noticeable for the strongest relief. The effect at its most bizarre can display a mountain overlaying a river or glacier (see Fig. 3.23b).

Related to layover is another effect typical of radar images: **foreshortening**. This occurs where the surface slope is less steep than that of the radar wavefront. The pulse reaches the base before the top, so that the sloped surface appears shorter on the image than on the ground (Fig. 3.22a). Where the surface is parallel to the wavefront all points on it are exactly the same slant distance from the platform, so that all fall together on the image as a single point (Fig. 3.22b). Examples of both phenomena can be seen in Figure 3.23b.

Perhaps the most obvious feature of radar images of variable relief is their **sidelit** character (Figs. 3.21 and 3.23). Slopes facing the platform are most strongly illuminated and reflect most of the energy back to the antenna, so showing up as bright. Slopes facing away receive least energy and appear darker. Where such slopes are steeper than the radar raypaths, then they are in radar shadow, receive no energy and appear totally black (Fig. 3.23). The farther the range, the lower the depression angle and the lower the relief needs to be to produce a radar shadow.

In a radar image, where depression angle varies greatly from near to far range, as in all images acquired from aircraft, layover, foreshortening and shadowing vary markedly in the range direction (Figs. 3.23a and b). This can be so grotesque in areas of only moderate relief that such images are of little use for detailed interpretation. One escape from this problem is to mosaic strips with the same

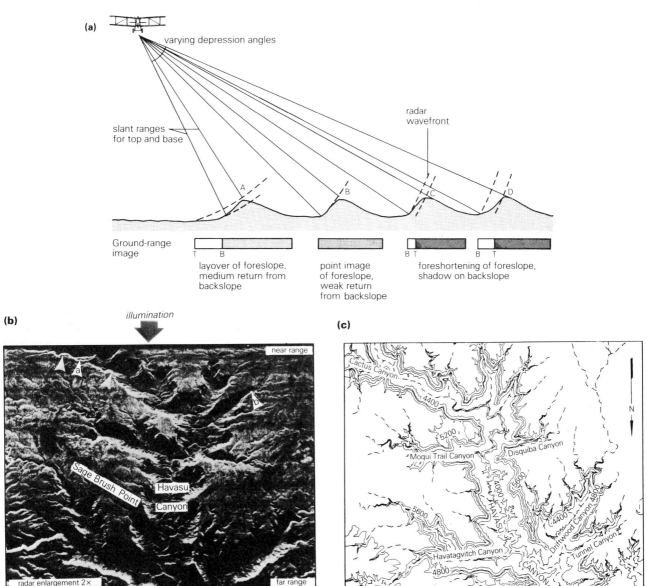

Figure 3.23 (a) This diagram summarizes the peculiarities of radar image geometry by showing the effects on mountains with the same shape at different ranges. Layover dominates slopes facing the platform at near range, and foreshortening falls from a maximum at medium depression angles to less significance in the far range. Wherever they are, slopes steeper than wavefronts always suffer layover, whereas shallower slopes are always foreshortened to some extent. Surfaces which slope away from the platform receive less energy and so always appear darker on a radar image. If their slope is greater than the depression angle they receive no energy and are in total shadow. Since depression angle decreases towards the far range, this part of an image is more likely to contain shadows than the near range. The airborne radar image (b) of the Coconino Plateau in Arizona, USA, when compared to the simplified topographic map (c), illustrates many of the distortions shown in (a). The image is in slant-range format, so that although scale parallel to the flight line – azimuth scale – is accurate scale is compressed at near range in the range direction. The contours on the map show that the walls of the canyons are roughly equal, around 50°. At near range the canyon walls facing the platform are grossly foreshortened so that they appear as bright lines (arrows). They are almost parallel to the radar wavefronts. Foreshortening decreases downrange, but shadowing increases. At near range slopes facing away from the platform are dark but have been illuminated. From mid-range onwards they have increasingly long, total shadows. However, the image shows the enhancement of topography by the sidelit nature of radar images, particularly on the almost featureless plateaus. Courtesy of H.C. MacDonald, University of Arkansas.

depression angle from overlapping swaths. A better solution is to make images from such an altitude that only a small range of depression angles covers a very broad swath on the ground. The best images are those from orbit. Despite their irritations, these peculiarities inherent in radar image have

one very useful advantage. Differential relief displacements caused by different depression angles and look directions cause image parallax. This, as in overlapping aerial photographs, enables stereoscopic viewing to be achieved (Ch. 7 and Appendix A).

3.6 Imaging spectrometers

The spectral curves shown in Chapter 1 were obtained using **spectroradiometers**, which direct radiant energy from a surface through a prism or diffraction grating so that it is spread into its constituent spectrum. Detectors appropriate for different wavelength ranges scan the spectrum, recording radiances for very narrow wavebands, so that accurate spectral curves can be constructed. While useful in establishing the spectral characteristics of materials, such instruments are not appropriate for mapping purposes.

While it is possible to carry spectroradiometers on remote-sensing platforms, the various factors discussed in Section 3.3 around Equation 3.5 limited them until recently to only a few narrow wavebands in producing profiles along flight lines. Carefully chosen bands could allow important information on the distribution of different minerals to be produced, but such systems are unwieldy and limited in the data that they produce.

The development of CCDs sensitive across the whole reflected region of the spectrum, and the ability to miniaturize them in large arrays, now means that much more flexible systems are possible. By exposing such an array, with different CCD elements 'tuned' to adjacent narrow wavebands, through appropriate optics, very detailed spectra can be produced for small areas along a profile. An example that has been digitally enhanced to visualize spectral features is shown in *Figure 3.24*.

The new CCD arrays have allowed a further development of **imaging spectrometers**, in which, instead of a few broad spectral bands for each pixel in an image, up to 210 very narrow bands can be captured in image form. One method uses a long linear array of CCDs, very similar to that in the pushbroom device described in Section 3.4. Instead of an image being constructed by sweeping the array across the ground, the line-scanning principle (Section 3.3) is adopted. Radiant energy collected by the mirror is focused through a dispersing element (a prism or diffraction grating) and the resulting spectrum carefully arranged to fall along the CCD array. Although very little different in principle from ordinary line scanners (Fig. 3.9), this combination of two technologies has been dubbed a **whiskbroom** imaging spectrometer.

By combining several linear CCD arrays, each tuned to adjacent narrow spectral bands, in an area array n bands long by m elements wide an even simpler pushbroom imaging spectrometer is possible. This operates in exactly the same general fashion as the system shown in Figure 3.14.

The many spectral channels, combined with millions of pixels in images from imaging spectrometers, pose problems of both data storage and analysis. Some of these techniques are covered in Chapter 5, and so discussion of examples of imaging spectrometry is delayed until Chapter 9.

3.7 Gamma-ray spectrometers

The naturally occurring unstable isotopes ^{40}K, ^{232}Th, ^{235}U and ^{238}U all emit **gamma-rays** when they decay. Each isotope (more precisely, various daughter isotopes in their decay schemes) emits a range with discrete energy levels that can be detected and measured using a gamma-ray spectrometer. Such instruments depend on the emission of bursts of light by certain crystals, such as sodium iodide doped with thallium, when they absorb gamma-rays. The intensity of the light is proportional to the energy and inversely proportional to the wavelength of the gamma-ray photons, whereas the frequency of light pulses is a measure of the amount of radioactivity. By filtering the discrete energy levels and measuring pulse frequency for narrow energy bands it is possible to estimate the proportion of each isotope in the surface which emits the gamma-rays. In practice the spectrometer comprises a very large crystal surrounded by photomultiplier tubes and appropriate shields, which amplify the bursts of light and block out cosmic rays respectively (Fig. 3.25). Measurements are made with respect to another crystal which receives continuous gamma-rays from a standard radioactive source.

Until recently this technique was capable of accurate analysis only under laboratory conditions, or for very crude analogue measurements from the air along survey lines. Improvements in electronics, photomultipliers and the size of suitable crystals now mean that quantitative airborne data can be acquired. Systematic overflights in a grid pattern, together with reformatting and interpolation of data to a raster, can produce pseudoimages of the apparent uranium,

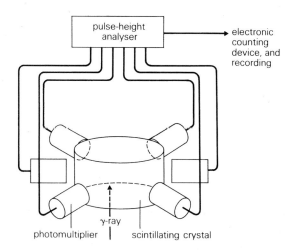

Figure 3.25 A gamma-ray spectrometer consists of a crystal in which gamma-ray photons induce scintillation. The light emitted is intensified by photomultipliers and measured by a pulse-height analyser. The amount of light produced by each photon is proportional to the gamma-ray energy level. The number of light pulses with a particular level are counted over a fixed time, and represent the intensity of gamma-rays with that energy level.

thorium and potassium contents of surface materials, to a high level of precision with moderate resolution (Ch. 8).

3.8 A short history of remote sensing

Remote sensing depends on the ability to get sufficiently far from the Earth's surface to obtain a worthwhile view and the invention of means of capturing an image. Although the first manned balloon flight was in 1783, daguerreotype photography only appeared in 1839. It was not until 20 years later that these two achievements were combined, when Gaspard Tournachon ascended in a balloon and photographed a village near Paris.

Military applications have always dominated the development of remote sensing since then. During the US Civil War (1861–65), the Union forces photographed Confederate defensive positions from captive balloons, and using remotely operated cameras flown on kites. Attempts were even made in Germany to use delayed-action miniature cameras carried by pigeons. Aerial photo-reconnaissance using powered aircraft during World War I (1914–18) systematized aerial photography, so enabling its first significant uses in cartography, forestry and geology during the 1920s and 30s. The first major geological applications were for oil exploration in what was then Persia, by the Anglo-Persian Oil Company. Aerial photo-reconnaissance dominated planning and execution of many operations during World War II. However, three new developments were achieved under the spur of military necessity. Radar was developed, together with VNIR-sensitive film for camouflage detection, and trials were made of thermal infrared sensing devices.

During the 1950s, colour infrared photography found uses in vegetation studies, side-looking airborne radar was refined and synthetic-aperture radar became possible with the development of a successful optical processor. In the same decade photographic technology and interpretation skills continued to develop, with the clandestine flights of US spyplanes such as the supersonic U2 over Soviet and other territory.

Since the early 1960s there have been large numbers of military surveillance satellites in orbit. Many of the earlier ones recorded images on film, which was either recovered on re-entry of the platform or ejected in canisters to be scooped up by recovery aircraft or located electronically on the ground. Increasingly, however, intelligence gathering has moved towards electronic means using line scanners and now pushbrooms, depending on ever-increasing spectral sensitivity of the solid-state detectors. These devices were at first military secrets, but as pressures grew for civil and commercial applications, the technologies were progressively declassified in the USA. In retrospect, it seems clear that the secrecy lay not in the technological

principles involved, but in the limits to which they could be pushed and the precise areas on which attention was directed. Various lines of indirect evidence suggest that satellite imagery with resolution better than 1 m has been available for two decades. The present estimate of 10–15 cm visible–VNIR resolution from the latest US 'Keyhole' satellite series (KH-12) may indeed have been superseded. Ultrafine resolution radar and thermal imagery is also indicated by such indirect evidence. Probable global coverage and certainly global potential is possessed by US and the former Soviet intelligence communities, but its release for civilian applications is likely to be slow. The reason for this is likely to be a mixture of diplomatic nicety and the advantage of potential opponents not knowing precisely what can be hidden and what can be seen.

In the next three sections remotely sensed data that can be acquired openly, albeit at some cost, and which are of use in geology are described.

3.9 Airborne data

Remote sensing from aircraft has several advantages over orbital remote sensing, but there are also disadvantages. It is easier to change sensors to suit a particular study, and to record at any time of day. The flying height can be varied, from less than 100 m above ground to 30 km to give flexibility of scale and to reduce various atmospheric effects. Major disadvantages are that an aircraft is subject to various perturbations which can cause distortions in the images, and that it is sometimes not possible for the aircraft to fly in sensitive areas.

3.9.1 Aerial photographs

Aerial photographs are the most easily available of all remotely sensed data, and have been acquired at various scales for much of the land area of the Earth. Their first widespread use was in World War I as a source of military intelligence. Soon afterwards oil companies began to use them in geological mapping. The basic theory and practice of making cartographic measurements from stereoscopic pairs of overlapping vertical aerial photographs were developed in the interwar years. Major advances in film and camera technology took place during World War II, again at the demand of the military. Since then their acquisition has become a matter of routine for a wide variety of agencies, following the transfer of technology from military to civilian applications.

Aerial photographic surveys are commissioned by both national and local government agencies and by consulting and exploration companies. In the first case they are acquired primarily for monitoring changes in land use and quality, and for updating topographic maps. In many cases the photographic campaigns are coordinated with conventional surveying, when requirements for different scales sponsor data acquisition from a variety of altitudes. Consequently, for any area of interest to the geologist, there may be photographs with different fields of view, scales and resolutions for a number of different years and seasons.

The basic form of an aerial survey consists of a number of approximately parallel flight lines, along which exposures are timed to give at least 60% overlap between successive photographs, and whose spacing is such that adjacent lines of images have sufficient **sidelap** to ensure complete coverage (Fig. 3.26). More often than not, an aircraft cannot maintain a perfect course, because of crosswinds and turbulence. If no correction is made for crosswinds the photograph edges remain parallel to the intended flight line, but they drift away from that line (Fig. 3.26). Correction normally means turning the aircraft's nose into the wind, which causes it to **crab**, and if the camera is not reoriented the photograph edges cease to parallel the flight line, although their principal points will lie along it (Fig. 3.26). Usually these deviations are not so severe as to affect seriously the usefulness of the photography. Turbulence does cause problems however. The aircraft may rise and fall, changing the scale of each image. It may pitch or roll, imparting a tilt to each image, which produces unreal slopes in the stereomodel (Fig. 3.8).

Finally, the ground speed may change, thereby altering the overlap between adjacent images. If the overlap is less than 50% there will be strips across the images for which stereoviewing is impossible. If it is greater than 70% the stereomodel will show insufficient relief for proper interpretation.

3.9.2 Other airborne data

Airborne scanners and pushbroom systems are flown commercially by a number of private companies and by national military and civil organizations. Some of them have been used in campaigns to give scientists experience in how to use and interpret similar data from future satellite systems. Table 3.2 shows some of the specifications for two such airborne systems operating in the reflected and emitted regions, each of which has produced large volumes of data for both public use and confidential exploration. The most interesting of these is the Geoscan, operated by Carr-Boyd Pty of Australia, which incorporates spectral coverage from both the reflected and emitted regions. The wavebands in the reflected region are sufficiently narrow and positioned to enable discrimination of specific mineralogical features in spectra. The bands in the emitted region are, likewise, targeted on molecular features of emission spectra. It combines fine spectral resolution within a strategically placed but limited number of wavebands that keeps data volume within manageable limits without sacrificing the systems potential for detecting and discriminating different surface materials.

More innovative airborne systems include the NASA imaging spectrometers. The first of these (1983) was the **Airborne Imaging Spectrometer (AIS)**, which used a pushbroom, area-array detector (Section 3.6). This was superseded by the **Airborne Visible/Infrared Imaging Spectrometer (AVIRIS)** based on the whiskbroom principle. Together with a number of similar, but less widely deployed imaging spectrometers, these devices are seen as precursors to the **High-Resolution Imaging Spectrometer (HIRIS)** intended to fly in orbit in the late 1990s (Section 3.13) Details of the specifications of AVIRIS and HIRIS are given in Table 3.3.

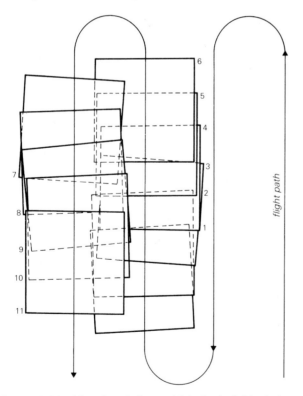

Figure 3.26 The aircraft from which the individual photographs outlined here were taken had to change its heading from the planned flight path because of wind effects. Many of the frames are therefore twisted out of alignment.

Table 3.3 Specifications of two imaging spectrometers.

	AVIRIS	HIRIS
Platform	Aircraft	Satellite
IFOV (mrad)	2.5	8.8 (30 m pixels)
Swath (pixels)	550	800
Spectral range	0.40–2.45 μm	0.40–2.45 μm
No. of channels	210	192
Bandwidth (nm)	10	10–20

Table 3.2 Spectral range of three commercial airborne multispectral imaging systems.

	Daedalus AADS 1268 IFOV 2.5 or 1.25 mrad			Geoscan AMSS Mk II IFOV 2.1 mrad			TIMS IFOV (2.5 mrad)		
Band no.	Central wavelength (µm)	Bandwidth (µm)	Band no.	Central wavelength (µm)	Bandwidth (µm)	Band no.	Central wavelength (µm)	Bandwidth (µm)	
1	0.435	0.030	1	0.522	0.042	1	8.4	0.4	
2	0.485	0.070	2	0.583	0.067	2	8.8	0.4	
3	0.560	0.080	3	0.646	0.071	3	9.2	0.4	
4	0.610	0.020	4	0.693	0.024	4	9.8	0.8	
5	0.660	0.060	5	0.717	0.024	5	10.7	1.0	
6	0.720	0.060	6	0.740	0.023	6	11.7	1.0	
7	0.830	0.140	7	0.830	0.022				
8	0.980	0.140	8	0.873	0.022				
9	1.650	0.200	9	0.915	0.021				
10	2.150	0.270	10	0.955	0.020				
11	10.500	4.000	11	2.044	0.044				
			12	2.088	0.044				
			13	2.136	0.044				
			14	2.176	0.044				
			15	2.220	0.044				
			16	2.264	0.044				
			17	2.308	0.044				
			18	2.352	0.044				
			19	8.640	0.530				
			20	9.170	0.530				
			21	9.700	0.530				
			22	10.220	0.530				
			23	10.750	0.530				
			24	11.280	0.530				

Airborne imaging radar is now routinely used by oil and mineral exploration companies in terrains, such as Indonesia Papua New Guinea and equatorial Africa, that are often cloud covered. Country-wide SAR surveys by governments are becoming widespread, the most notable being the Brazilian RADAM project in the 1970s and the current US Geological Survey programme for the whole USA. NASA has flown extensive multipolarized and multispectral radar surveys, principally in North America, as forerunners of possible Earth orbital systems and interplanetary probes. Examples of airborne SAR images are given in Chapter 7.

3.10 Basic characteristics of orbiting satellites

The orbit of a satellite is elliptical in shape, but remote-sensing satellites are usually put in orbits which are very close approximations to a circle. The laws of gravity dictate that a satellite in a higher orbit travels more slowly than one in a lower orbit, and since higher orbits are longer than lower ones this means that a high-orbiting satellite takes a good deal longer to circle the Earth than a low-orbiting satellite.

For a satellite in a circular orbit of radius R_o from the centre of the Earth, its velocity v is given by:

$$v = (GM/R_o)^{1/2} \qquad (3.10)$$

where G is the universal gravitational constant ($6.67 \times 10^{-11} \, \text{N} \, \text{m}^2 \text{kg}^{-2}$) and M is the mass of the Earth ($5.98 \times 10^{24} \, \text{kg}$).

The time taken to complete an orbit, the **orbital period**, P is given by:

$$P = 2\pi R_o/v \qquad (3.11)$$

The radius of the Earth (R_e) is 6371 km, and so the height (h) of the orbit about the Earth is:

$$h = R_o - R_e \qquad (3.12)$$

Below 180 km the Earth's atmosphere is too dense for satellites to orbit without burning as a result of frictional heating. Above 180 km there is still a small atmospheric drag on a satellite, causing its orbit to spiral downward gradually until eventually it reaches thicker atmosphere and burns. Satellites can be launched into such **low orbits**, but they do not last long. Above a few hundred kilometres there is so little atmospheric drag that a satellite will remain in **high orbit** indefinitely.

The plane of an orbit must always pass through the Earth's centre but can be in any orientation. If its orbit is inclined at more than 45° to the equatorial plane then a satellite is in **polar orbit**. An orbit that is less steeply inclined is called an **equatorial orbit** (Fig. 3.27). Various forces other than atmospheric drag can perturb an orbit,

such as the gravitational attraction of the Sun and Moon. The drift can be compensated using jets of gas to maintain the orbit and also to control the spin of the satellite.

An orbiting satellite normally changes its position in the sky continuously. However, if a satellite has an orbital period exactly the same as that in which the Earth rotates, and orbits in the same direction as the Earth rotates, it is in a **geosynchronous orbit**. To do this its orbital altitude must be 35 786 km. If a satellite is in a circular geosynchronous orbit with zero inclination (above the Equator) then it appears to remain stationary over the same point on the ground, and is in a **geostationary orbit**. Geostationary orbits are useful for communications and meteorological satellites which need to be sited sufficiently far from the globe that they can monitor almost a whole hemisphere on a nearly continuous basis. The altitude of geostationary satellites is so great that the ground resolution is low because the smallest IFOV of sensors in the reflected region is about 20 μrad, which at an altitude of 35 786 km gives about 720 m on the ground.

It is useful to obtain repeated images at the same time of day, to ensure similar illumination conditions. The time can be selected to avoid early morning mists or afternoon cloud in the tropics, to take advantage of the diurnal heating and cooling cycle in thermal infrared studies, or to ensure a low Sun angle that highlights topographic features. To do this a satellite must pass over all points at the same local solar time – it must be **Sun-synchronous**. A satellite placed in a steep polar orbit, whose motion carries it westwards over the ground at a rate comparable with the Earth's rotation, achieves this condition. Most Sun-synchronous polar orbiters pass from north to south over the sunlit hemisphere

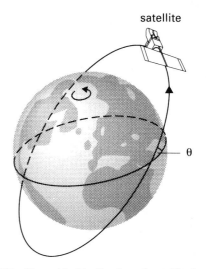

Figure 3.27 The orbital inclination of satellite is given by an angle θ between the plane of the orbit and that of the Equator. If the satellite passes directly over the poles then the inclination is 90°. For orbits that take the satellite around the globe in the same direction as the Earth's rotation then θ is less than 90°; if it travels in the opposite direction then θ is greater than 90°.

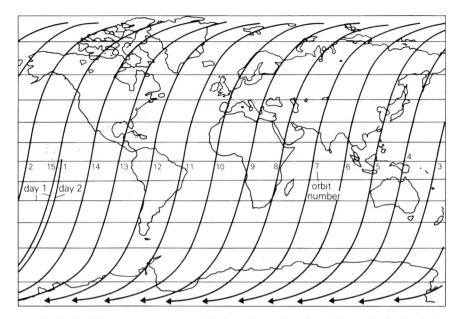

Figure 3.28 The groundtrack of a Sun-synchronous satellite (in this case Landsat-1) for a single day. In fact, the local solar time varies from 10.30 h at 60°N to 08.30 at 60°S, and a truly Sun-synchronous orbit is impossible.

and return from south to north over the night-time hemisphere. Because the Earth rotates beneath the orbital plane, successive orbits cover different groundtracks. Since the orbital period is much less than 1 day, images of several ground tracks can be acquired within 24 hours. Most Sun-synchronous remote-sensing satellites are placed in orbits with altitudes between 600 and 1000 km. At 800 km, a sensor with an instantaneous field of view of 20 μrad would have a ground resolution cell of 16 m, compared with the 720 m achieved from geosynchronous orbit.

The type of ground coverage offered by a Sun-synchronous satellite is shown in Figure 3.28. Unless the swath is very wide, there is a gap between the swaths imaged in successive orbits. Part of the design of orbiting systems is to calculate an orbital geometry that ensures that the gaps are filled as efficiently as possible. High-resolution systems with swath widths of 100–200 km can completely image the globe within about 20 days, whereas low-resolution systems, with swath widths of over 1000 km, can image the globe in the course of a single day.

One disadvantage of Sun-synchronous orbits is that it is not always possible to transmit an image to the ground as soon as it is gathered, in **real time**. To send a signal directly to the ground means that the satellite has to be above the horizon as seen from a **ground receiving station**. At typical orbit heights, the satellite has to be within about 3000 km of the station. If there is no ground receiving station in line of sight from the satellite then the image is either transmitted to the ground via a relay satellite in a higher, geosynchronous orbit or is saved on a tape recorder on-board the satellite to be transmitted to a ground station when it comes within range. Tape recorders use

power and make the satellite heavier to launch, so not all remote-sensing satellites carry them.

In the case of radar imagery a Sun-synchronous orbit is unnecessary, since the illumination is active. However, only polar orbits allow full global coverage.

Manned spacecraft are much heavier than unmanned ones, since they must carry life-support systems. This means that it is difficult to lift them into high orbits and expensive to put them in polar orbit. Equally important, it is difficult to arrange for them to land in convenient locations. Usually their orbital inclination is about the same as the latitude of the launch site. Most manned missions are of short duration, which makes them unsuitable for monitoring at a fixed solar time and incapable of acquiring comprehensive cover even within the limits of their orbital inclination. Manned missions, such as the Space Shuttle, tend to be used as test-beds for experimental systems. For example, spaceborne imaging radar was advanced considerably by Shuttle experiments.

3.11 Data from manned spacecraft

Manned satellites have provided platforms for a wide variety of remote-sensing instruments since the early days of space exploration. They have not, as yet, provided complete global cover on an operational basis, nor were they intended to. The presence of trained operators allows experimental systems to be tested from orbit, but demands on the crews' time from other activities has meant very limited coverage. In many cases the instruments have been directed repeatedly at geologically well-known targets to allow calibration and assessment of the information contained within the data. Except for data collected by Soviet cosmonauts, which are not readily available, all stem from United States' programmes operated by the **National Aeronautics and Space Administration (NASA)**. Archives for all the remotely sensed data of the Earth from manned NASA missions are held by **EROS Data Center** and at **NASA Goddard Space Flight Center**, from which catalogues and copies can be acquired (Appendix C).

The **Mercury** and **Gemini** programmes provided over a thousand normal colour and a few false-colour infrared photographs, taken from ports by hand-held 70-mm cameras. Many of them were directed at geologically interesting areas, and comprise oblique and near-vertical images. Both Gemini and Earth-orbiting **Apollo** missions were limited to orbits between 35°N and 35°S. As well as 70-mm colour cameras, Apollo 9 (1969) also carried the first orbital multispectral experiment (SO-65). This consisted of an array of four hand-triggered 70-mm cameras mounted in the port of the command module. Three of the cameras exposed black and white film to give images of the green (0.47–$0.62\,\mu m$), red (0.59–$0.72\,\mu m$) and near-infrared (0.72–$0.90\,\mu m$) regions, and the fourth used infrared colour film. Ground resolution proved to be about 100 m. This experiment was directed only at test sites in the southern USA and northern Mexico, and was coordinated with aircraft remote sensing flown at the same time as the mission. The experiment was designed as a test of the concept for an unmanned multispectral scanner, which became the Earth Resources Technology Satellite (July 1972), subsequently renamed Landsat-1 (Section 3.12.2).

The success of Landsat-1 prompted NASA to extend its remote-sensing ambitions by a series of experiments aboard **Skylab** (May 1973 to February 1974), a 100-tonne orbital workshop based on the third stage of a Saturn-V launch vehicle, which orbited between 50°N and 50°S. The S-190A experiment was an extension of the Apollo multispectral photography, and employed six synchronized cameras to produce colour infrared, natural colour and four black and white images in green, red and two near-infrared bands. The photographs cover $16\,km^2$ areas on the ground and have ground resolutions in the range 60–150 m. The S-190B **Earth Terrain Camera** experiment consisted of a single camera with an 11.4×11.4 cm frame and 45.7 cm focal length lens, sighted with the S-190A cameras, on ground areas $109\,km^2$. The films used were natural colour, colour infrared and minus-blue black and white panchromatic, yielding ground resolutions between 30 and 15 m. The most ambitious remote-sensing experiment aboard Skylab was a 13-channel multispectral scanner (S-192). This was a bizarre instrument, the data being gathered by a rotating mirror system which scanned circular swaths beneath the spacecraft. Only the forward 110° portion of each swath was recorded, so that images consist of 74-km-wide

strips made up of arcuate lines of pixels, instead of the straight lines from conventional line scanners. This makes the digital data difficult to input to most commercially available image-processing computers. The wavebands covered are five in the visible spectrum, seven in the near-infrared from 0.7 to $2.4\,\mu m$, and one in the emitted infrared. Only daytime images are available for the emitted infrared, recording differential solar heating and shadows, night-time data being required to estimate surface thermal inertia. Nominal ground resolution for the data is 79 m.

3.11.1 Space Shuttle data

The most recent development in NASA's manned spaceflight programme is the reuseable **Space Shuttle**, whose payload capacity and flexibility is enormous compared with its predecessors. The second flight in November 1981 (STS-2) carried two remote-sensing experiments of great importance to geologists, as well as several others. The first, the **Shuttle Multispectral Infrared Radiometer (SMIRR)**, was a non-imaging spectroradiometer. It measured reflectance in 10 wavebands over the range 0.5–$2.4\,\mu m$, including three with a width of $0.04\,\mu m$ in the vicinity of the Al–OH feature near $2.2\,\mu m$ (Fig. 1.9), to check in practice the theoretical possibilities for rock and mineral discrimination from orbit (Section 1.3.2). Its output enabled crude reflectance spectra for its IFOV on the ground (80 m) to be plotted and compared with data from targets of known composition.

The second system was the **Shuttle Imaging Radar (SIR-A)** experiment, employing a 23-cm (L-band) SAR system similar to that deployed on the unmanned Seasat in 1978 (Section 3.12.6). Unlike Seasat, whose main target was the ocean surface, SIR-A was designed primarily for land applications. To reduce layover problems (Section 3.5) in areas of rugged topography, without producing too much shadowing, the depression angle was fixed at 43°. The imaged ground swath to the side of the Shuttle was fixed at 50 km by the depression angle and the orbital altitude (259 km). Theoretical ground resolution was 40 m in both azimuth and range directions. Images were recorded on board as continuous holographic films which were optically correlated after the mission to reels of positive and negative film and positive prints. Some 8 hours of data were recorded, amounting to about 10 million km^2 of land and ocean between 41°N and 35°S (Appendix C). The results are one of the most fascinating archives of high-quality imagery of the planet (Fig. 3.29; see Ch. 7).

In October 1984 the Shuttle carried a system similar to SIR-A, called simply **SIR-B**. In this case, the depression angle could be varied from 75 to 30°. This flexibility allowed investigations of optimum depression angles for different kinds of application and several images with varying parallax for single areas, which permitted pseudo-

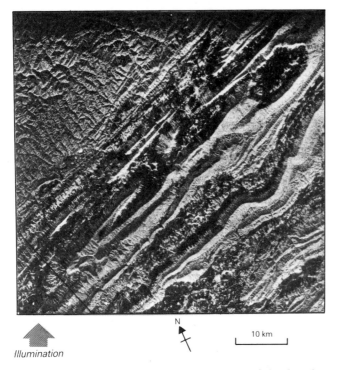

Illumination

N

10 km

Figure 3.29 This SIR-A L-band radar image of the Appalachian Plateau and the adjacent fold belt in Kentucky and Virginia shows the advantages over rugged terrain of a low depression angle. There is little distortion and many of the major geological features are displayed well. The same area is shown as Landsat MSS and RBV images in Figure 3.37 and as a Seasat SAR image in Figure 3.33. Courtesy of J.P. Ford, Jet Propulsion Laboratory, Pasadena.

stereoscopic viewing. The antenna was also pointable, so that test sites could be viewed from a variety of look directions. As well as various other advantages (Ch. 7), the pointability meant that small areas could be 'looked at' many times, thereby improving either resolution or image quality. Data were acquired in both optical hologram form and as digital records for swaths between 57°N and 57°S. Images were expected to be of even better quality than those from SIR-A, with an azimuth resolution of 25 m and a ground-range resolution between 17 and 58 m for the digital data. Image swaths were determined largely by the requirements of a large team of investigators, and in some cases comprised adjacent ground swaths with the same depression angle, which allow overlapping cover of ground strips up to 250 km wide (Appendix C). Unfortunately, technical problems during the mission thwarted many of the planned acquisitions, and only a few images are of usable quality. Future plans for Shuttle imaging radar involved the use of multispectral radar systems with various polarizations (Ch. 7), and polar orbits to give potentially complete coverage of the globe. However, the explosion in 1985 of the Shuttle *Challenger* shortly after launch caused this venture and many other scheduled remote sensing experiments to be shelved. Since the *Challenger* disaster, no publicly accessible remote-sensing experiments have been conducted.

In early 1984, a Shuttle mission carried two European imaging systems with potential for geological applications. One was a **Metric Camera**, for cartographic applications, with a ground resolution of 30 m and frame size of 23 cm square, which exposed false-colour infrared and panchromatic film. The other was the first test of the West German **Modular Optical-Electronic Multispectral Scanner (MOMS)** which used a pushbroom system with a ground IFOV of 20 m and two bands (0.58–0.63, 0.83–0.98 μm). Ultimately, MOMS was planned to consist of three pushbroom systems, two pointed fore and aft to give panchromatic stereoscopic capability and one aimed vertically downwards to gather data with 25-m resolution in four wavebands between 0.45 and 1.05 μm. This too has never been flown.

As well as the SIR-B system, the October 1984 Shuttle mission carried the **Large Format Camera (LFC)**, which produced panchromatic natural colour and false-colour infrared images. The LFC incorporated motion compensation, so that the effective resolution of the panchromatic photographs is between 8 and 15 m, depending on the altitude of the Shuttle orbits. The frame size is 23 × 46 cm, equivalent to ground areas of 250 × 500 to 350 × 700 km. A total of 2160 photographs, many of geologically interesting areas in arid and largely unknown terrains, was archived. Since the camera was operated in the same way as an aerial camera, with various overlaps between frames, the images can be viewed steroscopically for both interpretation and accurate cartography. This instrument was never flown again, and the archive of negatives was reported to have been sold by NASA for a peppercorn sum to a commercial distributor (Appendix C). Several LFC images are shown in Chapter 4. Figure 3.30 is an example of an LFC photograph for comparison with Landsat images of the same area later in this chapter.

Remote-sensing experiments scheduled for tests aboard the Shuttle until the *Challenger* disaster included the **Thermal Infrared Multispectral Scanner (TIMS)**, collecting emitted radiation in six bands between 8 and 12 μm (Table 3.2). Results from the aircraft-mounted version of this are discussed in Chapter 6. Another important but unflown candidate was an imaging spectroradiometer similar to AVIRIS (Section 3.9.2, Table 3.3). As in other manned missions, the astronauts took many photographs from the ports of the Shuttles with a variety of cameras. These are easily obtained from NASA (Appendix C).

3.12 Data from unmanned spacecraft

There are three overwhelming advantages of unmanned orbital platforms:

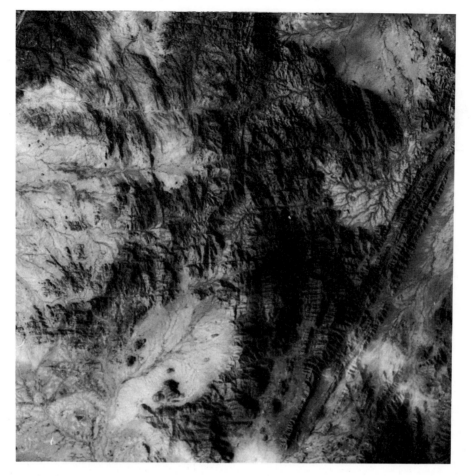

Figure 3.30 Large Format Camera image of semiarid mountains in Eritrea, northeastern Africa. The effective resolution is about 10 m. See Figure 3.36 also.

(a) Not requiring complex and heavy life-support systems, they are cheap to build and launch, and need not be recovered.

(b) They can be placed in Sun-synchronous polar orbits that guarantee the possibility of almost complete global coverage (Section 3.10).

(c) Subject to the deterioration of equipment and exhaustion of propellants required for orbit adjustments, they can operate for very long periods gathering repetitive data. Humans can endure the conditions of orbital travel for only a matter of months.

3.12.1 Meteorological and oceanographic satellites

The most enduring, successful and consistent production of remotely sensed images of the Earth has been from unmanned meteorological satellites. To describe and illustrate them all and the variety of devices which they have carried is beyond the scope of this book. Primarily, of course, they are designed to monitor global climatic features, and their instruments are tuned to cloud cover and patterns, atmospheric water content, precipitation and both land- and sea-surface temperatures. Some also carry instruments aimed at oceanographic features, such as the abundance of phytoplankton and particulate matter in sea water. Their prime objective has been monitoring of the entire planet on a day-to-day basis. Consequently their design and their orbits ensure coverage of vast areas at coarse resolution, between 800 m and 25 km. For many geological applications the features of interest are too small to be resolved. Their super-synoptic view, however, does make some of the data useful for gaining a gross overview of regional geology. In the same way that high-resolution satellite images help coordinate the information drawn from aerial photographs and field work, meteorological images can help draw together the findings from a study of better resolution satellite images.

The first image-gathering unmanned satellite was the US **Television and Infrared Observation Satellite (TIROS-1)**, launched on April 1 1960. It carried two miniature television cameras on an 800-km orbit between about 50°N and 50°S, with a period of about 100 minutes. This began an ongoing series of low-altitude environmental satellites launched from the USA. For administrative reasons a deep

N

Figure 3.31 The gross geomorphology of an area of about 4 million km², covering parts of Afghanistan, Pakistan, part of the former USSR and Tibet, is shown on this Channel 1 (red) image from the AVHRR aboard NOAA-7. The High Himalaya and Tibetan Plateau in the east are largely snow or cloud covered. The Himalayan foothills are densely forested and appear dark. The fertile plains of the Indus and its tributaries are dark, in contrast to the light-coloured desert areas. The geological advantages of a super-synoptic view are amply illustrated by the interconnected complexities of the Sulaiman and Salt Ranges of NW Pakistan. They are truncated in the far west by a huge strike-slip fault, along which the Indian Subcontinent has slipped during its collision with Asia.

well of confusion surrounds their naming, partly because before launch they had one name and then were rechristened in orbit. Their administering body also changed name. For simplicity they are known as the **TIROS/ESSA/NOAA** series, which were placed in near-polar orbits to gather data for most of the globe. They were first administered by the US Environmental Science Service (ESSA), which became the **National Oceanic and Atmospheric Administration (NOAA)**.

The first geostationary image-gathering satellite, with an orbit at about 41 000 km, was NASA's **Applications Technology Satellite (ATS-1)**, launched in December 1966. It provided a view of almost an entire hemisphere from a position above the Equator, and was succeeded by a series of similar platforms: Soviet **GOMS**, the Japanese **Himawari** (over the western Pacific), the European Space Agency **Meteosat** (over the eastern Atlantic), and the Indian **INSAT** (over the Indian Ocean). Together these make up the **GOES** family, administered by the World

Meteorological Organization in Geneva. The bulk of instruments aboard these platforms produce a range of data on a nearly real-time basis, but much is of too coarse a resolution to be geologically useful. However, the panchromatic visible sensors aboard the geostationary platforms have a resolution of 900 m, which does enable some gross geological detail to be seen.

The most geologically useful instrument aboard the current TIROS/ESSA/NOAA series is the **Advanced Very High Resolution Radiometer (AVHRR)**. This is a linescanning system, whose mirror sweeps through 56° either side of the nadir of the groundtrack. The system's IFOV together with the orbital altitude (833 km) leads to a ground resolution of about 1.1 km at nadir, degrading outwards because of the large scanning angle. Consequently, the uncorrected images become grossly distorted towards their edges, and must be geometrically corrected by computer (Appendix B). Each scan records data for 2048 pixels, which, together with the off-nadir distortion, means that images cover a swath width greater than 2500 km. All the NOAA series satellites operate from a near-polar, Sun-synchronous orbit, and cross the same ground area repeatedly at the same local time. Two satellites are always functioning, one passing over at 07.30 h the other at 14.30 h, on descending orbits (southwards). They cross the night-time side of the Earth 12 hours later on ascending orbits. The orbital period of 102 minutes results in 14.1 orbits per day, ensuring complete global coverage every 12 hours.

The AVHRR instrument has five channels sampling radiation from visible red to emitted infrared (Table 3.4). The detectors output intensity levels in digital form in the range 0–1023 (10-bit precision). Transmission to the ground takes two forms. Data are broadcast continuously at full resolution, when any suitably equipped ground receiving station can record and display it – **High-resolution picture transmission (HRPT)**. Five on-board recorders can each store 10 minutes of full-resolution data – **local area coverage (LAC)** – and a full orbit (110 minutes) of data which has been resampled to give 4-km resolution – **global area coverage (GAC)**. These stored data are transmitted to NOAA ground receiving stations in the USA, when the satellites are in line of sight with the receiving antennae. Figure 3.31 is an example of a visible-red LAC image from the NOAA-7 AVHRR. One advantage of the daily capture of images from the AVHRR is that eventually a cloud-free image or one with minimal cloud cover will be acquired. It therefore becomes possible to **mosaic** several such images to build up super-synoptic images of whole continents. This has been done for the whole world.

AVHRR imagery, though suited to investigations of very large geological features, is currently underused by geologists. However, two popular applications are: estimation of rainfall from cloud density and temperature and monitoring of snow masses. Both can be done on a daily basis and provide essential input to models of stream run-off used by hydrologists.

Between 1964 and 1978 various sensors were tried out on satellites of the **Nimbus** series, operated by NASA. **Nimbus-7** was the last of the series, launched in October 1978 into a 955-km Sun-synchronous orbit with an inclination of 99.3° and a repeat cycle of 6 days, and was retired in September 1984. Nimbus-7 carried a variety of radiometers ranging from the ultraviolet to microwaves, including the **Coastal Zone Color Scanner (CZCS)**. The CZCS covered a swath width of 1566 km, resulting in significant foreshortening towards the edges, with a pixel size of 825 m at nadir. There were six spectral bands, four of which were narrow channels (0.02 μm) in the visible region for mapping algal chlorophyll and other suspended material in the oceans, a VNIR channel for mapping surface vegetation and a thermal infrared channel aimed at ocean temperature variations. CZCS data had great potential for regional geological overview, but have rarely

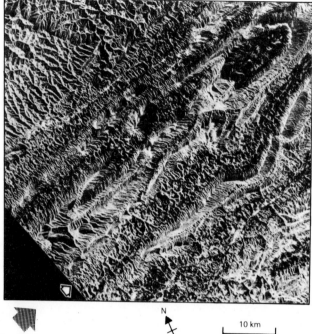

Illumination

N

10 km

Figure 3.32 This extract from a Seasat L-band radar image is of the same area in NE USA as Figures 3.29 and 3.36. The radar look direction is at 45° to that for the SIR-A image in Figure 3.29. This, combined with the steeper depression angle for the Seasat SAR compared with that for SIR-A, makes the image virtually unintelligible. The look direction is parallel to the main mountain ridges and valleys in the Appalachian fold belt and so they are suppressed. The rugged topography has resulted in the image being plagued by foreshortening and layover effects, which further disrupt its structure. However in the Appalachian Plateau – northern part of the image – there are advantages. The dominant southwards drainage is enhanced, allowing discordant linear features, probably major faults, to be picked out.

been used because of the patchy nature of the cover (Appendix C). There are plans to replace the CZCS with a similar, but finer resolution system known as the **Sea Wide-Field Sensor (Sea-WIFS)**. This may be carried by a future Landsat platform.

Seasat was launched into a 790 km, 108° inclination polar orbit in June 1978. It carried a variety of radiometers and a radar altimeter (Ch. 8), but more significantly it had the first SAR system to be used in orbit. This was an L-band (23.5 cm) system with a depression angle of 70°, giving a swath width of 100 km and a resolution of about 25 m. A steep depression angle results in topographic layover (Section 3.5) and other distortions in rugged terrains (Fig. 3.32), but is especially suitable for imaging the ocean surface to assess its roughness. In fact, as its name suggests, Seasat was designed to be used for oceanographic applications, but the radar also proved useful over land. The area of SAR coverage for Seasat was limited to North America and the northern Atlantic region by the available ground stations (Figure C.3) Unfortunately, a power failure terminated Seasat operations after only 105 days of operation. Nevertheless, it provided sufficient evidence of the advantages of all-weather, day or night orbital SAR imaging to increase the impetus for more geologically oriented systems, such as SIR-A and SIR-B.

3.12.2 The Landsat series

The experiments from manned satellites and the results and success of the semipermanent meteorological satellite systems encouraged NASA to initiate a series of high-resolution orbital systems aimed at the biological and physical resources of the Earth. The first **Earth Resources Technology Satellite (ERTS-1)** was launched by NASA on July 23 1972, using a Nimbus platform (Fig. 3.33a). It was subsequently renamed **Landsat-1**, to complement the oceanographic satellite Seasat, and eventually the administration of the Landsat series passed first to NOAA and then to a commercial company, **EOSAT** (Appendix C). The 918-km Landsat orbits passed within 9° of the poles, and circled the Earth once every 103 minutes. Descending orbits crossed the Equator at an angle of 9° at around 09.30 h local time. The Landsat series is Sun-synchronous, and images are illuminated by the mid-morning Sun at relatively low elevation. This arrangement was to avoid early morning cloud at mid-latitudes, but also to ensure highlighting of topography by a low Sun angle. Successive orbits were shifted up to 2760 km west from their predecessor (Fig. 3.34), so that the same point on the ground was crossed every 18 days, to a precision of about 37 km. Every part of the globe, except for the near-polar regions, which are never crossed, can therefore be imaged up to 20

times per year. Unlike the AVHRR, the Landsat imaging systems cover a narrow (185 km) swath, so there are gaps in the ground coverage in successive orbits (Figure 3.34). However, over an 18-day period (251 orbits) a complete set of groundtracks was covered by Landsats 1–3, spaced 159 km apart at the equator and giving a 14% sideways overlap, after which time the cycle repeated. The sideways overlap increased towards the poles, and reached 50% at 54° latitude, so that every point at this latitude was covered twice as frequently as most points on the Equator. The groundtrack of a Landsat 1–3 satellite over a single day is illustrated in Figure 3.28, and the relationship between adjacent orbits on successive days is shown in Figure 3.34. This repeated pattern of overpasses, common to all Sun-synchronous satellites, is the basis for the Landsat world-wide reference system (Appendix C) for individual scenes, whose principle is followed by other operational systems.

In 1982 a new orbital plan was adopted for Landsat-4 and -5 and their successors. This involved a new, heavier platform (Fig. 3.33b) and a lower orbit (705 km), which resulted in a shorter orbital period (99 minutes), a shorter repeat cycle of 16 days and a greater number of orbits to give global coverage. This was to give greater orbital stability and to help improve the resolution of the on-board sensors.

Landsat-1 and -2 were equipped with two imaging systems. One was a three-channel **return-beam vidicon (RBV)** system, the other a four-channel **multispectral scanner (MSS)**, both aimed at visible and VNIR bands containing features related to chlorophyll (Table 3.4). The original Landsat concept was clearly oriented towards monitoring of vegetation rather than geology. The one

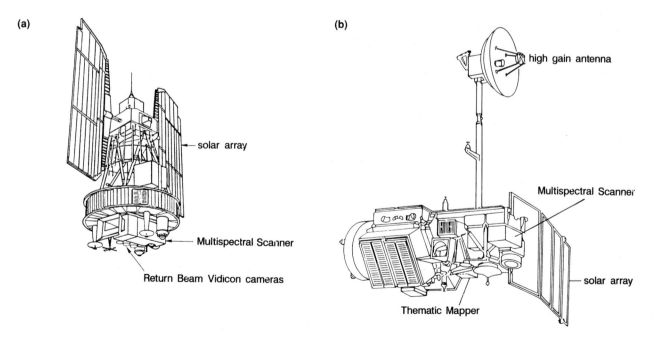

(a)

solar array

Multispectral Scanner

Return Beam Vidicon cameras

(b)

high gain antenna

Multispectral Scanner

solar array

Thematic Mapper

Figure 3.33 The first three Landsats occupied spare Nimbus platforms (a), while that for Landsat-4 and -5 is a modified TIROS platform (b).

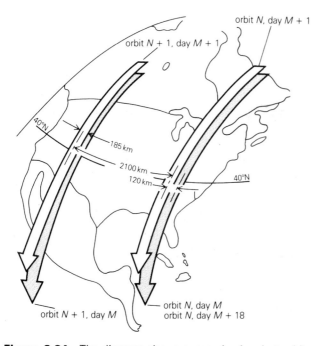

orbit N, day M + 1

orbit N + 1, day M + 1

40°N

185 km

2100 km

120 km

40°N

orbit N + 1, day M

orbit N, day M

orbit N, day M + 18

Figure 3.34 The diagram shows successive Landsat orbits on two days. On day M, orbit N+1 is shifted 2100 km west of orbit N at this latitude. Orbit N on day M+1 is only 120 km west of the same orbit of the previous day, so the images taken on both days overlap. The higher the latitude, the greater the overlap between adjacent scenes. The sequence repeated itself every 18 days for Landsat-1, -2 and -3. This revisit frequency was reduced to 16 days for Landsat-4 and -5. Very much the same principle applies to all Sun-synchronous. polar-orbiting systems. In the case of the NOAA AVHRR, the revisit frequency is every 12 hours to give day and night coverage.

concession to geologists was the low-Sun-angle illumination, which it was hoped would highlight appropriately oriented topographic features. There can be little doubt that Landsat was funded in order to maintain a permanent high-precision watch on world agriculture, particularly that of the USA's main customer for wheat, the Soviet Union. Nevertheless, the quality of the early Landsat data found its most exciting applications in geology.

The RBVs aboard Landsat-1 and -2 provided very few data. However, they left a legacy in the naming of the four MSS bands, which are designated bands 4, 5, 6 and 7, since they followed the RBV bands in sequence. The Landsat 1–3 MSS system had a scanning angle of about 12° using an oscillating mirror (Fig. 3.9). This collected radiation for banks of six sensors for each of the four wavebands, which was directed by a dispersing element to the detectors by optic fibres. The dimensions of the fibre ends determined the IFOV of the system, which was 109 μrad, resulting in a ground resolution of 79 × 79 m. The sampling rate, however, was such that each pixel overlapped those adjacent by about 11.5 m, resulting in an actual pixel size of 79 m depth and 56 m width. With the lower orbit of Landsat-4 and -5 the MSS scan angle was increased to maintain the swath

width at 185 km, and the optics were adjusted to preserve the approximately 80 m IFOV (actually 82 m). The spectral bands were identical to the old MSS, though renumbered as bands 1–4 as mentioned above, so that old and new MSS data are very closely comparable – essential to maintain data continuity through the whole programme.

The analogue data from each MSS detector are electronically chopped and digitized to a 0–63 range (6-bit precision). On Landsats 1–3 the data were either relayed directly to a ground receiving station or recorded by an on-board tape recorder until the platform was above a ground receiving station. On Landsat-4 and -5 there are no tape recorders and data are telemetered to the ground either directly or via a series of **tracking and data relay satellites (TDRS)**. The data are rescaled on the ground to 0–127 for bands 4, 5 and 6 (now 1, 2 and 3) and 0–63 for band 7 (now 4), and output either to film using a digital film writer or to computer-compatible tape (CCT). In both cases the data are used in the range 0–255 (8-bit precision), but of course only 64 different real levels are possible in the data. The detectors are calibrated by lamps built into the system in such a way that the darkest expected surface – deep clear water or black rock – and the lightest – cloud or snow – both give responses within the range. Because cloud or snow is so much brighter in the four bands than any surface vegetation, soil or rock, this means that cloud-free images generally have their data compressed into a relatively small range of low digital numbers and require contrast enhancement (Ch. 5).

The Landsat 1–3 MSS collected data for 3240 56-m-wide pixels during every sweep of the mirror, each 474 m deep – 79 m for each of the six detectors. The ground swath imaged on each overpass was therefore about 185 km wide. The continuous stream of data was sampled about every 25 seconds, giving a total of 2340 lines, so that each sample represents an area 185 × 185 km on the ground. This is termed a **scene**. Each scene acquired by Landsat does not represent a square area on the ground, but a parallelogram (Fig. 3.12h), because of the effect of the Earth rotating in the time taken to gather the data. Nor are the scenes oriented precisely relative to true north. This is because the orbits are inclined; in fact they are slightly curved (Fig. 3.28). Apart from data from Landsat-1 and -2, scenes have generally been corrected for Earth rotation effects, although the user must register them to local map coordinates (Appendix B). An extract from a Landsat MSS image is shown in *Figure 3.35a*.

Landsat-3, launched in May 1978 to continue the repeated MSS coverage, incorporated two modifications, though the MSS remained unchanged. The RBV was changed from multispectral to a high-resolution panchromatic mode. Although RBV image quality is variable, the two on-board cameras produced images corresponding to quarter scenes gathered by the MSS. Each is equivalent to 98 km² on the ground, giving 13 km overlap on adjacent

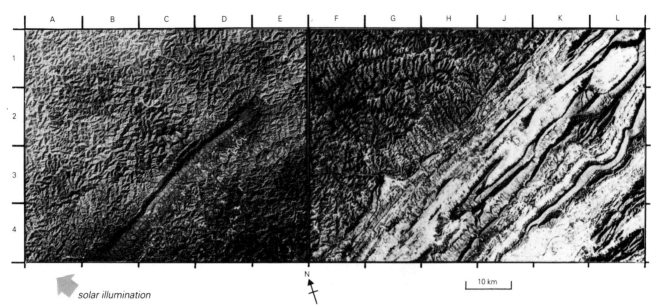

solar illumination

N

10 km

Figure 3.36 The left-hand part of this image was produced by the Landsat-3 RBV system and is effectively a panchromatic picture in the visible range. The right-hand part is of Landsat MSS band 5 data, and is a continuation of the same area. The area is the same as in Figures 3.29 and 3.32, the Appalachian Plateau and fold belt of Kentucky and Virginia, USA. Both were acquired in winter with a low Sun angle, which gives maximum accentuation of topography. Comparison between the two parts shows that considerably finer topographic detail is visible in the RBV image than can be resolved in the MSS image. Courtesy of the Jet Propulsion Laboratory, Pasadena.

images. The RBV imagery has a nominal 30-m resolution, achieved by doubling the focal length of the camera lens. The images were acquired instantaneously in pairs by the two cameras, twice during the capture of one MSS scene. The signals stripped from the RBV vidicon plate are formatted digitally, in much the same fashion as the MSS data, but incorporate the images of **reseau marks** in the form of crosses engraved on the plate. These were intended to aid in cartographic uses of the RBV data. The improved resolution had considerable advantages over MSS data for applications in structural geology (Fig. 3.36), given the best quality of the rather variable RBV imagery.

The other addition to Landsat-3 was a line-scan system for emitted infrared. This thermal data had a resolution of 120 m, with a similar structure to the MSS data. However, the thermal channel failed shortly after launch.

The gradual deterioration in the performance of all systems aboard Landsat-3, in particular increasing problems with the internal signals to start each line of the MSS, forced an early launch of its successor, Landsat-4, in September 1982. As well as a completely new platform design and the replacement of on-board recording capability with direct telemetry of data by multipurpose data-relay satellites, Landsat-4 carried an entirely new instrument – the **Thematic Mapper (TM)** – as well as an almost unchanged MSS. The TM is a line-scan system, but incorporates several innovations compared with MSS. Instead of using fibre optics to carry radiation to the detectors, they are placed directly at the focal planes of the optical system. One of these focal planes carries four banks

of 16 detectors for four wavebands in the visible to VNIR range. Another is refrigerated by a radiative cooler, and carries two banks of 16 detectors for two wavebands in the SWIR region, and one bank of four detectors for emitted infrared. (Table 3.4 shows the specifications for TM wavebands. There is an apparent anomaly in the numbering of the bands – band 7 is in the SWIR, while band 6 contains thermal data. This arose from the late addition of the SWIR band at the request of a powerful geological lobby.) This arrangement allows the mirror to scan a ground strip with approximately the same width as that scanned by the MSS, but radiation is collected by 16 instead of six detectors for the visible and near-infrared channels. The ground IFOV in these channels is therefore 30 m, an improvement of about 2.6 times compared with that of the MSS. Resolution for the thermal channel is 120 m. To match the IFOV to the platform's orbital velocity, the mirror gathers data in both forward and backward sweeps. This means that the actual scan lines are not exactly parallel on the ground because of orbital motion. Correction for this distortion results in an actual pixel size of 28.5 m.

Thematic Mapper scenes are almost the same size as those from the accompanying MSS, but because of the improved resolution and larger number of channels comprise 8.5 times as many digital numbers. This poses considerable difficulties for transmitting, receiving and handling the data. Considerably fewer TM scenes are available world-wide than those from the MSS, but the number in archive is still enormous. Landsat-4 ceased to operate early in 1983 because of problems with power

Table 3.4 Spectral bands covered by five geologically useful orbiting systems.

Landsat		AVHRR		SPOT		JERS-1 (Fuyo-1)		ASTER	
Band no.	Range (μm)	Band no.	Range (μm)	Band no.	Range (μm)	Band no.	Range (μm)	Band no.	Range (μm)
MSS 1 (4)	0.5–0.6	1	0.58–0.68	XS 1	0.5–0.59	1	0.52–0.60	1	0.52–0.60
MSS 2 (5)	0.6–0.7	2	0.73–1.10	XS 2	0.61–0.68	2	0.63–0.69	2	0.63–0.69
MSS 3 (6)	0.7–0.8	3	3.55–3.93	XS 3	0.79–0.89	3	0.76–0.86	3	0.76–0.86
MSS 4 (7)	0.8–1.1	4	10.5–11.5	P	0.51–0.73	4 (stereo)	0.76–0.86	4	1.600–1.700
MSS (8)	10.4–12.6	5	11.5–12.5			5	1.60–1.71	5	2.145–2.185
TM 1	0.45–0.52					6	2.01–2.12	6	2.185–2.225
TM 2	0.52–0.60					7	2.13–2.25	7	1.235–2.285
TM 3	0.63–0.69					8	2.27–2.40	8	2.295–2.365
TM 4	0.76–0.90							9	2.360–2.430
TM 5	1.55–1.75							10	8.125–8.475
TM 6	10.4–12.5							11	8.475–8.825
TM 7	2.08–2.35							12	8.925–9.275
								13	10.25–10.95
								14	10.95–11.65

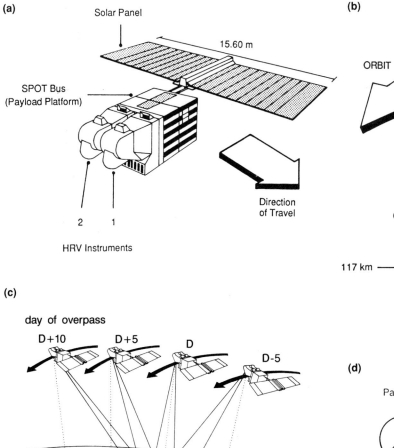

(a)

Solar Panel

15.60 m

SPOT Bus
(Payload Platform)

2 1

HRV Instruments

Direction
of Travel

(b)

HRV Instruments

ORBIT

HRV 1 HRV 2

60 km

117 km

60 km

3 km

(c)

day of overpass

D+10 D+5 D D-5

swath
observed

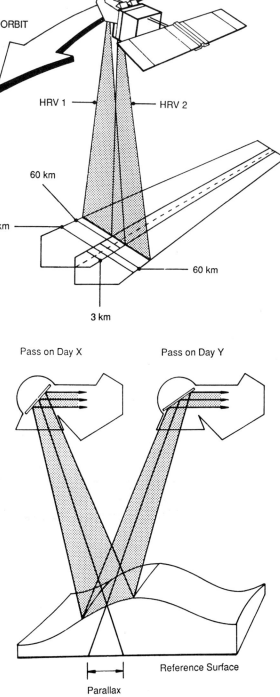

(d)

Pass on Day X Pass on Day Y

Reference Surface

Parallax

Figure 3.37 The SPOT platform carries two HRV sensors (a) that image two 60-km swaths directly below the satellite with 3 km overlap (b). Pointable mirrors in the HRVs allow viewing at various angles to the side to allow revisits at frequencies up to every 5 days (c) or stereoscopic imaging (d).

supply and serviceability of its relay system. Fortunately it was possible to replace it with an already prepared, but slightly modified, back-up system, now designated Landsat-5, in March 1984. *Figure 3.35* shows a Landsat TM image compared with one from the MSS system.

Because of the overlap between the image swaths for adjacent Landsat paths, which increases with increasing latitude, it is possible to view parts of the images stereoptically (Appendix A). A system designed to produce stereo pairs of images by pointing the detecting system off-nadir, thereby introducing parallax differences between images, is the French **Système Probatoire de l'Observation de la Terre (SPOT)**.

3.12.3 SPOT data

SPOT-1 was launched into an 830-km Sun-synchronous polar orbit (98.7° inclination) in February 1986 by the French **Centre National d'Études Spatial (CNES)** and is operated by **SPOT-Image**. The platform and its successor, SPOT-2, cross a point on the Equator on descending orbits at 10.30 h solar time every 26 days. The SPOT system employs two pushbroom devices (Section 3.4) (**Haute Resolution Visible – HRV**) comprising arrays of 6000 CCDs (Figs. 3.14 and 3.37a). These may operate in either a panchromatic mode with a ground IFOV of 10 m, or multispectrally to gather green, red and VNIR reflectance (Table 3.4) with an IFOV of 20 m. The imaged swath, when directly below the platform, is 60 km wide. In the panchromatic mode scenes comprise an array 6000 pixels square, and in the multispectral mode each scene is 3000 pixels square.

SPOT marked two significant advances in remote sensing; it was the first unmanned satellite to use a pushbroom system and was the first remote-sensing satellite to offer stereoscopic cover. By pointing both HRV sensors downwards it is possible to image a strip 117 km wide, with a 3-km overlap between instruments (Fig. 3.37b). Alternatively, by means of steerable mirrors that direct radiant energy onto the CCD arrays and point up to 27° either side of vertical, one or both HRV instruments can image a swath centred up to 475 km on either side of the groundtrack. This ability means that a stereoscopic pair of images can be acquired by imaging the same area from different directions, during different orbits (Fig. 3.37c). A steroscopic SPOT image is used to illustrate part of Section 4.4.1. The same area can also be revisited up to 11 times during the 26-day period, depending on the latitude (Fig. 3.37d). As well as providing routine high-resolution images, SPOT is also capable of responding to short-lived events, such as floods and volcanic eruptions.

SPOT platforms carry a tape recorder and transmit images recorded from around the world, as well as images of Europe in real time, to ground stations at Kiruna (Sweden) and Toulouse (France). In addition, many of the Landsat ground stations are also licensed to record and distribute SPOT data. The next in the series, SPOT-3, will be the same as the first two systems. It is planned that SPOT-4 will carry an additional spectral band at 1.58–1.75 µm and also a 1–4 km pixel vegetation-sensing system, using five spectral bands (blue, green, red, VNIR and SWIR), with a 2200-km-wide swath (extending 50° either side of nadir).

3.12.4 JERS-1 (Fuyo-1) data

In February 1992 the Japanese **National Space Development Agency (NASDA)** launched what is probably the most technically sophisticated, multipurpose remote-sensing system in the civilian domain. It was called simply the **Japanese Earth Resources Satellite-1 (JERS-1)** and renamed Fuyo-1 on reaching orbit. It carries two imaging systems, an **optical sensor (OPS)** and a **synthetic-aperture radar (SAR) system**. The JERS-1 orbit is at an altitude of 568 km with a 97.7° inclination, which allows a revisit period of 44 days.

The OPS is oriented to the reflected region of the spectrum and intended for detailed discrimination of vegetation, soils and rocks. It incorporates two radiometers, one carrying sensors for the visible and near-infrared, the other for the SWIR. Both can point vertically downwards, but the optics of that carrying visible and near-infrared sensors can also point 15.3° ahead of the nadir to obtain stereoscopic images. The seven spectral bands capturing data from the nadir (Table 3.4) each have a dedicated 4096-element CCD array capable of measurements with 6-bit (64 DN) precision. This configuration, together with an IFOV of 32.2 µrad, produces images 75 km across with a pixel size of 18.3×24.2 m. The forward-looking radiometer produces only a single VNIR band to be used with the corresponding one from the nadir-pointing mode for stereoscopic imagery.

The three bands in the 2.0–2.4 µm region are specifically aimed at Al–OH, Mg–OH and C–O bond transitions (Section 1.3.2) and should enable much more confident separation of clays, hydroxylated ferromagnesian minerals and carbonates than has been possible hitherto with operational remote-sensing systems. Technical considerations limit the dynamic range of the data to 64 DN compared with the 256 DN of Landsat TM data, which may trim this optimistic view somewhat. Also, early OPS data suffered from system noise, particularly in the SWIR region.

The JERS-1 SAR is also of considerable interest to geologists. It is a 23-cm L-band system with a depression angle of 55° aimed at suppressing layover and shadowing in high-relief areas that plague SAR images with larger and smaller depression angles respectively (Fig. 3.23, 3.38). The image swath will be 75 km across with a ground resolution of 18 m in both range and azimuth directions.

3.12.5 Other systems of interest

The **Heat Capacity Mapping Mission (HCMM)** experiment was launched by NASA in April 1978 into a near-polar orbit at 620 km (97.6° inclination) It ceased operation in September 1980. Its orbits were Sun-synchronous with times of equatorial passage of 14.00 and 03.00 h local time, chosen to match those of the average maximum and minimum daily soil temperatures. This offered the potential for estimating the areal variation in surface thermal inertia, when the day and night-time data werecorrectly registered (Section 1.3.2). Two sensors were carried, one covering visible and near-infrared (0.5–1.1 µm), the other emitted infrared (10.5–12.5 µm). The ground resolution of the thermal scanner was about 600 m, reduced to 480 m after on-board processing. The imaged ground swath was about 716 km wide. Because day and night orbits were inclined to one another, the shape of each scene of registered thermal data was that of a lozenge. For economy's sake, HCMM did not carry an on-board recording system. Consequently, data are available only for areas within range of suitably equipped ground receiving stations (Appendix C). However, the potential for extracting important information relating to rock types and to soil moisture is so great that HCMM results are discussed at some length in Chapter 6.

The Japanese **Marine Observation Satellite (MOS-1)** was launched into a Sun-synchronous 909-km 99° inclination orbit in February 1987. Its orbital repeat is 17 days, and Equator crossing time is between 10.00 and 11.00 h. Much of its coverage is limited to the region surrounding the Japanese ground station. MOS-1 carries three remote-sensing instruments. The only one of interest to geologists is the **Multispectral Electronic Self-Scanning Radiometer (MESSR)**, which is a pushbroom device recording 50-m pixels in four spectral bands similar to those used by the Landsat MSS (Table 3.4).

The **Indian Remote Sensing Satellite (IRS-1A)** was launched into a 904-km Sun-synchronous polar orbit by a Russian launch vehicle in March 1988. The orbital repeat is 22 days, with an equatorial overpass time of 10.00 h. The satellite carries three pushbroom **linear imaging self scanning (LISS)** cameras, each recording the same four visible and near-infrared spectral bands (0.4–0.5, 0.5–0.6, 0.6–0.7, 0.7–0.9 μm). LISS-1 covers a 148-km swath with a ground IFOV of 73 m. LISS-2A and LISS-2B are identical and image adjacent swaths on either side of the ground track at 36.5-m pixel size. Most data are transmitted to the Indian ground station in Hyderabad (limiting the coverage to India and its vicinity), but there are plans to receive some data at other receiving stations.

In 1988 images from part of the Soviet space programme, which had hitherto been shrouded in secrecy came onto the market. They stem from a satellite series known as **Resurs**, the first of which became operational in 1980 and which are in 250 km polar orbit. Resurs images can only be obtained in photographic form and are captured by four sensor systems. Three of these are line scanners operating in the visible and near-infrared (**Kate-140, Kate-200, MKF-6**). The fourth system is high-resolution (5 m) photography, using colour infrared film, ejected from the satellite and recovered on the ground (**KFS-1000**). Some of the data have stereoscopic potential. However, permission from the authorities of an overflown country is needed to gain access to the data.

In 1991 the **European Space Agency (ESA)** launched **ERS-1** in a blaze of publicity. Much of this was aimed at the geological community since ERS-1 carries a 5.3-cm C-band SAR imaging system, as well as a number of other instruments for marine applications. ERS-1 flies in polar orbit at 777 km altitude, but is not Sun-synchronous. The SAR imagery from ERS-1 has an 80-km swath width and is rated at a 30-m resolution for range and azimuth resolution. Its depression angle is the same as that for Seasat (67°), since it is largely oriented to monitoring the state of the ocean surface. Such a steep depression inevitably leads to layover in even moderately rugged topography. Although ERS-1 SAR imagery is of extremely good quality, the layover problem serves to highlight the deficiencies inherent in its design (Fig. 3.38a). It seems to offer little advantage in geological mapping in all but the most muted terrain because of this and its limited availability. Figure 3.38 also shows a JERS-1 SAR image of the same area, where the terrestrially more appropriate depression angle produces geologically more useful information.

3.13 Future prospects

For the period up to 2005 there are plans for enough civilian remote-sensing satellites to fill a separate chapter. Plans, however, only materialize given money, and many of the programmes are either unfunded or on shaky financial ground. Owing to technical difficulties, even funded ventures do not leave the ground on time. Some do not work properly, although only the SIR-B problems led to near-suicidal disappointment among scheduled investigators. Limiting the scope of this section is consequently not so difficult. Only those future systems that have a geological impact, and those which seem likely to fly, are discussed. The 1990s and the early years of the next century seem likely not to see great innovation in land-oriented remote sensing. At least, that is to be hoped, for the vast bulk of geologists are not 'up to speed' with Landsat, let alone with the hyperspectral capabilities of imaging spectrometers. The same cannot be said for atmospheric and oceanographic studies, which are far more advanced. The growing problems of global warming, pollution and environmental change have forced a change of focus from simple meteorological data to the application of rather arcane physical laws in the quest for means of understanding what the Earth is currently going through.

For most users of land-oriented remotely sensed data, the most pressing need is for assurance of continuity of tried and tested systems. The Landsat series is assured up to the launch of the sixth and seventh platforms in the series, with a few modifications. These include a 15-m-resolution panchromatic sensor to rival SPOT, an improvement of the TM thermal sensor to 60 m resolution and replacement of the MSS with improved dynamic range and 60 m resolution. The future of the extremely promising JERS programme depends largely on the demand for its products and the performance of an innovative and complex imaging system.

Illumination Direction

Illumination Direction

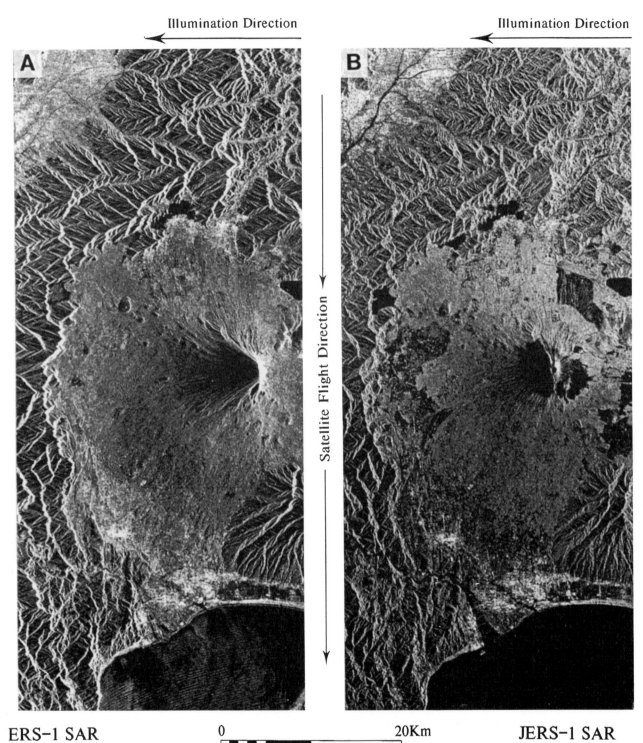

Satellite Flight Direction

ERS-1 SAR

0

20Km

JERS-1 SAR

Figure 3.38 ERS-1 (a) and JERS-1 (b) SAR images of part of Japan, showing the volcano Mount Fuji. The fact that Mount Fuji is a nearly perfect cone with a circular summit crater serves to demonstrate the inappropriate depression angle of ERS-1 SAR by its apparently lying on its side. Many other rugged topographic features are also completely distorted by extreme layover. The JERS-1 image preserves the shape of the volcano, but still contains layover.

The 1980s witnessed great activity with new ventures into multifrequency, multipolarization and selectable depression angles for SAR imagery, imaging spectrometry and multispectral thermal infrared systems, all tested using airborne platforms. Apart from the possible development of active systems aimed at exciting mineral fluorescence and improvements in gamma-ray spectrometry, there seems little likelihood of entirely new developments in the foreseeable future. Instead, much aspiring research depends on the carrying of experimental systems into orbit for further testing before truly operational satellites are launched. These ambitions centre on the joint US/European/Japanese **Earth Observing System (EOS)** which plans up to three unmanned polar-orbiting platforms starting in 1998.

The bulk of EOS plans are not high-resolution land-oriented systems, but three are of immediate interest to geologists, though not all are equally assured. The first EOS platform (EOS-A) is scheduled in 1998 to carry a development from the principle of the Geoscan and JERS-1 systems; that of using a few narrow wavebands strategically placed about useful spectral features. This is the **Advanced Spaceborne Thermal Emission and Reflection Radiometer (ASTER)**. This will incorporate three spectrometers: one for the visible and VNIR with three bands (15 m resolution), one for the SWIR region with six bands (30 m resolution), and one aimed at mineralogical features in the thermally emitted part of the spectrum with five bands (90 m resolution). Details of the band positions and widths are in Table 3.4.

The AVIRIS imaging spectrometer has had such success that a similar instrument is an ideal candidate for EOS. However, technical constraints in planning, mainly to do with weight and power requirements, have resulted in its deferment to EOS-B and EOS-C. These platforms are not yet assured. The instrument, called the **High Resolution Imaging Spectrometer (HIRIS)**, is planned to incorporate 192 bands, as shown in Table 3.3, sufficient for adequate discrimination of many important spectral features. The images will be 800 pixels wide at a resolution of 30 m, giving a swath 24 km wide. Similar technology will be incorporated in the **Moderate Resolution Imaging Spectrometer (MODIS)**, but this will have a 500-m ground IFOV that makes it of little interest to geologists. MODIS is assured to fly on EOS-A.

One of the experimental victims of the aftermath of the *Challenger* disaster was the testing of a follow-on to SIR-B, which was intended to deploy SAR systems with 3.0-5.3- and 24-cm wavelengths, that could operate in four different polarization modes and with variable depression angles. Airborne experiments of such complexity have had mixed success in geological applications, but have an extremely loyal following among vegetation specialists. Such a system was initially proposed for EOS, but is in limbo at the time of writing. There are considerable problems with SAR systems in orbit, not the least of which are sheer weight, high power consumption and extremely high demands on data transmission.

Many of the features of the SIR-C and EOS SAR have been incorporated into a Canadian operational spaceborne system, called **Radarsat**, which is scheduled for launch in 1994–95. The payload comprises a C-band SAR operating several modes with swath widths from 500 km at 100 m resolution to 40 km with 10 m resolution. To enable remote areas to be imaged Radarsat will carry on-board recorders as well as transmitting directly to suitably equipped ground stations. It will have variable depression angles from 20 to 70° optimizing its performance over terrains as diverse as oceans and rugged mountains. If it survives launch and operates as designed (by no means guaranteed because of the complex mechanics of unfolding SAR antennae from a compact spacecraft) Radarsat and JERS-1 SAR with their potential for global coverage, may take on many of the roles of airborne SAR, and displace ERS-1 imagery from the marketplace. Perhaps geologists will then have as good a chance of investigating our own planet as our neighbour Venus, which has global, geologically oriented SAR coverage from the recent Magellan mission.

Geologists seem to have rosy prospects in remote sensing for the next decade. This period is likely to be one of consolidation rather than innovation, giving the majority of geologists the time to get to grips with what has been happening over the last 20 years in geological remote sensing, apply the new data to exciting new geological problems instead of prowling over tiny test areas, and catching up with their colleagues in other fields served by the technology. The first step along this road is reviewing the basic methods of image interpretation using simple photographic data from both aircraft and satellites.

Further reading

Allison, L.J. and A. Schnapf (eds) 1983. Meteorological satellites. Chapter 14 in *Manual of remote sensing*, 2nd edn, Colwell, R.N. (ed.), pp. 651–679. Falls Church, Virginia: American Society of Photogrammetry.

Chavez, P.S. and J.A. Bowell 1988. Comparison of the spectral information content of Landsat Thematic Mapper and SPOT for three different sites in the Phoenix, Arizona, region. *Photogramm. Eng. Remote Sens.* **54**, 1699–1708.

Chiu, H.Y. and W. Collins 1978. A spectroradiometer for airborne remote sensing. *Photogramm. Eng. Remote Sens.* **44**, 507–517.

CNES 1982. SPOT *satellite-based remote sensing system.* Toulouse: CNES.

Doyle, F.J. 1985. The Large Format Camera on Shuttle mission 41-G. *Photogramm. Eng. Remote Sens.* **51**, 200.

Elachi, C. (ed.) 1983. Microwave and infrared satellite remote sensors. Chapter 13 in *Manual of remote sensing*, 2nd edn, Colwell, R.N. (ed.), pp. 571–650. Falls Church, Virginia: American Society of Photogrammetry.

Freden, S.C. and F. Gordon 1983. Landsat satellites. Chapter 12 in *Manual of remote sensing*, 2nd edn, Colwell, R.N. (ed.), pp. 517–570. Falls Church, Virginia: American Society of Photogrammetry.

Goetz, A.F.H. and M. Herring 1989. The high resolution imaging spectrometer (HIRIS) for EOS. *IEEE Trans. Geosci. Remote Sens.* **GE-27**, 136–144.

Goetz, A.F.H., G. Vane, J.E. Solomon and B.N. Rock 1985. Imaging spectrometry for earth remote sensing. *Science* **228**, 1147–1153.

Kahle, A.B., M.S. Shumate and D.B. Nash 1984. Active airborne infrared laser system for identification of surface rock and minerals. *Geophys. Res. Lett.* **11**, 1149–1152.

Hiller, K., 1984. *MOMS-01 Experimental Missions on Space Shuttle Flights STS-7 June '83, STS-11(41-B) Feb '84. Data Catalogue*. Oberpfaffenhofen: DFVLR.

Jensen, H., L.C., Graham L.J. Porcello and E.N. Leith 1977. Side-looking airborne radar. *Sci. Am.* **237**, 84–95.

Lowe, D. 1980. Acquisition of remotely sensed data. Chapter 3 in *Remote sensing in geology*, Siegal, B.S. and A.R. Gillespie (eds), pp. 91–115. New York: Wiley.

Lowman, P.D. 1980. The evolution of geological space photography. Chapter 4 in *Remote sensing in geology*, Siegal, B.S. and A.R. Gillespie (eds), pp. 91–115. New York: Wiley.

Moore, R.K. (ed.) 1983. Imaging radar systems. Chapter 10 in *Manual of remote sensing*, 2nd edn, Colwell, R.N. (ed.), pp. 429–474. Falls Church, Virginia: American Society of Photogrammetry.

NASA 1976. *Landsat data users' handbook*. GSFC Document 76SDS-4258, NASA Goddard Space Flight Center.

Norwood, V.T. and J.C. Lansing 1983. Electro-optical imaging sensors. Chapter 8 in *Manual of remote sensing*, 2nd edn, Colwell, R.N. (ed.), pp. 335–367. Falls Church, Virginia: American Society of Photogrammetry.

Slater P.N. (ed.) 1983. Photographic systems for remote sensing. Chapter 6 in *Manual of remote sensing*, 2nd edn, Colwell, R.N. (ed.), pp. 335–367. Falls Church, Virginia: American Society of Photogrammetry.

Vane, G. and A.F.H. Goetz 1988. Terrestrial imaging spectroscopy. *Remote Sens. Environ.* **24**, 1–29.

Most operational systems, such as Landsat and SPOT, are periodically replaced by new platforms and instruments, and new systems appear from time to time. The best means of updating information is to be on the mailing list for the various responsible institutions. Addresses for these are given in Appendix C.

CHAPTER FOUR | # *Photogeology*

Photographic images are the cheapest and most readily available remote-sensing data for geological interpretation. They may be acquired directly by cameras mounted on aircraft or satellites, or produced from digital image data. Images in this form, either black and white or colour, are available for all parts of the EMR spectrum accessible to remote-sensing systems. However, for simplicity this chapter deals only with those displaying information from the visible and near-infrared. Analysis of longer wavelength data and those in digital form is covered in Chapters 5, 6 and 7. The simple photogeological principles outlined in this chapter form the basis for interpretation of any images, whatever their origin.

The majority of images used here are vertical black and white photographs from aircraft, together with some single-band photographic hard copy from the Landsat MSS and RBV systems. For many users, colour photographs are a luxury, but they do have certain advantages stemming from the human eye's better chromatic discrimination. A few natural and false-colour photographs and some discussion of their information content are incorporated in the chapter. However, colour imagery is discussed at greater length in Chapter 5, because the results of computer processing of digital data are nearly always displayed in colour. Single photographs can be interpreted in two dimensions, indeed for Landsat images this is the only option, except for small strips of overlap between adjacent paths. However, stereoptic viewing of overlapping photographs adds the extra dimension of relief, usually exaggerated. As well as showing topography, stereoptic viewing permits the measurement of differences in altitude and the calculation of slope angles. These factors are of great importance both in highlighting geological features and in enabling field sites and traverses to be located accurately. Where possible therefore, the images in this chapter are in the form of stereo-pairs, set up for viewing with a pocket lens stereoscope. Appendix A contains some discussion of stereometry.

Interpretation of photographs for any purpose relies on several basic characteristics of surface. These are tone, texture, pattern, shape, context and scale. They are all more or less qualitative attributes, and their use is very much a matter of experience and personal bias.

Photographic **tone** refers to the colour or relative brightness of parts of the surface making up a scene. In a black and white photographs it is expressed as different shades or levels of grey. Without tonal variations the shapes, patterns, textures and context of objects could not be seen. Since it is related to the reflectance properties of surface materials, tone depends on the part of the spectrum covered by the imaging system and the composition of the surface itself. Tone may also be affected by processing and printing, and by the illumination conditions too. For example, the same surface will exhibit different tones on slopes facing the Sun, those facing away and those in shadow. As a result the absolute tone is of less use in interpretation than the relative tonal differences between different objects. For instance, a stand of deciduous trees in full leaf will have a lighter tone than conifers, irrespective of lighting conditions or the method of printing. Except under unusual circumstances in some arid or semiarid climates, rocks are generally masked by soil and vegetation. Even when outcropping at the surface they are frequently veneered with lichens, mosses or inorganic patinas. As a result rocks only very rarely show their true colour or tone. Nonetheless, tonal differences do play an important role in lithological discrimination on photographs (Section 4.2).

Texture is a combination of the magnitude and frequency of tonal change on an image. It is produced by the aggregate effect of all the many small features that make up a particular area of surface. The **texture** of a forest may be made up of the effect of branches, individual trees and stands of individual species. However, the scale and resolution of the image will determine which of these dominates texture. On a Landsat MSS image with 80 m resolution only stands of trees will affect texture, but on a low-altitude aerial photograph all the attributes of the forest except the leaves will contribute. Likewise, the texture associated with a particular rock type will change with scale and resolution.

Patterns on an image result from the spatial arrangement of the different tones and textures which make it up. They may be arrangements of vegetation, topographic features, drainage channels or different types of rock, which can be traced discontinuously over a significant area. The most commonly used patterns are those relating to drainage networks (Section 4.1.1), which are often related to underlying rock type or geological structure. Sometimes patterns on an image delineate specific **shapes** that can be related to familiar geological features, such as folds, igneous intrusions, faults, deltas and volcanic cones. Discerning and interpreting familiar shapes relies on the interpreter's powers of observation and experience.

Precisely how particular tones, textures, patterns and shapes are interpreted depends to a marked degree on their location relative to known attributes of the terrain under scrutiny. Their **context** is important. A U-shaped valley in the Sahara Desert is unlikely to have been formed by glacial action, and most probably results from water erosion during sudden floods. Similarly, a circular feature in an area of metamorphic rocks is unlikely to be a salt plug. By the same token, the **scale** of a feature may preclude some interpretations. A depression 40 km across bounded by arcuate faults is unlikely to be a karstic feature, but may well be a product of volcanic activity.

The criteria outlined in the following sections depend on various combinations of these basic characteristics of images. In photointerpretation they are usually combined with topographic relief expressed in stereoptic viewing, where possible. Obviously, tone, texture, pattern and shape, since they depend partly on illumination conditions and sometimes on vegetation cover, may change depending on the time of day and year of the imagery. In many cases there is an optimum time of day or a best season when geologically related features show up most clearly. Very subtle slope changes related to geology in a flat terrain may be highlighted by low Sun angles or by remnants of snow or frost occupying depressions. The same viewing conditions in a rugged terrain may degrade the interpretability of a scene because of too much shadow or snow relics, so that high Sun angles in summer give the best results. Because sedimentary rocks vary in their porosity, and since water content affects their reflective properties, it may be better to use images that were taken after rains rather than those from the dry season. However, in an intensely farmed area the post-wet season period may be characterized by the influence of dense crop canopies. These mask reflectance from rock and soil and disrupt natural patterns through the superimposition of field boundaries. In some parts of the world dry-season images are best since the only thriving vegetation is natural and may be related to the underlying geology (Section 5.6.3, Fig. 5.43).

4.1 Destructional landforms

The rock-sculpting activities of the various agents of weathering and erosion in different climatic zones determine both the textures and patterns of the surface. It is from these features that interpretations of bedrock geology are made. The transport and eventual deposition of erosional debris has the opposite effect. It masks features relating to the hard rocks buried by it. These two fundamental aspects of the Earth's surface processes produce two basic types of landform. **Destructional landforms** lay bare to some degree the structure and composition of consolidated and lithified rock, and indicate the dominant environmental influences over the development of landscape. **Constructional landforms** result from a superficial veneer of relatively recent rocks and sediments. Their surface attributes also give clues to environmental processes as well as to the nature of the veneers themselves.

In this section the emphasis is on destructional landforms, as they lead into the criteria for 'hard rock' interpretation covered in Sections 4.2–4.4. Constructional landforms and their associated superficial deposits are considered in Section 4.5.

Different rock types respond to weathering and erosion in different ways. This depends on many factors. The most important are the composition and degree of lithification of the rocks themselves, together with the type of weathering and erosion. These last two factors are mainly determined by climate, and sometimes by altitude. A region in the tropics may have a hot, humid climate near sea level, but mountainous areas experience conditions somewhat similar to those of temperate latitudes. Likewise, an arid or semiarid desert may be flanked by mountains with a moderate rainfall.

An important criterion in geological interpretation of images is the degree to which different rock types resist erosion. A sandstone strongly cemented with an inert compound such as silica will be resistant under virtually any conditions. However, a rock containing reactive minerals such as feldspars or carbonates will soon succumb to the agents of chemical weathering which predominate in hot humid climates. The same rock may respond in the opposite fashion in an arid or cold climate where chemical weathering is less significant. A rock's resistance to erosion is also relative. A basaltic dyke intruding soft mudstones may give rise to a prominent ridge, but where it cuts gneisses it may have a relatively low resistance and occupy a narrow trough.

There are four important types of erosion which can attack the products of weathering – those associated with flowing water, wind, wave action and moving ice. Marine and wind erosion can produce distinct destructional landforms, but they are of minor importance in image interpretation. Marine erosion is restricted, for obvious reasons, and most geological investigations are conducted well away from the sea. Aeolian erosion has a relatively minor effect at the scale normally used in remote sensing. The major sculpting agents are flowing water and ice. Water dominates, even in the most arid of modern environments, either because the main landforms were produced during more humid episodes or because water continues to flow at the surface after intermittent but spectacular rainstorms.

4.1.1 Landforms and drainage

Except in strongly glaciated areas, drainage patterns conform to some degree to the regional slope of the terrain and to its underlying geological structure. Because of this it is often possible, even where outcrop is poor, to recognize the gross structural elements. The first step in using drainage, usually the most obvious element of a landscape, is to seek genetic connections between stream patterns and the disposition of rocks. This involves assessment of the geomorphological history of the area and the stage of development of landscape dissection. It is not possible to catalogue all possible combinations of rock type, structure and stream development, or to outline all the many methods of describing drainage. This section uses a simple classification based on the direction of stream courses relative to geological controls.

A channel which has developed on some initial slope, and which continues to follow its original direction, is said to be **consequent**. The original slope may have been caused by regional tilting of an earlier peneplaned surface, or directly by the direction of dip of a stratigraphic unit. The point to remember is that the term relates only to the topographic and not to any structural aspect of a consequent stream's origin. Streams which clearly flow down the dip of a particular stratum or lithological boundary are termed **resequent streams**. They have developed on a surface already stripped by earlier, consequent streams and are structurally controlled.

Streams propagate themselves and develop tributaries by **headward erosion**. They tend to follow the lines of least resistance. On a surface underlain by dipping strata which resist weathering and erosion differently, some will follow lines determined by the least resistant layers. These are **subsequent** streams. By the same token, subsequent streams can follow and etch out the lines of fractured rock developed along faults. Consequently, the strike of strata and fault lines, so important in unravelling geological structure, is most likely to be reflected in subsequent stream courses.

Continued downward and headward erosion eventually begins to etch out the basic geological fabric of an area, in the form of cuestas, valleys and other topographic features. Slopes are produced on the valley sides of original consequent and subsequent streams in concert with the underlying geological diversity. They may be in several directions. Streams which follow them are **obsequent**. In areas of dipping strata, slopes develop in subsequent stream valleys, which are in the opposite direction to the local dip. Small obsequent streams frequently develop on such slopes. Others may flow down the sides of major consequent or resequent valleys, with a less obvious relationship to structure. By no means all streams conform to this simple classification. Most bear no obvious relationship to geology or former land surfaces. They are referred to as **insequent** streams.

The evolution of a landscape can be complex, particularly during protracted or episodic uplift and downward erosion. A stream system may begin by developing on a geologically simple surface of uniformly dipping strata, producing consequent, subsequent and other streams. This simple sequence may be merely a veneer unconformably above more complex older rocks. The older rocks may eventually be crossed by drainage which bears little resemblance to their structure but is inherited from an earlier, higher level system. This results in a **superimposed drainage system**. Relics of it may persist even after prolonged erosion establishes the control of the deep structure, leaving many insequent streams. Figure 4.1 shows the main classes of stream in a diagrammatic way. Figure 4.2 is a stereopair of aerial photographs illustrating real examples and their use in interpretation.

In areas where tectonic activity resumes after the establishment of a drainage system, the old streams may continue in their original courses across the axes of uplift or folding to produce **antecedent drainage**. This can happen if the uplift is quite slow or if the streams involved are sufficiently powerful to erode through the rising crust fast enough. The best-known examples of antecedent drainage are those of the Colorado River cutting through the Kaibab Uplift to form the Grand Canyon (*Fig. 4.3*), and the Indus

(a)

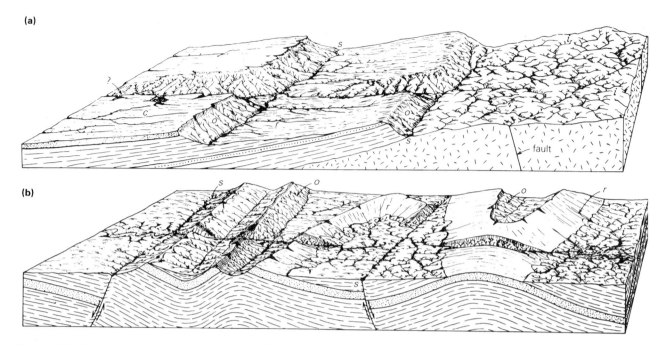

(b)

Figure 4.1 These two diagrammatic sketches of how underlying geology may control the trajectories and patterns of surface drainage are from Miller's classic, but out of print, textbook *Photogeology* (1961). The letters *c, s, r, o* and *i* refer to consequent, subsequent, resequent, obsequent and insequent streams respectively. That marked ? is possibly a consequent stream which developed upon a dipping planar surface, which has been incised into the underlying tilted strata during uplift. Reproduced with the permission of McGraw-Hill Books Inc.

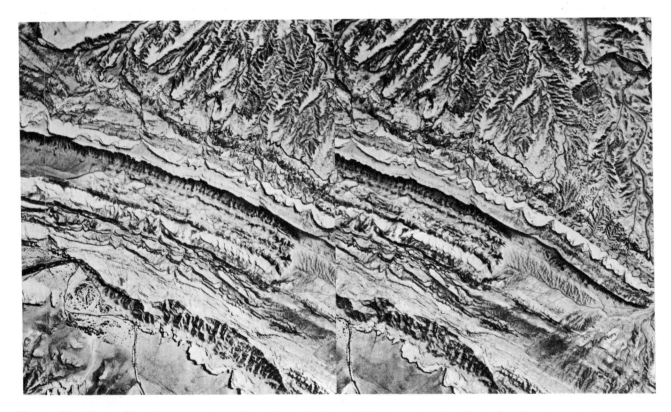

Figure 4.2 Many of the dry stream channels in this semiarid part of Utah can be classified using the scheme in Figure 4.1. A particularly important feature is the example of headward erosion in the major subsequent valley. Most of the gulley profiles are sharp, which is characteristic of intermittent stream erosion. Scale 1:40 000. Source: US Department of Agriculture, Agricultural Stabilization and Conservation Service (ASCS) UPRM-13 20+21.

and Brahmaputra, which flow southwards through the Himalaya, despite the phenomenally rapid rates of uplift in this tectonically active area. Active tectonic uplift in many cases is too rapid for antecedent drainage to develop, and streams may be reversed or ponded to form lakes.

Any cycle of stream erosion passes through various stages, which relate to how close the drainage system has adjusted to its erosional base level. The famous geomorphologist W.M. Davis compared these stages to those in a human life, and his general terminology is still in common use today. A cycle begins when the base level falls, through either uplift, tilting, fall in sea level, downcutting of a major river, increase in stream flow or various permutations. Such a change is referred to as **rejuvenation**. In the initial stages the previous drainage system remains or a new one develops in depressions in a newly emerged land surface. The **youthful stage** is characterized by active erosion and the formation of destructive landforms. Streams flow in V-shaped valleys, whose floors they almost completely occupy. **Maturity** begins as the stream system begins to develop wide valleys as a result of the destruction of ridges and the beginning of deposition. Mature streams have reached a lengthwise profile in equilibrium with the base level. **Old age** is characterized by the dominance of wide flat flood plains with meanders and redistribution of superficial sediments. The final result is a **peneplane** devoid of control by underlying geological structures. The mature and old-aged stages produce constructional landforms (Section 4.5).

How quickly an erosional cycle passes through these stages depends on a number of factors. The closer a stream is to the base level, the faster it reaches equilibrium. More remote areas pass from the initial to youthful stages at rates dependent on headward erosion in the main streams. Easily eroded rock types will achieve maturity more quickly than resistant ones. In an area of varied lithologies youthful features may be mixed with those of maturity. The rate of erosion, determined by both volume and rate of flow, and by the erosive content of solids in streams, plays its part too. Fall in base level is rarely instantaneous, and the rate of change also plays a role in the evolution of landscape. Episodic changes are common, and their interruption of the progress towards equilibrium can be marked by several levels in a drainage system, all characterized by youthful, mature and aged features. In such cases, the boundaries between levels can be marked by sudden changes in the longitudinal profiles of streams.

Adding to the complexity of landforms dominated by flowing water is the opposite of rejuvenation, when the base level rises. This hastens the maturation of a drainage system and the onset of depositional features. Such **aggradational episodes** may indeed be interspersed with those of rejuvenation. Further consideration of these complex geomorphological processes is beyond the scope of this book, but may be found in many modern texts on physical geology.

The shapes of valleys in cross-section, which are often apparent in stereoptic views of photographs, can be important criteria in identifying underlying lithologies. Similarly, the drainage density can play an important discriminatory role (Section 4.2). However, both are strongly affected by climate. Surprisingly, drainage density in an arid area on any particular rock type is usually greater than one developed under humid conditions. Less obvious is the contrast in valley profiles between humid and arid terrains. Humid conditions encourage the rapid formation of thick soil profiles. Lubricated by water, these tend to creep slowly downslope, thereby limiting slope angles and helping smooth the overall terrain. Under arid conditions neither soil nor lubrication is present to any marked degree. Consequently, much steeper slopes to valley sides can be sustained, even in rocks that are not strongly resistant to erosion. Moreover, most streams in deserts are intermittent, and when they do flow it is often during storms. Under these conditions downward erosion is rapid but short-lived. It produces slot-like gorges along main channels, and, because torrential rainfall contributes mainly to surface run-off, innumerable rilles and gulleys on the slopes. The soil and vegetation mantle in humid terrains slows surface run-off and encourages infiltration. Gulleying is therefore more subdued, if present at all. Figures 4.2, 4.7, 4.8 and 4.9 show the contrasts between typical humid and arid terrains for these two important characteristics.

As implied earlier in this section, the patterns developed in a drainage system as it evolves contain important clues to geological structure. They can also make some contribution to distinguishing some rock types. These aspects are considered in Sections 4.2 and 4.4. Here the main pattern types are described and illustrated with some typical examples.

Drainage patterns of all types may be found on a variety of scales, from those defined by major river systems to those associated with rilles and gulleys. They help define the textural features of a scene, and depending on the spacing of the individual streams may be defined as coarse-, fine- or intermediate-textured patterns. The streams which define the patterns can be of any genetic type: consequent, insequent, subsequent and so forth.

Areas drained primarily by insequent streams show a lack of any preferential channel direction. The streams flow in irregular, branching courses with many random bends. Tributaries enter larger streams usually at an acute angle to the general direction of regional flow, itself determined by regional slope. The pattern produced is like the complex branching of a tree, and because of this it is termed dendritic (Fig. 4.4a). **Dendritic drainage patterns** are characteristic of terrains showing lithological, structural and topographic homogeneity.

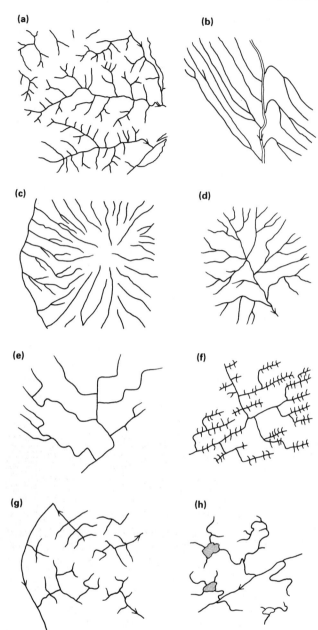

from a single point (Fig. 4.4c). The opposite case, in which streams flow radially towards a common point (Fig. 4.4d) is called **centripetal drainage**. Such simple patterns all derive from topographic features and cannot be assumed to reflect any particular structure or lithology, although this is often revealed by closer inspection.

Other categories of drainage pattern can be regarded as embellishments upon the last four. They include subsequent streams which have been controlled by lithological and structural weaknesses, and so give more geological information. Patterns dominated by many straight streams with a variety of trajectories may define **rectangular** or **angular patterns**, depending on their angular relationships (Fig. 4.4e). A particular variant of these two types, in which short tributaries connect to long straight major streams, produces a pattern reminiscent of trained vines (Fig. 4.4f) referred to as a **trellis pattern**. Subsequent streams developed on a radial pattern result in a concentric series of valleys defining an **annular pattern** (Fig. 4.4g).

In reality, the several basic pattern types are rarely developed to perfection. Several generally combine to give topologically complex systems, in which specific elements may be picked out by the interpreter. Typically, an overall pattern or series of patterns may contain streams which do not conform to the overall picture. They are anomalous, and attract attention simply because they are different. Such drainage anomalies in an area of clearly defined geology may highlight geological subtleties which would otherwise go unnoticed in a purely field study. On the other hand, in areas where geology is obscured because dissection is not well advanced or a thick blanket of superficial sediment masks the underlying structure, anomalies can give clues leading to geological revelations.

Whatever patterns are displayed on a photograph, it is always important to bear in mind that they reflect the full range of factors behind the development of landscape. Climatic, topographic, lithological and structural controls all combine with the stage reached in the evolution of the drainage system. In poorly exposed areas a crude idea of the structure can be appraised best simply by tracing the drainage patterns revealed by a photograph onto a transparent overlay. Sooner or later however, interpretations have to be confirmed and extended by field studies.

4.1.2 Glacially eroded landforms

Moving masses of ice are the most powerful landscape-sculpting agents imaginable. Although velocities of ice flow are very slow, even in the most active valley glaciers, the enormous masses involved ensure that their energy is enormous. During the Pleistocene glaciations it is estimated that some of the continental ice sheets exceeded 3 km in thickness. The process of glacial erosion begins with the plucking of debris from the substrate, often weakened by

Figure 4.4 Patterns formed by drainage networks can take on many distinct forms, often related to aspects of the underlying geology. A dendritic form is shown in (a), parallel in (b), radial in (c) and centripetal in (d). Minor variants on these four basic patterns include rectangular (e), trellis (f) and annular (g) systems. Areas with low, hummocky relief and few streams may develop deranged patterns (h). Many other subforms can be found, but nearly all conform to this basic subdivision.

In contrast, drainage may be dominated by a number of parallel or subparallel streams, indicating a unidirectional flow. For obvious reasons this is termed a **parallel drainage pattern** (Fig. 4.4b). Regular deviations of courses from this result in **fan patterns**, which reach their ultimate in a completely **radial pattern**, where streams all flow away freezing and thawing in advance of the ice front. The incorporation of this debris in ice provides the ice base with a renewable supply of abrasive material, which acts like a giant rasp. No rock type can resist for long the protracted passage of ice above it. The destructive landforms that result depend for their shapes and patterns on the type of glaciation involved. There are two main types – **valley** and **continental glaciation**.

Valley glaciation begins by the accumulation of permanent snow masses in depressions on mountain slopes. There it undergoes a transformation to ice through a series of stages. Once a certain mass of ice has accumulated it is able to flow downslope under its own gravitational potential energy. The climatic conditions suitable for ice accumulation ensure that exposed rock on peaks undergoes powerful physical weathering, dislodging angular fragments and thereby 'sharpening' the peaks. These fragments falling onto the ice, together with those plucked from the base of the ice, contribute to the abrasive capacity of the glacier. At its source the glacier carves a bowl-like depression or **cirque** by the local movement of ice through a vertical arc (Fig. 4.5). Once it has spilled over the lip of this bowl, the ice moves downslope, usually along a pre-existing valley.

Valleys are eventually remoulded to a **U-shaped cross-section** and straightened by the removal of interlocking spurs. Apart from their typical cross-section, glaciated valleys can be recognized easily by the abundance of **truncated spurs**. The other effect of glaciation is deepening of the earlier valleys, the amount depending on the energy of the glacier responsible. The pre-existing valley patterns determine to a marked degree the course of later glacial flow-ways, which comprise major valleys with tributaries. The energy differences involved in the glacier system result in the courses of less powerful glaciers being less deeply eroded than those of major ice streams. This produces **hanging valleys** at the confluences (Fig. 4.5). Because valley glaciation is generally superimposed upon pre-existing stream and river courses, except in the Arctic and Antarctica, the remaining patterns conform to some extent to those of their precursors. The difference is that the minor valleys are wiped out and those remaining are grossly straightened. The net result is to preserve some of the indicators of gross geological structure, but to erase those indicating the details.

Examination of large-scale photographs of glacially eroded uplands enables some of the smaller features typical of ice erosion to be recognized. Among these are **roches moutonnées** and major **ice striations** (Figs. 4.5 and 4.6). The typical shape of roches moutonnées, with smooth, rounded surfaces facing towards the former ice flow and

Figure 4.5 The Highlands of Scotland contain many examples of the products of upland glacial erosion. This stereopair shows typical cirques, aretes and hanging valleys, as well as the rugged bare rock surfaces resulting from subglacial plucking. Scale 1:25 000. Source: author.

steep, glacially plucked faces pointing downflow, enables estimates of ice flow directions to be made. Striations give similar information, but are ambiguous at these scales. In upland areas, ice-flow directions are generally obvious from the overall topography and the relative orientation of glaciated valleys, and these minor features are of more importance in glacial analysis of flat areas of continental glacial erosion.

During the Pleistocene, huge ice sheets, originating from snow accumulation at high latitudes and to a lesser extent from ice-capped mountain ranges spread southwards over large tracts of northern Eurasia and North America. They produced two main types of terrain, those dominated by glacial erosion and those where the products of erosion were deposited. The former are now the enormous rocky wastes of the Canadian, Baltic and Siberian Shields, from which most of the previous cover of Phanerozoic sediments was stripped. This revealed the underlying Precambrian basement. The areas dominated by glacial deposition occur further to the south where the impetus of the ice sheets waned. The forward movement of ice was balanced by the increased rate of melting at lower latitudes. As a result the ice sheets were relieved of their loads of debris. The typical

features of these depositional areas are considered in Section 4.5. Here a few comments about the erosional features of large, uniform ice sheets are required.

Unlike upland glaciers, whose erosional features are restricted to more or less narrow valleys, continental ice sheets have a uniform and dramatic effect on the areas which they have stripped bare. Although in a general sense they brook no obstacles and literally raze them to the ground, detailed examination reveals effects of great significance to the geologist. The all-pervading erosion by the debris-loaded ice base emphasizes every conceivable heterogeneity in the rocks over which it passes. The softer rocks and zones of structural weakness are etched out, sometimes completely, leaving the more resistant rocks as positive features. Pre-existing drainage patterns are obliterated, so that when the ice retreats new drainage is controlled by the intricacies of the newly scoured surface (Fig. 4.6). These patterns can be long-lived, simply because the grinding flat of the land surface reduces stream energy to a minimum. However, the transient but massive load of the former ice sheets was sufficient to depress the crust hundreds of metres below its original level. Slow post-glacial isostatic rebound, at different rates and to

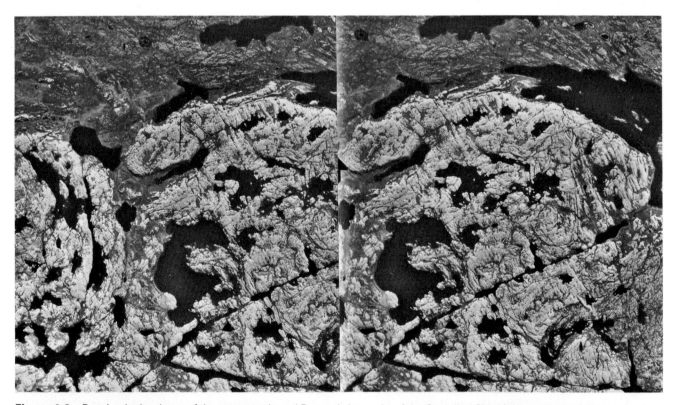

Figure 4.6 Despite the hardness of the metamorphosed Precambrian rocks of the Canadian Shield they were unable to resist the erosive action of the vast ice sheets which drove over them during the Pleistocene. This stereopair shows the typical low relief of such areas of continental glaciation. At top right can be seen grooves and ridges reflecting the ice-flow direction. There are two main rock types exposed, pale granite and darker metavolcanic rocks, the granite having resisted glaciation best. The intricate jointing in the granite, its intrusive contact and basic dykes cutting it have been selectively exploited by glacial action resulting in linear, vegetation-filled depressions and narrow lakes. Scale 1:50 000. Source: Department of Energy, Mines and Resources, Canada (EMRC) A13781 52+53. Copyright HM the Queen in Right of Canada (1953).

different extents depending on the amount of glacial depression, has imparted regional slope to the shields. These ensure that the drainage does have an overall orientation, albeit tortuous.

4.1.3 Other destructional landforms

Marine erosion is capable of producing landforms which are to some degree controlled by underlying geology. However, they are restricted to a narrow coastal swath, and in general are only obvious on large-scale photographs. In some cases, a rise in sea level and flooding of a landscape formed by other processes can reveal gross geological elements from the patterns of the islands left above sea level. Where geological interpretation of coastal areas is demanded, the reader is referred to existing texts on coastal geomorphology.

Erosion by wind in deserts is indeed an important process, but its products are generally visible only in the field. The reason for its relatively minor importance to the image interpreter is that wind energies are low compared with those of flowing water. Because of this only a small load of abrasive particles can be carried. Wind erosion is rarely powerful enough or at a sufficient rate to overwhelm the dominant effects of stream erosion in deserts, even though streams flow only intermittently.

4.2 The recognition of rock types

In order to recognize or distinguish between different lithologies on a photograph the geologist needs two prerequisites: a sufficient correlation between geology and landform and a combination of experience, patience, perception and ingenuity. The attributes of photographic tone, texture, patterns, context and scale need to be combined with a knowledge of how different rock types respond in different climates to weathering and erosion.

In this section the basic division is into sedimentary rocks, extrusive and intrusive igneous rocks and metamorphic rocks. To some extent the treatment pre-empts later sections by introducing some of the stratigraphic and structural criteria required in rock discrimination. Most of the distinguishing criteria, particularly those relating to textures and patterns, are equally useful in the interpretation of images of other parts of the EMR spectrum covered in later chapters. Because many rock types have different appearances under different climatic conditions, wherever possible they are illustrated with several images. It would be useful to give examples of the kinds of appearance most likely to be encountered by the interpreter – unspectacular and poorly expressed on the image. However, the world is a diverse place, this is an introduction and space is limited. The illustrations here are the best that could be found.

There is no rigid routine for the recognition and discrimination of lithologies in photogeological interpretation. However, a systematic approach of one kind or another is essential. It must be backed up by note-taking and annotation of the images, so that a permanent record is kept and experience is built up in a way that can be referred to at any future time. As a guide to this approach the following general scheme is recommended:

(1) The climatic environment has to be assessed – humid or arid, boreal, temperate or tropical.
(2) Is the vegetation, if any, natural or agricultural?
(3) The erosional environment must be assessed in terms of its energy, its stage of development and the relative contributions of stream, glacier and wind erosion estimated.
(4) The area should be divided into parts that are dominated by superficial deposits and those probably having bedrock at or close to the surface.
(5) Areas of outcrop or near-surface bedrock should be examined for signs of lithological banding or its apparent absence, and distinguished accordingly.

The next set of steps depends on the systematic description of the probable areas of bedrock. If possible, the terrain should be closely examined for any obvious boundaries between different types of surface. After a preliminary division of contrasted surface types, each can be described using the following key headings:

(a) The topography should be described, in particular noting the relative resistance to erosion of the unit and any anomalous features.
(b) What is the drainage pattern and what is the spacing between individual channels?
(c) If possible the cross-sectional shape of the smallest drainage features – gulleys – should be described.
(d) The vegetation cover and land use directly related to the unit must be noted.
(e) Finally, if bare soil or rock outcrop is visible its photographic tone or colour should be compared with other units, and any textural features should be described.

4.2.1 Sedimentary rocks

Sedimentary rocks are usually stratified owing to variations in the conditions of their deposition. As a result they typically display a banded appearance on photographs, although the width of the bands depends on their attitude as well as on the thickness of individual strata. Since volcanic lava flows and pyroclastics, some intrusive igneous rocks and most metamorphic rocks also show layering, there is considerable scope for confusion. Avoiding this relies on the geological context of the layered rocks being examined. In most cases this is obvious from previous knowledge of the study area. In relatively unknown areas the context must first be assessed by looking for signs of volcanoes, cross-cutting contacts and highly complex structures respectively. In their absence, layered rocks can be assumed to be sedimentary until field study proves the contrary.

The topographic expression of sediments depends on a variety of factors. Principally it is determined by the attitude of bedding, ranging from horizontal to vertical. This can result in a series of landforms from which estimates of dip and strike can be made, but this is considered in detail in Section 4.3. Topography is also governed by resistance to erosion, which itself depends on a variety of factors.

Sediments can exhibit various stages of compaction and cementation. For example, a compact but uncemented sandstone is less resistant to some types of erosion than one which is completely cemented. The porosity and permeability play a role too. A permeable rock will allow water to seep into it thereby lessening the effect of erosion by surface run-off compared with that on an impermeable rock. The main weak zones in all sediments are bedding surfaces. Their spacing makes an important contribution to relative resistance. So a thinly bedded rock is less resistant than one of the same composition with thick beds. For a sequence of equally well-cemented sediments, those comprising small particles will erode more easily than the coarser ones. This is because the energy required to dislodge small grains is less than that required for large ones. Finally, rock composition is a contributory factor. As well as the hydraulic action of moving fluids, their content of particulate and dissolved matter helps abrade and dissolve rocks. Rocks such as sandstone and siltstone composed dominantly of quartz, which is both hard and chemically inert, resist both mechanical and chemical erosion. Mudstones are composed mainly of soft clay minerals, which although inert are easily abraded. Rocks containing a high percentage of soluble or reactive compounds like carbonates or various salts respond easily to the effects of mildly acid rainwater containing dissolved carbon dioxide or organic acids.

The other morphological features of sediments, their associated drainage patterns, textures and gulley shapes, depend on exactly the same fundamental factors as resistance. Vegetation cover and outcrop tone or colour are controlled by subtler factors, and are described for each main sediment type. Only three main groups of sediment need be considered in photogeology: coarse clastics such as conglomerates and sandstones, fine clastics such as siltstones and mudstones, and biochemical and chemical sediments including limestones and evaporites.

Sedimentary sequences are nearly always composed of a variety of interbedded lithologies. The differences in their resistance to erosion impart a distinctive grain of parallel positive and negative features to the terrain. The appearance of bedding as patterns or textures depends on the attitude of the bedding.

Horizontal strata containing resistant units are generally expressed by distinctly stepped topography, especially when the resistors are more than 5 m thick. Each step is controlled by a resistant unit and separated by less steep slopes underlain by soft rocks. In arid climates, resistors frequently form plateaus incised by major streams flowing in steep-sided canyons with stepped walls. Headward erosion of tributaries can isolate buttes and mesas from the main plateau (Fig. 4.7a). Soil formation and its movement downslope under humid conditions mutes such topographic expression (Fig. 4.7b). The lack of original slopes in horizontally bedded terrain tends to encourage the development of dendritic drainage patterns. This, together with the tendency for major units to outcrop parallel to contours, results in complex patterns and textures (Fig. 4.7). Such complexities are often paralleled by vegetation communities which may differ from one lithology to another.

Tilted sediments which have been incised by stream erosion provide the conditions whereby consequent, subsequent and other stream classes can develop. The full exploitation of differences in resistance can then leave resistors as ridges of various kinds separated by parallel subsequent valleys in the less resistant units. The net result is a gross texture of more or less parallel elements of the landscape (Fig. 4.2), characterized by some form of trellis drainage pattern. The degree of parallelism becomes more nearly perfect the steeper the dip of the beds. In many humid terrains the ridges are wooded, whereas valleys are farmed.

Coarse clastic sediments

Sandstones and conglomerates are composed mainly of quartz grains, with varying proportions of other resistant minerals such as feldspars and rock fragments. Their degree and nature of cementation varies considerably, and so does their resistance to erosion. However, when interbedded with equally cemented finer clastics, they generally form positive features, often forming cliffs and steep escarpments. Cements based on iron compounds or silica are particularly strong, but carbonate cements are prone to attack by acids in rainwater.

In arid climates, quartz grains dislodged by weathering are easily removed by wind. Sandstones and conglomerates therefore tend to display bare surfaces under these conditions (Fig. 4.8). Except in tropical rain forest, where laterites may develop, coarse clastics in humid climates rarely develop deep, fertile soils. Their permeability makes them too well-drained to support extensive grass cover. As

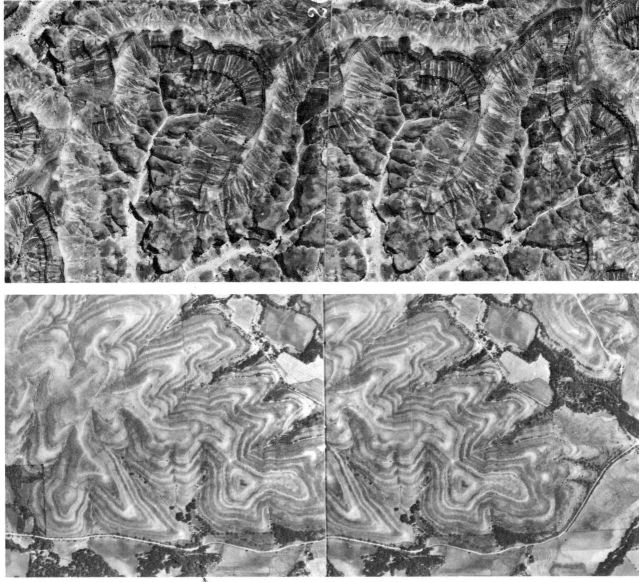

(a)

(b)

Figure 4.7 Both stereopairs show the most typical feature of topography developed upon horizontally layered rocks – outcrops which closely parallel topographic contours. In arid terrains (a) the intermittent violent erosion develops steep-sided gulleys and valleys. Variable resistance to erosion, in this case by sandstones and siltstones, leads to sudden changes in slope angle and step-like features on the valley sides. One noteworthy feature is the restriction of bushes to only one level in the succession. This is probably a boundary between water-carrying sandstone and underlying impermeable siltstone. In a more humid climate such as that of eastern Kansas (b) the topography is more muted. The spectacular 'candy-stripe' appearance results from interbedded white limestones and grey shales of Permian age. Scales: (a) 1:20 000, (b) 1:20 000. Sources: (a) Clyde Surveys Ltd, UK (CSL) Series B 3+4, (b) national Cartographic Information Centre, US Geological Survey (NCIC) Kans.2 A+B.

a result vegetation is relatively sparse and often dominated by trees with deep root systems (Fig. 4.8).

Since many sandstones are very permeable, rainfall infiltrates them, thereby reducing surface run-off. This helps ensure that they have relatively wide-spaced drainage textures (Fig. 4.8b). Gullies are relatively rare and small streams tend to develop V-shaped cross-sections owing to the well-supported nature of sandstone's granular structure.

Being unable to deform except by brittle dislocation, one of the most distinctive features of coarse clastic sediments is their abundance of joints, often in several tectonically related directions. The zones of weakness associated with jointing exerts a marked control on the finer structure of drainage on sandstones, which may take on a prominent rectangular or angular pattern (Fig. 4.8a). Cliffs and cuestas in sandstone are frequently joint controlled.

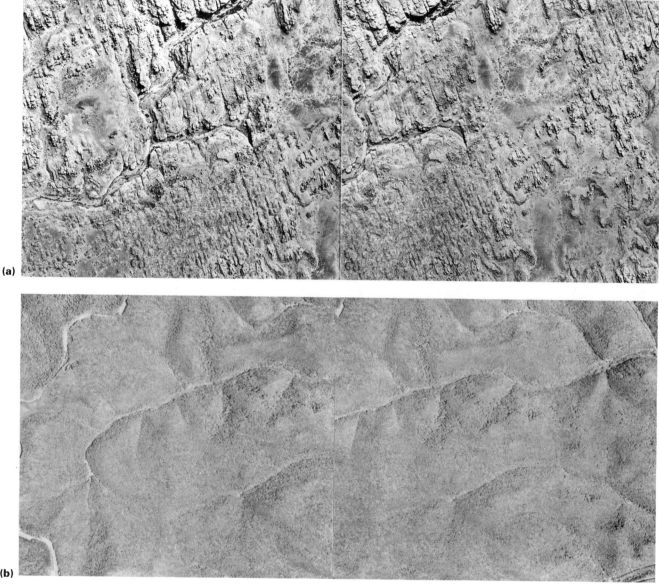

Figure 4.8 (a) Sandstones in an arid climate, in this case in Utah, are typically bare and display their internal regular jointing very well. Their excellent internal drainage reduces the number of streams at the surface. High resistance to erosion results in a rugged surface. (b) Sandstone in humid climates develops very poor soil on which the dominant natural vegetation is woodland as in this part of Pennsylvania. The main clue to the presence of sandstone is the wide spacing of drainage and the roundness of topography resulting from its often weak cement and susceptibility to chemical weathering. Compared with fine clastic sediments it is resistant to physical weathering and is not prone to solution like carbonates. Scales: (a) 1:20 000, (b) 1:33 000. Sources: (a) US Geological Survey (USGS) GS-WI-12 146+147, (b) ASCS APL-4V 98+99.

The bareness of sandstone outcrops in arid areas, combined with their well-drained nature, usually permits them to show their true photographic tone or colour, unaffected by near-surface pore water. Silica- and carbonate-cemented sandstones are usually pale, but those containing iron compounds can be any shade of yellow, orange, brown or red. In panchromatic black and white photographs red sandstones appear dark. The frequently dense forest cover of sandstones in humid climates also gives them a dark colour on panchromatic photographs.

Fine clastic sediments

Mudstones and siltstones contain a high proportion of clay minerals together with varying amounts of fine-grained quartz. They represent depositional environments with low energies. In many cases they contain fine laminations between 1 mm and a few centimetres thick. Because of this, such rocks frequently show a strong fissility parallel to bedding, that is accentuated by the reorientation of flaky clay minerals during lithification. It is this fissile nature which characterizes **shale**, a term which is commonly applied to both fissile mudstones and siltstones. Fine-grained clastic sediments may comprise a variety of grain sizes, sometimes in graded units, and show bedding on a scale from 1 cm to 1 m. However, except in detailed stratigraphic logs, they are usually lumped together as homogeneous units up to hundreds of metres in thickness.

Cements can be of various compositions, but even when totally uncemented rocks with a high clay content have a good cohesion owing to the electrostatic charges on the clay mineral particles. However, the poor permeability of fine clastics, means that in an unconsolidated sequence of fine and coarse sediments rainfall infiltration is at a minimum on the fine rocks and surface run-off has more chance of eroding them than the coarser materials. Therefore, irrespective of degree of cementation and climate, fine clastics are more prone to erosion than coarse. They tend to be poor resistors and form negative topographic features.

As well as promoting relatively rapid erosion, high run-off results in the development of closely spaced drainage textures. Clay-rich rocks are more able to deform plastically than sandstones, and as a result tend not to show prominent joint systems, although they may have finely spaced joints due to shrinkage. This encourages the development of randomly oriented streams in horizontal strata and an overall dendritic drainage pattern. Even in dipping sequences, fine clastic units often display a dendritic element within an overall trellis pattern of consequent and subsequent streams. The low resistance to erosion, particularly when cement has been dissolved or weakened, together with the continuous exposure to surface run-off means that gulleys in fine clastics soon develop. In an arid climate gulleys form during short-lived heavy rainfall and aggregate to form a minutely dissected terrain, the gulley walls retaining steep angles. The continuous run-off on fine clastics in humid climates encourages the degradation of gulley sides, the formation of less closely spaced drainage and a rounded topography.

Any rock with a high clay content is likely to contain a far higher complement of plant nutrients than those composed mainly of silica or carbonates. These are released for use by plants during weathering and soil formation. Clay soils are not only nutrient rich, but are able to retain the nutrients and high moisture contents because of the structure of clay minerals. In humid climates they therefore support dense vegetation and are often intensely farmed. In arid climates the converse applies. Unlike coarse clastics they do not receive much infiltrated rainfall and are consequently more barren.

Fine clastics can form under a wide range of conditions and may have very diverse chemistries, varying on a scale of metres. Iron, the main colouring agent in rocks, can be chemically bound in the clay minerals or exist in the cement. The low depositional energies of many mudstones encourages reducing conditions during deposition. This often results in a high proportion of iron sulphides in the cement. Weathering of sulphides produces a complex of iron oxides and hydroxides, collectively known as **limonite**, which can impart strong yellow, orange, brown and red coloration to outcrops. Unless they are composed of pure clay minerals like kaolinite, fine clastics generally show up as relatively dark surfaces on photographs. Provided that resolution is adequate, their heterogeneity may be revealed as fine colour or grey-tone banding. Because of dense vegetation cover and ease of erosion, fine clastics rarely outcrop over large areas in humid climates and must be distinguished on grounds other than photographic tone.

Figure 4.9 shows the typical appearance of horizontally bedded fine clastic sediments in humid and arid climates.

Chemically precipitated sediments

There are two main categories of chemical sediments: those precipitated by evaporation of restricted bodies of water, highly soluble **halite** (NaCl) and other salts, and those precipitated mainly as the hard parts of organisms – **calcite** and **dolomite**, the carbonates of calcium and calcium with magnesium – which form various limestones.

Being highly soluble in water, evaporites rarely outcrop in humid terrains. However, their presence in a sequence may be detected by the haphazard presence of a more or less circular depression where collapse into solution cavities has occurred. Where the evaporites are in the form of **salt diapirs**, such collapse structures may be arranged in distinctive patterns related to the shape of these gravity-driven structures. Near-surface salt may accumulate in soils as a result of capillary rise of saline solutions. Since few plants are salt tolerant, this may give rise to barren patches in otherwise fertile ground.

Evaporites are crystalline solids, and being devoid of pores do not allow infiltration of rainwater. In arid climates, where they are only attacked by infrequent rain storms, salt bodies may outcrop. They generally have distinctive textures composed of finely spaced gulleys with sharp profiles (Fig. 4.10). Patches of residual clastic rocks may protect the underlying salt to produce weird pillars and canyons. Being crystalline, evaporites in arid climates tend to resist erosion quite well compared with the fine clastics with which they are frequently associated. They generally stand out as positive topographic features. When in the form of diapirs, the domal nature of the intrusions often controls a distinctive radial drainage pattern, sometimes with an annular component related to the associated concentric fault structures.

Limestone, and to a lesser extent dolomite, is slightly soluble in rainwater with dissolved carbon dioxide – a weak

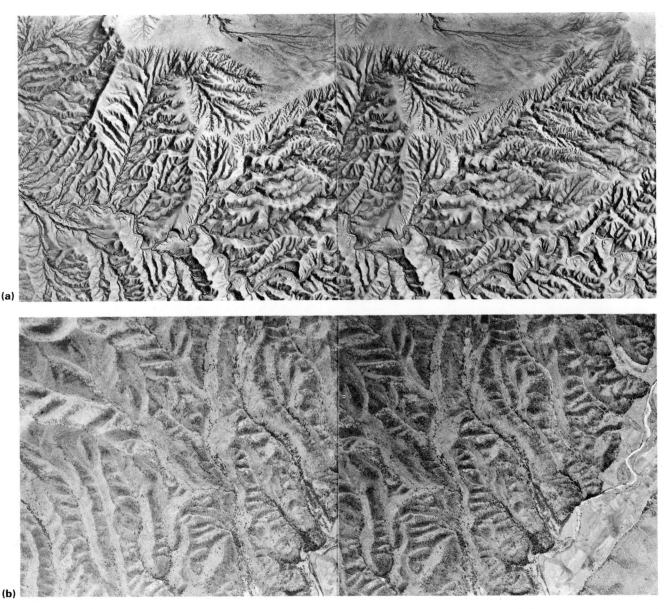

(a)

(b)

Figure 4.9 Gently dipping mudstones and siltstones typically develop dendritic and closely spaced drainage patterns because of their poor internal drainage. In arid areas, such as Utah (a), individual gulleys have a sharp V-shaped cross-section despite the low resistance to erosion of fine clastic sediments. Paradoxically, drainage on shales in humid climates (b) is often more widely spaced than under dry conditions. As shown clearly by the stereopair of part of Virginia, the smallest channels have vanished because of the ease of lateral erosion during continuous stream flow. Gulley profiles are smooth and shallow. The high content of nutrients in shales together with their poor internal drainage helps ensure that they have a luxuriant natural plant cover. Scales (a) 1:27 000, (b) 1:43 000. Sources: (a) USGS GS-WI-36 68+69, (b) USGS GS-AZ-2 119+120.

acid. In humid climates therefore, topographic features resulting from solution dominate areas underlain by carbonates. Since carbonates are generally very strongly cemented, shrink in the course of lithification and deform by brittle processes, they are strongly jointed. Dolomites, most of which form by the introduction of magnesium into the carbonate structure during or after lithification of a limestone, are yet more strongly jointed since the calcite to dolomite transformation is accompanied by a volume de-

crease. Solution is most easily achieved along joints or at their intersections. Once it begins, joints are accentuated, thereby increasing the already high permeability of lithified carbonates. Consequently infiltration of rainfall into carbonates is extremely efficient.

Above all else the distinguishing feature of carbonates in humid climates is the comparative absence of surface drainage. In the case of more easily dissolved limestones this feature is accompanied by abundant near-circular

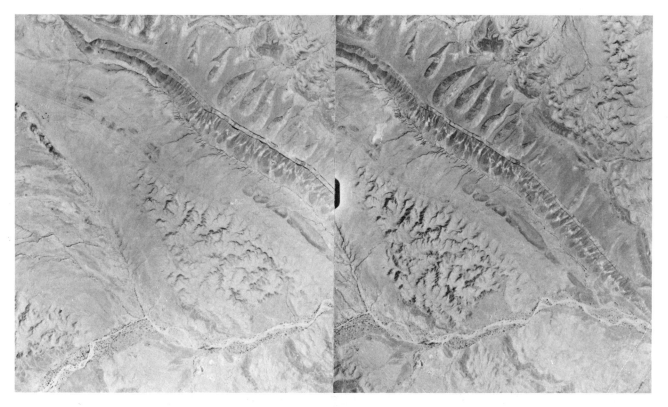

Figure 4.10 Anhydrite-rich evaporites in this area in Somalia display many of the peculiar landforms which make them so easy to recognize in semiarid terrains. The dip slope in the overlying limestones shows an excellent example of changing outcrop shapes controlled by varying valley-bottom slope superimposed on uniformly dipping strata. Scale: unknown. Source: unknown.

depressions where rainfall most easily seeps into the bedrock (Fig. 4.11a). These **sinkholes** may assume monumental proportions where underground drainage has carved large caverns which have collapsed. Such solution features sometimes control local centripetal drainage patterns. The net effect is an area of confused drainage on a landscape mottled by sinkholes and related features.

The solubility of limestone in areas subjected to warm humid climates for long periods results in their assuming a low-lying aspect. Dolomites under the same conditions are not so easily dissolved and therefore tend to form positive topographic features, but still have sparse surface drainage because of their high permeability. In humid areas that have undergone recent rejuvenation the hard and compact nature of carbonates, together with rapid headward erosion and the lack of surface drainage, leaves carbonates as long-lived uplands often with steep-sided major valleys.

Carbonates strongly resist glacial erosion. This combined with the closing of subterranean fissures by permafrost during subsequent periglacial conditions imparts a peculiar aspect to carbonate terrains in boreal areas. The preclusion of infiltration during periglacial conditions allows the development of extensive steep-sided valley systems in a glacially dominated topography of rugged carbonate scars

(Fig. 4.11b). Improvement of the climate 'unplugs' the subsurface drainage and the periglacial drainage is left as **dry valleys**.

Carbonates may vary in purity, but generally contain very little clastic material. As a result they are capped by very thin soils in humid climates, allowing their internal jointed structure to show up as distinctive patterns (Fig. 4.11b). The exception is in areas of very protracted and intense chemical weathering, as in a tropical rain forest, where residual material accumulates. Since the main clastic components are clay minerals, the resulting soils are poorly drained and dense vegetation may accumulate on a terrain almost completely lacking in large streams. In many cases the soil is washed into sinkholes, where particularly luxuriant vegetation may thrive.

In arid and semiarid terrains, carbonates become less easy to recognize on photographs. They resist erosion, have thin soil cover, are well drained and display prominent joint systems. It is easy to confuse them with coarse clastic sediments. On large-scale photographs with good resolution they can be discriminated by their lack of cross-bedding, their often thickly bedded nature and the peculiarities of their drainage. However, in most cases they can only be distinguished from coarse clastics by their

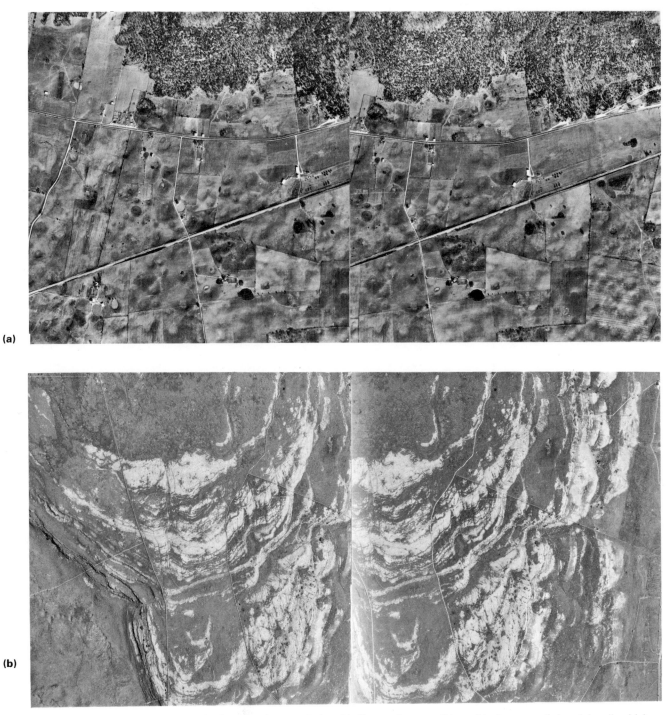

(a)

(b)

Figure 4.11 Prolonged chemical weathering of carbonates in humid climates leaves a thin residual veneer of clay-rich soil, which is often quite fertile, as in Kentucky (a). However, the extremely good internal drainage may preclude all but the largest surface streams. The often low-lying surface is generally pock-marked by many depressions over sinkholes. In recently glaciated areas, such as northern England (b), soil development has not been possible over limestones despite very humid conditions. Limestones have resisted glaciation better than associated sandstones and shales, to form prominent crags. Drainage is almost absent and the bare rock surface is rilled with innumerable solution-widened joints. Vegetation only occupies those surfaces veneered with glacial till. Scales (a) 1:25 000, (b) 1:10 000. Sources: (a) USGS GS-XS-6 38+39, (b) Metropolitan County of West Yorkshire 42-68, 176+177.

photographic tone or colour. Many carbonates are very pure, and being composed of white minerals generally appear light on photographs. There are anomalies though.

Some limestones have a high content of hydrocarbons and their dark coloration may be confused with that of basic igneous rocks. Such organic-rich limestones accumulated under reducing conditions and sometimes contain iron sulphide grains. Weathering and formation of limonite in these cases can impart strong reddish and brown stains to outcrops. Whatever the initial difficulties in arid terrains, the building up of general signatures for each of the dominant rock types will eventually produce sufficient differences for the carbonate component, if any, to be outlined.

4.2.2 Igneous rocks

Igneous rocks take on a variety of guises because they have a wide range of compositions and grain sizes and may be in various forms as extrusive or intrusive masses. Much effort in photogeology is assigned to establishing the relationships of intrusive bodies to country rocks, which is dealt with in Section 4.3. The most distinctive features of extrusive igneous rocks are those associated with their accumulation at the surface as constructive landforms (Section 4.5). The emphasis here is on distinguishing igneous rocks from sediments and from one another after they have been eroded.

Extrusive igneous rocks

The greatest problem in identifying the products of volcanic activity is that they are frequently interbedded with sediments as parallel-sided layers. The problems are removed if they are still associated with relics of volcanic landforms, such as dissected volcanic cones. Then the lavas and associated pyroclastic rocks form roughly circular features with radial and annular drainage patterns, and the only problem lies in discriminating between lavas and pyroclastics.

The classic cone-shaped volcanic edifice characterizes the viscous and explosive eruption of intermediate to acid magmas. With the exception of some areas of within-plate alkaline activity, magmatism of this kind is restricted to long, narrow zones near to destructive plate margins. As well as short-travelled viscous lavas, island-arc and Andean-type volcanism produces abundant pyroclastic materials of several kinds. The coarsest **agglomerates** travel only very short distances from vents. On photographs they show little difference from coarse clastic sediments, but may be recognized by their restricted outcrops and rapid changes in thickness. Finer grained **tuffs**, irrespective of their composition and grain size, travel long distances to settle as layered beds of fairly uniform thickness, either subaerially or in bodies of standing water. Because of this they are almost impossible to distinguish from clastic sediments. Their grain size and degree of later cementation determines their response to erosion, on which they can be subdivided in exactly the

same ways as clastic sediments. Identification as products of volcanism relies almost exclusively on context – whether or not they are associated with any distinctive volcanic feature.

The exception concerns those pyroclastic rocks which formed from incandescent clouds of volcanic debris whose heat was sufficient to maintain the particles in a near-molten state after they came to rest. In such **ignimbrites** the particles are annealed together to form a glassy rock, which may contain pumice fragments and abundant pores formed by residual gases. They are indeed tough rocks and form positive topographic features. They can be of any thickness up to several hundred metres. Their porosity ensures that they are well drained with widely spaced channels. The process of their formation – almost instantaneous deposition of thoroughly mixed debris – ensures that they are homogeneous and lack internal bedding. However, the resolution of photographs determines whether this feature can be discerned. In a dissected terrain ignimbrites can therefore be confused with sandstones and limestones.

Lavas, unless they are undissected and show distinctive surface features (Section 4.5), are difficult to distinguish from sediments with which they may be interbedded. Being crystalline rocks composed of hard silicate minerals, they are usually resistant to erosion and form positive topographic features. Unless highly jointed, they are impermeable compared with sandstones and carbonates and so develop closely spaced drainage textures. Highly jointed lava flows have excellent internal drainage and may have few surface streams. Joint systems are produced by shrinkage during cooling and tend to be closely spaced with a polygonal pattern, forming columns perpendicular to the flow bases. At the scales normally seen in photographs these patterns are not visible. This structural and compositional homogeneity ensures that dendritic patterns of minor drainage channels occur on their eroded surfaces, in contrast to the angular patterns of jointed resistant sediments.

The principal division of lavas in the field is based on colour, itself determined by the varying proportions of coloured ferromagnesian minerals in the rock. In the fresh state basic lavas are dark, intermediate compositions show as intermediate tones and acid lavas are always light toned. Except under conditions of extreme chemical weathering, the constituent silicates of lavas do not break down *in situ* to release the strong colouring agents of iron oxides and hydroxides. In arid and semiarid climates lavas therefore take on monotonous shades of grey. There is one important exception to this generalization. Some lavas may be altered soon after eruption by percolating hydrothermal fluids. Depending on original composition, the products may be strongly coloured by secondary minerals, including iron oxides and hydroxides. Such altered igneous rocks are of considerable importance in economic geology, since the hydrothermal fluids may have redistributed valuable metals to form ore deposits in association with the altered zones.

Under humid conditions the response of lavas to chemical weathering depends on the proportions of unstable minerals such as ferromagnesian minerals and feldspars relative to stable quartz. Acid lavas are clearly more resistant than basic, and the thickest residual soils form on basic lavas. The minerals quartz and feldspar, which dominate acid and intermediate compositions, contain relatively little in the way of plant nutrient, except in the case of potassium-rich alkali feldspar. Such lavas, except for alkaline varieties, form poor soils and are characterized by thin vegetation. Exposed soils are rich in

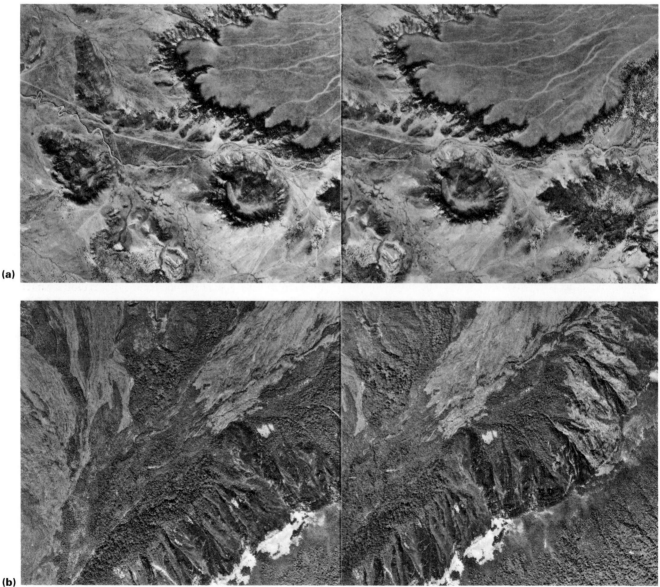

(a)

(b)

Figure 4.12 The high resistance of dissected lavas in arid terrains, such as that of Arizona (a), results in plateaus with flat tops and steep bounding cliffs. Isolated outliers often assume the form of spectacular mesas and buttes. Also shown are light-coloured buttes developed on diatremes, where the disruption of strata can be seen. In humid tropical areas, such as the Cameroons (b), the high nutrient content of weathered lavas results in luxuriant vegetation, which masks all but the most obvious primary features of the flows. The central part of the stereomodel shows subdued flow ridges in the pale grey area and possible flow fronts in the dark, jungle areas. Abundant drainage channels together with their association with clear volcanic features suggests that the deeply dissected parts of the area are underlain by lavas too. Scales: (a) 1:55 000, (b) 1:40 000. Sources: (a) NCIC Ariz.12 B+C, (b) CSL Series C 45+46.

quartz and clay minerals formed by feldspar breakdown and are pale coloured. Highly alkaline lavas, because of their abundance of potassium and sometimes phosphorus, often support anomalously luxuriant vegetation. More basic lavas break down to good iron-rich soils and support dense vegetation and intensive agriculture. Where soils are exposed they take on a distinctive brown or red hue reflecting high iron contents.

As well as their colour and resistance to chemical weathering, the composition of lavas determines their viscosity and the distance they can flow under gravity. Acid and intermediate lavas are very viscous, flow relatively short distances and as a result display rapid changes in thickness away from volcanic vents. Where thickness can be determined on a photograph, the most acid and viscous lavas often outcrop in the form of dissected domes.

The least viscous lavas are those of basaltic composition. They are commonly erupted from huge **shield volcanoes** or from long **fissures**, depending on the local tectonic controls over magmatism. They can flow for long distances over the gentlest of slopes to form thick piles of uniformly thick flows. For obvious reasons such lava piles are known as **flood basalts**. They form nearly level plains before dissection. Once erosion is under way the flood basalts, being resistant, produce plateaus, hence their other common name, **plateau basalts**. The time lapse between individual flows often allows soils and other sediments to develop between flows. The alternating contrasts in resistance then produce a stepped topography, each step representing an individual flow. However, this feature is equally common in alternating sequences of resistant and weak sediments. The pervasive columnar jointing in flood basalts makes them particularly well drained so that they have coarse dendritic drainage textures. Where incised by streams, they maintain steep slopes and often cliffs because of the vertical weaknesses induced by columnar jointing. The close joint spacing also ensures that cliffs maintain a very irregular serrated appearance, in contrast to the 'blocky' aspect of sandstone and limestone cliffs.

Because they are so like sediments when eroded, illustrations of dissected pyroclastic rocks are of little use here. Their more distinctive forms in volcanic landforms are shown in Section 4.5. Figure 4.12 shows some of the distinctive features of dissected lava flows in arid and humid climates.

Intrusive igneous rocks

The photographic tone or colour of intrusive rocks varies in the same way as that of lavas, and so too does their support of soils and vegetation. The main distinguishing features of intrusions derive from their shape, their internal structures and resulting photographic textures, and their structural relationships with the rocks which they intrude. These relationships are described in detail in Section 4.3. Here it is sufficient to state that they must in some way indicate that bodies of igneous rock post-date those surrounding them to be proven intrusions.

The shape of intrusions when they outcrop at the surface is as diverse as the means by which they were emplaced. They may be narrow, long strips resulting from the planation of vertical parallel-sided sheets or **dykes**. **Diapiric plutons** take on a variety of forms, ranging from elliptical bodies to irregular masses with outlying **stocks**, **bosses** and **apophyses**, depending on their three-dimensional shape and the depth of erosion. Various kinds of **ring intrusions** take on annular outcrops, as may **laccoliths** and **lopoliths**. There are numerous other minor variants. The most difficult to identify as intrusions are **sills**, whose emplacement parallel to sedimentary bedding allows them to be confused with lava flows or even resistant sediments. Whatever their form, to describe them fully from photographs the boundaries of intrusions with their country rocks must be continuously traceable. More often than not this is not possible. Estimates of outlines from photographs have to backed up by detailed mapping on the ground, including measurements of the attitudes of boundaries.

Figures 4.6 and 4.13 show a variety of the more common intrusive forms.

Since intrusions are emplaced at depth within the crust, where temperatures are elevated by the intrusions themselves and by the geothermal gradient, they cool more slowly than lavas. This enables them to develop coarser crystalline textures than lavas. Cooling also produces joints through shrinkage. The slower the cooling the more widely spaced are the joints. The orientation of the resulting joint systems is often complex, but is partly controlled by the outer surfaces of the intrusion through which heat flows because of temperature gradients. Dykes frequently illustrate this last factor very well, having regular joints perpendicular to their margins. Joint patterns therefore give valuable information on the depth of emplacement, the speed of cooling and the shape of the intrusion.

Grain size as well as composition of intrusive rocks is an important factor in controlling how they respond to weathering. Different silicates expand and contract to different degrees during heating and cooling. This is an important process during physical weathering. Similarly, some change volume as they are transformed to other minerals during chemical weathering, thereby assisting rotting of the rock. Both processes increase in effectiveness as the grain size increases. So a fine-grained intrusion may be more resistant to erosion than its coarse-grained counterpart.

The great variety of compositions, forms and grain sizes of intrusions precludes a comprehensive treatment here. As an illustration of most of the important points, an extensive description of granitic rocks, among the most common intrusions, is given here.

(a)

(b)

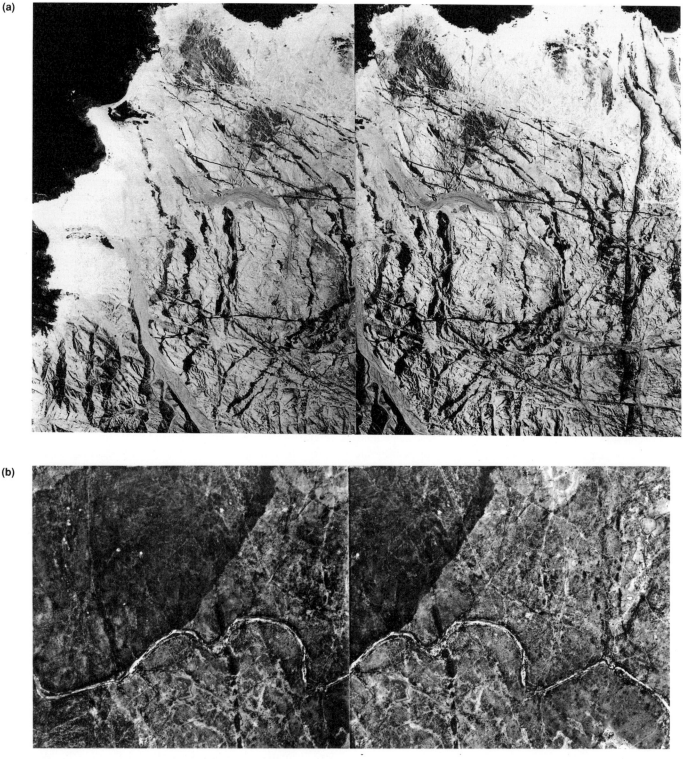

Figure 4.13 (a) This stereopair of aerial photographs shows an area of light-coloured Precambrian granitic rocks in the Sultanate of Oman. They are cut by several dark, minor basic intrusions. Those with a narrow and nearly straight outcrop are vertical dykes. Intrusive sheets with a low angle of dip are recognized by their sinuous trajectories and by their irregular outcrop widths. The greyish patches in the lower part of the pair are irregular ultrabasic intrusions. (b) The effects of spheroidal weathering of basic rocks in humid climates and rolling of boulders derived in this way often broadens and masks the outcrops of dykes. In this example from Zimbabwe the dyke is easily recognized where it cuts light Precambrian gneisses, but is only discernible from the dark metavolcanic unit when viewed stereoptically. Scales: (a) 1:20 000, (b) 1:40 000. Sources: (a) courtesy of Amoco Inc., (b) CSL Series C 39+40.

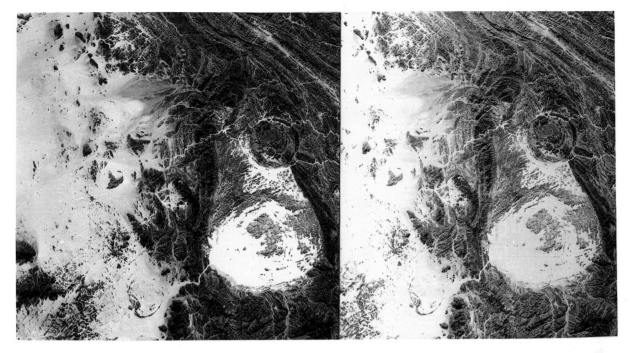

Figure 4.14 This stereopair of Shuttle Large Format Camera images of part of the Red Sea Hills in the Sudan shows circular granitic diapirs cutting deformed metasedimentary rocks in a late-Precambrian shear zone. Some of them have been deeply eroded to form sand-filled depressions, sometimes with an outer rim of resistant rock which is possibly gabbroic in composition. The small dark intrusion, clearly post-dating the nearby pale mass, is a composite alkaline body. Scale: 1:1 million.

Granitic rocks contain high proportions of the resistant mineral quartz. They are also homogeneous, as a result of the mixing processes involved in the convective uprise of granitic magmas. As a result, granites tend to resist erosion strongly. There is a notable exception. In arid climates, where weathering is dominated by physical processes, such as heating and cooling, the large differences in the coefficients of thermal expansion of quartz and feldspar rapidly cause crumbling of granite outcrops. Under these conditions granites may be expressed by depressions while related intrusions of different composition still form positive features (Fig. 4.14).

The homogeneity of granites tends to exert a strong control over drainage networks, which are dominantly dendritic. However, having cooled slowly at depth, granitic intrusions have frequently been fissured by large joints, which may show as controls of minor drainage. As both form light-coloured outcrops and are strongly jointed, granites and sandstones can be confused. The main distinguishing features are the irregular nature of granitic joint patterns compared with rectangular systems in sandstone and the irregular elevations of granite surfaces compared with those of sandstones which are controlled by bedding planes (Figs. 4.8 and 4.15a).

The crystalline nature of granite, together with its tendency to form poorly bound soils and its hardness, means that rainfall runs off efficiently, stripping the surface without forming gulleys. Soils may develop in joint-controlled depressions, so that in temperate humid climates bare surfaces criss-crossed with dark lines of thin vegetation are common. The overall effect is a rugged topography of rounded rocky knolls with widely spaced dendritic drainage (Figs. 4.6 and 4.15b).

Granites are capable of storing elastic strains produced in them during cooling. They are only released when erosion brings the rock close to the surface, when they are expressed by joint systems which closely parallel pre-existing topography. Further erosion exploits these weaknesses by a process known as **onion-skin weathering** or **exfoliation**. In its most extreme form, under humid tropical conditions, this results in the formation of immense domes known as **inselbergs**, typified by the Sugar Loaf of Rio de Janeiro in Brazil. Inselberg topography is characterized by arcuate drainage patterns between individual domes. Even in areas affected by intense chemical weathering and the development of substantial soils and vegetation upon granites, their distinctive landforms generally show up (Fig. 4.15c).

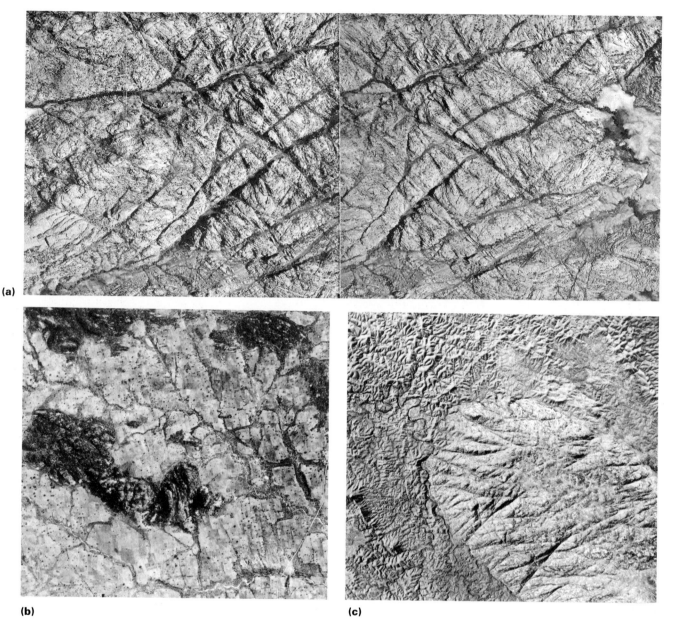

Figure 4.15 The stereopair in (a) is from an arid part of Wyoming, and shows the typical features of granites eroded under these conditions. The rugged, bare surface is reminiscent of sandstones under similar conditions, but the irregular nature of the more easily eroded joint system and the lack of layering are definitive. Drainage is controlled by the joints which contain the only vegetation in the area. Images (b) and (c) show the salient features of granitic rocks eroded under humid conditions in Nigeria and northern Australia respectively. Image (b) shows a typical inselberg surrounded by a flat pediment of debris derived from the granite. Scales (a) 1:37 000, (b) 1:30 000, (c) 1:25 000. Sources: (a) USGS GS-CMA-32 88+89, (b) Federal Ministry of Works, Nigeria 37-6 68+69, (c) Department of National Development and Energy, Australia (DNDE) CAB-151-2 5125+5126.

Basic and ultrabasic intrusions exhibit many of the characteristics of granites on photographs, particularly in temperate, humid climates. However, bare outcrops are, of course, much darker. Another distinguishing feature of basic intrusions and ophiolitic masses is their common banding (Fig. 4.27a), which results from the greater tendency of more fluid basaltic magmas to undergo efficient fractional crystallization. The jointing in such rocks is generally more closely spaced than in granites, and in arid climates this is expressed by extremely jagged topography (Fig. 4.16). All the minerals in basic and ultrabasic rocks are prone to decomposition under warm, humid conditions. This produces deep soils with luxuriant vegetation, and a tendency to more subdued topography than that underlain by granites.

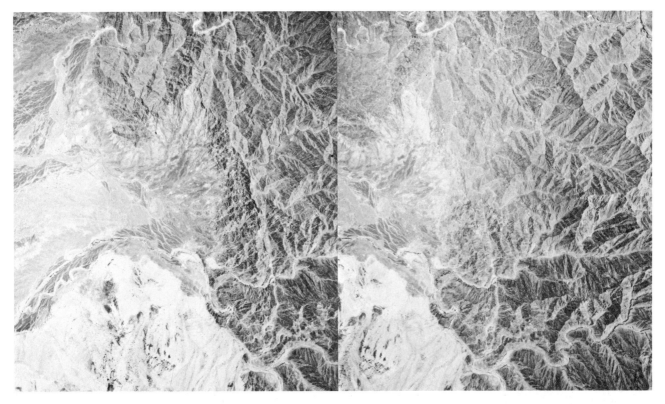

Figure 4.16 The mountains of NE Oman are dominated by exotic masses of oceanic lithosphere – mainly gabbros and peridotites – thrust over sediments of the continental margin. In this stereopair the Oman ophiolite shows as a dark jagged area with a complex and fine-textured drainage system. Its boundary with the block-strewn outcrop of white carbonates is a folded thrust. Scale: 1:40 000. Source: I.G. Gass, Open University.

4.2.3 Metamorphic rock types

Metamorphism is by definition the growth of new minerals in what were previously sediments and igneous rocks under the influence of elevated temperatures and pressures. Metamorphic rocks may therefore be of virtually any composition. However, the varied responses to erosion of sediments and igneous rocks by virtue of their composition and grain size is largely masked by the growth of new interlocking minerals during metamorphism. Except for moderately soluble marbles, metamorphic rocks are impermeable. Nor do they contain strong joint systems into which rainfall can infiltrate, having cooled slowly during uplift from the deep crust over millions of years. As a result drainage is both finely spaced and dendritic (Fig. 4.17a).

Being composed of strong interlocking crystals, metamorphic rocks are tough and so form positive topographic features. In humid temperate climates, where they are vegetated, very few distinctive characters show up compared with sediments (Fig. 4.17a). However, in areas of bare rock, in deserts or glaciated terrains, they have very distinctive attributes. Most metamorphic rocks contain compositional banding on a variety of scales, representing original layering of sedimentary or igneous origin. Alternatively, it may have resulted from the redistribution of the rocks' constituent elements during metamorphism, by the processes of **pressure solution** during deformation or **partial melting** at deep crustal levels. This can impart striking striped textures to bare metamorphic rock surfaces. The influence of the intense deformation that almost inevitably accompanies all but contact metamorphism modifies these patterns into even more distinctive shapes. Repeated folding and shearing results in complex structures, which may be etched out by weathering or glacial action (Fig. 4.17b and c).

It is only under conditions of strong chemical weathering that the compositional variations in metamorphic rocks manifest themselves in different resistances to erosion. As in the case of igneous rocks, the response is controlled mainly by the relative proportions of quartz and other stable silicates compared with the amounts of unstable, usually ferromagnesian, silicates. Siliceous metamorphic rocks are virtually inert and form strong positive features. In a sequence of metasediments these are not necessarily metamorphosed sandstones, but can equally be former siltstones or mudstones whose original clay minerals have become inert aluminosilicates. Layers with a high iron and

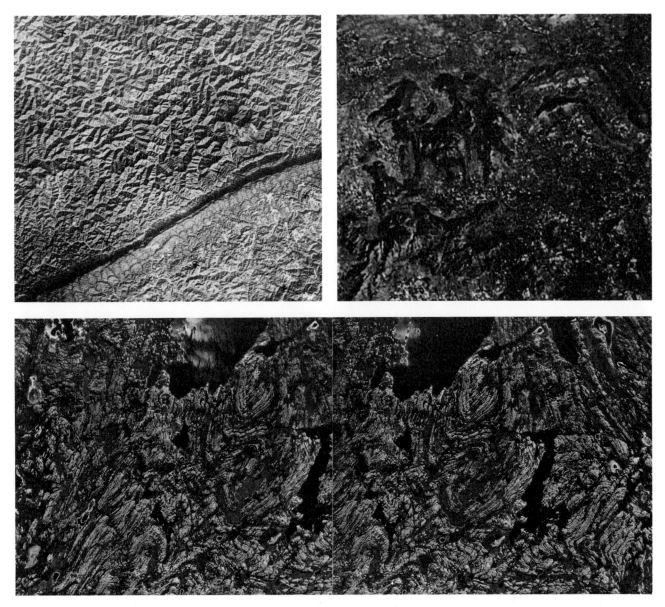

Figure 4.17 The dissected metamorphic rocks of the Cumberland Plateau in eastern Kentucky show an irregular pattern of dendritic drainage on a Landsat RBV image (a). Very few clues to the underlying structure are revealed at this scale, except in the younger sedimentary sequence running SW-NE across the image which shows V-shaped outcrops related to the direction of dip. A Landsat MSS band 7 image (b) of the Archaean metamorphic terrain of South India benefits from the selective weathering of rocks of different composition. Several of the resistant ridges define complex patterns of folding that typify metamorphic rocks. This diagnostic feature is far more obvious on aerial photographs, particularly of glaciated metamorphic terrains, such as the Canadian Shield (c). The stereopair shows an excellent example of fold interference patterns. Scales: (a) 1:500 000, (b) 1:250 000, (c) 1:50 000. Sources: (a) courtesy of J.P. Ford, Jet Propulsion Laboratory, (b) author, (c) EMRC A13781 19+20, copyright HM the Queen in Right of Canada (1953).

magnesium content tend to weather easily. These contrasting responses to chemical weathering are important, since they are the only means whereby the distinctive structural features of metamorphic rocks show up in densely vegetated rain forest (Fig. 4.17b).

Under the intense directed stresses involved in the folding of metamorphic rocks, newly forming platey and rod-like minerals tend to orient themselves, and small masses of rock slide by one another by shear deformation. Both processes result in **cleavage**, usually parallel to the axial surfaces of the folds. Cleavage forms on scales from millimetres to metres, and only shows clearly as strong parallel linear textures on photographs with the highest resolution. However, it frequently pervades large areas of metamorphic terrain, and may control minor topographic features and small-scale drainage, thereby masking the compositional banding and folds. This is particularly common in glaciated terrains, where the most subtle weaknesses are etched out by the scouring action of ice. Because glaciation produces finely spaced grooves it is easy to confuse these with cleavage (Fig. 4.6).

4.3 Stratigraphic relationships

The keys to successful interpretation of geological history from image interpretation are no more than a few rules used in stratigraphy and the interpretation of geological maps. As in rock identification, observations should be marked on images in some way and details of the criteria used noted down.

4.3.1 Dip and strike

In the field the angle and direction of dip on flat surfaces, such as bedding, joints, faults and intrusive contacts, can be measured with fair accuracy using a compass and clinometer. On photographs these measurements depend on such surfaces having some detectable topographic expression. In layered sequences, differences in resistance to erosion may result in the formation of cuestas of one kind or another (Section 4.1.1). They provide the best opportunities for estimates of dip.

Along a cuesta maintained by a resistant layer the slope which has the same direction as the dip is usually a consequent or resequent slope (Section 4.1.1). One whose direction is opposed to dip is an obsequent slope. Where dip is less than about 30° the obsequent slope is usually steeper than the resequent slope (Fig. 4.18). This can give a good indication of the direction of dip. However there are exceptions. Asymmetric cuestas can develop along faults (Section 4.4.1), but this is usually obvious. If the layers immediately above the resistant unit have been stripped from the resequent slope, then the resulting **dip slope** can provide a very good estimate of the average dip of the resistant layer. Making a dip estimate from photographs depends on being able to view the slope in a stereomodel.

As dip angle increases there is less chance that higher layers in a sequence are completely stripped from resequent slopes. As a result the cuesta becomes more symmetrical (Fig. 4.18). With steep dips the accumulation of talus on the obsequent slope and the increased opportunity for higher layers to slide under gravity down the resequent slope means that the asymmetry of a cuesta can be the reverse of that associated with shallow dips. Although angles of dip can be measured quite accurately from stereomodels (Appendix A), it is a tedious process. In most photointerpretation the stereomodel is used to estimate dips into broad ranges – <10°, 10–25°, 25–45°, >45° and vertical. Because of vertical exaggeration and radial relief

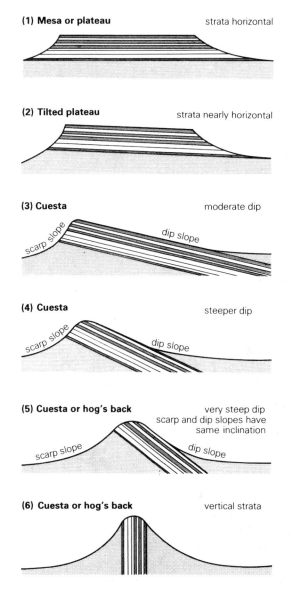

Figure 4.18 The relationship between the surface form of cuestas and the dip of underlying layered sequences.

distortion, care has to be taken to apply rough corrections to the apparent dips observed. Figure 4.19 illustrates dip estimation from cuestas and dip slopes. Appendix A includes details of how dips may be measured more accurately from stereopairs.

If stereoviewing is not possible, or if clear dip slopes are absent, accurate estimates of dip are not possible. However, topography superimposed upon sequences of dipping layers results in the outcrops of layer boundaries taking on shapes familiar to anyone who has studied a geological map. In valleys the boundaries assume V-shapes, the Vs pointing in the direction of dip. On interfluves the boundaries are more arcuate, concavities indicating dip direction (Fig. 4.20). In extreme cases, the landforms so produced take on the

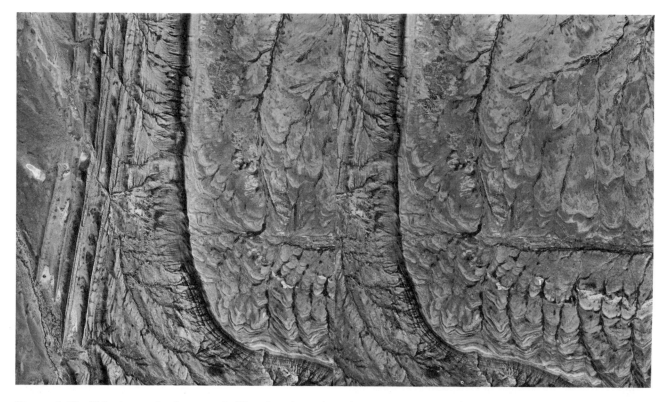

Figure 4.19 This stereopair of an area in Wyoming shows how the outcrop patterns of dipping strata are controlled by both angle of dip and topography. The structure displayed is a monocline with vertical strata to the west and shallow northward dips in the east. Scale: 1:32 000. Source: USGS GS-VHI-2 54+55.

appearance of **flatirons**. Using the **law of Vs** is essential in rapidly assessing the variation in direction of dip over large areas. Where folds are not expressed by distinct shapes it is often the only means of detecting them and distinguishing antiforms and synforms. Figure 4.19 gives an example of this useful technique. Occasionally it is possible to use the law of Vs on single satellite images.

Where dips are steep, or in areas of subdued relief, valleys do not result in V-shaped outcrops. Traces of layers and their boundaries only provide an indication of strike. This is not reliable in the case of shallow dips in subdued terrain, since the slightest slope has a marked effect on the trend of outcrops. Where resolution is poor or where suitable boundaries do not cross suitable valleys, strike determination is about the best that the interpreter can expect to achieve. Provided the elevation differences are small compared with the scale of the photograph, or provided visible units form ridges or valleys of roughly constant elevation, such estimates of strike are fairly accurate. This is generally the case for satellite photographs. However, in deeply dissected mountains even this aid to interpretation is notoriously unreliable.

Another method of assessing the direction of dip where valley Vs are absent is by examining drainage patterns. As Figures 4.1 and 4.18 indicate, where dips are less than about 45° consequent and resequent streams tend to be

longer than obsequent streams. Provided such streams are present, mapping them out can reveal a crude direction of dip.

Dip and strike estimations are not restricted to boundaries in layered rocks. Faults, the margins of igneous intrusions and unconformities are all surfaces whose geometry is important to geologists. Unconformities frequently form cuestas, and their dips can be estimated easily. Igneous intrusions, such as batholiths, generally form uniform positive features relative to the rocks which they intrude. Cuestas are rarely involved. However, the contact may display Vs in valleys and reveal its direction of dip, and perhaps clues to the dip angle. Since plutonic igneous contacts are often highly irregular, information of this kind may be misleading. Provided it is not vertical, the hade of faults may be revealed by V-shapes in valleys.

4.3.2 Superposition

If the dip direction of any geologically important surface is definable on a photograph then it is a simple matter to work out the vertical sequence of rocks outcropping on either side of it. In a layered sequence the rock outcropping in the dip direction is above the surface, that outcropping in the opposite direction is below. In most cases the rock above the surface is younger and the rock

(a) Upstream dip

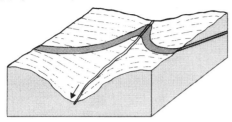

(b) Steep downstream dip

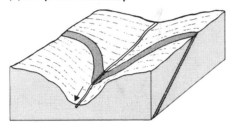

(c) Shallow downstream dip

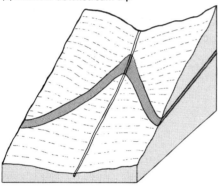

Figure 4.20 These block diagrams show how the interplay between topographic slope and the dip of strata control the shapes of outcrops in valleys and on spurs. Generally, V-shaped outcrops in valleys point in the direction of dip, but if topographic slope is locally greater than a dip in the same direction, the relationship is reversed (Fig. 4.10). The apical angles of the Vs become more obtuse as the dip becomes steeper, until no topographic displacement of outcrop occurs with vertical layers.

below is older. By using all the boundaries between layers that are expressed on a photograph it is therefore possible to build up a more or less complete stratigraphic column of the most obvious rock units. There is one obvious assumption, that there has been no major recumbent folding to invert the stratigraphy. Assessing this possibility is based on observations of structural complexity and on context. Field observations, which are vital to fill in the detailed stratigraphy, will in most cases show whether tectonic inversion is present from way-up indicators. Figures 4.2, 4.10, 4.17a and 4.19 gives some examples of simple stratigraphy which can be established once dip direction is known.

Identification of the relative age of important or prominent units in a layered sequence is not only useful in establishing a rough stratigraphic framework. It is able to help in recognizing the presence of folds and their sense of closure. The relative stratigraphic position of units juxtaposed across faults allows the sense of movement to be established, and in some cases the amount of throw too.

For faults with hades less than 90° exactly the same principle is used to discover the hanging wall and footwall. In terrains dominated by thrust tectonics, such as the Rockies of western North America and the European Caledonides, and by nappes as in the Alps, recognition of thrust surfaces and their dip directions is the key to establishing a vertical sequence of tectonic units (see Section 4.4).

4.3.3 Unconformities

Unconformities are among the most important stratigraphic features because they represent periods of time separating episodes of deformation, uplift and erosion from the re-establishment of deposition. They allow the geological history of an area to be subdivided into convenient episodes. By definition an unconformity separates older, more complex sequences from stratigraphically younger rocks with simpler structure which lie above the unconformity. This is usually revealed by the **overstepping** of the unconformity surface from one level in the underlying sequence to others. Overstep shows on photographs as an irregular and discontinuous line, marking the unconformity, which truncates traces of bedding and other structures which lie topographically below it (Fig. 4.21).

Unconformities are usually near-planar boundaries, marking the presence of erosion surfaces which have developed to completion. Where erosion is interrupted early in the cycle of denudation by a sudden increase in the local sediment load, a rugged landscape may be buried and preserved as a very irregular unconformity. Only examination of a stereomodel will allow such **buried landscapes** to be evaluated.

Although unconformities permit the ages and intensities of tilting, folding and faulting to be related to the overlying rocks, their most revealing relationships are to igneous intrusions. Since igneous rocks can be dated by radiometric means, their age relative to the unconformity, as well as to the rocks and structures divided by it, can place absolute time constraints on local geological history (*Fig. 4.22*).

Unconformities can be tilted and folded, in which case their attitude can be estimated using the same methods as those applying to dipping layers (Section 4.3.1). Because they are major time boundaries separating rocks of contrasted structure, unconformities can often be traced over huge areas. Satellite photographs with their super-synoptic cover are then very useful. Because elevation differences

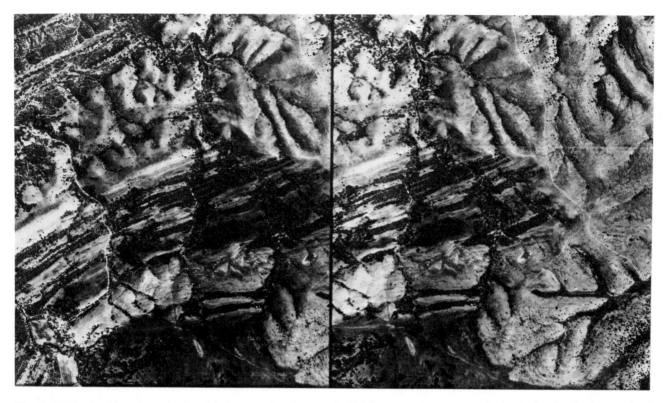

Figure 4.21 On this stereopair of aerial photographs of an area in Oklahoma can be seen two distinct units. One is characterized by a dendritic drainage pattern and is sparsely vegetated. Faint traces of bedding parallel contours suggest that it is horizontal. The other appears banded, with several almost straight, wooded ridges, which appear to be controlled by steep dips to the NNW. The boundary between the two clearly truncates the ridges, and the horizontal unit lies unconformably upon the steeply dipping strata. The wide spacing of drainage in the younger unit suggests that it is a massive, coarse clastic rock. The older unit comprises shales and limestones. Scale: 1:22 000. Courtesy of the Committee on Aerial Photographs, University of Illinois.

are effectively 'ironed out' at the small scales involved, the regional shape of the outcrop of an unconformity can be used to estimate quite subtle features relating to original basin extent, and the effects of regional warping and faulting younger than the unconformity (Fig. 4.23).

4.3.4 Cross-cutting relationships

As mentioned in Section 4.3.3, igneous rocks are generally the only units in an area which can provide reliable radiometric ages for calibration of the stratigraphy. Intrusions give the minimum age of the rocks which they cut and a maximum age for those which sit unconformably upon them. Similarly, they allow the time relations of structural features which they transect or which disturb them to be assessed. Sedimentary sequences are built up over millions of years, with perhaps very limited evidence of age such as fossils or radiometrically dated units. They provide only crude age limits for tectonic activity. Intrusions, however, are emplaced over geologically short periods of time and provide a more sensitive means of working out tectonic evolution.

Apart from sills and other intrusions with margins concordant to older layering, all intrusions have margins which cut across older structures, as shown in Figures 4.6, 4.14 and *4.22*. In the case of massive intrusions it is rare to find evidence of their later deformation. However, narrow dykes are particularly sensitive to distortion, and provide near-ideal markers for structural investigations.

4.4 Structural relationships

Folds, faults and thrusts, and their relations to features such as unconformities and intrusions, are used to work out a qualitative tectonic history for an area. They also help quantitative estimates of the displacements involved and the disposition of principal stresses to be made. Using structures as indicators of the mechanics of deformation is largely beyond the scope of this book. Only a few important comments are made, full details being available in standard textbooks on structural geology. In this section the emphasis is on detecting and describing major structures.

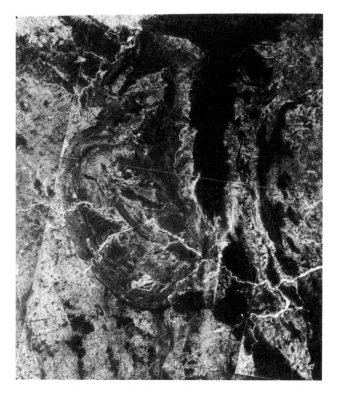

Figure 4.23 Mosaicing several of the Landsat MSS band 5 scenes surrounding the area in Figure 4.22 reveals the complete regional setting of the late-Precambrian Cuddapah Basin. In the west it is a shallow undeformed basin, but in the east has clearly been affected by strong deformation. Dark, forested ridge-forming units display complex fold patterns, and in fact the whole basin has been inverted and overthrust by Archaean basement from the east. Scale: 1:2.5 million. Source: author.

4.4.1 Faults, lineaments and arcuate features

Faults are surfaces across which blocks of crust have moved relative to one another. Identifying a feature on a photograph as a fault therefore means establishing that displacement has indeed taken place across it. Except for thrusts, most faults dip steeply and outcrop as more or less linear features, which are relatively unaffected by topography. There are, however, many ways in which obvious linear features may be formed. They may be faults, joints, dykes, steep to vertical strata and

cultural features, such as roads and boundaries between areas of different agricultural use. Certain defects in some images produce artificial lines too, known as **artifacts** (Ch. 5 and Appendix B). It may also be possible to link various elements of a scene by lines, such as isolated boundaries between surfaces of different tone, meanders in a number of streams, notches in ridges, truncated spurs and features relating to other geological structures. These may be purely fortuitous connections, but could have some genetic relationship to subtle or deeply buried faults.

With the increasing availability of small-scale, super-synoptic satellite images of the Earth there has been a tendency among some geologists to cover them with real, inferred and entirely imaginary lines. In some cases these extend across entire continents. Repeated analysis by the same person or by different interpreters often results in different arrangements of many of the lines. The near obsessive nature of this simplistic approach has provoked a measure of scepticism and cynicism towards the whole of remote sensing by many scientists. There can be no doubt that linear features of geological importance do occur, and that they are only visible on small-scale photographs because they form broad, subtle and very long connections. However, all potential lines need to be viewed with caution and subdivided into categories with different degrees of confidence (Section 2.6).

A note on nomenclature is necessary here, to avoid adding to the already burgeoning confusion surrounding lines on images. **Linear** is an adjective describing the line-like character of an object or array of objects. It is often misused as a noun designating clear, short lines on an image, in contrast to a **lineament**, which is correctly applied to long, often subtle, linear arrangements of various topographic, tonal, geological and even geophysical and geochemical features. **Linear feature** is used here to describe relatively short (less than 5% of the extent of the image being used) lines and regular arrangements of surface phenomena. It is used together with the term lineament in an entirely non-genetic sense. When either can be recognized or confidently inferred as a geological entity, then it is given its correct, geological name.

 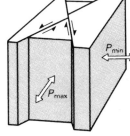

Figure 4.24 These block diagrams show the relationships between the three main classes of fault and the required arrangements of the maximum and minimum principal stress axes. Theoretically, for each arrangement of principal stresses, faults should develop with two orientations. The acute angle between them is bisected by the maximum principal stress direction, and the two sets form a conjugate pair.

Faults manifest the brittle response of the crust to stress. They are surfaces along which the crust has failed and which allow the stresses involved to be dissipated by crustal extension or shortening. The attitude adopted by faults is governed approximately by simple mechanical laws relating the orientation of the maximum, minimum and intermediate stress axes acting in the crust, the strength of rocks and the resulting surfaces of potential failure. Figure 4.24 illustrates these principles and shows the main classes of faults which develop. At the instant of failure one of two possible fault surfaces begins to break first and strain is concentrated and propagated across it. Thus, although faults should theoretically develop equally, parallel to two **conjugate** directions, in most cases one direction dominates. The conjugate set of faults to this is either suppressed or plays a relatively minor role in crustal deformation.

Heterogeneities in the crust and in the stresses involved during a period of crustal deformation mean that all the types of fault shown in Figure 4.24 may occur in an area. If they do, then estimates of their attitudes and the directions of movement along them allow the overall tectonics of the area, and its relation to major crustal forces, to be assessed (Fig. 4.25). An important parameter to assess from such composite fault systems is the overall sense of movement of blocks of the crust which the faults bound. This is often difficult for normal and thrust faults. For strike-slip movements, the relative dislacements visible may allow both dextral and sinistral movements to be recognized. **Dextral** means that the movement sense of a block on one side of the fault relative to an observer on the other side is to the right. **Sinistral** faults displace to the left. The orientation and sense of fault movement provides the basic information from which the disposition of the regional principal stresses can be worked out. This in turn gives a context within which other, subtler structural features can be sought.

The majority of faults that are easily visible on images have steep to vertical hades, as explained later. However, many change hade with depth in the crust to form what are known as **listric** surfaces, from the Greek for 'spoon-like'. As a result their surface expression may change with the depth of erosion. No fault continues indefinitely through the crust. It may die out, the strain being taken up along other faults. It may split or develop numerous minor **splay faults** along its length. Such splay faults result from the reorientation of principal stress axes in the close proximity to major faults. In turn, large splay faults have a similar but less widely distributed effect, and develop minor splays of their own. The result is a complex pattern of curved faults and tectonic joints of different sizes.

The photointerpretation of faults is often more reliable than their detection in the field. Because they are usually weaknesses, fault surfaces are rarely seen at outcrop. They often control low-lying features, from which views into the distance are difficult. Changes in vegetation and surface texture related to faults are difficult to see when the geologist is close to them. The synoptic view of photographs enables widely separated pieces of evidence to be linked as sharp and semicontinuous linear features or lineaments. The vertical exaggeration associated with stereoptic viewing accentuates even the most subdued topographic features and reveals clearly any vertical displacements associated with faulting. Despite the scepticism about 'linear geoart', image interpretation is the most powerful means of detecting crustal fractures and analysing their tectonic and economic significance.

As with all geological boundaries, the dip on fault surfaces governs how they are affected by landforms. The lower the angle, the more a surface tends to follow topographic contours and adopt complex outcrop patterns. Thrusts are controlled strongly by topography, and their expression is often identical to that of bedding surfaces. On occasion the floor of a thrust, which may be coated by tough **mylonite**, stands out as a prominent dip slope (Fig. 4.26c). Sometimes the tones, patterns and textures of rocks forming the roof of a thrust clearly indicate that they are older than the rocks forming the floor (Fig. 4.26c). The roof may be metamorphosed basement and the floor composed of sediments with simple structure. Distinct lithologies in the roof rocks, such as red beds, may also indicate an inverted sequence and the suspicion of thrusting. In the main, however, thrusts are notoriously elusive in photogeology: because they have low angles of dip their outcrop often parallels that of the layers that they have displaced. Often can only be inferred from the context of other observations. One of these is the identification of local truncation of compositional layering in the hanging wall or footwall (Fig. 4.27). These are known as **strike cut-offs**, and are more easily recognized on images covering large areas than on the ground, since

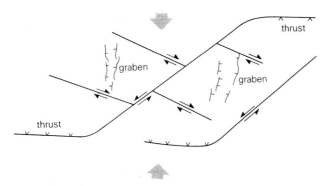

Figure 4.25 Because the Earth's crust is constrained in two dimensions one major episode of deformation, such as that characterizing the Tibetan Plateau today, can produce all three classes of faults. This cartoon shows how they might form relative to one another.

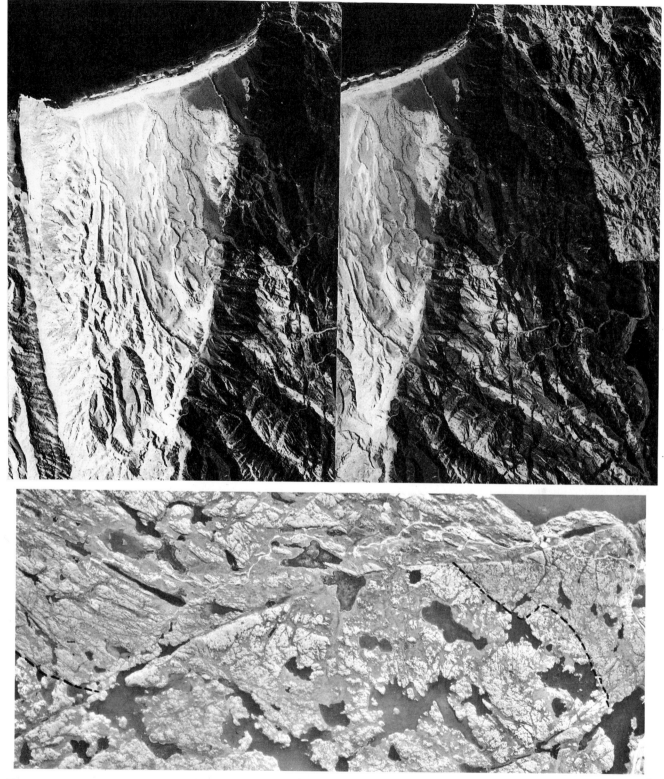

Figure 4.26 (a) The sharp boundary separating dark from light terrains is a very large normal fault in the Sultanate of Oman. The light unit consists of Tertiary limestones which were deposited upon the dark, late-Cretaceous ophiolite complex. The ophiolite here is composed of layered gabbros in which compositional banding is clearly visible. It has been thrust over the pale-grey Precambrian granites seen at top right. The thrust has itself been displaced by a small strike-slip fault on the right. (b) The sharp linear feature running diagonally across this aerial photograph of part of the Canadian shield is a strike-slip fault. The displacement across it can be judged from the relative disposition of the vertical contact between granite (light grey) and metavolcanic rocks (darker grey) marked by the pecked line. It is about 5 km.

(c)

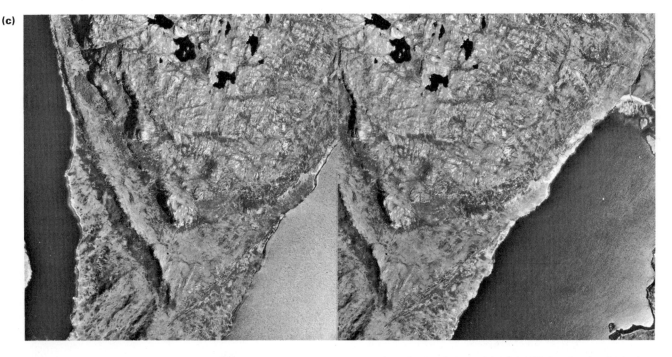

Figure 4.26 (*cont.*)   (c) This stereopair shows a spectacular thrust fault in the Caledonides of NW Scotland, which drove Archaean gneisses over Cambro-Ordovician sediments. The thrust plane is marked by the pronounced bench on the peninsula, which is coated with mylonite. The typical knobbly topography of the heavily glaciated gneisses is quite obvious in the upper part of the pair. Scales: (a) 1:20 000, (b) 1:50 000, (c) 1:20 000. Sources: (a) courtesy of Amoco Inc., (b) EMRC A13621 177, copyright HM the Queen in Right of Canada, (c) author.

the angle between thrust and local strike is often very small.

The steeper the angle of a fault, the less it conforms to topography. Steep faults are conspicuous on photographs because of their near-independence of valleys, ridges and uplands. The steeper they are the more they resemble regular lines. Because of intense fracturing along faults they often form local weaknesses, become eroded out and form linear depressions (Figures 4.26, *4.31* and 4.32). They are often followed by streams. The almost irresistible tendency of streams to meander means that any straight segments immediately raise the suspicion of fault control. There are relatively rare cases of faults which have been cemented by percolating fluids or followed by igneous dykes, in which case anomalous straight ridges can form.

The high permeability of fault zones means that they can be saturated by water. They provide easy access for root systems, and when forming depressions protect plants from wind and desiccation. Lines of vegetation encouraged by these conditions are also potential indicators of faults, but joints provide exactly the same conditions and other evidence is needed for confirmation. Where faults have thrown permeable rocks against impermeable, spring lines may form. In the case of limestone thrown against impermeable rocks, local drainage may disappear into lines of

sinkholes marking the fault. Where a fault juxtaposes rocks of grossly different resistance to erosion, the fault can be expressed as a line of cliffs, waterfalls or abrupt changes in slope.

Whatever linear features can be discerned on a photograph, they can only be identified as faults if other geologically significant features in the scene are displaced or truncated. Even truncation is a dubious criterion, since geological structures can terminate abruptly for a host of reasons. Normal and reverse faults displace the crust vertically. In terrains dominated by horizontal or gently dipping strata the displacement only shows up if there are changes in elevation of easily recognized beds or boundaries across the fault. Where dips are greater than about 5°, vertical displacements also produce apparent lateral displacements in outcrops. Features marking resistant units are truncated by the fault and reappear across it at another position, depending on the direction of dip and the sense of movement of the fault. Knowing the directions of dip of the unit and of the fault surface – perhaps from V-shaped outcrops – allows the sense of faulting to be worked out. Strike-slip faults produce true lateral dislacements. However, the resulting truncation and displacement of dipping resistant units can have exactly the same appearance as those associated with normal and reverse faults. The only reliable criterion is the displacement of vertical surfaces,

Figure 4.27 On this Landsat TM band 5 image of an area in Eritrea the presence of a fault almost parallel to compositional banding, probably a thrust, is indicated by a marked linear feature, to either side of which the strike of smaller linear features corresponding to layering is truncated. These are ramps in the hanging wall and footwall of the thrust. Scale 1:100 000. Source: author.

such as other faults, vertical strata, igneous dykes and the axial surfaces of upright folds.

As well as revealing the present tectonics of an area, **active faults** present major environmental hazards. Locating them and identifying their movement senses is doubly important to the geologist. World-wide monitoring of seismic events has provided such a wealth of data on the location of earthquake epicentres that all areas of major seismic activity are now known. Seeking active faults in them is therefore aided by known context. However, the world-wide increase in potentially hazardous and seismically sensitive nuclear installations means that even the smallest earthquakes pose a serious threat. Currently, many areas hitherto considered stable are being re-evaluated for **seismic risk**. This concentrates on delineating old fault systems which may be reactivated by minor tectonic processes, such as isostatic readjustment after glacial loading.

Large active faults are recognized in the same ways as old ones etched out by erosion. Their activity has extended for thousands if not millions of years, so that erosion has had time to pick them out. In many cases they are in areas of considerable relief due to rapid uplift and erosion which accompanies intense tectonic activity. They are easily seen in such terrains. An active tectonic zone may also contain faults which have ceased to move. So it is important to distinguish those which pose a threat from those which are probably safe. An active fault may remain dormant for tens and hundreds of years between earthquakes, stresses slowly being built up before explosive release. There may well be no records of seismic events related to them. Fortunately, faults which have been active in the last few thousand years still preserve unique features which can be seen on photographs.

The most obvious sign of a fault's activity is its disturbance of cultural features, such as roads and straight field boundaries. Equally as clear are displacements of Recent superficial deposits, often with the presence of clear breaks and low bluffs (Fig. 4.28). Small-scale tilting associated with fault movements produces depressions, often filled with water to form **sag ponds** (Fig. 4.28). Where streams cross active strike-slip faults they are periodically displaced. This produces sudden bends in their courses along the fault line. Such **offset streams** are often present in all drainage crossing the fault, and define both the line and the sense of most recent movement (Fig. 4.29). Physical disruption of topographic features, formed during periods of quiescence, by a major earthquake results in the formation of truncated or **faceted spurs** (Fig. 4.29). Such displaced ridges can be transported so far along a strike-slip fault that they block the upper ends of valleys whose formative streams have been shifted elsewhere. This produces **shutter ridges** and **headless valleys** (Fig. 4.29).

The super-synoptic view provided by satellite images is ideal for re-evaluating fault patterns and other reflections of brittle tectonics over large areas. Small, regionally insignificant features are suppressed and very large, subtle and previously unsuspected ones may show up. The smaller the scale the subtler, more completely connected and larger are the features that can be discerned. Individual scenes or mosaics of many scenes can be used to highlight the interconnectedness of tectonic features (Fig. 4.30). Bearing in mind the cautionary comments earlier in this section, linear features and lineaments can be mapped very quickly and related to notions of the tectonic evolution of an area. The best results are from areas of high relief and recent activity, where faults are well expressed and where evidence for movement directions is clearest (Fig. 4.31).

As well as their importance in tectonic analysis, faults have economic importance. Being zones of intense fracturing, they afford easy passage to various fluids. Because vertical faults ignore topography, where they cross from

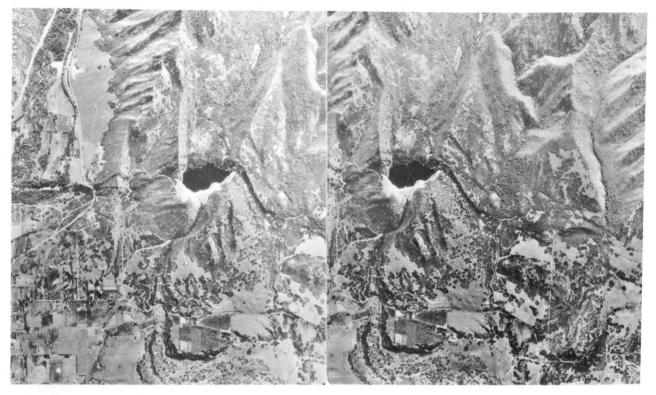

Figure 4.28 Running across the centre of this stereopair of an area in Utah are several connected scarps. They are developed within Pleistocene moraines, and resulted from normal displacements along an active fault. The body of water at the centre is a typical sag pond caused by fault-induced tilting. Scale: 1:28 000. Source: NCIC Utah 2 B+C.

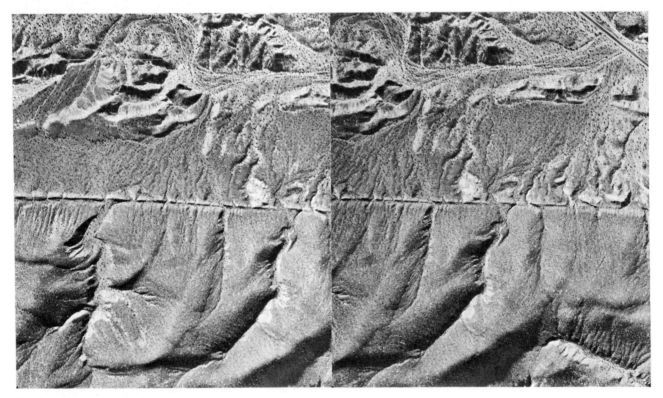

Figure 4.29 The linear feature running across this stereopair is one of many active faults in California. Along it can be seen good examples of off-set streams, headless valleys, a shutter ridge and faceted spurs. The sense of active movement appears to be sinistral strike-slip. Scale: 1:12 000. Source: USGS GS-GF-1 39+40 (colour original).

Figure 4.30 This NOAA-6 AVHRR band 2 image of West Asia shows the relationships between the tectonically linked Oman ophiolite (SW), the SSE–NNW Lut Block – a microcontinent which indented Iran – the E–W folded Makran Range and the N–S folded Kirthar and Sulaiman Ranges, which are bounded to the west by a large sinistral strike-slip system. All formed at roughly the same time in the late-Cretaceous to early-Eocene when the Tethys ocean closed and India impacted Asia. Scale: 1:15 million. Source: author.

(b)

0   50 km

Figure 4.31 (a, *colour*) This enhanced false-colour composite of Landsat MSS data shows an area in the central part of the Tibetan Plateau. Although it is of little use in this form for discriminating lithologies, the many linear features that it expresses are the key to understanding the region's active tectonics. Several of them clearly displace Recent superficial deposits, as at centre right and centre left. (b) This sketch map distinguishes between what are thought to be traces of compositional layering and major faults. The N–S faults bound a major pull-apart basin, possibly cored by Pleistocene volcanics. The NE–SW and WNW–ESE faults are conjugate strike-slip faults, the dominant set being the former. This pattern has been interpreted as reflecting northward crustal shortening and E–W extension. The crust in fact deforms as a framework of lozenge-shaped blocks bounded by strike-slip faults and which contain the grabens. Scales: (a) 1:1 million, (b) 1:1.8 million. Source: (a) courtesy of Dave Rothery, Open University.

Figure 4.32 In Eritrea the western lowlands contain large areas of potentially fertile, clay-rich soils yet they record much lower rainfall than the nearby upland areas to the east. Run-off from the uplands is heavily charged with sediment, and dams to harvest it for irrigation would soon become silted. Equally, the ephemeral streams are so powerful during storms that they would destroy channelled irrigation schemes. On this Large Format Camera image several marked linear features reflecting large crustal fractures trend from the high rainfall uplands to plains with clay-rich soils but low rainfall. Conceivably, they could be transferring large volumes of high-quality groundwater to the area of agricultural potential. These could be tapped quite easily. Scale: 1:700 000. Source: author.

areas of high elevation and rainfall to plains with shortages of drinking and irrigation water they may transfer large supplies to areas of need (Fig. 4.32). Fracturing of the crust can also focus the migration of hydrothermal fluids and magmas. Both may encourage mineralization. In the early years of Landsat image interpretation explorationists concentrated on the mapping of linear features and lineaments, and their relation to known mineral districts. This was encouraged by the long-held suspicion that some mines were focused on intersections of deep-seated faults. Further incentive stemmed from the synoptic analysis of regional patterns of mineralization that began to reveal linear arrangements of active mines and mineral prospects. One suggestion was that they lay over deep crustal weaknesses. Another was that they recorded the passage of the crust over mantle hot-spots. Theoretically, both mechanisms should be reflected in subtle tectonic and magmatic features visible at the surface, given a wide enough perspective.

Another regular and sharp type of feature that has attracted considerable attention from explorationists is the circle. The eye is very good at seeing circles. Indeed it is rather too good, and can pick out circles in nearly random patterns. Nevertheless, there are many nearly circular and elliptical features produced by crustal processes, and some of them are indeed related genetically to mineralization and hydrocarbon accumulations. The most obvious are salt domes produced by the diapiric uprise of low-density halite and the production of annular fault systems and overlying circular domes (Fig. 4.33a). They are well-known traps for oil and gas. Circular granite intrusions form in a directly analogous way, and when they are peralkaline have associated tin, niobium and rare-earth mineralization (Fig. 4.14). An important proportion of diamonds is found in **kimberlite pipes**, the products of cryptoexplosion structures associated with ultramafic magmas rising from the deep mantle. Such pipes too have a nearly perfect circular cross-section. However, kimberlite is very soft, and pipe formation often shatters the country rock so that circular features are suppressed. Within large igneous plutons of diorite to granodiorite composition, the patterns of convective flow of magma and hydrothermal fluids can result in circular cross-sections of flow cells. These may relate to mineralization of the porphyry type. Another type of real circular feature relates to the erosion of conical volcanoes and their frequently associated annular faults produced in **calderas**. Many porphyry-type ores are found at different levels in such structures, and may be exposed by erosion (Fig. 4.33b).

A view of the Moon reveals the most dramatic of circular features – the craters associated with the impact of large meteorites. There is no way in which the Earth could have escaped the bombardment responsible for the pock-marked lunar surface. However the vast majority of lunar impact structures arose during the period before 3.8 billion years ago. Since then the entire crust of the Earth has evolved and been reworked. All the truly enormous terrestrial impacts – theory suggests the largest to have had a diameter of 6000 km – have been obliterated. Such **impact structures** do exist where little has happened to the crust for a billion years or more. They are among the easiest features to spot from orbit (Fig. 4.33c). On an entirely different plane are circular features that are defined by mineral occurrences on a continent-wide scale, and which only show up, if at all, on satellite images encompassing millions of square kilometres. Several authors have interpreted such features as relics of the early bombardment of the Earth, and continually seek others as a regional guide to new mineral districts. This is an entirely illusory quest, since the thermal effect of even the biggest impact would last only about 50 million years. Moreover, the mineralization associated with such features affects rocks whose range of ages span up to 2.5 billion years. Whatever these giant features are – and if they are not imaginary – they probably reflect long-lived anomalies in mantle heat production, and their episodic effect on crustal uplift and thermal evolution. Finally, there are circular features which undoubtedly exist, but to which no mechanism can be assigned (Fig. 4.33d).

4.4.2 Shear zones

Near to the surface the crust deforms by brittle processes and by buckling. With increasing depth the influence of higher temperatures and hot fluids decreases the viscosity of rocks, so that they are more prone to deform plastically. Instead of crustal displacement being taken up across sharp fault surfaces, the shear strain is distributed through a large volume of rock, but the net effect is exactly the same. Such deep-seated, ductile fault movements produce **shear zones**, whose forms are very different from those of faults. Like faults, shear zones result in thrust, normal and strike-slip displacements of the crust. Their typical form is illustrated by Figure 4.34.

Deformation in a shear zone involves changes in angular relationships, so that linear features outside the shear system are seen to swing into it. This can be seen in Figure 4.34 to be accompanied by a narrowing in the spacing between the linear features as the shear zone is entered. The reason for this is simply the tectonic environment in which the shearing takes place. The crust is being compressed in the direction of the maximum principal stress and extended at right angles to it (see Figure 4.24). Some of this crustal deformation is taken up by the displacements along the shear zones, but because rocks are responding plastically local compressive and extensional strains develop along the shear zone itself. The rock is flattened in the plane of the shearing.

The more strain is taken up by a shear zone, the further displaced are once adjacent points either side of it, and the

(a)

(b)

(c)

(d)

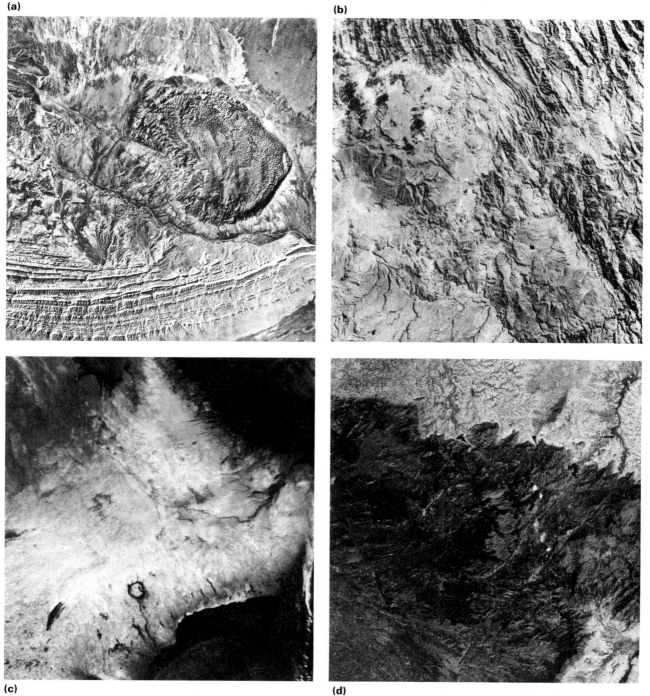

Figure 4.33 Circular and elliptical features, especially those so large that they are difficult to see on the ground, are easily seen on small-scale images. The smallest are commonly related to salt diapirism like that from Iran shown in (a). On (b), a Landsat MSS band 7 image of part of the Andes, can be seen a circular volcanic edifice some 40 km in diameter. Image (c) shows Labrador and parts of Quebec on a NOAA AVHRR near-infrared image. The obvious circular feature is the Manicouagan meteorite impact, about 70km across. The circular feature at the centre of (d), a Landsat MSS band 5 image, is located in the granulite-facies gneisses of the Anaimalai Hills in South India. Although it is bounded by a clearly defined boundary, on the ground there is no evidence for what may have produced the structure. Scales: (a) 1:90 000, (b) 1:1 million, (c) 1:14 million, (d) 1:1 million. Sources: (a) CSL Series B 11, (b) courtesy of P.W. Francis, Open University, (c) National Oceanic and Atmospheric Administration, Washington, (d) author.

wider the zone of flattened and stretched rocks becomes. If marker units are present then their displacement is immediately apparent. In most cases this is not possible, but theoretical methods allow the shear strain to be estimated from the width of the belt of flattening. Even if this is not measurable, the sense of strike-slip movement is quite obvious from the way in which linear features are rotated into the shear zone (Figs. 4.34 and 4.35).

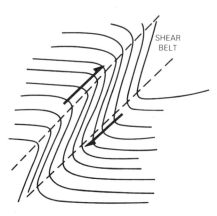

Figure 4.34 This sketch shows the main elements of a shear zone. Layers are displaced by shearing in the same way as in a fault. However, instead of a sharp break, the displacement is accomplished by rotation, extension and flattening of the layers, so that the shear zone itself comprises highly deformed, banded and often lineated rocks.

As well as deforming linear features, shear zones also rotate and flatten folds, often into unique and bizarre forms (Fig. 4.35b). Any relatively narrow belt of finely spaced linear features with flattened folds separating terrains with simpler structure can be suspected of being a shear zone with a strike-slip component. Thrust-like shear zones are not so obvious, but can be detected from their association with complex fold forms (Section 4.4.3).

4.4.3 Folds

Folding of the crust presents the most stimulating and challenging images to the geologist. As well as providing an element of variety for the interpreter, and another means of evaluating strain and stress patterns, folds are of great economic importance. Anticlinal structures form traps for oil and gas, whereas synclines often host artesian water supplies. Locating and analysing folds is an important element in predicting subsurface geology, and in reconstructing the geological history of an area.

Folds may be classified using a great range of geometric properties, for which there are excellent guides in standard texts on structural geology. In photointerpretation most of these criteria are not visible, so here a grossly simplified system is employed. It is based on three criteria: the **inter-limb angle** of folds (Fig. 4.36a), the **plunge** of fold axes (Fig. 4.36b) and the dip of a fold **axial surfaces** (Fig. 4.36c). Since the way-up of folded layers is not discernible from

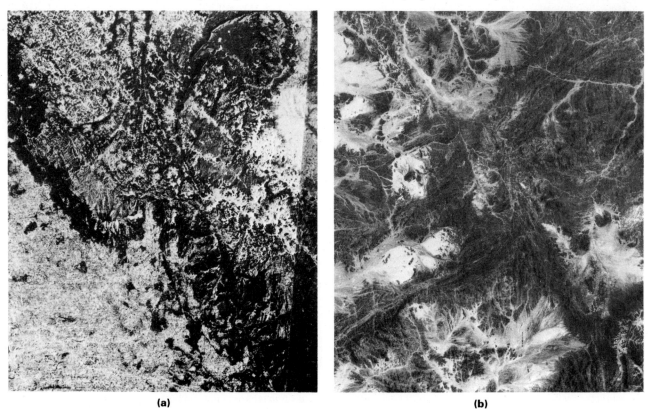

(a)   (b)

Figure 4.35 Large shear zones must be painstakingly mapped out in the field, but are often well displayed on satellite images such as those of Landsat MSS band 5 shown here. In (a) the curvature and narrowing of pairs of ridges controlled by Archaean ironstones defines a large sinistral shear belt in South India. In the Red Sea Hills of Sudan (b) an indistinct, NW–SE shear belt has sinistrally displaced an earlier WSW–ENE zone of shearing by about 30 km. Scale: 1:1 million. Source: author.

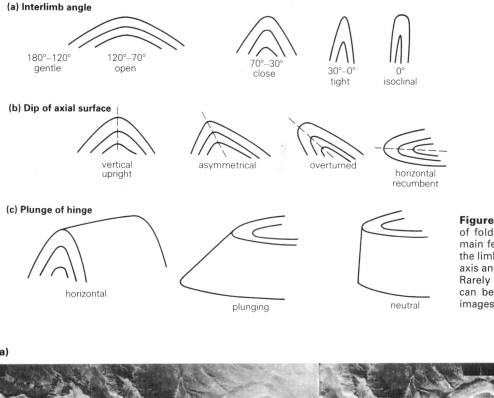

(a) Interlimb angle

180°–120°
gentle

120°–70°
open

70°–30°
close

30°–0°
tight

0°
isoclinal

(b) Dip of axial surface

vertical
upright

asymmetrical

overturned

horizontal
recumbent

(c) Plunge of hinge

horizontal

plunging

neutral

Figure 4.36 The nomenclature of folds is partly based on three main features – the angle between the limbs of a fold, the plunge of its axis and the dip of its axial surface. Rarely more than these features can be seen on remotely sensed images.

(a)

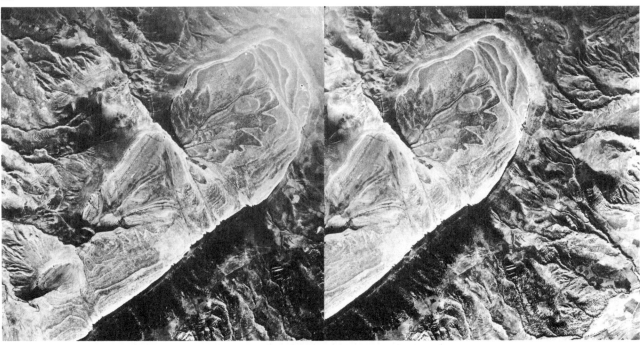

Figure 4.37 Folds are the most spectacular features on remotely sensed images, particularly when they are well exposed. Stereopair (a) gives an example of inverted topography in Algeria, where an asymmetrical, plunging synform folding Palaeozoic sediments controls high ground. The nature of the fold could be worked out using one image from the varying directions and angles of valley Vs.

photographs, an upward-closing fold is properly described as an **antiform**, the opposite being a **synform**.

Where a fold has a shallow plunge, closures are not common. The limbs outcrop as dipping series of layers, taking forms appropriate to the angle of dip and the topography (Section 4.3.1). Detecting folding and locating fold axes in such cases depends upon systematic observation of dip direction, using valley Vs (Figs. 4.37a and b). Like faults, however, folds do not propagate to infinity. At some point they die out, the strain being taken up by

(b)

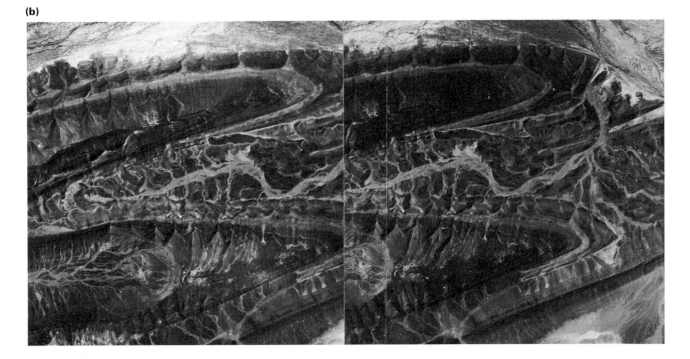

(c)

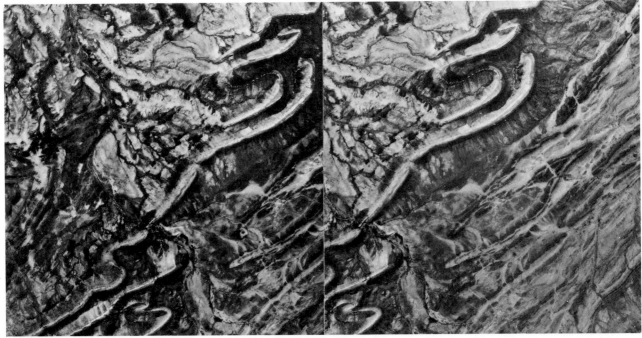

Figure 4.37 (*cont.*)   This would be possible on stereopair (b) too, which shows two plunging, asymmetrical antiforms separated by a synform in Morocco. Stereopair (c) contains several overturned folds in the Palaeozoic rocks of the Marathon Basin of Texas. The ridges are controlled by resistant carbonates and the sense of overturning is towards the NW. The area is also affected by thrusts which disrupt some of the folds, and a few normal faults. Scales: (a and b) 1:40 000, (c) 1:63 360. Sources: (a) Institute Geographique National, Paris (IGN) ALG-1952-231-233 123+124, (b) IGN Maroc-009 424+425, (c) NCIC Tex.1 A+B.

another fold. Even the most regular folds have a plunge on their axes somewhere, and this may show as a closure of outcrops of some distinctive unit. The more steeply fold axes plunge, the more obvious and more common closures are (Figs. 4.37a and b). The forms taken by folds on a photograph are strongly controlled by the asymmetry of the dips on the limbs. The limbs of an upright fold appear almost like mirror images of each other (Fig. 4.37b). In an extremely asymmetric fold the steeper limb is less controlled by topography than the shallow limb and adopts a more nearly linear form (Fig. 4.19). Overturned folds present problems. The tighter and the more nearly recumbent they are, the more complex are the outcrops of their limbs (Fig. 4.37c). Where stereoptic viewing is possible, the correct description of folds is relatively easy. For satellite images the process can be fraught with problems, the most common of which is confusion between antiforms and synforms (*Fig. 4.38*). The most painstaking search for evidence of valley Vs is the only solution.

Among the weirdest patterns that can be seen on remotely sensed images are those produced by the repeated folding of layered rocks. When a fold with one orientation is refolded by another with a different attitude a three-dimensional **interference structure** is produced. The distinctive patterns are produced when such structures are planed by erosion. They can adopt a bewildering variety of forms, but three types form the basic and most commonly seen end-members. Where upright folds are refolded by another set with a different axial trend, **domes and basins** result (Fig. 4.17c). Recumbent folds refolded by upright folds produce more or less **mushroom-shaped** interference patterns in horizontal section (*Fig. 4.39*). The effect of strike-slip shear zones on pre-existing folds is often to transform them into **hook-shaped** structures (Fig. 4.35). The presence of any of these fold forms, and even odder ones too, is sufficient to raise the suspicion of polyphase deformation. Caution is needed, however, as quite dreadful patterns can result purely by erosional means in the most innocuous terrains (see Fig. 4.55).

4.5 Superficial deposits and constructional landforms

More even than destructional landforms, those resulting from the constructive action of volcanism and from sediment transport and deposition are enormously varied. So many factors are involved that the number of permutations and combinations is near infinite. Space does not permit a comprehensive treatment, merely an account of some common and easily recognized features. Most texts on volcanic, desert, glacial, fluviatile and coastal geomorphology provide sufficient diversity of descriptions and photography for this brief account to be easily supplemented.

4.5.1 Volcanic landforms

The popular concept of an active volcanic landscape is that it is typified by symmetrical volcanic **cones**, each possessing a summit crater. This is only sometimes the case for areas dominated by viscous magmas of intermediate to acid composition. They cannot flow far from the vent from which they issue, and being unable to release their gas content easily are prone to explosive activity. The result is that lavas and ejecta from a vent build up close to it as a layered conical structure termed a **stratovolcano**, which may be as much as several thousand metres high. The sides of a stratovolcano typically slope at angles around 30°. The vent itself is kept relatively clear of debris by repeated explosions, so forming a crater. The strengthening of the volcanic edifice by lava flows ensures that the crater walls are steep and cliff-like. Figure 4.40 shows an example of the more typical, complex stratovolcano.

Minor explosive activity ejects solid debris in the 5 mm to 1 m size range and also produces cones. The fragments are frequently full of gas bubbles and look like cinders. As they are loose they come to rest at a natural angle of repose depending on their size and shape. Such **cinder cones** are therefore characterized by having a smooth surface – at most scales involved in remote sensing – and uniform slopes. The slopes in craters are approximately the same as those on the cone sides, giving them a funnel shape. This means that they are easily distinguished from stratovolcanoes (Fig. 4.41). Cinder cones are rarely more than 300 m high and 1 km in diameter.

Basaltic magmas are much more fluid than those of intermediate to acid composition. They tend to release their gas content with a minimum of explosive activity, and travel long distances down shallow slopes. They rarely build steep cones, though there may be a minor basaltic component in stratovolcanoes. Two major kinds of basaltic landform are produced. The magmas may issue from fissures induced by crustal extension. Such **fissure eruptions** (Fig. 4.42a) typify basaltic volcanism at constructive plate margins. Where basaltic magmatism is centrally controlled, as in a mid-plate setting, lavas flow in all directions to build up vast domes with very low slope angles – typically 5–10°. These **shield volcanoes** can be hundreds of kilometres across, as in the case of those in Hawaii.

Basaltic volcanism sometimes produces fire fountains as lava is forced violently to the surface by the pressure of rapidly rising magma. The lava forms droplets and globules which are still partly molten when they land. This ensures that they stick together to form **spatter cones** (Fig. 4.42a). These tend to be associated with fissure eruptions, but may also form on a minor scale when lava erupts from the flanks of shield volcanoes or squirts through the crust of a major flow because of the pressure head involved. Spatter cones have very steep sides as a result of rapid solidification. They are usually less than 20 m high.

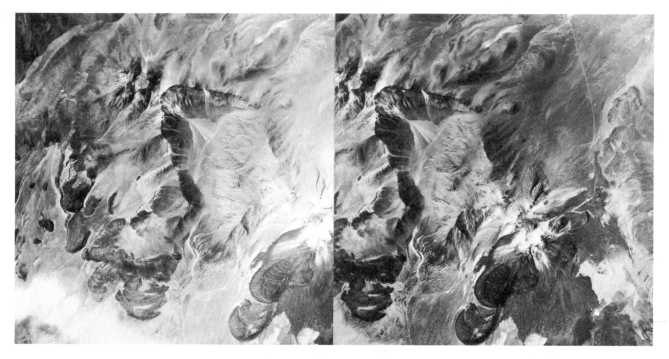

Figure 4.40 As a result of a sideways-directed explosion, this stratovolcano in the Andes of Chile has been breached to reveal its internal structure. The site of the blast is now occupied by a massive dacitic resurgent dome. The flanks of the original volcano are irregular as a result of marginal flows of viscous lava. Scale: 1:60 000. Source: Instituto Geographico Militar, Chile.

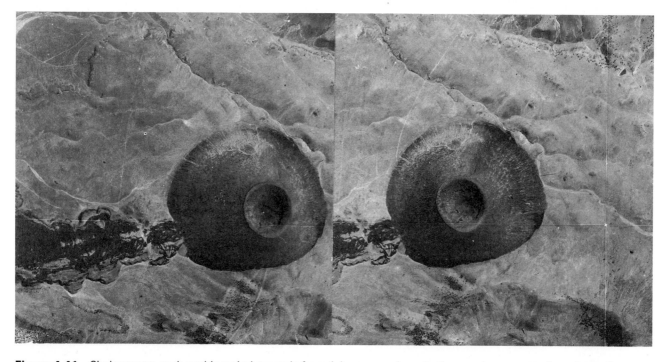

Figure 4.41 Cinder cones, such as this typical example from Arizona, are closer to the popular concept of a volcano than most stratovolcanoes. The cone is symmetrical, despite the apparent distortion due to radial-relief displacement. The funnel shape of the crater, owing to instability of unconsolidated ash, is clear. In this case, explosive activity succeeded earlier eruption of moderately fluid lava, whose typical morphology is obviously overstepped by the cone. Scale: 1:20 000. Source: ASCS BT 1952+1953.

Truly explosive activity with cinder and ash production is associated with basaltic activity only where water can enter the magma chamber. Basaltic cinder and ash cones are found in association with coastal volcanoes, and where volcanoes form beneath ice sheets, as in Iceland. In the last case truly bizarre structures called **jokulhaupfs**

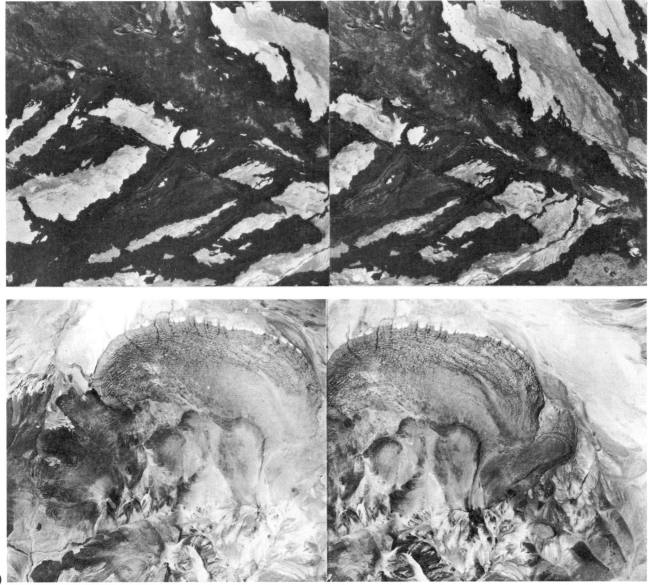

(a)

(b)

Figure 4.42 On the flanks of Mauna Loa shield volcano on Hawaii, eruptions of fluid, gas-charged basaltic lavas emanated from long fissures (a). Small spatter cones are aligned along some of the fissures, as are cinder cones. The black dots on a pale background are collapse pits above a lava tube. Silicic lavas tend to be far more viscous than those of basaltic composition. Stereopair (b) shows an excellent example from the Andes of Chile. It has not flowed far from the dissected stratovolcano which was its source. It has a distinct lobate form and shows ridges perpendicular to flow direction. Scales: (a) 1:41 000, (b) 1:60 000. Sources: (a) NCIC Hawaii 7, (b) Instituto Geografico Militar, Chile.

may form, which involve glacial collapse, catastrophic floods and mudflows as well as the formation of volcanic edifices.

Undissected lava flows have very distinctive appearances resulting from the process of flow itself. The most obvious is the formation of lobate margins, where the cool end of a flow is highly viscous and slowly spreads into topographic depressions. The solid crust buckles and breaks into blocks, which can produce **levée-like ridges** at the sides and ends of flows (Fig. 4.41). In viscous lavas, the formation of ridges perpendicular to flow direction extends right across flows (Fig. 4.42b). Such lavas flow only down steep slopes, and usually extend only short distances. Basaltic flows travel much further, and tend to develop **flow lines** parallel to flow direction (Fig. 4.42a). Sometimes late-stage lava movement is beneath an already solidified crust. The resulting **lava tubes** can collapse to form distinctive sinuous depressions on the flow surface (Fig. 4.42a).

In areas of repeated lava eruptions distinguishing between flows of different ages is sometimes a relatively simple matter. The stratigraphic rules of superposition and

111

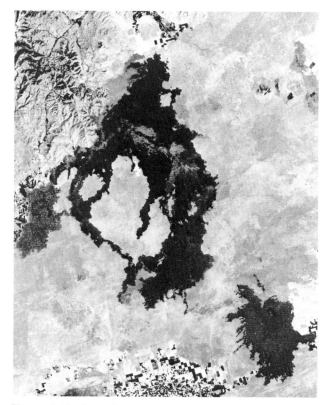

Figure 4.43 Lava flows of different ages are distinguished on this Landsat MSS band 7 image of part of Idaho by their different reflectances. The youngest flows are black and successively older flows are increasingly reflective owing to their masking by blown sediment and colonization by vegetation. The flows emerged from a NW–SE fissure, which can be seen faintly near the centre of the largest area of lavas. Scale: 1:1 million. Source: courtesy of Dave Rothery, Open University.

overlap can generally be applied. Moreover, the older a flow the greater the tendency for its surface roughness to be degraded by soil formation, and for it to become infested with vegetation (Fig. 4.43).

The issue of fine-grained pyroclastic material from volcanoes prone to explosive activity produces a blanketing effect over older landforms. The resulting tuffs smooth out the topography (see Fig. 4.46) and kill the local vegetation. They are, however, prone to rapid erosion, and are soon dissected. The most spectacular results of explosive activity relate to the flow of high-density, incandescent mixtures of ash and gases. These **nuées ardentes** are emitted from volcanoes with such viscous and gas-charged magmas that they cannot easily be extruded. Gas pressure builds up in the magma chamber until the entire contents are belched out in a single event. The dense mixture of hot ash and gas has a low viscosity, so that its immense gravitational energy causes the mixture to travel at velocities in excess of $100\,km\,h^{-1}$. It can therefore flow over and around large objects in its path to swamp vast areas and eventually solidify as an ignimbrite (Section 4.2.2). The high energy

of nuées ardentes results in deep fluting of the ignimbrite surface, parallel to the direction of flow (Fig. 4.44). Recent ignimbrites are thus easy to identify, even from satellite altitudes (see *Fig. 5.10*).

Stratovolcanoes, being formed by explosive magmatism, are prone to catastrophe. The expulsion of the contents of a magma chamber during a nuée ardente event leaves a cavity at depth, into which the superstructure may collapse. This is accomplished by annular systems of faults defining a **caldera** (Fig. 4.45a). The resulting circular depression is occasionally filled with a lake. Continued magmatism may exploit the caldera to form minor cones along the annular faults, and central domes of resurgent, viscous magma (see *Fig. 5.10*). Instead of resulting in nuée ardente activity, build-up of pressure within a volcano may cause the flanks to bulge alarmingly. If the bulge develops unstable slopes, the volcano flank may collapse to form a massive **debris flow** (Fig. 4.45b). The release of pressure on the flank can then allow the accumulated gas-rich magma to explode sideways, breaching the entire superstructure. This was the process associated with the May 1980 eruption of Mount St Helens in the northwestern USA.

Many stratovolcanoes reach high altitudes, and even in equatorial latitudes may be capped with snow and ice. This is a hazardous association. A combination of ice-bound ash and heat associated with episodes of activity can produce sudden melting and the formation of **mud avalanches**. These can assume nearly the same monumental proportions as ignimbrite and volcanic collapse events. The mud flows in much the same fashion as lava, usually faster and further. The energy of these volcanic mudflows is high enough to sweep all before them, leaving sinuous scars through vegetation, and blocking local drainage when they come to rest. Their process of solidification involves a fall in the velocity of turbulent flow, below which the mud ceases to behave as a liquid and assumes solid proportions. It sets, and slowly the water content seeps away to leave a resistant mass of ash and debris, which has many of the morphological features of a lava flow. Being soft, however, they are soon eroded away.

4.5.2 Fluviatile and lacustrine landforms

Deposition by flowing water to form constructional landforms results when flow velocity falls below that needed to retain sediment in suspension or to move it along the stream bed by bouncing or rolling.

High-energy streams issuing from uplands carry abundant coarse particles. Once the slope changes as they emerge from constricted valleys, this coarse load is quickly dumped to form low cones with their apices at the mouths of the mountain valleys. The streams are able to flow in any radial direction on these cones, and so split into numerous

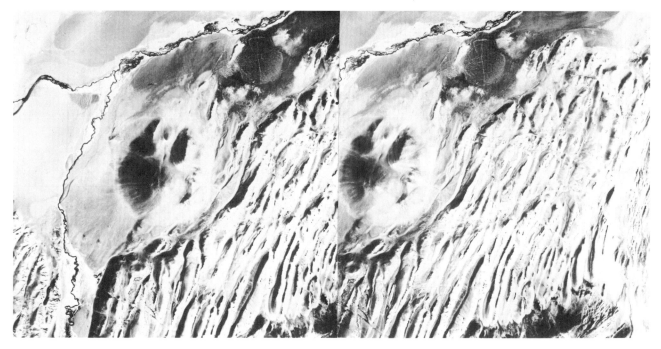

Figure 4.44 The most characteristic feature of the huge ignimbrite flows of the central Andes is their deep fluting. Associated with this flow in Argentina is a large dacitic dome. Scale: 1:60 000. Source: Instituto Geografico Militar, Argentina.

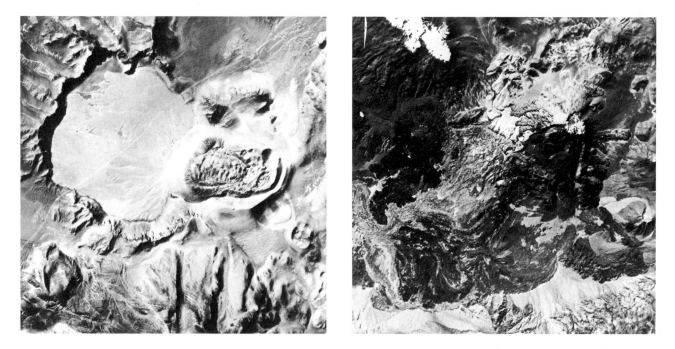

Figure 4.45 The caldera in the Argentinian Andes shown in (a) is partly filled with later silicic lava flows from a centre now occupied by a lava dome. The dome developed on the fault bounding the caldera. The Landsat MSS band 7 image in (b) shows the volcano Socompa in Chile, which underwent a catastrophic lateral blast which dwarfs the famous Mount St Helens event of May 1980. Most of the surface in the lower part of the image consists of a debris avalanche, formerly the southern flank of the volcano. The complex tonal and textural patterns in the debris can be used to identify the original location of the material in the volcanic superstructure and to reconstruct the mechanics of the avalanche. Scales: (a) 1:60 000, (b) 1:400 000. Sources: (a) Instituto Geografico Militar, Argentina, (b) courtesy of Dave Rothery, Open University.

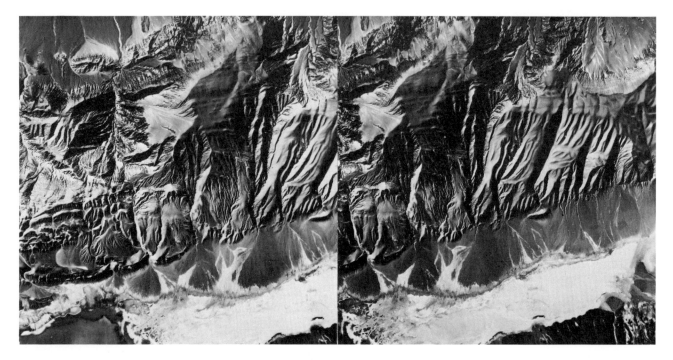

Figure 4.46 Alluvial fans typically develop at the exits of intermittent streams draining arid mountainous regions. In this part of the Andes of western Argentina, steeply dipping Palaeozoic strata have received a thin veneer of volcanic debris from a massive ignimbrite event resulting in a peculiar smoothing of the older topography. Erosion of the veneer has not long been under way, and is marked by localized, complex systems of sharp rilles. Scale: 1:60 000. Source: Instituto Geografico Militar, Argentina.

divergent channels. This gives rise to **alluvial fans**, which typify the flanks of upland in semiarid terrains (Fig. 4.46). Stream flow is sporadic and reaches a maximum during storms or rapid snowmelt at high altitude. The constricted flow spreads at the valley mouth to form **sheet floods**, which deposit and redistribute debris uniformly across the fans. The highly porous nature of the fans ensures that a high proportion of flow infiltrates to produce local groundwater supplies. Only where vegetation is unable to bind the debris and stabilize stream courses do alluvial fans in humid terrains develop on steep slopes as **screes**.

The lower reaches of a mature or old-aged stream have low slope angles. When the stream leaves its course during floods most of the suspended load is deposited on the flood plain as alluvium. Streams flowing across almost flat ground have an irresistible tendency to form meanders. The protracted migration of meanders across flood plains reworks the alluvium deposited there to produce several distinctive structures. The inside of each bend is the site for deposition, the outside being eroded. Meanders migrate towards their outside banks as well as downstream. This produces a system of low, arcuate features, known as **meander scrolls**, which represent deposition on the insides of bends (Fig. 4.47a). Sometimes meanders curve back upon themselves to such a degree that the narrow ground separating parts of a bend is cut through. The bend is cut

off to form a stagnant **oxbow lake** (Fig. 4.47a). Features such as these typify flood plains in which the alluvium, because it is sufficiently well-bound by vegetation or because of its fineness, can support discrete stream courses. In semiarid terrains or in flat valleys filled with poorly bound alluvium, stream courses are ephemeral. Flow may change from one course to another repeatedly, thereby forming a **braided stream** system (Fig. 4.47b).

Changes in erosional baselevel in a flood plain result in the stream system cutting into earlier alluvial deposits. This produces **terraces** of flat ground above the active flood plain, on which old fluviatile features may be preserved, and into which minor drainage may have been incised. It is often possible to recognize several terrace levels. Those with coincident heights on either side of the flood plain are the result of rejuvenation. Those which have different heights either side are the products of slow downward erosion and migration back and forth of the stream system.

Where streams flow into bodies of standing water, either lakes or the sea, the flow is halted and all sediment is deposited. The result is a **delta**. If the delta develops shifting distributory channels, similar to those in an alluvial fan, then it adopts an arcuate shape as a low-angled cone (Fig. 4.48a). Where persistent channels are maintained, deposition is from these and the delta propagates as a branching **birdfoot delta** (Fig. 4.48b).

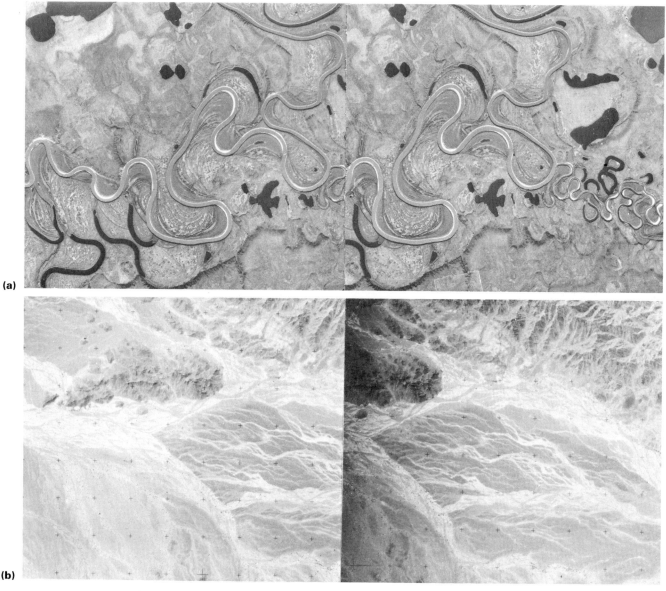

(a)

(b)

Figure 4.47 Continuous flow of streams over nearly featureless plains of unconsolidated sediments results in migrating meanders. In the example shown from the Canadian Arctic (a) traces of former meanders are preserved as meander scrolls on the insides of bends and abandoned channels in the form of oxbow lakes. Braided stream systems form on similar substrates when flow is intermittent. As in (b), they are best developed in semiarid terrains. Scales: (a) 1:70 000, (b) unknown. Sources: (a) EMRC A13139 82+83, copyright HM the Queen in Right of Canada (1951), (b) unknown.

Deposition in lakes, other than that associated with deltas, is in the form of horizontal layers or in beaches. Drainage of a lake results in almost perfectly flat topography, interrupted only by the relics of former islands. Old lake beds can be distinguished from abandoned flood plains by the absence of meander scrolls and oxbow lakes and by the presence of curvilinear features marking the sites of old beaches (see Section 4.5.4).

4.5.3 Aeolian landforms

The action of wind is not restricted to deserts, but can mould constructional landforms wherever sediments of a size small enough to be transported in air are not bound together. They may contribute to both coastal and glacial landscapes. The physics of wind and its means of transporting particles is complex and sensitive to many subtle

(a)

(b)

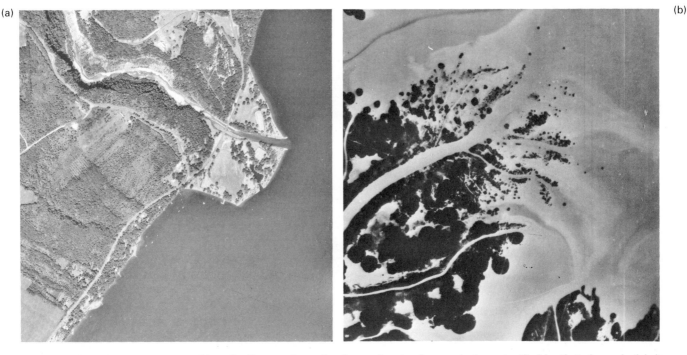

Figure 4.48 Deltas formed by shifting distributory channels take on the classic arcuate form, typified by that shown in (a). It results from the entry of a large stream into a lake in New York. Where sediment is deposited in standing water by a number of fixed distributaries, most material is deposited near the channels and builds up deltas of the birdfoot kind (b). This system is part of the Mississippi Delta in Louisiana. Scales: (a) 1:20 000, (b) 1:60 000. Sources: (a) ASCS ARU-IEE 74+75, (b) NCIC La.8.

factors. The dominant process is the efficient sorting of grain sizes into the bouncing and rolling load and that carried in suspension. For a particular wind speed the ranges of grain sizes present in both loads is very narrow. Aeolian deposits are therefore very well sorted. The rolling and bouncing load moves much more slowly than suspended material, and so the two size ranges are deposited in completely different areas.

Dunes result from the deposition of rolling and bouncing particles. Their form is determined by the amount of sand available in an area, the amount of vegetation cover and by the constancy of the wind. The classic migrating, horn-shaped dune or **barchan** (Fig. 4.49a) forms where sand supply is low, little vegetation is available to halt the movement of sand and wind direction is roughly constant. The horns point downwind. The lee slope, where deposition takes place, is steeper than the windward slope up which grains are blown. Barchans migrate slowly downwind. Where vegetation is able to bind sand as it accumulates, dunes with the same overall shape as barchans develop, but instead of the horns pointing downwind they are fixed by vegetation and point windwards.

An abundance of sand and a lack of vegetation encourage the formation of large dunes whose crests line up perpendicular to the prevailing wind. These **transverse dunes** are typical of the world's largest sandy deserts. However, where wind velocities are high, sand becomes stabilized in longitudinal or **seif dunes** running parallel to

the wind (Fig. 4.49b). These can extend for hundreds of kilometres, and are so large and stable that they can be preserved after the climate has become more humid, when the dunes become vegetated.

In deserts subject to seasonal fluctuations in wind direction, the dunes take on shapes conforming to the interfering effects of several directions of sand transport. They may have a random pattern, but sometimes develop distinctive star shapes.

The material carried in suspension by wind travels long distances until it reaches climatic regions with low wind speeds. These are usually associated with the high-pressure systems over continental interiors. Settling of windborne dust produces a peculiar sediment known as **loess**. It is exceptionally well sorted and homogeneous, and frequently lacks bedding. One consequence of this homogeneity and the process of deposition is that loess has a tendency to break along irregular vertical surfaces. This imparts a distinctive form of drainage pattern to loess-mantled areas in North America and Eurasia. They are dominated by dendritic networks of vertical-sided, U-shaped valleys and gulleys. Each stream network looks remarkably like a feather, so they are described as **pinnate** (Fig. 4.50). Most of the largest areas of loess stem from ablation of fine dust from glacial deposits during the Pleistocene, when wind systems controlled by high pressure over the ice masses blew from west to east in the northern hemisphere.

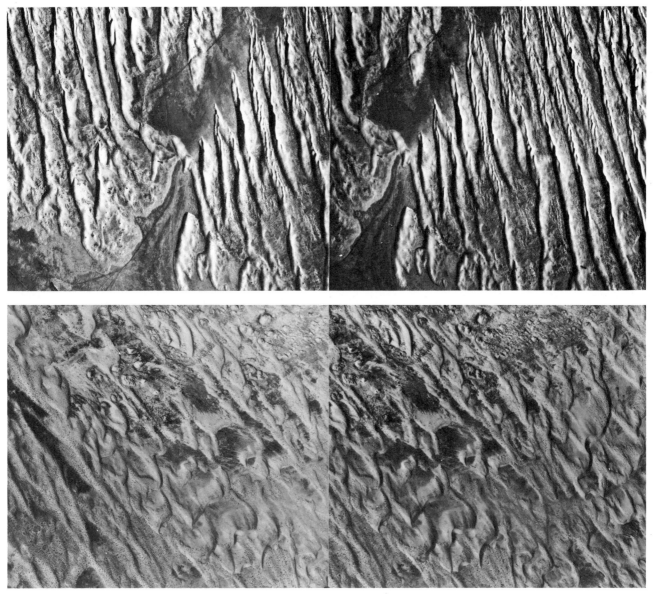

(a)

(b)

Figure 4.49 An abundant supply of sand, dry conditions and strong prevailing winds favour the linear or seif dunes shown from an area in the Middle East by (a). The major dunes are parallel to the prevailing wind and on their crests have small migratory dunes, the horns of which point downwind. Where sand supply is restricted, as on the Kaibab Plateau of Arizona (b), parabolic, transverse and barchan dunes dominate. Scales: (a) 1:20 000, (b) 1:40 000. Sources: (a) CSL Series B 9+10, (b) NCIC Ariz.7 B+C.

4.5.4 Glacial landforms

Constructional landforms resulting from glacial periods present the greatest variety of all. Their formation involved not only ice and its load of gouged-up sediment, but also meltwater and wind, which reworked the sediment and freezing temperatures which imposed various structures upon and within it. It is impossible to give a comprehensive account of all the possibilities here, only those distinctive enough to identify terrains dominated by glacial and related deposits. A thorough analysis of photographs of such areas requires reference to specialized texts.

The material deposited solely by melting ice during its retreat is given the catch-all name **till**. In an area of upland glaciation, till takes distinctive forms related to various kinds of **moraine**. Ice sheets in lowland areas deposit till in two distinct forms. At the ice front where supply is balanced by melting and ablation, debris is supplied continually. It is simply dumped and accumulates in a zone of exceedingly dirty ice. This forms an **end moraine** of one of several varieties that may mark the ultimate extent of the ice sheet or temporary halts during its retreat. Those associated with continental glaciation may extend as more or less continuous and sinuous lines for thousands of

117

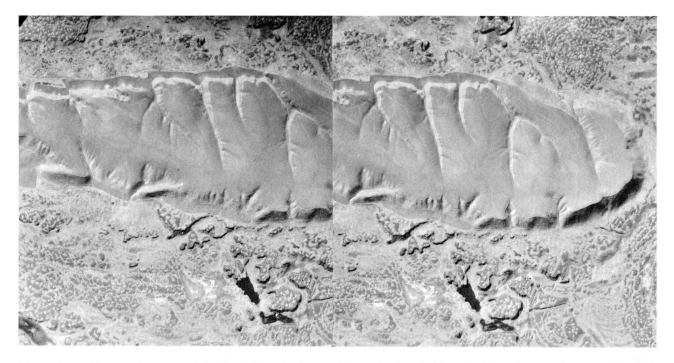

Figure 4.50 The very finest material stripped from dry, bare sediments by the wind is carried long distances in suspension to be deposited as homogeneous mantles of loess. Stream erosion of loess produces a characteristic pinnate or feathered drainage pattern well displayed by this stereopair of an area of Washington. The peculiar texture in the area stripped of loess, known as scabland, is a product of scouring and giant ripple formation by powerful stream action in glacial-lake overflow channels. Scale: 1:20 000. Source: ASCS AAP-1G 123+124.

kilometres. They are characterized by a narrow belt of hummocky topography in an otherwise almost featureless plain. Since till has a high content of fines, moraines are poorly drained and often have small lakes preserved in irregular depressions (Figs. 4.51a and 4.52). These result either from the irregular nature of the moraine or from the melting of buried ice masses and consequent collapse. Collapse structures of this kind are known as **kettle holes**.

Till deposited at the base of a moving glacier has often been planed almost flat. Apart from sporadic kettle holes it presents a depressingly boring prospect. Its uniformity, impermeability and low relief ensures poor drainage and the establishment of complex dendritic and deranged patterns. Subtle variations in relief and permeability help produce a mottled texture of vegetation, particularly in spring (Fig. 4.51b). The grinding monotony of basal till is relieved by features produced by the once overriding ice mass. The most impressive of these are rounded, oval-shaped knolls known as **drumlins** (Fig. 4.53). The typical 'basket of eggs' topography of drumlin country results from irregularities in ice flow, brought on perhaps by obstructions beneath or by confluence of several sheets. The long axes of drumlins are ambiguous indicators of ice-flow direction.

Melting of the Pleistocene continental glaciers provided huge volumes of water. Where this meltwater flowed within the ice, meandering tunnels formed. In them the glacial debris was sorted and transported. Some of it was deposited in the base of the tunnels, to result in sinuous ridges of well-drained sand and gravel, termed **eskers**, when the ice melted (Fig. 4.52). Somewhat similar tracts of well-drained sandy terrain formed from deposits in ice-margin streams, where the glacier abutted areas of high relief. These well drained **kame terraces** have a vegetation that contrasts with that of the impervious tills which they cross.

In front of the ice margin, water flowing from the top of the ice or from tunnels within it was heavily charged with sediment. The ice sheet, often up to a kilometre in thickness, formed prominent relief. The high-energy streams flowing from it slowed rapidly and deposited their sediment load to form **outwash deposits**. They are broad belts of sandy sediment which become progressively finer away from the ice front. In detail they are fans which coalesce, and on which braided streams flowed. This basic structure is still easily recognized in many cases (Fig. 4.54). Where outwash engulfed patches of ice left behind by glacial retreat, kettle holes formed, so that a pitted surface is sometimes seen. As

118

(a)

(b)

Figure 4.51 Glacial till deposited at the front of a continental glacier was riddled with pockets of 'dead' ice. Their melting produces an irregular, hummocky topography on ill-drained boulder clay. In the case of such end moraines in North Dakota (a), the depressions become filled with small lakes, and drainage is deranged. Also shown are areas of till with parallel linear ridges which represent deposition beneath a moving ice sheet. Well within the area mantled by ice, basal till is planed to an almost flat surface. Drainage takes no particular direction and rainfall eventually seeps into the till. The area of basal till in Indiana, shown in (b), is characterized by a mottled appearance as a result of variations in soil moisture controlled by the irregular but subdued topography. Scales: (a) 1:60 000, (b) 1:20 000. Sources: (a) NCIC N.Dak.2 B+C, (b) ASCS BWI-3BB 95+96.

they are so porous, outwash deposits are well drained and now have widely spaced surface drainage.

Preglacial drainage may have been temporarily dammed by ice so that large glacial lakes formed. The deposits resulting from such lakes are identical in most respects to those from any other drained lake. They are even flatter and more melancholy than ground moraine. Drained glacial lakes may even preserve relics of deltas

from meltwater streams which fed them. The sudden removal of the ice dam during glacial retreat released huge floods which carved out deep valleys. Once the lake had drained, these valleys became occupied by streams too small to have been capable of forming them. The valleys have a typical U-shaped cross-section, revealing that they were in fact the channels of these short-lived torrents. They are sometimes characterized by huge

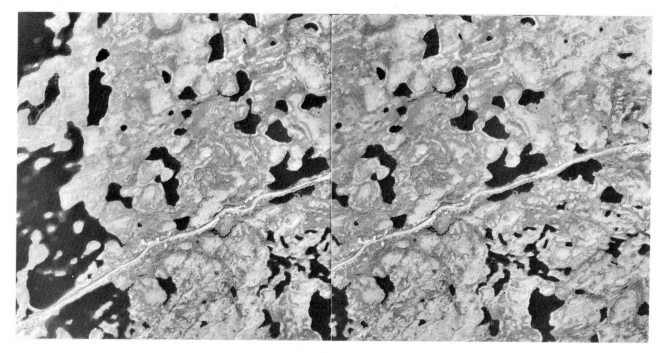

Figure 4.52 The dominant material beneath this area of northern Canada is till deposited in an area of 'dead' ice, with its typical knob and kettle topography. Running across this ill-drained landscape is a sharp ridge of light-coloured, well-drained sand, lacking vegetation. It is an esker deposited in a subglacial melt stream. Scale: 1:54 000. Source: EMRC A14887 102+103, copyright HM the Queen in Right of Canada (1955).

Figure 4.53 The masking effect of regular fields in this stereopair of part of New York completely obscures the topography until the scene is viewed stereoptically. Then a series of drumlins becomes quite obvious, which has the typical 'basket-of-eggs' landscape. Scale: 1:60 000. Source: NCIC N.Y.3 A+B.

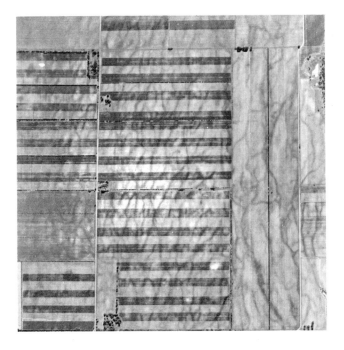

Figure 4.54 Glacial outwash plains formed in front of continental glaciers, such as this one in Wisconsin, are nearly featureless on the ground. However, from the air the variations in soil moisture due to different porosities show up the relic patterns of the former braided distributory channels. Scale: 1:27 000. Source: ASCS BRT-9V 38.

potholes and giant ripples producing **scabland** (Fig. 4.50). Episodic drainage of glacial lakes resulted in successive shore lines being preserved as more or less parallel **beach ridges** (Fig. 4.55).

The unifying feature of all glaciated terrains is that they were subject to intense cold for long periods. In common with modern boreal areas they were prone to **permafrost**. Among the many effects of permanently frozen ground, an easily recognized one is the formation of various kinds of **patterned ground**. The sediments most conducive to its formation are silts and clays, especially those of glacial lake beds and alluvium (Fig. 4.56). In now temperate latitudes, the patterns show up most clearly either in spring when vegetation is beginning to grow, or during periods of

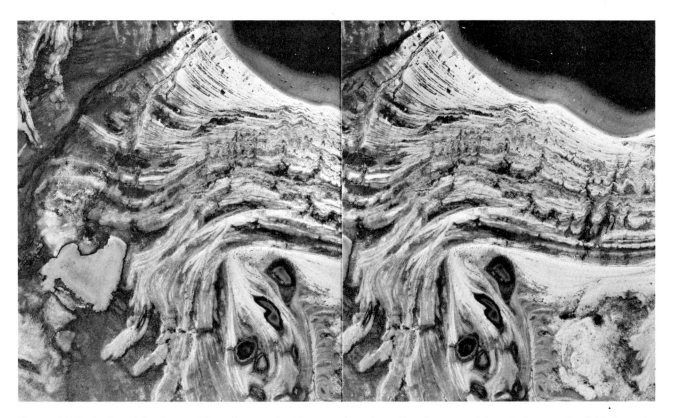

Figure 4.55 At first sight the curvilinear features in this area of northern Canada are reminiscent of a complex folded terrain. Stereoptic viewing reveals that the features are low ridges at successively higher elevations that were deposited as beaches, spits and bars during a period when the glacially depressed crust was slowly rebounding isostatically. Scale: 1:36 000. Source: EMR A16347 29+30, copyright HM the Queen in Right of Canada (1958).

121

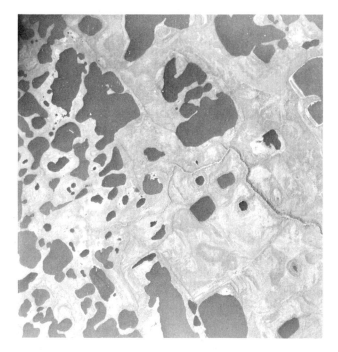

Figure 4.56 Where unconsolidated sediments in northern Canada and other boreal areas are permanently frozen at depth, the seasonal freezing and thawing of the upper soil layer produces regular patterns. This is accomplished by the volume changes involved in ice formation and melting, which slowly circulates and sorts grains of different grain sizes. Another contributory factor is the formation of ice lenses and doming of the surface, followed by melting and collapse. Scale: 1:36 000. Source: EMRC A16347 30, copyright HM the Queen in Right of Canada (1951).

drought. The former cracks, now filled with porous debris, are relatively dry so that crops growing over them become stunted or discoloured.

Further reading

These references comprise a useful compendium of examples of geomorphological, lithological and structural interpretation from aerial photographs and satellite images in the reflected region. Many of the selected references for Chapter 9 are also useful in geological interpretation.

Abrams, M.J., D.A. Rothery and A. Pontual 1988. Mapping in the Oman ophiolite using enhanced Landsat Thematic Mapper images. *Tectonophysics* **151**, 387–401.

Al Khatieb, S.O. and J.W. Norman 1982. A possibly extensive crustal failure system of economic interest. *J. Petrol. Geol.* **4**, 319–327.

Allum, J.A.E. 1966. *Photogeology and regional mapping.* London: Pergamon.

Allum, J.A.E. 1980. Photogeology – early days. *Geoscience Canada* **7**, 155–158.

Avery, T.E. and G.L. Berlin 1985. *Interpretation of aerial photographs*, 4th edn. Minneapolis, Minnesota: Burgess.

Babcock, E.A. 1971. Detection of active faulting using oblique infrared aerial photography in the Imperial Valley, California. *Geol. Soc. Am. Bull.* **82**, 3189–3196.

Bailey, G.B. and P.D. Anderson 1982. Applications of Landsat imagery to problems of petroleum exploration in Qaidam Basin, China. *Am. Ass. Petrol. Geol. Bull.* **66**, 1348–1354.

Baker, M.C.W. 1981. The nature and distribution of Upper Cenozoic ignimbrite centres in the Central Andes. *J. Volcanology Geothermal Res.* **11**, 293–315.

Bodechtel, M. Kley and U. Munzer 1985. Tectonic analysis of typical fold structures in the Zagros mountains, Iran, by the application of quantitative photogrammetric methods on Metric Camera data. *Proc. DFVLR-ESA Workshop Oberpfaffenhofen*, 193–197. ESA SP-209.

Crosta, A.P. and J.McM. Moore 1989. Geological mapping using Landsat Thematic Mapper imagery in Almeria Province, south-east Spain. *Int. J. Remote Sens.* **10**, 505–514.

Dikkers, A.J. 1977. Sketch of a possible lineament pattern in Northwest Europe. *Geol. Mijnbouw* **56**, 275–285.

Drury, S.A. 1982. A regional tectonic study of the Archaean Chitradurga greenstone belt, Karnataka, based on Landsat interpretation. *J. Geol. Soc. India* **24**, 167–184.

Drury, S.A. 1983. A Proterozoic intracratonic basin, thermal evolution and dyke swarms in South India. *J. Geol. Soc. India* **25**, 437–444.

Drury, S.A. 1990. SPOT image data as an aid to structural mapping in the southern Aravalli Hills of Rajasthan, India. *Geol. Mag.* **127**, 195–207.

Drury, S.A. and S.M. Berke 1993. Accretion tectonics in northern Eritrea revealed by remotely sensed imagery. *Geol. Mag.* (in press).

Drury, S.A. and R.W. Holt 1980. The tectonic framework of the South Indian craton: a reconnaissance involving Landsat imagery. *Tectonophysics* **65**, T1–T15.

Foster, N.H. and E. A. Beaumont (eds) 1992. *Photogeology and photogeomorphology*, Treatise of petroleum geology reprint series no. 18. Tulsa, Oklahoma: American Association of Petroleum Geologists.

Howard, A.D. 1967. Drainage analysis in geological interpretation: a summation. *Am. Assoc. Petrol. Geol. Bull.* **51**, 2246–2259.

Kronberg, P. 1984. *Photogeologie*. Stuttgart: Ferdinand Enke.

Lathram, E.H. 1972. Nimbus 4 view of the major structural features of Alaska. *Science* **175**, 1423–1427.

Marrs, R.W. 1974. Interpretative techniques in remote sensing. *Contributions to Geology* **12**, 23–32.

Marrs, R.W. and G.L. Raines 1984. Tectonic framework of Powder River Basin, Wyoming and Montana, interpreted from Landsat imagery. *Am. Ass. Petrol. Geol. Bull.* **68**, 1718–1731.

Mekel, J.F.M. 1978. The use of aerial photographs and other images in geological mapping. Volumes 8i and 8ii in: *ITC Textbook of Photo-interpretation*. Enschede: International Institute for Aerial Survey and Earth Sciences (ITC).

Miller, V.C. 1961. *Photogeology*. New York: McGraw-Hill.

Moore, J.McM. 1979. Tectonics of the Najd transcurrent fault system, Saudi Arabia. *J. Geol. Soc. London* **136**, 441–454.

O'Leary, D.W., J.D. Friedman and H.A. Pohn 1976. Lineament, linear and lineation: some proposed new standards for old terms. *Geol. Soc. Am. Bull.* **87**, 1463–1469.

Pandey, S.N. 1987. *Principles and applications of photogeology*. New Delhi: Eastern Wiley.

Qari, M.Y.H.T. 1991. Application of Landsat TM data to geological studies, Al-Khabt area, southern Arabian shield. *Photogramm. Eng. Remote Sens.* **57**, 421–429.

Ray, R.G. 1960. *Aerial photographs in geologic interpretation and mapping*. US Geol. Surv. Professional Paper 373.

Ricci, M. 1982. Dip determination in photogeology. *Photogramm. Eng. Remote Sens.* **48**, 407–414.

Rothery, D.A. and S.A. Drury, 1984. The neotectonics of the Tibetan Plateau. *Tectonics* **3**, 19–26.

Rothery, D.A. and R.H. Lefebvre 1985. The causes of age dependent changes in the spectral response of lavas, Craters of the Moon, Idaho, USA. *Int. J. Remote Sens.* **6**, 1483–1489.

Rowan, L.C. and P.H. Wetlaufer 1981. Relation between regional lineament systems and structural zones in Nevada. *Am. Ass. Petrol. Geol. Bull.* **65**, 1414–1432.

Short, N.M. and R.W. Blair Jr 1986. *Geomorphology from space*. NASA SP-486. Washington DC: US Government Printing Office.

Smith, J.T. and A. Anson (eds) 1968. *Manual of colour aerial photography*. Falls Church, Virginia: American Society of Photogrammetry.

Sultan, M., R.E. Arvidson, N.C. Sturchio and E.A. Guinness 1987. Lithologic mapping in arid regions with Landsat Thematic mapper data: Meatiq dome, Egypt. *Geol. Soc. Am. Bull.* **99**, 748–762.

Sultan, M., R.E. Arvidson, I.J. Duncan, R.J. Stern and B. El Kaliouby 1988. Extension of the Najd Shear System from Saudi Arabia to the central Eastern Desert of Egypt based on integrated field and Landsat observations. *Tectonics* **7**, 1291–1306.

Sultan, M., R. Becker, R.E. Arvidson, P. Shore, R.J. Stern, Z. El Alfy and E.A. Guinness 1992. Nature of the Red Sea: a controversy revisited. *Geology* **20**, 593–596.

Tapley, I.J. 1988. The reconstruction of palaeodrainage and regional geologic structures in Australia's Canning and Officer Basins using NOAA-AVHRR satellite imagery. *Earth Sci. Rev.* **25**, 409–425.

Venkatakrishnan, R. and F.E. Dotiwalla 1987. The Cuddapah salient: a tectonic model for the Cuddapah Basin, India, based on Landsat image interpretation. *Tectonophysics* **136**, 237–253.

Von Bandat, H.F. 1962. *Aerogeology*. Houston: Gulf Publishing Company.

Woldai, T. 1983. Lop Nur (China) studied from Landsat and SIR-A imagery. *J. ITC*, 253–257.

Zernitz, E.R. 1932. Drainage patterns and their significance. *J. Geol.* **40**, 498–521.

CHAPTER FIVE

Digital image processing

Many remotely sensed images exist in digital form (Ch. 3) as two-dimensional arrays or **rasters** made up of pixels. Each pixel is assigned a digital number (DN) that represents the energy of the EMR waveband being monitored. Using devices akin to line scanners or pushbrooms it is also relatively simple to reproduce photographs in digital form, including the additive, digital red, green and blue components of colour photographs. As explained in Chapter 8, non-EMR data, such as topographic elevation, gravitational and magnetic potential and geochemical data that are recorded at isolated points or semicontinuously along survey lines, can be converted to digital rasters by special computer software.

The DN are generally coded in the 8-bit (1 byte) binary range corresponding to 0–255, where each step corresponds to a range in the original real, or analogue, data. Digital images are degraded from the original data for convenience and economy of storage, but in most cases sufficient precision is preserved for them to be just as useful in practice.

Byte-format data are ideal for manipulation by image-processing software, either individually or within a whole array. Equally, the statistical distribution of the DN can be obtained and put to use in manipulations of the data, and in extracting information from them.

The design of digital imaging devices ensures that data from different parts of the spectrum are in perfect spatial register with one another. Thus, any pixel in a scene can be thought of as a stack of DN, each layer corresponding to one waveband. Data from different devices or processes can be registered to one another, particularly to a common cartographic base using geometric correction and rectification software (Appendix B), thereby increasing the depth of the 'stack'. This registration has two important advantages. First, three 'layers' (data sets) or combinations of them can be displayed together on a colour video monitor as colour images. This is possible because video pictures are themselves made up from exactly positioned pixels of red, green and blue phosphors on the screen. The phosphors glow in proportion to the electron flux from three colour guns, which is modulated on a pixel-by-pixel basis as the electron stream repeatedly sweeps from side to side and top to bottom to make up the picture. The guns are controlled by signals within the video electronics that correspond to the DN for each pixel, for the data chosen for red, green and blue additive components of the image (Ch. 2). The exact registration of pixels also enables the DN for different data 'layers' to be compared and combined in many different ways without disrupting the basic structure of the image.

In this chapter the objective is twofold: to introduce the methods of digital image processing and to show how they can be applied to geological remote sensing. Some of the tasks of an image-processing computer are directed at removing distortions and blemishes resulting from imperfect means of gathering data. They are introduced in Appendix B. Those covered here relate to enhancing the quality of images for improved visual interpretation, to extracting information that cannot be perceived and displaying it as an image, and to measuring and defining degrees of statistical similarity within a scene. This last topic involves the use of the computer as a trained but unbiased means of recognizing spatial and spectral patterns or classes within the image data.

As far as possible the treatment is descriptive rather than mathematical. There are many different image-processing software packages, and several approaches to the tasks which they are required to perform. The account is therefore general and does not venture deeply into computer hardware and software architectures. Any geologist using an image-processing package will have to become familiar with its individual foibles, its internal algorithms and the way in which it interacts with the user. This chapter provides a basis for understanding how image processing works, a guide to selecting appropriate means of processing images for various purposes, and some examples of their application.

5.1 The image histogram

An image of a single band of digital remote-sensing data is a representation of how the EMR energy reflected or emitted by the surface is distributed in two spatial dimensions. The energy is expressed as DN, which in a display are represented by a variation in brightness showing as different grey levels. Since the eye is capable of distinguishing only about 30 grey levels in a black and white image (Section 2.3), a display of up to 256 grey levels appears to be continuous. In fact it is made up of discrete steps. An image can also be expressed statistically as the probability of finding DN of a given value within it. For the 0–255 range of possibilities, this measure is properly termed the **probability density function (PDF)**. The PDF is most conveniently represented by a **histogram** of the number of pixels which, regardless of spatial position within an image, have a particular DN (Fig. 5.1).

The histogram of DN distributions is probably the single most useful measure in digital image processing. Its shape indicates the contrast and homogeneity of the scene. For instance, a scene of a homogeneous surface with a low contrast will produce a histogram with a single, sharp peak. A broad single peak suggests homogeneity but a wide range of contrast. Images containing several distinct types of surface cover may show multiple peaks. If each has a significantly different average brightness these peaks will be clearly separated. As their average brightnesses become more alike, so the peaks will begin to merge. Other shape attributes of the histogram give a kind of statistical shorthand for an image. The presence of 'tails' and the degree of asymmetry of the peak both indicate important structural features in an image that will rarely be obvious from the picture itself. Figure 5.2 shows examples of images and their associated histograms.

The PDF may also be displayed as a **cumulative** histogram, in which the cumulative frequency of pixels

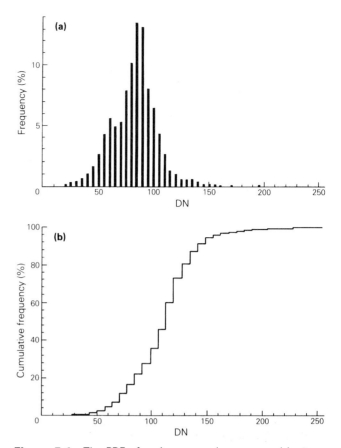

Figure 5.1 The PDF of an image can be expressed by two forms of histogram. In (a) the number or frequency of pixels assigned to each DN is plotted as bars against DN. Each division on the DN axis is termed a bin and is the width of one of the bars. In (b) the vertical axis is the cumulative frequency of pixels having DN less than a particular value. For example, the cumulative frequency for DN = 50 is $f_{50} + f_{49} + f_{48} + ... + f_0$, so that the cumulative frequency for the maximum DN is 100%. The same distribution of DN appears as peaks and sometimes troughs in (a) and as changes of gradient in a roughly S-shaped curve in (b).

with a particular DN is plotted against DN. For each DN the cumulative frequency is that of the DN plus the frequencies of all DN less than it. So the cumulative frequency at a DN of 128 is $f_{128} + f_{127} + f_{126} + ... + f_0$. In this case the steepness of the curve is a measure of the contrast and heterogeneities show up as kinks in the curve (Fig. 5.1).

It is of course possible to produce histograms for different parts of an image, so that the data structure in various types of terrain can be compared. These, together with the histogram of all the data, form the basic requirements for contrast stretching (Section 5.2), since it is effectively the histogram which is manipulated in this operation. A crude idea of the contribution of known types of surface to the histogram can be obtained simply by identifying known pixels and dumping their DN in different bands to a line printer or the computer console.

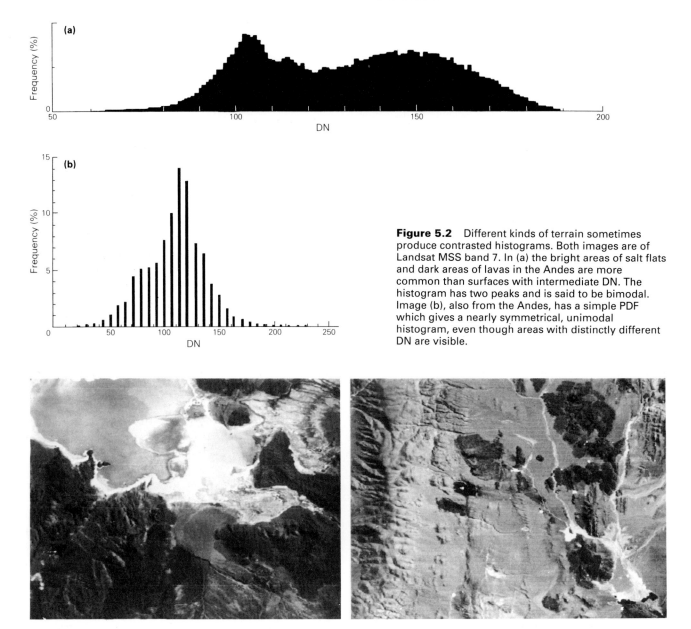

Figure 5.2 Different kinds of terrain sometimes produce contrasted histograms. Both images are of Landsat MSS band 7. In (a) the bright areas of salt flats and dark areas of lavas in the Andes are more common than surfaces with intermediate DN. The histogram has two peaks and is said to be bimodal. Image (b), also from the Andes, has a simple PDF which gives a nearly symmetrical, unimodal histogram, even though areas with distinctly different DN are visible.

Multispectral data can be expressed in multidimensional histograms, the simplest of which is the two-dimensional histogram (Fig. 5.3). These are simply bivariate plots of DN for one band against those for another. They display visually the degree of **correlation** between the two bands and identify instances where a surface has distinctly different kinds of response to the two bands. The density of plots of individual pixels is a measure of where peaks in the one-dimensional histograms coincide. Highly correlated data, or classes of surface materials which have similar appearances on images of the two bands, plot near-straight lines on the two-dimensional histogram. Poorly correlated data show as shapeless clouds of points (Fig. 5.3).

Histograms of multidimensional data are useful individually or combined in deciding on the contrast stretches needed to produce enhanced colour images. However, their greatest importance is that they can be described statistically and manipulated as the basis for image classification (Section 5.7) or multivariate analysis (Section 5.4).

5.2 Contrast stretching

The video screen of a digital image processor, or the light source in a digital film writer, expresses DN in a stepped range of intensities from 0 (black) to 255 (maximum intensity or **saturation**). The simplest function of image-

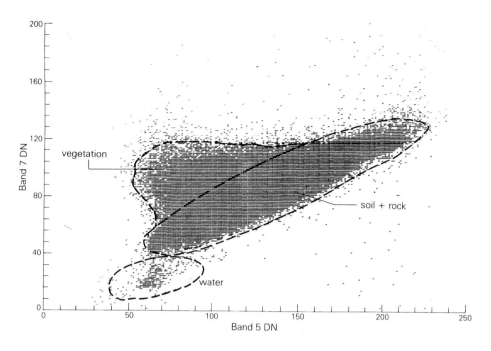

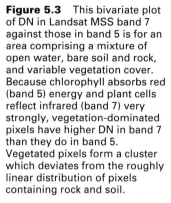

Figure 5.3 This bivariate plot of DN in Landsat MSS band 7 against those in band 5 is for an area comprising a mixture of open water, bare soil and rock, and variable vegetation cover. Because chlorophyll absorbs red (band 5) energy and plant cells reflect infrared (band 7) very strongly, vegetation-dominated pixels have higher DN in band 7 than they do in band 5. Vegetated pixels form a cluster which deviates from the roughly linear distribution of pixels containing rock and soil.

processing software is to change any DN in an image to any of these 256 intensity levels. It can also transform one range of DN to another. This is the basis of **contrast stretching**. There are many reasons why such a transformation may be required, but the most important stems from the way in which digital image data are acquired.

The objective of all land-oriented remote-sensing systems is to record the full range of reflectances possible from all conceivable surface materials. In other words, real differences in the darkest and the brightest surfaces should ideally be expressed as differences in DN. The dark objects should not appear totally black and the light objects should not be 'washed-out' by saturating the sensor. However, very few, if any parts of the Earth's surface express these extremes. As a result the histograms for most images are compressed into a relatively small part of the 0–255 range (Fig. 5.4a). This results in loss of data, although many land-oriented systems can be adjusted to compensate for un-wanted bright materials, such as clouds or snow. The human eye is only capable of discriminating about 30 grey levels in the black to white range, and those only if they are adjacent and sharply bounded. An unstretched image whose histogram is restricted to the lower half of the 0–255 range therefore appears to have very poor contrast to the human analyst (Fig. 5.4b), even though it might contain 100 different steps. For it to show sensible information the compressed histogram must be expanded to occupy the full range available in the display.

The simplest means of improving the contrast in an image is to change the range of data by spreading it equally over the 0–255 range. The minimum DN is set to 0, the maximum to 255. Each histogram bin relating to each DN

originally present is moved to a new position, and the new bins are equally spaced (Fig. 5.4d). This is a **linear stretch**. The computer accomplishes this by using a **look-up table (LUT)**. A LUT converts an input [DN(i,j)I] to an output [DN(i,j)O], where (i,j) expresses the position of a pixel in the image. For a linear stretch the function is the basic equation for a straight line relating DN(i,j)I and DN(i,j)O:

$$DN(i,j)I = m[DN(i,j)O] + c$$

where m is the gradient and c the intercept on the DN(i,j)O axis. The equation can be expressed as a graph of input against output (Fig. 5.4c). Because input and output DN have a limited range (0–255) the computer does not have to spend time performing the same calculation on each of the millions of pixels in an image. It simply replaces the input value with the corresponding output value from the LUT.

A simple linear stretch of the data in Figure 5.4a produces an image which at least shows some of the surface details (Fig. 5.4e). It still appears to have a rather poor contrast however – it appears hazy. The reason for this is twofold. First, each DN in the original data has a contribution from atmospheric scattering (Section 1.3.1), the amount decreasing as wavelength increases. The second is that the maximum DN is actually for small clouds in the image that are much brighter than the brightest part of the surface. The effect of the atmosphere is seen on the histogram of raw data (Fig. 5.4a), where there are no pixels with a DN of 0. On a planet with no atmosphere total or umbral shadows would be completely black, so one way of correcting for the scattered component is to identify shadowed pixels, find their DN and set all pixels with this and lower values to 0. The DN chosen is known as the

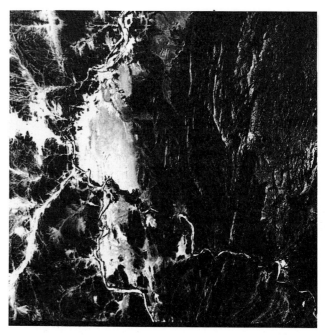

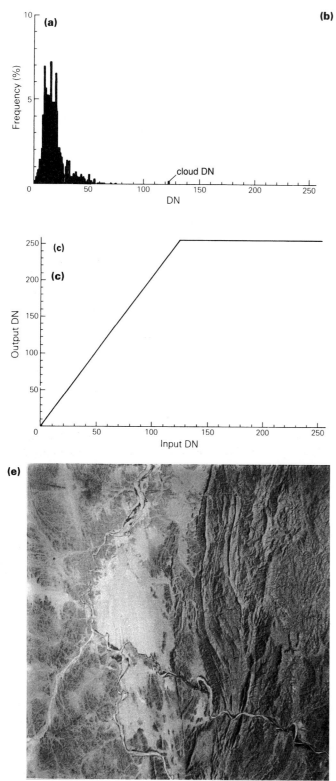

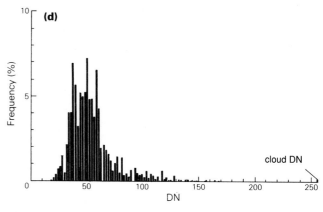

Figure 5.4 The raw Landsat TM band 3 data for a mixed terrain on the Sudan–Eritrea border are compressed towards low DN (a). Display of these data produces a dark, low-contrast image (b) in which few details can be seen. A linear contrast stretch is achieved by a simple straight-line LUT (c), which sets the minimum DN (in this case 0) to 0 and the maximum (128) to 255. This spreads out the histogram (d) and introduces discernible contrast in the resulting image (e). This image is approximately 30 × 30 km.

cut-off. This procedure is sometimes termed a **dark-pixel correction**. Care must be taken not to choose dark pixels in water for in the visible region their DN may be the result of suspended sediment not atmospheric effects. Using their value for cut-off may result in blacking out areas of dark but unshadowed surface. Another method of **atmospheric correction** is to plot DN for a high-wavelength band – usually in the infrared where scattering is at a minimum –

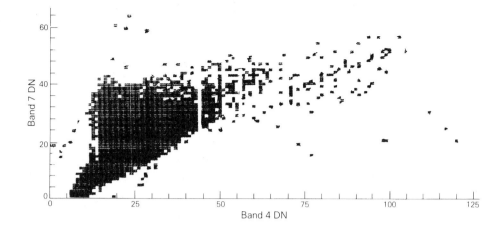

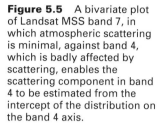

Figure 5.5 A bivariate plot of Landsat MSS band 7, in which atmospheric scattering is minimal, against band 4, which is badly affected by scattering, enables the scattering component in band 4 to be estimated from the intercept of the distribution on the band 4 axis.

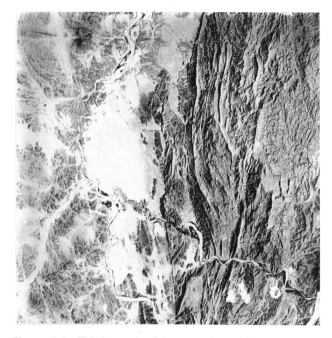

Figure 5.6 This image is of the same data as Figure 5.4b, but they have been corrected for atmospheric scattering and for small bright clouds (DN = 128 on Figure 5.4a). All the geologically valid data have been stretched linearly to occupy the whole 0–255 range.

information. Loss of information must be traded off against the improvement in image contrast resulting from atmospheric correction. Figure 5.6 shows the improvement in image quality resulting from atmospheric correction of Figure 5.4e. Since cloud, of little interest to the geologist, is present in the image, and has a DN of 128 (Fig. 5.4a), the contrast has been further increased by setting the maximum DN on soil or rock to 255.

A linear contrast stretch with atmospheric correction is in most cases sufficient to produce an image of high quality, the removal of haze and increased contrast sharpening the high-spatial frequency features in the image (Section 5.3). Enhanced images of single bands or false-colour images comprising three contrast-stretched bands can then be interpreted geologically with a fair measure of success. They can be improved further using the interactive possibilities of the computer to suit the aesthetic preferences of the interpreter. More contrast can be introduced by increasing the value of the cut-off DN and decreasing the value of DN above which all values are set to 255 or saturation. Increasing the cut-off will darken a larger percentage of a scene. Decreasing the saturation value increases the amount of the image with light tones. However, some information is lost in both cases.

Occasionally a scene has areas dominated by both light and dark surfaces, as in the example used here, both of which contain geologically interesting information. A simple linear contrast stretch will not perform an enhancement ideally suited to both. Contrast in the central part of the range will be enhanced at the expense of the low and high ends of the range. Again the imperfections of human vision will not allow a complete interpretation. There are many ways of overcoming these limitations by more complex methods of stretching. The simplest is to select cut-off and saturation for linear stretching of the dark and light parts of the scene, to produce two separate images. Figure 5.7 illustrates this. The image in which dark areas are stretched

against those for a band in the visible region where scattering has a greater effect. A line of best fit drawn through the distribution will intercept the short-wavelength axis at a DN approximating the scattered component (Fig. 5.5). This value is then used as the cut-off. A third method is by inspection of the histograms for all the bands and estimating the shift attributable to scattering in each. Whichever method is chosen, some care is needed. Valuable information can be present in shadowed areas because they are lit by the scattering effect of the sky. Correction will lose this

(a)

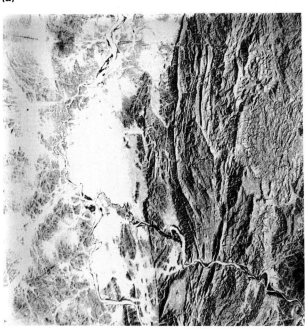

(b)

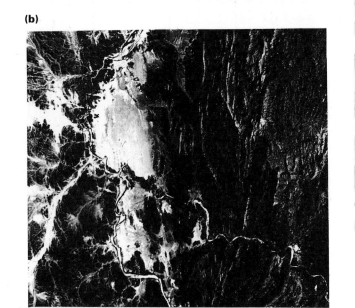

Figure 5.7 In (a) the low DN of Figure 5.6 have been stretched linearly to occupy the full 0–255 range. The dark terrain now shows more detail, but the light areas are washed out. Image (b) has had all the low DN set to 0, so that maximum contrast in the light alluvial flats allows their variation to be seen.

(a)

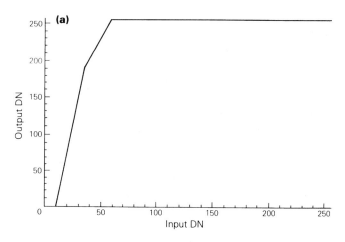

(b)

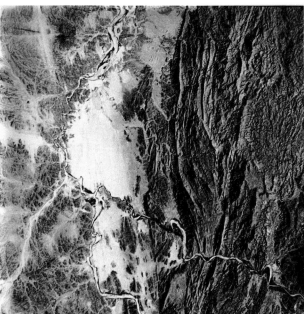

Figure 5.8 The LUT (a) for a piecewise stretch of Figure 5.4b shows two different linear stretches for the low range and the high range of geologically important DN. The resulting image (b) has improved contrast in both dark and light terrains. In a clearly bimodal image, such as Figure 5.2a, the best strategy would be to stretch the peak of low DN, compress the trough of intermediate DN and stretch the peak of high DN. In the LUT shown in (a) this would introduce a low-angle segment between the two stretched components.

(Fig. 5.7a) has all the light areas washed out. The converse holds for the enhancement of the light areas (Fig 5.7b). This is an expensive, time-consuming and inconvenient approach in all but the most extreme cases. A compromise is to investigate the histograms for the contrasted areas of geological interest and to devise a **piecewise stretch**. In this operation the geologically unimportant parts of the overall histogram are compressed, and the remaining space is occupied by linear stretches of the light and dark ranges selected. Sensible contrast is thus introduced into both light and dark areas. The LUT for such a manipulation and the resulting image are shown in Figure 5.8.

More sophisticated stretches involve creating LUTs using **non-linear** transformations. To avoid the loss of contrast in the tails of the original histogram, inherent in linear stretches, the raw data can be forced to resemble a normal distribution. This obeys Gaussian laws of statistical distribution, produces a symmetrical, bell-shaped histogram with its peak at a DN of 127, and results in a **Gaussian stretch**. The manipulation of bins in the raw histogram to produce an equal population density of pixels along the DN axis results in the spacing of bins becoming inversely proportional to the number of pixels that they contain. This is achieved by forcing the cumulative histogram (Section 5.1) to become a straight line (Fig. 5.9a), and because of this the operation is known as a **ramp stretch**. Ramp stretches result in the greatest contrast stretch being applied to the middle, most populated, range of DN, with compression in the less densely populated low- and high-DN tails. Sometimes it may be necessary to stretch the dark part of an image as much as possible while still retaining some contrast in the light range. This is possible using a **logarithmic stretch** (Fig. 5.9b). The converse is achieved by an **exponential stretch** (Fig. 5.9c). Virtually any mathematical transformation can be devised for contrast stretching, but in most cases the results are not a sufficient improvement over the simpler options to warrant the time involved.

Figure 5.10 is an example of a false-colour image whose component bands have been interactively stretched to produce the optimum contrast and colour balance for the geological information of interest.

5.2.1 Choosing bands for colour images

The Landsat MSS and SPOT systems record data from only three regions in the visible and VNIR parts of the spectrum. Effectively, only one kind of false-colour composite image can be generated, where VNIR controls red, visible red controls green and green controls blue, to give the familiar rendition of vegetation in reds and approximately natural colours for other kinds of surface. Contrast stretching can improve the range of colours in such an image, but there are limits imposed by the strong correlation between the MSS and SPOT bands (Section 1.2.2). Newer systems, such as the Landsat Thematic Mapper, JERS-1, various airborne multispectral scanners and imaging spectrometers, provide more bands in the visible, SWIR and thermal infrared regions, centred on particular spectral features due to different kinds of surface material. The data in these regions are less correlated and the number of possible false-colour images is increased. An example of just how useful

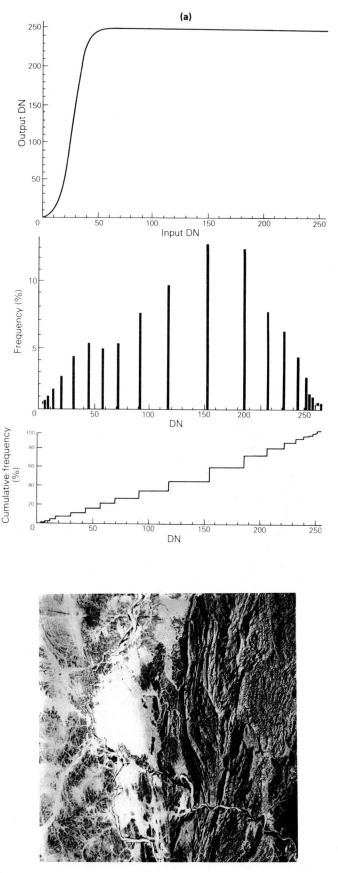

Figure 5.9 The effects of (a) an equipopulation or ramp stretch, (b) a logarithmic stretch and (c) an exponential stretch on Figure 5.4b are shown as the LUT, histogram, cumulative histogram and resulting image from top to bottom.

131

(b)

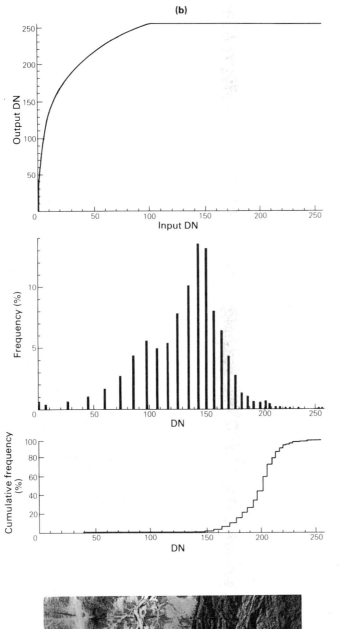

(c)

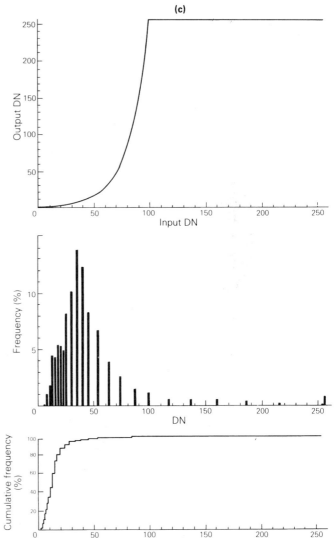

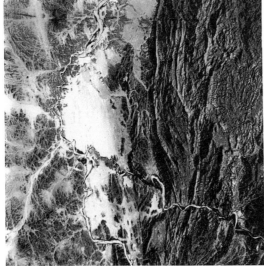

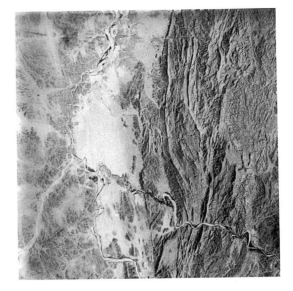

(a) (b) (c)

(d) (e) (f)

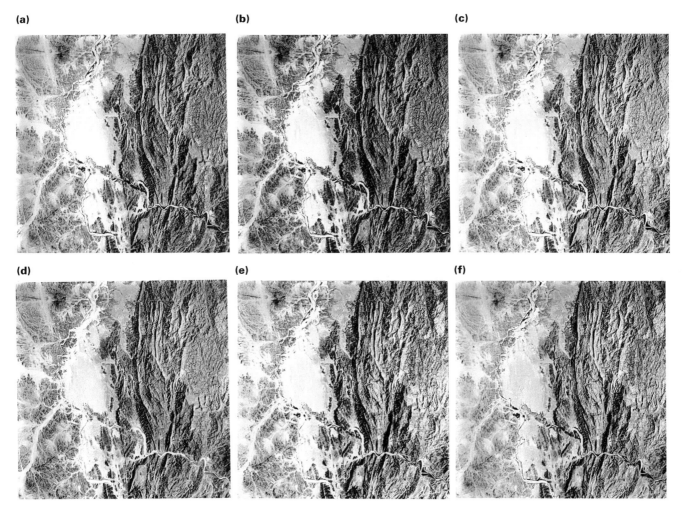

Figure 5.11 Images (a) to (f) are of the six reflected Landsat TM bands (1, 2, 3, 4, 5 and 7 respectively) for the area at the Sudan–Eritrea border used in earlier figures.

this flexibility can be is shown in *Figure 5.10*, comparing a natural colour Landsat TM image with a standard false-colour image and one in which red, green and blue (RGB) are controlled by SWIR, visible red and blue wavebands. However, the more bands that are available the greater is the choice of possible three-band combinations, including the order of their rendition in RGB. Considering the last point involves attention to the proclivities of human vision, aesthetics in particular. Quite simply there is usually a single rendition of three particular bands that is more visually stimulating (and therefore more readily interpreted) than the other five possible RGB combinations, even though the information content in all six RGB renditions is identical. Figure 5.10c and d illustrates this point. Although the reasons for this are not fully understood, a simple rule of thumb is to render the most informative band for a particular purpose in red, the next in green and the least informative in blue.

Choosing three bands, when an important objective is to use as few images as possible in interpretation, is an increasingly difficult task for data with large numbers of bands. For the six reflected bands in a Landsat TM image there are 20 combinations, for each of which there are six RGB orders, compared with only six possibilities for three-band SPOT data. Clearly the potential for confusion with 120 possible colour images, let alone a variety of enhancements for each, is enormous. The numbers involved in imaging spectrometry data are more appropriate to telephone directories. Selecting two or three combinations for a particular objective can be aided by statistical analysis of the correlation between the bands. Inspection of Figure 5.11, showing all six Landsat TM bands, reveals that all are very similar, owing to the high correlation inherent in the reflected part of the spectrum due to the dominance of albedo. They do contain differences, but they are quite subtle. Computer analysis of the correlation can identify groups of three bands in order of their non-redundant information content.

However attractive, such an automatic procedure makes no distinction between the reasons for the order, which in the

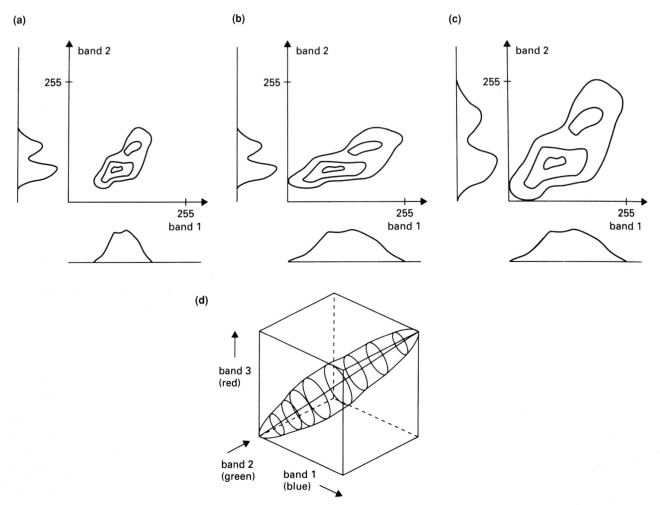

Figure 5.12 Bivariate plots of two bands, showing (a) the raw data, (b) the data after linearly stretching band 1 only and (c) the data after stretching both bands. The high correlation between the two bands is retained. (d) Perspective view of RGB colour space, showing the volume occupied by DN from three correlated bands of reflected data in the form of an ellipsoid with its principal axis along a line where red, green and blue DN are equal.

vast majority of cases arises from the spectrally distinct nature of vegetation (Fig. 5.3), even when it forms only a very sparse cover to an area. While RGB combinations that emphasize vegetation differences can be useful in geological mapping, a better choice is to select bands on the basis of whether or not they contain spectral features due to mineral content in soil and rock. Compared with the effects of vegetation, such features will have a very muted influence, but if the minerals involved are present their influences will be there in the data, unless vegetation cover is total. Section 5.5 discusses inspection of mineral spectra in designing uses of ratio images, but a few guidelines are appropriate here.

In the reflected region only a few groups of minerals have marked effects on band response. The dominant ones are Fe^{3+} oxides and hydroxides that govern 'redness' and absorption around 0.9 μm, overall reflectivity or albedo of common rocks that peaks around 1.6 μm, OH^- minerals that have absorptions around 2.1–2.1 μm and carbonates with absorptions around 2.35–2.4 μm (Section 1.3.2). The reason that *Figure 5.10c* is far more geologically useful than *Figure 5.10a* or *b* is that it expresses albedo and redness well, and the overall reflectivity and iron content of the local rocks are more variable than any other mineralogical characteristics. The narrower the spectral bands, the more strategically placed they are relative to spectral features of mineral; and the more features that are covered, the greater the possibilities for lithological discrimination.

In the thermal infrared many more minerals, including the bulk of rock-forming minerals as opposed to minor minerals and surface coatings, influence the details of emission spectra (Figs. 1.12 and 1.13). Consequently, given multispectral thermal data such as TIMS or those likely to become available from ASTER, the direct mapping of true petrographic categories becomes a distinct possibility (Ch. 6).

In both emitted and reflected data, high correlation between bands (Fig. 5.11) is a major hindrance for two reasons. First, it means that there is a great deal of **redundant data**, that is each band contains more or less the same information apart from subtleties, and for general purposes any one band could be substituted for any other. The greater the number of bands and the narrower they are, the more the redundancy. This is a problem for computer storage as well as a source of confusion. A seven-band Landsat TM scene occupies 250 megabytes of magnetic storage. An equivalent area of imaging spectrometry data from the HIRIS instrument would occupy about 7 gigabytes before any enhancement of it. Clearly some means of **data reduction** are needed (Section 5.4) to extract the wheat from the chaff. High correlation between bands is impossible to remove by simple methods of contrast stretching. The full range of 256^3 colours possible in an RGB cannot be exploited, and the bulk of colours are pastel shades that the eye finds difficult to subdivide. Some means of removing the correlation must be sought for some applications.

5.2.2 *Contrast stretching in different colour spaces*

Figure 5.12a demonstrates schematically the way in which high correlation between two bands is retained during linear contrast stretching, while Figure 5.12d expresses the limit

of such stretching in RGB space. Using any of the methods of contrast enhancement discussed so far would produce the same result. The stretched data fall within an elongated ellipsoid, thereby producing only a very limited range of the colours that are possible. The full range would occupy the entire volume of the colour cube in Figure 5.12b. To fill that range would involve drastically reducing the degree of correlation in the data, which is the object of **decorrelation stretching**. This is discussed in Section 5.4 since it relies on statistical manipulation of data. The methods covered here depend on changing the coordinate system used to represent colour.

The major axis of the ellipsoid in Figure 5.12b defines those points where the red, green and blue components are equal, thereby producing shades of grey. This is the grey or **achromatic axis** in RGB space, and the rest of the ellipsoid represents pastel shades and the colour limits of the associated image. A position on the achromatic axis, or a projection onto it from a coloured pixel, is a measure of the **intensity** (Section 2.4), or the brightness of the colour. The actual colour can be expressed by two other measures. The closer to the achromatic axis, the more pastel the colour; the further away, the more vivid or pure the colour. This measure is the **saturation**, at right angles to the axis. The third measure of colour in relation to the achromatic axis is the **hue**, and this varies around a circle also at right angles to the axis. Hue is essentially a measure of the dominant colour Figure 5.13a shows the relationship between the descriptions of colour in the RGB and **intensity–saturation–hue (ISH)** coordinate systems. The ISH system is in the form of a symmetrical cone with its apex at the black point of RGB coordinates. *Figure 5.13b is a section at right angles to the achromatic axis, showing the relationship between hue and saturation in the form of a **colour wheel**.

Intensity is a number from 0 at the apex of the ISH cone to an arbitrary 255 at the limit of RGB space. Saturation is an angle between 0° and half the apical angle of the cone. Hue is also an angle between 0° and 360° around the colour wheel. Red is chosen as the hue corresponding to 0°, blue is at 120°, green at 240° and the circle is completed by 360° at red again. To enable ISH space to be exploited in image processing, the RGB coordinates of each pixel are converted to ISH measures by a mathematical transformation. Rather than leaving saturation and hue in the form of angles, they are expressed in the 0–255 range, when their ranges, and that of intensity, can be modified independently by simple stretching. Stretching intensity is akin to using the same contrast stretch on the red, green and blue bands in RGB space. Stretching hue leads to a complete modification of colour, and is to be avoided. Stretching saturation is the most important manipulation, for this is the same as inflating the RGB ellipsoid of highly correlated data to fill a greater proportion of available colour space. After such manipulation the modified intensity, saturation and hue

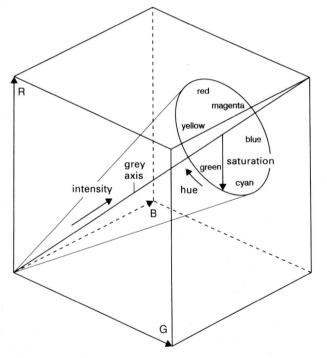

Figure 5.13 (a) Intensity, saturation and hue (ISH) defined in RGB space. (b, colour) Cross-section through the conical representation of HSI colour space, or colour wheel, showing how pure spectral hues on the perimeter grade through pastel shades to grey at the axis of the cone. Courtesy of LogE Ltd.

measures are converted back again to RGB space by the inverse of the mathematical transform, so that the enhanced image can be displayed on a video monitor. *Figure 5.14* shows the result of using an ISH transform, involving stretching of intensity and saturation only, on *Figure 5.10c*. The result is a far more vivid image, but one in which essentially the same colours are present – of great importance in making geological sense of an interpretation.

Very similar results can be achieved by transforming RGB images into the CIE coordinate system (Section 2.4), but the ISH transform is simpler and takes less time. Many variants of the ISH technique are possible. Among them are performing other manipulations on intensity, such as spatial frequency filtering, substituting a single band of better resolution for intensity, combining different sorts of imagery, one as intensity another as hue. Some examples are to be found in Chapter 8.

5.3 Spatial frequency filtering

The concept of spatial frequency distribution of grey tones within a photograph was introduced in Section 2.2. Exactly the same concept applies to digital images, with the difference that scene brightness variations are expressed in DN distributed as rectangular pixels in a raster. The varia-

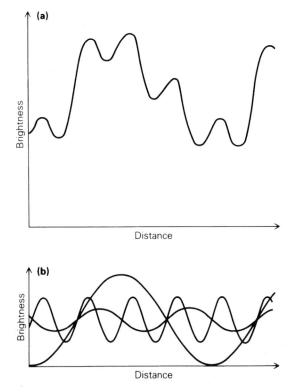

Figure 5.15 Variations in DN along a line on an image (a) can be expressed as a range of sine waves (b) with different amplitudes and frequencies. Their cumulative effect is the same as the real spatial frequency distribution of the image.

tion can be expressed as a graph of DN against distance along a line on the image. The fluctuations on such a graph can be reconstructed as a series of sine waves with different frequencies and amplitudes. When they are superimposed they interfere with one another to give the same effect as the graph (Fig. 5.15). In reality the variation in DN is expressed by sine waves in two dimensions rather than in the single dimension shown by Figure 5.15.

All images contain boundaries between surfaces with different interactions with EMR. They may constitute boundaries between different cover types, such as vegetation, soil types or rocks of different composition. Another kind of boundary separates areas with different amounts of illumination resulting from topographic effects. Those between brightly lit and shadowed areas are an important example. In a single-band image the boundaries mark changes from one range of DN to another. In the most extreme case a boundary is an abrupt change from an area of uniform DN of one value to a uniform area with another DN. On a graph of DN versus distance this is represented by a steep or even vertical gradient. Boundaries of this kind are known as **edges**. They occupy only a small area and are thus high-frequency features. They are narrower than they are long, and can define lines of various shapes and lengths. Good examples are the boundaries between fields with different crops, roads and rivers and their surroundings, and between shadows and well-lit slopes. Gradational boundaries, as might be expected where natural vegetation changes with altitude, have low gradients, occupy large spaces and are therefore low-frequency features. Any linear attributes they may have are vague and difficult to define.

There is of course a complete range from high-frequency features through medium to low frequency. The scale and gradient associated with changes in DN within an image are closely interwoven, and both help in recognizing different types of boundary. For geological purposes the most important boundaries are often the edges. They may be shadow effects giving information on topographic features, some of which represent rock types with different resistances to erosion, or tectonic weaknesses such as faults and joints. Some edges are boundaries between rocks with different reflective properties, soils derived from different rock types, or vegetation boundaries that have an underlying geological control. Edges may occur in isolation, as in the case of faults or other boundaries separating large masses of uniform but different rock types. They may also be closely spaced, especially when they represent compositional banding or joints.

Whereas edges may represent small-scale geological features, medium- and low-frequency spatial features often show the gross geological features of an area. Many folds repeat stratigraphic sequences on the scale of kilometres. They define medium frequency features. Phenomena such as batholiths, major fault blocks, sedimentary basins and orogenic belts control low-frequency features with dimensions in tens or hundreds of kilometres. The lower the frequency of a feature on an image the subtler it tends to be, and the more difficult it is to perceive, depending on the associated contrast (Section 2.2).

The spatial frequency of any feature is determined by the scale of the image. With decreasing scale, the frequency of a particular kind of feature will tend to become higher. As resolution coarsens, the highest frequency features disappear altogether because they are smaller than an individual pixel. What would be undetectable subtle variation on a large-scale image often becomes clearly distinguishable on a small scale. Features are in some cases transformed from low-frequency features to edges. The human visual system responds to varying spatial frequencies in images in a complex way, depending on the scale and viewing distance of an image and on the eye's MTF, which is different for black and white and colour images (Section 2.2, Eq. 2.1).

The process involved in improving the appearance and the interpretability of the spatial distribution of data in an image is **spatial frequency filtering**. It consists of selectively enhancing the high-, medium- and low-frequency variations of DN in an image. It is not always necessary. Simply by manipulating the contrast of an image the properties of the human MTF (Section 2.2) can be exploited. Reducing the contrast leaves visible only the low- and medium-frequency features, whereas increasing it accentuates the sharp changes in contrast associated with edges. However, there is a limit to which either of these simple contrast transformations can be taken, when the visual quality of the image breaks down and interpretability begins to degrade. A more powerful technique is to use various mathematical transforms to extract selectively the high-, medium- and low-frequency variations.

A mathematical technique for separating an image into its various spatial frequency components is Fourier analysis, the details of which are beyond this book. The basic principle is illustrated by Figure 5.15 for a single dimension. The **Fourier transform** of an image, the result of such a separation, expresses the spatial attributes of an image in terms of their frequencies, amplitudes and their orientation. It is a transform that enables certain groups of frequencies and directions to be emphasized or suppressed by algorithms known as filters. Those which emphasize high frequencies and suppress low frequencies are **high-pass filters**. Similarly, there are **medium-** and **low-pass filters**. Moreover, selected ranges of spatial frequencies can be removed or retained in the resulting image, using **band-stop** and **band-pass filters**. The process is analogous to the electronic filtering in amplifiers to reduce hiss and rumble, enhance the bass or treble and so on in a sound recording. Filtering can be implemented through the Fourier

transform, when it is said to operate in the frequency domain, or in the spatial domain of the image itself by a process known as **convolution**. Frequency-domain filtering is more powerful, but is also the more expensive in terms of computer time and involves highly complex mathematics. Most image-processing systems employ convolution filters.

The easiest way to understand convolution is to follow the actual process which takes place in the computer itself. Convolution is accomplished by what is known as a **box filter**. An image can be represented by the expression or function $P(i,j)$, the original DN at every coordinate in the raster, where i and j are the line and pixel (row and column) coordinates. A box filter is a matrix of dimension $2M+1$ rows by $2N+1$ columns, so the number of rows and columns is odd and one cell always lies at the exact centre of the matrix. Each cell in the box filter has a weighting C, and the whole matrix can be expressed by the function

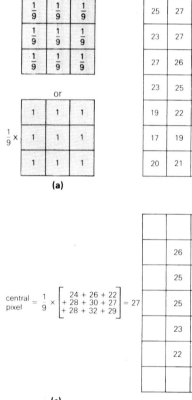

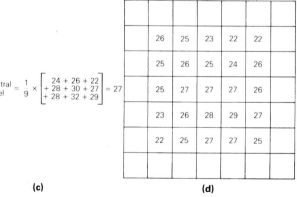

Figure 5.16 The convolution matrix for a low-pass filter (a) comprises a 3 × 3 matrix of equally weighted cells. The data from a raw image consist of a matrix of pixels, each with its own DN (b). During convolution, the value assigned to the pixel overlain by the central cell of the convolution matrix, shaded in (b), is the sum of the products of the cell weights and the DN of pixels which they lie over, for the whole convolution matrix. This calculation is shown in (c). The result of convolution for part of the image is shown in (d). All convolution works in this way and the results depend on the shape, dimensions and weightings of the convolution matrix.

(a)

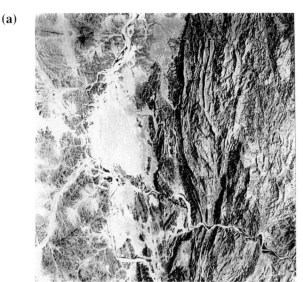

$C(k,l)$, k and l being the cell coordinates within the box. An output image $O(i,j)$ is computed by convolving the image $P(i,j)$ with the matrix $C(k,l)$. This operation is mathematically expressed by:

$$O(i,j) = \sum_{k=-M}^{M} \sum_{l=-N}^{N} P(i+k,j+l)C(k+M+1,l+N+1) \qquad (5.1)$$

$O(i,j)$ = the sum from $k = -M$ to M of the sum from $l = -N$ to N of $P(i+k,j+l)$ multiplied by $C(k+M+1,l+N+1)$

In operation this means that the matrix C is overlain on the image with its central cell $(M+1,N+1)$ on top of a pixel (i,j), and the other cells lying on top of the immediately surrounding pixels. The DN for each pixel overlain by the convolution matrix is multiplied by the corresponding weighting factor and the products are summed. It is this sum of the local area operations which is used to compute the value to be used in place of the DN of the pixel beneath the centre of the convolution matrix. An output image is produced by the convolution matrix being moved over every pixel in the image.

(b)

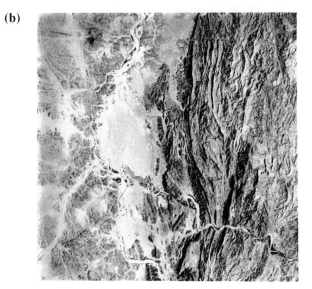

The simplest convolution is that used to generate a low-pass filter. This functions by replacing the DN of each pixel with the average DN of the pixels surrounding it. Figure 5.16a shows a convolution matrix that could be used. In this case it is a 3×3 matrix; each cell has an identical positive weighting and the sum of the weights adds to 1.0. This ensures that the overall statistics of the image are not changed by the convolution. Figure 5.16b–d shows how a portion of an image is converted to a low-pass version. The dimensions of the convolution filter – sometimes called its kernel or window size – determine the extent to which the image is smoothed. Put another way, the bigger the filter, the lower the frequency of spatial variations in DN that are expressed in the resulting image. Figure 5.17 shows the results of two low-pass convolution filters with different dimensions compared with the original image.

(c)

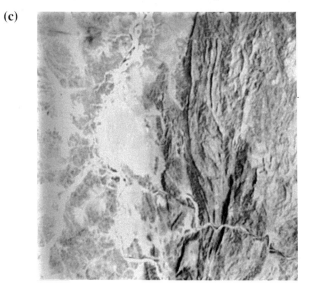

The simplest means of high-pass filtering is accomplished by subtracting a low-pass filtered image from the original image. This shows all the deviations in DN from the local mean. It can be achieved directly by convolution. A simple high-pass convolution filter producing differences from the local mean is given in Figure 5.18a. In this case the sum of the weightings is zero. The deviations from the local mean may be either positive or negative. Moreover, they most often have smaller values than the original DN.

Figure 5.17 Image (a) is a linearly stretched image of Landsat TM band 5 data for the Sudan–Eritrea area used previously. Images resulting from 3×3 and 13×13 low-pass convolution are shown in (b) and (c). As the dimensions of a low-pass filter increase the smoothing effect becomes more obvious.

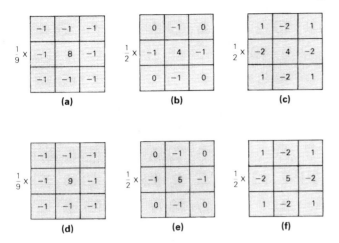

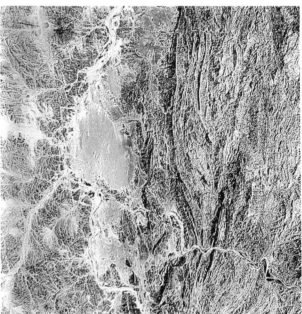

Figure 5.18 Convolution matrices for edge detection or high-pass filtering can be achieved by subtracting the results of a low-pass convolution from the original image (a), or by devising matrices based on more complex algorithms (b and c). Edge-enhancement matrices result from adding the edge detector to the original image (d, e and f).

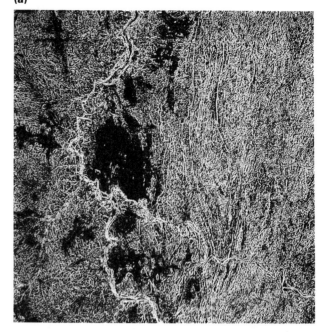

(a)

(b)

So that the high-pass filtered image can be displayed, its DN must be rescaled to occupy the 0–255 range. As with low-pass filters, the size of a high-pass convolution matrix has an effect on the resulting image. In this case, the smaller the matrix, the more finely spaced are the differences which show up, and vice versa. An example of a high-pass filtered image of this kind is shown in Figure 5.19a. One of its functions is a means of **edge detection**. Many other types of convolution filter can be devised for edge detection, and some of them are shown in Figure 5.18. They may be used in cases where the simple mean difference matrix does not give satisfactory results.

A user generally hopes to perform all interpretations on a single image, using both tone and colour variations together with textural features represented by edges. The image of detected edges in Figure 5.19a is noticeably lacking in contrast. Producing an image with both tonal and enhanced spatial information means adding the results of edge detection to the original image. Such **edge enhancement** can also be achieved by a single convolution with a suitably designed filter. Figure 5.18 shows three edge-enhancement matrices corresponding to the three edge-detection matrices. In each case the weighting of the central cell of the matrix is increased by 1, thereby adding the DN of each pixel automatically to the convolution. The sum of the weights in each edge-enhancement matrix is thus 1. Figure 5.19b is an edge-enhanced version of Figure 5.17a produced by this method.

A high-pass spatial filter normally enhances features which are less than half the dimensions of the convolution matrix used. In the case of geological features of regional

Figure 5.19 Image (a) is the result of a simple edge-detection convolution (Figure 5.18a) for the data displayed in Figure 5.17a. This was added to the original image to produce the edge-enhanced version shown in (b).

dimensions, such as major faults and intrusive contacts, very large matrices must be used. These are time-consuming and expensive to implement. Figure 5.20 is an example of the use of a large filter to detect regional fault patterns.

(a) **(b)**

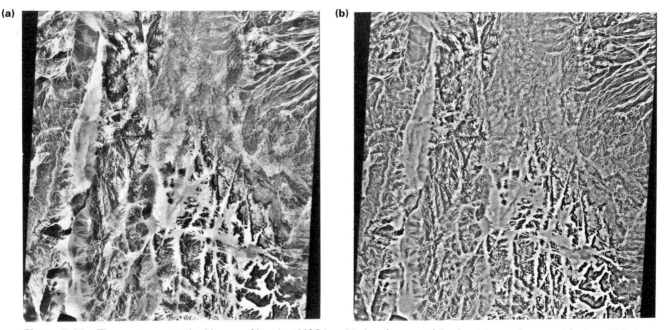

Figure 5.20 The contrast-stretched image of Landsat MSS band 7 data for part of Jordan (a) reveals several faults which do not appear on local geological maps. However, many more are discernible on an image of medium-scale edges detected by a 31 × 31 mean-difference matrix (b). Courtesy of Pat Chavez, US Geological Survey.

Since edges and other spatial boundaries in an image are expressed by changes in DN over a small distance, they can be detected in images of the gradient of DN. Gradient is defined as the magnitude of the **first derivative**, and this measure can also be calculated by convolution techniques. Changes in gradient are related to edges too, but in a more complex way. They are displayed by the rate of change of the gradient, or the **second derivative**. Derivative techniques usually produce images of remotely sensed data which bear little resemblance to the landscape in a scene, and are difficult to use as a result. Such images of remotely sensed data are not illustrated here. However, in geophysics it can be very useful to render aeromagnetic data as images (Ch. 8) and then convert these into images of the variation in magnetic gradient, or gradient of the gradient over an area.

So far, all the convolution matrices employed have involved symmetrical distributions of weightings. Sometimes asymmetrical weightings are required for specific applications. The most important of these are for enhancing spatial features arranged in different directions. Figure 5.21 shows two asymmetrical filter designs that produce approximately the value of the first derivative in two different directions. Using 3 × 3 matrices it is possible to achieve **directional filtering** to the eight principal points of the compass. Figure 5.22 shows an example of directional filtering to enhance edges running north to south across an image. In fact, edges between 22.5° either side of the chosen direction are preferentially enhanced. Figure 5.22 also demonstrates the suppression of broad tonal variations

1	2	1		0	−1	−2
0	0	0		1	0	−1
−1	−2	−1		2	1	0

(a) **(b)**

Figure 5.21 Directional filters based on square convolution matrices depend on the symmetrical distribution of positive and negative weightings about a particular direction in the image. The results of convolution approximate to the first derivative or gradient in the direction at right angles to the axis of symmetry in the matrix. Positive gradients are normally converted to high DN and negative gradients to low DN. Matrix (a) produces an image of gradient in a northward direction, matrix (b) in a southwestward direction.

and the rendering of edges as if they were shaded topographic features. In this case this helps overcome the directional bias in satellite images due to illumination by the Sun. The **pseudo-shadowing** effect of directional filters is extremely useful in enhancement of non-image data that lack the clues to depth that actual shadows give (Ch. 8).

A danger in convolution filtering is that the filter-weighting designs are only approximations to those that would be feasible in frequency-domain filtering. Moreover, the filters are restricted to rectangular matrices. These deviations from the ideal result in spurious features or **artifacts** appearing in some filtered images. Figure 5.19 contains examples of a common type of artifact, known as **ringing**. In the raw image (Fig. 5.17a) a dark line crossing

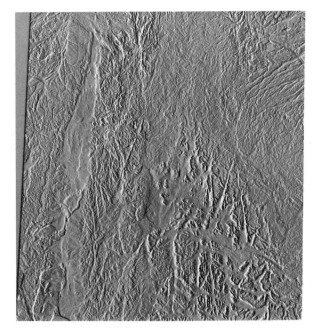

Figure 5.22 The image of Jordan shown in Figure 5.20a has been subjected to an eastward directional first-derivative filter. The resulting image has been smoothed by a 3 × 3 low-pass filter and shows many faults more clearly than Figure 5.20b. However, this enhancement of linear features is at the expense of tonal variations in the original image, which relate to different kinds of surface material. Courtesy of Pat Chavez, US Geological Survey.

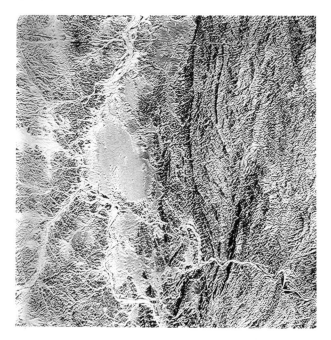

Figure 5.23 Directional filtering by a one-dimensional mean-difference matrix – 1 pixel wide and 27 deep in this case – does highlight N–S edges in this image (see Figure 5.19b for comparison). However, it has produced regular artifacts in two directions, roughly NNE and NNW, which could easily be misidentified as geologically significant features.

pale ground at bottom left is an igneous dyke. On Figure 5.19a this is represented by a dark line with bright fringes on either side, as are other linear features. This is ringing, which in some cases can help detect small edges, but can introduce imaginary features to the interpreter. An even more disturbing type of artifact results from the geometry of the convolution matrix, which can introduce totally new geometric features (Fig. 5.23).

5.4 Data reduction

Apart from the effects of spectral features due to various transitions (Section 1.3), the spectral reflectance curves of natural materials are relatively smooth in the 0.4–2.5 μm range. In most cases a high reflectance in one waveband is matched by similarly high reflectances in the others, which is the result of the overall albedo of the surface. In such cases the data are said to be highly correlated. High correlation indicates that there is a high degree of redundancy among the data – for many purposes the information in one band is very much the same as that in the others. This is illustrated graphically in Figure 5.11, which shows all six reflected bands of Landsat TM data for a scene largely bare of vegetation. A very high proportion of interband variability in scenes with abundant vegetation is caused by the unique and very broad spectral features associated with living plant cells (Section 1.3.3) High correlation between the three bands used to produce a false-colour composite results in little improvement over a single-band image. There is little colour variation. Even where bands have been selected to highlight the effects of known spectral features redundancy can still be a major problem to the interpreter because of the lack of colour contrast and the exploitation of only a limited region in RGB space. Very similar strong correlation between different wavebands can characterize any part of the EM spectrum where the bands are close to one another. In the thermal infrared the correlation is even stronger than in the reflected region because of the close approximation of many natural surfaces to blackbodies. To some extent redundancy in colour images can be overcome by manipulations such as the ISH transform (Section 5.2.2). There are, however, methods that use powerful statistical analysis to re-express the information contained in multispectral data according to its variability, so achieving a full description of the information in fewer variables. This is **data reduction**. Inherent in these methods is the possibility for inflating the data to fill more fully the multidimensional space that they occupy, thereby achieving **decorrelation**. This section explores some of the possibilities.

If DN from one band are plotted against those from another band near to it in the EM spectrum, the majority of points lie on, or near to, a diagonal line passing through the origin of the graph (Fig. 5.12a). The closer the data are to the diagonal, the greater their correlation. Poorly correlated data plot away from the diagonal. The result is an elliptical distribution. Extending this to three bands often reveals the data to be mainly contained within a cigar-shaped ellipsoid (Fig. 5.12b).

A means of improving the spread of data is to redistribute them about another set of axes in multidimensional space, which maximizes the separation of differences in the data (in this case the transform is in Cartesian space, rather than the spherical system of coordinates used in the ISH transform). The most commonly used procedure is **principal component (PC) analysis**, also known as the **Karhunen–Loeve transform** after its originators. In the bivariate scatter shown by Figure 5.24a, the distribution of points can be expressed by the means and variances of the data from the two bands. The **variance** of a single variable expresses the spread of its values about the mean. A measure of the joint variation of two variables is known as their **covariance**. When covariance is positive the data are positively correlated, when negative an inverse relationship is present. When the covariance is zero, the two channels of data are completely independent of each other. For multispectral data the full statistical relationship between all the data is expressed as a **covariance matrix**. This can be expressed in another way as a matrix of **correlation coefficients**.

The first step in a PC transformation is to set the means to zero (Fig. 5.24b) by shifting the axes. At this stage the axes can be rotated so that one coincides with the line along which the data have the greatest spread, that is along the principal axis of the ellipse of data. This new, rotated axis is the first PC (Fig. 5.24c), and the values associated with it are orthogonal projections of the 'raw' data points onto it.

An axis at right angles to this now defines a line along which all the remaining variation is expressed, again by orthogonal projection to the axis from the data points. This is the second PC. In space with more than two dimensions this operation continues to define orthogonal axes that progressively consume all the variation that does not project onto lower order PCs, giving as many PCs as there were original channels of data. The mathematics to achieve this uses an expression of the intervariability of the constituent 'raw' data bands, either the covariance or the correlation matrix. The results from the two alternative 'driving' statistics are slightly different, though the reasons need not be explained here (for simplicity the covariance matrix is used). In short, PC analysis is a little like finding the axes of a deformed pebble and measuring them for strain analysis, one big difference being that it deals with hyperspace.

The original n bands of data are projected onto n new PCs as linear, additive combinations by using **eigenvectors** that are derived from the 'driving' statistics. Each eigenvector is a loading factor for the contribution of each band to a component. Table 5.1 includes a matrix of eigenvectors for each band and each new PC. The value assigned to a

Table 5.1 Eigenvectors for each principal component of the Landsat TM data shown in Figure 5.25 indicate the relative loadings of the different bands in each component. The eigenvalues indicate the relative proportion of the overall scene variance encompassed by each component.

Band/PC	Eigenvalues	Eigenvectors					
		1	2	3	4	5	7
PC1	2242	0.27	0.21	0.37	0.31	0.68	0.42
PC2	284	0.58	0.32	0.40	0.27	−0.48	−0.32
PC3	18	−0.48	−0.11	0.11	0.67	0.18	−0.52
PC4	11	−0.44	0.01	0.37	0.23	−0.50	0.60
PC5	6	0.31	−0.14	−0.67	0.57	−0.16	0.29
PC6	1	−0.27	0.91	0.32	0.00	0.00	0.00

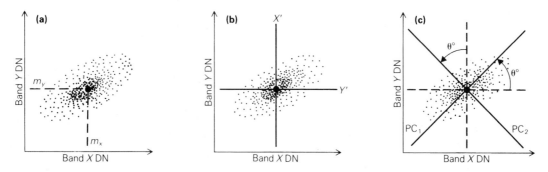

Figure 5.24 Bivariate plots of data from any two bands in the visible and near-infrared generally produce an elongate ellipse of points (a) because of strong correlation. Principal component analysis begins by shifting the origin of the plot to the point defining the means (m_x, m_y) of the two sets of data (b). The axes are then rotated through an angle θ so that one is aligned with the maximum variance in the data (c). This axis becomes the first principal component onto which new values of the data, combining contributions from both bands, are projected. The second axis expresses the variance that cannot be expressed by the first principal component. When these residual data are projected onto this axis they comprise DN for the second principal component.

pixel's PC is simply obtained by adding together the results of multiplying the DN for each band with its associated eigenvector (the rows in Table 5.1). As well as transposing the axes through the *n* bands of data, the covariance matrix is transformed too, so that the covariances between the resulting PCs are set to zero. In other words, the PCs are decorrelated. The variation within the 'raw' data is recast as variances on the PCs, which are known as **eigenvalues**. The

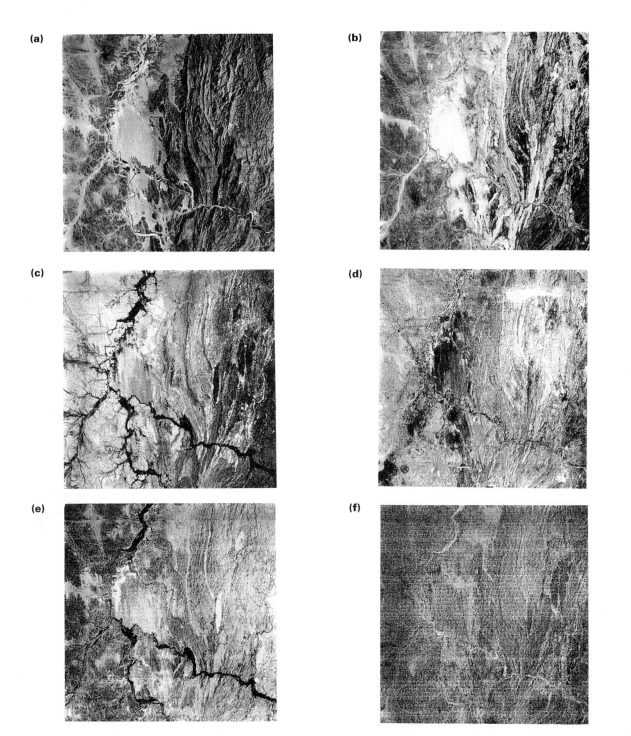

Figure 5.25 Images (a) to (f) represent data in the six principal components that are possible for Landsat TM reflected data. They cover the same area as Figure 5.11. The high quality of the image of the first principal component results from the expulsion of noise to higher order components, and from combination of highly correlated contributions from all six TM bands. The bulk of noise resides in the sixth PC (f). The other PCs are additions of each band weighted by the respective eigenvectors as explained in the text. A false-colour image derived from these data is shown in *Figure 5.26*.

highest eigenvalue is associated with the first PC, and progressively lower eigenvalues are associated with each higher order PC. From Figure 5.24c it is clear that the values assigned to a PC can be positive or negative. For them to be displayed as an image means expressing the range of values in the familiar 0–255 range using a look-up table of some kind.

The result from highly correlated data is that the first PC is generally a weighted average of all the data, and in the case of reflected data approximates an image of the albedo and topography in the range covered by the remote-sensing system. For thermal data the first PC is dominated by surface temperature variations. Because they are often highly correlated, atmospheric effects reside in the first component. The higher order components express deviations of various kinds from this average, and contain information relating to the geological and vegetation variations in the scene. Any noise in the data, being the only completely uncorrelated component, is contained in the higher order components. Figure 5.25 shows the six PCs derived from the data shown in Figure 5.11, after they have been scaled to the 0–255 range. The decrease in variance and increase in noisiness as the order of the components increases is obvious. The great question is: 'What do these new images mean, after such a convoluted process?'

Some sense can be made of the images by examining the eigenvectors or the relative loadings of each input band for each component. As Table 5.1 shows, the loadings are all positive and high for the first component, indicating that it expresses the average of all the bands quite closely. However, for the other components there is a mixture of positive and negative, and low and high eigenvectors. Understanding these patterns means returning to specific features in spectra (Ch. 1). Considering vegetation first, this has a uniquely high reflectance in band 4 and a low one in band 3, relative to soils and rocks (Fig. 1.15). A component that has a high positive eigenvector for band 4 and a high negative value for band 3 (e.g. PC5 in Table 5.1), or the converse, is clearly expressing variations in vegetation density. Figure 5.25e shows bright features along drainage that relate to vegetation as predicted. In the first case it would appear as bright, in the second as dark. The reflectance high in band 5 and the absorption by clay minerals in band 7 (Fig. 1.9), would be characterized similarly in a component containing information about clay variability (e.g. PC4 in Table 5.1). Figure 5.25d shows dark areas, but to know if the prediction is correct would mean field checks in this case. Much the same argument for the spectral characters of ferric iron minerals in the visible and VNIR (Fig. 1.7) can help identify a component that expresses iron variability. Unfortunately, things are rarely that simple, and the eigenvectors are generally only a guide to understanding PC images.

Because the effect of PC analysis is to compress the variance of the original data into the lower order components, it can be used to reduce the number of variables that must be analysed. This is useful for data from systems which produce several channels, such as Landsat TM and airborne systems. However, since important information for very small parts of a scene may lurk in the higher order components, it is important to check all components carefully. The PC approach will undoubtedly be essential in analysing the huge volumes of hyperspectral data from AVIRIS and HIRIS imaging spectrometers. With such a wealth of data there are many possible combinations to examine, and confusion is inevitable using simple band techniques. Various strategies can be devised that perform separate PC analyses in different parts of the spectrum to cram information from many bands that are specific to single-surface variables into one or two components. These then become 'indicators' of individual spectral features and minerals of interest.

Principal components may be displayed in any combination as red, green and blue to produce a false-colour image. Instead of the frequently limited range of colours resulting from normal band composites, a vivid array is common (*Fig. 5.26*). This effect of the decorrelation process can be extremely useful in separating subtly different categories of surface. However, the colours bear little relation to the true composition and EM properties of the surface. To explain them would mean grappling with the intricacies of the eigenvector matrix. Moreover, no two scenes are alike, and the covariance matrices, for each produce unique sets of components. So, images of different terrains and images of the same scene acquired on different dates will not show similar geological materials in the same way. Rather than attempting to identify the reasons for the appearance of specific divisions of the surface that are not seen in conventional images, it is better to use colour PC images to map those divisions and the structures that they reveal arbitrarily, and then seek reasons for their separation in the field. There are other strategies though.

5.4.1 Decorrelation stretching

Figure 5.27 shows in two-band form the principle of **decorrelation** or **D-stretching**. Figure 5.27a shows two highly correlated bands relative to original band axes and to new PC axes. Figure 5.12a and Section 5.2.2 explain why there are limits to the exploitation of RGB colour space by simple contrast stretching. The rotation of axes involved in PC analysis enables the cloud of data to be stretched in two direction at right angles, instead of just along the major axis of the original elliptical distribution. The space defined by the new axes can be filled more efficiently (Fig. 5.27b and c). Simply by rotating the axes back to their original position in band space (Fig. 5.27d) results in an extreme, and otherwise impossible, stretch of the data. Moreover, this procedure retains the relative position of the pixels in the original cloud. This means, in a three-dimensional case, that a colour image can be stretched by this means to give nearly all conceivable colours, without altering the basic colours of each type of surface in the scene. This is achieved by stretching the PCs to the full 0–255 range and then reversing the transform. Complex as it might seem, in practice this merely involves adding together the products of all the stretched PCs and their associated eigenvectors – the rows in Table 5.1 – for each band to produce the new D-stretched bands. As an example, band 1 is reconstructed by adding the products of each PC and its associated eigenvector in the first column. *Figure 5.28* shows a D-stretched version of *Figure 5.10c* for comparison with *Figure 5.14*. The effect is quite similar. However, some of the unique possibilities presented by this technique have been used to sharpen the image and to reduce the noise that is inevitable in extreme stretches.

As in the manipulation of intensity in the ISH stretch, the first PC can be sharpened by edge enhancement (Section 5.3) and all atmospheric haze removed by careful contrast stretching. However, since noise is distributed in the higher order PCs, especially in the last one (Fig. 5.25f), noise reduction is possible. This can be achieved by using **median filters** (Appendix B) on noisy PCs before the inverse transform. Because the highest PC rarely contains any meaningful information, it can simply be omitted from the inverse transform, thereby achieving a dramatic reduction in speckle and striping resulting from sensor malfunctions.

5.5 Band ratioing

Just as the data in an image can be displayed as grey-tone images of single bands, or as three-band colour images, they can be shown as various arithmetic combinations. The most useful of these combinations is the **ratio** of one band to another. It is prepared simply by dividing the DN of each pixel in one band by that in another band. Theoretically this should produce a range of new values for the pixel from zero to infinity, since some DN will have zero values. Because of the restricted range in each band of data and the strong correlation between bands, in practice ratios seldom fall outside the range 0.25–4.0. In order to display the ratio these values must be rescaled to the 0–255 range.

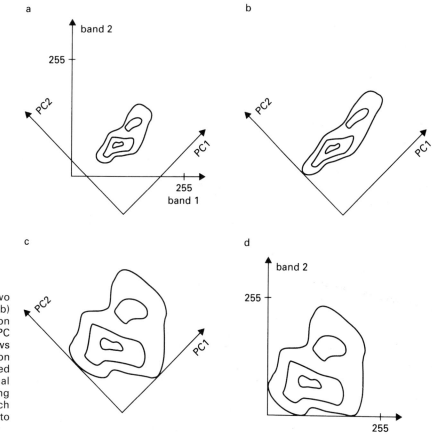

Figure 5.27 (a) A bivariate plot of two bands with PC axes superimposed. In (b) the first PC has been stretched after rotation of the axes to PC space, the second PC having been stretched in (c). This shows how it is possible to produce a decorrelation of the data in PC space. (d) The decorrelated data have been rotated back to original band space, the original correlation having been drastically reduced, although each pixel is still in its original position relative to all the others. Compare with Figure 5.12.

145

Because random noise in different bands is often uncorrelated, ratios for pixels with spurious DN in either the numerator or denominator band produce extreme values. This enhances noise and most ratio images suffer from strong speckling and striping. They can be 'cleaned up' using the digital processes described in Appendix B. Because the contribution from atmospheric effects (Section 1.3.1) varies with wavelength, ratioing also tends to accentuate its degrading effects on images. So, before ratios are calculated the bands involved should be corrected for atmospheric scattering (Section 5.2).

A common problem on remotely sensed images is the effect of varying illumination caused by topography. A flat horizontal surface is illuminated homogeneously by the Sun. Where there is any appreciable relief, slopes facing the Sun are more strongly lit than horizontal surfaces, and those facing away from the Sun receive less radiation. As a result a surface with uniform reflectance properties will show varying DN across a scene. In a scene with many different surface types this can lead to added confusion in both detailed visual interpretation and computer-assisted classification (Section 5.6.1) using bands by themselves.

Theoretically any surface should receive the same proportions of energy in all wavebands irrespective of its orientation to the Sun. It should also reflect energy in the proportions controlled by its spectral reflectance properties. Therefore, the ratio between two bands for pixels containing the same kind of surface should be the same, no matter in which direction the slope faces. For this to be true the surface must reflect radiation equally in all directions. In nature this behaviour is uncommon and reflection

reaches a maximum in a direction controlled by the structure of the surface and the angle of illumination. Another disruptive factor is the effect of illumination by diffuse radiation from the atmosphere. The radiation from this source, which is responsible for the illumination in deep shadow, has a variable contribution to the whole scene. As its spectral range is different from direct solar radiation, because it stems from wavelength-dependent scattering, it changes the ratios from different slopes in a subtle fashion. Nevertheless, a ratio image reduces the effects of slope and shadows to a marked degree (Fig. 5.29), and atmospheric correction before ratio generation reduces the effect considerably. Very much the same arguments hold for surfaces that vary in their albedo but have similar spectral properties. They will appear very differently in band images, but are expressed in the same way in a ratio image (Fig. 5.30).

In these advantages lie some of the disadvantages of ratioing. In its 'ironing-out' of topographic effects and the suppression of differences in albedo, ratioing can also hide important information. However, image processing is one endeavour in which it is possible to get a free lunch, or maybe even two. By using the ISH transform (Section 5.2.2), the colour in a ratio image is expressed by saturation and hue. The 'lack' of spatially important information and the wealth of noise inevitable in ratioing finds its way into intensity. One ruse to restore spatially important information is to replace the intensity from the ISH transformation of three ratios with a suitably stretched and edge-enhanced band. An example of this technique is shown in *Figure 5.31*.

The most important property of a ratio image is that features in the spectral signature curve of a particular

(a)   **(b)**

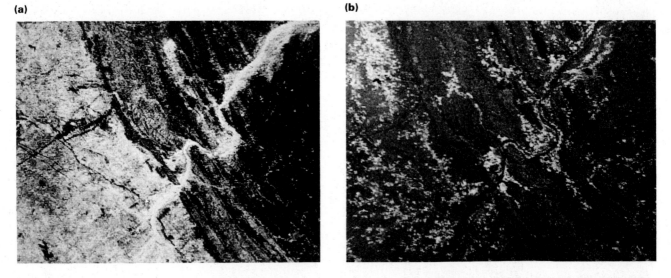

Figure 5.29 An image of enhanced Landsat MSS band 7 data for an area in South India (a) shows patches of strong reflectance which could be either bare soil or healthy vegetation. Displaying an image of the band 7/band 5 ratio (b) exploits the spectral properties of vegetation to highlight vegetated areas and to give some indication of the proportions of plant cover to bare soil. Pixels devoid of vegetation have the lowest value of the ratio and appear dark, whereas the brightest pixels have dense green vegetation cover.

surface material are accentuated. If the bands used are chosen to cover peaks, absorption troughs and changes in slope on the curve then they can be combined in pairs as ratios to express aspects of the material's spectral signature. The simplest example relates to vegetation. Plant spectra are characterized by a combination of the chlorophyll absorption feature in the red part of the spectrum and the strong reflection of infrared in the 0.7–1.2 μm range by living cells (Section 1.3.3). In images of Landsat MSS,

band 5 and band 7 pixels containing a high proportion of plants will appear dark and light respectively. In a standard false-colour composite image they will stand out from bare soil or rock as strongly red-coloured areas. Within these fairly obvious areas may be all sorts of variations. The proportion of a single species relative to soil may change from place to place. Soil moisture or other environmental variations may affect the health and spectral properties of the species. The type of vegetation may vary, and there

(a)

(b)

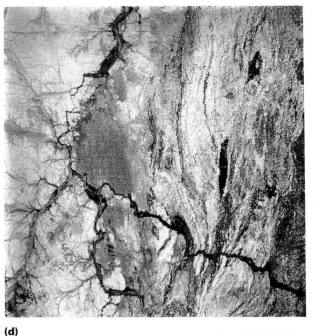

(c)

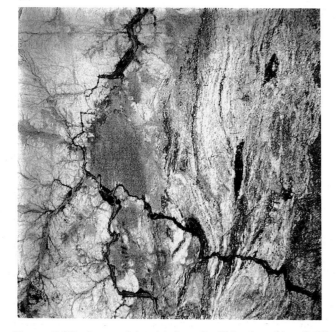

(d)

Figure 5.30 Images (a) to (c) show the TM ratios of bands 5/4, 3/1 and 7/5 compared with a band 3 image (d) for the area on the Sudan–Eritrea border used previously.

may be all manner of combinations of these important factors. In images expressing only data from various wavebands these differences are often concealed, simply because the human eye has a limited range of perception. However, the effect of the surface variations is to change the structure of the spectral reflectance curve. In particular, the depth of the chlorophyll absorption feature, the peak height of infrared reflectance and the gradient of the curve between red and infrared will change. Very small changes in these parameters have a disproportionately large effect on the ratio of band 7 to band 5 (Fig. 5.29). They become easier to evaluate on the ratio image. In vegetation studies ratio images of different kinds are used to estimate the proportion of leaf cover and to help in discriminating between and classifying different species.

In the widest sense ratios between bands describe the 'colour' of an object, although this 'colour' only corresponds to that perceived by humans when the visible range is considered. An important geological example does relate to perceptible colour. The Fe–O charge-transfer transition (Section 1.3.2) is characterized by a broad absorption band at wavelengths less than 0.55 μm. It is responsible for the strong red coloration of rocks rich in iron oxides and hydroxides. Sometimes this coloration is masked by the mixture of iron minerals with large amounts of minerals, such as quartz, which reflect strongly at all wavelengths. The albedo of such a material will be so high that it appears white in a natural- or false-colour image. However, the ratio of red to blue reflectance will enhance the small contribution of iron minerals, giving pixels of iron-bearing rocks a higher value than those composed of pure quartz. In Landsat TM data this corresponds to the band 3/1 ratio. Iron also produces an absorption band between 0.85 and 0.92 μm, owing to a crystal-field effect (Section 1.3.2). This feature falls within the range of Landsat TM band 4, while a reflectance high for all minerals is found in band 5. The ratio of band 5 to band 4 therefore shows higher values for oxidized iron-rich rocks than for other types. The Al–OH and Mg–OH rotational effects associated with clays and other hydroxylated minerals result in absorptions within Landsat TM band 7. By ratioing this band against band 5, clay-rich rocks show up as dark areas. Using Landsat TM data these four spectral features form the practical limit to surface discrimination using ratio techniques even though there are 30 possible ratio combinations of the six reflected bands. Moreover, the large bandwidths mean that only gross differences are separable. Many other features can be investigated using narrower bands within the same reflected range, as from JERS-1 and AVIRIS. Even better control is provided by measurements of spectral reflectance of each of the major surface categories in the field, although this is often impractical. However, to show the potential of the technique the ratios of Landsat TM 5/4, 3/1 and 7/5 are shown in Figure 5.30, together with a single band to show spatial features of the area of study. *Figure 5.31* shows these ratios in colour.

Plants depend on the underlying soils and rocks for their supply of water and nutrients. In their natural state they are sometimes excellent indicators of geology in humid terrains. This may be because certain rocks provide favourable conditions for growth of restricted plant communities, but in some cases the substrate actually threatens the health of plants. This may be caused by anomalously high concentrations of toxic elements, as might be the case in the vicinity of certain mineral deposits. More commonly, however, **stressed vegetation** is merely a response to either waterlogging or a shortage of water, in which case it is generally a seasonal phenomenon. Different plants have different tolerances to environmental stress, so another geologically related feature of vegetation is the development of plant communities specific to particular geological conditions. Both types of biological indicator can be examined most successfully using ratio techniques based on careful scrutiny of field reflectance spectra.

Figure 5.32 shows how the reflectance spectrum of a plant changes with the moisture content of its leaves. The progressive deepening of the absorption features at about 1.45 and 1.9 μm as leaf moisture increases is very clear. Although this portion of the spectrum is masked by atmospheric effects, the related changes in the regions around 1.6 μm relative to the shorter infrared plateau and in the 2.2 μm region suggest that ratios could be devised to highlight variable moisture stress. With Landsat TM data the 4/5 and 5/7 ratios should increase as leaf-moisture content increases. **Geochemical stress**, resulting either from shortages of essential nutrients or from the presence of toxic compounds, sometimes results in the near absence of vegetation over the offending rocks and soils (*Fig. 5.33*). More common is the stunting and discoloration of plants growing on them. Disruption of the pigmentation in plants produces shifts in the position of the chlorophyll absorption features associated with the red and blue parts of the

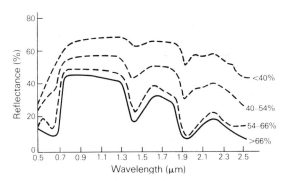

Figure 5.32 The leaves of Indian corn have reflectance spectra which show considerable changes with increasing moisture content. Similar curves have been obtained from various plant species. After Hoffer and Johannsen, 1969.

spectrum. It may also affect the shape of the spectrum near to these features. These signs of geochemical stress are often most discernible at particular stages of plant growth, commonly just before the onset of leaf senescence (Fig. 1.17). At present the wavebands most readily available from satellite and airborne systems are too broad to exploit these changes using ratioing techniques. However, the shifts and distortions are definable by ratios between very narrow bands of data gathered by spectroradiometers (Section 3.9).

The search for plant communities specific to different rock and soil types, and to various agents of stress, can exploit the differences between reflectance spectra of different species. Ratios are an appropriate technique once again. The greatest contrasts between species occur seasonally for only short periods, usually as buds are beginning to break and just before leaf fall (Fig. 1.17). The use of remote sensing for geobotanical investigations is discussed in Chapter 9, but the subtlety of many of the features which are sought requires instruments that are not widely available, and more importantly careful field and laboratory studies of the spectral effects of stress on vegetation.

5.6 Pattern recognition

Research in military and various scientific fields since about 1970 has developed several mathematical means of automatically extracting information from digital images. The techniques fall under the general heading of **artificial intelligence**. They were originally devised to aid in the recognition of specific objects, such as tanks or engineering components, to speed up intelligence gathering and develop robotic vision. Such **pattern recognition** is focused on three main aspects. First is the detection of different kinds of surface materials, such as camouflage or colour-coded objects, which relies on the tonal or spectral characteristics of images. Of equal importance is the discrimination of distinctive shapes, such as warships or tanks, from natural spatial patterns. Third is the recognition of changes in an area with time, as in the case of the progressive build-up of military forces or the redeployment of missile silos. Although most of the software involved stemmed from the military, medical and engineering communities, much of it is very useful in environmental science applications.

Because geological features are so variable and since they are often masked by soils and vegetation, visual interpretation, even by an experienced person, is often ambiguous. This is made even more of a problem by the sheer number of theories which a geologist can use in assessing the context of features on an image, together with individual bias. Artificial intelligence and pattern recognition now open up the possibility of geologists training computers to make some geological decisions in a less biased way.

5.6.1 Spectral pattern recognition

The computer-assisted recognition of surface materials, commonly called **classification**, is based on their spectral properties. These are best expressed by spectral reflectance curves (Fig. 5.34). These are semicontinuous spectra produced by narrow-waveband spectroradiometers, but the digital data in most easily available multispectral images are from discrete, usually quite wide, bands. Consequently the subtle features of a material's spectrum are degraded to average DN for spaced-out portions of the range in question. As explained earlier, the wavebands are usually selected to highlight specific kinds of spectral feature for specific materials. Instead of a complete spectrum, the variation of a material's reflectance with wavelength can be represented crudely by a simple bar chart for each band (Fig. 5.35).

Inspection of Figures 5.34 and 5.35 suggests that a crude discrimination between some of the different surface types could be achieved using data from only one band. For instance, vegetation and rocks have low and high reflectances respectively in Landsat TM band 3. There are also differences between the different rock types in this band and the other four bands. The rock differences can be enhanced further by ratio techniques (Section 5.5). However, things are never as simple as they might seem. The bars and spectral curves relate only to specific localities within a scene, and are average results. Over the whole scene the reflectance properties of the different surface categories vary within limits determined by natural variations in the materials themselves and mixtures between materials. If small areas known to be composed of each class were examined, the DN of pixels within them would themselves be distributed in different histograms expressing this variation in each of the bands concerned. Figure 5.36 shows that the overall histogram in one band is built up from many individual peaks. Many of these 'sub-histograms' overlap. Some are narrow and others are broad. Each may be described by the mean DN for the category which it represents and the variance, which expresses the spread of DN within a category.

Inspection of the histograms for different surface categories allows different ranges of DN in the overall histogram to be assigned to those categories or groups of categories which can be separated by this means. These ranges can be highlighted on an image by assigning a colour to each and displaying each pixel whose DN falls within the range as the appropriate colour. This simplification of the data, in effect a crude classification, is called **density slicing** (*Fig. 5.37*). Where an area is composed of only a few, very distinct surface types, this can be a rapid and accurate means of mapping the distribution of each

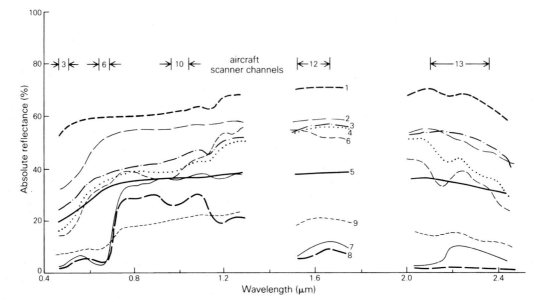

Figure 5.34 Superimposed on the reflectance spectra of a number of surface materials from Utah are some of the wavebands available from an airborne multispectral scanner. From Podwysocki *et al.* (1983).

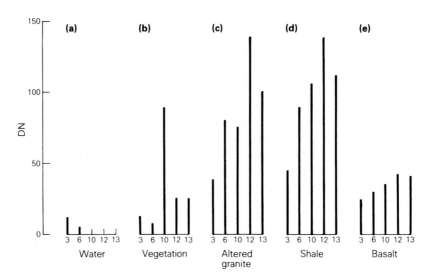

Figure 5.35 Spectral reflectance curves can be represented crudely by bar charts corresponding to DN in the restricted number of wavebands covered by most imaging systems. In this case (a) represents water, (b) vegetation, (c) hydrothermally altered granite, (d) shale and (e) basalt. The waveband numbers shown are those in Figure 5.34.

type. More often it is used to simplify a scene to assess gross variations, or to express continuous variation in a single type of surface. One example of the last application is density slicing of the Landsat MSS band 7/band 5 ratio to express variations in density of vegetation cover. Another is slicing the DN range of blue or green reflected radiance from the bed of a body of clear water to express bathymetric variations (Section 1.3.4, *Fig. 1.18*).

Figures 5.34 and 5.35 show that some surface categories display contrasted reflectance at different wavelengths. For example, vegetation has high DN in band 4 and low in band

3. Using two bands of data, selected because of such contrasts, can enhance differences between categories and improve their separability. This is shown diagrammatically in Figure 5.38a. To train a computer to make these separations means giving it a set of rules on which to base 'yes' or 'no' decisions. The simplest means of doing this is to divide the bivariate distribution into rectangular boxes (Fig. 5.38b). The boundaries of the boxes represent the ranges of DN for the two bands within small, known areas of the interesting surface categories. Such areas are selected during field work and are termed **training areas**, because

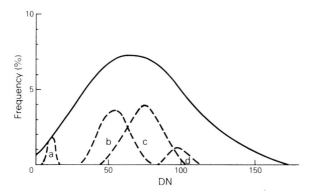

Figure 5.36 The histogram of one band for a whole scene conceals within it smaller histograms for particular classes of surface. In this case (a) to (d) are hypothetical classes.

they are used to train the computer. The computer compares the DN of unknown pixels with the boxes. If they fall within one they are assigned to the relevant class. If they fall in none then they remain unclassified, and possibly indicate a need to refine the means of classifying or increase the number of classes. The same principle can be applied to any number of dimensions, and usually is. This is known as **parallelpiped** or **box classification**. An important limitation is that natural categories generally plot as ellipsoids in N-dimensional space, and parallelpipeds are only a crude representation of this. A refinement is to represent the volume occupied by the data from training areas by an assembly of smaller parallelpipeds (Fig. 5.38c).

Providing the computer with a more sophisticated set of rules for decisions of the 'yes, if' type means employing the statistics of data from training areas. The simplest of these classification routines is to identify the mean DN for each training-area category in each band being used. The distance from each of these means in N-dimensional space of an unknown pixel can then be calculated. The pixel is assigned to the class with the closest mean. This **minimum distance to means classification** is shown for the two-dimensional case in Figure 5.38d. A refinement of this is to bring the variance of DN within training areas into play. If the DN within a training area are assumed to form normal distributions for each band, the histograms can be considered to be bell-shaped. Depending on the variance (a measure of the width of the distribution), the further a DN is from the mean the less the probability that it represents the category in question. In the two-dimensional case (Fig. 5.38e) DN from a training area define an elliptical cluster. Each cluster can be contoured to show how the probability decreases away from the mean point. This is expressed more graphically as a 'topography' of probability in Figure 5.38f. The plot of DN from an unknown pixel can then be assessed in this probabilistic context by the computer. It calculates the likelihood of the pixel belonging to each of the predefined classes and assigns it to that class where

the likelihood is maximized. This method is known as **maximum-likelihood classification**. The three basic spectral classification methods shown in Figure 5.38 form the basis for more sophisticated methods that are beyond the scope of this book, but more information can be gained from the further reading at the end of the chapter.

Before making a maximum-likelihood classification, an interpreter may be able to assess roughly how much of a scene is likely to be occupied by each surface category. This may result from field observations or from a rapid inspection of an image. This crude estimate can then be used to **weight** the probabilities involved in the classification. For example, beach sand will be limited to narrow strips around bodies of water. The probability of any randomly selected pixel being beach sand is therefore low, and its calculated probability in that context is given a low weighting. Conversely, vegetation in a humid climate is very common, so the probability of any pixel being classified as such is given a high weighting. Another anticipated factor is that not all real surface categories are represented in the training areas. The classification can be weighted accordingly so that the computer does not try to force 100% of the scene into classes. Both these refinements help to ensure that the classification is as close to reality as permitted by the quality of the data and the precision of the classification method.

All the above classification methods rely on the operator making decisions about the areas on the ground which are most representative of the surface categories of interest. This approach is termed **supervised classification**. It is possible to allow the computer to examine the data in each band and sort out particular correlations amongst them. This in effect means dividing the N-dimensional histogram into arbitrary segments purely on the basis of heterogeneities in the distribution of DN. The operator can control the sharpness and number of the divisions, but basically leaves the computer to its own devices in assigning pixels to different classes. This is **unsupervised classification**, and expresses differences purely on the basis of spectral properties. It is useful in totally unknown areas, when it provides the operator with a means of identifying spectrally different kinds of terrain. This can then orient the future field work, or be used as an adjunct to more conventional visual interpretation of the image.

Usually, the more independent variables, or dimensions used in a classification, the more easily spectrally distinct classes can be separated. However, in the 0.4–2.5 μm range there is a high degree of correlation between bands. This is quite clear from the spectral reflectance curves in Figure 5.34, particularly those for rocks. Differences are expressed in only one or two bands – that around 0.8–0.9 μm with an absorption feature related to electronic transitions in iron minerals such as limonite and that around 2.2 μm for the OH^- vibrational transition. These bands are the main means

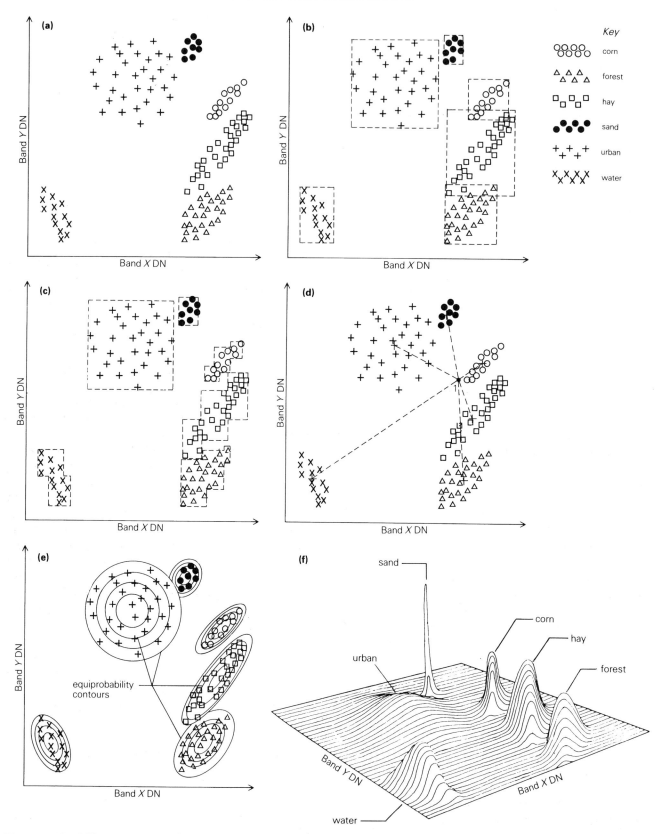

Figure 5.38 Different methods of spectral classification can be represented diagrammatically by reference to bivariate plots of two of the bands employed. In (a) several clusters in the data correspond to areas with different kinds of surface. The simple parallelpiped classification is shown in (b), that based on more precise boundaries for each class in (c), and (d) represents the minimum-distance-to-means method. The contours in (e) express the probability that any point belongs to a particular class, which is the basis of the maximum-likelihood method of classification. The probabilities are illustrated more graphically as a three-dimensional topology in (f).

of discriminating iron-rich and clay-rich rocks from others. By themselves these bands would perform a reasonably precise classification. It might seem that using all the bands available from a remote-sensing system would sharpen the discrimination even further. However, the effect of strong interband correlation is to dilute the contribution of the most discriminating data. What happens in practice in this part of the EM spectrum is that as the number of bands used for classification increases beyond a certain limit the accuracy of the results actually declines. A strategy needs to be devised to use only those bands which do the job well. In the case illustrated by Figure 5.35, the best approach using just raw data would be to employ bands 4 and 7 to separate the rocks and band 3 to separate rocks from vegetation. This approach also speeds up the operation of the software involved.

An irritating problem with classification based on spectral data alone is the variation in DN due to varying illumination. In terrain of high relief or where Sun elevation is low, the presence of many shadows disrupts the process. Moreover, the spectra of rocks contain only subtle features which can be hidden in the natural variations. Variation in illumination is reduced by ratioing, and if the bands involved are chosen carefully ratios can enhance these subtleties (Section 5.5). Another advantage of ratio techniques is that they combine data from several bands in a smaller number of parameters, thereby improving classification. A disadvantage is that they have a low signal to noise ratio, which tends to counteract some of their advantages, noise pixels being misclassified.

It can be seen from Figure 5.38e that four of the six categories overlap completely in the bands defining the horizontal and vertical axes, even though the overall separation looks good. Unfortunately, computers do not have eyes and work systematically with Cartesian coordinates in this case. A classification based on Figure 5.38e would not be very good. If, however, the data could somehow be plotted on other axes, so that differences are maximized, it would improve the classification based on two bands alone. A far more powerful approach is to perform a PC analysis before classification. This not only derives new axes, but also expands the data to fill *N*-dimensional space as fully as possible. More important still, it combines together the highly correlated parts of the *N*-dimensional distribution along the different axes (Section 5.4). Thus the number of axes containing significant data is reduced automatically. Each axis has a contribution from all the bands and the new data sets are uncorrelated. This can be improved still further by a deliberate attempt to arrange the new axes to maximize separation between the fields of known classes. Normal analysis relies on the covariance matrix from the complete range of data. It is also possible to restrict the range of DN to known parts of the scene which contain surface types which the interpreter wishes to discriminate

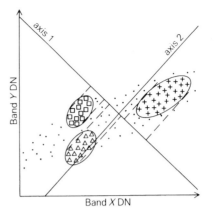

Figure 5.39 Lying within the highly correlated ellipse of data on this bivariate plot of DN for two bands are three classes of surface that need to be separated. It is clear that classification based on the two axes shown would produce confusion between the classes. However, by basing a PC analysis on the means and covariances of data from within training areas of these classes produces new canonical axes which maximize the differences between them.

over the whole scene. The means and covariances from such a training area are used to perform the transformation. Figure 5.39 shows PC axes placed to maximize the ability to discriminate three types of surface by such a **canonical analysis**.

Spectral pattern recognition for geological applications may be divided into two main approaches. One is to map surface classes that correspond to several different kinds of underlying rock. This can be useful in producing a reconnaissance lithofacies map of a whole area, to be refined by field checking. In other words, the common rocks are sought. An example of this approach is given in *Figure 5.40*. Another strategy is to use classification to pick out those small, usually imperceptible, areas on an image that contain rare but distinctive rock types. This is of great importance in commercial mineral exploration. First, ore deposits are unusual rarities by definition. Second, to find them by painstaking field survey is slow and expensive, especially in poorly known areas. If the area of exploration can be narrowed by classification of remotely sensed data, even if it is quite imprecise, so much the better for all concerned. The geologists, geochemists and geophysicists in particular are then able to concentrate their talents much more cost-effectively.

Whether or not a particular patch of a surface category can be classified accurately depends on its size relative to the spatial resolution of the imaging system. It also depends on its contrast to the surrounding surface. In many cases an individual pixel's DN is contributed to by several surface components whose sizes are less than that of the pixel itself (Fig. 3.11). The DN of such a mixed pixel is an average of those of each of its components weighted by their relative size and their contrast. Strongly contrasted components may have such an effect on the pixel that their contributions to its DN are disproportionately large compared with their actual size. Under certain conditions very small isolated areas can therefore be detected and classified.

All this may seem to suggest that the geologist is becoming a redundant part of the analysis, except as a computer supervisor. That is hardly the case. Except in the most arid terrains with little superficial cover, rock outcrops are really quite rare, though often very prominent. They are mantled to various degrees by soil and vegetation (Fig. 5.41). Although vegetation and soils may be related to rock type, even uniquely in some cases, the geologist requires an outline of where different rocks are present beneath the veneer. Even in areas of complete exposure classification faces problems in the range of wavelengths covered in this chapter. In deserts thin surface veneers of manganese and iron oxides known as desert varnish coat rock surfaces which, irrespective of their composition, appear dark in visible and near-infrared images. A similar problem is encountered with highly reflective encrustations of salts formed by evaporation. In some areas of diverse vegetation and soil cover the only possibility in classification is to select subclasses within each lithological category, such as bare rock, derived soil and vegetated surfaces with different degrees of plant cover. More often than not so many classes would be required that the results are so confusing as not to repay the effort expended. The only option is to visually interpret enhanced images of different kinds on the traditional basis of colour, texture, pattern and geological context. In the majority of applications this is the dominant approach, aided only where appropriate by judicious use of spectral pattern recognition.

5.6.2 *Spatial pattern recognition*

The surface texture of different rock types, as expressed by drainage networks, colour banding and mottling for instance, is an important parameter in photointerpretation (Ch. 4). It represents the spatial distribution of tone variations. It predominates where tone or DN in an image varies with a high frequency. Where low frequencies dominate, textural analysis is secondary in importance to evaluation of tone. As introduced in Chapter 2, human vision is very perceptive in recognizing textural features. However, it is very difficult for an interpreter to make accurate decisions on the boundaries between areas of subtly different texture – different interpreters would place the boundaries in different places. The use of computer-assisted measures of image textures, although very difficult and time-consuming, may add to the power of image classification. One method is to calculate the **variance** of DN within predetermined square boxes across an image. High variance suggests fine, sharp textures, whereas low variance indicates coarse, smooth textures. Another approach is to extract different spatial frequencies from an image using a variety of filters. Each expresses different kinds of texture, and the different images can form the basis for a semiquantitative classification of texture (Ch. 7).

One approach is to use statistical measures of the spatial frequency of variations in DN. To do this means that limits have to be set on gradients of DN and the spacing between changes in gradient must be represented in some way. This approach is likely to become increasingly useful in geological applications. Another line of attack is to use mathematical expressions of the spatial structure of the data. Basically, a sort of mathematical grammar is devised to describe each spatial pattern in the image data in terms of its parts. Each subpattern is broken down to its components, the smallest distinguishable category of which comprises **primitives**. Primitives may be the result of some kind of statistical approach to textural features. They are signified to the computer by a mathematical 'sentence', and each class of patterns is described by a set of such sentences. So far the use of pattern recognition of this kind has focused on simple or predictable patterns such as print characters in document image processing, chromosomes and military objects. Simple pattern recognition has been applied to geometric features in geology, such as the detection of circular and linear features. While these are of considerable importance, the fact is that such features are found equally as easily by visual inspection (Ch. 2), and the automated methods often find spurious features.

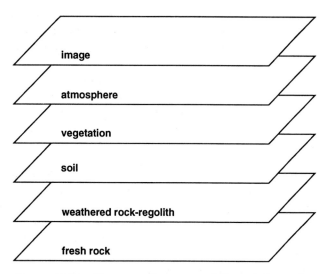

Figure 5.41 Diagrammatic representation of the various possible layers that obscure or cryptify true geological relationships. To this may be added the limited number of mineral types that easily acquired remotely sensed data can distinguish. Even if completely bare of cover rocks can rarely be classified on standard petrographic grounds by remote sensing alone.

Where a precise classification scheme exists for extremely complex patterns and textures, as in the case of fingerprints, considerable advances have been made. The problem with geological patterns is that, as well as being complex in their own right, they are also part of a complex whole. They have to be detected as well as being described and classified. Fingerprints are not detected by computers, they are sought, found and photographed by detectives. Elegant though automated spatial pattern recognition may be, it remains to be seen if it can be developed for new geological applications. More important is the question of whether it will repay the effort in comparison with the biased, but extremely effective, analysis by trained geological interpreters. One great difference between the military pattern analyst and the geologist is that the former is generally not permitted to visit the site of interest!

The spatial variation of DN in an image can be used in another way that might pay dividends for geological interpretation, that is by extending the methods of spectral pattern recognition using the concept of context. A particular pixel on a surface may be classified better if there is some knowledge of the classification of its surroundings. **Contextual classification** at its simplest consists of using the classification of other neighbouring pixels to weight the classification algorithm. The computer performs a check of results within a specified radius in order to achieve this. Conceivably it could be improved to take into account the context of other associated classes. Thus a pixel which could be either granite or sandstone on the basis of its spectral properties would be most likely to be sandstone if it were near to pixels identified unambiguously as limestone.

Any classification seeks to locate the boundaries between surface areas of different types and the extent of areas of each class as accurately as possible. A means of doing this is **image segmentation**. It consists of creating areas of several pixels that show spectral similarities. In a simple example a box of predetermined size passes over the image and tests the pixels falling within it for similarity according to the analyst's instructions. It is a technique that finds a ready use in analysis of imaging spectrometer data, such as those from AVIRIS, where the spectra of individual pixels are compared with spectral libraries of diagnostic minerals, such as different hydroxyl-bearing minerals (*Fig. 5.42*). Either the spectra are matched directly or a kind of mathematical shorthand for the spectral shapes is devised to speed up the comparisons. If they fall within predetermined bounds of similarity they are grouped together as members of a class. The effect is to cause areas with similarity to spectral categories to grow to their predetermined spectral limits. By combining this approach with a means of edge detection (Section 5.3), the growth of areas of each class can be stopped at what are hoped to be natural boundaries in the scene. This approach is most successful in images where the surface categories are distinct and spectrally homogeneous, as in agricultural land. As emphasized in Section 5.6.1, geological classes are often spectrally heterogeneous.

5.6.3 Change detection

The monitoring of changes at the Earth's surface by the use of images recorded on several dates – **multitemporal analysis** – has been important for studies of vegetation, cultural and military features throughout the history of remote sensing. With photographic data it consists simply of visual comparison. The advent of regular repetitive digital imaging, first from meteorological satellites then from the early Landsats, meant that more automated methods became possible. Most applications have been for analysis of the evolution of weather systems, crop rotation and diseases, changes in land-use patterns and many other topics for which these satellites were designed. One of the two main methods of analysis is based on detection of spectral changes in fixed surface materials. One example exploits the seasonal changes in vegetation canopy which can discriminate between different species, if the correct times for comparison are chosen. Another is detection of spatial change at the surface, such as the replacement of agricultural land by buildings, or the development of military installations. At its simplest the comparison is achieved by flicking from an image taken at one time to that taken at another.

Early in the Landsat programme it became clear that there was considerable potential for exploiting images taken at different times of year in geological investigations. As seasonal climates become more contrasted so lithologically controlled variations in soil moisture and vegetation become more variable during the year. Increasing soil moisture in bare areas results in lower reflectance in all bands, whereas increasing vegetation cover increases infrared reflectance and diminishes that in red and blue bands. The differences are clearest between dry- and wet-season images (*Fig. 5.43*). For most purposes geologists exploit these differences in selecting an optimum time of year when geological information content is highest. In some climates the dry season is best because wet-season images are masked by vegetation, often with agricultural patterns. Others show geology better just after the wet season when soil and rock moisture varies most, according to porosity, and natural vegetation is strongly controlled by it.

Highlighting differences by using data from two or more seasons can be a very powerful technique. As well as expanding the variety of geologically related information it can show up geobotanical anomalies related to different kinds of geochemical stress and selective growth of plants. Since the spectral effects may be at a maximum for only short periods, dates of imagery need to be chosen carefully. Sometimes particularly severe weather in one year is the only reason why such phenomena are detectable, and comparison is made between several years as well as several seasons.

A special case of multitemporal analysis of spectral change is the use of diurnal variations in surface temperature to estimate the thermal inertia of the surface. This is considered separately in Chapter 6.

Short-lived geological and hydrological events can be detected, monitored and assessed by multitemporal analysis. Among these spatial changes are volcanism, faulting, slumping, floods, snow accumulation, glacial advance and retreat, shifts in drainage, sand bars, beaches and dunes, the progress of mining and the spread of subterranean fires. The data used are of the 'before and after' variety. With Landsat data the minimum frequency of imaging of an area of interest is every 16–18 days. The pointability of the SPOT system increases this frequency to once every four days. For really vast events and those of short duration the TIROS-N/NOAA satellites produce coarse resolution data every 6 hours.

The simplest means of automated change detection involves the subtraction of data for one day from that for another. However, this can present problems. Unless the two images have nearly the same structure – similar vegetation and atmospheric conditions – the new data sets can be overwhelmed by non-geological differences. It is best applied to data from the same season for different years. Another method depends on changes being poorly correlated with the rest of the data. They comprise anomalies on plots of DN from the same bands for different dates. Principal component analysis (Section 5.4) of selected bands for two or more dates casts the highly correlated data from the separate images into the first and second components. The major differences due purely to gross seasonal changes in vegetation appear in the second and third components. The unusual, small-scale differences are generally found in higher order components. Although the potential for becoming lost in a labyrinth of decorrelated data sets is high, careful selection of components and their display can highlight small but important changes very strongly.

Further reading

These references are a framework for extending understanding of techniques of digital image processing.

Anuta, P.E. 1977. Computer-assisted analysis techniques for remote sensing data interpretation. *Geophysics* **42**, 468–481.

Berhe, S.M. and D.A. Rothery 1986. Interactive processing of satellite images for structural and lithological mapping in north-east Africa. *Geol. Mag.* **123**, 393–403.

Blodget, H.W. and G.F. Brown 1982. *Geological mapping by use of computer-enhanced imagery in western Saudi Arabia*. US Geol. Surv. Professional Paper 1153.

Buchanan, M.D. and R. Pendgrass 1980. Digital image processing: can intensity, hue and saturation replace red, green and blue? *Electro-Optical Systems Design* **12**, 29–36.

Cañas, A.A.D. and M.E. Barnett 1985. The generation and interpretation of false-colour principal component images. *Int. J. Remote Sens.* **6**, 867–881.

Castleman, K.R. 1977. *Digital image processing*. Englewood Cliffs, New Jersey: Prentice-Hall.

Chavez,. P.S. 1988. An improved dark object subtraction technique for atmospheric scattering correction of multispectral data. *Remote Sens. Environ.* **24**, 459–479.

Chavez, P.S. 1989. Radiometric calibration of Landsat Thematic Mapper multispectral images. *Photogramm. Eng. Remote Sens.* **55**, 1285–1294.

Chavez, P.S. and B. Bauer 1982. An automatic optimum kernel-size selection technique for edge enhancement. *Remote Sens. Environ.* **12**, 23–38.

Chavez, P.S., G.L. Berlin and L.B. Sowers 1982. Statistical method for selecting Landsat MSS ratios. *J. Appl. Photographic Eng.* **8**, 23–30.

Condit, C.D. and P.S. Chavez 1979. *Basic concepts of computerised digital image processing for geologists*. U.S. Geol. Surv. Bull. 1462.

Crippen, R.E. 1988. The dangers of underestimating the importance of data adjustment in band ratioing. *Int. J. Remote Sens.* **9**, 767–776.

Davis, P.A. and G.L. Berlin 1989. Rock discrimination in the complex geologic environment of Jabal Salma, Saudi Arabia, using Landsat Thematic Mapper data. *Photogramm. Eng. Remote Sens.* **55**, 1147–1160.

Drury, S.A. 1985. Applications of digital image enhancement in regional tectonic mapping of South India. *Proc. 18th Int. Symp. Remote Sensing Environment, Paris*, pp. 1895–1904.

Drury, S.A. 1986. Remote sensing of geological structure in temperate agricultural terrains. *Geol. Mag.* **123**, 113–121.

Drury, S.A and G.A. Hunt 1988. Remote sensing of lateritized Archaean greenstone terrain: Marshall Pool area, northeastern Yilgarn Block, Western Australia. *Photogramm. Eng. Remote Sens.* **54**, 1717–1725.

Drury, S.A and G.A. Hunt 1989. Geological uses of remotely sensed reflected and emitted data of lateritized Archaean terrain in Western Australia. *Int. J. Remote Sens.* **10**, 475–497.

Dykstra, J.D. and R.W. Birnie 1979. Reconnaissance geological mapping in Chagai Hills, Baluchistan, Pakistan, by computer processing of Landsat data. *Am. Assoc. Petr. Geol. Bull.* **63**, 1490–1503.

Evans, D. 1988. Multisensor classification of sedimentary rocks. *Remote Sens. Environ.* **25**, 129–144.

Evans, D. and H. Lang 1985. Techniques for multi-sensor image analysis. *Proc. 18th Int. Symp. Remote Sensing Environment, Paris.*

Fabbri, A.G. 1984. *Image processing of geological data.* New York: Van Nostrand Reinholt.

Gillespie, A.R. 1980. Digital techniques of image enhancement. Chapter 6 in *Remote sensing in geology*, Siegal, B.S. and A.R. Gillespie (eds), pp. 139–226. New York: Wiley.

Gillespie, A.R., A.B. Kahle and R.E. Walker 1986. Colour enhancement of highly correlated images. I. Decorrelation and HSI contrast stretches. *Remote Sens. Environ.* **20**, 209–235.

Gillespie, A.R., A.B. Kahle and R.E. Walker 1986. Colour enhancement of highly correlated images. II. Channel ratios and chromaticity transformation techniques. *Remote Sens. Environ.* **22**, 343–365.

Gonzalez, R.C. and P. Wintz, 1977. *Digital image processing.* Reading, Massachusetts: Addison-Wesley.

Hord, R.M. 1982. *Digital image processing of remotely sensed data.* New York: Academic Press.

Hunt, G. A. 1988. Improvements in the forward and inverse principal component transformations for geological mapping in a semi-arid terrain. *Proc. IGARSS Symposium 1988, Remote Sensing: Moving towards the 21st Century.* ESA SP-284, pp. 1061–1062.

Jensen, J.R. 1986. *Introductory digital image processing.* Englewood Cliffs, New Jersey: Prentice-Hall.

Knepper, D.H. Jr and G.L Raines 1985. Determining stretch parameters for lithologic discrimination on Landsat MSS band ratio images. *Photogramm. Eng. Remote Sens.* **51**, 63–70.

Lang, H.R., S.L. Adams, J.E. Conel, B.A. McGuffie, E.D. Paylor and R.E. Walker 1987. Multispectral remote sensing as a stratigraphic and structural tool, Wind River Basin and Big Horn River Basin areas, Wyoming. *Am. Assoc. Petrol. Geol. Bull.* **71**, 389–402.

Mather, P.M. 1987. *Computer processing of remotely-sensed images: an introduction.* New York: Wiley.

Moore, G.K. and F.A. Waltz 1983. Objective procedures for lineament enhancement and extraction. *Photogramm. Eng. Remote Sens.* **49**, 641–647.

Podwysocki, M.H., D.B. Segal and M.J. Abrams 1983. Use of multispectral scanner images for assessment of hydrothermal alteration in Marysvale, Utah, mining area. *Econ. geol.* **78**, 675–87.

Pratt, W.K. 1978. *Digital image processing.* New York: Wiley.

Rothery, D.A. 1984. Reflectances of ophiolite rocks in the Landsat MSS bands: relevance to lithological mapping by remote sensing. *J. Geol. Soc. Lond.* **141**, 933–939.

Rothery, D.A. 1985. Interactive processing of satellite images for geological interpretation. *Geol. Mag.* **122**, 57–63.

Rothery, D.A. and P.W. Francis 1985. A remote sensing study of a sector collapse volcano. *Proc. 18th Int. Symp. Remote Sensing Environment, Paris.*

Rowan, L.C., A.F.H. Goetz and E. Abott 1987. Analysis of Shuttle multispectral infrared radiometer measurement of the Western Saudi Arabian shield. *Geophysics* **52**, 907–923.

Schowengerdt, R.A. 1983. *Techniques for image processing and classification in remote sensing.* New York: Academic Press.

Siegal, B.S. and M.J. Abrams 1976. Geologic mapping using Landsat data. *Photogramm. Eng. Remote Sens.* **42**, 325–337.

Siegrist, A.W. 1980. Optimum spectral bands for rock discrimination. *Photogramm. Eng. Remote Sens.* **46**, 1207–1215.

With the breadth of uses of digital image processing in such fields as astronomical, medical and engineering imagery, as well as in the fields served by remote sensing, the 1980s saw an unprecedented explosion in image-processing software aimed at users of many different types of computers. The most widespread can be subdivided into the VMS, Unix, MS-DOS and Apple operating systems, serving DEC VAX, Sun, IBM-compatible PCs, and Macintosh computers respectively. I do not intend to venture any suggestions for 'ideal' image-processing systems for geological users, and readers must carry out their own investigations. Virtually any trade periodical on computers will contain numerous advertisements for such software. Perhaps the most convenient source of information is to scan any copy of *Photogrammetric Engineering and Remote Sensing* for the numerous trade advertisements, and request information directly from suppliers. Occasionally, this journal carries reviews of systems, as does *Geobyte*. A safe source of advice for any newcomer to the field is always colleagues who are well established in the field, although they will nearly always complain that there is no ideal system, and wish that they had waited before purchasing their own. Prices fell dramatically as functionality and speed increased, during the late 1980s and any system that survived the 1980s will almost certainly be a useful purchase.

CHAPTER SIX | # *Thermal images*

This chapter builds on concepts about the thermal behaviour of natural materials, which were introduced in Section 1.3. Any reader who has little background in physics is advised to re-read that section before proceeding. Section 3.3 also contains useful information about the imaging devices used in remote sensing of the mid-infrared part of the EM spectrum.

Beyond about 4 μm in the EMR spectrum energy from the Earth's surface is almost exclusively due to radiant emission from natural materials. Just how much energy is emitted is governed by the fourth power of a material's absolute temperature. This energy is distributed among a range of wavelengths, rising to a maximum determined by absolute temperature. These relationships are quantified by the Stefan–Boltzmann law and Wien's displacement law respectively (Section 1.2, Fig. 1.3). Both laws relate to the ideal behaviour of blackbodies – perfect absorbers and emitters of EM energy. Since natural materials are not blackbodies they only approximate these relationships. The Earth's average surface temperature of 300 K means that maximum energy is emitted at a wavelength of 9.7 μm. Gases in the atmosphere absorb energy in distinct wavebands, so that only a small proportion of the emitted spectrum is transmitted. The main atmospheric window within which detectors can be deployed is between 8 and 14 μm (Fig. 1.5).

Thermal infrared radiation is usually detected in image format using line-scan systems (Section 3.3). These employ cooled solid-state detectors onto which radiation is directed by a rotating mirror and a system of diffraction gratings.

The resulting images are available in two forms. The earliest were of the analogue type, signals from each scan being used to modulate the brightness along a line on a cathode-ray screen. Film moving across the screen built up an image from a succession of lines. Modern systems record energy levels as DN for individual pixels along each scan line, to form a digital image. These can then be enhanced and analysed by the image-processing methods described in Chapter 5.

One great advantage of thermal infrared images is that they can be acquired at any time of day or night. The Earth's surface is always far above absolute zero and emits thermal radiation equally well at night as it does during the day. This adds another dimension to the possibilities for geological interpretation. The reason for this is that different materials lose heat at different rates during the night, and show up in quite different ways compared with their daytime appearance. The only limitations are the degree of cloud cover, which this radiation cannot penetrate, and the atmospheric window within which it is not severely attenuated.

The thermal properties of surface materials which control energy transfer are very different from those in the 0.4–2.5 μm region of the EM spectrum. As a result thermal images are often poorly correlated with those from the visible and near-infrared range. They provide an extra dimension for the discrimination of different rocks, soils and vegetation. They can be used in three main ways for investigating geological features. First, they may be interpreted in just the same way as photographs, provided

159

that the thermal properties of the surface are understood. Second, images of the same area taken at different times of day give semiquantitative information about how different materials respond to heating and cooling. This is the basis of estimating variations in thermal inertia, introduced in Section 1.3.2. The third application depends on quantum mechanics and laboratory investigations, which show that troughs in the emission spectra of minerals, related to Si–O bond stretching and other phenomena, occur at different wavelengths depending on chemical composition and molecular structure (Section 1.3.2). It relies, therefore, on gathering thermal infrared data in narrow wavebands to highlight these distinctive features in emission spectra.

6.1 What a thermal image shows

The variations in tone or DN in a thermal image are measures of the surface's radiant emission (Section 1.3.2). In the 8–14 μm waveband natural materials are efficient absorbers of solar radiation and very little is reflected (Fig. 6.1). If the surface was a blackbody the image tone or DN would be an accurate measure of the true surface temperature. Radiant emission is controlled by a property of matter known as emissivity (Section 1.3.2). A blackbody has an emissivity of 1, whereas all natural materials have values less than 1. Most natural materials are selective emitters rather than true greybodies and their emissivity varies with wavelength (Section 1.3.2). The temperature derived from thermal infrared measurements by applying the Stefan–Boltzmann law – the apparent blackbody temperature of the surface – is therefore always less than the true surface temperature.

Materials with high emissivity absorb and emit larger proportions of incident energy and heat energy transmitted

into them than those with low emissivity. Whether the temperature of a surface increases or decreases depends on increase or decrease in the heat content of the surface material. The heat balance at the surface is determined by the law of energy conservation. Heat may be transferred to and from the surface by many different means. Geothermal heat is added from below by conduction through rock and soil from the Earth's interior. Except in volcanic areas, this component is more or less constant over very large areas. Solar radiation transmitted through the atmosphere is absorbed at all wavelengths, including a proportion in the visible and near-infrared. Downward radiation contains a component of solar energy originally absorbed by the atmosphere in the form of wavelengths between the atmospheric windows but re-emitted at longer wavelengths. Energy is lost from the surface by an even more complex set of mechanisms. Most important is radiation away from the surface. However an important loss involves the transfer of heated gases in the atmosphere.

Heat transfer by radiation dominates the heat balance at the surface. The distribution of energy is described in terms of reflectance, absorptance and transmittance by Equation 1.5. The same relationship holds for the normalized versions of these variables – **reflectivity**, **absorptivity** and **transmissivity**. They must sum to 1 because of the law of energy conservation. For opaque materials that do not transmit EMR to any significant extent – most surface materials except standing water – reflectivity and absorptivity alone must sum to one (Eqn 1.8). Absorptivity is, according to Kirchoff's law (Section 1.3.2), interchangeable with emissivity. So, if reflectivity of a surface changes then its emissivity must also change, as described by Equation 1.9. This theoretical relationship is amply illustrated by a motorist wearing shorts sitting on a black seat on a hot day. A white seat is distinctly more comfortable. The black surface has low reflectivity and high absorptivity – it heats up very efficiently – and vice versa. Most solar energy which penetrates the atmosphere is carried by visible and near-infrared radiation (Fig. 1.5a). Heating of the surface is therefore due mainly to absorption of these wavelengths and transformation to thermal vibration of the material's component molecules. Solar radiation in the mid-infrared is completely absorbed by any surface, but contributes relatively little to heating. A major factor in the heat balance of a surface is therefore its ability to reflect radiation over the whole visible and near-infrared range. This is the **albedo** of the surface, which controls its reflectivity.

To appreciate the surface heat balance and how the surface temperature of an area changes with time the heat added to and removed from the surface must be considered. Since it is usually constant and low compared with the heating effect of solar radiation, geothermal heat can be disregarded outside volcanic areas. The amount of solar

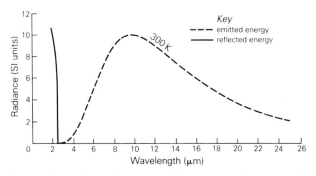

Figure 6.1 The radiance of EM energy reflected by the Earth's surface falls rapidly towards zero beyond about 2.5 μm. Absorption is virtually complete. Energy received from the Earth at wavelengths longer than this is almost entirely that emitted because of the temperature of the surface.

radiation at all wavelengths which is available to heat the surface depends on:

(a) The elevation of the Sun above the horizon – a function of latitude, time of year and time of day.
(b) Atmospheric conditions, such as cloudiness, humidity and air density – a function of weather and altitude.
(c) The topography in relation to solar azimuth and elevation – slopes facing the Sun intercept more radiation than those facing away. If slopes are steep enough or the Sun is low enough there may be shadows only receiving radiation from the sky.

Removal of heat from the Earth's surface is controlled by three main processes:

(a) Radiation of thermal infrared.
(b) Heat transfer by convection – this depends on the movement of heated air, either by convection cells or by wind. Cool air is heated by a hot surface, but equally a cold surface may receive heat from warm air. The amount of heat transferred by convective means depends on temperature gradients in the atmosphere, wind speed and turbulence, the area of surface exposed (this depends on the surface roughness) and on the density of the air and hence altitude.
(c) Transfer of **latent heat**. Evaporation of water from the surface involves adding the latent heat of vaporization from the surface to the water to form water vapour. This depends on the same variables as convective heat transfer, together with the moisture content of surface materials and the atmospheric humidity. It is complicated by the transpiration from any vegetation cover. The reverse is dew formation when latent heat is added to the surface as water condenses on it.

The relative importance of these factors varies according to the prevailing conditions.

Clearly, interpretation of thermal images is not a task to be undertaken lightly. As well as the addition and loss of heat at the surface, the heat balance is affected by the movement of heat just below the surface, how it changes the temperature of rocks and soils and the time factor involved. In addition to the albedo and emissivity of the surface, there are other factors at work.

The ability of a volume of material to store heat is expressed by its **thermal capacity** *(c)*. This is the amount of heat required to raise the temperature of a unit volume of material by one degree Celsius. Thermal capacity is the product of **specific heat** and density (ρ) and is expressed in heat units per unit volume per degree Celsius. Specific heat varies very little for rocks and soils, so density differences have most effect on their ability to store heat. The higher the density, the more heat can be absorbed by the surface with only a 1°C rise in temperature. Low-density materials undergo a greater change in temperature as heat is added or lost.

The ability of a material to pass heat by conduction is given by its **thermal conductivity** (**K**). It is defined as the amount of heat passing through unit area for a unit distance in unit time for a temperature difference of one degree Celsius. Rocks and soils are poor conductors of heat, but vary over an order of magnitude. Since water and air have even lower values of K, their presence in porous rocks extends the range further.

The rate of change in temperature in a material is controlled by its **thermal diffusivity** (κ). This combines thermal capacity, thermal conductivity and density in the relationship:

$$\kappa = K/c\rho \qquad (6.1)$$

Thermal diffusivity is the most convenient measure of a material's ability to transfer heat from the surface to the interior during heating and vice versa.

Thermal inertia (**P**) is a measure of the resistance of a material to change its temperature in response to a change in the temperature of its surroundings. It is derived by the relationship:

$$P = \sqrt{\rho c \kappa} \qquad (6.2)$$

Since the Earth's ambient temperature varies fairly systematically throughout the 24-hour diurnal cycle, thermal inertia is an appropriate measure of the thermal properties of surface materials. It is also relatively simple to estimate from digital thermal images captured at different times of day (Section 6.3.1). Values for thermal inertia together with other parameters measured for various surface materials in the laboratory are given in Table 6.1.

How the layer of soil and rock immediately beneath the surface heats and cools is a complex interplay between all these parameters. Heat flows from hotter to cooler regions in this layer at a rate determined by thermal conductivity. Daytime heating of the surface causes heat to be conducted downwards. Once surface cooling begins in the afternoon the heat stored at depth flows back to the surface. During the diurnal cycle the temperature profile in the top layer therefore changes. The shape of the profile and how it changes with time are governed by the surface heating and the various thermal properties of the materials involved.

Calculations have been made to simulate this process. Figure 6.2 shows a time sequence of temperature profiles modelled for varying surface heat input and a typical set of thermal parameters for a uniform near-surface layer. The profiles show how temperature changes down the layer as a heating wave from dawn to the hottest part of the day and a cooling wave as solar heating wanes after noon. Beyond a certain depth temperature stays the same throughout the daily cycle. For a given material, this depth varies over the course of a year because of seasonal variations in solar elevation. The shapes of such profiles vary with the values of the different thermal parameters of the near-surface

Table 6.1 Thermal properties of rocks and water measured experimentally at 293K.

Material	Thermal conductivity, K (J m^{-1}s^{-1}K^{-1})	Density, ρ (kg m^{-3})	Thermal capacity, C (J kg^{-1}K^{-1}) ($\times 10^{-2}$)	Thermal diffusivity, $\varkappa$ (m^{2}s^{-1}) ($\times 10^{-6}$)	Thermal inertia, P (J m^{-2}s$^{-1/2}$K^{-1}) ($\times 10^{-3}$)
Peridotite	4.6	3200	8.4	1.7	3.5
Gabbro	2.5	3000	7.1	1.2	2.3
Basalt	2.1	2800	8.4	0.9	2.2
Granite	3.1	2600	6.7	1.6	2.2
Pumice (dry)	0.3	1000	6.7	0.4	0.4
Ignimbrite	1.2	1800	8.4	0.8	1.3
Serpentinite	2.6	2400	9.6	1.3	2.6
Quartzite	5.0	2700	7.1	2.6	3.1
Marble	2.3	2700	8.8	1.0	2.3
Slate	2.1	2800	7.1	1.1	2.1
Shale	1.8	2300	7.1	0.8	1.4
Limestone	2.0	2500	7.1	1.1	1.9
Dolomite	5.0	2600	7.5	2.6	3.1
Sandstone	5.0	2500	8.0	1.3	2.3
Gravel	2.5	2100	8.4	1.4	2.1
Sandy soil	0.6	1800	10.0	0.3	1.0
Clay soil	1.3	1700	14.7	0.5	1.8
Water	0.5	1000	42.3	0.1	1.5

materials. An increase in conductivity allows the heating wave to penetrate further so distributing the solar energy through a greater volume. As a result, surface temperature does not rise so high or so quickly and changes more slowly with depth. An increase in thermal capacity – controlled mainly by density – means that more heat is required to raise the temperature of the topmost part of the layer. Less is left to penetrate to depth. Temperature at the surface does not rise so high or so quickly, but changes more rapidly with depth. Both these parameters are combined as a product in thermal inertia (Eqn 6.2) and so conspire to magnify these two effects as thermal inertia increases. One result of this modelling is that, although the shapes of profiles change for materials with different conductivities and thermal capacities, if they have the same thermal inertia their surface temperatures at any time are the same. Because of this, thermal inertia can be estimated from digital images with a fair degree of confidence.

An extension from thermal modelling of the near-surface is the prediction of how surface temperatures vary through the diurnal heating and cooling cycle (Section 1.3.2, Fig. 1.14) depending on the thermal properties of the materials involved. Figure 6.3 shows diurnal variations in surface temperature calculated for different values of two important thermal parameters – thermal inertia and albedo – with other parameters held constant. The family of curves for different thermal inertias show clear **thermal crossovers**. The reason for them is that a material with low thermal inertia – resistance to change in temperature – heats up quickly to a high temperature during the day and

cools in a similar fashion. Conversely, materials with high thermal inertia heat and cool more slowly to less extreme temperatures. The least diurnal change in surface temperature is experienced by metals and any materials containing water, which have very high thermal inertias. Although the curves for different albedos have different positions on the graph, they are essentially the same shape. Curves derived for all other parameters are like this too. This confirms the importance of thermal inertia in thermal remote sensing. The cross-overs imply that measuring the difference be-

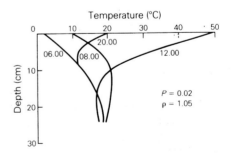

Figure 6.2 The results of modelling the thermal behaviour of a thin layer at the Earth's surface show that temperature varies with depth. The profiles of temperature against depth change according to the time of day down to a depth of about 30 cm. The greatest variation occurs in the top 10 cm or so. Examining the curves in a time sequence shows that a heating 'wave' rises through the ground from dawn to noon. Cooling then progresses downwards, becoming slower during the night. The curves were modelled for relatively low thermal inertia and density, so that they represent extreme rates of heating and cooling. After Kahle (1980).

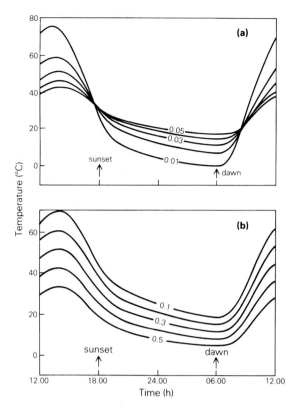

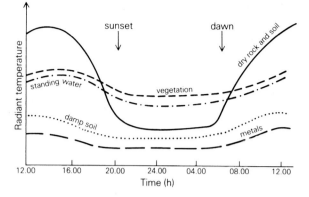

Figure 6.4 The shapes of diurnal temperature curves of different natural materials depend largely on their thermal inertias, to which moisture content makes an important contribution. The actual temperatures that they achieve depend mainly on albedo and, to a lesser extent, on geothermal heat flow. The curves are merely sketches of relative behaviour.

Figure 6.3 The diurnal variations in temperature of surfaces underlain by materials of different thermal inertia (a) show different rates of heating and cooling. As a result, they cross one another about 2 h after dawn and 1 h before sunset. Temperature–time curves for similar materials with different albedos (b) are approximately parallel. Those with low albedo (dark surfaces) consistently have higher surface temperatures than those with higher albedos (light surfaces). Both sets of curves are based on mathematical models rather than actual measurements. After Watson (1975).

tween surface temperatures at night and during the day gives a clue to thermal inertia only. A large difference implies a low thermal inertia and a small variation suggests the converse. For materials with the same thermal inertia but very different values of all other parameters this difference will not vary much.

Figure 6.4 is a sketch of the diurnal temperature curves for a number of surface materials. It allows the relative grey levels relating to these materials on thermal infrared images taken at different times of day to be predicted (Section 6.2). It is also useful in selecting the times when greatest contrast exists between different materials.

6.2 Qualitative interpretation of thermal images

This section discusses day- and night-time images of energy emitted in the 8–14 μm waveband, in either analogue or digital format. They are considered first as greytone images, and then combined with other data as false-colour images.

6.2.1 Greytone thermal infrared images

Single-channel thermal infrared data are widely available as greytone images. Like those of visible and near-infrared wavebands, the main elements of interpretation rely on tone, texture, pattern, shape and context. Unlike images of shorter wavelength radiation, the tone of a thermal image expresses surface temperature and not reflectance. Cooler areas have dark tones and warmer areas appear light. The greatest and most common problem in interpreting images of reflected visible and near-infrared radiation occurs in areas of monotonous albedo. These are typically terrains with a thin skin of soil, vegetation or desert varnish. In such cases, thermal images can be of great use since they should reveal differences in surface temperature related to various thermal properties down to depths of 30 cm or so.

During daylight hours, as well as the differential heating effect of direct sunlight on materials with different thermal properties, images are affected by topography. Areas in shadow are cool and appear dark in much the same way as they do in more conventional images. Sunlit slopes are differentially heated according to their orientation. South-facing slopes are heated most strongly in the northern hemisphere. Exactly the same enhancement of topographic features normal to the Sun's azimuth and suppression of parallel features occur as they do in images of shorter wavelengths. Daytime images express topography and geological structure very well, but in doing so obscure variations due to different thermal properties of the surface.

After sunset the effects of differential solar heating remain for a time. Loss of heat by radiation is controlled by both thermal inertia and surface temperature. For materials with the same thermal inertia, the hottest surfaces cool most quickly, and topographic effects are gradually removed. As Figures 6.3 and 6.4 show, surface temperatures at night become very stable, particularly in the few hours before dawn. During the day temperature fluctuates rapidly as the Sun rises to its zenith and then begins to fall. Because topographic effects are suppressed and temperatures are stable, night-time images are often preferred for lithological interpretation. However, both types complement each other and are interpreted together, when available. Figure 6.5 shows the different attributes of day and night-time images of the same area. Since the properties which control the temperature of the surface are complex and unfamiliar, interpretation is best achieved with as much ground control as possible. The identity of some features, such as water bodies, can be suggested by their shape and image texture.

Planning the time of day to acquire images with the greatest information content relies very much on the nature of the problem. Figures 6.3 and 6.4 reveal that there are two brief periods during the day, 2–3 hours before sunset and 2–3 hours after dawn, when no matter what the variations in thermal inertia of materials surface temperature should be quite uniform, according to theory. These times of thermal cross over are unsuitable for any applications. The same figures show that maximum temperature contrasts prevail during the hottest part of the day and before dawn. These times are those normally chosen for thermal imaging.

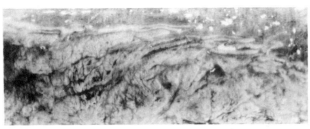

Figure 6.5 The top image shows the emitted infrared energy at 11.00 h from an area in the Front Range of Colorado, USA. The effect of solar shadowing is clear and highlights the local topography. The lower image is of the same area, but was acquired at 04.00 h, when surface temperatures are very stable. There is virtually no topographic effect and the image shows clear distinction between warm (bright) areas of dry outcrop and soil, and darker areas of cool damp soil. The bright patches on both images are small ponds. North is to the left in both cases and the scale is about 1:100 000. Courtesy of Ken Watson, US Geological Survey, Denver.

Dry rocks and soils have relatively low thermal inertias, whereas vegetation, standing water and wet soils have high values (Fig. 6.4). Merely to discriminate between these types of surface cover should be possible using day or night images. The effects of topography during daytime help to delineate geological structures, but hinder lithological discrimination. Although the contrast in surface temperatures over rocks of different thermal inertias is lower during the night, the suppression of topographic effects means that night images are best for discrimination.

The thermal inertia of dry rocks is strongly affected by variations in density (Table 6.1). A high-density crystalline rock, such as peridotite, has a high thermal inertia, and its surface temperatures remain fairly stable compared with less dense rocks such as granites. In sediments and pyroclastic volcanic rocks density and thermal inertia are determined mainly by porosity. A highly porous rock such as pumice displays rapid diurnal variations in temperature because of its low thermal inertia. Less extreme differences help distinguish between, for instance, sandstones with various porosities. The mineralogical composition of rocks also contributes to thermal inertia because of differences in thermal conductivity. The carbonates calcite and dolomite provide an interesting case. Dolomite is both denser and more conductive than calcite, the combined effect being to give dolomites a thermal inertia roughly twice as high as those in limestones. Although the two carbonate rock types appear identical on shorter wavelength images, they are contrasted on thermal images (Fig. 6.6). Since quartz has a very high conductivity compared with clay minerals there should be a good contrast between otherwise similar clayrocks and siltstones.

These observations suggest that thermal images aid lithological discrimination where dry rocks and soils are near to the surface. However, the actual surface temperatures and image tones achieved by different rocks are not controlled entirely by thermal inertia. The other important factor is the interplay between albedo, emissivity and absorptivity. If two rocks have identical thermal inertia, but one has a higher albedo, areas underlain by that rock will show the lower temperatures and darker tones at any time of day. Since rocks with other combinations of thermal inertia and albedo may well achieve similar temperatures there is ample opportunity for confusion if only one image is interpreted. The rocks in Figure 6.6 all have similar albedo. Figure 6.7 shows examples of day and night thermal images from a dry terrain, where albedo varies markedly.

In humid terrains complications relating to water begin to make their presence felt. The diurnal temperature curve for standing water on Figure 6.4 does not have much to do with the thermal inertia of water, which in the laboratory is of the same order as those of rocks. The apparently high value in nature is caused by the fact that water is a liquid. It

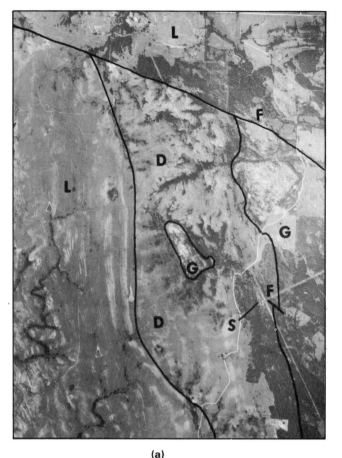

(a) **(b)**

Figure 6.6 The aerial photograph (a) of an area in Oklahoma, USA, shows mapped boundaries between limestone (L), dolomite (D) and granite (G). Apart from variations in texture, there is little to distinguish between the three rock types, and the dolomite appears identical to the granite. A thermal image acquired just before dawn (b) reveals the differences in the thermal inertia between the three rock types with equal albedo. The high thermal inertia of the dolomite ensures that it remains warm during the night, whereas the limestone and granite, with lower thermal inertia, lose more energy and appear darker. Irregular dark patches in the dolomite are due to wet soils in dry valleys. Courtesy of Ken Watson, US Geological Survey, Denver.

convects when temperature varies with depth. During the daytime the surface water in a lake achieves the highest temperature. This cools at night to be replaced by warmer water rising from below, thus stabilizing the surface temperature to some extent. This effect is magnified because water has a very high thermal capacity and can therefore store heat very efficiently. The net effect, as shown by Figure 6.4 and illustrated by Figure 6.6, is that relative to dry rock and soil water appears cool (dark) during the day and warm (light) at night.

Vegetation introduces other complexities and anomalies. Because of its high water content, green deciduous vegetation stores heat efficiently and appears warm on day images. During the night, water vapour is transpired from the leaves thereby shedding latent heat. This gives a relatively cool signature (Fig. 6.6b). Overall, the diurnal temperature pattern is similar to that of water (Fig. 6.4). Curiously, the composite effect of the needles on coniferous trees is to simulate a blackbody. This results in

such vegetation having a brighter night-time signature than that during the day. Dead vegetation, such as grasses or agricultural stubble, has a low water content and a very high content of air, both in stems and trapped between the foliage. It forms such a good insulating layer that the ground retains heat and has a brighter night-time signature than bare soil.

Moisture contained in soils at or near the surface has a profound effect on the thermal behaviour of rocks. This has nothing to do with its intrinsic thermal properties but results from the cooling effect of evaporation. The more porous a rock is, the greater the effect. Areas of damp terrain appear cool on images taken at any time (Fig. 6.7). The amount of cooling increases with air temperature and decreases as humidity rises. The greatest contrast between damp and dry soil is therefore during the daytime, particularly when the weather is hot and dry. Another enhancing factor is the speed of the wind as this 'blow-dries' the surface as well as increasing the convective loss

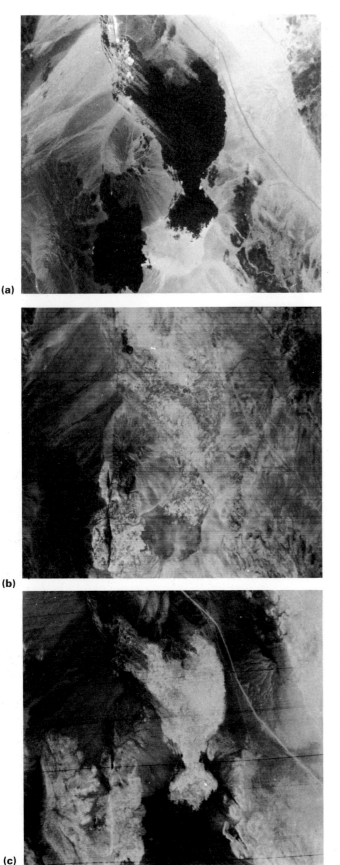

(a)

(b)

(c)

of heat. However, wind above a certain speed however produces curious patterns on thermal images because of turbulence. Local variations in speed produce differential evaporative cooling of damp soil and vegetation. Figures 6.8 and 6.9 illustrate some of the typical features of thermal images in humid terrains.

The thermal images shown up to this point have been gathered from aircraft. They cover narrow swaths of ground at a large scale. Small-scale thermal images with low resolution are also available from a variety of satellites. These include images from the Landsat-3 MSS and Landsat TM with resolutions of 240 and 120 m respectively. They are acquired at 09.30 h local time, which is close to the cross-over point on Figure 6.3a. As surface temperature shows the least contrast at that time and topographic effects are marked because of low Sun elevation, these images are of little use for geological interpretation – they appear like images of shaded relief. Although night-time TM thermal images can be acquired, this requires special requests and higher costs, and in any case the overpass time is not pre-dawn, but at around 21.30 to 22.30 h when differential heating effects have not had time to subside. Because of the usefulness to fisheries of global estimates of sea temperature, and to meteorology of land-surface and cloud temperature, nearly all meteorological satellites carry a thermal imaging system. That with the best resolution (1.1 km) is the AVHRR aboard the TIROS-N/NOAA series (Section 3.12.1). Since 1978 there has been continuous day and night coverage of the whole globe at 4 km resolution and selective imaging at full resolution. The system has a

Figure 6.7 The area of Recent volcanic activity and intense desert erosion at Pisgah in the Mojave Desert, California, USA, is a classic test site for remote-sensing techniques. The digital image of reflected visible radiation in (a) – equivalent to albedo – shows very little information in the nearly black areas of lava flows, or in the very bright areas of superficial sediments and the evaporites in the dry lave at the bottom centre of the image. Images (b) and (c) are, respectively, of day- and night-emitted infrared. Comparison between the three images enables the effects of albedo on energy absorption, and of thermal inertia variations, to be assessed qualitatively. For example, the high albedo lake deposits are cooler during the day than the less reflective alluvial deposits surrounding them, as expected. However, the black lava flows have not achieved much higher daytime temperatures than the surrounding reflective sediments, which is contrary to first expectations. On the night image the lavas are much warmer than the sediments. This suggests that the lavas heat up and cool down more slowly than the sediments, and therefore have a higher thermal inertia. Some details of the lavas appear in the thermal images, but a fuller analysis is reserved for the images in Figures 6.14 and 6.15. The thermal images also reveal a clear linear feature running from top to bottom, just to the left of centre, which is not visible on the albedo image. This is probably an active fault cutting both lavas and sediments. Courtesy of Anne B. Kahle, Jet Propulsion Laboratory, Pasadena.

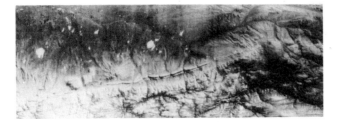

Figure 6.8 The top of this pair of thermal images of the Front Range in Colorado, USA, was acquired at 11.00 h, the bottom just before dawn, and they show much the same contrasts as noted for Figure 6.5. On both, but particularly on the day image, the complex folds at the mountain–plain boundary are clear, as are many linear features (probably faults) in the Rockies proper. The night image shows more clearly the different sedimentary units along the mountain front, and distinguishes between them and the dominantly granitic rocks of the Rockies in this area. The particularly bright folded layers at the front are quartzites, which have a very high thermal inertia. Courtesy of Ken Watson, US Geological Survey, Denver.

ground swath about 2500 km wide and has great but underused potential for regional studies of geology and hydrology. An example of NOAA thermal imagery is shown in Figure 6.10. One of the two constantly operating NOAA platforms has overpasses at 14.30 and 02.30 h, which are better suited to geological interpretation of the thermal bands.

The Heat Capacity Mapping Mission (HCMM) (Section 3.12.5) was specifically designed for measurement of thermal inertia and thermal discrimination of surface materials. Although the amount of data and their coverage was limited by termination of the mission in 1980 after 2 years and data were received by only a few ground stations, HCMM data form a valuable resource for small-scale geological applications. The resolution is 600 m for swath widths of 716 km. Data were acquired during the day in a broad band between 0.55 and 1.1 µm to estimate surface albedo (Day-VIS) and in a 10.5–12.5 µm thermal band both at night (Night-IR) and in daytime (Day-IR). Because of the timing of day and night orbits and variation in cloud cover only a limited number of areas have both kinds of thermal image close enough in time to be compared meaningfully. Examples of these are shown in Figure 6.11. Although they show features of great geological interest, they are by no means as useful as combinations of the data with those from other systems as false-colour composites (Section 6.2.2) and images of thermal inertia derived from the HCMM data (Section 6.3).

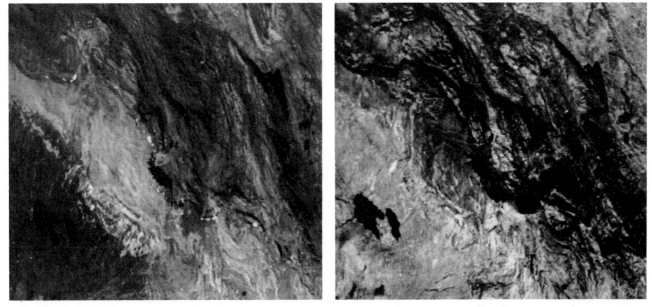

(a)   (b)

Figure 6.9 This pair of daytime digital images contrasts reflected visible radiation (a) with emitted infrared (b) from an area of complex Precambrian and Lower Palaeozoic rocks in northern Scotland, which are largely blanketed by vegetation, boulder clay and peat. The albedo image shows very little detail. In contrast, the thermal image is affected by subtle differences in vegetation, soil moisture content and thickness of the thin superficial veneer. This reveals several interesting structural features that would otherwise go unnoticed. Source: Open University, courtesy of NERC, Swindon.

(a) **(b)**

Figure 6.10 The TIROS–NOAA series of meteorological satellites provide coarse-resolution image data in the visible and near-infrared, and in the thermally emitted part of the spectrum, using the on-board AVHRR system. Image (a) shows AVHRR red reflectance (band 1) over part of southeastern Iran, taken approximately 1 h after dawn. This is equivalent to an albedo image, and shows considerable variation over this tectonically complex area. The image of emitted radiation in the thermal band 4 (b) is much simpler. The most obvious feature is the zone of relatively cool rocks extending roughly north–south along the Dasht-e-Lut. This represents an exotic block of old continental crust which was impacted into this geologically young terrain during the closure of Tethys. The younger, folded sediments of the Makran Range, running east–west in the south, and the less deformed sediments flanking the Lut Block have relatively high surface temperatures. Considering the time of day, the younger rocks possibly have higher thermal inertia than the crystalline rocks by the Lut Block, although there will be some confusion as a result of the time of the image being close to that of cross-over on Figure 6.3a.

6.2.2 *The use of thermal data in false-colour images*

Despite the complexities of interpreting thermal infrared data in the form of greytone images, various methods have been devised to display them in colour. The attraction of doing this stems from the contrasted appearance of day and night images and the lack of correlation between thermal data and those from other parts of the spectrum. In theory, poorly correlated data displayed together as components of a colour image should produce a very wide range of hues.

There are various options for colour display. The simplest is to use suitably contrast-stretched raw data to control red, green and blue components of an image. An example of this is shown in *Figure 6.12*. Despite the poor resolution the result is a much stronger discrimination among the rock types present than in Figure 6.11.

A means of adding fine topographic detail to low-resolution HCMM data is to combine them with better resolution data from another system. Merely to use, say, 80 m resolution Landsat MSS data to control one of the three primary colours adds little. The coarser HCMM data dominate the other two colour components, still resulting in an image with poor spatial resolution. To avoid this requires that the brightness or intensity of the image is controlled by the data of better spatial quality, while the colour incorporates thermal information. *Figure 6.13* is an image using ISH colour space (Section 5.2.2). It combines Landsat MSS band 7 data with HCMM Day-IR and Night-IR.

A more complex and powerful means of colour display involving thermal data involves combining them with many sets of data from other parts of the spectrum. A convenient means of doing this is by principal component analysis (Section 5.4). In a display, those components loaded strongly by thermal data are combined with components with a strong loading for other data sets. *Figure 6.14* is an image where red and green are controlled by PCs loaded with visible and near-infrared information, whereas blue is driven by a PC containing most of the thermal information. Although vivid in colour and clearly discriminating different kinds of surface, such images are difficult to interpret in terms of the spectral properties of different types of surface.

6.3 Semiquantitative analysis

Extraction of information relating to surface thermal properties from images relies on their being in digital format. Fortunately, most modern thermal systems produce digital images. Semiquantitative analysis has two main thrusts. First, it exploits the diurnal changes in surface temperature at surfaces with different thermal properties to express them as thermal inertia. Second, it uses thermal information, either of one time or combined for day and night as thermal inertia, together with data from other spectral regions to improve the separability and therefore classification of surface materials.

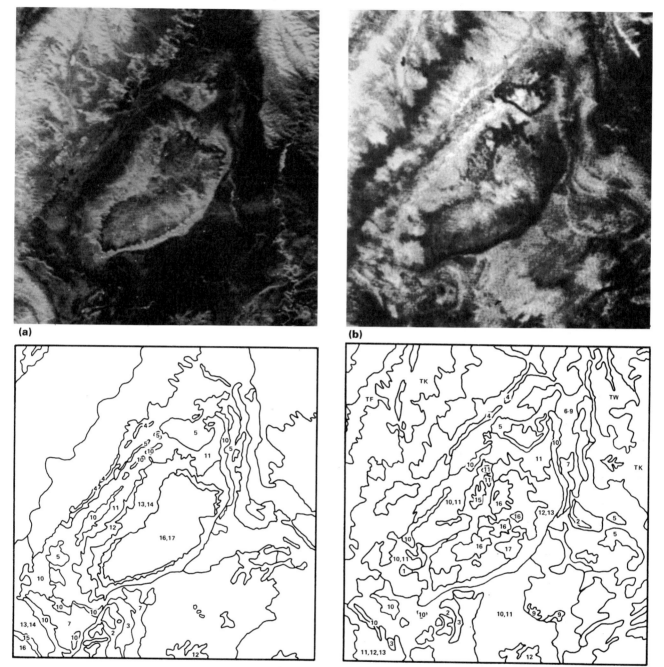

Figure 6.11 Both images are of digitally processed HCMM data for the San Rafael Swell in Utah, USA, which is an eroded asymmetrical anticline. It exposes Permian sediments in its core, which are succeeded outwards by Triassic, Jurassic and Cretaceous sediments, mainly sandstones, shales and carbonates. Image (a) shows Day-IR data and (b) Night-IR data. Below each image is an interpretation based on the thermal data and the known stratigraphy. Units 17 and 16 comprise Permo-Triassic limestones and red shales. Unit 15 is a Triassic sandstone. Units 14, 13 and 12 are all pale, massive sandstone of Triassic to Jurassic age. Units 11 and 10 are Jurassic shaley limestone and fine red sandstone. Units 5, 3 and 2 are Cretaceous shales, and unconsolidated Tertiary strata are represented by TF and TK. On each image all are crudely distinguishable. An important feature is that Units 12, 12 and 14 show cool day and warm night signatures, compared with the similar-looking Unit 10, which is warm during the day and cool at night. Units 12, 13 and 14 have high thermal inertia, whereas Unit 10 has a low thermal inertia. Courtesy of Anne B. Kahle, jet Propulsion Laboratory, Pasadena.

Table 6.2 Guide to interpretation of colours in Figure 6.13, showing their relationship to apparent thermal inertia of near-surface materials. After Short (1983). H = high, M = medium, L = low.

Day-Vis (albedo)	H	L	L	H	H	L	L	H	M
Day-IR	L	H	L	H	L	H	L	H	M
Night-IR	L	L	H	L	L	H	L	H	L
ΔT	M	H	L	H	L	M	M	M	M
ATI	M	L	H	L	H	M	M	L	H
Image colour	Blue	Green	Red	Blue-green	Purple	Yellow	Black	White	Pink

6.3.1 Thermal inertia estimates

Only sophisticated laboratory experiments can obtain accurate measurements of thermal inertia. However, estimates are possible by combining information on albedo and the temperature change of the surface during the diurnal heating cycle. Because it is impossible to measure the true surface temperature precisely using thermal data, the values used in calculations of thermal inertia are those derived from the emitted energy, assuming that the surface acts as a blackbody. The mathematical relationship for this is fairly simple, and the conversion from DN to equivalent blackbody temperature is done using look-up tables for the instrument employed. The albedo is estimated from the average DN in the visible and near-infrared reflected from the surface during daytime.

Although expensive, it is quite easy to acquire the three data sets needed for thermal inertia estimations using airborne line-scan systems. Finding suitable data from a satellite is by no means so simple. The only orbital system designed for this purpose was the HCMM. Its 600-m resolution data for albedo and day and night temperature are only available for areas covered by a few ground receiving stations (Appendix C). Global data is available at 1.1 to 4 km resolution from NOAA-7 and -8. Although Landsats-3, -4 and -5 gathered thermal data, they were only acquired routinely during daytime overpasses. By special request it is possible to turn on the sensors at night. However, the unfortunate timings of the Sun-synchronous Landsat orbits (9.30 a.m. and p.m.) coincide with the times of least contrast in surface temperatures (Fig. 6.3).

The first step in calculating the pixel-by-pixel variation of thermal inertia over an area is to register the images of albedo, day and night thermal data using a computer. An irksome problem, particularly with airborne data, is accurate registration of the images from two times. This is because of complex variations in scale and distortions due to topographic relief between the two images that cannot be completely overcome by geometric rectification (Appendix B). Satellite data for day and night during the same 24-hour cycle are captured from ascending and descending orbits, so that only lozenge-shaped areas where both groundtracks intersect are available for study. In the case of the short-lived HCMM experiment, from which data were recorded at only a few ground stations, the scope for study of thermal inertia is very limited. The continuous, world-wide recording of thermal data from the NOAA AVHRR system offers much greater potential, though it has been little used.

The simplest measure of the rate of heat loss from the surface by radiation is the difference between day and night temperature (ΔT). This does not give an accurate estimate of thermal inertia because of the albedo effect. A surface with a high albedo heats up relatively slowly, has less heat to lose at night and so has a small value of ΔT. Low-albedo surfaces soak up more heat, achieve higher day temperatures and lose heat very rapidly at night to give a high ΔT. A more meaningful estimate of **apparent thermal inertia (ATI)** combines albedo (a), ΔT and a correction factor for varying solar energy input to the surface (C), as follows:

$$\text{ATI} = C(1-a)/\Delta T \qquad (6.3)$$

The correction factor C depends on season, latitude, altitude and the angle and direction of slope. For most purposes corrections are made only for season and latitude. To remove topographic effects requires a digital image of elevation and extensive computations. In most cases the results show no striking improvement on uncorrected ATI. Values for a and ΔT are derived from the average visible to near-infrared reflectance, and from day and night temperature estimates based on thermal image data. For HCMM these are Day-VIS, and Day-IR and Night-IR respectively. The relevant AVHRR data are daytime Channels 1 and 2 for albedo, and Channels 4 and 5 for thermal data. The calculation is performed for each pixel in the registered scene of day and night data. The ATI values for each pixel are rescaled to the conventional 0–255 range, when ATI itself can be displayed as an image. Figure 6.15 compares images of ΔT and ATI derived from the aircraft data for the area shown in Figure 6.7.

Like conventional day and night thermal images, from which they are derived, ATI images contain anomalous features. As well as being affected by topography, they contain features due to variations in soil moisture content, varying wind speed, air temperature, humidity and various other factors. Since it is not possible to correct for all these factors, interpretation must be backed up by surface observations on the day of the image acquisition.

(a)

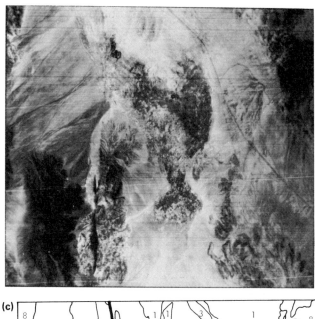

(b)

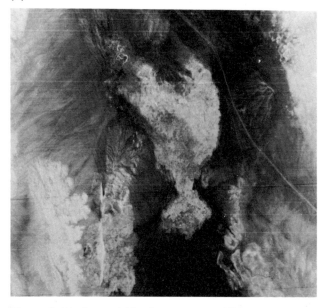

(c)

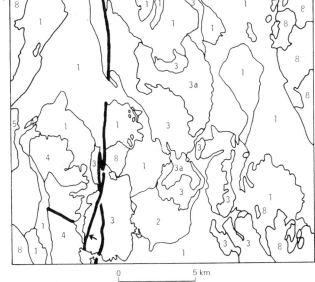

0   5 km

Figure 6.15   Image (a) is of temperature difference between day and night derived from aircraft data of the same volcanic area in the Mojave Desert of California, USA, as Figures 6.7 and *6.14*. Image (b) is of apparent thermal inertia. The map (c) shows rough outlines of the major outcropping rock units. Unit 1 is alluvium, 2 represents saline flats on a playa lake, 3 is basalt (3a with an aa surface), 4 indicates rhyolite intrusives, 5 is granite and 8 is andesite. The image helps to discriminate igneous rocks with high thermal inertia from alluvium with low, and identifies a division between aa and pahoehoe surfaces within the central Pisgah flow. However, it makes no clear distinction between igneous rocks such as 3, 4 and 8 with very different compositions. Courtesy of Anne B. Kahle, Jet Propulsion Laboratory, Pasadena.

6.3.2 Thermal data in classification

Images of thermally emitted infrared and their derivatives express variations in density, porosity, moisture content and thermal inertia of surface materials. These have little if any effect on images of reflected radiation. Apart from the effects of narrow absorption bands, visible to near-infrared images are dominated by variations in albedo. Thermal infrared images contain an albedo effect, so that bright areas on an image of reflected energy are relatively dark (cool) on a thermal image. There is a negative correlation between the two types of image. The albedo effect is removed by the calculations involved in producing an ATI image and so they are more or less uncorrelated with images in the visible to near-infrared spectrum. Clearly, this improves the potential for discrimination between different types of surface.

Images of ATI allow discrimination in areas of uniform albedo, where visible and near-infrared images are least effective (Fig. 6.16). Examining the range of thermal inertias for some common rocks (Table 6.1, Figure 6.17) shows several interesting features that help orient the use of thermal data in classification. Igneous rocks of widely different composition are not well separated by thermal data, with the exception of ultrabasic rocks. They are best discriminated by reflected radiation. Sedimentary rocks on the other hand show an excellent range of values, reflecting large variations in their porosity, density and mineralogy. Of particular importance is the strong contrast between limestone and dolomite, which are virtually indistinguishable by any other remote-sensing technique. Thermal data are also useful in distinguishing between crystalline, partly cemented and uncemented sediments, because of variations in porosity and density. Quartzite, sandstone and sand are all composed mainly of quartz and are therefore difficult to distinguish on images of short-wavelength radiation. They show strong contrast on thermal inertia images. Even where the available data do not permit calculation of thermal inertia values, as with Landsat TM band 7, a single thermal dimension can be employed as a powerful discriminant in

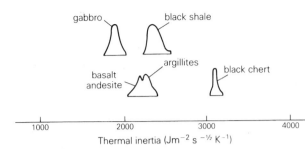

Figure 6.16 Landsat MSS data fail to discriminate between rock types with similar, low albedos. In thermal imaging constant albedo is a distinct advantage, as variations in surface temperature then relate only to differences in density, thermal capacity and conductivity. These differences are best expressed by thermal inertias, shown in these histograms, where the spread among dark rocks is very wide. Data from Watson (1978).

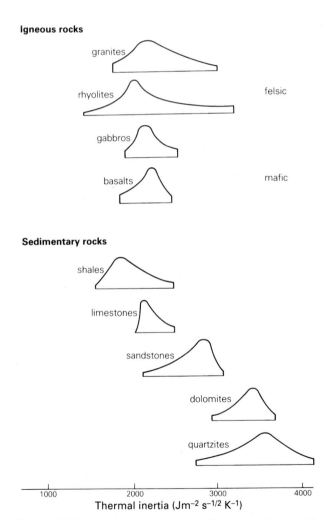

Figure 6.17 A comparison between histograms showing the range of thermal inertia in igneous and sedimentary rocks shows that thermal imagery is more helpful in mapping sedimentary basins than areas of crystalline rock. Metamorphic rocks show much the same overlaps as igneous rocks. Data from Hummer-Miller and Watson (1977).

classification, simply because of low correlation with other dimensions.

6.4 Multispectral thermal data

Within the range 8–14 μm the emission spectra of silicate minerals contain a prominent, broad absorption trough and associated features caused by Si–O bond stretching. The position of this trough and the shape of its shoulders are controlled by the coordination of silicon with oxygen. As the proportion of silicon in a silicate increases, the absorption feature shifts to shorter wavelengths. Since silicates are subdivided according to Si–O coordination, this shift is potentially a means of discriminating between them using remote sensing (Section 1.3.2, Fig. 1.12). Similar features characterize carbonates (C–O bond stretching), iron minerals (Fe–O), clay minerals (Si–O–Si, Si–O, Al–O–H) and various other groups of minerals (Section 1.3.2, Fig. 1.13). The wealth of different, compositionally controlled, features in the thermal infrared part of the spectrum suggests a bright future for multispectral analysis within the 8–14 μm band. It is the region most likely to provide direct discrimination between rock types, since the most prominent features relate directly to rock-forming minerals rather than minor components such as limonite and clay minerals. Figure 6.18 shows spectra for a wide range of igneous and sedimentary rocks.

Despite the great attraction of multispectral thermal data, the difficulties in separating narrow wavebands in the emitted region has enabled only two experimental imaging devices to be produced to date – the TIMS and the Geoscan systems. Their spectral ranges are shown in Table 6.3. Both have only been operated from aircraft, though plans exist to capture multispectral thermal images using the ASTER system (Table 3.5) aboard the first EOS polar orbiter in the late 1990s.

In theory, choosing an appropriate combination of bands based on laboratory spectra and suitable ratios should highlight the effects of different minerals. In practice, the radiance emitted by the surface is dominated by temperature and hence topography, albedo and thermal inertia.

Table 6.3 Wavebands in the 8–14 μm region of the mid-infrared spectrum measured by experimental line-scanning systems.

Bendix (defunct)	TIMS (JPL – Daedalus)
8.3–8.7	8.2–8.6
8.8–9.3	8.6–9.0
9.4–9.9	9.0–9.4
10.1–11	9.4–10.2
11–12	10.2–11.2
12–13	11.2–12.2

There is a very high degree of correlation between thermal bands. Colour composites of raw bands or ratios, even with contrast stretching, are very bland. The best approach is using the decorrelation stretch discussed in Section 5.4. This fully exploits colour space and produces images whose colours can be related to laboratory spectra and interpreted in terms of different rock types.

Experimental work on a number of test sites has shown up several interesting results, a few of which are highlighted by *Figures 6.19* and *6.20*. There seem to be two major roles for this approach. The first relates to igneous rocks, which of course contain a blend of various silicate minerals. Figure 6.21 shows the progressive shift of the Si–O bond-stretching feature in rock spectra towards longer wavelengths as bulk silica content decreases. *Figure 6.19* shows how powerful this line of attack could be. Were ultrabasic rocks present in the area even better results would have been possible. The other approach concentrates upon the differences in quartz,

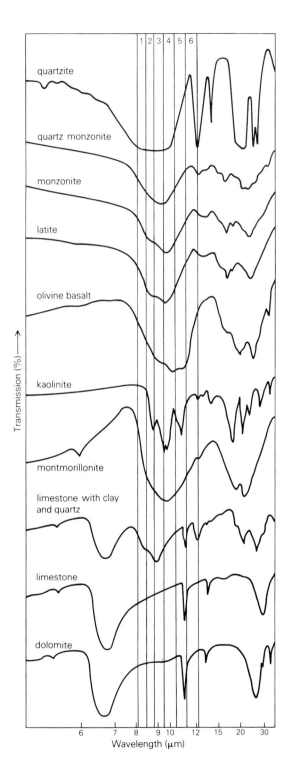

Figure 6.18 These thermal-infrared transmission spectra of igneous and sedimentary rocks depend on the component minerals in each rock (Figs. 1.12 and 1.13). The vertical bars indicate the wavebands detected by the experimental Thermal Infrared Multispectral Scanner (TIMS). The spectra are stacked to show relative shapes. From Kahle and Rowan (1980).

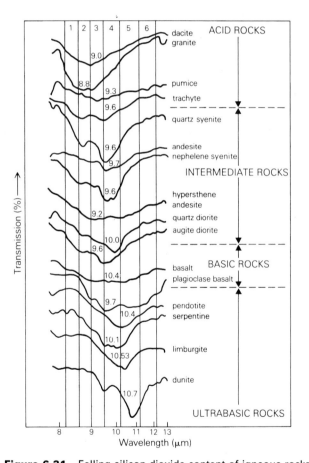

Figure 6.21 Falling silicon dioxide content of igneous rocks (and metamorphic rocks of the same range of compositions) results in a progressive shift to longer wavelengths of the Si–O bond-stretching absorption feature in thermal emission spectra. The positions of the TIMS channels (vertical bars) suggest that multispectral thermal studies could become an extremely powerful tool in geological mapping of crystalline terrains. The spectra are stacked to show relative shapes. Data from Vickers and Lyon (1967).

clay mineral and carbonate spectra and their effects on the signatures of sedimentary rocks. *Figure 6.20* gives an example of sedimentary discrimination using this method.

Further reading

Abrams, M.J., A.B. Kahle, F.D. Palluconi and J.P. Schieldge 1984. Geologic mapping using thermal images. *Remote Sens. Environ.* **16**, 13–33.

Byrne, G.F. and J.R. Davis 1980. Thermal inertia, thermal admittance and the effect of layers. *Remote Sens. Environ.* **9**, 295–300.

Eberhardt, J.E., A.A. Green, J.G. Haub, R.J.P. Lyon and A.W. Prior 1987. Mid-infrared remote sensing systems and their application to lithological mapping. *IEEE Trans. Geosci. and Remote Sens.* **GE-25**, 230–236.

Hummer-Miller, S. and K. Watson 1977. Evaluation of algorithms for geologic thermal inertia mapping. *Proc. 11th Int. Symp. on Remote Sensing of Environment*, pp. 1147–1160.

Kahle, A.B. 1980. Surface thermal properties. Chapter 8 in *Remote sensing in geology,* Siegal, B.S. and A.R. Gillespie (eds), pp. 257–273. New York: Wiley.

Kahle, A.B. and A.F.H. Goetz 1983. Mineralogic information from a new airborne thermal infrared multispectral scanner. *Science* **222**, 24–27.

Kahle, A.B. and E. Abbot (eds) 1986. *The TIMS data users' workshop.* Pasadena, CA: JPL Technical Publications.

Kahle, A.B. and L.C. Rowan 1980. Evaluation of multispectral middle infrared aircraft images for lithologic mapping in the East Tintic Mountains, Utah. *Geology* **8**, 234–239.

Kahle, A.B., M.J, Abrams, R.E. Alley and C.J. LeVine 1981. *Geological application of thermal inertia imaging using HCMM data.* JPL Publication 81–55.

Kahle, A.B., F.D. Palluconi, C.J. LeVine, M.J. Abrams, D.B. Nash, R.E. Nash and J.P. Scheildge 1983. *Evaluation of thermal data for geologic applications.* JPL Publication 83–56.

Nash, D.B. 1985. Detection of bedrock topography beneath a thin cover of alluvium using thermal remote sensing. *Photogramm. Eng. Remote Sens.* **51**, 77–88.

Offield, T.W. 1975. Thermal-infrared images as a basis for structure mapping, Front Range and adjacent plains in Colorado. *Geol. Soc. Am. Bull.* **86**, 495–502.

Pohn, H.A., T.W. Offield and K. Watson 1974. Thermal inertia mapping from satellites – discrimination of geologic units in Oman. *U.S Geol. Surv. J. Res.* **2**, 147–158.

Pratt, D.A. and C.D. Ellyett 1979. The thermal inertia approach to mapping of soil moisture and geology. *Remote Sensing Environ.* **8**, 151–168.

Rowan, L.C., T.W. Offield, K. Watson, P.J. Cannon and R.D. Watson 1970. Thermal infrared investigations, Arbuckle Mountains, Oklahoma. *Geol. Soc. Am. Bull.* **81**, 3549–3562.

Sabins, F.F. 1969. Thermal infrared imagery and its application to structural mapping in Southern California. *Geol. Soc. Am. Bull.* **80**, 397–404.

Sabins, F.F. 1980. Interpretation of thermal infrared images. Chapter 9 in *Remote sensing in geology,* Siegal, B.S. and A.R. Gillespie (eds), pp. 275–95. New York: Wiley.

Short, N.M. and L.M. Stuart 1982. *The Heat Capacity Mapping Mission (HCMM) anthology.* NASA Special Publication 465.

Vane, G. (ed.) 1987. *Proceedings of the 3rd airborne imaging spectrometer data analysis workshop.* JPL Publ. 87–30. Pasadena, CA: JPL Technical Publications.

Vickers, R.S. and R.J.P. Lyon 1967. Infrared sensing from spacecraft – a geological interpretation. *Proc. Thermophysics Spec. Conf.,* American Institute of Aeronautics and Astronautics, Paper 67-284.

Watson, K. 1975. Geological applications of thermal infrared images. *IEEE Trans. Geoscience and Remote Sens.* **GE-63**, 128–137.

Watson, K. 1978. Thermal phenomena and energy exchange in the environment. In *Mathematical and physical principles of remote sensing* pp. 109–174. Toulouse: CNES.

Wolfe, E.W. 1971. Thermal IR for geology. *Photogramm. Eng. Remote Sens.* **37**, 43–52.

Wood, J.A., M. Lasserre and G. Fedosejevs 1990. Analysis of mid-infrared spectral characteristics of rock outcrops and an evaluation of the Kahle model in predicting outcrop thermal inertias. *Remote Sens. Environ.* **30**, 169–195.

CHAPTER SEVEN

Radar remote sensing

The microwave region of the EM spectrum presents two opportunities for gathering remotely sensed data. First, like radiation in the 8–14 µm range, microwaves are emitted by the Earth's surface as a result of its temperature according to the Stefan–Boltzmann relationship and Wien's law (Section 1.2). Second, microwave radiation can be generated artificially as coherent waves. Not only does the atmosphere fail to attenuate microwaves to any great extent beyond about 0.3 cm, but electronic systems can detect very low energies. The first opportunity relates to passive microwave remote sensing, the second to radar, the only operational active remote-sensing system. Radar plays the dominant role in this chapter because passive microwave methods, although promising, are still at an early stage of development.

Passive microwave sensors are very similar in concept to radio telescopes, and comprise a horn-like antenna. Data in the form of profiles of emitted microwave energy are easily produced by simply flying a downward-pointing antenna along lines above the surface. The resolution of a passive microwave antenna is inversely proportional to its diameter (Eqn 3.5). Sheer size therefore poses much more stringent limits than with other systems. The effect is compounded in producing images by scanning the antenna across the surface being flown over. As well as suffering from coarser resolution than images produced by other systems, passive microwave images contain all the geometric distortions of a line-scan system. The larger the antenna, the greater the mechanical problems in ensuring smooth scans. Developments in electronic separation of the microwave 'beam' gathered by a static passive antenna into segments representing pixels of the surface are beginning to improve the potential for adequate resolution.

Passive microwave images have many of the attributes of thermal images (Ch. 6). The intensity of radiation is proportional to the surface temperature, so that warm areas are bright and cool areas dark. Not only can images be acquired at any time of day, but the cloud-penetrating properties of microwaves beyond 0.3 cm mean that passive microwave imaging is an all-weather system. By careful selection of wavelengths it is possible to choose whether to 'look' through the atmosphere, or to 'look' at it to measure its temperature and estimate its content of ozone or water vapour. It is easily possible to gather data in several wavebands simply by using antennae with different shapes and sizes. Thus multispectral images are more easily acquired than with thermal systems.

The energy of thermally generated microwaves is much weaker than in shorter wavelength parts of the spectrum – the microwave region is far into the 'tail' of the blackbody radiation curve for the Earth (Fig. 1.3). Microwaves emanating from the Earth contain components emitted by both the surface and the atmosphere, solar and atmospheric radiation reflected from the surface, and energy transmitted from below the surface. These factors mean that passive microwave images are noisy and difficult to interpret, as well as having poor resolution. For the geologist the greatest interest lies in the subsurface component of radiation. The transmittance properties of rocks and soils vary with microwave wavelength. Multispectral microwave remote sensing therefore offers a unique means of penetrating overburden to delineate changes in materials and moisture content, and to detect subsurface voids. It will be some time however before this potential is translated into an operational system with resolution to match other methods of gathering geologically important information.

Radar imaging possesses many advantages relating to the control that is possible with an active system. The principles were covered in detail in Section 3.5. It too has a day or night, all-weather capability and can be directed at the surface or at the atmosphere. It depends on the scattering of energy by materials that lie in the path of an artificial microwave beam, known as **backscatter**, and reception of the proportion of energy that returns back to the antenna. Radar waves are generated in coherent form, that is as radiation with a single wavelength where all waves are in phase. Coherent radar makes possible the use of Doppler shift in generating synthetic-aperture radar (SAR) images, where resolution is fine and independent of range (Section 3.5). Any microwave wavelength can be generated with any polarization. The angle at which the surface is illuminated can be varied by adjusting the antenna. The direction of radar propagation can be changed simply by changing the flight line of the platform. These controls allow a choice of optimum illumination conditions for many kinds of application. Flexibility and complete control is essential, since the interactions between radar waves and the surface are both complex and completely different from those for shorter wavelengths.

7.1 Interactions between radar and surface materials

What happens to the electromagnetic energy in a radar pulse when it meets the surface is controlled by four main factors:

(1) The attitude of the surface – dealt with at length in Section 3.5.
(2) The **roughness** and heterogeneity of the surface and of subsurface materials.
(3) The wavelength, polarization and depression angle of the radar. These are controlled variables.
(4) The electrical properties of the surface – the **complex dielectric constant** of surface materials.

In decreasing order of importance, all help determine the proportion of incident microwave energy that is scattered back from the surface directly to the antenna aboard an aircraft or orbiting platform. This governs the tone of the radar image. The brighter the tone the larger the proportion of backscattered energy. As with images acquired from any part of the spectrum, the fundamental basis of interpretation lies in the spatial distribution of tones to give familiar textures, shapes and patterns. The tone at any point gives information relevant to the actual nature of the surface itself. This section considers the effects on backscatter of variations in surface electrical properties and roughness and how these effects change with wavelength, polarization and depression angle. Before going further a couple of important definitions must be introduced.

A measure of the intensity of energy that is backscattered from a point target is its **radar cross-section**. This is the area of a hypothetical surface which scatters radar energy equally in all directions and which would return the same energy to the antenna as the real point target. A measure of the energy backscattered from a target with a large area, such as a field, is its radar scattering coefficient. This is the average radar cross-section per unit area. It is a dimensionless quantity, and since it varies over several orders of magnitude it is expressed as ten times its logarithm in decibels (dB). The **radar scattering coefficient** is a fundamental measure of the radar properties of a surface, and governs the tone of the surface on a radar image.

7.1.1 Complex dielectric constant

A material's dielectric constant controls the proportion of radar energy reflected by a material and that penetrating into it. Materials with a high dielectric constant, like metals and water, are excellent reflectors and absorb very little energy. The lower the dielectric constant the more energy is absorbed, leading to penetration beneath the surface. The dielectric constant is not a simple function of wavelength, but varies relatively little for most rocks and soils over the range of commonly used wavelengths.

Dry soils and rocks have dielectric constants in the range 3–8. These are low enough to permit penetration of a significant proportion of incident radar energy into dry materials to depths up to 6 m using L-band or 25-m radar. Penetration is only possible, however, where the topographic surface is radar smooth. Subsurface returns are detected only when the subsurface has a radar-rough component (Section 7.1.2). Since water has a maximum dielectric constant of 80, the greatest cause of variation in this parameter in rocks and soils is moisture content. As moisture content increases the dielectric constant increases in a roughly linear fashion. However, the dielectric constant of water increases as wavelength increases (Fig. 7.1), and this also has an effect on the radar-related properties of damp soil. Since even a saturated soil contains relatively little water the effect is not marked.

Penetration of radar into soil is expressed in terms of the number of wavelengths. The complex equations governing this behaviour suggest that for constant dielectric properties the same number of waves penetrate, irrespective of wavelength. Thus, the longer the wavelength the greater the penetration. Recent studies indicate that moisture content

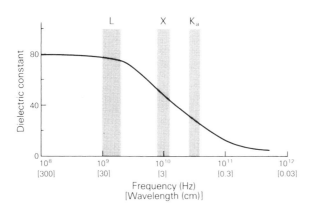

Figure 7.1 As the wavelength of microwave radiation increases, so too does the effective dielectric constant of water. At the wavelengths of Ka- and X-band radar the dielectric constant is between 30 and 45, whereas for L-band radar it is at its maximum of about 80. Rocks and soils rarely contain more than about 15% water, so the effect of moisture on their dielectric properties is considerably reduced compared with that suggested by the graph. It might appear from the graph that, since the dielectric constant of water decreases at shorter wavelengths, Ka-band radar is most likely to penetrate beneath the surface. However, the physics of the phenomenon show that roughly an equal number of radar waves penetrate material with the same moisture content, irrespective of wavelength. So, contrary to expectations, it is L-band radar which is most effective at revealing subsurface features. Experiments, now backed up by theory, indicate that unless the moisture content is less than 1%, penetration is negligible.

greater than 1% effectively rules out any penetration, so this phenomenon can only be exploited in hyper-arid terrains.

Because the leaves of growing plants have a high moisture content, vegetation has a higher dielectric constant than dry natural materials. Plants are therefore excellent radar reflectors. As a result, only a proportion of radar energy is able to penetrate to the surface beneath, depending on the nature and density of the vegetation canopy. Figure 7.1 suggests that longer wavelength radar is more capable of penetrating vegetation to give information about the surface than that of short wavelength.

Except for its effect on penetration, dielectric constant is a minor factor in controlling the tone and texture of radar images. They are dominated primarily by slope effects (Section 3.5) and by surface roughness.

7.1.2 Roughness

A perfectly smooth surface of a material with a high dielectric constant acts as a mirror to radar, as it would to all forms of EM radiation. As radar pulses are directed to the side of the platform they meet a horizontal surface at an acute angle and are reflected away from the antenna at the same angle, without being scattered. This is known as **specular reflection**, and results in a totally black signature

for a smooth surface (Fig. 7.2a). When a smooth surface is oriented at right angles to the radar beam, the reflection is directly towards the antenna, giving an intensely bright response. This is commonly shown by faces of sand dunes and ocean waves. Smooth reflectors with facets arranged at right angles result in multiple reflections between the facets. This is the principle behind the **corner reflectors** placed at the mastheads of small boats so that they are detectable by navigational radar. Regardless of the incidence angle at which a radar wave enters the cavity of a corner reflector, reflections between the facets ensure that the energy is returned directly to the antenna (Fig. 7.2b). Corner reflectors occur naturally at the intersections between bedding and rectangular jointing in rocks like sandstones, limestones and lavas. They give rise to bright speckles within the area of more uniform tone which characterizes such rocks.

A rough surface is made up of countless irregularities, some of which mimic corner reflectors and others that give rise to more complex interactions. The net effect is to scatter radar energy diffusely in all directions. Some returns to the antenna as a measurable signal (Fig. 7.2c). Roughness, for the purpose of interaction with EM radiation is a relative term depending on wavelength and angle of incidence. Two relationships allowing roughness to be quantified are given by Equations 7.1 and 7.2. In them the height of irregularities – the roughness (h) – is determined by the wavelength λ and the angle of incidence θ. A surface which appears smooth to radiation satisfies the **Rayleigh criterion**:

$$h < \lambda/25\sin\theta \qquad (7.1)$$

One that is rough satisfies the criterion:

$$h < \lambda/4.4\sin\theta \qquad (7.2)$$

The behaviour of radar waves at natural surfaces is quite complex. Rough surfaces scatter energy diffusely in all directions, whereas surfaces of intermediate roughness combine specular and scattered components (Fig. 7.2d). The tone of a horizontal natural surface on a radar image is therefore a combined result of its roughness and to a much lesser extent of the dielectric constant of the materials from which it is formed.

Quite clearly the Rayleigh criterion implies that radar wavelength helps determine what is rough or smooth. Table 7.1 shows limiting values of the mean height of surface irregularities associated with different categories of roughness for three radar wavelengths in common use. They were derived using the Rayleigh criterion. Roughness also depends on the angle of incidence of radar waves at the surface. For radar images gathered from aircraft this is a major problem. Since the depression angle changes markedly from near to far range (Section 3.5) so that the antenna can record from a wide swath of surface, the incidence angle changes too. The apparent roughness of a surface of

Figure 7.2 How radar is backscattered depends on the incidence angle and on surface roughness. Four possibilities are shown: (a) for a perfectly smooth horizontal surface; (b) for a corner reflector; (c) for a rough surface and (d) for a smooth natural surface.

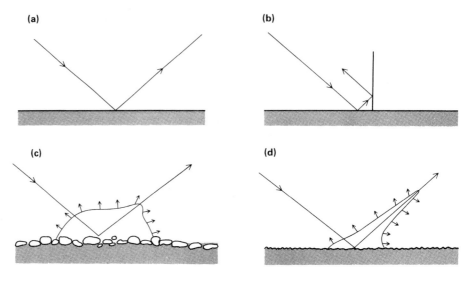

uniform roughness therefore changes across the swath. Since only a narrow range of depression angles can encompass a very broad swath from orbital altitudes, this effect on image tone is not apparent on Seasat and SIR images (Section 3.10.2). Depression angle can be varied systematically on orbital SAR systems. It is theoretically possible to exploit the variation of apparent roughness with incidence angle to gain more detailed information about the nature of the surface, or to select a depression angle which gives the greatest discrimination between surfaces of different roughness.

Figure 7.3 shows how the radar scattering coefficient depends on surface roughness and incidence angle. For low incidence angles smooth surfaces reflect a large proportion of energy directly back to the antenna. As the incidence angle increases, more and more energy is reflected away from the antenna, until at about 40° nearly all energy is reflected away. Smooth horizontal surfaces therefore show as bright on images taken with a steep depression angle and dark on those taken looking further to the side of the platform. Since rough surfaces scatter energy diffusely in all directions, the proportion returning to the antenna is virtually independent of incidence angle. Their brightness

on an image usually does not change much with the angle at which radar waves are received at the surface. They appear dark relative to smooth and intermediate surfaces when incidence angle is steep (depression angle shallow), but form bright features at all incidence angles less than about 20°. Figure 7.3 implies that images taken with a judicious selection of depression angles can give a powerful discrimination of variations in roughness of a horizontal surface. This is very useful where the tonal variation of a single image is controlled by an unknown variation of both roughness and dielectric constant.

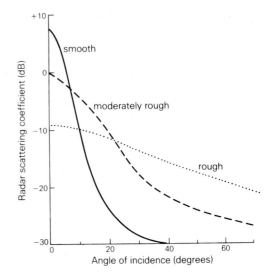

Figure 7.3 The proportion of emitted energy backscattered from a surface to the antenna – the radar scattering coefficient – depends on both the surface roughness and the angle of incidence. Both the depression angle and the surface slope control the incidence angle.

Table 7.1 Surface roughness (in cm) relative to radar wavelengths, derived from the Rayleigh criterion.

Roughness	Ka-band ($\lambda = 0.86$ cm)	X-band ($\lambda = 3$ cm)	L-band ($\lambda = 25$ cm)
Smooth	<0.05	<0.17	<1.41
Intermediate	0.05–0.28	0.17–0.96	1.41–8.04
Rough	>0.28	>0.96	>8.04

As well as scattered energy from the ground surface or the top of a vegetation canopy, the radar returns from the Earth's surface contain components from within the soil and the vegetation canopy itself. These comprise the results of complex **volume scattering**, mainly multiple reflections from electrical inhomogeneities within the soil and plant structures such as branches. Some of the energy penetrating the soil surface may be reflected and scattered from soil layers, and even from the buried soil–rock interface. In many cases it is impossible to separate all the different components, and all form part of the overall roughness of the surface. However, in relatively simple terrains it has proved possible to identify effects due to subsurface features (Fig. 7.4).

7.1.3 Polarization

Like visible light, radar can be transmitted and received in different modes of polarization. Polarized radiation has its electrical component of wave vibration in a single plane perpendicular to the direction of propagation. For radar transmission and reception this is usually arranged to be either horizontal (H) or vertical (V). The most common combination is to transmit horizontally polarized radar and receive the horizontally polarized component of back-scattered radiation. This is assigned the coding HH, and gives **like-polarized** images. Horizontal transmission and vertical reception (HV) produces a **cross-polarized image**. There are four possibilities – HH, VV, HV and VH. The

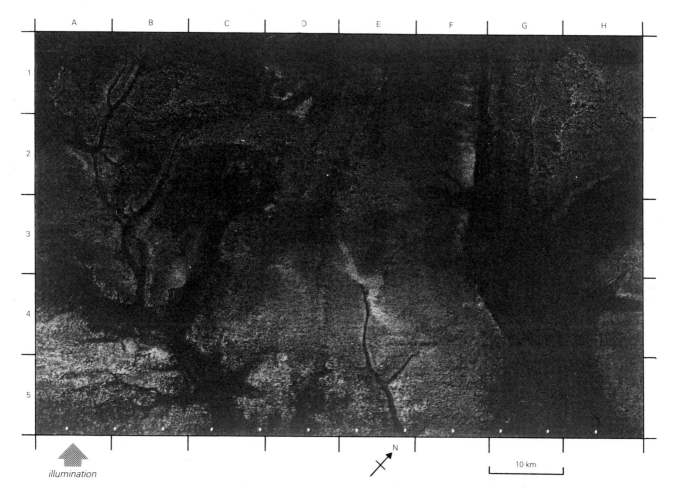

illumination

N

10 km

Figure 7.4 This widely publicized SIR-A image of the Eastern Sahara Desert in the Sudan caused a major stir in remote-sensing and climatological circles when it first appeared. Landsat images show that the area is a nearly featureless sand and gravel plain. The image shows patterns which suggest a drainage network, and since tributaries of the main channel 'V' towards the south water flow which produced the network was southwards. The Nile system, which is some 250 km to the east of this area, flows to the north, as do most of the widely spaced wadis in this area. The drainage pattern is thought to date from a Pleistocene wet period and to have been preserved beneath sand. Several nearby archaeological sites confirm that the area was humid enough 6000 years ago to support agriculture. Now it is extremely arid. One theory holds that the patterns result from radar penetration and backscatter from subsurface variations in grain size. An alternative is that the radar is picking up subtle variations in surface roughness related to the old stream courses. This SIR-A image, together with most of those illustrating this chapter, was supplied by NASA NSSDC/World Data Center A (Rockets and Satellites). The Principal Investigator for the SIR-A experiment was Dr Charles Elachi, of the Jet Propulsion Laboratory, Pasadena.

most usual strategy is to transmit horizontally and receive both horizontal and vertical components – HH and HV. Circular and elliptical polarizations are also possible and under active consideration.

Interaction between the surface and radar waves usually leaves the sense of polarization unchanged. However, it can cause depolarization and rotation of the plane of polarization. So the mode of polarization can influence how objects appear on images. A proportion of the depolarized compon-

ent of backscatter and that rotated through 90° are detected in a cross-polarized image. How these effects are produced is not perfectly understood, but a widely held view is that some of these phenomena are the result of multiple reflections at or beneath the surface. Multiple reflections are at a minimum with bare rock or soil with a high dielectric constant. Where vegetation is thick and varied in structure there is a greater chance of multiple reflections between leaves, twigs and branches. Depolarized returns are com-

illumination

Figure 7.5 This 1:35 000 image of an area near Pittsburgh, Pennsylvania, USA, is from an airborne X-band SAR system looking from west to east. It is 50 km wide, has a resolution cell of 6 × 12 m (azimuth × range) and is a digitally processed product of the real-time STAR system. Its very high quality enables not only the gross folding patterns in this part of the Appalachians to be mapped, but shows up many fine details. At D2 and F2 the two folds are clearly anticlines plunging towards each other. In the synclinal zone at E3 the doubly plunging structure has created a triangular interference pattern. The bright ridge at D5 Vs to the southeast, suggesting that the band of ridges from A3/4 to E6 are strata dipping steeply to the southeast. The eastern limb of the syncline at F4 has been displaced by a fault trending southwest–northeast. Displacement of ridges suggests that it has a downthrow to the southeast. The ridges are densely wooded, hence their relatively bright signatures. A power line cut through the forest between A6 and B5 shows up clearly. Backscatter is dominated by the vegetation canopy, and does not relate to variations in surface roughness. Nevertheless, the wealth of textural information is useful in identifying different rock types. The ridges are well-drained sandstones, and the valleys are floored mainly by shales and carbonates, which are less resistant to weathering and erosion. The impermeable shale units from A3 to E6 and B1 to H3/4 are characterized by a much finer drainage network than the more permeable strata. Courtesy of Intera Technologies Ltd. Calgary.

mon from vegetated surfaces, so supporting this view. It is possible that subsurface backscatter by soil particles or rock heterogeneities may give rise to similar effects.

7.2 Interpretation of radar images

The processes which produce the tonal and textural features on radar images are varied and complex. A general account of how the full range of rock types and geological structures respond to radar illumination requires a book in its own right. Only an impression of the possibilities is given in this section. The strategy adopted is first to apply some of the photogeological principles introduced in Chapter 4 to a series of radar images showing a few important geological phenomena (Section 7.2.1). Section 7.2.2 then discusses the advantages for structural geology of images taken with different radar look directions. Images taken with different depression angles enable more information about surface roughness to be gleaned (Section 7.2.3). Pairs of radar images with different look directions or different depression angles introduce parallax, and this, as in over-

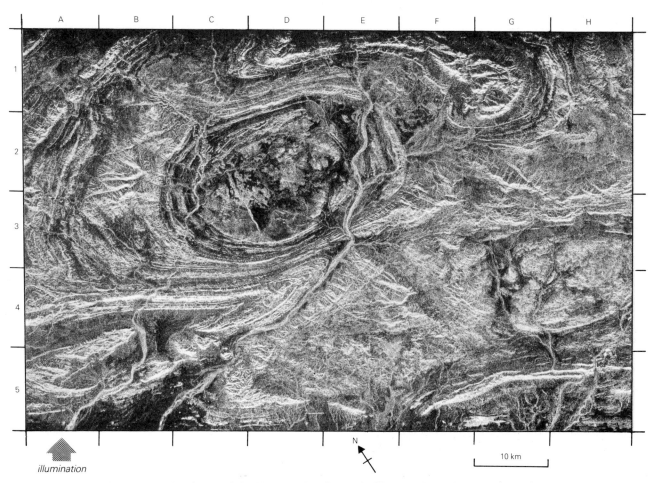

illumination

N

10 km

Figure 7.6 This SIR-A image is of part of the Hammersley Range in Western Australia, at a scale of 1:500 000. The area is underlain by Lower Proterozoic volcanics which are interbedded with some of the world's largest iron ore deposits, in the form of banded ironstone formations. The largest structure is the Rocklea Dome (C2 to E2 and C3 to E3) whose core is Archaean granite. A similar basement-cored dome occurs at H3/4. The bright linear feature from D3 to C2 is a dyke cutting the granite, but which is unconformably overlain by the Proterozoic volcanics. Other fine lines in the granite are also dykes. The dark unit with bright ridges surrounding the dome is an easily weathered sandstone. Succeeding it to the west and between D2, E5 and F4 are pillowed metabasalts, whose rough surface results in a bright signature. The synform with an axial trace from D4 to A5 contains a layered sequence of ironstones, shales and carbonates. The radar-smooth unit in the synform consists mainly of shales, and is veneered by alluvium. From D1 to G1/2 is a rugged area underlain by a massive ironstone, weathering of which has produced the huge iron ore deposits of Mount Turner (D1) and Mount Tom Price, which is just north of H1. As well as defining the major fold structures and lithological divisions magnificently, SIR-A also shows up many hitherto unmapped geological features. The most obvious form a series of wide bright linear features in the area from C1 to B3. These are thick quartz veins, many of which follow minor faults. The image fails to detect pisolitic Tertiary limonite and hematite deposits which form the main iron ores, except near Mount Turner (D1), where they show as a bright patch.

lapping aerial photographs, allows stereoscopic viewing (Section 7.2.4). Multifrequency (Section 7.2.5) and multi-polarized radar images (Section 7.2.6) provide additional information about the composition and texture of surface materials. Radar image data are sometimes available in digital form. They contain quantitative information and can be analysed by image processing-techniques to extract concealed information (Section 7.2.7) or combined for comparative purposes with other kinds of data (Section 7.2.8).

7.2.1 Geological features on radar images

Radar images combine the attributes of tone, texture, pattern, shape, context and scale in much the same way as do greytone images of shorter wavelength radiation. They differ in the way these interpretable attributes are produced, but the same photogeological principles apply (Ch. 4).

The most striking feature of a radar image is how it accentuates surface topography. To a large extent the

Figure 7.7 One of the most striking SIR-A images is of the Kalpin Tagh mountains in northwestern Xinjiang, China. The area comprises Lower Palaeozoic carbonates and clastics accreted to Asia by plate tectonic events in the Triassic period. Their structures were reactivated and disrupted during the Cretaceous to Eocene collision of India with Asia which formed the Himalaya far to the south. The rugged terrain has resulted in some layover. The best displayed of the older structures is a thrust from C2 to G2 which is expressed as a bright line representing a slope angled steeply to the radar beam. It transgresses the layering to the south, especially near the southward lobe at G2, and dips to the north. Determining the dip in the layered strata is difficult because of the prominence of layover flatirons (B/C5, F/G4). Clear Vs in escarpments at E4 and E/F2 show that the two blocks dip north and may be separated by another east–west thrust. Dips in A/B/C4 are northward and are to the south in A/B/C5, indicating an east–west striking antiform. The east–west structure from G2 to H2 is a synform. The difficulty in assessing the older structures is magnified by the effects of later faulting. The linear feature from C1 to C5 clearly displaces structures on either side in a left-lateral sense and is a major strike-slip fault. Another important fault trends from F4 to G2. In both cases the faulting also affects drainage and alluvium, and has obviously been active recently. An earthquake of magnitude 6.8 on the Richter scale occurred in the area in 1961. In some places (F/G4) huge rock slides, possibly induced by seismicity, have obliterated the layering in the mountains. In the alluvial deposits tone decreases towards the valley axes as granularity decreases, and the distributary gulleys are well defined.

amount of energy backscattered to the antenna is governed by the attitude of slopes. Those normal to the direction of wave propagation return nearly all incident radiation and appear very bright. Those sloping away at a steeper angle are in shadow. They are totally black. All other slope angles produce returns whose intensity combines influences of slope together with those stemming from the properties of surface materials. Slope attitude does however produce distortions of layover and foreshortening (Section 3.5), so topography is sometimes displayed in an unusual form. Despite this, the overall effect is to sharpen topography to a

much greater degree than is present in other kinds of image. Radar images are analogous in this respect to edge-enhanced, low-Sun-angle images of visible and near-infrared reflectance. The strong shadowing helps the eye appreciate topography because of the pseudostereoscopic effect (Section 2.5).

Topographic emphasis is most important for interpretation of the geological structures underlying major destructional landforms. They are often controlled by strike and dip of compositional layering, folds, faults and the boundaries of igneous intrusions. Figures 7.5 and 7.6 show

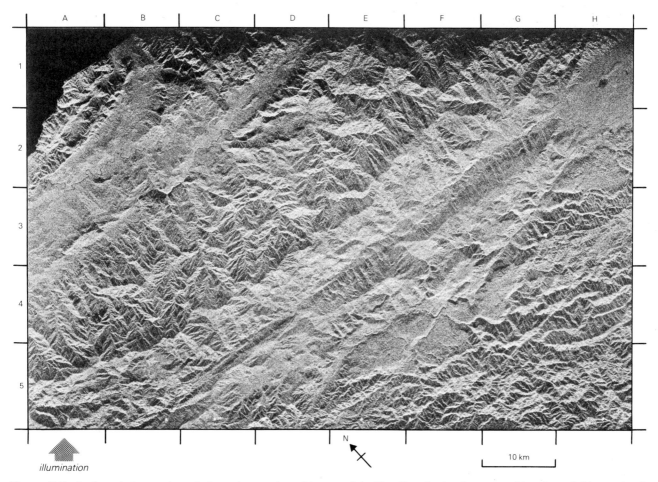

illumination

N

10 km

Figure 7.8 In densely forested tropical terrains, such as this part of the Vogelkop Region in western Irian Jaya, field mapping is hindered by the terrain. Aerial photography and other means of gathering data in the visible and infrared spectra are thwarted by near-continuous cloud cover. Although radar provides useful images, like this one from SIR-A, they are not nearly so sharp as those over arid terrains, since the vegetation canopy intercepts a high proportion of the energy and only a muted representation of the ground surface emerges. However, given experience it is possible to recognize many geological features. The most prominent here is a linear feature trending roughly east–west from H1 to B5. Careful examination of the feature around D/E4 reveals truncated valleys, deflected drainage and shutter ridges, all reminiscent of an active fault. Its sense of movement is left-lateral strike-slip. Another prominent, possible active fault trends from H2 to E/F2, and many others can be picked out, especially if the image is viewed obliquely from several directions. Oblique viewing also helps to distinguish different surface textures related to the bedrock. Three units can be distinguished easily. The dissected terrain (H5) is underlain by a Lower Palaeozoic metamorphic complex. The flat surface at E/F4/5 is almost devoid of drainage and is probably underlain by limestone. Along the major fault is a rugged bright area of thrust blocks, but to the north and south are dark, smoother terrains which have developed on sandstones.

examples of the enhancement of layering and folds. Some of the most spectacular examples of topographic enhancement relate to faulting (Figures 7.7 and 7.8). Recognition of igneous intrusions often relies on tonal and textural differences as well as on the expression of cross-cutting contacts. Figure 7.9 gives some particularly good examples of both plutonic diapirs and dykes.

Enhancement of structures is also aided by another special property of radar. Topographic features with sharp angular boundaries are in fact natural corner reflectors (Section 7.1.2). When the angles are illuminated by radar, all the energy returns to the antenna. Even where a corner

reflector is much smaller than a resolution cell its backscatter can saturate the response from the cell which contains it and thereby show up on an image. Sometimes the backscatter swamps several cells, producing a star-like **bloom**. Aligned corners along a small fault or dyke help highlight a linear feature that would be invisible on an image of reflected short-wavelength radiation, unless it had an extraordinary contrast (Fig. 7.9).

Topographic sharpening also magnifies the contrast associated with smaller scale features, such as drainage patterns and other textural attributes of the surface. They become easier to distinguish and to interpret in lithological

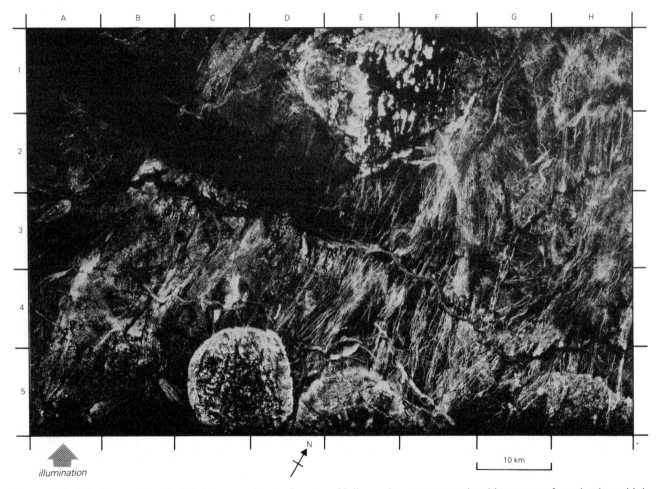

illumination

N

10 km

Figure 7.9 Like Figure 7.4, this SIR-A image of part of eastern Mali may have penetrated a thin veneer of sand, whose high reflectivity swamps Landsat MSS images with large areas of bright tones. The dark area in the top left corner is a sand-filled, possibly fault-controlled valley, which is so smooth that all energy is reflected away. The large circular feature at C5 is a diapiric granite penetrating late-Proterozoic metamorphic rocks. Its bright rim and dark interior suggest that its outer zones are more resistant than the now sand-covered core. Other granites occur at D/E5, G/H5 and E1. The last one consists mainly of huge inselbergs set in a sand and gravel pediment, but the roughly circular shape can be picked out. At its southwestern boundary it is truncated by a straight linear feature – probably a fault. The scene is dominated by hundreds of dykes, which show as bright lines. Most are oriented nearly parallel to the look direction, and are at least partly buried by sand. The fact that they show so clearly suggests that they consist of aligned joint-bounded blocks buried by sand, each of which acts as a corner reflector. Careful mapping shows a complex pattern with a variety of orientations, including an arcuate set at F2. The granites do not seem to have been cut by the dykes and may be later intrusions. The dykes are useful in identifying less obvious granite bodies. At A/B4/5 a swarm of about 10 east–west dykes are not seen in an area bounded by a vaguely circular set of features. This could be another granite. The dominance of dykes in the image obscures most details of the older metamorphic complex which they cut, probably because the older rocks have radar-smooth surfaces. Some curvilinear features around B/C3/4 may define folded banding in the basement.

terms. Figures 7.8 and 7.10 show examples of various rock-related textures in tropical rain forest, enhanced by radar.

A further result of the highlighting effect of radar is to make shapes which characterize erosional or constructive processes more distinctive. This is particularly useful in glacial terrains, where strong reflection from snow and ice swamps images of shorter wavelengths. Radar images show variations in surface roughness and are therefore grey over snow and ice. The topography shows quite clearly (Fig. 7.11). Volcanic cones and the effects of dissection are well displayed by Figure 7.12. Much smaller and more intricate

drainage channels show up on radar images than on those from other systems (Fig. 7.13). Figure 7.14 shows various desert landforms.

Some terrains present problems for geological interpretation of images in the visible and near-infrared range. The worst are those with low relief and monotonous reflectivity, and where natural patterns are masked by regular agricultural fields. Both are common in all parts of the world. Included among them are areas with thin highly reflective sand cover, dark desert varnish, burn scars and thin vegetation. The partial dependence of radar backscatter

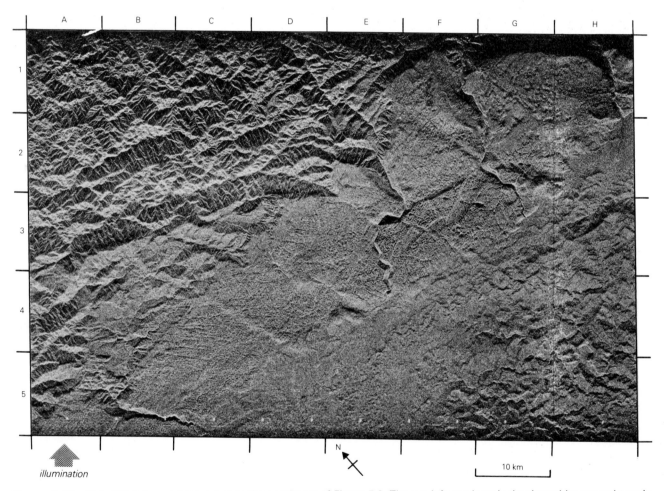

illumination

N

10 km

Figure 7.10 This SIR-A image begins just to the southeast of Figure 7.8. The top left quadrant is dominated by rugged terrain developed on metamorphic rocks. They are overlain by a small tongue of clastic rocks trending northwest–southeast from A4. The clastics are less rugged, and they have a coarser drainage texture. They are succeeded to the southeast, beyond a line roughly from B/C5 to H1, by rocks on which there is virtually no drainage, and whose surface is pitted with large depressions. They are particularly noticeable in the area G/H1/2. Surfaces like these are typical of tropical karst developed on carbonates. Only three major streams drain the area in deep gorges, and most rainfall, of which Irian Jaya has no shortage, disappears into sinkholes. A low NNW–SSE scarp between D4 and E4/5 possibly defines a major fault through the carbonates. Indeed, a whole series of muted linear features are visible in this monotonous terrain. A roughly east–west line from D/E5 to H2/3 separates the carbonates from a subtly different kind of landscape to the south. Along the boundary can be seen several small scarps with clear V-shaped (G/H3/4). These are clastic sediments which dip to the south. The line of Vs is, in fact, a zone of locally steepened dip – a monocline – flanking a major sedimentary basin to the south. Within the basin the drainage becomes clear once more because the rocks which fill it are impermeable.

on surface roughness allows normally invisible differences in microrelief and vegetation cover to show through such optical masks. In many cases patterns of great geological significance are revealed, as the following examples show.

Basaltic lavas are dark in the visible and near-infrared. Radar is potentially capable of discriminating rough aa flows from smooth pahoehoe flows, and between flows of different ages whose roughness is variably modified by vegetation, soil cover and degradation (Fig. 7.15). The granularity of soil is often controlled by the response to weathering of the rocks from which it formed. Different grain sizes of alluvium and other superficial deposits relate directly to the varying energies of transport and deposition. Chemical sediments, such as salt and gypsum, in enclosed

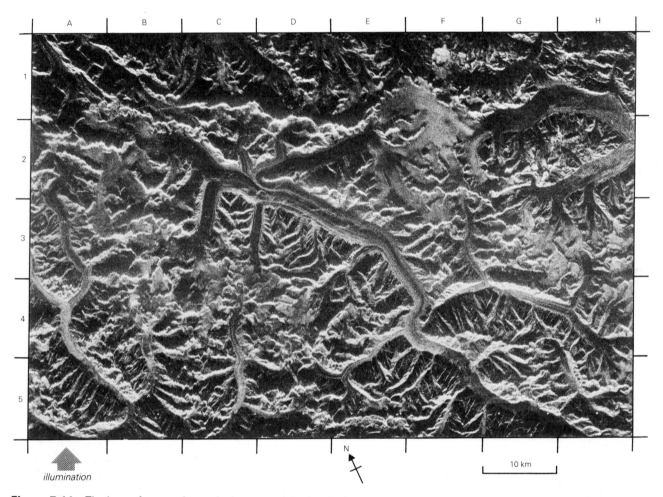

illumination

N

10 km

Figure 7.11 The knot of mountains at the juncture of the Pamir, Salt and Karakoram Ranges was formed by the indentation of Tethyan marine sediments, island arcs and microcontinents when India finally collided with Asia some 90–70 Ma BP. Together they form one of the most rugged terrains on Earth, with the most active erosion known. This SIR-A image of part of the Karakoram on the India–Pakistan border is, as a result, dominated by layover and shadow effects. Very few, if any, details relating to geological structure can be seen because of these distortions. However, it contains probably the most spectacular features of mountain glaciation to be seen anywhere. Huge snow and ice caps at B2/3 and E/F1/3 show as relatively homogeneous grey areas through which the major peaks show as bright foreshortened slopes facing the antenna and dark shadows on the opposite side. The relatively bright returns from the ice fields indicate moderately rough surfaces. Each ice field forms the source for major valley glaciers several kilometres across. The glacier in the centre is about 50 km long. In it dark and light stripes corresponding to ice and rougher medial moraines can be seen. Each of the moraines can be traced to the entry points of tributary glaciers. Bright streaks running across the central glacier are probably ice falls riven with huge crevasses, those normal to the look direction being preferentially highlighted. The snout of the main glacier is at E/F5, which is vaguely defined as a down-valley lobe. Below it the valley has a dark signature, suggesting that it is flat-bottomed. As the snout is approached, the glacier becomes brighter and more uniform in tone as melting and ablation reveals more debris and disrupts the pattern of medial moraines. Two tributary glaciers at C3 and D3 appear anomalous, with a uniform black signature. This probably results from their sloping steeply away from the antenna and receiving very little incident radar energy. Although distorted, the radar image shows far more topographic detail than images of other parts of the spectrum do. They would be overwhelmed by the uniform reflectivity and low temperatures of snow and ice, which formed a near total cover in the area at the time of the SIR-A overpass (November 1981)

186

evaporating basins often show great variations in roughness due to shrinkage and erosion. All these differences can show up as tonal patterns on radar images (see Fig. 7.20). They are added to by the changes in dielectric constant induced by different moisture contents. Therefore, in flat-lying areas the tonal variations on radar images can be used directly for geological mapping (Fig. 7.16). However, in more rugged terrains the same effects, though present, are modified by the influence of slope. The radar signature of a uniform surface type changes with the angle and direction of slope. If slopes are chosen carefully, it is possible to see through this and map lithologies with a fair measure of accuracy.

Under conditions of extreme dryness, soils are penetrated by a proportion of the incoming radar energy. By the same token they permit its return to the surface after subsurface scattering. In very arid deserts this means that radar images may give direct information about buried features. Radar is the only remote-sensing method where this is possible, but only field studies can confirm that penetration has taken place. A possible example was shown in Figure 7.4, but in that case the significance of the patterns related only to buried river courses. They probably stemmed from variations in subsurface grain size of the sand. Of more importance to the geologist is energy scattered back to the surface from the interface between sand and bedrock. This allows

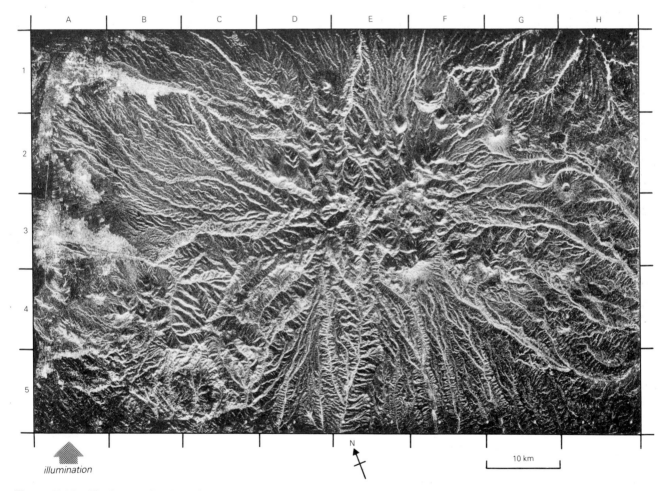

Figure 7.12 The huge volcanic edifice of Kuhha-ye Sahand, south of Tabriz in northwestern Iran, clearly reveals its structure on this SIR-A image. The marked radial drainage is a common feature of dissected andesitic stratovolcanoes. The valleys radiate outwards from what was a central caldera complex at D/E3, but which is now barely discernible because of deep erosion. Each major valley has an intricate dendritic system of tributaries, in which no annular element can be seen. This suggests a relatively homogeneous structure, perhaps dominated by pyroclastic rocks. Thick lava units separated by more easily eroded tuffs could tend to impart a concentric element to the drainage. Several younger, parasitic volcanoes can be seen on the flanks of the major edifice from E2 to H3, and around the central zone. Each is clearly cone, and one has preserved a summit crater (H2/3). On the flanks of these small volcanoes dissection has also begun to impart a radial drainage pattern. In several cases the development of parasitic cones appears to have deflected drainage on the flanks of the main volcano.

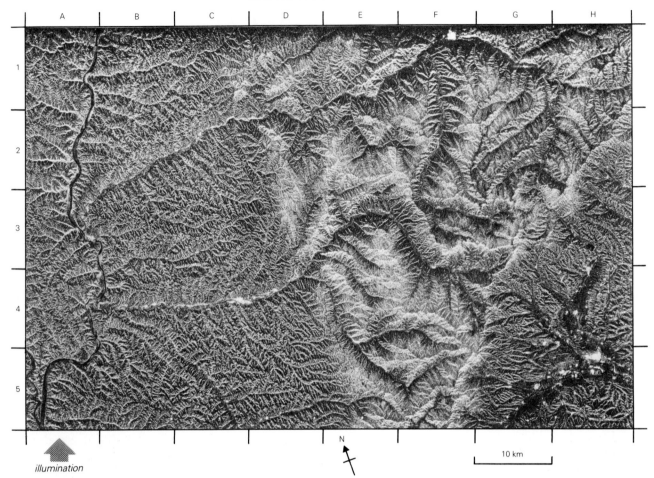

illumination

N

10 km

Figure 7.13 The Huang He (Yellow River) in Shanxi Province, China (A1 to A5) carries an extremely high load of suspended sediment, owing to its catchment from large areas mantled by wind blown dust, or loess. This SIR-A image illustrates the complex dendritic patterns of the innumerable tributaries of the Huang He flowing westwards from the mountains in the centre of the image. The changes in structure of drainage from the Hei-ch'a Shan and Luliang Shan mountains to the lower terrains on either side mark major lithological boundaries. The mountains are complex Palaeozoic basement unconformably overlain by Triassic sediments in the lowlands to the east and faulted against the Triassic rocks to the west. The brighter returns from the mountains are due to volume scattering from the dense forest canopy above 1500 m. The lowlands have sparse vegetation except in the valleys, and they show typical badland topography. Many of the smaller tributaries to the west of the mountains display a pinnate drainage pattern. This is typical of areas mantled by thick, homogeneous loess deposits. In some areas this mantle remains, but much of the drainage is probably inherited from a now-eroded loess cover. Although little geological structure is immediately apparent in the lowlands, there is a hint of a roughly north–south grain immediately west of the mountains. Several major valleys have nearly straight courses which may reflect faults cutting the Triassic (A2, A4 to D4). The bright areas from A4 to D4 and round H4 are major towns in this otherwise sparsely populated region.

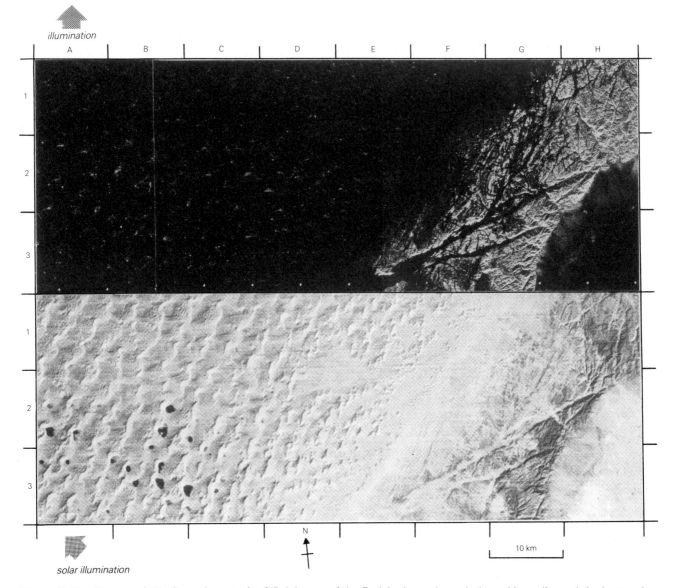

Figure 7.14 The top of this figure is part of a SIR-A image of the Badain Jaran desert in Inner Mongolia, and the bottom is a Landsat MSS band 5 image of the same area. The comparison is quite instructive. The Badain Jaran contains the world's largest sand dunes, up to 300 m high. On the Landsat image they show clearly, together with smaller dunes superimposed on them. In the west they are huge composite dunes with a crescentic or barchan-like component. Towards the mountains they grade into sharp-crested ridges with a northwesterly trend. Some of the interdune depressions contain spring-fed lakes. On the SIR-A image very little information on dune structure is visible. This is because sand is smooth to L-band radar, and only dune slopes facing south return energy to the antenna. The main trend of dunes is parallel to the look direction, so the whole area appears mainly dark. The bright patches are favourably oriented dune faces and thickets of reeds surrounding the interdune lakes. The low information content of radar images of sand-covered areas is in sharp contrast with the response from areas of outcrop. There, the Landsat image is 'washed out' by highly reflective thin sand cover, whereas the radar image is sharp and informative. This is a result of low returns from deep sand-filling depressions, and high returns from both bare rocks and surfaces with only thin, dry sand cover, which the radar has penetrated. Much more structural information is present in the radar image. Rock surfaces in deserts are generally rough because of wind erosion. At E/F3 on the radar image can be seen evidence for this in the form of narrow ribs of rock trending northeast for about 10 km. These are *yardangs*, or aerodynamic ridges sculpted by sand-laden prevailing winds.

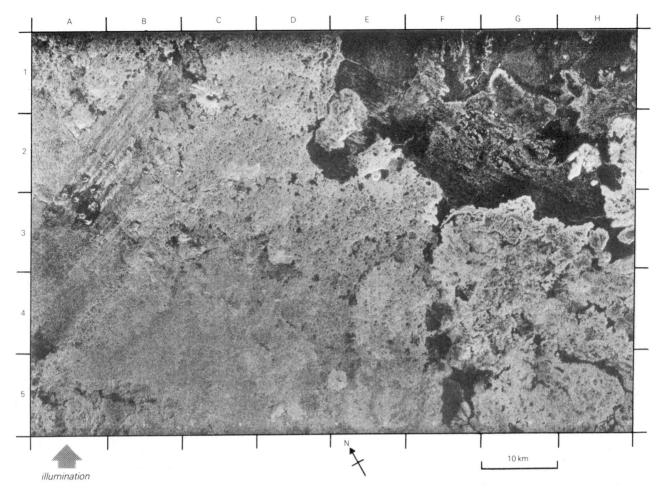

illumination

N

10 km

Figure 7.15 The Jebel al Druz in western Syria is a large Quaternary volcanic field dominated by basaltic lavas, the northwestern part of which is shown on this SIR-A image. Much of the surface is extremely rough, so the lava field shows up as medium to light greytones. On Landsat MSS images it is very dark. Here the boundary between lavas and the smooth, dark, older surface onto which they flowed is sharply defined. Its lobate form from E1 to H3 is typical of the flow fronts of fluid lavas. Much of the lava surface is speckled with black patches. These are pits and depressions in the flows, now partly filled with wind-blown sand. As a general rule, lava surfaces become smoother with age as surface processes degrade their original morphology, so the youngest lavas should be the brightest on radar images. At D/E5, E2 and C1 are particularly bright surfaces. In each case a small cone is associated with these rough surfaces, and at C1 the area is made up of many tongue-shaped lobes, confirming the presence of young flows. In the area from A2/3 to C2/3 are a number of small, young cones with vents. Those at A2/3 are surrounded by a dark patch, suggesting that they produced pyroclastic deposits which form a locally smooth surface. Streaks running to the northeast from this area show how the finer ashes have been transported by the prevailing southwesterly wind. To the southeast of this cluster of cones is a northwest–southeast line which proves to be an array of small cones on closer inspection. These are probably controlled by a fault in the basement. A similar feature extends between A1/2 and C3. These northwest–southeast arrays of minor vents are common throughout the Jebel al Druz, and they are found as far south as southern Jordan. They seem to be connected to faults which splay out from the major left-lateral strike-slip system along the Jordan valley and the Gulf of Aqaba.

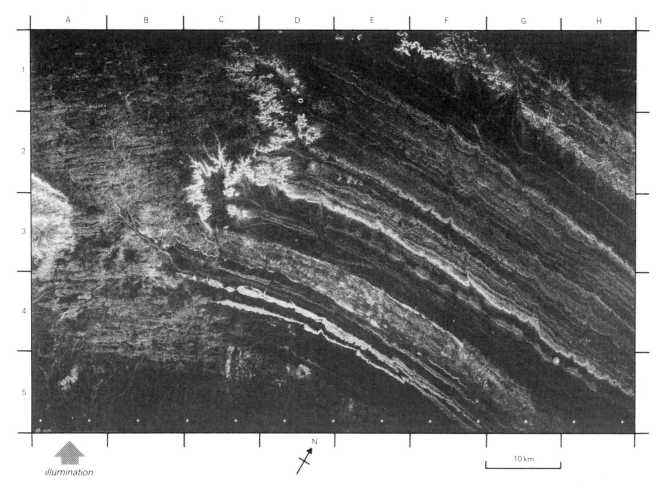

A B C D E F G H

illumination

N

10 km

Figure 7.16 The Devonian sediments of Western Sahara, which are shown on this SIR-A image, are mainly siliciclastic, ranging from conglomerates to siltstones. They are approximately the same in composition, and present similar signatures on images in the visible and near-infrared. Here they are magnificently divided into easily mapped units on the basis of their radar backscattering properties. The desert surface is nearly flat, and the tonal banding represents variations in outcrop roughness. Because individual beds can be mapped, small-scale structures show up well, such as the folds from D4 to E5 and small faults from F2 to F4 and G2 to G5. The presence of V-shaped outcrops controlled by small valleys shows that dip is to the north and the oldest rocks are at C/D5. The bright, irregular boundary from C1 to C3 is an escarpment, facets of which act as corner reflectors to give specular returns. The escarpment truncates the Devonian bedding and represents a nearly horizontal unconformity, above which are much younger sediments. Their radar signature is monotonous since they are undissected. Lines running southwest–northeast on the surface may be sand streaks parallel to the prevailing wind. Another possibility is that they are related to joints. This would explain the uniformly bright signature of the escarpment, irrespective of its orientation. Joints with this direction would produce many facets on the escarpment which are perpendicular to the radar look direction, and would ensure specular returns. Another interesting feature is that the very few drainage channels in the area have bright signatures. This suggests that they are filled with pebbles and bouldery material. The supply of fine-grained material in such a rocky desert is probably low.

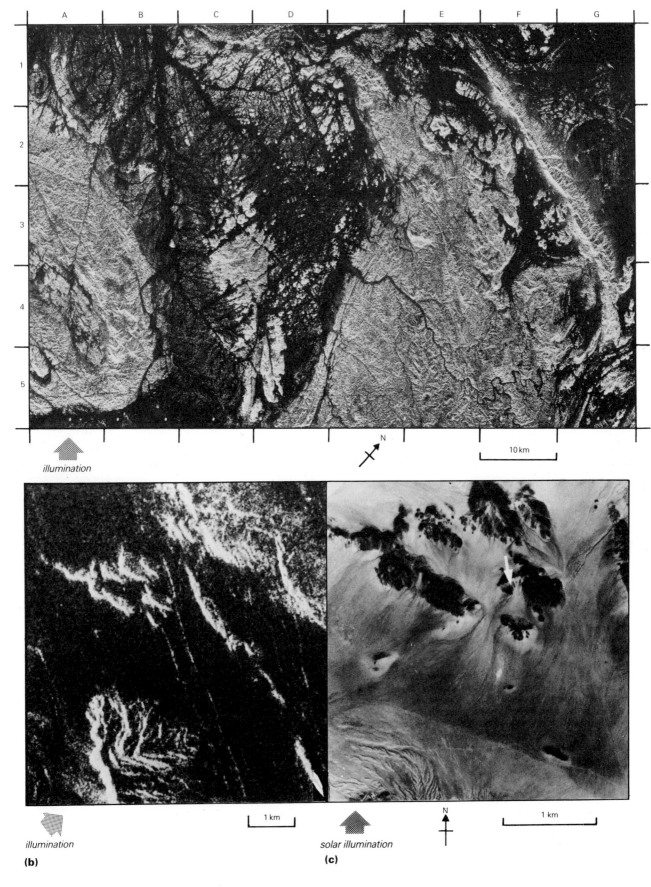

(a)

illumination

N

10 km

(b)

illumination

1 km

(c)

solar illumination

N

1 km

the topography of the buried surface to be analysed. Erosional patterns predating the inundation by sand can reveal the same structural information as bare rock surfaces. The only difference is that energy scattered beneath the surface is often attenuated and the patterns appear relatively dark on radar images (Fig. 7.17). However, since the incidence angle and wavelength are reduced by refraction at the surface, the backscatter can sometimes be increased as more of the subsurface satisfies the roughness criterion (Eqn 7.2).

7.2.2 Varying look direction

The path of the Sun restricts the illumination directions which can be exploited by other remote-sensing systems. Radar is potentially subject to no such hindrance because it is pointable. Topographic enhancement by low Sun angle is limited to early morning and late afternoon. Landsat and other unmanned satellite systems gather data at fixed times of day. This means that topographic features more or less oriented along the solar illumination direction are suppressed. Airborne radar systems can look in any direction. Although the degree of suppression of features parallel to illumination is greater than with other methods, only two or three carefully planned sorties can reveal everything that is detectable. Orbital systems are not so flexible, but still permit four look directions – to either side from both ascending and descending orbits. Selective pointing of the antenna by electronic means can increase the range of directions even further.

There are two main advantages of multiple look directions. First and foremost is the selective enhancement of differently oriented topographic features. Careful planning allows the analysis of structural features with all trends and geometries. Moreover, features hidden in shadow from one look direction are revealed from another direction. Figure 7.18 shows examples of SIR-A and Seasat imagery of the same area taken from orbits inclined at about 45° to each other.

The other advantage relates to directional features at the surface which are too small to be resolved. Examples are parallel corrugations in ploughed fields and on weathered outcrops of finely banded or foliated rocks. Radar looking along the corrugations responds as though the surface is smooth – it appears dark. A look direction across them gives the effect of roughness – the surface appears bright – provided the amplitude and wavelength of the corrugations satisfy the criterion in Equation 7.2. For sand ripples these conditions are not met – they are not sharp enough. Although some research has been directed at detecting hitherto undiscovered potato crops, the potential for geological analysis so far remains untapped. Figure 7.19 shows this effect in a rather unusual agricultural context.

There is one major disadvantage of using different look directions. As illustrated in Section 3.5 and in Figure 7.18, the appearance of rugged topography is very different on radar images looking in two separate directions. It can disrupt interpretation quite considerably.

7.2.3 Varying depression angle

Whereas any radar image can give information on surface roughness, radar science presents two possibilities for finer division of this attribute. Section 7.2.5 examines the potential of different radar frequencies. This section concentrates on what may be possible with different radar depression angles. Figure 7.3 implies that steep angles give a maximum response from surfaces which are smooth for a particular wavelength, according to the Rayleigh criterion. Shallow angles eliminate backscatter from all but the roughest surfaces. Angles between 30 and 40° give different responses from all sorts of surface.

Variations in depression angle also accentuate surface topography in different ways because of the different degrees of layover, foreshortening and shadowing (Section 3.5). In particular, steep angles maximize the discrimination of subtle changes in areas of low relief. This has to be traded against the distortion of high relief features, which

---

Figure 7.17 (a) The Red Sea Hills, a narrow swath of which is shown by this SIR-A image running southwest–northeast near the Sudan–Egypt border, are composed of a complex assemblage of Precambrian and Lower Palaeozoic metamorphic and igneous rocks. The bright areas are free of sand cover, and they are very rough. They are almost black in the field, owing to desert varnish. The darker areas are mantled by high-albedo sand. As the sand is very dry, radar has penetrated it to show features at the sand–rock interface, but has been attenuated. Large numbers of linear features show up, some of which control subsurface extensions of the wadis which cut the exposed rock surface. As well as aiding geological mapping of the areas, the penetrating capacity of radar provides a unique means of predicting where groundwater may have accumulated in the subsurface channels. (b) The left-hand image was produced after digital processing and enlargement of Seasat radar data for part of the semiarid Mojave Desert in California, USA. That on the right is an aerial photograph of the left-central part of the area covered by the Seasat image. The radar image shows several NNW–SSE-trending bright lines, whereas the photograph shows no sign of these features, which are in a monotonous area of alluvium. Detailed field mapping, and geophysical surveys across the radar features showed them to be buried quartz–monzonite dykes. That they show up no the Seasat image is the result of four factors: the dryness of the sand cover at the time the image was acquired, the fortuitous orientation of the dykes across the radar look direction, marked subsurface relief on the dykes which caused them to act as elongated corner reflectors and the rubbly nature of the products of dyke weathering compared with those derived from country rock. Courtesy of Ron Blom, Jet Propulsion Laboratory, Pasadena.

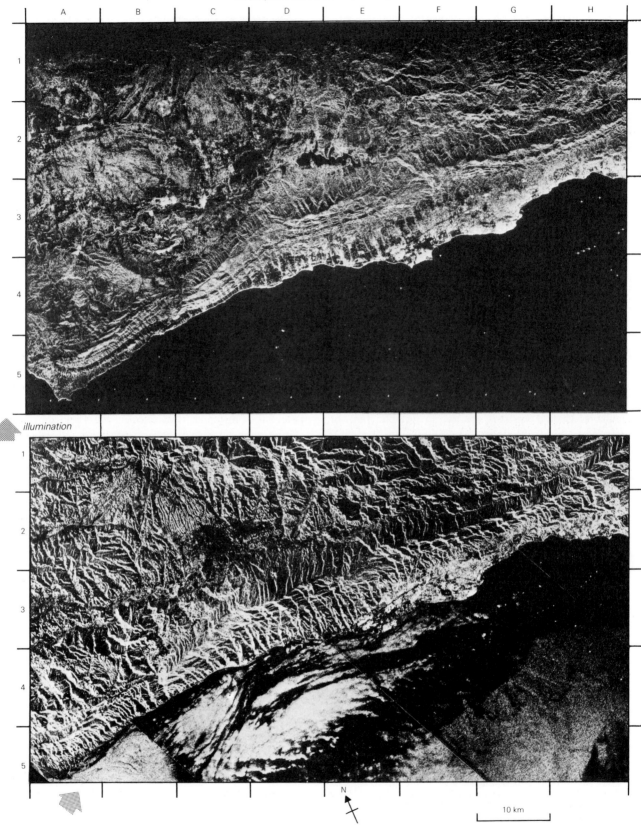

illumination

10 km

are better expressed by shallow depression angles. In turn, low-angle illumination may miss gentle features in the landscape.

Using different depression angles is then a means of increasing information related potentially to both lithology and structure. Although most research has been conducted with aircraft data, the most widely available comparisons come from the Seasat and SIR-A orbital missions – depression angles of 70 and 43° respectively. Figure 7.20 gives some idea of the potential from these two experimental systems, and from the SIR-B mission which incorporated multiple depression angles.

7.2.4 Stereoscopic radar images

One of the inherent characteristics of side-looking radar is the introduction of relief displacement on images (Section 3.5). Since it measures the downrange distance of an object in terms of time taken for energy to reach and return from the object, the displacement is towards the nadir of the system. In images relying on optical systems, relief displacement is away from the nadir. Both phenomena introduce the element of parallax when images taken from different positions are compared. Parallax is the basis of stereoptic vision (Section 2.5, Appendix A). How it is produced makes little difference to the observer.

There are several radar configurations which produce stereoscopic potential (Fig. 7.21). Images acquired from each side of an area with the same depression angle or from the same side with different depression produce stereoscopic convergence. Theoretically, radar images from any combination of look directions should produce stereopairs, but there are problems.

Depression angle and its geometric effects vary considerably across airborne radar images from near to far range. On a pair of images the conditions for stereoptic fusion and for vertical exaggeration change from place to place. The observer may need to be an ocular athlete. This variation is almost absent from orbital images, so they are potentially much easier to use. Worse problems are associated with steep slopes and rugged relief, and their influence on layover, foreshortening and shadow effects. Provided these effects all have the same sense, as they do on pairs of images acquired from the same side of an area, information is sensible and can produce photogrammetric-quality stereopairs. Images taken with opposed look directions are all

illumination   N   10 km

Figure 7.19 The circular patches on this SIR-A image of northern Libya are fields irrigated by centre-pivot sprinkler systems, supplied by deep boreholes. The bright lines oriented parallel to the radar look direction are caused by the concentric ploughed furrows in the fields. Only furrow slopes normal to the radar illumination are able to reflect energy back to the sensor. Closer examination shows that the lines are, in fact, shaped like bow ties because the curvature of the furrows becomes less extreme towards the perimeters of the fields. The effect is due to corrugations far smaller than the image resolution and may also occur on ribbed rock outcrops.

◀ **Figure 7.18** The top image is from SIR-A and the lower from Seasat. The image swaths were gathered from orbits inclined at about 45° to each other. The area is the Santa Ynez Mountains of coastal California, USA, centred on Santa Barbara at E/F4. There are obvious differences between the two images, owing to the different depression angles of the two systems. The Seasat image has stronger layover, and it shows subtle features at the sea surface. However, many of the differences stem from the contrasted look directions. The strike of layered rocks along the coast is shown well by SIR-A, to whose look direction it is favourably oriented. This attribute is disrupted on the Seasat image by strong returns from north–south valley sides. Running from D1 to B/C5 is the Santa Ynez Fault, which is clear on the SIR-A image, together with indications of the displacement of bedding. It is nearly undetectable on the lower image. Seasat, however, highlights a major fault from B1 to A/B4 which is not visible on the top image because of its unfavourable orientation. The smaller depression angle of SIR-A results in a much clearer expression of variations in surface roughness. Courtesy of J.P. Ford, Jet Propulsion Laboratory, Pasadena.

illumination

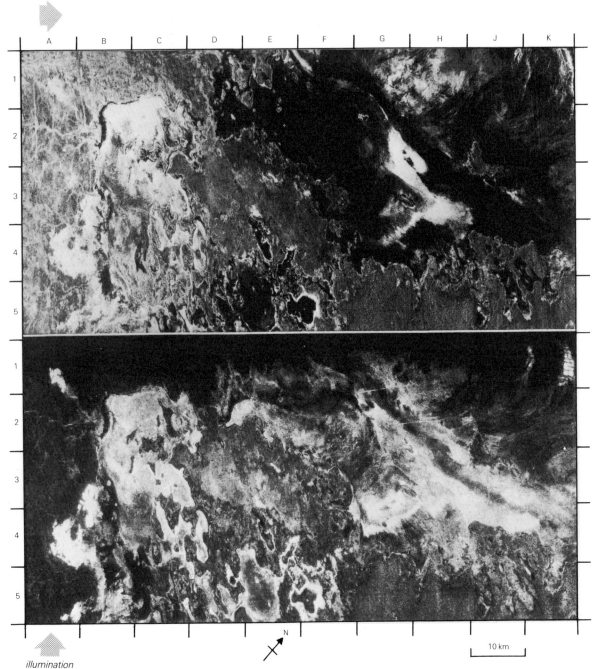

illumination

N

10 km

Figure 7.20 The top image is from Seasat and the lower from SIR-A, using L-band radar in both cases. Although the illumination directions are at right angles, the area has too little relief for this to have any significant effect. The obvious differences between the two images derive mainly from the different depression angles (70° and 43° respectively). The area is the Sahara Desert of northeastern Algeria, and is dominated by evaporite basins which are below sea level (B2 to C2 through B5 to C5, and D2 and G2 through F4 to K4). They are known locally as *chotts*. The western chott has roughly the same brightness on both images, suggesting a moderately rough surface; however, the Seasat image appears monotonously dark apart from a swirling bright band on the Seasat image, whereas the SIR-A image shows stronger and more variable returns. The differences could result from subtle variations in the roughness of the salt deposits which floor the chotts, and which are variably enhanced by the different depression angles. Courtesy of J. P. Ford, Jet Propulsion Laboratory, Pasadena.

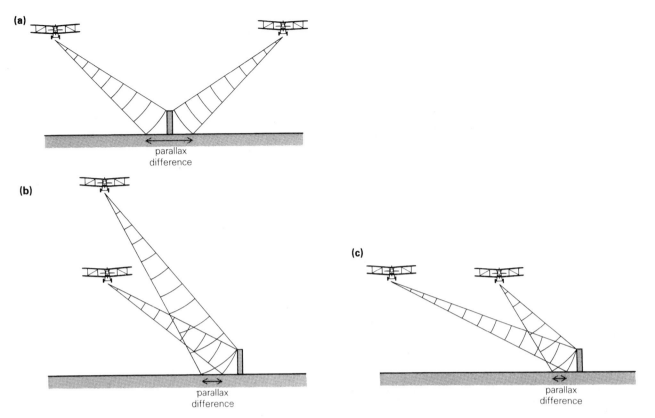

Figure 7.21 Radar parallax suitable for stereoscopic viewing can be produced successfully in three main ways: (a) illumination from opposite sides; (b) illumination from the same side but from different altitudes and (c) illumination from the same side, at the same height. Configurations (a) and (c) are possible from orbit. The method which produces best stereoptic models is (c).

but useless in areas of high relief. For this reason, the majority of stereo radar missions adopt the same-side, same-height configuration (Fig. 7.22c).

Despite the difficulties, and expense, stereo radar imagery offers the geologist the advantages of both overlapping aerial photographs and radar's terrain discrimination. However, measurements are rarely possible and interpretation is usually qualitative. Figures 7.22 and 7.23 give examples of stereo radar images from aircraft.

7.2.5 Multifrequency radar

The most powerful means of discriminating between surfaces with different degrees of roughness is to exploit the wavelength dependency of the Rayleigh criterion (Section 7.1.2, Table 7.1). This requires the illumination of an area by radar of several frequencies. As well as aiding the mapping of different lithologies and superficial deposits in terrain bare of vegetation, images of backscattered energy for a range of frequencies can provide interesting information from densely vegetated areas such as jungles.

At relatively short wavelengths (Ka- and X-bands) the returns are mainly from any plant canopy that is present, rather than from the surface. The high dielectric constant of vegetation makes all parts of plants highly reflective to these wavelengths. Radar is therefore scattered primarily by leaves, and to a lesser extent by twigs and branches. At longer wavelengths (L-band) the dielectric constant is smaller and greater penetration is possible. This means that the backscatter is influenced by the ground surface beneath grasses. In forests, even L-band radar fails to penetrate the canopy, and backscatter is mainly from twigs and branches. Combining the different wavelengths should therefore give information relating to three attributes of the surface – its topography, its roughness and the density of vegetation cover. This is potentially of great interest in the search for geobotanical features related to geochemical anomalies. It is certainly a means of looking at the different vegetation covers that sometimes distinguish one lithology from another.

Clearly, multifrequency radar is expensive, involves complex equipment, large amounts of data and imperfect

Figure 7.22 In southern Venezuela, near to the Guyana border, the spectacular plateaus formed by fault-bounded blocks of the Cambrian Roraima Formation were the inspiration for Conan Doyle's 'Lost World'. Although not infested with dinosaurs, they are generally shrouded in cloud and comprehensive field work is not possible. This L-band stereopair, produced from an aircraft by the same-side, same-height method, reveals many details of the local structure, including evidence for an unconformity where the Roraima Formation oversteps a dyke in the crystalline basement in the left-hand part of the pair. Courtesy of Earl Hajic, University of California, Santa Barbara. Images produced by Goodyear Aerospace Corporation.

theory on radar backscatter. Consequently, few studies have been made. Plans are afoot eventually to fly a polar-orbiting, unmanned system (SISEX) with the potential for global coverage as part of the Earth Observing System (EOS), although at the time of writing such a system had not been operated from the Space Shuttle and an EOS slot had not been allocated. Figure 7.24 gives a flavour of what might ultimately be possible.

7.2.6 Multipolarization radar

A variety of interactions between radar, the surface cover and subsurface materials can alter the polarization of radar waves (Section 7.1.3). By examining different combinations of transmitted and received polarizations it should therefore be possible to add yet more flesh to geological interpretation of radar images. In an analogous way to multifrequency radar it helps discern subtle differences in surface roughness, vegetation cover and subsurface granularity that are not visible on single radar images or on those from other parts of the spectrum. Information of this kind is useful in an empirical sense for rock discrimination and highlighting anomalies. It is of more value to the botanist

or agricultural specialist in quantitative measures of the kinds and densities of vegetation cover.

Different send–receive combinations can be compared as separate images but, as always, their combination as false-colour images makes far better use of the eye's acuity in comparative studies. Figures 7.25 and 7.26 show examples of the potential of multipolarization radar images applied to the study of varied sequences of bedrock.

7.2.7 Digital processing of radar images

As well as permitting geometric correction and noise removal, radar data in digital form can be processed to extract geologically important information. Variation in DN, resulting partly from surface roughness can in its own right contribute to classification when combined with other data. However, the dominant control over DN on all scales is topography. This has a much greater contribution than in images of reflected and emitted radiation. Consequently, it tends to disrupt seriously the accuracy of classification in all except the most subdued terrains.

The greatest opportunity with radar data lies in texture enhancement and analysis. There is far more textural in-

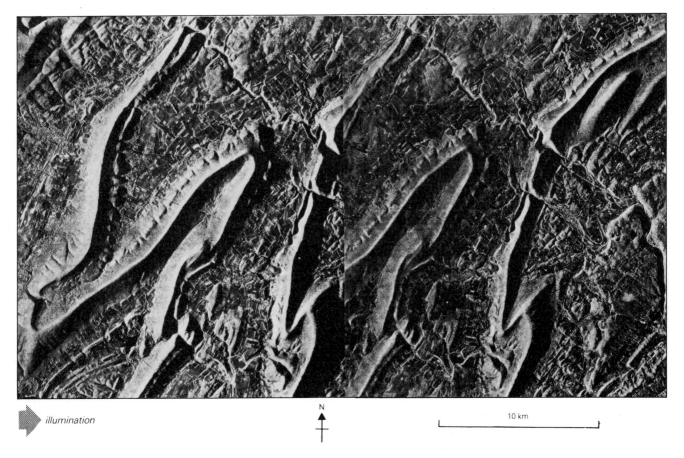

illumination

N

10 km

Figure 7.23 This same-side, same-height stereopair of X-band airborne radar images is of part of the same area shown in Figure 7.5. It shows considerable detail of the folding and faulting in the Carboniferous sediments of the Appalachians near Pittsburgh, Pennsylvania, USA, and its quality is good enough for accurate photogrammetry. The images were produced by the STAR digital SAR system, and are provided by courtesy of Intera Technologies Ltd. Calgary.

formation in a radar image than the eye can handle and sort into categories. So, considerable effort has been spent in processing radar image textures by computer to simplify and categorize them. The most obvious treatment is to use edge enhancement and directional filtering (Section 5.3) to extract the maximum amount of information about curvilinear features that are present in an image. But this ignores a lot of variation in the image which lies between linear features and is distributed in more or less homogeneous patches. To extract information from this segment of the data requires a more quantitative approach.

There are two main ways of quantifying spatial information, of which texture forms a major part. The simplest is spatial frequency filtering (Section 5.3). Tonal variations with low spatial frequencies are most usually influenced by the overall changes in roughness in an area. This is fundamental lithological and vegetation information. The higher frequency variations stem from all the different topographic features – scarps, ridges, valleys, gulleys, pits and hummocks. They contain much of the structural and textural information. Separating the two gross components by low-

and high-pass filtering (Fig. 7.27) enables a colour rendition to be extracted from a monochrome image, often with spectacular results. The filtered data are expressed in the HSI system (Section 5.7), where different hues are more easily interpreted in terms of their control by terrain features (*Fig. 7.28*). Separation into high-, medium- and low-frequency components is also possible, when the image can be reconstructed in colour through red, green and blue filters.

A more complex option is to express texture as a statistic. Since texture amounts to the spatial variation of tone or DN in an image, an appropriate measure is the variance of DN within an area. The higher the variance, the more widely and rapidly DN vary, and the finer and more contrasted the texture. Relatively smooth textures should be expressed by low variance. The procedure involves measuring the variance in a square box surrounding each pixel, and assigning that to the pixel as a DN. The art lies in choosing boxes of the right size to express different textures properly. With the radar data in this form it is possible to display an image of variance. It is important to note that

199

(a)

near range   *look direction* →   far range

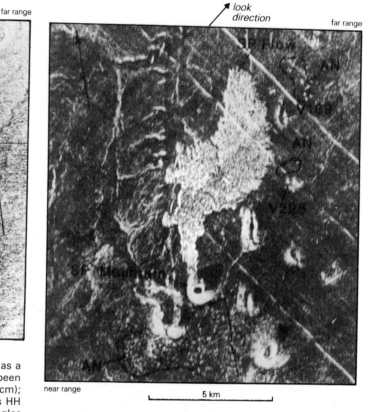

(b)

look direction   far range

near range   5 km

Figure 7.24 The volcanic area in Arizona, USA, shown as a panchromatic aerial photograph in Figure 4.41 has also been imaged using three radar wavelengths: (a) Ka-band (0.86 cm); (b) X-band (3 cm); and (c) L-band (25 cm). Each image is HH polarized, but three different resolutions and depression angles are involved, which add to the complexities. For instance, each image shows differently highlighted topographic features. There are four important points to note, remembering that as radar wavelength increases so too does the criterion for what constitutes a rough surface. First, although the lava flow – SP flow on (a) and (b) – is rough to all wavelengths, being a blocky basaltic andesite, on (c) can be seen a darker salient about halfway along the flow. This is a patch covered by cinders and vegetation, which has a more subdued surface. Secondly, on (a) the flow is shown equally as bright as the north–south-trending, fault-bounded zone to the east. On (b) and (c) there is a clear distinction between the flow and this zone of what are, in fact, limestones. Thirdly, (a) highlights lava levées (L) just north of SP Mountain, partly because of its more favourable look direction. Finally, (b) shows up a field of lava blisters or pushups (AN) which appear on neither of the other images. Courtesy of Gerald Schaber, US Geological Survey, Flagstaff, Arizona.

(c)

look direction ↓

near range

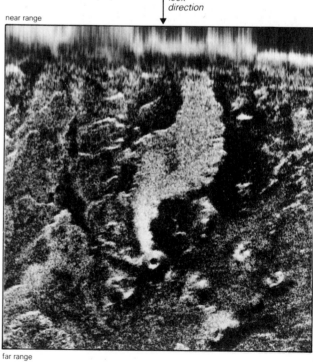

far range   5 km

(a)

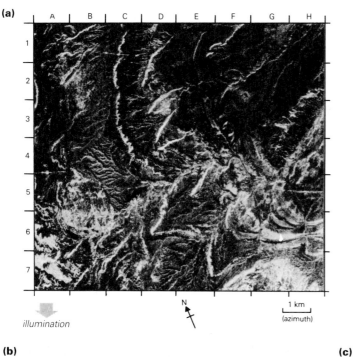

illumination

N

1 km
(azimuth)

Figure 7.25 These images are from an airborne L-band radar study of variations in backscattered energy using various modes of polarization: (a) HH, (b) VV and (c) VH. The target area is in the Wind River Basin of central Wyoming, USA, and comprises a uniformly dipping sequence of Triassic to late-Cretaceous limestones, siltstones, shales and sandstones. The oldest rocks outcrop in the west of the image, and the dip is roughly eastwards. The illumination direction was chosen to minimize the effects of topography, mainly north–south escarpments. At first sight there appears to be little difference between the images of different polarization arrangements. Indeed, in this form the data are so highly correlated as to make any one image as useful as the others. However, when the data are expressed in a false-colour image the effect is dramatic (*Fig. 7.26*).

(b)

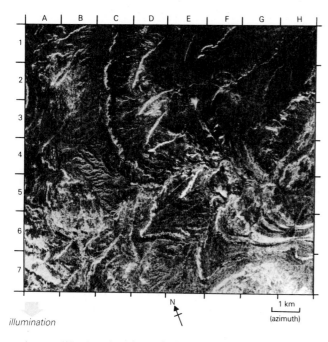

illumination

N

1 km
(azimuth)

(c)

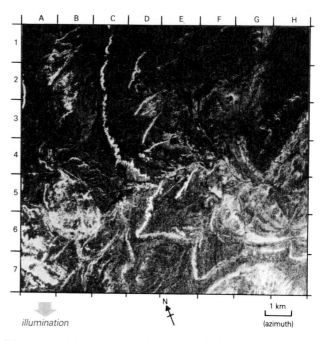

illumination

N

1 km
(azimuth)

variance, like band ratios of shorter wavelength data, is little affected by variations in the angle of illumination.

The final step is to express differences in texture by several images which have been spatially filtered to enhance a range of spatial frequencies. Each is then recast as a variance image in its own right. The images are then treated as independent spectral bands, but part of a spatial spectrum rather than an EM spectrum. These can be displayed together as colour images or used as an objective means of texture classification by multivariate methods (Section 5.8).

Elegant as this approach might seem, little success has yet been achieved.

7.2.8 Radar combined with other data

Since radar images are so different from those of other spectral regions, it might seem appropriate to use them in the raw form together with other data sets as an uncorrelated dimension in classification. This is not a fruitful option. The great sensitivity to topography would

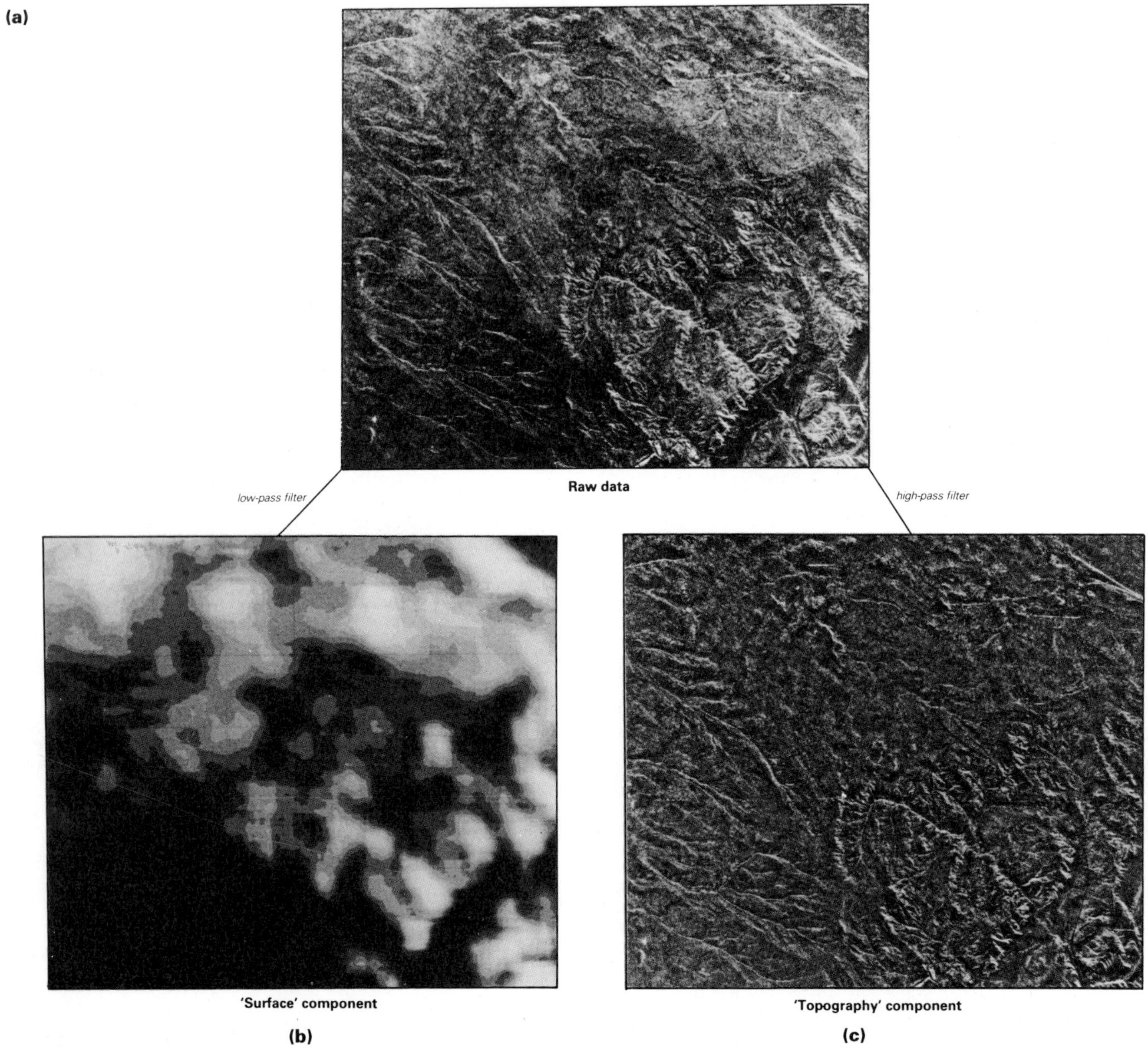

(a)

Raw data

low-pass filter   *high-pass filter*

'Surface' component

(b)

'Topography' component

(c)

Figure 7.27 Digital separation of different spatial frequency components from a Seasat image of the Wamsutter Arch in Wyoming, USA (a) results in the production of (b) an image of low-frequency variations related to gross variations in roughness and possibly rock type, and (c) an image of high-frequency variations containing topographic and textural information. The high-pass image can be used to control intensity and the low-pass image to express hue in colour HSI image (*Fig. 7.28*) where saturation is assigned a constant value to give the best colour rendition. Courtesy of Ronald Blom and Michael Daily, Jet Propulsion Laboratory, Pasadena.

mean that landforms played a greater role in classification than differences in surface properties. There would be gross misclassification. One option is to use measures of topographic texture taken from radar images, such as the variance data described in Section 7.2.7. However, uses of this kind discard most of the visual information content inherent in radar images. An important use of radar images is therefore as a means of introducing or enhancing topography and texture into colourful, but unsharp, combinations of other wavebands. The radar contributes a mass of structural information, the other data provide the distinction between different rocks (*Fig. 7.29*).

Further reading

Berlin, G.L., G.G. Schaber and K.C. Horstman 1980. Possible fault detection in Cottonball Basin, California: and application of radar remote sensing. *Remote Sens. Environ.* **10**, 33–42.

Blom, R.G. and M. Daily 1982. Radar image processing for rock-type discrimination. *IEEE Trans. Geoscience and Remote Sens.* **GE-20**, 343–351.

Blom, R.G., R.E. Crippen and C. Elachi 1984. Detection of subsurface features in Seasat radar images of Means Valley, Mojave Desert, California. *Geology* **12**, 346–349.

Blom, R.G., L.R. Schenk and R.E. Alley 1987. What are the best radar wavelength, incidence angles and polarization for discrimination among lava flows, and sedimentary rocks? A statistical approach. *IEEE Trans. Geosci. Remote Sens.* **GE-25**, 208–212.

Curlis, J.D., V.S. Frost and L.F. Dellwig 1986. Geological mapping potential of computer-enhanced images from the Shuttle Imaging Radar: Lisbon Valley anticline, Utah. *Photogramm. Eng. Remote Sens.* **52**, 525–532.

Daily, M. 1983. Hue–saturation–intensity split-spectrum processing of Seasat radar imagery. *Photogramm. Eng. Remote Sens.* **49**, 349–355.

Daily, M., C. Elachi, T. Farr and G. Schaber 1978. Discrimination of geologic units in Death Valley using dual frequency and polarization imaging radar data. *Geophysical Res. Lett.* **5**, 889–892.

Daily, M., T. Farr, C. Elachi and G. Schaber 1979. Geologic interpretation from composited radar and Landsat imagery. *Photogramm. Eng. Remote Sens.* **45**, 1109–1116.

Dellwig, L.F. 1969. An evaluation of multifrequency radar imagery of the Pisgah crater area, California. *Modern Geology* **1**, 65–73.

Dellwig, L.F. and R.K. Moore 1966. The geological value of simultaneously produced like- and cross-polarised radar imagery. *J. Geophys. Res.* **71**, 3597–3601.

Elachi, C. 1983. Microwave and infrared satellite remote sensors. Chapter 13 in *Manual of remote sensing*, 2nd edn, Colwell, R.N. (ed.), pp. 571–650. Falls Church, Virginia: American Society of Photogrammetry.

Elachi, C., W.E. Brown, J.B. Cimino, T. Dixon, D.L. Evans, J.P. Ford, R.S. Saunders, C. Breed, H. Masurski, G. Schaber, L. Dellwig, A. England, P. MacDonald, P. Martin-Kaye and F. Sabins 1982. Shuttle imaging radar experiment. *Science* **218**, 996–1003.

Elachi, C., L.E. Roth and G.G. Schaber 1984. Spaceborne radar subsurface imaging in hyperarid regions. *IEEE Trans. Geoscience Remote Sens* **GE-22**, 382–387.

Evans, D.L., T.G. Farr, J.P. Ford, T.W. Thompson and C.L. Werner 1985. Multipolarization radar images for geologic mapping and vegetation discrimination. *IEEE Trans. Geoscience Remote Sens.*

JPL 1980. *Radar geology, an assessment.* JPL Publication 80–61.

JPL 1982. *The SIR-B science plan.* JPL Publication 82-78.

Kasischke, E.S., A.R. Schuchman, R.D. Lysenga and A.G. Meadows 1983. Detection of bottom features on Seasat synthetic aperture radar imagery. *Photogramm. Eng. Remote Sens.* **49**, 1341–1353.

Lowman, P.D., J. Harris, P.M. Masuoka, V.H. Singhroy and V.R. Slaney 1987. Shuttle imaging radar (SIR-B) investigations of the Canadian Shield: initial report. *IEEE Trans. Geosci. Remote Sens.* **GE-25**, 55–66.

McCauley, J.F., G.G. Schaber, C.S. Breed, M.J. Grolier, C.V., Haynes B. Issawi, C. Elachi and R. Blom 1982. Subsurface valleys and geoarcheology of the Eastern Sahara revealed by Shuttle radar. *Science* **218**, 1004–1020.

Martin-Kaye, P.H.A. and G.M. Lawrence 1983. The application of satellite imaging radars over land to the assessment, mapping and monitoring of resources. *Phil. Trans. R. Soc. Lond. A* **309**, 295–314.

Pravdo, S.H., B. Huneycutt, B.M. Holt and D.N. Held 1982. *Seasat synthetic-aperture radar data user's manual.* JPL Publication 82–90.

Sabins, F.F. 1983. Geologic interpretation of Space Shuttle radar images of Indonesia. *Am. Ass. Petrol. Geol. Bull.* **67**, 2076–2099.

Sabins, F.F., R. Blom and C. Elachi 1980. Seasat radar image of San Andreas Fault, California. *Am. Ass. Petrol. Geol. Bull.* **64**, 612–628.

Schaber, G.G., G.L. Berlin and W.E. Brown Jr 1976. Variations in surface roughness within Death Valley, California: geologic evaluation of 25-cm wavelength radar images. *Geol. Soc. Am. Bull.* **87**, 29–41.

Schaber, G.G., C. Elachi and T.G. Farr 1980. Remote sensing of SP Mountain and SP Lava Flow in North-Central Arizona. *Remote Sens. Environ.* **9**, 149–170.

Wadge, G. and T.H. Dixon 1984. A geological interpretation of Seasat-SAR imagery of Jamaica. *J. Geol.* **92**, 561–581.

CHAPTER EIGHT

Non-image data and geographic information systems

Earlier chapters have dealt almost exclusively with data that in one way or another were gathered in the form of images. These contain a wealth of information from which geological inferences can be made and synthesized in the form of maps. However, they are restricted to the use of EMR emanating from the Earth's surface, and the spectral response of rocks poses fairly tight limits on geological interpretation. Except where structural features can be extrapolated in three dimensions, it also limits interpretation to, at most, a few kilometres of the crust where uplift and erosion have produced extreme relief. Increasingly, geologists are becoming concerned with ever-deeper levels, partly because the search for resources has to extend its scope as near-surface deposits become depleted, and partly because other kinds of data enable deep levels to be investigated. Indeed, the one presupposes the other.

Data giving clues to subsurface geology include well logs, seismic reflection sections, potential-field data from gravity and magnetic surveys, and results from various kinds of geophysical survey oriented at the electrical properties of rocks, soils and minerals. There are many other kinds of data with an indirect bearing on surface geology, such as measurements of emitted gamma-radiation, and geochemical surveys of rock and soil samples, vegetation, stream sediments and water. To these 'raw' data can be added information carried on existing maps. As well as definition of lithological and stratigraphic units, and geological structures, maps may include sites of resource extraction, finds of economically interesting mineral associations (prospects or showings) and the whole range of information on surface

elevation, hydrology, communications, habitations, land use and ownership generally associated with conventional topographic maps.

For decades geologists have used many of these other data sources in particular tasks, such as general mapping, geomorphological studies, exploration for hydrocarbons, metals and water, site investigations for engineering projects, and assessing environmental constraints on various operations, as well as in fundamental research (Ch. 9). The unifying factor among all these types of information is that they are geographical in nature. They relate to points, lines or areas on the Earth's surface expressed in various cartographic coordinate systems. As paper maps, such data present a number of problems in manually assembling them. They may be at a variety of scales and in different projections. Even as transparent overlays, the space required and the geologist's finite powers of mentally retaining information pose limits to integrating the information properly.

The symbolism used in maps can vary (Section 8.1), and is frequently out of tune with human visual perception. Many maps show variations in a third dimension as contour lines. Human vision treats lines and tonal variations in different ways (Ch. 2). Our view of a contour map is partly one of tonal variation that depends on the spacing of contours: the closer the lines are, the darker the perceived tone. But the spacing of contour lines relates to gradients in the third dimension, not actual values. So even if contours are carefully labelled there is conflict between what is learned about contour maps and their interpretation and innate human perception. Contour maps are notoriously difficult to relate to the real world. Section 8.2 centres on converting information that is generally rendered as contour maps into image form. Images are more readily understood and amenable to enhancement using digital image processing.

The variety of data that a geologist may need to assemble, brood over and interpret can be represented as a series of layers (Fig. 8.1). Each layer contains information pertinent to a specific element of the task. For an assessment of water resources for domestic and agricultural uses a hydrogeologist might need layers for geology, soil type, rain fall, land use, hydrology, water table in wells, topography, land ownership, transportation routes and settlements. From these basic layers it would be necessary to extract information on the distribution of aquifers, well yields, stream gauging data, faults, topographic slope, the facing direction of slopes (**slope aspect**), and so on. This is a daunting body of conventionally separate information. An agriculturalist working on the same programme would need some of this information too, plus more detail on, say, soil texture, soil depth, drainage properties, content of nutrients and pH. Map information in paper form clearly poses problems for both, indeed some information may well not appear on maps. Inevitably the analysis is slow and largely dependent on intuition and arbitrary selection of information.

A layered view of geographic information is the basis for management and interrogation of map data in digital form as a **geographic information system (GIS)**. Not only are data rationalized in a GIS, using a computer as a tool greatly speeds access to data. They become amenable to a variety of objective and efficient means of analysis, which involve all pertinent information and thereby broaden the scope for interpretation, planning and execution. Section 8.3 introduces some of the basic concepts and techniques in GISs.

8.1 Forms of non-image data

The raw data available for use in geological and many other kinds of investigation can take a variety of forms:

(1) Values for some variable at a point (e.g. elevation, geochemical and gravity data, borehole records, dip angle and direction).
(2) Continuous records of a variable along a line (e.g. seismic profiles, airborne geophysical data, ground electrical surveys).
(3) Areas designated as homogeneous categories (e.g. lithostratigraphic, soil and vegetation maps, and results of classification).
(4) Lines expressing relationships or linear categories (e.g. faults, intrusive contacts, roads, property boundaries).
(5) Continuous or semicontinuous greytone or colour images of remotely sensed data.

Types 1, 3 and 4 often involve information that is not part of some continuous variation, but expresses defined categories or **attributes**. Obvious examples are the metal-bearing minerals found at a mining prospect, names of rock types, different soil classes and various senses of fault movement. However, a named category often has other associated attributes. A stream will have a particular order in relation to its connections with other larger and smaller streams – the higher the order the greater the number of tributaries – and will have a unique catchment size. It may be named in its own right or as a tributary of a larger system. A particular soil type may have variable colour, texture and drainage properties, and can also be categorized in terms of how prone to erosion it is. Roads can have different numbers of lanes and various paving surfaces, as well as a designated code. Rocks have many attributes, a few being mineralogy, chemical composition, radiometric age, porosity and even associated plant community.

There are two basic models that can encode or format geographic information, known as **raster** and **vector** models. In the raster model the real world is represented by a regular division of two-dimensional space into cells with a definite shape arranged in a regular fashion. Cells may be rectangular, triangular, hexagonal or any other shape that allows a systematic tiling or mosaic to cover the surface. That most commonly used involves rectangular cells arranged in a grid of rows and columns. Position is defined by Cartesian (x,y or column, row) coordinates. This means that precision is limited by the size chosen for the cells. Objects and conditions or properties referring to the surface

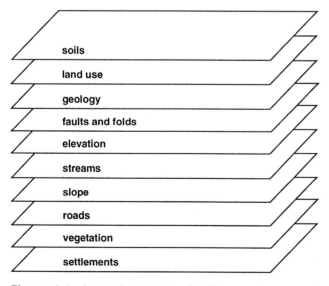

Figure 8.1 Layered structure of primary geological and related data.

are represented by attributes assigned to each cell. The cell attribute applies to every location within the cell, and the cell cannot be divided. In raster format every category of attribute requires a separate file, the discussion above suggesting that used alone raster-format data can occupy vast volumes of computer storage. The clearest examples of raster-format data are provided by digital images, including paper maps captured by various scanning devices. Other types are renditions of numerical non-image data recast in the form of a grid of values (Section 8.2.1), and conversions to a raster from vector format.

In the vector model, objects or conditions are represented by the points and lines that define their boundaries, much as if they were drawn on a map. Vector-format data are represented by points, and by lines and closed loops (polygons) made of straight-line segments. Line segments are defined by their end points. Since any point on the Earth's surface has a unique coordinate, the accuracy of vector-format data is limited by the precision of surveying, the encoding length of computer words (now at least 16 bits) and the number of points used to define curved lines and polygons in the real world. Primarily, vector format represents spatial entities, but many attributes can be recorded for and assigned to each point, line or area within a single file. Data input to vector format can take many different forms, by keying in location and attributes at a terminal from field records, through data logging and positional devices such as a satellite positioning system used in the field, by manually digitizing existing maps, using complex pattern recognition to extract vectors from raster-format images, by line-following scanners, and by input of previously compiled vector files.

How raster- and vector-format data are encoded digitally is beyond the scope of this book, and a number of methods with various efficiencies and uses have been devised. Figure 8.2 shows the essential differences between raster and vector formats. Raster data files, since they cover the whole of an area, each contain millions or tens of millions of cells. In this regard vector-format files are much more compact, comprising up to tens of thousands of elements. Each model has other advantages and disadvantages. The raster model has a far simpler data structure than the vector model. It allows much easier combinations of different data than the vector model, represents spatial variability much more efficiently, and permits a great variety of digital manipulations and enhancements. Vector-format data, as well as being the more compact, encode topological relationships, while rasters do not. Being very precise representations of definite spatial features, vector files are better suited to graphic representation than rasters, which present boundaries with a blocky structure because they are represented by arrays of cells. Both raster and vector data are used in geographic information systems (Section 8.3), but raster-format renditions of non-image data have many uses in purely visual interpretation and combination with the information in remotely sensed images.

8.2 Non-image data in raster format

The simplest raster-format data are those produced when generating colour separates in digital form from paper geological maps. Facsimiles of the red, green and blue components are produced as raster files by a scanning or

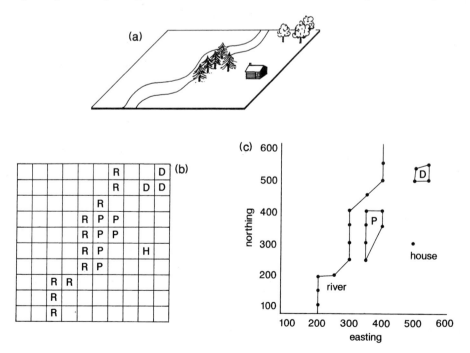

Figure 8.2 Differences between raster- and vector-format data. A simple scene of reality (a) is represented as a raster by (b), where each element of the scene is made up of square pixels, and in vector format (c) by points, lines and polygons labelled with an attribute.

CCD device. Although in theory three-colour maps can be classified into categories comprising lithological units, boundaries and structural features, in practice the cartographic use of hachured tones, similar colours for different features and the presence of symbols such as dip arrows tend to thwart such efforts. A better representation of the information content in the map is achieved by using the vector model. The appeal of raster maps lies in their retention of the cartographer's art and the ability to combine them with other kinds of raster data in composite images (Section 8.2.6).

All other data involving quantifiable attributes that in nature vary continuously over an area initially require conversion from records at points or along survey lines to the regular grid that is the hallmark of the raster model. This involves interpolation from the values at surveyed positions to areas for which there are no data.

8.2.1 Interpolation and gridding

Producing a raster rendition of non-image data gathered at more or less irregularly spaced positions involves mathematically predicting from nearby measured values and the overall variation what values might be found within regularly spaced cells covering the whole area occupied by the data. This is **interpolation**. Predicting values that lie outside the surveyed area is **extrapolation**, which is rarely used, except in predicting values that are at the boundaries of the area of cover.

Interpolation relies on expressing the known data in the form of a three-dimensional mathematical model. The simplest model is to assume that the value at any point is the same as that at the nearest surveyed station. This divides the area into polygons containing survey locations, whose sides are equidistant between adjoining positions. The model consists of steps, and unless the original data were gathered in a rectangular grid the polygons are more akin to a vector representation than a raster. This method is rarely used in geological applications, models embodying predictions of gradual change being preferred.

The simplest of these predictive models is that involved in **regression analysis**, which fits surfaces to a data distribution to minimize the sums of squares of the distances between real points and the surface. Figure 8.3a shows a best-fit line to the variation of a property z with distance x, which can be considered as a cross-section of a planar surface in three dimensions. The distance in question is that between the points and the line in the z direction – there is no need to interpolate the distance which is implicitly correct. The method can be extended to polynomial surfaces of any order (Fig. 8.3b). This method, which is also termed **trend-surface analysis**, predicts the long-range variation of the third, non-spatial dimension and effectively smoothes local variations, rarely passing

exactly through the original data points (Fig. 8.4). Effectively, trend-surface analysis treats the 'raw' data as though they contain errors. A raster produced in this way degrades the information content, but the deviations or **residuals** involved with trend surfaces of different orders are often extremely useful in some applications (Section 8.2.5). A similar surface-fitting interpolation involves Fourier analysis (Section 5.3), but this too omits deviations from smooth surfaces.

Before computers could be used to fit curves to distributions of data on a graph, it was achieved using flexible rulers. Technically, these were called **splines**. The important feature of a spline is that it can be fitted to curves whose form varies from place to place. Trend surfaces and Fourier series accommodate the whole in one complex function and the points often deviate from the computed prediction. A spline fit can be perfect, and the joins between one part of a curve and other different parts are continuous. This does not mean that a spline exactly

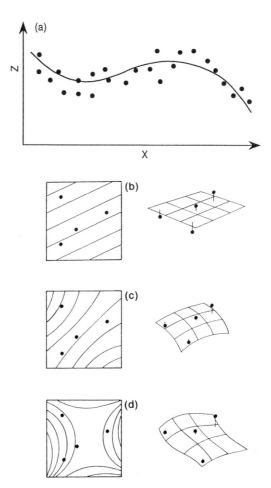

Figure 8.3 (a) Best fit line through points showing the variation of Z with X. First-, second- and third-order trend surfaces fitted to four points are shown as contoured maps and three-dimensional surfaces in (b), (c) and (d) respectively.

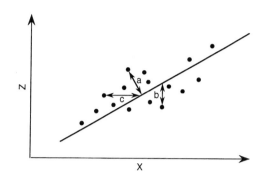

Figure 8.4 Deviation of a best-fit line from the actual data points.

predicts values of the third dimension at unsurveyed points, but adding extra points merely allows the spline to become a more precise reflection of reality. However, a spline ruler makes no allowance for errors in the data. It can be shown that a line drawn using a spline is approximately made up of segments defined by different cubic polynomials, and has continuous gradients and gradients of gradient (first and second derivatives in calculus terms). Consequently, it can be expressed mathematically and applied to two- and three-dimensional data sets using a computer. For lines it is known as a **cubic-spline function**, and for surfaces as a **bicubic-spline function**. Mathematical splines can be used to fit data exactly, or, if errors are suspected, to incorporate a degree of smoothing to allow for imprecision. Figure 8.5 shows a spline fit to several points and the modification that must occur if one point is subsequently revised, emphasizing the limitations of this approach.

One of the problems with using bicubic splines in gridding, as implied by Figure 8.5, is that they can introduce artificial anomalies because of the way that they work. One means of avoiding this is to assign to an unsurveyed cell the average value from actual points in its local neighbourhood. This is a **moving-average** approach, and

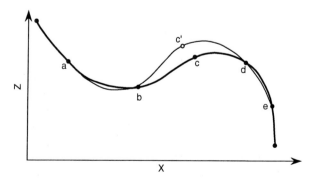

Figure 8.5 Cubic-spline function exactly fitted to data points, the dashed line showing how the fit changes with the modification of one point.

the size of the neighbourhood or 'window' can be varied. It is possible to incorporate means of weighting the contribution of each point according to its distance from the unknown cell. However, this leaves several difficulties: What is the optimum size for the 'window'? What shape and orientation should it have? Is distance the best control over weighting? What errors are associated with the interpolated values. These were addressed by a mining engineer, D.G. Krige, in attempting to optimize predictions of spatial factors in mine planning. He and mathematicians working in parallel recognized that many properties vary too irregularly to be modelled by smooth functions based solely on three-dimensional geometry. They require knowledge of some of the statistics involved. The mathematics involved is complex, but **kriging**, as this approach is known, has become widely employed where great control on the precision and accuracy of gridding is required, as in mapping variations of metal grade in ore bodies and in the production of digital elevation data (Section 8.2.4). However, it is much more expensive in terms of computer time than methods based on splines and weighted moving averages, which are the most frequently encountered means of producing rasters.

8.2.2 Geophysical data

Today, virtually every geophysical survey records data in computer-readable digital form, with extremely precise geographic positioning thanks to inertial and satellite navigation systems. The raw data are therefore immediately accessible – given permission or the payment of the appropriate fee – for interpolation using the methods outlined in the last section. Gridding may already have been done and the results stored, because this is essential in the computer production of conventional contour maps. Given the raw data there are, however, a few problems. Since point measurements are generally produced with a fairly even spacing, problems are minimal with ground gravity data and similar information. However, many surveys are conducted along survey lines, either continuously, as with aeromagnetic surveys, or at regular along-line sampling intervals, as in airborne gamma-ray spectrometry and electrical ground surveys.

The main problem with line surveys is that the sampling interval along lines is generally smaller than the separation between lines – there is a distinct linear bias to the data. Moreover, in terms of the variability encountered, some segments contain far greater deviations from regional trends than others. By using all the data two problems are encountered. First, the quality of the interpolation decreases away from the lines, imparting artificial geometric features parallel to the lines. Second, the same weight is given to 'smooth' areas as to complex areas, involving much redundant information and tending to extend smoothness into areas that predictably should be complex. Some means of reducing redundancy and avoiding bias has to be sought.

There are two strategies to follow. The line spacing limits the degree of spatial accuracy in areas between the lines, and so an appropriate grid cell size must be chosen. In general, a size between a quarter and an eighth of the line spacing is required to avoid artifacts parallel to the lines. With regard to the raw data themselves, some strategy for sampling along the lines is needed. If the spacing is much smaller than the eventual cell dimensions then directional bias remains. If sampling is infrequent, then some of the information is lost. Clearly a compromise is needed. Wide sampling in smooth areas loses little information, and the sampling in complex areas seeks to identify local minima and maxima, and more importantly to define the shape of the variation where there are changes in gradient (breaks in slope). To do this automatically means that the software must incorporate measures of local complexity, such as variance and the second derivative, plus identification of maxima and minima and an upper limit imposed on sampling density. Inevitably information is lost to be replaced by mathematical interpolation, but this is a trade-off with the advantages of rendering the data in raster form.

Of course, a very large proportion of geophysical information was gathered before the current opportunities presented by computing became available. Raw data may no longer be available, or may be in the form of analogue profiles along survey lines. In the latter case digital data can be generated by manual input from the profiles. Most information will be in the form of contour maps that may well have been produced by manual interpolation. As well as the visual disadvantages of contour maps discussed earlier, their very nature in expressing continuous variations in discrete steps degrades the original data. In such cases the only option is to extract information by one of several means. Figure 8.6 shows three methods. All can be achieved using a digitizing table, the differences being in the sampling strategy. The first systematically estimates a value for the variable at points in a regular grid (Fig. 8.6a). Using the reasoning that more points are needed to define areas of increasing complexity means sampling with variable spacing (Fig. 8.6c). Both methods 'second guess' the methodology used in compiling the original map, inevitably assuming linear variation between contours in manual digitizing. The third method assumes that the contours are accurately positioned, and samples along them (Fig. 8.6b). This maintains, and even extends, the degradation implicit in contouring. However, the last method can be partly automated by using line-following devices, and variable contour spacing assists the gridding software in fitting a better surface to the data than is possible using the other methods. None has particular advantages, but since producing raster maps often involves input from many

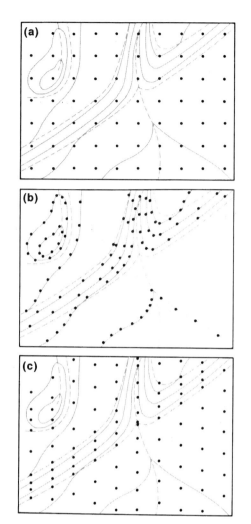

Figure 8.6 Three methods of digitizing data from contour maps.

original contour maps when a method is chosen it must be adhered to so that the product has a consistent mathematical basis.

8.2.3 Geochemical data

Measurements of the concentration of an element in a sample of rock, soil or vegetation relate only to the geographical location of the sampling. Consequently they can be treated in exactly the same way as geophysical data from point surveys, and converted by interpolation to raster images. However, such surveys are slow and expensive to conduct and are rarely undertaken for regional evaluation. A much quicker, cheaper and convenient approach is to exploit the natural sampling of soils and rocks associated with erosion, transport and deposition by flowing water. Most of the continental surface has been subject to such processes and is criss-crossed by drainage channels that are easy to locate on maps or aerial photographs, and easy to sample. Results of **drainage geochemical surveys**, as analyses of stream sediments or stream water, are by far the most widespread basis for geochemical exploration. However, they present a particular kind of problem in conversion to raster format.

The concentration of a chemical element in stream sediment of water does not represent the composition of the soil or rock in the immediate vicinity of the sample point in a stream channel. Instead, the natural sampling represents the area from which all the water and sediment moving past the sample point has been derived. That is, it represents the **catchment area** upstream of the sample point. Figure 8.7 illustrates the difficulty. The area represented by each sample increases the further down the drainage the sample is collected. This relates to the **order** of the stream – the more tributaries entering a stream, the higher is its order and the larger is its catchment area. Consequently, if samples are taken from all streams, each sample has not only its own unique concentration but a unique significance in terms of the area that it represents. In such a case it is impossible to interpolate the results to a regular raster with any meaning. In fact it would be grossly misleading to do this. The only valid representation would be assigning the measured values to the associated catchments. If there are several sample points along a drainage this clearly leads to great confusion. Furthermore, as the order of a stream increases, so the chances of anomalous values decrease owing to the diluting effect of water and sediment being contributed from a wider area. Although many drainage geochemical surveys have been conducted for metal exploration, the original style of seeking anomalies low in a drainage and then tracing them upstream to their source largely rules out the data being used in a raster form.

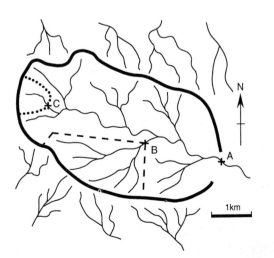

Figure 8.7 Map showing the variation in size of catchments (dotted, pecked and bold lines) for points on streams of different order.

However, there is a strategy to overcome this problem.

The lower a stream's order, the smaller is its catchment and the more likely are the concentrations of chemical elements in stream samples to represent nearby rocks and soils. Provided only streams of the same order, and preferably the first or second order, are sampled and grid cells similar in size to that of the associated catchments are used, interpolation to raster format is realistic. Because of the wealth of possibilities for display and enhancement of geochemical data as images, and their combination with other kinds of data, either in raster images or GISs, this form of sampling is becoming the norm for drainage geochemical surveys.

Multi-element geochemistry is a powerful means of discriminating rock types and gaining insights into petrogenetic relationships, because of the different behaviours of various suites of elements during chemical fractionation related to different geological processes. So, one use of raster-format geochemical data is in basic geological mapping, when the full range of variability is employed. Geochemical exploration, primarily for metals but sometimes for hydrocarbons, relies on locating areas where concentrations of some elements rise well above the general levels or **backgrounds** associated with common rock types to form **anomalies**. A problem lies in deciding which values constitute anomalies within the full range of variation. A variety of solutions centre on statistical analysis of the frequency of occurrence of ranges of values found in the data. The most frequently occurring ranges can be considered as background and infrequent occurrences may constitute anomalies. Background values generally form a more or less distinct and broad peak in the histogram with a clear maximum and minimum. Anomalies lie outside this range, and usually only abnormally high values are considered in exploration, for obvious reasons (Fig. 8.8a). The maximum expected value within the background range is sometimes termed the **threshold**, and it is possible to separate anomalies from the normal by setting all cells with values below the threshold to an arbitrary level and using contrast enhancement to highlight anomalies. More sophisticated statistics help refine this screening. One is to use the cumulative histogram and density slice at a variety of percentile levels (Fig. 8.8b). Since many elements show a log-normal distribution of values – many occurrences over a restricted range (such as 10–50 parts per million) and a few occurrences over a very wide range (such as 100–1000 parts per million) – the histogram is often used with a logarithmic axis. Another approach is to use some arbitrary rule that, for example, expresses cells with values below the threshold (t), between t and t plus the average value (a), $t + a$ to $t + 2a$, $t + 2a$ to $t + 3a$, and greater than $t + 3a$ with different intensities or colours, each constituting anomalous cells of increasing potential significance. Because of the wide variation in

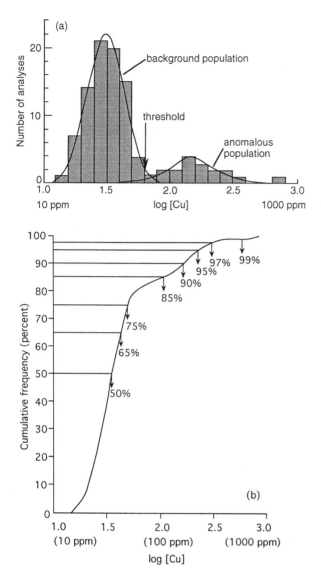

Figure 8.8 (a) Histogram of copper concentrations in a geochemical survey with a smooth curve fitted to the variability. (b) Cumulative frequency distribution for the copper data in (a) showing different percentile levels.

chemical composition of common rocks, particularly for some trace elements, a concentration that is anomalous for one rock type may be within normal bounds for another. So, a further complicating factor in using geochemical data is screening them according to the known distribution of different lithological units.

8.2.4 Elevation data

The Earth's surface is the most familiar example of continuous variation in three spatial dimensions, and is almost universally represented by contoured maps of topographic elevation. As well as containing accurate representations of topography, in which may dwell clues to geological features that exert a control over landforms, topographic data have immense potential for the extraction of other information with a variety of uses. Topography controls the rates and directions in which surface water flows, and drainage networks can be established in the absence of any hydrological survey. If planar geological boundaries are known, perhaps from interpretation of remotely sensed images, their trends in relation to topography enable the dip and strike and even structure contours of the boundaries to be estimated using the simple three-point solution. Topographic slope can be estimated, from which stem measures of the likelihood of soil erosion or risk from landslip. The topographic data can be incorporated with others for a variety of purposes, such as perspective visualizations of unknown terrain, introduction of relief displacement into remotely sensed images to give stereoptic viewing potential and the correction of remotely sensed data for variable solar illumination.

Topographic elevation values expressed in digital form are known as **digital elevation models (DEMs)**, which can be in a variety of forms. The simplest are as raster arrays, but as these employ the same density of cells irrespective of the complexity of the topographic surface they occupy large storage volumes. A number of methods employ variable densities of data points to reduce storage space, but all must be gridded if the data or derivatives from them are needed in raster format. Capturing elevation data from existing contour maps can employ any of the methods described in Section 8.2.2, and raster DEMs are produced using the interpolation methods in Section 8.2.1. For some areas DEMs are available from state mapping agencies in various forms. The US Department of Defense's Defense Mapping Agency (DMA) maintains a global archive of DEMs derived from surveillance satellites and aircraft for most of the planet at very high resolution. This is known as Digital Terrain Elevation Data (DTED) Level-1. At the time of writing DTED Level-1 for areas outside the USA was only accessible to US government agencies or those of allied powers, but this may change if pressure from potential users is applied strenuously and continuously.

A very large proportion of topographic maps have their elevation data derived from stereoscopic measurements of aerial photographs, using a variety of manual and semi-automatic photogrammetric instruments, backed up by precise geodetic surveying. The methods rely on measurement of the parallax differences inherent in the relief displacement present in different forms in stereoscopic image pairs (Appendix A). As satellite systems, such as SPOT and JERS-1, produce digital stereopairs, and as photographic images can be digitized accurately, it is possible through the use of complex software to derive DEMs automatically. The parallax estimation that is essential in such automated cartography relies on the computer being able to recognize the same features on each image of the stereopair. An operator identifies a number of points on the stereopair that act as 'seeds' for the necessary pattern recognition on both images that allows the parallax differences or disparities in position to be calculated in multiples of the images' pixel dimensions. Surveyed ground-control points are used to rectify and calibrate the disparities to elevation values at precise ground positions. Inevitably, a variable proportion of the area covered has featureless terrain, so halting the automated process. Interpolation, such as kriging (Section 8.2.1), is then used to fill the gaps or to improve the spatial resolution of the DEM. Since elevation precision depends on that associated with parallax, the spatial resolution of the imagery is crucial, since parallax can only be measured in multiples of pixels. For 10-m resolution SPOT data elevation precision is around 20–30 m – too poor for all but qualitative use of the resulting DEMs. Aerial photographs have resolutions in the 0.1–1 m range, which approximates the reported elevation precision of the DTED Level-1 data.

Theoretically, use of satellite positioning systems in ground surveys can provide elevation and position accuracies at the submetre level, but so many survey points would need to be visited to produce a DEM of useful size that the time involved would be prohibitive. In the absence of readily available, precise DEMs, the best means of producing them for detailed, quantitative applications is by painstaking digitization of contours on large-scale (>1:25 000) maps and then interpolation. This should ensure vertical precision of the order of 1 m.

Because the travel time of radar waves scattered from the surface can be measured very precisely, it might seem reasonable to expect that radar could be used for measurements of surface elevation to within a few centimetres. Such **radar altimeters** have been deployed on Seasat and ERS-1, but results are only available for the ocean surface. The problem over land lies in both the difficulty in focusing the radar beam and in the response from rugged surfaces. From orbital altitudes the radar beam spreads to several kilometres, thereby limiting the resolution in the horizontal plane. Within this 'footprint' the highest features reflect the radar wave first and the lowest give a later return of the radar pulse. Consequently, all that can be measured in the vertical dimension is the average elevation and the range of elevations. For such a wide 'footprint' that information over all but the gentlest terrain is of little use. Radar altimetry is therefore of little use over land. However, waves at the ocean surface are rarely higher than 1–20 m and the average ocean-surface elevation can be measured to within a few centimetres within the wide radar 'footprint'. Wave height is obviously an interesting measurement for oceanographers and meteorologists, but the usefulness of ocean-surface elevation is not immediately apparent.

Being a fluid, the level of sea water is closely controlled by gravitational factors, hence the diurnal and monthly patterns of tides. But the Earth's gravitational field also plays a role, as well as those of the Moon and Sun. Averaged over several months the ocean-surface elevation is mainly related to variations in terrestrial gravity. Over the oceans the gravitational field, and therefore the surface elevation, is dominated by variations in ocean depth. Because water is about a third as dense as the rocks constituting the oceanic lithosphere, the shallower the water the higher the gravitational potential and vice versa. This means that water is attracted to shallow areas to form a bulge, and conversely the surface is depressed over deep ocean basins, thereby restoring a constant surface gravitational potential. A feature on the ocean floor with a relief of 1 km results in a 2-m disturbance of the surface. With a vertical precision of 5 cm, radar altimetry can therefore represent features as small as 25 m, provided that they extend over several kilometres. So, as a result of this convoluted relationship, images of radar altimetry data over the oceans form bathymetric maps of such precision that subtle features of the ocean floor are readily apparent (Fig. 8.9). Because conventional bathymetric maps are compiled from soundings taken by ships, their quality varies according to the density of marine traffic. Over most of the oceans bathymetry derived from radar altimetry is far more informative. It is possible to use conventional bathymetry to remove the effect of varying water depth to analyse changes in gravitational potential resulting from variations in the density of the underlying crust and mantle. This can be used to map features possibly related to thermal convection in the mantle, and to locate deep sedimentary basins in areas of continental shelf.

While radar altimetry appears unlikely to generate useful DEMs over land, because of beam focusing problems, laser altimeters can potentially produce very high resolution in all three dimensions over land. Indeed, laser methods are used from orbit for precise site positioning in studies of plate dynamics. There is one major difficulty of a non-scientific nature associated with very precise DEMs. They are essential for the guidance systems of cruise missiles, as well as other military applications, and are therefore shrouded in secrecy. Cruise missiles have been around for well over a decade, and thus so have DEMs with the requisite precision. Quite probably these are of the US DMA DTED Level-1 type, and possibly generated by highly secure laser altimetry.

It is possible to extract some information on surface elevation from the complex signals received by synthetic aperture radar (Section 3.5), because in the separation of signals from objects ahead of and behind the platform, each element of the surface is 'looked' at several times. The arrival times for each look incorporate information on the shape of the surface, but in such a complex way that the resulting DEM is rarely a precise representation of the

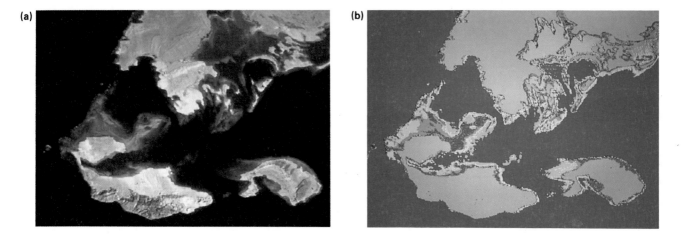

Figure 1.18 The clear water of the Red Sea off Saudi Arabia allows green light to penetrate to depths of 20–30 m. In image (a), a Landsat Multispectral Scanner false-colour image, the blue colours of the near-shore waters are the result of reflection from coral reefs and sand in shallow water. Image (b) shows colour bands assigned to narrow ranges of green reflectance to produce a representation of the variation in bathymetry. Grey is above sea level, red is the shallowest water and the progression towards dark blue is from shallow to deep water.

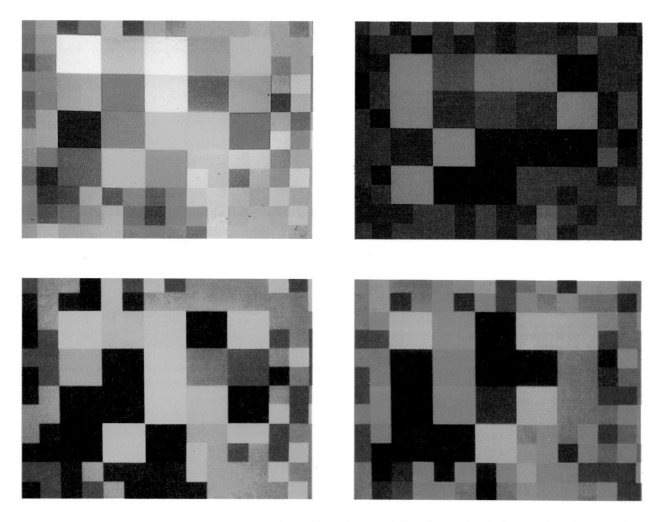

Figure 2.14 The 'paint box' of colours has been produced by combining the three additive primary colours in the proportions shown as red, green and blue.

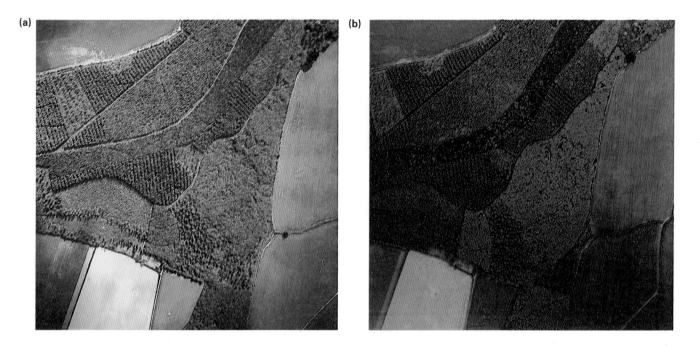

Figure 3.5   In this pair of vertical aerial photographs of a rural scene in Devon, UK, (a) is natural colour and (b) false-colour infrared. Although the natural colour image is more pleasant to look at, because it is dominated by wavelengths near the peak of human visual sensitivity, it contains less information than the false-colour infrared image. This is particularly striking in the wooded area, where not only are the conifers sharply distinguished from the sparse, bright-red broad-leaved species in the dark swath of trees, but many stands of different broad-leaved species, different stages of growth and different canopy types can be separated too. On the natural colour image these features are by no means obvious. Copyright Aerofilms Ltd.

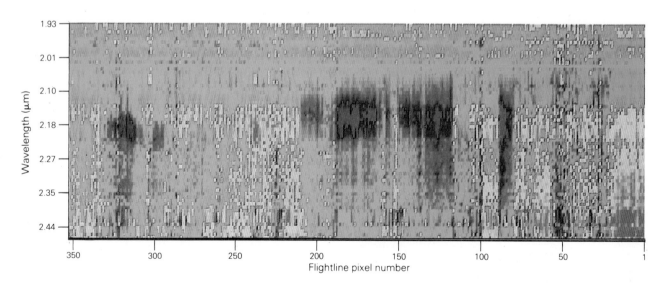

Figure 3.24   This figure consists of many spectra from an airborne spectroradiometry campaign. The spectra are stacked for individual ground resolution cells along a flight line from left to right. The vertical axis spans wavelengths from 1.93 to 2.44 μm in 20 nm bands. For each narrow spectral band the radiance for a single ground resolution cell is colour coded from red (high value) through a rainbow sequence to violet (low value). The colour patterns indicate the distribution along the flight line of peaks and troughs in the surface reflectance spectrum. These, in turn, may indicate the abundance of minerals which have distinctive absorption bands. The blue patches between 2.1 and 2.3 μm suggest abundant clay minerals (Fig. 1.9) at the surface from samples 70–80, 120–210 and 300–330 along the flight path. Courtesy of Stuart Marsh, Sun Oil, Houston.

(a)

(b)

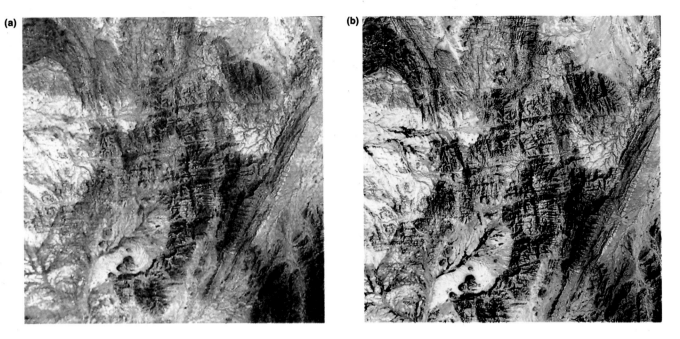

Figure 3.35 Landsat-2 MSS false-colour image for part of Eritrea (see Fig. 3.30). Image (b) shows enhanced Landsat-5 TM data for the same area, where red is band 5 data, green is band 3 data and blue is band 1 data. The 28.5-m resolution of the TM data produces a sharper image than the MSS data, helping delineate finer drainage and topographic textures. The extension of the range in the near-infrared by TM allows variations in surface composition to be expressed in a wider range of colours than is possible with MSS data.

Figure 4.3 The Colorado River of Arizona, USA, is a classic example of antecedent drainage. In this false-colour Landsat TM image at a scale of about 1:3 million it has carved the spectacular Grand Canyon through the rising Colorado Plateau because its rate of downward erosion exceeded the rate of crustal uplift.

Figure 4.22 The curved dark bands on this enhanced Landsat MSS false-colour composite of part of Andhra Pradesh in South India are outcrops of sediments which filled the huge Cuddapah Basin between 1.7 and 1.3 Ga BP. The yellow area in the south-west comprises 2.6 Ga BP Archaean granitic gneisses. Dykes cutting the Archaean show up very clearly as intersecting dark lines, but stop at the boundary with the late-Precambrian rocks. This boundary is clearly an unconformity. Recent dates on the dykes show that they are about the same age as the oldest of the basinal sediments. Scale: 1:1 million. Source: author, written to film by Michael Smallwood, Optronix Inc.

Figure 4.31a This enhanced false-colour composite of Landsat MSS data shows an area in the central part of the Tibetan Plateau. Although it is of marginal use in this form for discriminating lithologies, the many linear features that it expresses are the key to understanding the active tectonics of the region. Several of them clearly displace Recent superficial deposits, as at centre right and centre left. Scale: 1:1 million. Source: courtesy of Dave Rothery, Open University.

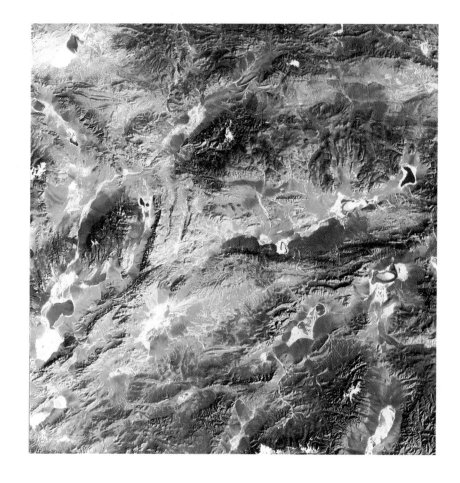

Figure 4.38 The western part of the Qaidam Basin in Qinhai Province, People's Republic of China, shown on this Landsat MSS false-colour composite, is floored by folded lacustrine and other non-marine sediments of Tertiary to Quaternary age. They occupy the mainly grey texturally flat area. The basin is bounded to the north-west by the sinistral Altun strike-slip fault, which forms a prominent linear valley. The rugged area in the north is an uplifted massif of older, Mesozoic rocks. Scale: 1:1 million. Source: author.

Figure 4.39 Superimposition of intense shear strains and upright folds on an earlier set of recumbent folds has produced several fold interference structures in a Precambrian metamorphic complex in NE Sudan. They show up well on this enhanced Landsat TM false-colour composite because the different lithologies are strongly contrasted in colour. The image is 30 km across. Source: author.

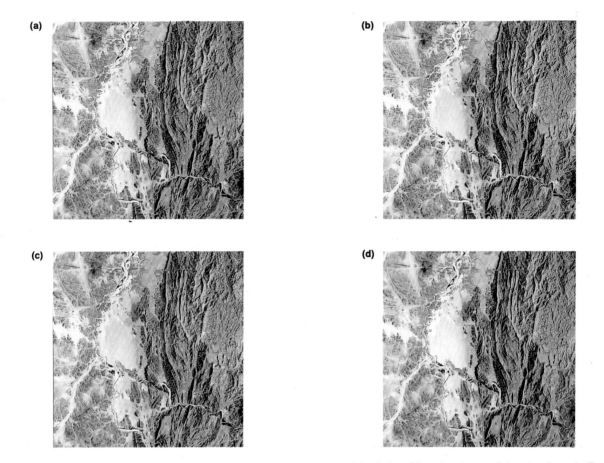

(a)

(b)

(c)

(d)

Figure 5.10   These linearly stretched false-colour Landsat TM images of part of the Sudan–Eritrea border are of the area shown in Figures 5.4 to 5.9. They reveal more details than the band 3 images in both light and dark terrains, but each band combination contains different information. The natural colour image (bands 3, 2 and 1 as RGB) (a) is least informative. The standard false-colour composite (bands 4, 3 and 2 as RGB) (b) shows vegetation in shades of red, but little more than (a). Combining bands 5, 3 and 1 in RGB (c) reveals better detail of the distribution of different rock types, while suppressing vegetation as dark tones. The importance of a correct assignment of bands to colour components is shown by (d), which has bands 3, 1 and 5 in RGB. Exactly the same information as in (c) is shown, but the choice of colours prevents the eye from appreciating the full range of variability. The geology is of a major boundary between a high-grade metamorphic terrain with granite intrusions and basaltic dykes to the left, and a very complex, younger terrain of peridotites, metabasalts and metasediments to the right. The boundary is marked by deep alluvium along a major river controlled by a huge shear zone. Each image is 30 km across.

Figure 5.13 (b)   This cross section through the conical representation of HSI colour space shows how pure spectral hues on the perimeter grade through pastel shades to grey at the axis of the cone. Courtesy of LogE Ltd.

Figure 5.14   The Landsat TM band 5, 3 and 1 data in *Figure 5.10c* have been transformed to ISH coordinates, with the intensity and saturation files stretched and the hue unchanged. The results have been transformed back to RGB space to produce a vivid range of colours. Comparison of the two images reveals that the basic colour differences in the image have not been changed, so that colour can still be related easily to spectral properties.

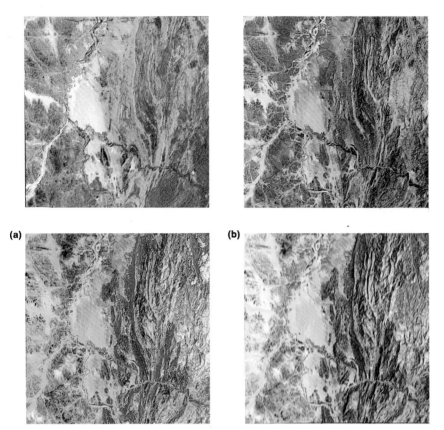

(a)

(b)

Figure 5.26 This image combines the first-, second- and third-order principal components from the area of *Figures 5.10* and 5.11 in red, green and blue. The result is a vivid colour representation of surface variations in which much geological detail is visible, particularly different kinds of rock. However, the colours are not easily related to the rocks' spectral properties, and the compression of most of the variance into the first PC means that the other PCs are noisy and noise interferes with interpretation in the false-colour image.

Figure 5.28 Decorrelation- or D-stretched image of Landsat TM bands 5, 3 and 1 in RGB for the same area as *Figure 5.10c*. The first PC was stretched and edge enhanced, and higher order PCs filtered to remove noise before rotation back to original band space. It shows little difference compared with *Figure 5.14*, but the D-stretch technique offers more opportunities for cosmetic improvement than the ISH transform.

Figure 5.30 (a) False-colour ratio image of the area of Figure 5.31, using TM 5/4 as red, 3/1 as green and 5/7 as blue. Though producing an excellent discrimination of rock types, the image lacks some topographic detail and is noisy. By using the ISH transform and substituting a contrast-stretched TM band for the ratio intensity, (b) both defects can be avoided without changing the colour rendition of different rocks, which is dependent on spectral features related to iron minerals, albedo and hydroxy-bearing minerals. Both should be compared with *Figures 5.14* and *5.26*.

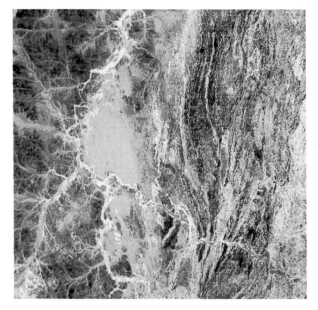

Figure 5.33 Vegetation in the humid climate of northern California is luxuriant over most rock types. However, ultramafic rocks produce soils that inhibit growth. On this colour composite of Landsat MSS band ratios—4/5, 4/6 and 6/7 as red, green and blue – the bluish area have sparse vegetation compared with the red areas. They correlate very well with known outcrops of ophiolites–black outlines. Courtesy of Gary Raines, US Geological Survey.

Figure 5.37 This image is a density-sliced version of the ratio of Landsat TM bands 5/7 (see Figure 5.31). This ratio should be correlated with the proportion of hydroxyl-bearing minerals in surface rocks and soils. The colours are assigned to ranges of ratios, the 'cool' colours representing low hydroxyl-mineral contents, the 'warm' colours higher contents.

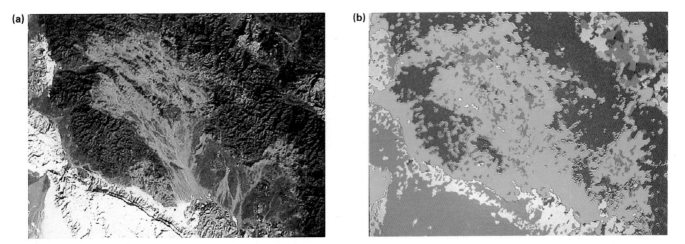

Figure 5.40 The Cretaceous ophiolite complex of the Sultanate of Oman is difficult to interpret from a false-colour Landsat MSS image (a). Most of the ophiolite is very dark. However, careful manipulation of the data and use of supervised maximum-likelihood classification techniques allows a crude discrimination between the different major lithologies to be made. In (b) the colours turquoise, green and dark blue are assigned to the hartzburgite, layered gabbro and sheeted basaltic dykes which comprise the ophiolite. Red indicates zones of pervasive serpentinisation in the hartzburgite, and the pink, yellow and orange relate to volcanic rocks and limestones which are tectonically overlain by the ophiolite. Courtesy of Dave Rothery, Open University.

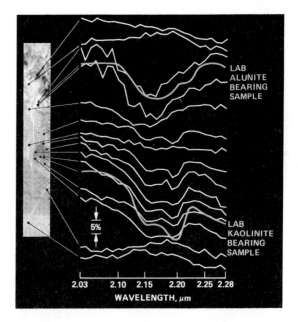

Figure 5.42 An Airborne Imaging Spectrometer (AIS) developed at the Jet Propulsion Laboratory in Pasadena, USA, gathers radiance data for 128 10 nm channels in the 1.2 to 2.4 μm region of the EM spectrum from a swath 32 pixels wide. The image shown is of part of the Cuprite mining district in Nevada and is of the first three principal components extracted from the 128 channels. The narrow bandwidths of the channels allow spectra to be constructed for each pixel in the image with sufficient precision that the subtle difference between many minerals can be discriminated. In the examples given (the white spectra), both alunite- and kaolinite-bearing surfaces can be identified by comparison with the laboratory spectra (shown in yellow). On the image, kaolinite-rich material shows up as magenta. Courtesy of Mike Abrams and Alex Goetz, Jet Propulsion Laboratory, Pasadena.

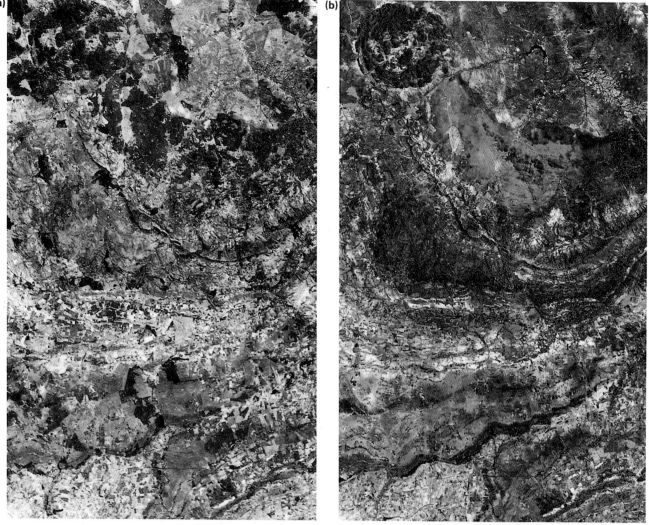

Figure 5.43 Southern Africa has a strongly seasonal climate which has a marked effect on the appearance of remotely sensed images. Image (a) is an enhanced false-colour composite of Landsat MSS data for an area in the Transvaal, South Africa, during the dry season. Although some geological features show up, they are muted by the effect of dead vegetation and dry soil. The same area imaged just after the wet season (b) shows a spectacular improvement. This is the result of strong geological control over vegetation and variations in soil moisture. Important features are the Bushveldt layered basic–ultrabasic intrusion in the NE, the circular Pilansberg intrusion at top centre and previously unsuspected stratigraphic variations in the Precambrian Transvaal dolomites – lower half. Courtesy of ERIM, USA.

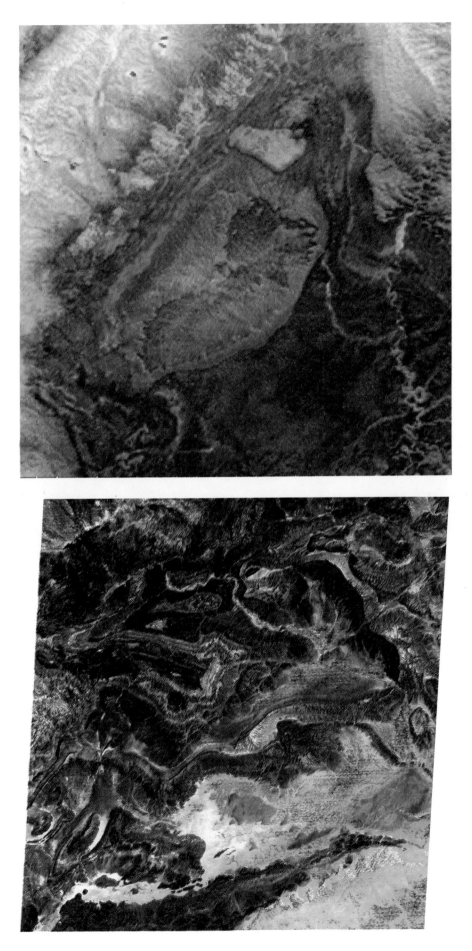

Figure 6.12 This colour image of HCMM data is of the same area as that shown in Figure 6.11. The red, green and blue components are controlled by negative images of Day-IR, Night-IR and Day-VIS, so a warm area during the day imparts a dark red to the image, a cold area at night contributes bright green, a surface with high albedo is represented by a dark blue addition, and so on. The resulting colours combine information on albedo and thermal inertia in a striking way. As well as a much better discrimination between many different major rock units compared with Figure 6.11 (see Units 15, 2, 3, TK, Km) there are several important points to note. Sandstone Unit 10 shows up as blue. It has low albedo, and is warm during the day and cold at night, implying a low thermal inertia. This is related to its red colour and high silt content. Other sandstones, such as Units 12, 13 and 14, appear dark orange (high albedo, low daytime temperatures, warm at night, and hence high thermal inertia). They are pale, coarse-grained, massive sandstones. Courtesy of Anne B. Kahle, Jet Propulsion Laboratory, Pasadena.

Figure 6.13 This image was produced by displaying Landsat MSS band 7 data (representing albedo) with HCMM Day-IR and Night-IR as intensity, saturation and hue, respectively. The area is of the High Atlas Mountains in Morocco, which are formed by a fold belt of Permo-Triassic sandstones and Jurassic to Cretaceous carbonates resting on a Precambrian and Palaeozoic igneous and metamorphic complex. The valleys are partially filled with Tertiary to Recent sands and alluvium. The various colours can be interpreted in terms of thermal properties by reference to Table 6.2. Courtesy of Rupert Haydn, University of Munich.

Figure 6.14 Combining data from visible, near- and thermal-infrared parts of the spectrum through principal component analysis and RGB display results in spectacular colour images. In this case, red and green are controlled by components loaded with visible and near-infrared data, whereas blue represents a component containing most of the day and night thermal information. It covers the same area as Figures 6.7 and 6.15, Pisgah crater and associated lava flows in the Mojave Desert of southeastern California, USA. It is impossible to relate image colours to a multitude of contributing surface properties, and the image must be interpreted empirically. The central dark-red and orange units are aa and pahoehoe flow from Pisgah Crater, which is brighter orange – it is a cinder cone. The yellow and magenta area at bottom centre is a playa lake. Different igneous units are clearly discriminated in the lower-left and lower-right quadrants, and many subtle differences in the alluvium at the top left also show up well (see the map in Fig. 6.15). Courtesy of Anne B. Kahle, Jet Propulsion Laboratory, Pasadena.

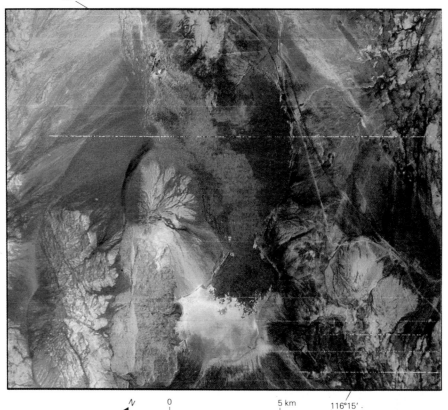

(a) 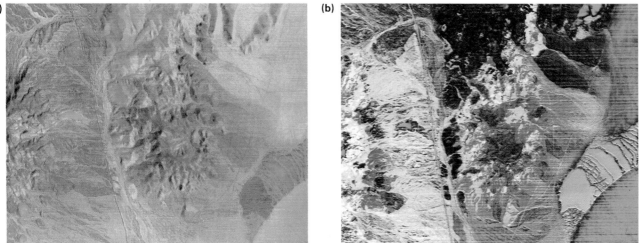 **(b)**

Figure 6.19 Image (a) is a false-colour image of TIMS bands 5, 3 and 1, displayed as red, green and blue after contrast stretching of principal components and re-rotation into the original data space (Section 5.7). Image (b) is a colour ratio composite of 1.6/2.2 μm (red), 1.6/0.48 μm (green) and 0.6/1.1 μm (blue) reflectances from an airborne multispectral scanner. Both are of the Cuprite mining district in Nevada, USA. The TIMS image is much better than the ratio image in distinguishing tuffs (T), basalts (B), carbonates (C) and siltstones (SS). The ratio image is better for separating alluvial deposits (A). The area contains rocks which have suffered two different kinds of alteration during hydrothermal activity and mineralisation, in a roughly circular zone just left of the centre, which both images highlight in mainly red colours. In the ratio image clay-rich parts of the altered zone have a high 1.6/2.2 ratio and appear bright red. Those with a high iron content and a high 1.6/0.48 ratio appear green. Silicified rocks have lost their clay content and are dark red, brown and bluish. Yellow patches reflect zones rich in both iron and clay minerals. The TIMS image expresses these variations rather differently, and the colours are most affected by silica content – either quartz or opal. Silicified rocks are bright orange, and clay-rich opalised rocks are magenta. Both types of image complement each other in the search for this type of mineral deposit. Courtesy of Anne B. Kahle, Jet Propulsion Laboratory, Pasadena.

Figure 6.20 This TIMS image was produced in the same way as that in *Figure 6.19.* It is of part of the Mesozoic Wind River sedimentary basin in central Wyoming, USA. From the spectra shown in Figure 6.18, silica-rich sediments are portrayed in red to red-orange, and carbonates in green and blue-green. Compared with the Thematic Mapper image of the same area (*Fig. 7.27*), many significant variations in stratigraphy, which are invisible in the reflected part of the spectrum, are quite evident in this image. The blue-green carbonates contain sporadic patches and discontinuous layers of red sandstones. The brightly coloured, dominantly arenaceous rocks on the left owe their variation in colour (pinks, greens and yellows) to variable proportions of carbonate and silica in their cement. Courtesy of Harold Lang, Jet Propulsion Laboratory, Pasadena.

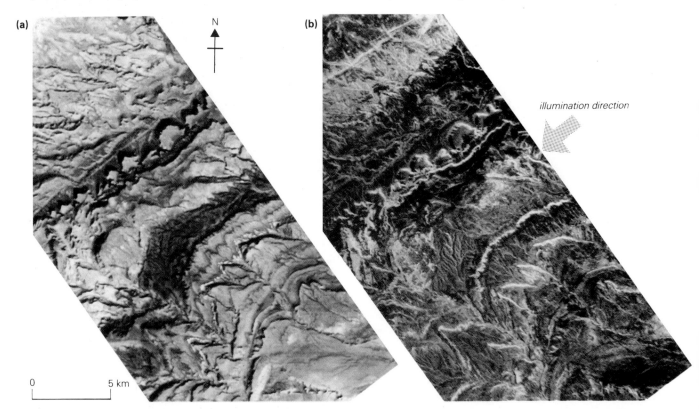

Figure 7.26 The images here cover a larger area of the Wind River Basin than do those in Figure 7.25. Image (a) is a false-colour composite of Landsat TM bands 4, 3 and 2 as red, green and blue. The same primary colours in (b) are controlled by the VH, HH and VV SAR data shown in Figure 7.25. The colours in (b) therefore show the effects of surface morphology on backscatter and of matter–radar interactions on the polarity of radar pulses. Those in (a) represent electronic and vibrational transitions. Of particular interest are the red-hued areas in the south-east of (b), where strongly depolarised returns were produced. The lack of vegetation revealed by (a) in this area means that subsurface volume scattering may be responsible, possibly as a result of significantly deeper weathering in the rock unit there. The other, more subtle, hues in pinks, creams, browns, greens and blues relate more closely to variations in surface roughness, Compared with the TM image, the multi-polarised radar image does not show such clearly defined geological boundaries and lithological distinctions. However, it does show additional boundaries and units that are not seen on any other kind of image, particularly in the north-west. An advantage of the control possible with radar is the suppression of shadows resulting from illumination parallel to the main ridges in the area. Both images clearly complement each other. Courtesy of Tom Farr, Jet Propulsion Laboratory, Pasadena.

Figure 7.28 Recasting a frequency-filtered digital Seasat image in the HSI colour system restores the full information content of the image, but adds more easily interpreted colours relating to varying roughness and dielectric constant. In this case the Wamsutter Arch of Wyoming, USA, is more clearly defined by rock-related colour bands than in the original greytone image (Fig. 7.27a). Courtesy of Ronald Blom and Michael Daily, Jet Propulsion Laboratory, Pasadena.

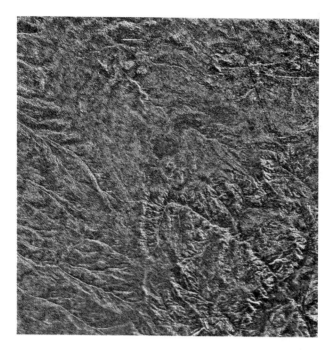

Figure 7.29 The San Raphael Swell of Utah, USA, has been the target to test the geological usefulness of many remote-sensing systems (Figs. *6.14* and *6.15*). In this image Seasat radar data have been combined with Landsat MSS data. The first, second and third principal components of Landsat MSS data have been modulated by the Seasat SAR data and displayed as red, green and blue. The extent to which the radar data have improved the image can be judged by comparing the four corners of the image, which Seasat did not cover, with the central parts. There are three distinct advantages with this method. The better resolution of the Seasat data resolution sharpens the expression of the Landsat data, topographic features are enhanced by radar, and variations in backscatter due to surface properties control the brightness of the colours stemming from the decorrelated MSS data. A much more detailed geological interpretation is possible than would be the case with any single imaging system. Courtesy of Ronald Blom and Bill Stromberg of the Jet Propulsion Laboratory, Pasadena.

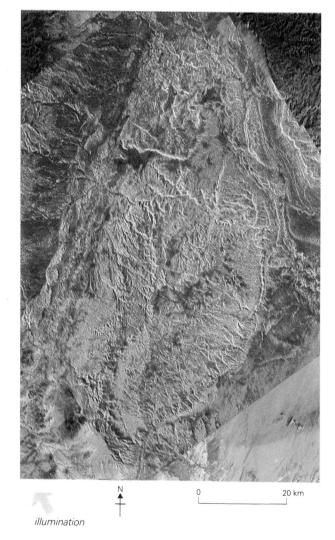

N

0   20 km

illumination

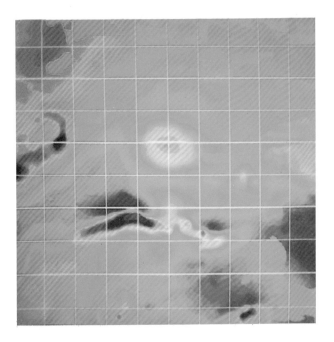

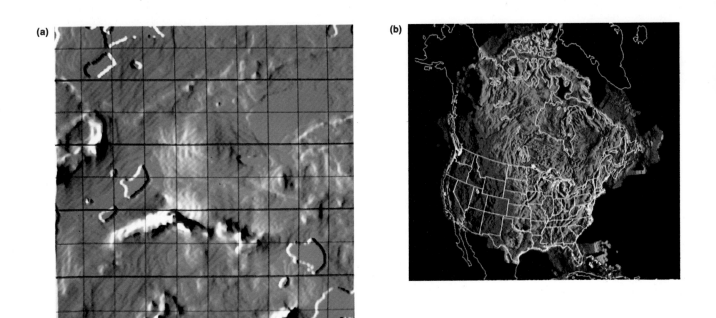

(a)

(b)

Figure 8.15 (a) 'Illuminated' aeromagnetic data from *Figure 8.14* combined with a coloured rendition. (b) Gravity anomaly data for North America colour coded from magenta through blue, green and yellow to red and 'illuminated' from the northwest. The large negative anomaly over the western USA is associated with active crustal thinning in the Basin and Range Province. Much detail of deep crustal structure is revealed for the central plains, which are veneered by almost featureless Mesozoic sediments. Courtesy of the Earth and Planetary Remote-Sensing Laboratory, Washington University, St Louis.

(a) 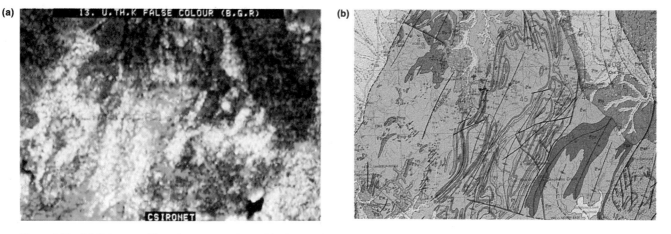 **(b)**

Figure 8.18 (a) Colour rendition of gamma-ray intensities for uranium, thorium and potassium as red, green and blue components for an area in Australia. Reds, greens and blues show areas that have high values for uranium, thorium and potassium respectively, and low values for the other two elements. Equally high values for all three elements are shown by grey tones and pastel shades. Dark areas have low radioactivity. Courtesy of BMR and CSIRO, Canberra. (b) Geological map of the corresponding area. Black lines indicate important faults and fold axes. Yellow areas are Quaternary unconsolidated sediments and all other shades relate to various Precambrian rocks. The brownish units at top right are glacigenic sediments resting unconformably upon high-grade metamorphic rocks, the bulk of which are aluminous metapelites (pale purple), together with green amphibolites and various granitic rocks, shown in blue, red and orange. Courtesy of the Geological Survey of New South Wales. Comparing the radiometric image with the map reveals some interesting features. Sharp boundaries on the image at top left and bottom right relate to major faults. The red to pink body on the image towards top left links to the red granite on the map, but extends over a larger area, perhaps indicating associated permeation of the metapelites by uranium-rich pegmatites. Some of the amphibolites show as dark streaks. The blue granite appears to be equally rich in all three radioactive elements, while the glacigenic sediments have low radioactivity. The bulk of the metapelites appear to be thorium rich. Possibly more detail is revealed by the image than by the map.

Figure 8.19 Image combining digital elevation data with Bouguer gravity anomaly data for the same area as Figure 8.17, using the DEM illuminated from the northwest as intensity, a constant saturation and gravity as hue in an ISH transform. The colour range from blue for negative anomalies through a rainbow spectrum to magenta for the highest gravity anomaly. The green to yellow transition, being the most easily perceived spectral boundary, is keyed to the zero Bouguer anomaly.

Figure 8.20 This image including the area in Figure 8.18 was produced using the ISH transform, with aeromagnetic data as intensity, a constant saturation and hue derived from uranium, thorium and potassium data in Figure 8.18. While the faults are well displayed in both magnetic and radiometric data, the unconformity beneath glacigenic sediments has no effect on the magnetic data, though it is prominent in the radiometric data.

Figure 9.4 Enhanced Landsat TM image (bands 7, 4 and 2 as RGB) of an area in Eritrea showing a major shear zone with clearly differentiated lithologies that have been displaced by a set of sinistral strike-slip faults. Size: 30 by 30 km.

Figure 9.5 Image of part of Nova Scotia combining airborne SAR imagery with a geological map, using the ISH transform. The greens are Ordovician metasediments, reds indicate Devonian granites and the brown areas are mixed Carboniferous sediments. The radar adds considerable detail to the relatively uninformative geological map, particularly with respect to faults. Courtesy of J. Harris, Canadian Centre for Remote Sensing.

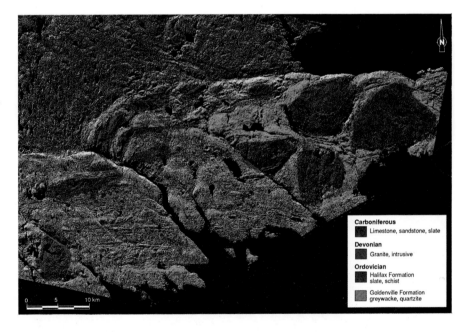

Carboniferous
Limestone, sandstone, slate

Devonian
Granite, intrusive

Ordovician
Halifax Formation
slate, schist

Goldenville Formation
greywacke, quartzite

0   5   10 km

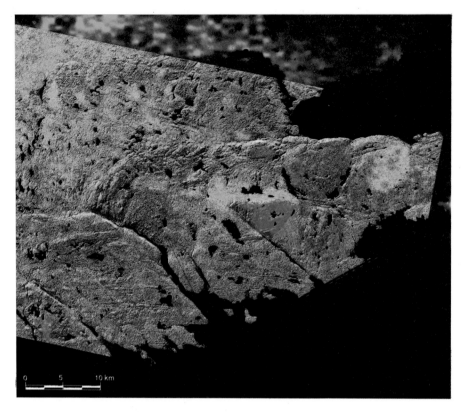

Figure 9.6 By combining SAR data as intensity and airborne gamma-ray spectrometer data as hue, as IHS transform reveals considerable structural and lithological variation for this area in Nova Scotia. Comparison with *Figure 9.5* shows that the granites that were mapped as similar bodies have considerable differences in uranium, thorium and potassium content.

Figure 9.8 This false-colour ratio image of a geologically unknown area in Eritrea uses the ratios 5/4, 3/1 and 7/5 in RGB order to exploit the spectral features of ferric minerals and hydroxyl-bearing minerals, in which hydrothermally altered rocks are often rich, to assign a yellow colour to areas bearing them. The small yellow areas at left were found to be hydrothermally altered. The much bigger yellow zone running north–south in fact proved to be an area of slumped and relic lateric soils found on a high ridge, thereby showing that remote sensing has to be used with field verification. Size: 30 by 30 km.

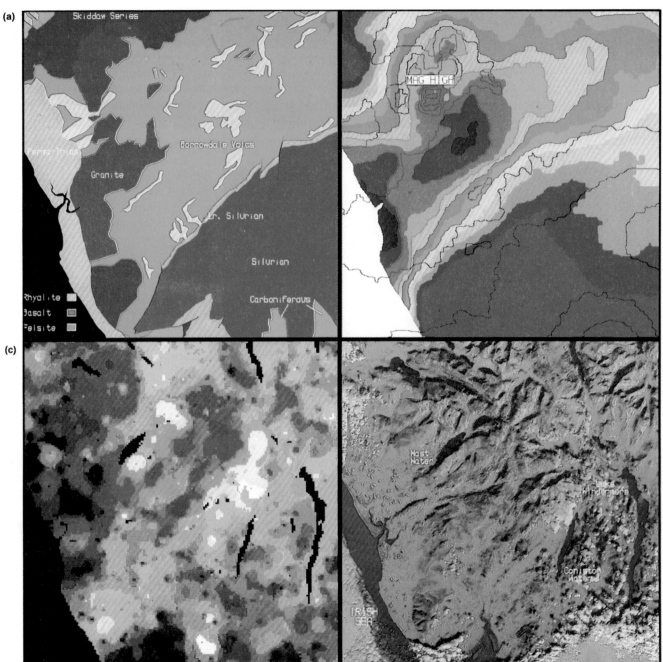

Skiddaw Series

Perno-Trias

Borrowdale Volcs

Granite

Lr. Silurian

Silurian

Carboniferous

Rhyolite
Basalt
Felsite

(b)

MAG HIGH

(c)

(d)

Wast
Water

Lake
Windemere

IRISH
SEA

Coniston
Water

Figure 9.9 Data and results from an image-oriented GIS exercise in targeting tin mineralization in the English Lake District. (a) Geological map: within the Borrowdale Volcanics greens are basalts and yellows rhyolites. (b) Colour-sliced map of Bouguer gravity anomaly, ranging from magenta for lowest negative anomalies through blue to red at highest positive anomalies. Superimposed are contours for magnetic field intensity. (c) Tin, copper and zinc values sliced at 50–75–95–99 percentile levels (Figure 8.8b) and displayed in RGB order. (d) Landsat TM 742 image showing the dominant vegetation cover in green. (e) Landsat TM band 5 and tin values combined through the ISH transform, with magnetic field intensity shown in contours. (f) Side-illuminated Landsat TM band 5 image (to enhance fractures–white) combined with Bouguer gravity anomaly data through the ISH transform. Superimposed in red and green are areas with significant tin and zinc–bismuth anomalies respectively. The last two are spatially associated with fractures at the margin of the negative gravity anomaly associated with buried granite.

(e)

(f)

Figure 9.10 Stand of prematurely senescent maple trees (orange) related to seepage of natural gas. Courtesy of Harold Lang, Jet Propulsion Laboratory, Pasadena.

Figure 9.11 Landsat TM 742 image of part of the East African Rift in Kenya, with vegetation related to springs near faults showing green in an otherwise arid terrain. Width: 40 km. (Courtesy of EOSAT).

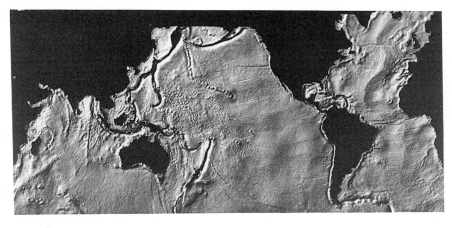

Figure 8.9 Image of sea-surface elevation derived from Seasat radar altimetry data, showing details of ocean-floor topography due to the effect of gravitational potential on the sea surface.

variation in elevation. Nevertheless, it can contain sufficient information for qualitative analysis of the surface.

8.2.5 Raster processing methods

Raster data of the kind discussed so far in this section contain a wealth of information, from which geologically oriented interpretations can be made and which can be combined with other kinds of data for analysis in a GIS (Section 8.3). While GIS methods provide awesome analytical power, for many applications interpretations of non-image data in raster form are most easily and effectively achieved by visual interpretation of images, to which raster format lends itself admirably. Figure 8.10 shows the great improvement in visual accessibility of information inherent in the conversion of contoured data to a raster image. In this case the data are aerial measurements of anomalies in the total magnetic field potential, which have been converted from negative and positive values of nanotesla (i.e. real numbers) to an 8-bit (0–255) range of positive integers for display.

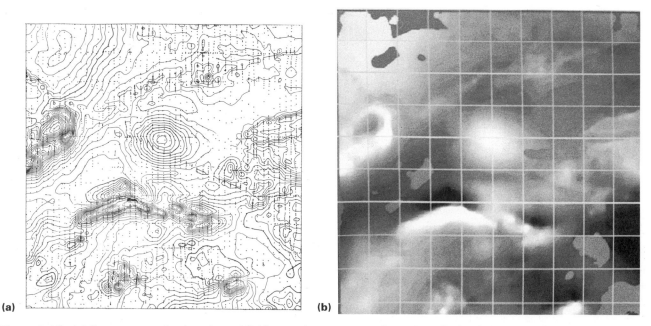

(a) (b)

Figure 8.10 (a) Contour map of magnetic total field anomaly over an area in northern England. (b) Image of the data shown in (a). The area is 100 × 100 km.

Although a vast improvement over contoured data, the image in Figure 8.10b suffers from two main problems. Human vision only distinguishes between 16 and 32 grey levels, and the image lacks depth and therefore appears bland. Because of these factors high-frequency spatial features are not visible. Using contrast stretching (Section 5.2) allows some improvement to be made, but the full 256 values for magnetic anomaly can only be expressed graphically if the data are displayed in colour. This is most conveniently achieved by creating three different versions of the data to combine as red, green and blue. Each is stretched differently using LUTs that focus on different DN ranges (Section 5.2). Figure 8.11 shows three LUTs whose outputs when combined produce a 'rainbow' range of colours, where low values are in blues and greens, intermediate values appear as greens and yellows, and high values are expressed by orange to red and magenta. The resulting **pseudocolour** image of the data in Figure 8.10 is shown in *Figure 8.12*. Most magnetic and gravity data are of deviations from the average potential field, and the anomalies may be positive or negative. Careful use of the LUTs can ensure that the zero anomaly coincides with the green to yellow transition in the rainbow spectrum, which is perceptually the most distinct boundary, so that 'cold' colours are associated with negative anomalies and 'warm' colours with positive.

Although pseudocolour renditions express more fully the data's information content, as discussed in Section 2.2 colour masks high-frequency spatial features in the data. The degrading effect of a lack of depth and loss of spatial

detail is well shown by unenhanced images of topographic elevation (Fig. 8.13a). A most important cue to depth in images of topography is shadowing caused by solar illumination, as seen in all aerial and satellite imagery. Solar shading can be simulated on non-image raster data by a variety of algorithms, the simplest of which are the directional filters discussed in Section 5.3, which simulate a constant Sun elevation from the eight principal points of the compass. Figure 8.13b shows the dramatic improvement and realism resulting from such a transform of a

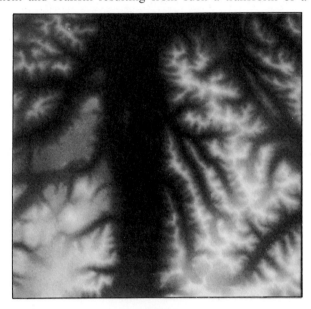

(a)   20 km

(b)   20 km

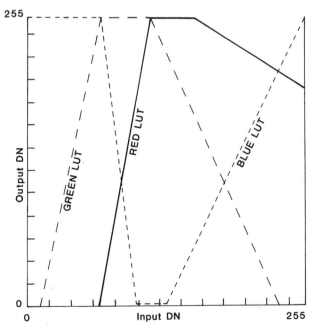

Figure 8.11 Look-up tables to produce red, green and blue versions of a single input image, resulting in a pseudocoloured image.

Figure 8.13 Digital elevation data of part of Alaska expressed as an image (a), which in (b) has been filtered to simulate the shadowing by solar illumination from the southeast. Courtesy of Charles Trautwein, EROS Data Center.

(a) **(b)**

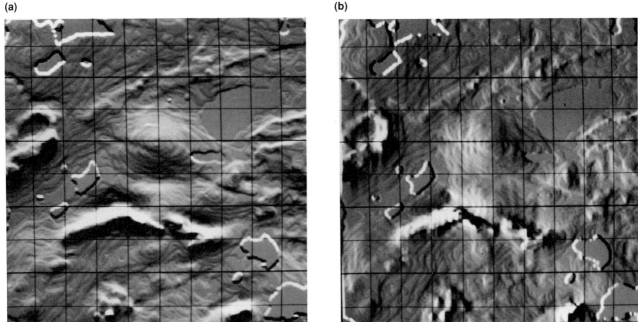

Figure 8.14 Aeromagnetic data shown in Figure 8.10b 'illuminated' from the north (a) and west (b).

DEM. More sophisticated algorithms allow various illumination angles and types of lighting to be selected.

Raster renditions of any spatial variable are in effect maps of the 'topography' of the variable, and can just as easily be enhanced by simulated shading to tune an image to the proclivities of human vision. Figure 8.14 shows shaded images of magnetic 'relief' incorporating illumination from two directions at right angles. This shows how high-frequency spatial features with different orientations can be separately highlighted. By combining oblique 'illumination' with pseudocolour, using multiplicative or ISH methods (Section 5.2.2), the advantages of both can be exploited in astonishingly graphic images, ideally suited to interpretation (*Fig. 8.15*).

As well as different renditions of raw raster data after enhancement, information can be extracted from them by a variety of mathematical functions. These methods include differentiation to produce various derivatives and trend-surface analysis (Section 8.2.1).

The magnitude of the first derivative of a spatial variable expresses the gradient of the topological surface. It is of particular use in analysing and applying DEMs to various problems by providing estimates of topographic slope. This can be used in assessing slope stability and rates of run-off, as well as in geomorphological analysis. In some geological applications, derivatives of geophysical data are needed. Figure 8.16 shows an image of gravity data together with an image expressing the slope of the gravitational field. The latter allows sudden changes in gravitational potential to be visualized, which may correspond with subsurface density boundaries.

The magnitude of the second derivative expresses the rate of change of gradient of a topological surface, and is thereby a measure of the roughness of the surface. Inflections in the surface by definition have a value of zero for the second derivative, and so are uniquely defined. In force-field data the main element in contributing to high-frequency variations is the crystalline basement, in which magnetic susceptibility and density vary considerably in contrast to their relative uniformity in the overlying veneer of sediments. The more deeply buried basement features are, the smoother is their expression in gravity and magnetic data. In magnetic data, the relationship between anomaly patterns and the bodies responsible for them is often complex owing to bipolarity. Many magnetic anomalies due to a single body have both negative and positive features, and the source of the anomaly frequently resides beneath the line of inflection in the anomaly. Consequently, second-derivative images can be used qualitatively to express depth to basement from gravity and magnetic data, and to locate the sources of magnetic anomalies. Quantitative use of force-field data involves complex three-dimensional modelling, in which geologically reasonable bodies of different density and magnetic susceptibility are manipulated to simulate the observed gravitational or magnetic field anomaly patterns. They are beyond the scope of this book.

Another approach to analysing deeply buried features, especially from gravity data, is trend-surface analysis (Section 8.2.1), in which polynomial surfaces are fitted to the original point data. A first-order fitted surface expresses the gross trends as a dipping plane, while higher order surfaces assume more complex shapes to express regional

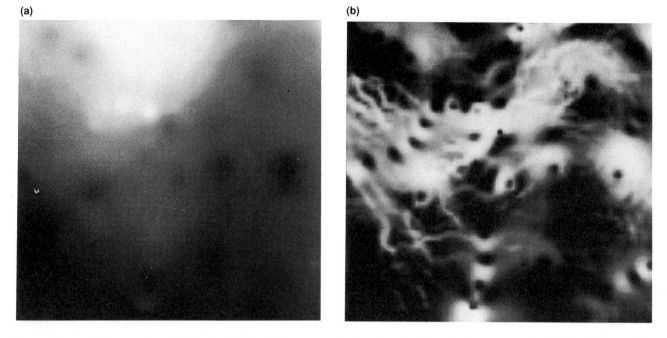

Figure 8.16 (a) Image of gravitational potential in the area of Alaska shown in Figure 8.13, compared with (b) an image of the first derivative of the gravitational potential.

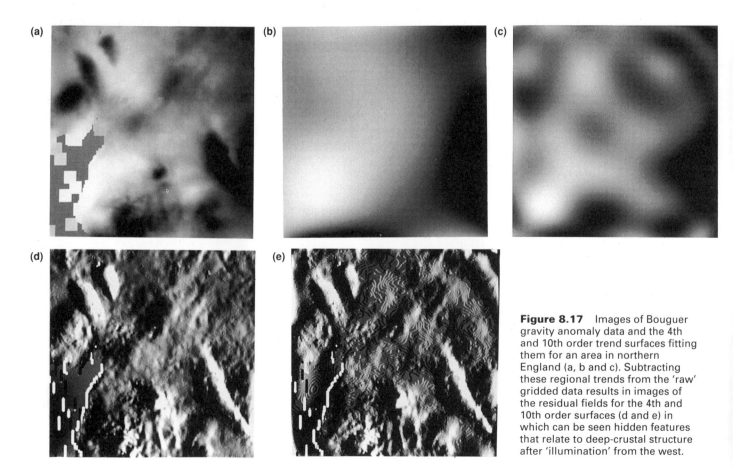

Figure 8.17 Images of Bouguer gravity anomaly data and the 4th and 10th order trend surfaces fitting them for an area in northern England (a, b and c). Subtracting these regional trends from the 'raw' gridded data results in images of the residual fields for the 4th and 10th order surfaces (d and e) in which can be seen hidden features that relate to deep-crustal structure after 'illumination' from the west.

patterns. The higher the order of trend surface, the more closely it matches the actual variation in the data. However, even for 10th-order surfaces, the patterns are grossly smoothed compared with surfaces interpolated by spline or kriging functions, and represent the low-frequency spatial variations contained within the data. Low-frequency variations in gravity data stem from broad variations in the deep crust and upper mantle and from the relatively uniform but variably thick veneer of surface sedimentary cover. As mentioned above, the higher frequencies are derived from variations within near-surface basement, or perturbations in the depth to the cover–basement interface, often related to deep faulting. Subtracting the trend surface or **regional field** from the interpolated field topology results in a **residual field**, in which may reside important and previously indiscernible information about cover–basement relationships. Figure 8.17 shows the results of trend-surface analysis and production of the associated residual fields from Bouguer gravity anomaly data for the area shown in Figures 8.10, *8.12*, 8.14 and *8.15a*.

8.2.6 Multivariate raster images

Data sets of single variables in raster format expressed as suitably enhanced images are eminently suited to interpretation, using all the skills and intuition embodied in a trained geologist. However, there is a wealth of data types that can be rendered in this form, and using them singly does present the same problem mentioned in the introduction to this section. There is a danger of assembling a welter of interpretations that need to be coordinated in some way as a coherent product. One approach is to transfer them to a GIS, where a variety of computer applications can assist in this task (Section 8.3), but this relies on mathematical means of seeking relationships. Human vision is by far the most flexible means of assembling connections between disparate sets of information, and it makes sense to exhaust the full range of possibilities presented by images before resorting to dominantly machine-led analysis.

There are a variety of methods whereby several data sets can be combined as images, most relying on techniques covered in Chapter 5. The simplest of these is the combination of three sets as the red, green and blue components of colour images. Seeking relationships between the sets relies on Young's theory of additive colour. Where all three variables are strongly correlated, the DNs employed in colour display are all similar, so that the result is a shade of grey, ranging from white to dark grey depending on whether all the values are high or low. If two of the variables are well correlated and the third is unrelated or anticorrelated, this is signified by the area being rendered in shades of yellow, magenta or cyan, depending on the colour assignment of the variables and their DN. Areas showing the three additive primary colours suggest that there is no significant correlation between any of the variables, and one is high while the other two have low values. Pastel and non-spectral colours result from partial correlation among the variables.

Because RGB images assign the same weight to all three variables displayed, low information content in one variable tends to swamp that in the others, particularly if there are gross disparities in the spatial resolution of the data sets. Therefore, a simple rule is to combine data sets with approximately the same spatial resolution. Nor is it wise to combine data that have fundamentally different relationships to geological features. Consider an image made up from a Landsat band, gravity and magnetic data. By no stretch of the imagination can any meaningful correlation in an RGB image be expected, for the properties being displayed relate to spectral reflectance, density and magnetic susceptibility, which are not related. Although all three may contain vital information on the distribution of, say, major faults, the resulting image will inevitably be a mess. A second rule is therefore to combine data in RGB form where there is reasonable expectation of some real correlation between the variables. For most geological applications, the unifying factor is likely to be different relations to rock type.

If they are available, a good combination of variables to express in RGB order for lithological discrimination might be nickel, chromium and gravity anomaly. Since ultramafic rocks are rich in nickel and chromium and have high density, then areas underlain by peridotites would show as bright grey tones on the image. Basalts generally have lower Ni/Cr ratios than ultramafic rocks and slightly lower densities. They might be revealed by greenish or cyan areas. Granites and sediments have low values for all three variables, and would consequently show as dark patches. Ironstones, with high density and low chromium and nickel would be distinguished by blue signatures. Occurrences of nickel sulphide ores, being depleted in chromium but associated with dense ultramafic rocks, should be revealed as magenta or red areas.

Because much is now known about the affinities of different chemical elements for different lithologies, and their behaviour relative to one another in geological fractionation processes, geochemical data are ideally suited for simple RGB combination as a route to lithological discrimination. In particular, the common association of restricted ranges of elements during mineralization episodes of different kinds makes this approach extremely powerful in metal exploration. Some granites with which a variety of pegmatite, skarn and hydrothermal deposits are frequently associated consistently carry tin–tungsten– lithium–fluorine. In exploration for gold mineralization the pathfinder elements arsenic–bismuth–antimony are routinely sought in drainage and soil surveys. However, geochemical survey data are not commonly available outside of mining companies.

More readily available, particularly in arid and semiarid terrains, are the results of airborne gamma-ray spectrometry (Section 3.7), often flown together with magnetic surveys. Gamma-radiation data relate to the abundances of radio-active isotopes of uranium, thorium and potassium in soils and rock. Fortuitously, these three elements behave very differently in a great variety of geological processes, are found in a large range of concentrations and assume quite different relative abundances in a wide variety of common rock types. Though often noisy because of the blocking of radiation by vegetation and air, RGB images comprising uranium, thorium and potassium estimates from spectro-metry are very colourful, the colours relating well to the surface distribution of different rocks and soils, as *Figure 8.18* shows. Interpreting such images relies on both an understanding of additive colour theory and knowledge of the common relative abundances of the three elements in rocks. Granites usually contain all three elements in abundance, whereas basic and ultrabasic igneous rocks are strongly depleted. Sandstones are often depleted in both uranium and potassium, being dominated by quartz grains, but can have high Th contents locked in stable heavy minerals such as zircon and monazite. Clay-rich rocks generally contain high potassium contents bonded within clay minerals, and if deposited under reducing conditions generally have elevated uranium contents due to precipita-tion and adsorption of the insoluble U^{6+} ion. They contain little thorium due to its retention in inert heavy minerals that rarely reach the low-energy environment associated with the deposition of clays. Limestones are usually depleted in all three, but if rich in organic remains appreciable uranium may have been precipitated from sea water or hydrothermal solutions because of the reducing conditions that accompany hydrocarbons.

Provided that the results can be understood easily, it is possible to combine information from up to six variables in an RGB image by using ratios. This is most suited to geochemical data, where ratioing is commonly used in expressing petrogenetic differences.

Despite the earlier warning about unwise combination of data in RGB form, it is possible to perform a meaningful fusion between variables with fundamentally unrelated structures but important geological content. The appropriate method is the intensity–saturation–hue (ISH) transform (Section 5.2.2). While this was devised for the enhancement of RGB images by manipulation of the intensity and saturation derived from them, it is possible to substitute data of different kinds for the intensity and hue in the inverse (ISH to RGB) transform. The simplest application is using a single data set, such as aeromagnetic raster data. The raw data are used as the hue and a synthetic solar-shaded version incorporating high-frequency spatial features is used as the intensity, with saturation set to a constant (in the range 64–255) to ensure vivid colours in the result. This is another means of producing images similar to *Figure 8.15*.

Combining two data sets using the inverse ISH transform employs the strategy of using the data with the greatest spatial information content, often some kind of remotely sensed image, as the intensity input. This ensures that the spatial information is best rendered for visualization as brightness variations in the output colour image. Hue is controlled by the data with the greatest contribution to understanding lithological variation, such as gravity or geochemical data, so that the resulting colours are meaning-ful. Saturation is again set to a constant. *Figure 8.19* gives an example of this approach.

Because an RGB image comprising three variables can be converted to intensity, saturation and hue values using the ISH transform, the colour information can be separated as the saturation and hue to be combined with another data set that is substituted for the intensity. Again, the best strategy is employing data with potential for lithological discrimination as a source of colour and allowing intensity to be controlled by a variable containing high-frequency spatial information.

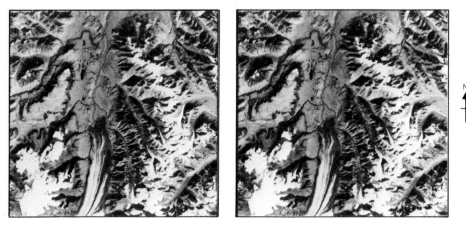

20 km

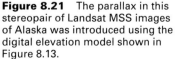

N

Figure 8.21 The parallax in this stereopair of Landsat MSS images of Alaska was introduced using the digital elevation model shown in Figure 8.13.

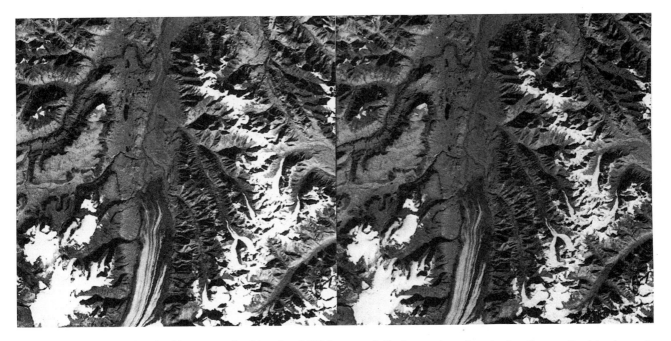

Figure 8.22 The parallax in this stereopair of Landsat MSS images of Alaska was introduced using the gravity data shown in Figure 8.13, and though the stereomodel looks odd it helps resolve evidence from both the surface and subsurface.

Figure 8.20 incorporates side-illuminated aeromagnetic data as intensity and uranium, thorium and potassium estimates from airborne radiometric data as saturation and hue for the same area as *Figure 8.18*. By careful use of ratios, this method allows the combination of up to seven variables, but at the expense of increasing the difficulty of interpretation. Usually such extreme methods employ variables that are selected on the basis of a well-understood model relating to the task in hand. For instance, epithermal gold mineralization is often associated with faults, generally results in clay-mineral alteration of host rocks, has elevated concentrations of arsenic–bismuth–antimony and the hydrothermal fluids often deplete the hosts in a number of alkali metals. From that model a sophisticated use of the ISH method could be based on high-resolution imagery for intensity and a mixture of geochemical data and spectral ratios as the source of hue and saturation controls, but it may be less confusing to use GIS methods.

As parallax can be derived from stereopairs of images as a route to modelling variations in topographic elevation, so the inverse is possible. In the absence of stereoscopic images, which greatly improve the detection of geological structures and lithological boundaries, synthetic stereopairs can be generated from satellite images by adding parallax derived from a DEM. Figure 8.21 was produced in this way using Landsat data and the DEM shown in Figure 8.13a. This approach is not limited to the use of elevation data since any spatial variable can be employed to transfer its three-dimensional topology into parallax shifts in synthetic stereopairs. Figure 8.22 shows an example of using gravity anomaly to introduce relief into the Landsat image used in Figure 8.21. Nor is this method limited to a pair of data sets, but synthetic stereo pairs can be produced in colour images that already may incorporate information from up to seven variables, as discussed above. Although such a large amount of data could be confusing, astute application of data to a particular geological model can produce images that fully exploit the geologist's powers of observation and mental synthesis (Ch. 9).

8.3 Data analysis in geographic information systems

Like different wavebands in multispectral remote-sensing data, the data layers residing in a GIS are registered, but with the additional advantage that the registration base is a geodetic coordinate system of some kind. A GIS is **geocoded**. Both raster and vector data, together with stacks of attributes for each vector category, are likely to be present and used in a geologically oriented GIS. Unlike remotely sensed data, the contents of each file may not be directly related to the others. As will be shown, the purpose of a GIS is to enable new, topic- or task-oriented attributes and layers to be derived from interrogation of the original data. Consequently, large numbers of newly derived files are likely to be generated, many of which may be intermediate steps to some ultimate goal.

The most important general cautionary note is that using a GIS demands a far more ordered approach than does digital image processing. Its analytical potential should not simply be explored in the quest for visually stimulating images. It requires a carefully thought-out strategy that exploits information in the context of well-defined goals, and is constrained by the analytical functions that reside in the system itself. Without this discipline, the user will undoubtedly experience acute confusion and results that have no significant meaning.

Geographic information systems form a major growth area in software development for information technology, and there are several different architectures. These boil down to two main types: those having a dominantly vector-based approach and those that are oriented to raster format. The first type is mainly oriented to the handling of existing map data in digital form, and is more or less a kind of digital mapping system of interest to planners and cartographers. Raster-handling capabilities are essential when remotely sensed and other semicontinuous, spatial variables form an important proportion of the source data, as is undoubtedly the case in geological applications. Fortunately, there are now many GISs that combine both raster and vector capabilities. The link between the two kinds of function is the ease of conversion of vector files to raster format with various cell sizes, so that vector data can be treated as rasters. Obviously this means that several orders of magnitude more storage and computing capacity is required than with a vector-based system, but the downward spiral of cost per unit of storage and number-crunching power largely obviates these problems.

Much of the output from a GIS is in the form of maps that result from data fusion and analysis, and it is often necessary for these to be displayed or printed to acceptable cartographic standards. For this, vector format has the distinct edge of sharp, accurate boundaries and ease of graphical modification. So, the most appropriate GISs for geology incorporate means of conversion from raster to vector format, at least for the simple boundaries and their contained categories that result from analysis.

The functions available in a GIS are numerous and often complex. Many were devised with the planner or manager in mind, not the geologist. The following sections summarize some of the most relevant functions, and more detailed accounts can be found in a number of specialist texts. Functions relevant to geological applications in a GIS break down to: retrieval and measurement (Section 8.3.1); overlay operations (Section 8.3.2); neighbourhood operations (Section 8.3.3); operations involving DEMs (Section 8.3.4); operations involving faults and fractures (Section 8.3.5)

8.3.1 *Retrieval and measurement functions*

Retrieval operations are the simplest functions in a GIS, involving the search for specific attributes, values or ranges of values residing within the available data, and the transfer of the relevant points, lines, polygons or raster cells to a new file. Examples would be extracting all areas where granite outcrops, points where gold has been found, fold axes, and areas of positive Bouguer gravity anomalies or where the abundance of a chemical element exceeds the threshold plus three times the average concentration. More complex categories, such as all granites with high zirconium in stream sediments and low topographic relief, can also be retrieved by specifying the data layers within which the relevant information lies. It is also possible to use retrieval operations to combine several classes as a means of simplifying information. An example would be combining all granites, adamellites, granodiorites, tonalites and monzonites of any age in an area as a general class of granitoids. The purpose of retrieval functions is to isolate specific features of interest, usually so that they might be combined with other information at a later stage. One possibility is setting all found cells or polygons to the value of 1.0 and other areas to zero. Multiplying other data sets by the retrieved file would lead to actual values only remaining for the retrieved class. This is a form of **masking**.

Measurement of the distance between points, the lengths of lines, perimeters and areas of polygons, the areas occupied by raster cells conforming to some limits, and volumes of specified segments of a DEM are functions common to any GIS. Potential uses in geology may be as a first step in analysis of faults and fractures, assessing the relative importance of different rock types that may contribute toxic elements to drainage in a catchment area, measuring the areas and volumes of potential sources of aggregates, or even the road travel distances from one important locality to the next.

8.3.2 *Overlay operations*

Overlay operations can involve both arithmetic and logical approaches, and seek to combine information from two or more layers of data to derive another. Combinations involving arithmetic overlays can become extremely complex, so logical overlays are considered first. Both require considerable forethought and planning in the context of some model.

Logical operations involve the rules of simple **Boolean algebra**, which use the operators **AND**, **OR**, **XOR** and **NOT** to determine whether a particular condition is true or

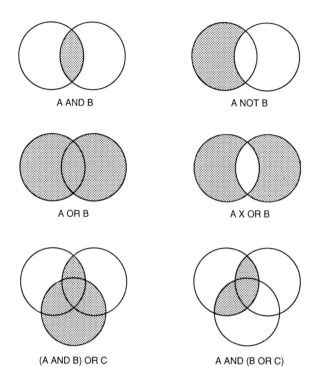

A AND B

A NOT B

A OR B

A X OR B

(A AND B) OR C

A AND (B OR C)

Figure 8.23 Venn diagrams showing shaded areas that correspond to the Boolean logical statements AND, OR, XOR and NOT, and two more complex statements.

false. These logical relationships are most easily understood using **sets** and **Venn diagrams**. Figure 8.23 shows a number of sets of attributes as Venn diagrams for a variety of logical statements, the shaded portions indicating the conditions where the statements are true. As an example of a simple but realistic model, consider a search for areas of potential hydrothermal mineralization in an area containing limestone. Limestones are prone to various types of hydrothermal mineralization, since they are attended by reducing conditions and are subject to easy solution by hydrothermal fluids. A common hydrothermal mineral in limestone country is fluorite (CaF_2). Given a geological map and stream-sediment fluorine determinations, an indicator of possible areas of mineralization would be derived by using the statement (limestone AND F > 100 p.p.m).

To illustrate the OR operator, consider a model for the location of useful wearing-course aggregate. In an area dominated by weak shales and sandstones there are small outcrops of basalts and slightly metamorphosed greywackes that would be ideal. The statement (basalt OR greywacke) would find all mapping units that are either basalt or greywacke, or both together.

For the NOT operator a useful illustration could be conditions for constructing a road. Areas of low slope would be ideal, but those occupied by peat deposits would be potentially disastrous. The statement (slope < 2° NOT peat) would show all gentle slopes except those infested by peat.

The XOR operator is a little more complicated, and is equivalent to 'either A or B, but not both together'. This operator is rarely employed in geological applications, but is useful in selecting areas for specific land uses.

Logical operators can be applied to more than two attributes or conditions, but the operators must be in some form of priority. Figure 8.23 shows the different results of A AND B OR C, the primary operator in parentheses. Consider the example of a search for mineralization in limestones. As well as fluorite, baryte ($BaSO_4$) is a common hydrothermal mineral in such terrains, and areas of limestone with either fluorine or barium anomalies might be prospective. The statement [limestone AND (F > 100 p.p.m. OR Ba > 200 p.p.m.)] would narrow the search, but that with the AND operator prioritized would also include areas with high fluorine and barium that are not associated with limestones, but perhaps with barren shales.

Results of logical overlay operations can be the end product of a search or the basis for masking, but may be a step in a more complex sequence involving other functions.

Arithmetic overlay operations can be used when considering data that combine both attributes and variables, generally assembled to exploit some conceptual model. The general idea is to use the data and the model to rate or score areas or cells according to how well they satisfy the model. A good example is provided by targeting possible sites of porphyry-style copper mineralization. These always occur in association with intermediate to acid granitoid intrusions, so information about their distribution is needed, perhaps combining areas where they outcrop with measures of proximity to them (Section 8.3.3). Since porphyry deposits occur near the top of such intrusions, buried intrusions need to be sought, when their low density and low magnetic susceptibility relative to country rocks produces negative anomalies on gravity and magnetic maps. Copper concentration in drainage or soil geochemistry data are an obvious part of the model, but high copper can be associated with unmineralized basaltic rocks, so some means of screening such false signals is needed. Basalts contain far higher chromium concentrations than granitoids, so high Cu/Cr ratios should characterize mineralized granitoids. Porphyry mineralization is formed by the transport of metals in hot, watery late-stage fluids derived from the granitoid magma. Typically they result in alteration of feldspars to clay minerals, which have distinctive spectral signatures on remotely sensed images covering the SWIR. Porphyry deposits also contain large volumes of disseminated iron and copper sulphides, which are broken down to brightly coloured ferric hydroxides during weathering to give gossans. The model should therefore include data from remote sensing that highlight such alteration. Suitable data sets would be Landsat TM 7/5 and 3/1 band ratios.

Each criterion in the model must be assessed in terms of how the values of the variable involved can be divided into ranges that carry a score in favour of the presence of porphyry–copper mineralization. It is useful to set thresholds for some critical factors, values beyond which definitely militate against a satisfactory conclusion, so that the relevant cells are excluded from the model. In developing the model, some criteria will be more encouraging than others, so the scoring often involves weighting the data sets employed differently. The complex overlay operation then sums the weighted scores for each cell, resulting in a map that prioritises the region for more detailed exploration and expenditure of funds. Virtually every kind of mineral deposit, hydrocarbon play or groundwater source could be expressed in such a form, so that the search is narrowed and rationalized.

8.3.3 Neighbourhood operations

Neighbourhood operations evaluate the characteristics of the area surrounding a specified location. One function is to count the number of specified elements within a particular distance from a point, line or boundary. An example would be to count the number of mines within an economic trucking distance of every cell in an area as a means of deciding on possible sites for ore-processing plants serving several mines. In that case, other considerations would also be used to indicate the most favourable sites.

A second function that might help in this siting exercise would be measuring the distance of every cell from established transport routes. In the porphyry–copper example above, this would be the means of establishing proximity to granite outcrops.

Many geological applications of GISs employ proximity analysis in relation to various types of boundary. For example, many mineral deposits produced by movement of solutions through rock, such as hydrothermal, contact metasomatic and pegmatite types, are spatially related to faults, unconformities and contacts of igneous intrusions. There is a higher probability that they lie close to such features than in homogeneous rock. **Corridors** or **buffer zones** of a specified width astride boundaries of these kinds can be generated, within which more complicated overlay operations can be conducted.

Many other neighbourhood operations rely on moving search areas that produce statistical summaries, including averages, totals, maximum and minimum values, and measures of diversity, for the immediate vicinity of points or cells in vector or raster data. Specialized texts will contain accounts of other neighbourhood operations that are more appropriate for land-use and other non-geological applications.

8.3.4 Operations involving DEMs

As well as estimations of topographic slope and simulation of solar shading using first-derivative filters (Section 8.2.5), DEMs in raster format allow the extraction of specific geomorphological features, such as lines of drainage, stream order, ridges and catchments. Such operations perform a search outwards from a starting location using a specific decision rule. In seeking the path of water flow over a DEM the rule used might be to start at the highest elevation in the area and then move to the nearest cell among the eight surrounding cells that has the lowest elevation. The operation would then be repeated until either the edge of the area was reached, or a cell in a depression surrounded by cells with higher elevation. This would trace one drainage path. Starting again at the next highest elevation would trace another, and so on, until all topographically defined drainages had been defined. Using the connectivity between tributaries then allows the number of tributaries and thus stream order to be defined for all the drainages. Catchments above specified points can be defined by spreading only to adjacent cells with the same or higher elevation, until there are no adjacent higher cells, thereby defining watersheds. Such operations are potentially useful in hydrological and hydrogeological applications, where the land unit of interest is the catchment basin.

Although mainly of interest to land-use planners, DEMs can be used with **intervisibility** functions that define the areas in direct line of sight from specified locations. This uses the topography to find features that screen straight-line connections between the target location and parts of the surrounding landscape. This might be of use in satisfying the ever-increasing environmental and amenity constraints placed on development of extractive industry and route orientation, with which geologists might easily become involved.

8.3.5 Operations involving faults and fractures

As well as the quest for hitherto undiscovered potato fields, lost cities and hidden oceans, it is tempting for the geologist to relax by drawing dense masses of straight lines on remotely sensed images. This is often supported by the misguided belief that all apparent linear connections between elements of terrain represent faults or fractures that surface mapping has missed. In truth, this once popular practice owes much to imagination and the line-seeking predilection of human cortical cell assemblies (Section 2.1), for individuals rarely agree on all linear features observed on images. Nonetheless, suitably enhanced images do reveal many known and unsuspected real faults and fractures, the trick being to devise means of ascertaining their reality.

Now, the presence of fractures in the crust, particularly those involving dilatation, has considerable significance for the channelling of various kinds of fluids. The fluid dynamics of fractured rocks as opposed to those in porous and permeable media are not well known. What is abundantly clear is the strong economic connotation of fracture-controlled mineral deposits, hydrocarbon migration paths and groundwater resources, as well as leakage potential from fractured waste-disposal sites and seismic risk in heavily faulted terrain, hence the near obsession of some remote-sensing geologists with fracture analysis and the growth of a not inconsiderable cottage industry. Geological remote sensors are sometimes regarded with a jaundiced eye in consequence of a welter of learned papers in the 1970s and 80s, which rested on masses of tedious, web-like maps and largely meaningless rose diagrams indicating the length, density and azimuth of lines on images.

Given that it is possible to weed the illusory from the real, the digitization of mapped and interpreted faults and fractures in vector format now allows useful statistical information to be extracted. Software is available to define fracture spacing and density, the density of fracture intersections, spatial trends and a variety of more sophisticated measures. These derivatives can then be combined with other data layers using operations covered in Sections 8.3.1 to 8.3.3.

8.4 Concluding note

The use of non-image data in raster form and application of GIS methodology to multivariate information is at the high end of image interpretation in terms of costs in time and money. Set against this are a number of mitigating factors. Many non-image data are initially generated for limited uses, and if they fail to deliver the 'goods' they are often discarded, despite the frequently high costs of acquisition. For many of them, ingenuity can easily devise other applications. Indeed, in their original form important information with unexpected connotations is sometimes hidden. Recasting data in digital form, either as rasters or in vector format, helps reveal these surprises, particularly if now fairly routine enhancement techniques are applied. Because of potential multiple uses, original and data-processing costs can be divided among several projects. The basic element in GIS methods is integration of data, and there is no reason why this should not lead to integration of seemingly unrelated projects. As an example, it requires no stretch of the imagination to see that drainage geochemistry can serve mineral exploration, human and livestock environmental risk monitoring, and in some cases

help explain features of natural vegetation. All three have other common links, such as soil type.

By establishing an ethos of employing spatial databases and GIS methodology for all aspects of the environment in its broadest sense, public administrations from the local, through national to regional and global levels can foster closer links between all the disciplines involved. Each has contributions to make to all the others. Social, economic and environmental problems are not unrelated in reality. Treating different problems separately often leads to unsuspected difficulties in another field. So such a fusion of effort as well as data can chart a course that takes as its starting point the interconnectedness of all things.

Further reading

Anfiloff, V. and A. Luyendyk 1986. Production of pixel maps of airborne magnetic data for Australia, with examples for the Roper River 1:1 000 000 sheet. *Exploration Geophysics* **17**, 113–117.

Aronoff, S. 1989. *Geographic information systems: a management perspective*. Ottawa: WDL Publications.

Arvidson, R.E., E.A. Guinness, J.W. Strebeck, G.F. Davies and K.J. Schultz 1982. Image processing applied to gravity and topographic data covering the continental United States. *EOS* **63**, 261–265.

Batson, R.M., Edwards, K. and Eliason, E.M. 1976. Synthetic stereo and Landsat pictures. *Photogramm. Eng. Remote Sens.* **42**, 1279–1284.

Bolivar, S.L., S.H. Balog and T.A. Weaver 1982. Resource characterization for uranium mineralization in the Montrose 1° × 2° Quadrangle, Colorado. *Proc. 5th Annual Uranium Seminar*, pp. 37–48. New York: American Institute of Mining, Metallurgy and Petroleum Engineering.

Bonham-Carter, G.F., F.P. Agterberg and D.F. Wright 1988. Integration of geological data sets for gold exploration in Nova Scotia. *Photogramm. Eng. Remote Sens.* **54**, 1585–1592.

Burrough, P.A. 1986. *Principles of geographical information systems for land resources assessment*. Oxford: Oxford University Press.

Campbell, A.N., V.F. Hollister, R.V. Dutta and P.E. Hart 1982. Recognition of a hidden mineral deposit by an artificial intelligence program. *Science* **217**, 927–928.

Drury, S.A. and A.S.D. Walker 1987. Display and enhancement of gridded aeromagnetic data of the Solway Basin. *Int. J. Remote Sens.* **8**, 1433–1444.

Drury, S.A. and A.S.D. Walker 1991. The use of geophysical images in subsurface investigations of the Solway Basin, England. *Surveys in Geophysics* **12**, 565–581.

Guinness, E.A., R.E Arvidson, C.E. Leff, M.H. Edwards and D.L. Bindschadler 1983. Digital image processing applied to geophysical and geochemical data for Southern Missouri. *Econ. Geol.* **78**, 654–663.

Harrington, H.J., C.J. Simpson and R.F. Moore 1982. Analysis of continental structures using a digital terrain model (DTM) of Australia. *BMR J. Aust. Geol. Geoph.* **7**, 68–72.

Hastings, D.A. 1983. Synthesis of geophysical data with space-acquired imagery: a review. *Adv. Space Res.*, **3**, 157–168.

Hoffman, P.F. 1987. Continental transform tectonics: Great Slave Lake shear zone (ca. 1.9 Ga), northwest Canada. *Geology* **15**, 785–788.

Jenson, S.K. and J.O. Domingue 1988. Extracting topographic structure from digital elevation data for geographic information system analysis. *Photogramm. Eng. Remote Sens.* **54**, 1593–1600.

Junkin, B.G. 1982. Development of three-dimensional spatial displays using a geographically based information system. *Photogramm. Eng. Remote Sens.* **48**, 577–586.

Kowalik, W.S. and W.E. Glenn 1987. Image processing of aeromagnetic data and integration with Landsat images for improved structural interpretation. *Geophysics* **52**, 875–884.

Lee, M.K., T.C. Pharaoh and N.J. Soper 1990. Structural trends in central Britain from images of gravity and aeromagnetic fields. *J. Geol. Soc. Lond.* **147**, 241–258.

McGuffie, B.A., L.F. Johnson, R.E. Alley and H.R. Lang 1989. IGIS: computer-aided photogeologic mapping with image-processing, graphics and CAD/CAM capabilities. *Geobyte* (October 1989), 8–14.

Marble, D.F. and D.J. Peuquet 1983. Geographic information systems and remote sensing. Chapter 22 in *Manual of remote sensing* 2nd edn, Colwell, R.N. (ed.), pp. 923–958. Falls Church, Virginia: American Society of Photogrammetry.

O'Sullivan, K.N. 1983. The role of image processing in mineral exploration: why stop at Landsat? *Adv. Space Res.* **3**, 169–171.

O'Sullivan, K.N. 1986. Computer enhancement of Landsat, magnetic and other regional data. *Pub. 13th CMMI Cong. Singapore, Vol. 2 Geology and exploration*, pp. 1–10.

Paterson, N.R. and C.V. Reeves 1985. Application of gravity and magnetic surveys: the state of the art in 1985. *Geophysics* **50**, 2558–2594.

Reeves, C.R. 1985. Airborne geophysics for geological mapping and regional exploration. *ITC Journal* **1985-3**, 147–161.

Seemuller, W.W. 1989. The extraction of ordered vector drainage networks from elevation data. *Computer Vision, Graphics Image Processing* **47**, 45–58.

Wadge, G., P.A.V. Young and D.C. Mason 1992. Simulation of geological processes using an expert system. *J. Geol. Soc. Lond.* **149**, 455–463.

With the breadth of uses of GISs in geography and social science applications as well as in geology, the 1980s saw an unprecedented explosion in GIS software aimed at users of many different types of computers. The most widespread can be subdivided into the VMS, Unix, MS-DOS and Apple operating systems, serving DEC VAX, Sun, IBM-compatible PCs, and Macintosh computers respectively. I do not intend to venture any suggestions for 'ideal' GIS for geological users, and readers must carry out their own investigations. One note of warning is appropriate, however, for GIS systems range from automated cartography and design, vector-based GISs to systems combining both vector and raster data. The latter are essential for geological applications, since many of the data will be in raster format. Ideally, both image processing and GISs should be linked in the best systems. Virtually any trade periodical on computers will contain numerous advertisements for GIS software. Perhaps the most convenient source of information is to scan any copy of *Photogrammetric Engineering and Remote Sensing* for the numerous trade advertisements, and request information directly from suppliers. Occasionally, this journal carries reviews of systems, as does *Geobyte*. A safe source of advice for any newcomer to the field is always colleagues who are well established in the field, although they will nearly always complain that there is no ideal system, and wish that they had waited before purchasing their own. Prices fell dramatically as functionality and speed increased during the late 1980s, and any system that survived the 1980s will almost certainly be a useful purchase.

CHAPTER NINE

Geological applications of image data

Most applications of remote sensing in geology involve the delineation of structures and the discrimination of different rock and soil types, often in spite of, or exploiting, variations in natural vegetation cover. Many techniques have been described earlier, so this chapter examines the contexts and potential roles for remote sensing in the day-to-day activities of professional geologists. Obviously, much can be learned from case studies of individual ventures, but such is the range of possibilities that to illustrate them well would require a book on each application area in its own right. Each project has its own internal logic, geared to the nature of the terrain, the availability of image data, costs and efficiency, and the specific objectives of the investigation. In case studies many of the generalities are skated over or omitted for the sake of brevity, or because readers can be assumed to have some geological knowledge. Occasionally, some of the details of specific methodology are omitted deliberately for reasons of commercial confidentiality.

Selecting a remote-sensing strategy for any geological assignment requires consideration of the specific circumstances involved. Part of the strategy is linked to the way geological models are built from a number of general components, part to the means whereby information from images or other graphic data can assist in assembling these components. This chapter covers several types of activity in which geologists play a crucial role, examines the kinds of information that they need to contribute in helping to achieve the objectives of a particular programme, and suggests the kinds of data and the way that they can be handled appropriately to provide this information. It is not a 'cookbook' but a guide to orientation of the relatively new skills and opportunities involved in remote sensing to the observational and analytical skills that have long been the geologist's stock in trade. Can remote sensing supplant field observations? The answer is a resounding 'No!', for a number of reasons. First, many of the features that are essential in building up a geological picture, such as petrographic texture, minor tectonic and sedimentary structures, and detailed relative time relationships are far too small to be resolved by any conceivable remote-sensing instrument. Second, truly fresh rock is rarely exposed, being covered by weathering patinas, soil and vegetation of different types. The hammer, hand lens and ultimately the microscope and geochemical analytical techniques have to be applied to ferret out the mineralogical and textural features that are used in classifying rocks and understanding their genesis. Third, even if fresh rocks were exposed completely, detailed knowledge of the spectra of rock-forming and accessory minerals reveals that not all can be identified and separated uniquely, nor can their proportions be precisely assessed because of variations in the strength of their associated spectral features. In the reflected region detectable minerals are restricted mainly to those carrying ferric, hydroxyl and carbonate ions, together with differences in overall reflectivity stemming from a multitude of factors. The thermally emitted region holds out greater promise because of the shifts in spectral features due to variations in silicon and aluminium coordination with oxygen and other molecular features that give information on rock-forming minerals.

While giving some guide to rock composition, overlaps and different intensities of spectral features still mean that multispectral thermal data are unlikely ever to provide a comprehensive petrographic mapping capability. Radar data provide information on the weathering texture of rocks, the variations in roughness of the surface and the presence of corner reflectors smaller than the method's resolution dimensions. Though helpful in some cases by providing another dimension to image interpretation, radar too is not an all-purpose geological mapper in its own right.

So information provided by remote sensing has to be verified and amplified by field work, in much the same way as the subsurface information provided by geophysical surveys needs to be interpreted in the light of surface observations. However, remote sensing permits viewing of the surface in a detailed map-like form with the advantage of providing a synopsis of areas that are far larger than can be encompassed by a ground view. In doing so it reveals features that are difficult to map at the surface and allows features and characteristics observed in the field to be extrapolated into unvisited areas. In this regard remote sensing enables the amount of field work needed to achieve project objectives to be reduced, and also directs field investigations to areas containing the most critical evidence. So it helps increase a geologist's efficiency. By venturing into non-visible parts of the spectrum and through digital image processing, remote sensing increases the chances of making discoveries that would be overlooked in conventional field work. So it amplifies the geologist's powers of observation and detection.

Rather than being an area for topic-specific research, remote sensing provides a kit of tools that a geologist can deploy as and where necessary. Making a selection from this toolbox involves several considerations:

(1) *Application definition.* What are the geological features and processes that serve the application? Is it possible to extract information about them from image data?

(2) *Resolution and scale needed.* What is the minimum spatial resolution needed to detect the required geological information? Over what range of scales do the geological features and processes manifest themselves? In general, the finer the resolution the larger is the scale of presentation. The maximum scale needed is often a guide to the minimum resolution size. If the requirement involves a maximum scale of 1:1 million then there is little point in using data with a resolution of 10 m or less. As Equation 2.1 reveals, what the eye can see in an image depends on the scale and viewing distance, and there are definite limits. For a project involving products at 1:10 000 scale a resolution less than 5 m will be needed.

(3) *Spectral coverage.* Is multispectral, single-band or panchromatic imagery required, and what regions of the spectrum are appropriate for the features being sought? The answers depend on the main emphasis being on lithological discrimination, mapping geological structures or evaluation of terrain. The first depends to a great extent on the degree to which rocks or soils derived from them are free of vegetation cover, but obviously benefits from selection of wavebands that are affected by mineralogically determined spectral features. Structural mapping and examination of geomorphology depend to a large extent on the interpretation of high-frequency topographic features or edges. So, the better appreciation by human vision of fine detail in greytone images (Section 2.2) than in colour images often means that single-band or panchromatic images are more appropriate than false-colour composites. However, structural geology and lithological mapping are complementary, and some tectonic features can be inferred only by their displacement of or relationship to lithological boundaries, when colour images can be useful. Similarly, geomorphology involves considering the relationship between physical processes of landscape development and the effects of vegetation cover, when false-colour images are the best means of providing information on plant distribution. For some applications non-image data are appropriate, such as topographic elevation or potential-field data in a form suitable for use in image processing or GIS operations.

(4) *Data processing.* Chapters 5 and 8 discussed a wide range of possible manipulations that can be used in enhancing or extracting the information contained in images. Because all involve time and therefore cost, and in some cases produce new images that require varying depths of insight into the meaning of the features that they reveal, a choice of techniques is an important consideration in planning an application. Some are aimed at improving the visual qualities of images, such as contrast stretching and edge enhancement, others at expressing hidden information and relations between different data sets, such as ratioing and principal component analysis. A further suite extracts information from many spatially related data sets, as in classification and GIS operations.

There are other considerations of a more mundane character, such as whether the required data are indeed available, how much they would cost, and if they have acceptable cloud cover and atmospheric haze. An important point concerns the time of year for data acquisition, as emphasized in Section 5.6.3 and Figure 5.43. This involves both the presence of living vegetation – sometimes it is a distinct aid, sometimes a hindrance, depending on the local climatic conditions – and the Sun angle at the time of overpass. At moderate to high latitudes the winter Sun is much lower in the sky than in the summer, so that the shadows of muted topographic features are more apparent. In a few applications involving short-lived phenomena, such as studies of volcanoes, changing river courses and environmental changes associated with resource-based industry, repetitive cover is all important. However, for most geological applications a single image with favourable atmospheric and vegetation conditions is often all that is needed. Moreover, the age of the image is frequently immaterial. There are, of course, areas that are so plagued by perpetual cloud cover that reflected and thermal images rarely reveal the surface. Whatever the application in such an area, only radar remote sensing provides any assistance to the geologist.

9.1 Geomorphology

The study of landforms and landscape involves description, classification and analysis of the evolution of the planet's surface. Though it is currently emerging from being a marginalized topic within geology, geomorphology is of fundamental importance because it is one of the driving forces of biological evolution, and controls habitability. In landscape studies the element of detail is essential, for landforms are enormously complex and diverse on all scales. The information base has to match reality, and images at different scales are the only realistic base for interpretation.

Remotely sensed images lend themselves ideally to geomorphological studies, for all is revealed at any required scale and area of coverage. As well as specific topographic and hydrological features, images can provide details on vegetation type and cover, on which landscape evolution depends, together with climatic variations, underlying geology and time.

Until the widespread accessibility of satellite images the science had drawn in on itself, after the falling into disfavour of the megascopic ideas of W.M. Davis. It focused on the small scale, the short term and the study of process, becoming almost divorced from geology. This trend coincided with the rise of ideas on systems analysis and the application of statistical methods, to which detailed information on small areas lent itself. The landscape became idealized as elements linked by flows of mass and energy. Such an approach found itself incapable of extrapolation to large features and timespans of geological magnitude. It was an exclusively 'bottom upwards' approach. Studies of other planetary bodies, such as the Moon, Mars and satellites of the Outer Planets based themselves entirely on images of successively increasing scale, forcing a 'top downwards' approach and much different methodologies that relied largely on stratigraphic rules of observation. Elements concerned with planetary evolution grew to dominance. As well as discovering features of gigantic dimensions, considerable ingenuity was required to interpret the processes involved. Planetology found an echo in geomorphology, with the focus shifting once again to grand theories.

Climatic geomorphology builds on Davis' stageist theories of evolution. It is based on the notion that today's relief-forming mechanisms vary according to zoned climatic conditions, and this can be extrapolated to the past. Much of the terrestrial landscape is seen as being inherited from past climatic periods. Since climate is currently in transition from a major warming only 10–15 000 years ago, this seems quite reasonable. Before the end of the last glacial period the world was a much different place from today over a period of perhaps 100 000 years, and imposed features that have not yet reached a steady state under modern climatic conditions. Indeed, the last 2–4 million years have been a period of great climatic instability, with glacial and interglacial periods succeeding each other with high frequency in comparison with geological timescales. The period prior to this episode of rapid change seems to have been one of greater climatic stability, and elements of a steady-state pre-Pliocene set of landscapes still play an underlying role in setting today's geomorphological scene. But climate is not the only dynamic in the evolution of the Earth's surface.

Structural geomorphology focuses on the fundamental control of geology and tectonics over landscape, partly by different resistances of rocks to erosion (long known in geomorphology) and partly because of active vertical movements of the crust through different mechanisms. Climate plays a role but its effects are conditioned by the rocks and their movements. A unity of the two strands of terrestrial planetology (**mega-geomorphology**) is suggested by the growing recognition that rapid erosion by glaciers and powerful rivers unloads the lithosphere, thereby allowing uplift. Since such unloading is achieved by removing mass mainly from valleys, the remaining peaks and higher ground are subject to continued rise, to generate in the extreme mountains of Himalayan and Alpine magnitude. This recognition stems from the discovery that much of the rapid Himalayan uplift took place in the Pliocene and Pleistocene, whereas the underlying tectonic forces that generated thick, buoyant continental crust were initiated long before. The most rapid uplift was delayed until rapid erosion became possible when climate changed and glaciers and the meltwater derived from them could sculpt the landscape at an accelerated rate.

Clearly, geomorphology is scale dependent, and unification is only possible by studies at all scales from that of the minor gulley to continent wide. From a lower limit of around 1:10 000 enabled by aerial photography, remotely sensed data now support scales down to 1:10 million or less through platforms like Landsat and SPOT and the coarse-resolution meteorological satellites such as the NOAA and geostationary series. Even terrain features on the submetre scale, as expressed by surface roughness, are amenable to radar imaging. Although many landscapes change at rates that are too slow to be monitored within the 60-year history of systematic remote sensing, some processes are quick enough for change detection to be possible. These include aeolian, coastal, glacial, volcanic, lacustrine, mass-wasting and some fluvial processes. Judicious selection of time series of an area, if available, can help monitor the dynamics involved in landscape change.

Since landscapes are three-dimensional, stereoscopy is of great importance in geomorphology. Where organized agriculture camouflages topographic features with patchwork patterns (Fig. 4.52) it is essential. Gradually the SPOT programme, and latterly that of JERS-1, is providing global stereoscopic coverage that was previously only possible through large-scale aerial photographs, which do not allow continuity of three dimensional visualization. Although several million square kilometres are covered by stereoscopic Large Format Camera images, sadly the deployment of this low-cost instrument on the Space Shuttle was limited to just one mission in 1984.

In rigorous statistical analysis of landform, stereoscopic images include extraneous clutter due to variations in the reflective properties of the surface at a wide range of spatial frequencies. Moreover, proceeding from a mental stereomodel to actual measurements of relief is a tedious process. The base for quantitative landform analysis is accurate expressions of the variation in topographic elevation through DEMs (Section 8.2.4), derived either from topographic contour maps or by automated parallax estimation from digital stereoscopic imagery. Such DEMs enable the scale dependence of terrain features to be monitored, amounts and rates of mass transfer to be estimated and drainage channels and watersheds to be extracted automatically.

Geomorphological mapping poses considerable problems because of the many different approaches that are in vogue and the sheer complexity of landforms. All mapping involves simplifying the complex continuum of reality through symbols, categorization and areal division – a sort of data reduction in its own right. Three possible general approaches to division of landforms are: purely as functions of shape and pattern; according to interpretation of the genetic mechanisms involved; and by recognizing landforms of different ages using simple stratigraphic rules. It is difficult, if not impossible, to avoid welding the three approaches together, since evidence for all three manifests itself to the interpreter on images. Ready examples of the confusion are provided by drainage systems. These can be categorized purely on form (Fig. 4.4), but the forms always have some underlying cause, sometimes geological controls, and may have been induced by an earlier fluvial episode but subsequently been incised into an uplifting block of crust. It is quite common in any climatic zone to find meandering drainages that developed on an early planation surface, which are now incised into rugged, rising mountains (Fig. 4.32).

It is unrealistic to expect any but the most grossly generalized geomorphic categories to be widely agreed upon. In practice no two geomorphic maps produced by different interpreters can be compared in detail, and few that correspond except in a very general way. Producing maps is a graveyard for many a geomorphologist with a bureaucratic bent! Essentially, such a map caters for specific needs, not for all. Attempts have been made to map **geomorphic units**, which are genetically homogeneous landforms produced by specific constructional or destructional processes. But all land-forming processes tend to overlap, and many landforms owe their features to several processes of different age. A more productive line of attack relies on a hierarchy of forms depending on scale. In such a **multitiered approach** one tier of map units at large scale disappears or blurs as scale and perceptual detail decreases, to be replaced by a succession of tiers at increasingly smaller scales. In this way links can be made between manifestations of process and evolution from the scale of the smallest element of interest to those that characterize entire continents. This encourages a unification between understanding of detailed dynamics of currently active systems, through the interplay between fundamentally different types of erosional and constructional processes in an evolutionary context, to the grandiose relations between surface and internal processes that involve the lithosphere as a whole, areas the size of continents and timespans of tens, hundreds and perhaps even thousands of million years. Trying to achieve such a symbolic relationship, full of understanding of the dynamics involved, is the challenge posed to geomorphologists by planetologists working on extraterrestrial bodies.

Even if this systematization were to be achieved, there is still the likelihood that geomorphic maps are made by experts for experts. There is no problem or harm in the context of academic research, but it often seems that remotely sensed images themselves are the most useful geomorphic maps, since all the information is there for producing thematic maps of any type for any purpose. However, in practical life decisions have to be made and boundaries drawn. Consequently, geomorphologists are often called on to make interpretations and maps to assist a specific social, environmental or economic programme. Coordinating image interpretation involves isolating the elements of the landscape that are relevant to the programme's objectives. Geomorphology with an end other than human curiosity is often termed **terrain analysis**. It can form an input to environmental and resource management, land-use and route planning, military strategy, and engineering applications (Section 9.?). The resulting thematic maps are increasingly combined through GIS with other types of information, some from image interpretation too, such as variations in vegetation cover, soil type, geology and hydrology.

Chapters 4 and 7 contain many useful guidelines for geomorphological image interpretation, which can be amplified by some of the Further Reading for this chapter and modern textbooks on geomorphology. Images from the reflected region are quite sufficient for most geomorphological purposes, and it is rarely impossible to achieve substantial results with single-band images alone. However, false-colour images, if affordable, can add significantly to interpretations. Since the dominant features on images are geomorphological in origin, little enhancement is necessary, except for cosmetic improvement by contrast stretching and edge enhancement (Figs. 5.20 and 5.22).

Thermal data and radar images increase the breadth of detectable features, radar adding information on microrelief that forms a direct link to field observations. Where cloud cover is dominant, as in equatorial regions, radar sometimes forms the only source of information about terrain, because of its all-weather capabilities. Attempts have been made in such obscured regions to produce radar mosaics, such as Project RADAM in Brazil. Of the existing orbital SAR instruments, that carried by ERS-1 is inappropriate for geomorphology in all but areas of low relief because of its steep depression angle and the dominance of images in rugged terrain by layover (Fig. 3.39). The JERS-1 SAR has a less steep depression angle and produces images as useful as those from SIR-A. Radar has another important attribute to offer geomorphologists, in the form of shallow penetration of very dry sand and ice. Figure 7.4 gives a dramatic example of the potential for discovering completely hidden geomorphic information using SAR, where an extinct system of drainages in the eastern Sahara flowing in the opposite direction to present ephemeral drainage is revealed. The potential global coverage of JERS-1, ERS-1 and eventually RADARSAT promises an upsurge in geomorphological discovery, although it should be noted that only JERS-1 carries on-board recording that ensures images from anywhere (the others can only transmit data to suitably equipped receiving systems in line of sight).

It is often forgotten that the 70% of the Earth's surface covered by oceans has landforms too. Conventional bathymetry is limited in its contribution to mapping the morphology of the ocean floor through its restriction to shipping lanes. The Seasat and ERS-1 radar altimetry data, through measurement of sea-surface elevation, contain information relevant to water depth through gravitational effects (Fig. 8.9). More detailed images of the sea bed are produced by side-scanning sonar that reveals many unsuspected features (Fig. 9.1).

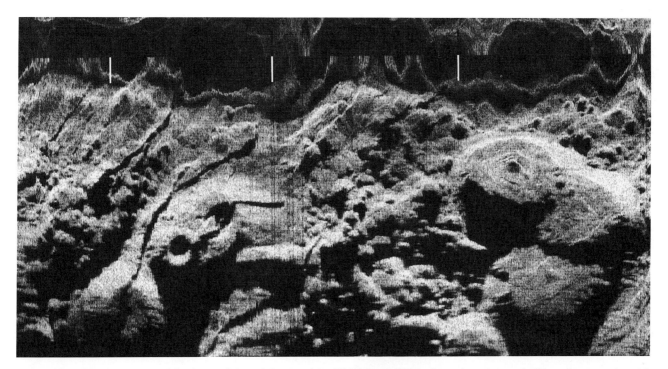

Figure 9.1 Sidescan sonograph of part of the axial zone of the Mid-Atlantic Ridge. Sonar images are similar to those produced by radar, looking sideways from the platform track and responding to timed acoustic returns. They are both shadowed and vary in tone according to surface roughness. In this case, the dark upper strip is directly beneath the platform – a submersible. Prominent on the image are flat-topped shield volcanoes at right and a conical volcano with a funnel-shaped crater at left. Separating these features is a hummocky terrain of huge pillow-like flows along the axial rift. A fault scarp is prominent at left. The image is 3 by 4 km. Courtesy of Bramley Murton, Institute of Oceanographic Sciences, UK, and Roger Searle, University of Durham, UK.

9.2 Geological mapping

The bulk of this book is oriented towards extracting geological information from images, but the main responsibility of geologists is rationalizing this information in the form of graphic maps. How such maps are designed and produced is mainly outside the book's scope. Essentially, mapping consists of defining boundaries between rock units of different type, expressing their disposition relative to each other and to time, and delineating the tectonic structures about which they are disposed. Geological maps are two-dimensional expressions of four-dimensional systems, and incorporate cues to the understanding of earth history and the interplay between internal and surface processes. Remote sensing is unable to provide a great deal of this information unless it is blended with field work and laboratory investigations. As emphasized many times, image data do not directly provide conventional divisions between rock types, which are and will remain dependent on mineralogy, texture in hand specimen and thin section, and geochemistry. There are two main, general approaches to mapping from images, one based on **image units** and the other on **lithofacies units**.

Image units combine the textural and pattern attributes of the surface with the way it interacts with EM radiation – most frequently in terms of albedo or spectral characteristics expressed in different ways on false-colour images. It is a more or less objective approach to mapping, implying no genetic connotations. For extraterrestrial surfaces with little if any chance of ground verification such an approach cannot be avoided. The relative ages of the units can be inferred from simple stratigraphic rules, such as discordant relations. In studies of many planetary bodies variations in the distribution of impact craters are often useful (Fig. 9.2). This is based on the observation, initially from the Moon, that the older the surface the greater the chance of craters having formed, the rate of impacting having decreased with time throughout the solar system. Other such signs of relative age include the masking of features by transported debris, such as ejecta from impacts or aeolian dust (Fig. 4.43). Occasionally there is sufficient detail to recognize general shapes reminiscent of processes on the Earth involved in the flow of fluids of different viscosity, including water, ice, lavas and landslips (Fig. 9.3). Using image units has the appeal of being definable in terms of the available data, but different units emerge from using different data (Fig. 6.11). More importantly, such units are of little use to other geologists, and the main requirement of a geological mapping programme is to lay out information that has a practical use, without the user having to go through the rigmarole of understanding the particular means of subdivision.

In terrestrial mapping, there are few cases where field data or earlier geological maps are not available. Consequently there are often opportunities to assign lithologies to recognizable image units, extrapolate from known to unvisited areas and to trace structural features over broad areas. Even in cases of completely unknown terrain – now becoming very rare – image interpretation can proceed directly to a reconnaissance map of conventional type. Enough will be known from adjoining terrains that have been visited and mapped to make an educated guess as to

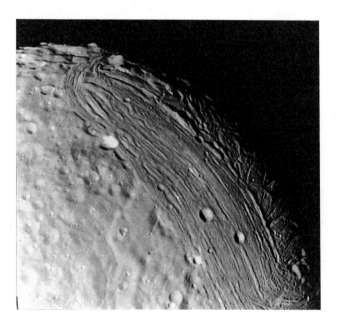

Figure 9.2 Voyager-2 image of Miranda, a moon of Uranus, showing a grooved terrain next to an older cratered terrain which has been partially resurfaced to mute the craters. Younger impact craters clearly show as sharp circular features. Courtesy of JPL, Pasadena, USA.

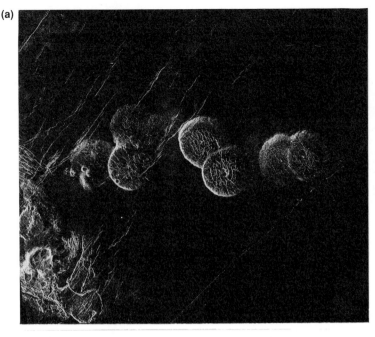

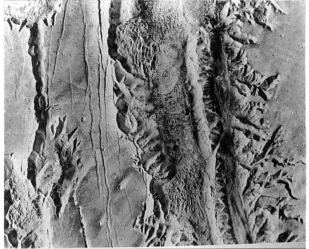

Figure 9.3 (a) Magellan SAR image of the Alpha Regio region of Venus showing volcanic domes, around 25 km across, formed by extrusion of viscous magma. The curious fracture patterns on the domes suggest extrusion after the formation of a solid skin. Courtesy of JPL, Pasadena, USA. (b) Viking image of Valles Marineris on Mars, in which the branching form of some of its side valleys suggests the former action of flowing water on this now dry planet. Courtesy of JPL, Pasadena, USA.

the likely rocks and structures expected, backed up by spectral knowledge and the appearance of different rocks in climatically similar terrains. Geologists are unlikely to find many surprises in terms of rock composition that require a complete revision of terrestrial petrogenesis, such as vast flows of sulphur lava or methane ice. In new areas mistakes can be made during image interpretation unsupported by field data, but where there is no information virtually any new observation is valuable, and new ideas help guide field work to test them out. Armed with experience of the ways in which geological boundaries are modified by topographic relief it should be possible to predict where hidden boundaries trend and reappear.

In general, the vast majority of geological boundaries reflect either roughly parallel compositional layering or discordances that cut across that layering, such as faults, igneous contacts or unconformities (Figs. 4.21, 4.26a and 7.10). Recognition of layer-parallel features on images, conforming to the relationship between dip and strike of layering or other planar fabrics and relief, is of primary importance, for this enables folding and angular discordances to be discovered, evaluated and mapped. Occasionally, layers with distinctive texture or spectral properties (Figs 6.20 and 7.27) can be used as marker horizons that help in more accurate delineation of fold structures and relative displacements on faults (*Fig. 9.4*). Although the amount of information that permits such photogeological mapping varies with vegetation and soil cover, this more subjective approach based on inferred genetic relationships leads to

results that have a predictive content of immediate use to any geologist. It forms the bones on which more geological flesh can be sculpted as investigations proceed. Achieving this often depends on experimentation with digital image processing to reveal the best combination of data, and access to a variety of renditions helps glean all the available clues.

Of all possibilities, the availability of stereoptic potential is undoubtedly the single most important, where the relative disposition of lithological units and the dip of surfaces can be visualized in relation to relief. Estimates of the attitude of layers and their thickness are immediately possible, and using a minimum of instruments they can be quantified accurately. The law of Vs (Section 4.3.1) can be used on single images to judge the direction of dip, but where topographic elevation data are available the attitude can be quantified using the simple three-point solution for elevations on an assumed plane. Where DEMs are registered to images, such dip and strike determinations can be partly automated by the selection of appropriate locations on an identified boundary. Alternatively, the DEM can be used to introduce parallax into a single image, so that when viewed stereoptically with the original three-dimensional relief is combined with the image features (Fig. 8.22). Many existing geological maps were constructed on the basis of field work and aerial photograph interpretation, often with generalization about lithological variation, or to suit a specific purpose that limited the number of divisions. Very often the 'nose-to-the-ground' approach prevented the recognition of large or subtle features. Important divisions were frequently missed, simply because they were invisible. For huge tracts at small scales (1:100 000 and smaller) such mapping is based on traverses where the terrain permits easy and rapid access, rather than by systematic visits to every outcrop and the following of boundaries. Inevitably, much detail will have been omitted, but a general framework already exists. Rather than remapping the whole area, what is needed is revision based on remotely sensed data. The simplest revision involves marking newly observed features onto the old maps, but digital methods open up new possibilities. An existing colour geological map can be digitized into red, green and blue separates, registered to an image, and then combined with it using techniques such as the ISH transform (Section 5.2.2) (*Fig. 9.5*).

Just the boundaries from existing maps can be digitized as vectors, either automatically or manually using a digitizing table. These are then merged with suitably enhanced imagery as guides to the distribution of lithologies and structures. Interpretation of the image allows these vectors to be edited and new ones to be added as the first step in conversion from paper maps to **digital cartography**. Comprehensive interpretation of all conceivable and accessible geological attributes in an area is extremely difficult to express graphically in a single paper map without resulting in distracting clutter and confusion. The high costs of mastering and printing lithographic paper maps generally mean that much of this information, though available, is rarely accessible except by consulting archives. If the wealth of attributes are stored as vectors, polygons and points in a digital mapping system, the basis is laid for entirely new styles of map production. Instead of trying to fit as much information as possible onto a conventionally published map, which results in compromises, omissions and simplifications, maps that extract detail pertinent to specific applications from the mapping database can be generated on demand as 'one-offs' using a suitable graphics device, such as an ink-jet or wax-thermal printer. Moreover, all information is available for further integrated analysis using GIS approaches.

Geological mapping, since it aims at understanding the subsurface as well as surface geological features, benefits from using geophysical data, such as those from magnetic and gravity surveys (Section 8.2.2, Figs 8.10 to 8.15). Not all means of subdividing rocks are provided by field or image observations. As Figure 8.19 demonstrated, gamma-radiometric surveys contain a wealth of information related closely to lithological and petrogenetic variation. *Figure 9.6* shows the potential of merging such data with more spatially 'clean' remotely sensed images.

9.3 Exploration

Although the guidelines for finding mineral deposits, hydrocarbon reservoirs or water are geological in nature,

exploration itself is primarily an economic activity. Water exploration may in many cases be initiated for social or political reasons rather than in the quest for profit, but no anomaly is sought merely out of curiosity. Abnormally high concentrations of metals, oil or water beneath the surface do not necessarily constitute resources. To become economic entities, they must satisfy a large number of criteria. They must have a ready market, and be extractable and refinable to a useful product at a total cost that is less than their intrinsic value, thereby ensuring their exploitation for profit. They are unlike any other commodities in that production inevitably depletes the assets of the operating organization – other ventures either increase assets or at least maintain them at a stable level. Moreover, they are often hidden beneath the surface. As with all commodities, the intrinsic value or market price of physical resources is subject to largely unpredictable fluctuations, some of which is linked to changes in the available supplies. Consequently, successful exploration can rebound on the market, as in the case of the discovery of large petroleum reserves outside the ambit of the OPEC cartel, which since 1973 has attempted to maintain oil prices at a high level. Together with other economic forces and measures to conserve energy in the 1980s, these discoveries led to a depression in the world price of oil that continues to this day, and means that exploration is continually subject to stringent limits. At the time of writing (July 1992) these limits are so rigid that major oil companies are in the process of disbanding the large teams of remote sensors that had been built in their exploration departments since the mid-1970s. Much the same observation could be made for virtually every metal and lower value resource. The concept of what constitutes a resource or a reserve changes with time. Water is rather different, for it is a vital requirement for survival and for the development of the largely agricultural economies of the 'Third World', as well as for the smooth running of the social and industrial systems of the developed countries.

More than any other industrial activity, exploitation of and exploration for physical resources is bound up with risks to invested capital. The attraction of capital depends on these higher risks being offset by the opportunity for a greater return on investment. No-one will seek even gold if the required capital can be more profitably and safely invested elsewhere. Exploration is akin to research and development – it carries no prospect of profit in its own right, and certainly its successful outcome after evaluation is not immediate. Most resource operations require a lead time of between 1 and 15 years before the costs of exploration can be offset against production. However, the depletion of assets demands that exploration continues, except in periods of fundamental economic depression, such as the 1930s. This is not the place for a full account of the non-geological factors relating directly and indirectly to a decision to explore. Suffice it to say that it centres on a decision about what to look for, where the search is to be concentrated, a minimum quantity of the resource in question, a minimum unit value, depending on the concentration of the commodity being sought and its unit price, and a minimum rate of profit. This, in a nutshell, is an **exploration objective**. Note that only the location of the search area involves geological considerations, and they are mixed up with other factors, such as varying fiscal conditions, accessibility and communications, and political stability. To a variable extent exploration involves a gamble – at the outset only a set of optimistic notions is available, particularly when most of the deposits of the 'trip-over' variety have long been discovered. The greatest risk therefore is that of '**gambler's ruin**', or the loss of capital through a string of unsuccessful ventures. Avoiding this disagreeable situation means estimation of the probability of satisfying the exploration objective and assigning funds in proportion to the degree of risk to each stage in the whole operation. Exploration is therefore conducted in stages, so there is every opportunity to proceed according to the accumulation of information, not as a blind gambler would. Each stage involves a review of information gained and the degree to which the risk of not satisfying the exploration objective has changed. The expected value of the informa-

tion from the next stage is set against the cost of getting it. When the value exceeds the cost exploration continues. When cost exceeds the value of expected information then the decision to abandon exploration must be taken. The repeated decision whether to continue or not sets lost opportunities against the chances of lost investment. Figure 9.7 shows the kinds of exploration method available to a metal-oriented venture and the stages at which they are often deployed, in relation to growing costs. Table 9.1 shows some approximate figures for costs and efficiencies of various exploration techniques involved in metal exploration.

The low cost and high efficiency of remote sensing makes it a favoured method in the early stages of exploration. It both reduces early costs and helps narrow the focus of later stages. This is important because at the end of each exploration stage the area of search as well as the degree of risk to investment must be reduced.

As well as helping in reconnaissance geological mapping, remote sensing is useful in **targeting** smaller areas for more detailed follow-up using more costly methods. Moreover, its use does not end with the preliminary stage. The interpretation can be updated in the light of other data, and imagery forms an ideal base upon which to coordinate this later information through a GIS approach.

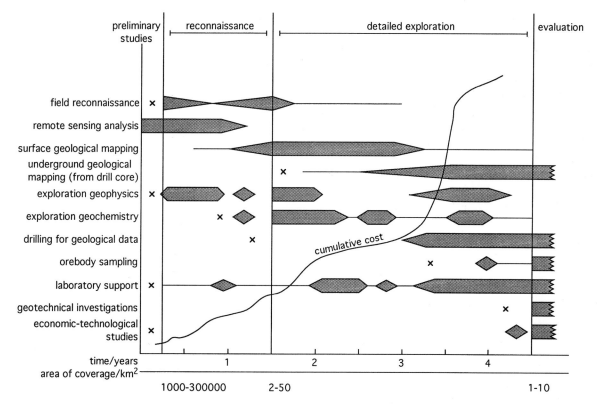

Figure 9.7 Chart showing the general stages involved in a mineral exploration programme. The graph of costs is only an indication of the way cumulative costs mount.

233

Table 9.1 Approximate costs and average efficiencies of some exploration methods (1988 data).

Methods	Cost (US dollars)	Efficiency km^{-2} day^{-1}
Preliminaries		
Satellite remote sensing	0.02 km^{-2}	>10^6
interpretation and map	0.7 km^{-2}	10^4
Airborne remote sensing	10 km^{-2}	500
interpretation and map	5 km^{-2}	50
Airborne geophysics		
(magnetic and EM)	25 km^{-1}	500
interpretation and map	10 km^{-2}	25
Literature search	250 day^{-1}	—
Field studies		
Geological reconnaissance	160 km^{-2}	10
Detailed geological mapping	600 km^{-2}	1
Geochemical surveying	15 km^{-2}	50
orientation		
drainage survey	50 km^{-2}	25
soil or biogeochemical	750 km^{-2}	2
survey		
Geophysical surveying		
resistivity and SP	160 km^{-1}	10
IP	5000 km^{-1}	0.5
Diamond drill cores	40 m^{-1}	—
Shaft sinking	5000 m^{-1}	—

Exploration is no longer a haphazard process based on intuition, individual experience and luck, although all three still play a role. As easily found resources become scarcer and economic viability of production becomes subject to increasing stringency a much more scientific basis is required. This is expressed in targeting or play generation. A geological model is based on the fund of knowledge about regional and local structural controls on known mineralization, hydrocarbon or other resource accumulations. It is added to by what is known from research about the processes involved in their formation and the blend of geological features commonly associated with such processes. Targeting not only sets out the regional and local geological settings which favour formation of some resource, it also helps define the physical and chemical peculiarities and associations involved. These indicate the kinds of information which are needed by the explorationist to narrow down the search and eventually pin-point a deposit. This blend of critical information, either to hand before exploration begins in earnest or acquired at various stages during the campaign, forms the basis for both planning and interrogating a GIS.

9.3.1 Metal exploration

Deposits of metalliferous ores can form by a host of processes within the igneous and sedimentary parts of the rock cycle. There are few, if any, examples of ores originating through exclusively metamorphic processes. A large proportion of deposits evidence the concentration of metals to ore grade through the agency of watery fluids moving beneath the surface, such as pegmatite, porphyry, contact-metasomatic, hydrothermal and secondarily enriched deposits. Such fluids commonly carry **hydrogen ions**, as measured by their **pH**. Hydrogen ions are the general agency whereby the covalent bonds in many silicates are broken, so inducing alteration in the common rocks associated with these deposit types. Moreover, the freedom for electrons to move in watery fluids means that they have a wide variety of **redox potentials (Eh)**, play a major role, together with pH variations, in variable oxidation and reduction, and the solution and precipitation of many compounds including ore minerals. This broad group of mineralizing processes then induces considerable changes in the common rocks with which the ores are sometimes associated.

Ore formation from which the influence of subsurface watery fluids is largely excluded, such as magmatic segregation and placer deposits, takes place during the formation of the igneous or sedimentary rocks hosting the ore. Consequently, the primary process leaves products that are part and parcel of their host. This renders them difficult, if not impossible, to discern on remotely sensed images, because they are orders of magnitude smaller than common features in the host. In their unaltered state, such ores often blend imperceptibly into the background. Occasionally, spectral features peculiar to the ore minerals, as with those of chromite, make it theoretically possible to highlight them using image processing. But this is only feasible if the ore bodies are similarly sized or larger than the spatial resolution of the sensor. Most commercial chromite ores are tabular and rarely more than a few metres in thickness, and few have been discerned using remote sensing alone.

However, the geochemical affinities of metals commonly sought in magmatic segregations, such as titanium, chromium, nickel and platinum-group metals, means that it is easily possible to reduce the area of search to likely host rocks. In all four cases these are basic to ultrabasic igneous rocks. In lightly vegetated terrain these are readily distinguished on images from other igneous lithologies, and from sedimentary and metamorphic rocks. In areas of dense natural vegetation rocks rich in ferromagnesian minerals produce fertile, clay-rich soils and carry different plant associations and densities. High concentrations of metals may even suppress vegetation, giving rise to geobotanical anomalies that form easily identified targets for ground follow-up.

Placer deposits are even more intractable to remote sensing, for they are often buried beneath ordinary sediment by virtue of their content of high-density minerals. However, experience suggests many likely sites for placer accumulation in drainage, shoreline and aeolian environments. Careful analysis of geomorphological features from imagery thus helps in locating potential targets.

Remote sensing becomes an extremely powerful exploration tool in its own right when the primary and secondary processes of mineralization result in the formation of spectral anomalies. This is especially so when the anomalies extend well beyond the extent of the ore itself. Deposits formed or modified through the influence of migrating watery fluids frequently exhibit such **alteration haloes** spread through large volumes of rock because of pervasive fluid migration. These can quite literally appear as targets, hopefully with a paying bull's eye at the centre.

The most common style of alteration is the breakdown of feldspars and ferromagnesian minerals to a variety of clays and other hydroxyl minerals, where the SWIR range of their spectra exhibits absorptions with patterns that are unique to each species (Fig. 1.9). The general presence of hydroxylated minerals in lightly vegetated terrain, but little potential for their identification, is provided by the contrast between Landsat TM bands 7 and 5, usually expressed by a ratio image. The three SWIR bands of JERS-1 provide more opportunity for discrimination, but the most useful data are those from hyperspectral imaging radiometers, such as AVIRIS.

A considerable number of ore deposits contain abundant sulphide minerals, particularly pyrite (FeS_2), if their deposition was associated with the availability of sulphide ions and reducing conditions. Under the oxidizing conditions of surface weathering and in migrating groundwater iron-rich sulphides are unstable. They break down to sulphuric acid and a number of ferric hydroxides and complex sulphates, which are both strongly coloured and possess crystal-field absorptions in the VNIR (Fig. 1.7). As well as **gossans** formed over secondarily enriched sulphidic deposits, simple surface weathering imparts these spectral features to soils. Moreover, the ferric compounds are often in the form of colloids that are transported to affect broad areas. Such anomalies are characterized by higher red reflectance than in green or blue, and can be identified using ratios of Landsat TM bands 3, 2 and 1. The crystal-field absorptions in the VNIR express themselves in ratios of TM bands 4:3 and 5:4, although the positioning of MSS bands 4 and 3 is more appropriate for these features.

Occasionally the geochemistry of hydrothermal fluids induces the solution and reprecipitation of silica around ore deposits. While quartz has no unique spectral features in the reflected region, cryptocrystalline and opaline silica contains abundant water. As well as the high albedo of siliceous surfaces, cherty or opaline alteration may exhibit absorption in TM band 5 on the flank of the 1.4-μm water feature (Fig. 1.8).

This suite of alteration features has proved extremely useful in targeting a variety of hydrothermal deposits,

notably porphyry and hot-spring epithermal types. *Figure 6.19* shows dramatically how the combination of all three alteration types near a copper–porphyry deposit can be expressed using carefully selected combinations of both reflected and thermally emitted data. *Figure 9.8* uses three Landsat TM band ratios selected to express ferric minerals, clays and albedo to highlight possible zones of hydrothermal alteration in a completely unknown area. The yellow areas at left centre proved to coincide with hydrothermal alteration of metavolcanic rocks in which scheelite ($CaWO_4$) was found in quartz veins.

The effect of fluid migration on rocks is not restricted to alteration and oxidation. If conditions are reducing to slightly oxidizing and very acid then iron in its ferrous state and a number of other transition metals are soluble. They can be leached from rocks through which the fluids pass, producing **bleached zones**. This is commonly associated with the formation of roll-type sedimentary uranium and vanadium deposits. Formerly iron-rich sandstones, either grey because of finely divided pyrite or red to orange from their contained ferric minerals, become white. The anomalous colour contrast thereby allows extremely efficient detection of areas affected by potentially mineralizing fluids of this kind.

The presence of vegetation does not necessarily preclude a search for mineralization using images alone. The high concentrations of metals, the peculiar soil Eh and pH associated with many ore deposits, and the leaching of nutrients due to migration of acid from sulphide oxidation is often inimical to the proper development of common plants. They become stunted, discoloured or simply fail to grow, thereby forming **barrens**. Such geobotanical anomalies form yet another focus for image processing and analysis in target generation. Another occasionally encountered type of anomaly is where common plants burgeon because of extremely favourable levels of nutrients. This is particularly the case with sedimentary phosphate deposits and carbonatites containing abundant apatite ($CaPO_5$).

Potentially useful as remote sensing is, there are very few ore deposits whose discovery is the result of the use of images alone. In fact, much of the literature on remote sensing in metal exploration focuses on features associated with well-known deposits. Exploration more generally employs specific mineralization models, such as that outlined for porphyry-style deposits in Section 8.3.2. These fuse many kinds of data bearing on the model, either in the form of complex image products or within a GIS. The products of a GIS are so numerous and often have no immediate meaning outside the exploration team that they are not illustrated here. Instead an example of graphic combination of various data sets for visual interpretation is given in *Figure 9.9*.

The area is part of the English Lake District, whose physiography is shown by *Figure 9.9d*. It is clearly dominated by dense vegetation. The generalized geology emerges from *Figure 9.9a*, while the gravity and magnetic anomaly patterns are shown in *Figure 9.9b*. The exploration model is oriented to hydrothermal tin, zinc and copper mineralization associated with the granite intrusions. *Figure 9.9c* is a colour image combining stream-sediment tin, copper and zinc analyses as RGB. Where all three elements have high values is signified by white and cream colours – these are areas of potential interest. However, experience suggests that significant mineralization of this type is closely associated with granite contacts, particularly in the roof zone. In *Figure 9.9e* and *f* the focus shifts to the vicinity of the geochemical anomaly near the granite at left of centre on the regional images, where there is also a prominent magnetic anomaly and a negative gravity anomaly that extends beyond the outcrop of the granite. *Figure 9.9e* is an RGB image using Landsat TM data as intensity, a constant saturation and gridded tin values as hue, with magnetic contours overlaid. The magnetic high is probably due to magnetite formed during contact metamorphism at the roof of the buried granite. The high tin values are spatially related to two indistinct linear features – possibly fracture zones related to deep-seated faults – trending WSW–ENE and NW–SE. *Figure 9.9f* supplements this by combining directionally filtered TM data as intensity, gravity anomaly as hue and significant tin and bismuth anomalies as red and green overlays. The purple area indicates where the granite is lurking at shallow depths. The conclusion is that tin anomalies here are spatially related to the buried granite and arranged along deep-seated fractures, and so constitute an ideal target for detailed follow-up in this poorly exposed area.

9.3.2 Hydrocarbon exploration

Oil and natural gas fields form much larger targets than metal ore deposits, but for obvious reasons they are always buried and therefore hidden. Locating them relies on detailed interpretation of seismic reflection sections and, at the end of the day, a commitment to the drill. The focus on a particular area on which to expend the often vast resources demanded by seismic surveys and drilling relies almost entirely on **play generation**. A hydrocarbon play is a combination of favourable geological circumstances for the likely presence of oil or gas, conditioned by the economics involved in developing any finds in a particular region. The geological aspects of a play can be summarized as the coincidence of a number of favourable factors: the presence of an organic-rich **source rock**; its burial to a depth where local geothermal conditions permit the maturation of organic compounds in the source to oil and gas; a path whereby migration from source to reservoir can occur; the presence of rocks with sufficient porosity and permeability to act as a reservoir; the presence of a suitable **trap**

with an impermeable **cap** of some kind where the hydrocarbons can accumulate and be preserved. Many of these factors are assessed in existing oil fields from previous drilling records together with stratigraphic and structural interpretation of seismic sections and exposed geology. The huge amounts of data of many different kinds in known hydrocarbon basins, including those from fields that have already been discovered, are now routinely handled and analysed in what are really three-dimensional GISs. Remote-sensing methods sometimes complement such analyses, but assume a more important role in unexplored, or **frontier areas**. That is the main focus here. All significant hydrocarbon fields are found in or near sedimentary basins that subsided sufficiently for thick and varied sedimentary sequences to be deposited. There are many different tectonic situations where these basins might have formed, and probably most large basins are already known. Without expensive seismic surveys, however, the details of their architecture are sketchy. Thick accumulations of sediments with densities and magnetic susceptibilities lower than crystalline basement give rise to negative gravity anomalies. So a first approximation of their innards arises from examination of gravity and magnetic data. Using gridded data and derivatives from them in image form, as in Figures 8.10 to 8.15, helps locate variations in basin depth. With a knowledge of rates of subsidence and geothermal conditions the location of zones within the oil and gas maturation 'windows' can be assessed. Sometimes, important deep fracture zones that may have focused sedimentary facies variations and fluid migration can be visualized. Nor are actual gravity measurements always essential. The radar altimetry of the oceans discussed in Section 8.2.4 (Fig. 8.9) contains information on regional variations in gravitational potential. This can locate offshore basins.

Many clues to the internal structure of sedimentary basins can be derived by analysis of surface exposures. Chapters 4, 6 and 7 are replete with examples of the structural and lithological information that can be won directly from remotely sensed images. While this is unlikely to directly locate oil fields, it provides a basis for basin analysis and an understanding of the tectonic controls over basin evolution. Figures 4.31, 4.38, 6.20, 7.5, 7.8, 7.10 and 7.26 are particularly instructive in this respect.

A number of oil fields, both onshore and at sea, were initially located by finding natural oil and gas seepages, sometimes flaring as a result of ignition by lightning. Every oil explorationist hopes to make such an 'easy' discovery, for little remains other than to investigate by drilling. Now, it is well known that there is no such thing as a completely 'tight' trap, particularly with respect to light hydrocarbons and gas. Every hydrocarbon field undergoes some leakage, or has leaked in the past. Whether or not this reaches the surface, and, if it does, has a sensible effect, is a matter of chance. Remote sensing for **seep detection** is consequently a topic in which considerable resources have been invested. At the outset it must be emphasized that evidence for seepage is rarely a trigger to 'drill here'. Light petroleum and gas migrate along the line of greatest permeability, either a suitable sedimentary stratum or a zone of fracturing. Sometimes these might be directly above a trap, but equally they may be oriented laterally. Also, the signs may indicate past leakage, and the source may have been exhausted or contain only highly viscous tars. A good example of the latter are oil sands, from which the light fraction has escaped, and which require mining and heat treatment to win useful products.

The most obvious seepages contain liquid oil and tarry residues from evaporation, and everyone knows that tar is black. Good examples are the La Brea tar ponds of the Ventura Basin in Los Angeles, and the major Iranian fields, which were found from flaring seeps known for centuries by local people. Dark signatures on images from the reflected region in prospective basins are always worth noting. However, most seeps are far subtler. There have been reports of a sort of physical blurring of minor physiographic features above several major oil fields in unvegetated terrains. This has not yet been explained, but may caused by periodic upwelling of formation water charged with gas to create quicksand conditions. Of more use are the potential effects of such fluids on the chemical and physical properties of the materials through which they have passed.

Accumulations of hydrocarbons evidence extremely reducing conditions, and the formation waters associated with them have low Eh values. The passage of reducing fluids through rocks containing oxidized iron minerals, such as hematite, induces the reduction of ferric (Fe^{3+}) to ferrous (Fe^{2+}) ions, which are far more soluble. One of the possible effects of seepage of hydrocarbons and the movement of formation water is bleaching, particularly of redbeds in the sequence. Not only iron can be mobilized in this way, but many other metals too. So, seepage zones can be associated with anomalous soil geochemistry at the surface. Geochemical soil surveys, for hydrocarbons as well as metals, can form a part of hydrocarbon exploration, where the methods described in Section 8.2.3 are appropriate.

One of the most controversial methods in hydrocarbon exploration centres on another likely phenomenon in highly reducing environments. The common ferric iron oxides and hydroxides that act as colorants in many sediments can be partly reduced to magnetite (Fe_3O_4 or $Fe_2O_3.FeO$). Little imagination is required to surmise that seepages with which such **diagenetic magnetite** is associated may induce high-frequency magnetic anomalies. The controversy lies in whether it happens at all, and if it does whether the anomalies can be screened from others with different

sources. In active exploration areas the ground will be cluttered with all sorts of ironmongery that would produce very similar anomalies. That it does occur is partly confirmed by increased magnetic susceptibility in core from productive wells to depths as great as 1 km compared with that in dry holes. This has been backed up with the discovery of tiny magnetite spherules in the cores. Their form encourages the idea that as well as reducing conditions some kind of biological activity is involved, of which more shortly. Conceivably, the diagenetic magnetite phenomenon adds more value to the use of high-resolution aeromagnetic surveys in oil exploration, in which sophisticated spatial-frequency filtering and image enhancement may isolate the predicted seepage-related anomalies. Since unconsolidated sediments on the sea floor have more potential for the passage of seeping fluids, and offshore exploration is dominated by high-cost seismic surveys, related methods, including remote measurements of magnetic susceptibility, are under development.

Far less controversial are methods related to the effects of noxious seeping fluids on terrestrial plant life. Plants obtain their nutrients and water through complex symbioses of bacteria and fungi at their root tips. If these are damaged then the plants fail to thrive or die. Enhanced hydrocarbon content in groundwater encourages the growth of anaerobic bacteria that reduce sulphate (SO_4^{2-}) ions to sulphide (S^{2-}). This is the source of hydrogen sulphide or 'sour gas' in many oil fields, and its presence encourages the precipitation of heavy-metal sulphides carried by groundwater or seeping formation water. Sour-gas generation is the reason for the association of geochemical anomalies with some seeps, and is possibly involved in diagenetic magnetite formation. It and the 'dumping' of heavy metals wreaks havoc on root-tip symbioses, with a range of effects on overlying plant life. They may become stunted or discoloured, wholesale die-off may occur, and the timing of seasonal colour change in the canopy (Section 1.3.3, Fig. 1.17) may change, commonly resulting in premature senescence (*Fig. 9.10*). In vegetated areas remote sensing provides a wide range of opportunities to locate such seep-related geobotanical anomalies.

Hydrocarbon seepage is not restricted to land areas, but it would be easy to dismiss as a focus for offshore exploration because the sea floor is not usually accessible to remote sensing. But consider for a moment what gas seepage beneath water might do. It forms rising plumes of bubbles. Bubbles do not rise passively, but induce a slow upward component of movement in the water. This is the principle of the air-lift dredge used in marine archaeological excavations. Such plumes can draw cold, nutrient-rich bottom water to the sea surface. Of course, other phenomena such as tidal and current activity result in upwellings, but these change position with time. A seep-related upwelling should remain in the same place. Theoretically, therefore, images of sea-surface temperature and colour due to phytoplankton blooms, taken over a period, should reveal fixed cold spots and planktonic blooms possibly related to seepage. Since offshore interest is in large hydrocarbon fields with commensurately large seeps, such an indirect exploration method can be conducted on a daily basis using very low-cost meteorological data with coarse resolution. Research along such lines has been conducted under conditions of secrecy by a number of major oil companies. Related to it is the deployment of low-level airborne surveys of aerosols at the sea surface that result from the bursting of small bubbles. The hydrocarbon chemistry of the sucked-up samples is monitored using gas chromatography.

9.3.3 Water exploration

In the midst of a world economic depression, many of the talents of remote-sensing geologists are being shed by oil and mining companies, as the demand for and price of their products stagnate or fall. At the same time, in both developed and underdeveloped regions, the problems of water shortage and decline in its quality grow to disastrous proportions. A sage once commented that the first provision in any human society is that of a safe and dependable water supply, yet this basic need is under considerable threat. To a large extent geologists can assemble the basic information needed to alleviate, if not solve, these problems.

Water supply is served by two main options, outside of desalination and other technological fixes. These centre on surface water and that stored in rocks and soils as groundwater. The use of remote sensing in hydrogeology and hydrology relates mainly to suggesting favourable areas for development in terms of the relative amounts of water available and the spatial characteristics that might condition development. Except indirectly, it has less bearing on water quality. An example would be the identification of zones of hydrothermal alteration and beds of marine shales, both of which can contribute potentially toxic compounds to waters flowing over or through them. Screening for biological pollution would in most cases be served through a GIS by data layers on habitations and land use. A geologically or hydrologically favourable site may not necessarily be useful. To evaluate it in economic and social terms requires information on the type and location of usage, as well as on various engineering considerations. Again, a multifaceted GIS is required, of which geological information from remote sensing and other spatial data would form a part.

The surface water regime in an area can be expressed by the relationship between the four factors of precipitation, surface flow, evapotranspiration and infiltration. Only when channelled or in lakes does surface water become a potential resource. Aside from losses by evapotranspiration and infiltration, the flow through a channel or entering a lake depends on the area of upstream catchment together with precipitation. The quality of the water, in terms of sediment load, depends mainly on the slope angles in the catchment and the density of vegetation cover that binds soil.

The precipitation information needed can be derived from the use of monthly averages of cloud-top temperature on metsat images as a gauge of the likelihood of rain falling, and by the use of multitemporal images showing snow cover and snow melt rates. Evapotranspiration rates can be estimated from surface temperature averages from metsats, and by models based on vegetation density derived from the use of VNIR and red reflectance contrasts on multispectral imagery. Infiltration is a thornier problem and is discussed later. Catchment area and slope estimation, together with analysis of drainage networks, can be derived from DEMs, as covered by Section 8.2.4. Combined with remotely sensed estimates of vegetation cover, each catchment can then be assessed qualitatively for likely levels of turbidity due to soil erosion.

The main input by geologists to studies of surface water as a resource focuses on the location and evaluation of sites for capturing flow and harvesting it for drinking water, irrigation or hydropower generation. Whereas long earth barrages can be used to pond water in broad valleys in gently undulating terrain, the best sites are where valleys narrow as they pass through more resistant rocks. These **thresholds** are often floored by only thin mantles of permeable alluvium, and construction of dams or barrages is aided by the small volumes required and firm footings. Thresholds are easily located on stereoscopic aerial photographs or satellite images (Fig. 4.14).

Hydrogeological assessment of groundwater resources involves primarily the mapping of surface lithologies and structures to help assess the subsurface disposition of sedimentary aquifers. This is akin to basin analysis for hydrocarbons, with the difference that groundwater migrates laterally and downwards. The conditions for subsurface water accumulation, involving various kinds of trap, are familiar to most geologists. Images of various sorts provide abundant information that can be blended with observations on run-off versus infiltration potential in recharge areas. Here the intention is to concentrate on specific advantages offered by remote sensing. Among the many sites for groundwater accumulation are those provided by **subsurface dams**. These include faults that juxtapose aquifers with aquitards and igneous dykes, whose crystalline nature blocks flow where the dyke trends across the direction of subsurface flow. Both exhibit discontinuous linear features at the surface that are often more easily seen and extrapolated on images (Figs. 4.13, 4.22, 4.26, 4.31 and 7.9) than on the ground. Radar is particularly useful in locating small dykes because it highlights the aligned corner reflectors formed by jointing (Fig. 7.9), even when the dykes are buried by veneers of alluvium in very arid areas (Fig. 7.17). Because dykes are frequently more resistant than their hosts, when a landscape becomes mantled by superficial soft sediments older dykes may form corrugations at the interface, upflow of which groundwater can be ponded.

Unconsolidated sediments, especially piedmont fans, alluvium, aeolian sand and beach deposits (Figs. 4.46, 4.47, 4.49 and 4.55), provide limited supplies of groundwater that are easily accessible. In semiarid climates the water table in such sediments may be deeper than the extent of the potential host, and estimates of thickness are needed. Aside from geophysical surveys at the surface, the only means of visualizing this parameter is the use of radar images. Provided soil moisture is low, radar can penetrate as deep as 4 or 5 m to give a signal from subsurface features (Section 7.1.1). Figure 7.17a shows a dramatic example from the Red Sea Hills of Sudan, where otherwise completely hidden intricacies of a drainage system buried by alluvium indicate the most likely sites for obtaining water from the main distributaries of the old drainage. Conversely, in areas of variable soil moisture – a good guide to deeper groundwater – radar scatterometry gives a guide to moisture content.

While faults in sedimentary sequences provide opportunities for subsurface dams, in areas dominated by impermeable crystalline rocks the shattering associated with faulting provides the only opportunity for infiltration and eventual recovery of groundwater. Remote sensing is preeminent in delineating such zones. Of special interest is the extrapolation of large fracture systems from elevated areas of high precipitation to lower, drier ground. The fractures potentially can transfer water laterally over tens to hundreds of kilometres. Because the secondary porosity involved in fracturing can become sealed by fines, evaluating fracture zones requires consideration of the rock types involved and the nature of weathering. In all climates micaceous rocks are easily sealed. In humid areas, or those once subject to high chemical weathering, feldspars in granitic and gneissic rocks, and ferromagnesian minerals in more mafic rocks, break down to clays that clog the potential pathways. In dry climates many granites break down by mechanical means to form gravelly regoliths and fracture zones still retain their permeability. In all climates, inert quartzites and soluble carbonates are the ideal hosts for fracture-controlled aquifers. As discussed in Section 4.2, most images carry clues to the general distribution of lithologies, while multispectral data can help further distinguish rock types.

Because **phreatophyte plants** can put down roots to depths in excess of 100 m to reach the water table, the presence of vegetation in arid areas is a sure guide to the presence of water, though not necessarily to its quality. *Figure 9.11* shows an example of the discontinuous distribution of vegetation in an arid, faulted area, and clearly

indicates areas favourable for development of subsurface supplies. Phreatophytes in fact consume large volumes of water. One estimate is that 1 km^2 of dense desert scrub transpires sufficient water vapour in a year to supply all the needs of a village of 1000 inhabitants.

9.4 Engineering applications

Geologists have long made important contributions to the siting of major constructions, such as roads, dams, power plants and waste disposal sites. Much of this has centred on aspects of safety and stability in relation to various kinds of slope failure, seismicity and flooding, as well as to the engineering properties of foundations and sources of potential construction materials.

Slope stability and risk from landslip is most appropriate to routing of roads and railways. While a variety of factors contribute to instability, the factor common to all such hazards is variation in topographic slope. Slope can be visualized using stereoscopic images, but these generally incorporate a degree of vertical exaggeration. Painstaking use of photogrammetric instruments is required to produce accurate estimates of slopes and slope profiles. If a DEM is available, or can be constructed from digital stereoimages, it is a simple matter to extract gradient values and separate those so steep as to pose a hazard from those with less risk attached.

In humid tropical areas, where thick soil and regolith pose potential problems of mudflows and arcuate slips, it is common to see extremely steep slopes that are stabilized by dense vegetation and the associated root mat. Vegetation cover, or rather the lack of it, is an important parameter in slope-stability assessment in soil-covered areas. Together with gradient data, multispectral means of vegetation classification from images clearly forms an important input to planning. In areas largely free of soil, vegetation is likely to give little assistance to the engineer. The rock type and associated structures govern the likelihood of rock falls and landslips. The riskiest combination is that of interbedded permeable and impermeable strata which dip parallel to the topographic slope. Both gravity and lubrication by water along bedding surfaces conspire to encourage detachment and mass wasting. Generally, the resolution of satellite imagery is too coarse resolution to permit detection of such features, though multispectral data may assist in delimiting lithologies with contrasted engineering properties. Stereoscopy using aerial photographs is a decided advantage in locating potential hazards and, equally important, evidence of previous slope failure.

Steep slopes are not the only areas posing potential hazard to heavy construction. Soft sediments, such as peats and clay-rich rocks, are easily compacted as water is expelled during loading. If the compaction varies laterally, the differential subsidence can cause failure. Former lake beds, glacial tills and flood-plain alluvium are replete with such hazards, yet they are often signified on images by the distinctive landforms associated with their formation (Figs. 4.47, 4.51 and 4.54) that are not detectable on the ground.

Section 4.4.1 illustrated several of the features associated with active faults, most of which require the fine resolution of aerial surveys. It would be a foolish geologist who failed to recognize a project entering seismically active terrain, because virtually all sizeable earthquakes above magnitude 4 are readily and systematically located by a global network of seismographs. A first call would be to delineate all potential faults that might fail, using aerial photographs. But most damage in seismically active areas occurs not in high-relief areas of hard rocks, where faults are easily spotted, but in areas of unconsolidated sediment that behave plastically during earthquakes, even when the seismic event is far distant. The catastrophes of San Francisco and Mexico City bear grim witness to this. Areas of silts and clays, often associated with former lake beds and estuarine deposition, need to be delimited. This is often no easy task, as all low-lying flat areas are suspect. Careful searches for morphological features, such as strand lines (Fig. 4.55), that indicate such sediments must be conducted.

Equally, it would be an extremely foolhardy engineer who wilfully built a bridge, a dam or a power plant straddling a fault of any age, for the loading itself could induce movement. Also, old lines of weakness are often exploited by modern earth movements, such as those related to post-glacial unloading. Displacements of centimetres could cause catastrophic events in structures containing moving parts with low tolerances, such as the control rods in a nuclear plant. However, it is not always easy to recognize old fractures on the ground, or even on images, since their active control over landforms is long extinct. In areas of low relief and intensive agriculture the patchwork of fields with different crops produces an efficient camouflage for muted topographic features that might indicate faults (Fig. 4.53). Various image-processing methods are available to reduce this cultural camouflage and reveal previously unsuspected features of tectonics (Fig. 9.12).

Whether they move or not, fractures form pathways for the large-scale movement of fluids (Sections 9.3.2 and 9.3.3). This is the last thing that is desired in a waste-disposal site, particularly one for long-lived nuclear debris. Besides using images to screen areas with faults from consideration, many of the techniques deployed for water exploration are useful in selecting waste-disposal sites. Apart from methane generation, which vents upwards and laterally, leakage follows exactly the same rules as the movement of groundwater, and hydrogeological interpretation of image data is essential in siting.

Figure 9.12 Enhanced early-spring Landsat TM band 5 image of part of an intensely farmed area in southern England. At this time of year grasses and winter cereals have similar moisture contents and the field patterns that generally obscure topographic features (Fig. 4.52) are uniquely removed to reveal many major fault zones that are unreported by conventional geological mapping.

9.5 Geochemical hazards

Statistical analysis of medical records, particularly those of morbidity and mortality (sickness and cause of death), are beginning to reveal disturbing evidence for health blackspots that correlate with a variety of environmental parameters. These are in addition to the known associations of mental retardation with lead pollution, leukaemia and other cancers with nuclear plants, and a variety of horrible afflictions with mercury and cadmium pollution, but seem to stem from purely natural environmental variations.

Some environmental hazards have been known for a long time, such as the associations of goitre with areas deficient in iodine and fluorosis with areas with an abnormally high soil fluorine content. However, new relationships are appearing regularly. Some cancers are more frequent over certain uranium-rich granites and shales, and have been traced to radon-gas emissions from the soil accumulating in houses. There is some evidence for an increased incidence of multiple sclerosis in fluorine-rich areas. Men living in areas supplied with water from limestones are more at risk from heart disease than those in soft-water areas. High contents of organic pigment from peat in water correlates with increased risk of stomach cancer. To these few examples of human risk from geochemical anomalies can be added incidence of ill thrift in livestock from excess molybdenum, copper deficiency and lead anomalies. Whereas the associations are known, currently the geo-chemical data to assess variable risk are lacking for most parts of the world.

The most useful information would be results from geochemical surveys of soil, as carried out routinely but in restricted areas for metal exploration. This is extremely expensive (Table 9.1), and unlikely ever to be conducted globally. At much lower cost, and available now for many developed countries, are data from drainage surveys (Section 8.2.3). In image form (Fig. 9.9) they provide an extremely efficient means of screening for geochemical hazards, as they are for exploration, and could easily be incorporated in health-oriented GISs to be assessed with the many other variables. Risk from naturally high radio-activity is readily assessed by reference to images of gamma-ray emissions derived from airborne radiometry (Fig. 8.19).

In the absence of analytical data, the known concentra-tion or depletion of some of the geochemical culprits with specific rock types and with relatively unusual processes, such as those involved in mineralization, means that geo-logical maps are a rough guide to potential problems. Maps derived from images are in some cases even more useful in this regard than those compiled by more conventional means. The discussion in Section 9.3.1 on the signatures of hydrothermally altered areas and those where sulphides have been oxidized to products including sulphuric acid shows that remote sensing has a unique contribution in this respect. Hydrothermal and other types of mineralization involving pervasive fluids boost the levels of many hazardous elements in rocks and their associated soils. The natural release of acids takes some of these elements into solution, further dispersing them in the natural environment.

There is one important point of an ethical nature that is often overlooked in assessment of hazards of whatever kind. It may well be possible to establish a previously unsuspected risk. The problem lies in informing the people exposed to it. If there is no remedy, other than migration at great cost and carrying perhaps yet other risks, should they be told?

A final point with ethical content is perhaps obvious, but rarely stated. As well as intelligence analysts, industrial and academic geologists in the developed countries are privy, through remote sensing and digital image processing, to a great deal of strategic economic information about less-fortunate areas of the world. Often they are able to learn more about resources and terrain than their counterparts in the so-called Third World because of their technological advantage. In an ideal world, such information should be transmitted on a completely equitable basis, but frequently it is not. The simplest recourse is the spread of the enabling technology of remote sensing. Costs of hardware and software to achieve what is outlined in this book have now been reduced to levels that are affordable by any government.

Further reading

These references are but a few of the many relating to applications of remote sensing and GISs in geology. The *Proceedings of the Thematic Conferences on Remote Sensing for Exploration Geology*, sponsored by the Environmental Research Institute of Michigan (ERIM), are the best source of papers in this very general area. Occasionally, trade journals, such as the *Mining Magazine* and the *Oil and Gas Journal*, will contain review articles on this topic. Journals such as *Economic Geology and the Bulletin of the American Association of Petroleum Geology*, often carry papers on remote sensing in exploration.

Abrams, M.J., R.P. Ashley, L.C. Rowan, A. Goetz and A.B. Kahle 1977. Mapping of hydrothermal alteration in the Cuprite mining district, Nevada, using aircraft scanner images for the spectral region 0.46 to 2.36 μm. *Geology* **5**, 713–718.

Abrams, M.J., D. Brown, L. Lepley and R. Sadowski 1983. Remote sensing for copper deposits in Southern Arizona. *Econ. Geol.* **78**, 591–604.

Abrams, M.J., J.E. Conel and H.R. Lang 1985. *The joint NASA/Geosat test case study.* Tulsa, Oklahoma: American Association of Petroleum Geologists (two volumes).

Allum, J.A.E. 1981. Remote sensing in mineral exploration – case histories. *Geoscience Canada* **8**, 87–92.

Bailey, G.B. and P.D. Anderson 1982. Applications of Landsat imagery to problems of petroleum exploration in Qaidam Basin, China. *Am. Ass. Petrol. Geol. Bull.* **66**, 1348–1354.

Baker, M.C.W. and J.A. Baldwin 1981. Application of Landsat multispectral classification for locating gossans in North Chile. In *Remote sensing in geological and terrain studies*, Allan, J.A. and M. Bradshaw (eds), pp. 25–33. London: Remote Sensing Society.

Berhe, S.M. 1988. A regional tectonic study of NE and E Africa and its implication for mineral exploration: a synoptic view from satellite imagery. *Proc. IGARSS '88 Symp., Edinburgh*, pp. 363–366. ESA SP-284. Paris: European Space Agency.

Billings, W.P. 1950. Vegetation and plant growth as affected by chemically altered rocks in the Western Great Basin. *Ecology* **30**, 62–74.

Birnie, R.W. and J.R. Francica 1981. Remote detection of geobotanical anomalies related to porphyry copper mineralization. *Econ. Geol.* **76**, 637–647.

Bolviken, B., F. Honey, S.R. Levine R.J.P. Lyon and A. Prelat 1977. Detection of naturally heavy-metal-poisoned areas by Landsat-1 digital data. *J. Geochem. Exploration* **8**, 457–471.

Chang, S.H. and W. Collins 1983. Confirmation of the airborne biogeophysical mineral exploration technique using laboratory methods. *Econ Geol.* **78**, 723–736.

Cole, M.M. 1982. Integrated use of remote sensing imagery and geobotany in mineral exploration. *Trans. Geol. Soc. S. Afr.* **85**, 13–28.

Collins, W., S.H. Chang and J.T. Kuo 1981. *Detection of hidden mineral deposits by airborne spectral analysis of forest canopies.* NASA Contract NSG-5222, Final Report.

Collins, W., S.H. Chang, G. Raines, F. Channey and R. Ashley 1983. Airborne biogeochemical mapping of hidden mineral deposits. *Econ. Geol.* **78**, 737–749.

Conradsen, K and O. Harpoth 1984. Use of Landsat multi-spectral scanner data for detection and reconnaissance mapping of iron oxide staining in mineral exploration, central East Greenland. *Econ. Geol.* **79**, 1229–1244.

Darch, J.P. and J. Barber 1983. Multitemporal remote sensing of a geobotanical anomaly. *Econ. Geol.* **78**, 770–782.

Deutch, M. and J.E. Estes 1980. Landsat detection of oil from natural seeps. *Photogramm. Eng. Remote Sens.* **46**, 1313–1322.

Donovan, T.J., R.L. Forgey and A.A. Roberts 1979. Aeromagnetic detection of diagenetic magnetite over oil fields. *Am. Ass. Petrol. Geol. Bull.* **63**, 245–248.

Drury, S.A. 1990. Satellite aid. *New Scientist* **126**, 50–53.

Drury, S.A and S.M. Berhe 1991. Remote sensing in groundwater exploration in arid regions: examples from the Red Sea Hills of NE Africa. *AGID News* **No. 67/68**, 17–20.

Ellyett, C.D. and D.A. Pratt 1975. *A review of the potential applications of remote sensing techniques to hydrogeological studies in Australia.* Australian Water Research Council Technical Paper 13.

Feder, A.F. 1986. Integrated interpretation for exploration. *Oil Gas Journal* (May 5 1985), 180–184.

Feldman, S.C. and J.V. Taranik 1988. Comparison of techniques for discriminating hydrothermal alteration minerals with airborne imaging spectrometer data. *Remote Sens. Environ.* **24**, 67–83.

Fookes, P.G., M. Sweeney, C.N.D Manby and R.P. Martin 1985. Geological and geotechnical engineering aspects of low-cost roads in mountainous terrain. *Eng. Geol.* **21**, 1–152.

Francis, P.W. and S.L. De Silva 1989. Application of the Landsat Thematic Mapper to the identification of potentially active volcanoes in the Central Andes. *Remote Sens. Environ.* **28**, 245–255.

Francis, P.W. and D.A. Rothery 1987. Using the Landsat Thematic Mapper to detect and monitor active volcanoes: an example from Lascar volcano, northern Chile. *Geology* **15**, 614–617.

Gupta, R.P. and J. Bodechtel 1982. Geotechnical applications of Landsat image analysis of Bhakra dam reservoir, India. *Remote Sens. Environ.* **12**, 3–13.

Gupta, R.P. and B.C. Joshi 1990. Landslide hazard zoning using the GIS approach – a case from the Ramganga catchment, Himalyas. *Eng. Geol.* **28**, 119–131.

Halbouty, M.T. 1976. Application of Landsat imagery to petroleum and mineral exploration. *Am. Assoc. Petrol. Geol. Bull.* **60**, 745–793.

Halbouty, M.T. 1980. Geological significance of Landsat data for 15 giant oil and gas fields. *Am. Ass. Petrol. Geol. Bull.* **64**, 8–36.

Harding, A.E. and M.D. Forrest 1989. Analysis of multiple geological data sets from the English Lake District. *IEEE Trans. Geosci. Remote Sens.* **GE-27**, 732–739.

Horler, D.N.H., J. Barber and A.R. Barringer 1980. Effects of heavy metals on the absorbance and reflectance spectra of plants. *Int. J. Remote Sens.* **1**, 121–136.

Huntington, J.F. and A.A. Green 1988. Recent advances and practical considerations in remote sensing applied to gold exploration. In *Bicentennial Gold 88, Melbourne*.

Keighley, J.R., W.W. Lynn and K.R. Nelson 1980. Use of Landsat images in tin exploration, Brazil. *Proc. 14th Symp. Remote Sensing of Environment, San Jose*, pp. 341–343.

Kezheng, B. 1980. The application of remote sensing techniques to prospecting for metal deposits. *Proc. 14th Symp. Remote Sensing of Environment, San Jose*, pp. 135–142.

Kruse, F.A. 1988. Use of airborne imaging spectrometer data to map minerals associated with hydrothermally altered rocks in Northern Grapevine Mountains, Nevada and California. *Remote Sens. Environ.* **24**, 31–52.

Kruse, F.A., K.S. Kierein-Young and J.W. Boardman 1990. Mineral mapping at Cuprite, Nevada, with a 63-channel imaging spectrometer. *Photogramm. Eng. Remote Sens.* **56**, 83–92.

Labovitz, M.L., E.J. Masuoka, R. Bell, A.W. Siegrist and R.F. Nelson 1983. The application of remote sensing to geobotanical exploration for metal sulphides – results from the 1980 field season at Mineral, Virginia. *Econ. Geol.* **78**, 750–760.

Labovitz, M.L., E.J. Masuoka, R. Bell, R.F. Nelson, E.A. Latsen, L.K. Hooker and K.W. Troensegaard 1985. Experimental evidence for spring and autumn windows for the detection of geobotanical anomalies through the remote sensing of overlying vegetation. *Int. J. Remote Sens.* **6**,195–216.

Lattman, L.H. and R.R. Parizek 1964. Relationship between fracture traces and the occurrence of groundwater in carbonate rocks. *J. Hydrol.* **2**, 73–91.

Legg, C.A. 1990. *Remote sensing, an operational technology for the mining and petroleum industries.* London: Institute of Mining and Metallurgy.

Liggett, M.A. and J.F. Childs 1976. An application of satellite imagery to mineral exploration. *Proc. 1st Ann. William T. Pecora Mem. Symp., Sioux Falls, South Dakota*, pp. 253–270.

Loughlin, W.P. 1990. Geological exploration in the western United States by use of airborne scanner imagery. In *Remote sensing, an operational technology for the mining and petroleum industries*, Legg, C.A. (ed.), pp. 223–241. London: Institute of Mining and Metallurgy.

MacDonald, H.C., B.C. Clark, D.S. Taylor, G.L. Rainwater, V.H. Kaupp and W.P. Waite 1989. Assessment of shuttle imaging radar and Landsat imagery for groundwater exploration in arid environments. *US Army Corps of Engineers Misc. Pap.* EL-79-6.

Marsh, S.E. and J.B. McKeon 1983. Integrated analysis of high-resolution field and airborne spectroradiometer data for alteration mapping. *Econ. Geol.* **78**, 618–632.

Milton, N.M., W. Collins, S.-H. Chang, and R.G. Schmidt 1983. Remote detection of metal anomalies on Pilot Mountain, Randolph County, North Carolina. *Econ. Geol.* **78**, 605–617.

Missalati, A., A.E. Prelat and R.J.P. Lyon 1979. Simultaneous use of geological, geophysical and Landsat digital data in uranium exploration. *Remote Sens. Environ.* **8**, 189–210.

Norman, J.W. 1980. Causes of some old crustal failure zones interpreted from Landsat images and their significance in regional mineral exploration. *Trans. Inst. Min. Metall. (Sect. B: Appl. Earth Sci.)* **89**, B63–B72.

Offield, T.W. 1976. Remote sensing in uranium exploration. In *Exploration of uranium ore deposits*, pp. 731–744. Vienna: International Atomic Energy Agency.

Offield, T.W., E.A. Abbott, A.R. Gillespie and S.O. Loguercio 1977. Structural mapping on enhanced Landsat images of southern Brazil: tectonic control of mineralization and speculations on metallogeny. *Geophysics* **42**, 482–500.

Peters, D.C. 1983. Use of airborne multispectral scanner data to map alteration related to roll-front uranium migration. *Econ. Geol.* **78**, 641–653.

Plant, J.A., D.G. Jones, G.C. Brown, T.B. Colman, J.D. Cornwell, K. Smith, A.S.D. Walker and P.C. Webb 1988. Metallogenic models and exploration criteria for buried carbonate-hosted ore deposits: results of a multidisciplinary study in eastern England. In *Mineral deposits within the European Community*, Boissonnas and P. Omenetto (eds), pp. 321–377. Berlin: Springer-Verlag.

Podwysocki, M.H., D.B. Segal and M.J. Abrams 1983. Use of multispectral scanner images for assessment of hydrothermal alteration in the Marysvale, Utah, mining area. *Econ. Geol.* **78**, 675–687.

Prost, G. 1980. Alteration mapping with airborne multispectral scanners. *Econ. Geol.* **75**, 894–906.

Raines, G.L. and J.C. Wynne 1982. Mapping of ultramafic rocks in a heavily vegetated terrain using Landsat data. *Econ. Geol.* **77**, 1755–1769.

Ramos, V.A. 1977. Basement tectonics from Landsat imagery in mining exploration. *Geol. Mijnbouw* **56**, 243–252.

Richards, D.M., V.T. Jones, M.D. Matthews, J. Maciolek, R.J. Pirkle and W.C. Sidle 1986. The 1983 Landsat soil-gas geochemical survey of Patrick Draw area, Sweetwater County, Wyoming. *Am. Ass. Petrol. Geol. Bull.* **70**, 869–887.

Rothery, D.A., P.W. Francis and C.A. Wood 1988. Volcano monitoring using short-wavelength infrared data from satellites. *J. Geophys. Res.* **93**, 7993–8008.

Rowan, L.C., P.H. Wetlaufer, A.F.H. Goetz, F.C. Billingsley and J.H. Stewart 1974. *Discrimination of rock types and detection of hydrothermally altered areas in South-central Nevada by the use of computer-enhanced ERTS images.* US Geol. Surv. Professional Paper 883.

Saraf, A.K., A.P. Cracknell and J. MacManus 1989. Geobotanical applications of airborne Thematic Mapper data in Sutherland, NW Scotland. *Int. J. Remote Sens.* **10**, 545–555.

Schmidt, R.G. 1976. Exploration for porphyry copper deposits in Pakistan using digital processing of Landsat-1 data. *J. Res. US Geol. Surv.* **4**, 27–34.

Schmugge, J.T. 1983. Remote sensing of soil; moisture: recent advances. *IEEE Trans. Geoscience Remote Sens.* **GE-21**, 336–344.

Segal, D.B. 1983. Use of Landsat multispectral scanner data for the definition of limonitic exposures in heavily vegetated areas. *Econ. Geol.* **78**. 711–722.

Short, N.M. and R.W. Blair Jr 1986. *Geomorphology from space*. NASA SP-486. Washington DC: US Government Printing Office.

Siegal, B.S. and A.F.H. Goetz 1977. Effect of vegetation on rock and soil type discrimination. *Photogramm. Eng. Remote Sens.* **43**, 191–196.

Simpson, C.J. 1978. Landsat: developing techniques and applications in mineral and petroleum exploration. *BMR J. Australian Geol. Geophys.* **3**, 181–191.

Vincent, R.K. 1977. Uranium exploration with computer processed Landsat data. *Geophysics* **42**, 536–541.

Vogel, A. 1985. The use of space technology in earthquake hazard assessment. *Proc. 18th Int. Symp. Remote Sensing Environment, Paris.*

Wang, Q.M., T. Nishidai and M.P. Coward 1992. The Tarim Basin, NW China: formation and aspects of petroleum geology. *J. Petrol. Geol.* **15**, 5–34.

Whitney, G., M.J. Abrams, and A.F.H. Goetz 1983. Mineral discrimination using a portable ratio-determining radiometer. *Econ. Geol.* **78**, 688–698.

Williams, R.S. (ed.) 1983. Geological applications. Chapter 31 in *Manual of remote sensing*, 2nd edn, Colwell, R.N. (ed.), pp. 1667–1953. Falls Church, Virginia: American Society of Photogrammetry.

APPENDIX A | *Stereometry*

Viewing remotely sensed images in three dimensions relies on the stereoptic capabilities of the human visual system. As outlined in Section 2.4, for an object to be perceived in three-dimensional space the absolute parallax of its images on the retinas of both eyes must be greater than the minimum resolution of the visual system. For two objects to be discriminated in three dimensions similarly means that their relative parallax or parallax difference at the eyes must also exceed this minimum. If the positions of an imaging platform at high altitude or in orbit are spaced widely enough during the capture of two overlapping images, then the resulting absolute and relative parallaxes on the images can be large enough for them to be resolved visually. This being the case, a stereoptic model of the surface topography is seen if each image can be viewed separately by each eye. The adjacent images are substituted for the natural views using both eyes, and the effective eye base is increased from 6 or 7 cm to as much as 100 km. Relief is perceived because a continuum of parallax difference exists for all of the points that constitute the surface.

Parallax is normally achieved in images by different positions of the platform as in overlapping aerial photographs taken from adjacent positions along the same flightline, or from different flightlines with different viewing geometries, as in the case of radar and line-scan or pushbroom systems (Chs 3 and 7). Landsat images from adjacent paths have between 15 and 80% overlap, from the Equator to the highest latitudes covered by the system. Stereoptic potential is available from both the SPOT and MOMS systems (Section 3.8.3) by selective pointing off-nadir and a combination of forward- and nadir-looking devices respectively. It can also be introduced synthetically into a single image from other two-dimensional data, such as those for digital elevation or geophysical and geochemical variables (Ch. 8). When the unchanged image is viewed with one eye and the transformed image with the other, the result is a synthetic stereoptic model of the artificial topology. For both kinds of image pair the trick is to persuade the visual system that the eyes are being used in a normal way.

For two overlapping aerial photographs to be viewed stereoptically, they must first be oriented so that the eye base is parallel to the flight direction. Secondly, the traces of the flightline on both images must coincide. This is necessary because of radial relief displacement and distribution of parallax parallel to the flight direction. This means identifying the principal points of both images on each image and aligning the four points (Fig. A.1). For line-scan and pushbroom images which overlap, and radar images which contain parallax differences, apparent relief displacement and relative parallax between image swaths are parallel to the scan lines and the look direction respectively. There is neither relative parallax nor relief displacement parallel to the flight direction. The images must be arranged so that the two flightlines are parallel. Finally, the separation of the two images must be adjusted to suit the method of viewing.

The normal reaction to unaided viewing of two separate objects at close range is for the eyes to converge on only one of the objects at one time. For the untrained observer, therefore, only one of a pair of images can be seen at one

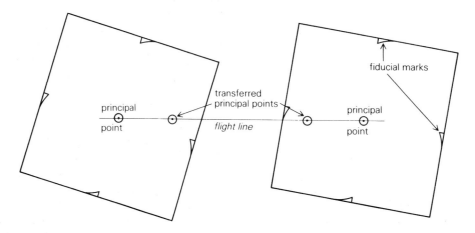

Figure A.1   This figure shows how an overlapping pair of aerial photographs is set up for stereoptic viewing using a reflecting stereoscope. The principal point of each photograph is located by the crossing of lines ruled between the fiducial points on the margin of the frame. The objects on the ground to which the principal points are related are then located on the adjacent photographs to give the four points which define the flightline and its direction. Separation of the images is determined by the amount of overlap and the geometry of the stereoscope.

time. Stereoptic fusion of the two images means overcoming the natural tendency for close-range convergence. When looking into the far distance the eyes assume a parallel orientation of their optic axes, as well as the necessary focal length for clear vision. One method of achieving unaided stereopsis of an image pair is to stare 'through' them, as in a daydream, and then to coax the eyes to regain focus without convergence. With luck, a blurred stereoptic model is achieved, which becomes sharper with perseverance. Of course, to accomplish this means that common parts of both images must have roughly the same separation as the eyes. A simple aid for the unsuccessful beginner is to separate the two views physically with a card held at the bridge of the nose. Once fusion and focus can be achieved, then the card can be dispensed with. As useful as unaided stereoptic viewing of image pairs is, only a minority of people can manage to do it. The majority require some kind of optical assistance – a **stereoscope**.

In a simple lens stereoscope (Fig. A.2) the lenses refract rays from an object portrayed on both images in such a way that they correspond to the convergence normally experienced with close-range vision. The two images of the object are focused on the left and right retinas with no strain, and the stereoptic model of relief quickly springs into being, as can be tested with any of the stereopairs of images in Chapters 4, 7 and 8. The problem is that only a portion of the overlap between the two images as wide as the eye base can be viewed. To view the full area of overlap means using a system of lenses together with prisms or mirrors, or both, in a reflecting stereoscope (Fig. A.3). This combines the refraction of rays to the normal convergence angle with an increase in the effective eye

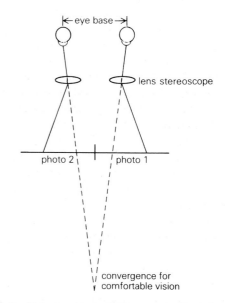

Figure A.2   This simple ray diagram shows how the lenses of a lens stereoscope optically straighten the line of sight from each eye when the eyes are focused at and converge towards a point at the normal distance for comfortable reading. The effect is to enable each eye to see a separate image and to create the illusion of viewing the stereoptically fused pair of images from a great distance.

base, in much the same way as binoculars. All stereoscopes, including those incorporated in sophisticated plotting and measuring instruments, are based on these simple principles.

The stereoptic potential of image pairs with parallax differences can also be exploited by other optical prin-

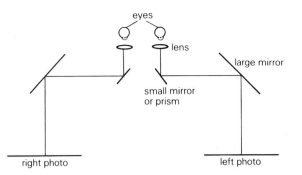

Figure A.3 The lens system in a reflecting stereoscope optically straightens the line of sight, as in a lens stereoscope. The prisms and mirrors enable the pair of images to be separated sufficiently for the whole area of overlap to be viewed stereoptically.

ciples. One involves projecting both images onto a screen, one through a filter which polarizes light in the horizontal plane, the other through a vertically polarizing filter. The screen is viewed through spectacles with filters having corresponding polarities. Each eye only receives light from one of the two projected images, and stereoptic fusion results. This is a handy method of presenting and teaching the principles of stereoptic photogeological interpretation. Another way of ensuring that each eye only sees one of a pair of images is to print or project the images in separate primary colours. Viewing with spectacles having filters with the same arrangement of primaries ensures that only light from the left image is received by the left eye, and vice versa. Coloured light from the other image is absorbed by the filter. This is the principle of the **anaglyph**, once popular in children's books and three-dimensional movies.

Viewing most of the pairs of images in Chapter 4 with a lens stereoscope reveals a marked degree of **vertical exaggeration** of the topographies involved. This phenomenon is very useful for highlighting subtle topographic features which would otherwise go unnoticed. However, it also causes all slopes to appear steeper than they really are. This is particularly irritating when dips of geologically important surfaces need to be estimated. In most cases vertical exaggeration means that estimates can be made only in terms of horizontal, gentle, moderate or steep dip. The amount of vertical exaggeration depends on the geometries of both the imaging and viewing systems.

To ensure complete stereoptic cover aerial photographs generally have a 60% overlap or more along a flightline. Two factors contribute to the overlap. First, the focal length of the lens governs the field of view and, for a fixed frame size, the scale of the image. The shorter the focal length, the wider the field of view and the smaller the scale. The distance flown by the platform between successive exposures – the **air base** – is the obvious second factor. At a fixed altitude, therefore, 60% overlap is achieved by a larger air

base for a lens with short focal length than for one with a longer focal length. The two images in the first case contain a greater relative parallax for two objects with different elevations. This produces an enhanced three-dimensional effect when the two images are viewed stereoptically. From these simple relationships the degree of vertical exaggeration can be deduced to be directly proportional to the ratio between the air base and the altitude.

Because of the advantages of vertical exaggeration for interpretation, and since slope angles can be measured by other methods, aerial photographs usually have an air base/altitude ratio of between 0.4 and 0.6. This gives exaggeration factors of between three and four times normal. Beyond exaggeration factors of 4, the amount of relative parallax between objects with high and low elevation may be larger than the visual system can accommodate. To view the whole scene stereoptically requires different image separations for the low and high parts. The field of view of orbiting systems, although large in absolute terms, is small relative to altitude to ensure that distortions at the margin of images are kept to a minimum. As the equivalent of air base for overlapping Landsat images decreases towards the poles from a maximum at the Equator, the vertical exaggeration changes from about 1.2 to 0.2. A useful stereoptic model is only possible for latitudes below about 50°. The stereoscopic imaging arrangements for SPOT and MOMS aim at exaggeration factors of around 2.

The parallax differences between overlapping images provide the basis for quantitative measurements of the relative elevations of objects. Where b is the air base of the images, H is the altitude of the platform and Δp is the parallax difference between the images of two objects, their vertical separation h is given by:

$$h = H\Delta p/b \qquad (A.1)$$

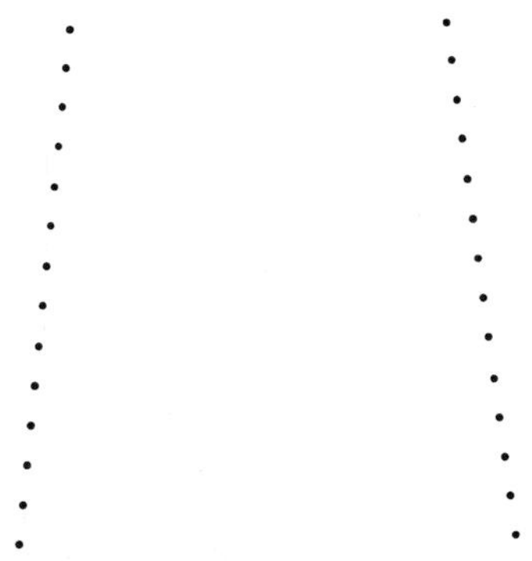

Figure A.4 Viewing these converging rows of dots with a lens stereoscope produces a stereoptic illusion that they form a single row which dips into the page. This is the principle behind both the parallax wedge and the stereometer. In a parallax wedge, each pair of dots is accompanied by a scale division indicating the absolute parallax between the dots. In a stereometer this distance is measured using a micrometer to which the plates carrying the dots are attached.

provided measurements of Δp and b are in the same units. Converting the parallax differences between objects on pairs of overlapping radar images to relative elevations involves different equations which depend on the particular configuration of the sensors. For the commonly used same-side, same-height arrangement the elevation difference h is given by:

$$h = \Delta p/(\tan \theta_2 - \tan \theta_1) \qquad (A.2)$$

where θ_1 and θ_2 are the depression angles from the antenna to objects on the two images.

Because parallax differences in most images are small, they cannot be measured precisely using a ruler. It is more convenient and useful to employ the principles of stereopsis during stereoptic viewing itself. The simplest method is to use a transparent plate engraved accurately with two converging rows of dots, crosses or other marks, known as a **parallax wedge** (Fig. A.4). When viewed with a lens stereoscope the two converging rows of marks appear as a line dipping through the stereoptic model, because of the regular variation in absolute parallax between adjacent marks. By moving the wedge over the stereopair at right angles to the flightline, one of the fused pairs of marks can be 'sat' on a particular topographic feature. The corresponding absolute parallax of the two marks is read from the scale. Another pair of marks is fused so the floating mark 'sits' on a feature at a different elevation, to give the absolute parallax at that point. The difference between the two readings is then used in Equation A.1 to give a difference in elevation between the two points. Clearly, a parallax wedge together with a lens stereoscope is a useful tool in the field.

The parallax bar or **stereometer** employs the same principles as the parallax wedge does. It consists of two small transparent plates, each engraved with a dot or a cross, which are linked by a micrometer screw so that their separation can be measured precisely. With the bar aligned parallel to the flight direction the separation of the spots is adjusted so that the fused sot 'sits' on the surface, first at one position and then at another. The parallax difference is read from the micrometer, and is converted to a difference in elevation.

More sophisticated instruments used in stereometry incorporate means of calculating elevation differences, together with mechanisms for removing tilt produced in the stereopairs during flying and for transferring information from the images to a base map. A pair of marks similar to those used in the parallax bar are on linked arms, so the fused mark can be moved along topographic or geological features. Another linkage incorporating the appropriate scale conversion drives a pencil across a base map to record the features. If the fused mark is maintained apparently on the surface, then it is possible to map topographic contours directly. Further refinement combines the results from such plotters and measuring systems through microprocessors to produce digital maps. Further details of the various instruments used in photogrammetry are beyond the scope of this book.

The angle between the horizontal and a line which joins two points can be defined by ratio between their difference in elevation and their horizontal separation. This ratio is the tangent. The angle can therefore be estimated by stereometric measurement of parallax difference for the two points and their horizontal separation. If the two points lie on the same dipping surface, such as a topographic slope or a bedding plane, then this angle is the true dip of the surface. The advantages of this possibility for the geologist equipped with aerial photographs, a stereoscope and a parallax wedge or bar are obvious. One in particular is that the minor variations in dip which plague field measurements are removed to give a local average.

Relative elevations of objects on images can be measured without involving parallax, but with less precision by using the lengths of shadows which they cast. If the angle θ at which the object is illuminated by the Sun or by radar is known, then the elevation of the top of the object above its base h is related to the length of its shadow l by:

$$h = l\tan \theta \qquad (A.3)$$

Useful as this method may be for estimating topographic elevations of landforms, it is of little use in estimating dips, since the very presence of shadows obscures geological features.

Image correction

Most kinds of remote-sensing device produce unavoidable geometric distortions in the images which they produce. These departures from the normal cartographic projection of the Earth's surface are added to by the warping effects of deviations in the flight direction and attitude of the platforms on which the devices are mounted (Ch. 3). As well as distortions, defects in the radiometric fidelity of the images are also common. These range from mistakes in the exposure, processing and printing of photographic film to the results of systematic foibles in an individual imaging device.

Section 5.2 covered defects in contrast resulting from atmospheric scattering and compression of the contrast range in digital images, and also the means of compensating for them. Other common blemishes in digital images produced by electronic imaging systems are caused by malfunctions in the hardware, or are peculiarities of the method itself. The manufacture of line-scanning devices and, to a lesser extent, pushbroom systems fails to achieve a perfect match between the responses of individual detectors to the same stimulus. Each detector may also drift or deteriorate with time, especially if its temperature fluctuates. The net result is the production of **striping** parallel to the scan lines on the image. In the Landsat MSS and TM instruments detectors for visible and near-infrared radiation are mounted in banks of 6 and 16 respectively. The effect of mismatches between the detectors is repeated patterns of striping, each stripe being 6 or 16 lines deep.

Brief failures in the circuits of a detector result in spurious signals during a scan cycle. This may produce lines without data or, where the data have uniformly high values, which appear as black or white lines respectively. They are known as **line drop-outs**. Probably the most disturbing defect in line-scan systems relates to malfunctions of the electronic signals to begin recording data from a single sweep. A line may not begin until well into a scene. Such **line-start problems** plague images from the Landsat-3 MSS. Worse still, the line starts may be out of phase between the individual detectors. This leads to **offsets** between lines, which disturb the continuity of surface features. Build-up of minute electrostatic charges in the circuits of the system and their eventual discharge can result in a spurious response for a single pixel. This noise effect is generally distributed as random speckles in an image. A very similar result stems from the complex returns of microwave signals, so that radar images are often infested with speckle. In fact, the speckle does contain valid information relating to attributes of the surface, but this is rarely of much interest to the geologist, and it disturbs the topographic patterns of interest.

Not only do defects degrade the visual quality of an image, but many of them have spatial frequencies close to where the achromatic MTF of the human visual system rises to a maximum (Section 2.2). They are noticed more readily than more natural variations are, and even a slight defect disturbs interpretation severely.

B.1 Geometric rectification

All images contain geometric distortions of some kind. There is a large number of combinations of effects due to different kinds of platform instability, optical and mechanical distortions in the radiation-gathering set-up, Earth rotation beneath the platform, and both parallax and scale effects resulting from topographic relief. Apart from the last two effects, these are amenable to quite simple corrections. Where precise information about platform attitude and track relative to the Earth's rotation is available, this can be built into automatic correction programmes. In Landsat images the correction for Earth rotation is simply a systematic line-by-line displacement of pixels, very much like giving a slant to the edge of a pack of cards.

At large scales the Earth's surface can be regarded as a plane on which the topography is superimposed. Rectification of an image essentially restores objects to their correct relative disposition in two-dimensional space as if they were all viewed from directly above. Small-scale images contain effects due to the Earth's curvature. They are projections of a spherical surface into two dimensions. All maps have similar distortions. However, different scales and different uses call for different kinds of projection, such as stereographic, conical, cylindrical and more complex renditions. All aim to maintain a common scale over a whole map, a minimum of distortion, and a uniform representation of shapes and areas. Because maps are the stock-in-trade for all users of remotely sensed images, geometric manipulations of images attempt to register images to the map projection required for a particular project. Since most digital images consist of rectilinear arrays of DN for columns of pixels in rows of lines, rectification consists of a transformation from one set of Cartesian coordinates to another. In cartographic projections the spherical coordinates of points, expressed as latitude and longitude, do not conform to a rectilinear array. Points must be expressed as a metric grid of eastings and northings. Sometimes a grid of this kind is an integral part of the map, as in the Universal Transverse Mercator (UTM) projection and other relatively modern projections. Where more archaic projections are found, a false grid must be used to register the image to the map.

All image distortions, except those caused by differences in surface elevation, can be removed by registration of a digital image to a map base. The process begins by identifying topographic or cultural features visible on both the image and the map. The map coordinates are assigned to the pixel and line coordinates of a number of these **ground-control points** on the image. A very similar procedure can be used to register an image of one type to another. Depending on the number of control points, a pair of polynomial equations, such as:

$$X_m = a + bX + cY + dX^2 + eXY + fY^2 + gX^2Y + hXY^2 + iX^3 + jY^3$$

$$Y_m = z + yX + xY + wX^2 + vXY + uY^2 + tX^2Y + sXY^2 + rX^3 + qY^3$$

where X_m and Y_m are map coordinates and X and Y are image coordinates, can be generated which describe the deviation in two dimensions of the image from the map projection. The pair of **polynomial transforms** is used to warp the image to register with the map by treating mathematically like a rubber sheet. In the production of a new rectified array of pixels for the image, it is possible to change the dimensions and shapes of pixels. In the case of the rectangular pixels of the Landsat MSS system the output pixels are commonly given a square format.

Each new pixel in a rectified image must have a DN derived from those in the raw image assigned to it. As the new pixels are displaced relative to the raw array of DN, simply assigning the original DN of a shifted pixel will produce errors in the new image. The simplest means of allowing for this effect is to assign the DN of the nearest raw pixel to a pixel in the new array. This is the nearest-neighbour **resampling** method (Fig. B.1a) Because it is a crude approximation it results in a blocky appearance in the resampled image. However, it retains the original statistics of the data, and is thus commonly employed when the resampled image is intended for multispectral classification. A more geometrically precise approach is to assign the distance-weighted mean DN of several raw pixels immediately surrounding the position of a rectified pixel using convolution (section 5.3). Best results involve the mean of the 16 surrounding raw pixels using a method

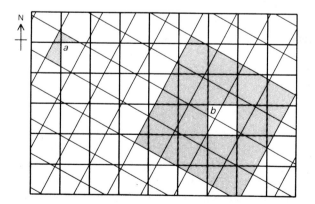

Figure B.1 In the nearest-neighbour method of resampling the DN for an output pixel (*a*) is taken unchanged from the input pixel (shaded) lying nearest to the new one. Resampling by cubic convolution produces an output DN at *b* which is the mean value of the DN from those 16 input pixels grouped around the position of the output pixel (shaded). A more sophisticated version weights the contribution of the DN of each input pixel to the mean according to its distance from the new pixel position.

known as cubic convolution (Fig. B.1b). This reduces the blockiness in the rectified image, while keeping disturbance of the original frequency distribution of DN to a minimum.

The parallax and scale variations which cannot be removed from an image by its digital registration to a map depend on both elevation differences and position of features relative to the nadir of the imaging system. For most satellite images these do not produce distortions that are much greater than the imprecision inherent in surveying and printing small-scale maps. For instance, an elevation difference of 1 km at the edge of a Landsat image gives a displacement equivalent to only 160 m. Parallax does introduce important distortions in aerial photographs with scales greater than 1:1000 000.

To overcome parallax and scale distortions, interpretations from stereopairs of aerial photographs are transferred to maps using various optical–mechanical plotters. Where maps do not exist at a scale suitable for the interpretation they must be constructed from the photographs using triangulation methods which allow for radial-relief displacements. The parallax involved in radial-relief displacement can be removed from aerial photographs using an **orthophotoscope**. In this instrument the image is rephotographed through a narrow slit. The operator views the stereomodel and attempts to keep an image of the slit at the ground surface (see Appendix A) as the image is scanned in one direction as a series of narrow swaths. Through various mechanical linkages this manipulation is translated into up-and-down movements of the film onto which the image is projected. This controls the local scale of the new image on the film. The process can involve direct rephotography, or the three-dimensional coordinates controlling the film and slit positions can be stored and replayed through the orthophotoscope when the task is complete. The final product is an **orthophotograph**, which represents each point as though it has been viewed from directly above, just as in a map. Where digital elevation data are available complex computer programs can remove parallax from digitized photographs, again resulting in an orthographic image.

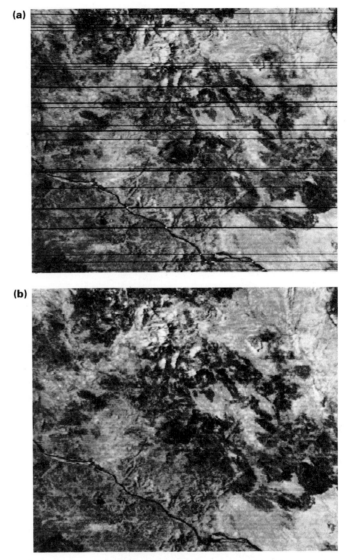

Figure B.2 The Landsat-2 MSS image of an area in the Ethiopian Highlands (a) is severely affected by lines of spuriously high data. In image (b) the spurious lines have been replaced by data derived from those in the adjacent lines. At the scale the defect is hardly noticeable.

B.2 Replacing dropped lines

Figure B.2a illustrates graphically the disturbing effects of a relatively few lines in images which contain spurious data. The problem can be reduced by replacing each line with data derived from those adjacent to it. Each pixel in the dropped line is assigned the DN of the mean value of the pixels immediately above and below it. Although the new line is entirely artificial, it is so similar to its neighbour that it becomes barely noticeable, except under high magnification. The degree of cosmetic improvement that can be achieved is clear from Figure B.2b.

B.3 Destriping

Where **image striping** stems from different responses from each detector in a bank, as in Landsat MSS and TM images, it appears as a regularly repeated defect throughout an image (Fig. B.3a). A simple and rapid means of cosmetic treatment in this case begins by comparing histograms for all of the detectors in a bank over a representative part of the scene. The histogram with the highest mean DN and the greatest variance is selected as the standard, and the others are then normalized to it. Individual DN for pixels contributing to each histogram are changed to fit the 'master'

251

(a)

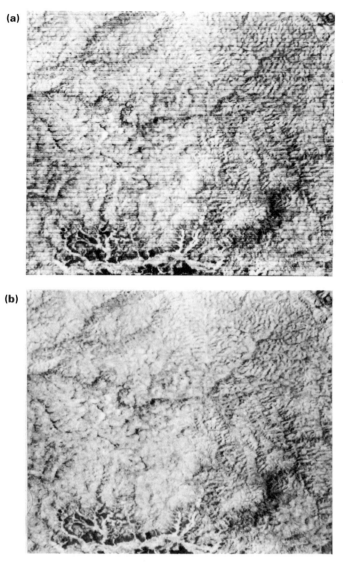

(b)

Figure B.3   Unequal responses of the six band 7 detectors in the Landsat MSS system have produced severe striping in an image of part of the Ethiopian Highlands (a). In image (b) the stripes have been almost eliminated by equalizing the histograms for the six sensors.

histogram using look-up tables (Ch. 5). The improvement in quality is shown by Figure B.3b.

Histogram-matching methods remove stripes effectively from images of relatively homogeneous scenes. Where scenes contain large areas with very different overall brightness, the correction may leave residual stripes in particularly dark and light areas. More comprehensive destriping methods involve more complex, and thus more costly, computations. One is to use convolution filtering based on matrices whose dimensions mathchthe number of sensors in the imaging system. The filter effectively smoothes out the striping. Other methods rely on identifying the frequency

and amplitude of the striping which is superimposed on the real variations, usually by analysing the appearance of areas known to be homogeneous. The periodic noise is then removed by subtractive methods.

B.4   Removal of random noise

Because noise, such as speckle, is randomly distributed it is uncorrelated with the real data in a multispectral image. In the decorrelation process involved in principal component analysis such poorly correlated data are relegated to the highest order components. This leaves the first principal component virtually devoid of noise, including striping too. For interpretation of the spatial attributes of a scene the first principal component therefore forms an excellent image, which can be selectively enhanced to maximize its interpretability.

For some noisy images, such as those produced by band-ratioing techniques or by radar systems, principal component analysis is not an appropriate means of noise removal. The interesting information is best retained in the original data set. However, speckle degrades the visual impact of the raw images (Fig. B.5a), and should therefore be removed by other means. A hypothetical DN due to noise is represented in Figure B.4 by the number 255, which is surrounded by valid DN. Calculation of the mean of the nine DN to replace the DN of the central noisy pixel by a high-pass filter produces a value of 51. This is still sufficiently different from its neighbours to appear as a speckle in the image. However, selection of the median DN of the sequence 24, 25, 26, 26, 27, 27, 255 gives a value of 26. As this is more representative of the surrounding DN, the resulting image is effectively cleared of noise. **Median filtering** of this kind, like other spatial filtering, is most economically achieved by convolution in the spatial domain. It is usually accomplished using a 3×3 square convolution matrix. More comprehensive noise filtering can be performed in the frequency domain using Fourier methods. Both types of filter have little effect on most of the real data, and the cleaned images can be interpreted alone or combined with other data sets in classification with

24	26	25
27	255	26
26	25	27

Figure B.4   This array of DN for a 3×3 part of an image consists of eight valid DN surrounding a spuriously high DN which constitutes system noise. Replacing the value of 255 with the median DN for all nine pixels removes the noise effect.

(a)

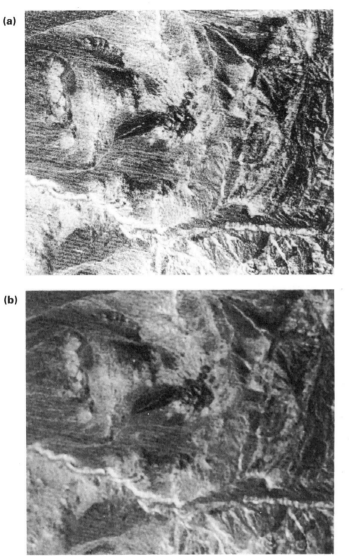

(b)

reduced likelihood of classes being assigned to spurious data. The efficiency of median filtering by convolution is demonstrated by Figure B.5b.

B.5 Scan-line offsets

The degradation of an image by irregular start positions for scan lines is a serious, though rare, problem. Natural patterns, particularly those defined by narrow linear features, are badly disrupted. If the offsets are systematic the correction algorithms involving displacement of pixels along the offset line are possible. If the problem is irregularly distributed in an image, then the effects can only be removed by manually by changing the pixel coordinates in each affected line.

Figure B.5 An image of the ratio between Landsat MSS bands 4 and 5 for an area in the Chilean Andes (a) is plagued by an increase in the signal-to-noise ratio, which is inevitable in ratio images. By convolving the raw image with a 3 × 3 median filter the speckle and residual striping is virtually removed (b).

253

Sources of remotely sensed images

C.1 Aerial and satellite photographs

Aerial photographs are readily available for a large proportion of the continental land area. In many countries a single national body is responsible for collating the various survey records and maintaining an archive. However, several agencies may have produced the photographs. The main reason for flying photographic sorties is cartographic mapping, and updating of maps often ensures a wide choice of dates and scales. However, some sorties are specifically for resource inventories, particularly relating to monitoring agriculture and soils. As well as national archives, there are libraries of photographs for ex-colonial countries, now usually quite old, that are maintained by the former colonial power. Most aerial surveys are conducted by commercial contractors, who also maintain records and archives. To give a comprehensive world-wide list of suppliers is obviously impossible here. An excellent guide to sources of information is given by:

US Geological Survey 1981. *Worldwide directory of national earth-science agencies and related international organizations.* USGS Circular 834.

This is now out of print, but copies can be obtained from:

US Geological Survey
507 National Center
Reston
Virginia 22092
USA

In the circular each agency is coded according to its main function. Those coded 'C' are involved in cartography, and are the most likely sources of information on aerial photography.

Access by the public to aerial surveys varies from country to country, but is generally possible given the correct procedure. The first step is usually obtaining official authorization for purchase, which is essential when ordering copies from non-indigenous sources. The second is to ascertain the date, scale and coverage of a survey, generally by specifying the limits of the area of interest. In some cases the response will be supply of reduced mosaics of the photographs for the area, but more frequently a map showing flightlines and information on overlap and sidelap, with details of the camera used, flying height and purpose.

Photographs are usually supplied as contact prints from large negatives around 22×22 cm, and scales can vary from greater than 1:1000 to 1:100 000. In this form overlapping vertical photographs can be viewed easily using a lens or mirror stereoscope. Because the grain of aerial survey film is very fine, enlargement beyond ten times rarely degrades the visual quality of the prints, so scale is rarely a problem for most geological applications. Enlargements can be ordered directly from suppliers, but can be achieved at little extra cost by rephotographing, even with a 35-mm camera. Enlargements can be viewed stereoptically only by cutting one frame of a pair into strips perpendicular to the flight direction.

As a general rule, the best images for geological work have low cloud and snow cover, low-angle illumination –

either morning or late afternoon sorties – and good contrast. Most photographs obtained since the 1970s have been printed using an electronic 'dodging' process that balances the contrast and removes the vignetting inevitable with optical cameras. It is usually possible to specify the contrast qualities, weight and gloss of the prints, the best being high contrast, double weight and matt finish for minus-blue, panchromatic photographs. Natural-colour or false-colour infrared photographs are sometimes available. Whether these have advantages that outweigh the increased cost depends on the use to which they will be put. For mapping of lithological boundaries and geological structures most geologists find panchromatic prints quite adequate, particularly because of the eye's excellent visualization of high-frequency spatial features in achromatic images (Ch. 2). However, in subdued terrain colour photographs often have decided advantages.

In the absence of easily available photographs, there is little option but to commission an aerial campaign, usually with a commercial contractor. Costs can be high, and are divided between fixed costs for photography and processing and variable costs for the flying. Most contractors require a minimum contract price, and charge for both the cost of reaching the area and aircraft hire even if weather delays or postpones the campaign. Since the variable costs depend on actual distances flown, they increase with the scale required for the survey.

As indicated in Chapter 3, photographs are available from a number of manned spacecraft missions. Most prominent among these are those from the Apollo missions, Skylab and the Space Shuttle, but there are signs that some surveillance photographs from intelligence satellites are becoming available from formerly Soviet satellites, and possibly from their US equivalents.

Information about photographs from the US manned spaceflight programme – mainly Apollo missions – is available from:

National Space Science Data Center (for US enquiries), or World Data Center A for Rockets and Satellites (for international enquiries).
NASA
Goddard Space Flight Center
Greenbelt
Maryland 20771
USA

Products from Skylab and the Large Format Camera carried on the October 1984 Space Shuttle mission can be sought from:

EROS Data Center
US Geological Survey
Mundt Federal Building
Sioux Falls
South Dakota 57198
USA

Metric Camera images obtained on a 1983 Space Shuttle mission can be obtained from:

DFVLR
Oberpfaffenhofen
8031 Wessling
Germany

Manned and unmanned satellites of the former Soviet Union provided a range of photographic products that were originally only obtainable outside the Soviet Union by nationals of the overflown country, are now marketed worldwide on normal terms of trade. Information is available in Britain from:

Nigel Press Associates, Edenbridge, Kent

Astronauts aboard the Space Shuttle are usually provided with hand-held cameras to photograph 'targets of opportunity' during their free time. A very large archive, mainly of oblique natural-colour photographs, has been assembled at:

Media Services Branch
Still Photograph Library
NASA/ Johnson Space Center
PO Box 58425, Mail Code AP3
Houston
Texas 77258-8425
USA

C.2 Digital images in the reflected and emitted regions

The very high capital cost of digital imaging systems, together with the small number of contracting companies equipped with them means that airborne data are far more expensive to acquire than aerial photographs. This is despite the fact that reproduction of the data on magnetic or optical storage media now has similar costs per unit area as photographic printing. As a result, much airborne digital imagery is commissioned by mining or oil companies, or acquired speculatively by contractors for sale to such organizations. In the first case it is held in confidence, in the second it is available only for high licence fees. However, various governmental institutions commission campaigns for a variety of reasons, either for simulation of forthcoming satellite systems or to allow fundamental research into the uses of multispectral imagery.

Although every country with ambitions in remote sensing will undoubtedly hold experimental data of this kind, the following institutions are known to offer low-cost digital copies of airborne data sets to the academic and industrial communities:

Media Services
Jet Propulsion Laboratory
California Institute of Technology
4800 Oak Grove Drive
Pasadena
California 91109
USA

Canadian Centre for Remote Sensing
2464 Sheffield Road
Ottawa
Ontario
Canada K1A 0Y7

Division of Mineral Physics and Mineralogy
CSIRO
Delhi Road
North Ryde
NSW 2113
Australia

Scientific Services
NERC
Polaris House
North Star Avenue
Swindon
Wiltshire
SN2 1EU
UK

Laboratoire d'Études et de Recherches
CNES
18 Avenue Eduoard Belin
31055 Toulouse CEDEX
France

National Space Development Agency (NASDA)
Earth Observation Center
Hatoyama-machi
Hiki-gun
Saitama-ken, 350-03
Japan

US Geological Survey
EROS Data Center
Mundt Federal Building
Sioux Falls, South Dakota 57198
USA

The most extensive archive of satellite remote-sensing data in digital form is that of the Landsat programme, which has been in continuous operation since 1972. Originally launched by NASA, handed over to NOAA after commissioning, the Landsat programme is now a joint venture of the US Government and a commercial agency called EOSAT. The act of commercialization took effect from September 1985. Data from areas world-wide are currently transmitted by data relay satellites to ground stations in the USA, and are available from both EOSAT and EROS Data Center (pre-September 1985). Because of limits on data transmission rates, US archives do not represent a complete cover for all available dates outside the USA. For any area the existence of some images is guaranteed, but for many areas images are available for only a limited number of years and seasons. However, rights to receive Landsat data through payment of licence fees are held by a growing number of satellite receiving stations (Fig. C.1) that decode the continuous data signals transmitted by the satellite when it is above the local horizon. The chances of obtaining more recent or more frequent coverage outside the USA are higher through these stations, though Figure C.1 shows that some areas are still dependent on reception in the USA. Many countries that do not have an independent reception ability maintain national points of contact, where information on existing imagery and ordering facilities are available. Through EOSAT and the international receiving stations it is possible to request special acquisition of data, though at greater cost. The most readily available information on US data holdings from Landsat emanates from EROS Data Center and:

EOSAT
4300 Forbes Boulevard
Lanham
Maryland 20706-9954
USA

For Europe, North and West Africa, similar information is available from:

Earthnet User Services
ESA-ESRIN
Via Galileo Galilei
00044 Frascati
Italy

Addresses for other Landsat suppliers are given in Cracknell and Hayes (see below).

Landsat data, as with all polar-orbiting, high-resolution data, are digitally divided along each orbit into segments in the form of parallelograms covering individual scenes of the Earth's surface. This is illustrated in Figure C.2, which shows the **Worldwide Reference System (WRS)** of **paths** along orbits, and **rows** roughly parallel to latitude. Ordering data requires path–row coordinates and specific scene codes, so the first step in getting Landsat data is to request a search in the area of interest, specifying either latitude and longitude, or path and row limits to the area. Any authorized supplier will provide the information on availability in the form of a computer listing. The listing comprises scene code, date, precise centre and corner coordinates, estimated cloud cover and data quality, and the media in which the data can be purchased, for each path–row location. Maps of

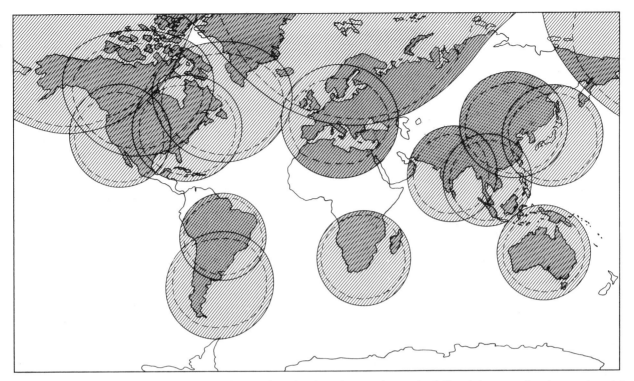

Figure C.1 The shaded areas on this map indicate where Landsat data can be received directly by operational ground receiving stations. They represent the areas where the satellites are over the horizon. The solid lines apply to Landsat-1 to -3 and the pecked lines to Landsat-4 and -5.

the WRS for the whole world can be obtained from EROS Data Center and EOSAT.

Prices of Landsat data vary, depending on whether MSS or TM is specified and on the level of processing. At the time of writing, when the issue of global environment change was perceived as important, MSS data more than 2 years old were marketed by EOSAT at the prices applying in 1972–76. For data that predate the act of commercialization in September 1985, no copyright applies and the data may be freely exchanged. An excellent service aimed at encouraging swapping is maintained by: Nebraska Remote Sensing Center, University of Nebraska, Lincoln, Nebraska 68588–0517, USA. The issue of Landsat data copyright after commercialization is not completely clear, but it is believed that it applies only to the original data, and that on irreversible changes to the data, such as convolution or non-linear contrast stretching, copyright passes to the originator of the changes. This loophole to pass on and exchange post-commercialization Landsat data should only be used with legal advice.

The second most important source of image data is the SPOT programme, in which handling of data is organized in much the same way as those from Landsat. Again, Cracknell and Hayes is the best source of information on distributors.

Detailed information is available from:

SPOT Image
18 Avenue Eduoard Belin
31055 Toulouse CEDEX
France

Copyright for SPOT data is very much tougher than that for Landsat. Effectively, SPOT images are permanently leased to users for a fee and remain the property of SPOT Image. Technically, reproducing even specially enhanced images and making them available to other users or printing them in a book or paper is subject to payment of royalties and requires the explicit permission of SPOT and CNES. In many cases the royalties may be waived, but permission and explicit acknowledgement of copyright is obligatory.

Other important sources of digital satellite imagery are from the Japanese (MOS-1 and JERS-1) and Indian (IRS-1) programmes. Information is available from NASDA (above) and:

ISRO
Cauvery Bhavan
Kempegowda Road
Bangalore 560 009
India

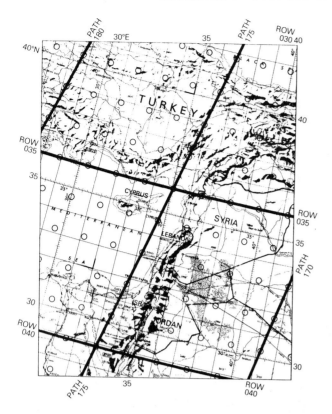

Figure C.2 Extract from Landsat WRS map showing path/row coordinates for Landsat-4 and -5. The scene covering southern Cyprus is referred to as 176/036. The path/row coordinate for the same area for Landsat-1 to -3 would be 189/036 because of their different orbit heights.

Occasionally geologists find images from coarse-resolution meteorological systems useful. The most useful of these are the TIROS/NOAA AVHRR, Nimbus CZCS and the pending SeaWIFS. Data are received by a large number of stations listed in Cracknell and Hayes (below), and information is available from:

NOAA/NESDIS
US Department of Commerce
Satellite Data Services Division (E/CCGI)
World Weather Building, Room 10
Washington, DC 20233
USA

The Heat Capacity Mapping Mission data were received by only seven stations, but may be useful. They are available from NASA, Goddard SFC and Earthnet (above). MOMS data can be obtained from DFVLR (above).

Perhaps the most useful source reference for obtaining national and international contacts, sources of data and software information on all aspects of remote sensing is:

Cracknell, A. and L. Hayes (biannual). *Remote sensing yearbook*. London: Taylor & Francis.

Watching briefs on the main operational programmes can be maintained by being on the mailing lists of the originating organizations. Several issue regular bulletins at no charge, including the *Landsat Data Users' Notes* (EOSAT) and *Nouvelles de SPOT* (SPOT Image). In fact there is a growing number of such bulletins issued by national and regional remote-sensing centres. Using sources in the *Remote sensing yearbook* should help establish a regular flow of useful information.

An exciting period of development in remote sensing is scheduled for the late 1990s and the early part of the 21st century, with the planned launch of the Earth Observation System (EOS) series of satellites. Notable geologically useful systems are the ASTER and HIRIS systems, scheduled for early deployment, but other systems may be of interest. NASA has a weighty range of information packs that can be obtained freely from:

EOS Project Science Office
Code 900
NASA
Goddard Space Flight Center
Greenbelt
Maryland 20771
USA

Of these, the most important for early examination are the *EOS reference handbook* and the regular bulletin *Earth Observer*.

C.3   Radar image data

Radar imagery, because of its independence of time and weather and its sensitivity to textural features of the surface, is of great value to geologists. However, its availability is limited at the time of writing.

Airborne radar imagery is costly for the same reasons as digital imagery. Moreover, there are now very few commercial contracting companies and only a handful of governmental institutions equipped to deploy SAR systems. These include JPL and the National Aerospace Laboratory of the Netherlands. Commercial contractors have been involved in regional SAR surveys of cloud-infested tropical areas in Central America, Brazil and Indonesia, and a programme for complete coverage of North America is in progress. Information on the latter is available from EROS Data Center and the Canadian Centre for Remote Sensing. A consortium of research establishments in Europe has sponsored multifrequency SAR campaigns aimed mainly at agricultural applications.

Until 1991 public-domain SAR images from satellites were limited to those from the Seasat mission and the SIR-A and -B experiments carried on the Space Shuttle. These were extremely limited in coverage (Fig. C.3), but nonetheless form an important source of geologically useful

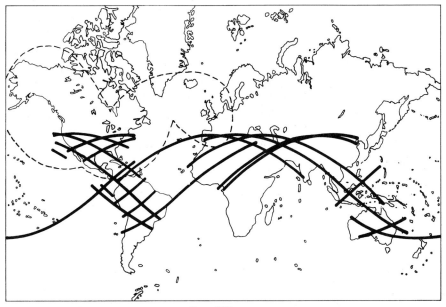

                    ——————— SIR–A coverage   — — — — Seasat SAR coverage

Figure C.3 Orbital synthetic-aperture radar data from the Seasat and SIR-A missions are only available for the areas and swaths indicated. The SIR-A swaths are approximately 55 km wide. Reception of Seasat SAR data was restricted to only three ground receiving stations in Alaska, the eastern USA and England.

data. Seasat data, in both optically correlated and digital form, are available at moderate cost from NOAA Satellite Data Services Division and Earthnet (above). Few SIR-B images are of interest, but those from the more successful SIR-A can be obtained from NSSDC at NASA Goddard SFC, who make no charge to *bona fide* research workers. They are only available in photographic form. With the launches of ERS-1 in 1991, JERS-1 in 1992 and Radarsat scheduled for 1994, this limited coverage has been transformed to a world-wide potential. Aside from its inappropriate depression angle for land applications in all but low-relief areas, ERS-1 has no on-board recording facilities. The complexity of receiving stations for SAR data therefore limits coverage to areas in line-of-sight of a few stations in North America, Europe and Australia. Both JERS-1 and Radarsat SAR systems have smaller depression angles and on-board recorders, so are potentially of far more significance to geologists. Information for ERS-1, JERS-1 and Radarsat can be obtained, respectively, from:

European Space Agency
8–10 rue Mario-Nikis
75738 Paris CEDEX 15
France

National Space Development Agency (NASDA)
Earth Observation Center
Hatoyama-machi
Hiki-gun
Saitama-ken, 350-03
Japan

Canadian Centre for Remote Sensing
2464 Sheffield Road
Ottawa
Ontario
Canada K1A 0Y7

C.4 Non-image data

The trend to archiving information in digital databases, using geographic coordinates, is making data that can be converted to images and used in GISs more widely available. The most commonly available gridded data are those for topographic elevation, and enquiries about their availability should be addressed to national mapping agencies. The US Defense Mapping Agency is the repository of a global, high-resolution digital elevation data set (DTED Level-1) compiled from surveillance aircraft and military intelligence satellites. At the time of writing DTED was still classified, but there were clear signs that pressure for its public release was growing. Enquiries and requests for the release of this environmentally crucial data should be addressed to:

The Director
Defense Mapping Agency Aerospace Center
3200 South Second Street
St Louis
Missouri 63118-3399
USA

Less widely available are sets for airborne magnetic and radiometric surveys, measurements of gravity and the results of various types of geochemical survey. National geological surveys will be able to provide information on their availability. The Australian Bureau of Mineral Resources, British Geological Survey, Bureau de Recherche Geologiques et Minieres, Geological Survey of Canada and the US Geological Survey are known to be compiling such databases for wider dissemination. Potentially the most fruitful source of global and North American data of many kinds is the:

National Geophysical Data Center
NOAA E/GC3
325 Broadway (code 895)
Boulder, Colorado 80303-3328
USA

GENERAL FURTHER READING

These references comprise the main sources of information on remote sensing in general and a number of geologically oriented texts.

Beaumont, E. A. and N.H. Foster (eds) 1992. *Remote sensing*, Treatise of petroleum geology reprint series no. 19. Tulsa, Oklahoma: American Association of Petroleum Geologists.

Colwell, R.N. (ed.) 1960. *Manual of photographic interpretation*. Falls Church, Virginia: American Society of Photogrammetry.

Colwell, R.N. (ed.) 1983. *Manual of remote sensing*, 2nd edn. Falls Church, Virginia: American Society of Photogrammetry. (two volumes).

Curran, P.J 1985. *Principles of remote sensing*. London: Longman.

Drury, S.A. 1990. *A guide to remote sensing*. Oxford: Oxford University Press.

Drury, S.A. and D.A. Rothery 1989. *Remote sensing*. (Distance-learning course jointly produced by the Dutch and British Open Universities. British Open University code PS670.) Heerlen, Netherlands: Open universiteit.

Goetz, A.F.H. and L.C. Rowan 1981. Geologic remote sensing. *Science* **211**, 781–791.

Goetz, A.F.H., B.N. Rock and L.C. Rowan 1983. Remote sensing for exploration: an overview. *Econ. Geol.* **78**, 573–590.

Gupta, R.P. 1991. *Remote sensing geology*. Berlin: Springer-Verlag.

Henderson, F.B. and B.N. Rock (eds) 1983. *Frontiers for geological remote sensing from space*. Rep. Fourth Geosat Workshop. Falls Church, Virginia: American Society of Photogrammetry.

Hord, R.M. 1982. *Remote sensing – methods and applications*. New York: Wiley.

Lillesand, T.M. and R.W. Kiefer 1987. *Remote sensing and image interpretation*, 2nd edn. New York: Wiley.

Reeves, R. (ed.) 1975. *Manual of remote sensing*. Falls Church, Virginia: American Society of Photogrammetry. (two volumes).

Sabins, F.F. 1987 *Remote sensing: principles and interpretation*. 2nd edn. San Francisco: Freeman.

Short, N.M. 1982. *The Landsat tutorial workbook*. NASA Reference Publication 1078.

Siegal, B.S. and A.R. Gillespie (eds) 1980. *Remote sensing in geology*. New York: Wiley.

Smith, J.T. and A. Anson (eds) 1968. *Manual of colour aerial photography*. Falls Church, Virginia: American Society of Photogrammetry.

Swain, P.H. and S.M. Davis 1978. *Remote sensing: the quantitative approach*. New York: McGraw-Hill.

The most fruitful volumes in which to seek literature on every conceivable application of remote sensing in geology are the *Proceedings of the Thematic Conferences on Remote Sensing for Exploration Geology* sponsored by the Environmental Research Institute of Michigan (ERIM). There have been nine of these conferences up to 1993, and their proceedings contain hundreds of excellent, though unrefereed papers, which of course are too numerous to list here. ERIM also sponsors the annual *Conferences on Remote Sensing of the Environment*, which cover all aspects of remote sensing, including sections on geological applications. Other conference proceedings should be sought by using remote sensing as a keyword in bibliography searches. The main journals for remote sensing are *The International Journal of Remote Sensing, Photogrammetric Engineering and Remote Sensing, Remote Sensing of Environment* and *IEEE Transactions on Geoscience and Remote Sensing*. Many geological journals contain papers on the results of remote-sensing studies. A convenient means of seeking more recent papers on remote sensing is to look for references to older publications within a specific field in the Science Citation Index.

Image atlases

Ford, J.P., R.G. Blom, M.G. Bryan, M.I., Daily T.H. Dixon, C. Elachi and E.C. Xenos 1980. *Seasat views North America, the Caribbean, and Western Europe with imaging radar*. JPL Publication 80–67.

Ford, J.P., J.B. Cimino and C. Elachi 1983. *Space Shuttle Columbia views the world with imaging radar – the SIR-A experiment*. JPL Publication 82–95.

Hamblin, W.K. 1980. *Atlas of stereoscopic aerial photographs and Landsat imagery of North America*. Minneapolis, Minnesota: Tasa.

Institut Geographique National 1984. *I'Atlas des Formes du Relief*. Paris: Institut Geographique National.

Mollard, J.D. 1974. *Landforms and surface materials of Canada: a stereoscopic airphoto atlas and glossary*. Regina, Saskatchewan: J.D. Mollard.

Sheffield, C. 1981. *Earthwatch: a survey of the world from space*. London: Sidgwick & Jackson.

Sheffield, C. 1983. *Man on Earth*. London: Sidgwick & Jackson.

Short, N.M. and R.W. Blair Jr 1986. *Geomorphology from space*. NASA SP-486. Washington DC: US Government Printing Office.

Short, N.M. and L.M. Stuart 1982. *The Heat Capacity Mapping Mission (HCMM) anthology*. NASA Special Publication 465.

Short, N.M., P.D. Lowman, S.C. Freden and W.A. Finch 1976. *Mission to Earth: Landsat views the world*. NASA Special Publication 360.

GLOSSARY

This glossary defines many terms and concepts with which readers may not be familiar and which crop up in the book and in other remote-sensing literature. It should be used in conjunction with the index, which shows where the terms are defined more fully and in context.

absolute temperature Temperature measured on the Kelvin scale, whose base is absolute zero (−273°C). 0°C is expressed as 273 K.

absorptance A measure of the ability of a material to absorb EM energy at a specific wavelength.

absorption band A range of wavelengths in the EM spectrum where a material absorbs EM energy incident upon it, often resulting from various energy–matter transitions.

achromatic line A line in red, green, blue image display space, running at 45° to the axes. A three-channel combination from most images tends to be correlated, and so the multispectral data will plot close to this line, and the image will not be strongly coloured unless special image-processing techniques (such as decorrelation stretching) are applied.

achromatic vision The perception by the human eye of changes in brightness, often used to describe the perception of monochrome or black and white scenes.

active remote sensing A system based on the illumination of a scene by artificial radiation and the collection of the reflected energy returned to the system. Examples are radar and systems using lasers.

acuity A measure of human ability to perceive spatial variations in a scene. It varies with the spatial frequency, shape and contrast of the variations, and depends on whether the scene is coloured or monochrome.

additive primary colours The spectral colours red, green and blue, which Thomas Young (1773–1829) discovered to be capable of reproducing all other colours when mixed by projection through filters, and each of which cannot be produced by mixtures of the other two.

albedo The fraction of the total EM energy incident on a material which is reflected in all directions.

analogue image An image where the continuous variation in the property being sensed is represented by a continuous variation in image tone. In a photograph this is achieved directly by the grains of photosensitive chemicals in the film, in an electronic scanner the response in, say, millivolts is transformed to a display on a cathode-ray tube where it may be photographed.

artifact A feature on an image which is produced by the optics of the system or by digital image processing, and sometimes masquerades as a real feature.

ASTER Advanced Spaceborne Thermal Emission and Reflection Radiometer to be carried by EOS-1, scheduled for launch in 1998. ASTER will acquire images in 14 spectral bands in the reflected and thermally emitted regions, selected particularly for geological applications.

atmospheric shimmer An effect produced by the movement of masses of air with different refractive indices, which is most easily seen in the twinkling of stars. Shimmer results in blurring on remotely sensed images, and is the ultimate control over the resolution of any system.

atmospheric window A range of EM wavelengths where radiation can pass through the Earth's atmosphere with relatively little attenuation.

AVHRR Advanced Very High Resolution Radiometer, a multispectral imaging system carried by the TIROS-NOAA series of meteorological satellites.

azimuth In general, this is the compass bearing of a line given in degrees clockwise from north. In radar terminology it refers to the direction at right angles to the radar propagation direction, which is parallel to the ground-track in a sideways-looking system.

band In remote sensing, a range of wavelengths from which data are gathered by a recording device.

bin One of a series of equal intervals in a range of data, most commonly employed to describe the divisions in a histogram.

binary A numerical system using the base 2. Examples are $0 = 0$, $1 = 2^0 = 1$, $10 = 2^1 = 2$, $11 = 2^1 + 2^0 = 3$.

bit An abbreviation of binary digit, which refers to an exponent of 2. A bit is represented by 0 or 1 for 'on' or 'off' in a digital computer.

blackbody A perfect radiator and absorber of EM energy, where all incident energy is absorbed and the energy radiated from the body at a particular temperature is at the maximum possible rate for each wavelength, as governed by the Stefan–Boltzmann law. No natural material has these ideal properties.

blind spot The point of entry of the optic nerve to the retina where no radiation is detected by the eye.

box classification A classification technique in which the decision boundary around the training set is a rectangular box. The term parallelepiped classification is synonymous.

byte A group of 8 bits of digital data in binary form. A byte represents digital numbers up to 255, and is the standard adopted by most digital remote-sensing systems where the range of energies is coded from 0 to 255.

cell assemblies The linked receptors, retinal neurons and neural cells in the visual cortex of the brain which enable interaction between perception and past experience.

change detection A range of techniques to identify important differences between scenes recorded on different dates.

channel The range of wavelengths recorded by a single detector to form an image. A multispectral image is recorded in several channels simultaneously. The term can also be used to refer to a synthetic channel (i.e. not a simple spectral band as originally recorded), such as one created by ratioing or principal components transformation.

charge-coupled device (CCD) A light-sensitive capacitor whose charge is proportional to the intensity of illumination. They are able to be charged and discharged very quickly, and are used in pushbroom devices, spectroradiometers and modern video cameras.

charge-transfer A mechanism of spectral absorption of EMR, when an electron is transferred across a chemical bond.

chromatic vision The perception by the human eye of changes in hue.

classification The process of assigning individual pixels of a multispectral image to categories, generally based on spectral characteristics of known parts of a scene.

Coastal Zone Colour Scanner (CZCS) A multispectral imaging system carried by the Nimbus series of meteorological satellites.

coherent radiation Electromagnetic radiation whose waves are equal in length and are in phase, so that waves at different points in space act in unison, as in a laser and synthetic-aperture radar.

cones Receptors in the retina which are sensitive to colour. There are cones sensitive to red, green and blue components of light.

context The known environment of a particular feature on an image.

contrast The ratio between the energy emitted or reflected by an object and its immediate surroundings.

contrast stretching Expanding a measured range of digital numbers in an image to a larger range, to improve the contrast of the image and its component parts.

corner reflector A cavity formed by three planar reflective surfaces intersecting at right angles, which returns radar directly back to its source.

cut-off The digital number in the histogram of a digital image which is set to zero during contrast stretching. Usually this is a value below which atmospheric scattering makes a major contribution.

decorrelation stretching A way of making a three-band multispectral image more colourful by stretching the data distribution along axes related to the natural elongation of the data distribution (the principal component directions). After stretching, the data are displayed on the original red, green and blue axes, thus retaining the original, straightforward colour relationships.

density slicing The process of converting the full range of data into a series of intervals or slices, each of which expresses a range in the data.

depression angle In radar usage this is the angle between the horizontal plane passing through the antenna and the line connecting the antenna to the target. It is easily confused with the look angle.

diffuse reflection Reflection of light (or other EMR) from a surface approximately evenly in all directions, as opposed to specular (mirror-like) reflection. A diffuse reflector has a surface that is rough on the scale of the wavelength of EMR concerned.

digital image An image in which the property being measured has been converted from a continuous range of analogue values to a range expressed by a finite number of integers, usually recorded as binary codes from 0 to 255, or as 1 byte.

digital number (DN) The value of a variable recorded for each pixel in an image as a binary integer, usually in the range 0–255. An alternative term used in some texts is brightness value (BV). The plural of its acronym is DN.

directional filter A spatial-frequency filter which enhances features in an image in selected directions.

Doppler shift A change in the observed frequency of EM or other waves caused by the relative motion between source and detector. Used principally in the generation of synthetic-aperture radar images.

edge A boundary in an image between areas with different tones.

edge enhancement The process of increasing the contrast between adjacent areas with different tones on an image.

electromagnetic radiation (EMR) Energy transported by the propagation of disturbances in the electric and magnetic fields. Detection and measurement of natural or artificial EMR is the basis for remote sensing.

electronic transition A mechanism of spectral absorption of EMR, when an electron is moved from a lower orbit to a higher, as the result of absorption of a photon. Also a mechanism of generation of EMR, when an electron goes from a higher orbit to a lower, and emits a photon in the process.

emissivity A measure of how well a surface emits, or radiates, EMR thermally, defined as the ratio of the thermal exitance from the surface to the thermal exitance from a blackbody (perfect emitter) at the same temperature. A blackbody therefore has an emissivity of 1 and the emissivity of natural materials ranges from 0 to 1.

emittance A term for the radiant flux of energy per unit area emitted by a body, now obsolete.

EOS Earth Observing System, a proposed multinational series of heavily instrumented remote-sensing satellites to be deployed in the decade beginning in the mid-1990s. It will probably include American (NASA), European (ESA) and Japanese polar orbiting platforms and a manned space station.

EOSAT Earth Observation Satellite Company, based in Lanham, Maryland, USA. A private company contracted to the US Government since September 1985 to market Landsat data and develop replacements for the Landsat system.

equatorial orbit An orbit of a satellite around the Earth in which the orbital plane makes an angle of less than 45° with the Equator.

EROS Earth Resources Observation System, based at the EROS Data Center, Sioux Falls, South Dakota, USA. Administered by the US Geological Survey, it forms an important source of image data from Landsat-1, -2 and -3 and for Landsat-4 and -5 data up to September 1985, as well as airborne data for the USA.

ESA European Space Agency, based in Paris. A consortium between several European states for the development of space science, including the launch of remote-sensing satellites.

ERS-1 Earth Remote Sensing Satellite-1, a European (ESA) satellite scheduled for launch in 1992, targeted principally on marine applications by the use of active and passive microwave techniques.

exitance The radiant flux density (of EMR) leaving a surface.

false-colour image A colour image in which parts of the non-visible EM spectrum are expressed as one or more of the red, green and blue components, so that the colours produced by the Earth's surface do not correspond to normal visual experience. Also called a false-colour composite (FCC). The most commonly seen false-colour images display the very near-infrared as red, red as green and green as blue.

flatiron A term used to describe roughly triangular features seen on images, derived from their similarity to the household appliance used for smoothing cloth. On aerial photographs they result from dipping rock layers. On radar images they may be an artefact caused by high relief and steep depression angle.

fluorescence A property of some materials whereby EM energy of one wavelength is absorbed and then re-emitted at a longer wavelength.

foreshortening A distortion in radar images causing the lengths of slopes facing the antenna to appear shorter on the image than on the ground. It is produced when radar wavefronts are steeper than the topographic slope.

fovea The region around that point on the retina intersected by the eye's optic axis, where receptors are most densely packed. It is the most sensitive part of the retina.

frequency The number of waves that pass a reference point in unit time, usually one second.

geographic information system (GIS) A data-handling and analysis system based on sets of data distributed spatially in two dimensions. The data sets may be map oriented, when they comprise qualitative attributes of an area recorded as lines, points and areas often in vector format, or image oriented, when the data are quantitative attributes referring to cells in a rectangular grid, usually in raster format. Also known as a geobased or geocoded information system.

geostationary orbit An orbit at 4100 km in the direction of the Earth's rotation, which matches speed so that a

satellite remains over a fixed point on the Earth's surface.

grid format The result of interpolation from values of a variable measured at irregularly distributed points, or along survey lines, to values referring to square cells in a rectangular array. It forms a step in the process of contouring data, but can also be used as the basis for a raster format to be displayed and analysed digitally after the values have been rescaled to the 0–255 range.

ground-control point A point in two dimensions which is common to both an image and a topographic map, and can be represented by (x,y) coordinates based on the map's cartographic projection and grid system. Used in geometric correction of distorted images, and their registration to a convenient map projection.

ground truth Observations made on the ground that can be used to verify the interpretation of an image. Ground truth includes field-based identification of surface types and their distribution (to help perform and verify classification). Similar observations at sea (e.g. phytoplankton concentration, wave height) are usually known as sea truth.

heat capacity A measure of how much energy it takes to warm up a given mass of a material through 1°C.

Heat Capacity Mapping Mission (HCMM) NASA satellite launched in 1978 to observe thermal properties of rocks and soils. Remained in orbit for only a few months.

high-pass filter A spatial filter which selectively enhances contrast variations with high spatial frequencies in an image. It improves the sharpness of images and is a method of edge enhancement.

HIRIS High Resolution Imaging Spectrometer, possibly to be carried by the Space Shuttle.

histogram A means of expressing the frequency of occurrence of values in a data set within a series of equal ranges or bins, the height of each bin representing the frequency at which values in the data set fall within the chosen range. A cumulative histogram expresses the frequency of all values falling within a bin and lower in the range. A smooth curve derived mathematically from a histogram is termed the probability density function (PDF).

HRV Haute Resolution Visible, the visible and very near infrared pushbroom imaging system carried by SPOT: 20-m pixels in colour and 1-m pixels in panchromatic mode.

hue One of the three characteristics that define the colour of a pixel in an image in terms of intensity, hue and saturation. Hue is a measure of the relative amounts of red, green and blue contributing to the colour.

image dissection The breaking down of a continuous scene into discrete spatial elements, either by the receptors on the retina or in the process of capturing the image artificially.

image striping A defect produced in line-scanner and pushbroom imaging devices produced by non-uniform response of a single detector, or amongst a bank of detectors. In a line-scan image the stripes are perpendicular to flight direction, but in a pushbroom image they are parallel to it.

imaging radar A radar that constructs an image of the terrain or sea surface by complex processing of the echoes reflected back to the antenna.

imaging spectrometer A sophisticated remote-sensing instrument that records an image in a large number of narrow spectral channels.

incidence angle The angle between the surface and an incident ray of EM radiation – most usually referring to radar.

infrared radiation EMR of wavelength between 0.7 μm and 100 μm, comprising reflected infrared 0.7–3.0 μm and thermal infrared 3.0–100 μm.

instantaneous field of view (IFOV) The solid angle through which a detector is sensitive to radiation. It varies with the intensity of the radiation and the time over which radiation is gathered, and forms one limit to the resolution of an imaging system.

intensity A measure of the energy reflected or emitted by a surface.

intensity–hue–saturation (IHS) processing A way of enhancing the visibility of colours in an image by stretching the saturation, without altering the hue.

irradiance The radiant flux density falling on a surface.

IRS-1 Indian Remote Sensing satellite launched in 1988, which carries two pushbroom scanners covering four bands in the visible and VNIR, one with 73-m resolution, the other creating pixels half that size. Most data are restricted to the Indian subcontinent.

JERS-1 Japanese Earth Resources Satellite, launched in 1992, when it was renamed 'Fuyo-1' (the acronym JERS-1 seems to have stuck outside Japan). JERS-1 carries four sensors. Pushbroom sensors in the reflected region produce two bands in the visible range, two in the VNIR, one being a forwarding pointing band to produce stereoscopic images, and four bands in the SWIR. Each band has a pixel size of 18.3×24.2 m. The fourth sensor is an L-band SAR system with a ground resolution of 18 m. Data are available globally through on-board recording facilities.

Lambertian reflector A perfectly diffuse reflector, which reflects incident EMR equally in all directions.

Landsat A series of remote-sensing satellites in Sun-synchronous, polar orbit that began in 1972. Initially administered by NASA, then NOAA, and since 1985 by EOSAT. Carried MSS, RBV and TM systems.

laser Light amplification by stimulated emission of radiation. A beam of coherent radiation with a single wavelength.

layover A distortion in radar images when the angle of surface slope is greater than that of radar wavefronts. The base of a slope reflects radar after the top and, since radar images express the distance to the side in terms of time, the top appears closer to the platform than the base on an image, giving the impression of an overhanging slope.

line drop-out The loss of data from a scan line caused by malfunction of one of the detectors in a line scanner.

line scanner An imaging device which uses a mirror to sweep the ground surface normal to the flight path of the platform. An image is built up as a strip comprising lines of data.

look angle The angle between the vertical plane containing a radar antenna and the direction of radar propagation. Complementary to the depression angle.

look direction The direction in which pulses of radar are transmitted.

look-up table (LUT) A mathematical formula used to convert one distribution of data to another, most conveniently remembered as a conversion graph.

luminance A measure of the luminous intensity of light emitted by a source in a particular direction.

Mach band An optical illusion of dark and light fringes within adjacent areas of contrasted tone. It is a psycho-physiological phenomenon which aids human detection of boundaries or edges.

maximum-likelihood classification A classification technique in which unknown pixels are assigned to a class according to statistically defined probabilities.

median filter A spatial filter, which substitutes the median value of DN from surrounding pixels for that recorded at an individual pixel. It is useful for removing random noise.

Meteosat The European (ESA) member of the GOES geostationary weather satellite series.

microwaves EMR of wavelength between 100 μm and 1 μm.

mid-infrared (MIR) The range of EM wavelengths from 8 to 14 μm dominated by emission of thermally generated radiation from materials. Also known as thermal infrared.

Mie scattering The scattering of EM energy by particles in the atmosphere with similar dimensions to the wavelength involved.

minimum-distance-to-means classification A classification technique in which unknown pixels are assigned to the class whose mean they are closest to, in multispectral space.

minus-blue photograph A panchromatic black and white photograph from which the blue part of the visible range has been removed using a yellow filter.

mixed pixel A pixel whose DN represents the average energy reflected or emitted by several types of surface present within the area that it represents on the ground. Sometimes called a mixel.

MOMS Modular Optical-electronic Multispectral Scanner, a German imaging system carried experimentally by Shuttle missions, and which is based on a pushbroom system.

modulation transfer function (MTF) A measure of the sensitivity of an imaging system to spatial variations in contrast.

MSS Multispectral Scanner, a remote-sensing instrument carried on all the members of the Landsat series, recording pixels about 80 m across.

multispectral scanner A line scanner that simultaneously records image data from a scene in several different wavebands. Most commonly applied to the four-channel system with 80-m resolution carried by the Landsat series of satellites.

multispectral space The multidimensional space (sometimes known as feature space) represented mathematically by plotting the DN in each spectral band of an image on an orthogonal set of axes. If there are six spectral bands under consideration (for example when using the six reflected bands in Landsat TM data), then the multispectral space is six-dimensional.

nadir The point on the ground vertically beneath the centre of a remote-sensing system.

NASA National Aeronautics and Space Administration, USA.

near-infrared (NIR) The shorter wavelength range of the infrared region of the EM spectrum, from 0.7 to 2.5 μm. It is often divided into the very-near infrared (VNIR) covering the range accessible to photographic emulsions (0.7–1.0 μm), and the short-wavelength infrared (SWIR) covering the remainder of the NIR atmospheric window from 1.0 to 2.5 μm.

Nimbus-7 An experimental polar orbiting satellite launched in 1978, notable for carrying the Coastal Zone Colour Scanner (CZCS), the Scanning Multichannel Radiometer (SMMR) and the Total Ozone Mapping Spectrometer (TOMS).

NOAA National Oceanic and Atmospheric Administration, USA.

noise Random or regular artifacts in data which degrade their information-bearing quality and are caused by defects in the recording device.

non-selective scattering The scattering of EM energy by particles in the atmosphere which are much larger than the wavelengths of the energy, and which causes all wavelengths to be scattered equally.

non-spectral hue A hue which is not present in the spectrum of colours produced by the analysis of white light by a prism or diffraction grating. Examples are brown, magenta and pastel shades.

normalized difference vegetation index (NDVI) A vegetation index that calculates how far a pixel plots from the soil line, using the relationship: NDVI = (VNIR–red)/(VNIR+red).

orbital period The time taken by a satellite to complete an orbit.

orthophotograph A vertical aerial photograph from which the distortions due to varying elevation, tilt and surface topography have been removed, so that it represents every object as if viewed directly from above, as in a map.

orthophotoscope An optical-electronic device which converts a normal vertical aerial photograph to an orthophotograph.

parallax The apparent change in position of an object relative to another when it is viewed from different positions. It forms the basis of stereopsis.

parallax difference The difference in the distances on overlapping vertical photographs between two points, which represent two locations on the ground with different elevations.

parallelepiped classification A classification technique in which the decision boundary around the training set is a rectangular box. The term box classification is synonymous.

passive microwaves Radiation in the 1 mm to 1 m range emitted naturally by all materials above absolute zero.

passive remote sensing The capture of images representing the reflection or emission of EM radiation that has a natural source.

pattern A regular assemblage of tone and texture on an image. Often refers to drainage systems.

photographic infrared That part of the near-infrared or reflected infrared) spectrum to which photographic films respond, i.e. wavelengths between $0.7\,\mu m$ and about $1.0\,\mu m$. Virtually synonymous with very near-infrared.

photon A quantum of EM energy.

photopic vision Vision under conditions of bright illumination, when both rods and cones are employed.

pixel A single sample of data in a digital image, having both a spatial attribute – its position in the image and a usually rectangular dimension on the ground – and a spectral attribute – the intensity of the response in a particular waveband for that position (DN). A contraction of picture element.

Planck's law An expression for the variation of emittance of a blackbody at a particular temperature as a function of wavelength.

point spread function (PSF) The image of a point source of radiation, such as a star, collected by an imaging device. A measure of the spatial fidelity of the device.

polarized radiation Electromagnetic radiation in which the electrical field vector is contained in a single plane, instead of having random orientation relative to the propagation vector. Most commonly refers to radar images.

polar orbit An orbit that passes close to the poles, thereby enabling a satellite to pass over most of the surface, except the immediate vicinity of the poles themselves.

principal component analysis The analysis of covariance in a multiple data set so that the data can be projected as additive combinations onto new axes, which express different kinds of correlation among the data.

principal components Directions, or axes, in multispectral space, defined by approximating the data from a whole image, or selected area in an image, to a multidimensional ellipsoid. The first principal component direction is parallel to the longest axis of this ellipsoid, and the other principal components are orthogonal to it. The first principal component of the image is the data displayed relative to an axis parallel with the first principal component direction.

principal point The centre of an aerial photograph.

probability density function (PDF) A function indicating the relative frequency with which any measurement may be expected to occur. In remote sensing it is represented by the histogram of DN in one band for a scene.

pushbroom system An imaging device consisting of a fixed, linear array of many sensors which is swept across an area by the motion of the platform, thereby building up an image. It relies on sensors whose response and reading is nearly instantaneous, so that the image swath can be segmented into pixels representing small dimensions on the ground.

quantum The elementary quantity of EM energy that is transmitted by a particular wavelength. According to the quantum theory, EM radiation is emitted, transmitted and absorbed as numbers of quanta, the energy of each quantum being a simple function of the frequency of the radiation.

quantum theory A theory about EMR that dictates that there is a minimum amount of energy that can exist (or be emitted) at any particular wavelength. This minimum amount is a quantum, or photon.

radar The acronym for radio detection and ranging, which uses pulses of artificial EMR in the $1\,\mu m$ to $1\,\mu m$ range to locate objects which reflect the radiation. The position of the object is a function of the time that a pulse takes to reach it and return to the antenna.

radar altimeter A non-imaging device that records the time of radar returns from vertically beneath a platform to estimate the distance to and hence the elevation of the surface. Carried by Seasat and the ESA ERS-1 platforms.

radar cross-section A measure of the intensity of backscattered radar energy from a point target. Expressed as the area of a hypothetical surface which scatters radar equally in all directions and which would return the same energy to the antenna.

radar scattering coefficient A measure of the back-scattered radar energy from a target with a large area. Expressed as the average radar cross-section per unit area in decibels (dB). It is the fundamental measure of the radar properties of a surface.

radar scatterometer A non-imaging device that records radar energy backscattered from terrain as a function of depression angle.

radial relief displacement The tendency of vertical objects to appear to lean radially away from the centre of a vertical aerial photograph. Caused by the conical field of view of the camera lens.

radiance The radiant flux density falling on a surface measured per solid angle. A useful concept because we rarely measure the radiant flux density leaving a surface in all directions; instead we collect it with a detector responding to EMR arriving at the detector from a finite solid angle.

radiant flux The power incident on or leaving a body in the form of EMR.

radiant flux density The power incident on or leaving a body in the form of EMR per unit area of surface.

range In radar usage this is the distance in the direction of radar propagation, usually to the side of the platform in an imaging radar system. The slant range is the direct distance from the antenna to the object, whereas the distance from the groundtrack of the platform to the object is termed the ground range.

range resolution In a radar image, the resolution in the down-range direction, i.e. at right angles to the flightline, as distinct from azimuth resolution. Range resolution depends on the pulse length and the incidence angle, and is not made worse by flying at high altitude.

raster The scanned and illuminated area of a video display, produced by a modulated beam of electrons sweeping the phosphorescent screen line by line from top to bottom at a regular rate of repetition.

raster format A means of representing spatial data in the form of a grid of DN, each line of which can be used to modulate the lines of a video raster.

ratio The DN of one band of a multispectral image divided by the DN of another band usually rescaled onto an 8-bit scale. This emphasizes the relative differences between the two channels while ignoring brightness/intensity/albedo.

Rayleigh criterion A way of quantifying surface roughness with respect to wavelength of EMR, to determine whether the surface will act as a specular (smooth) reflector or as a diffuse (rough) reflector. A surface can be considered rough if the root mean square height of surface irregularities is greater than one eighth of the wavelength of EMR divided by the cosine of the incidence angle.

Rayleigh scattering Selective scattering of light in the atmosphere by particles that are small compared with the wavelength of light.

RBV The Return-Beam Vidicon system aboard Landsat-3 which produced panchromatic digital images with a resolution of 40 m.

real-aperture radar An imaging radar system where the azimuth resolution is determined by the physical length of the antenna, the wavelength and the range. Also known as brute-force radar.

red edge The sharp increase in spectral reflectance of healthy leafy vegetation that occurs with increasing wavelength between about 700 nm and 750 nm wavelength, i.e. in the red/very near-infrared part of the spectrum.

redundancy Information in an image which is either not required for interpretation or cannot be seen. Redundancy may be spatial or spectral. Also refers to multispectral data where the degree of correlation between bands is so high that one band contains virtually the same information as all the bands.

reflectance/reflectivity The ratio of the EM energy reflected by a surface to that which falls upon it. It may be qualified as spectral reflectance. The suffix -ance implies a property of a specific surface. The suffix -ity implies a property for a given material.

reflected infrared That part of the infrared spectrum that, in terrestrial remote sensing, is mostly made up of reflected solar EMR, as opposed to thermal infrared, which has longer wavelengths. The reflected infrared is defined as wavelengths from $0.7\,\mu m–3.0\,\mu m$, and is synonymous with the near infrared.

resampling The calculation of new DN for pixels created during geometric correction of a digital scene, based on the values in the local area around the uncorrected pixels.

resolution A poorly defined term relating the fidelity of an image to the spatial attributes of a scene. It involves the IFOV and MTF of the imaging system, and depends on the contrast within the image, as well as on other factors. It is usually expressed as line pairs per millimetre of the most closely spaced lines that can be distinguished, and therefore depends on human vision, scale and viewing distance.

ringing Fringe-like artifacts produced at edges by some forms of spatial-frequency filtering.

rods The receptors in the retina which are sensitive to brightness variations.

rotational transition A mechanism of spectral absorption of EMR, when a photon is absorbed of the correct wavelength to cause a gaseous molecule to undergo a change in its rotational energy state.

saturation In a digital image this refers to the maximum brightness that can be assigned to a pixel on a display device, and corresponds to a DN of 255. In colour theory it means the degree of mixture between a pure hue and neutral grey.

scale In cartography this refers to the degree of reduction from reality that is represented on a map, usually expressed as a ratio (e.g. 1:250 000), a representative fraction (e.g. 1/250 000) or an equivalence (e.g. 1 cm = 2.5 km). A large-scale map represents ground dimensions by larger cartographic dimensions than a smaller scale map In common usage a large-scale feature has larger dimensions than a smaller scale feature.

scattering An atmospheric effect where EM radiation, usually of short visible wavelength, is propagated in all directions by the effects of gas molecules and aerosols. See Rayleigh, Mie and non-selective scattering.

scene The area on the ground recorded by a photograph or other image, including the atmospheric effects on the radiation as it passes from its source to the ground and back to the sensor.

scotopic vision Vision under conditions of low illumination, when only the rods are sensitive to light. Visual acuity under these conditions is highest in the blue part of the spectrum.

Seasat Polar-orbiting satellite launched in 1978 by NASA to monitor the oceans, using imaging radar and a radar altimeter. It survived for only a few months.

short-wavelength infrared (SWIR) That part of the near or reflected infrared with wavelength between 1.0 μm and 3.0 μm. These wavelengths are too long to affect infrared photographic film.

signal-to-noise ratio (S/N) The ratio of the level of the signal carrying real information to that carrying spurious information as a result of defects in the system.

signature In remote sensing this refers to the spectral properties of a material or homogeneous area, most usually expressed as the range of DN in a number of spectral bands.

SIR Shuttle Imaging Radar, synthetic-aperture radar experiments carried aboard the NASA Space Shuttle in 1981 and 1984.

SMIRR Shuttle Multispectral Infrared Radiometer, a non-imaging spectroradiometer carried by the NASA Space Shuttle covering 10 narrow wavebands in the 0.5–2.4 μm range.

soil line A diagonal line at 45° on a plot of red DN against very near-infrared (VNIR) DN. Bare soil plots close to this line, but leafy vegetation plots away from this line, having much higher VNIR reflectance.

spatial-frequency filtering The analysis of the spatial variations in DN of an image and the separation or suppression of selected frequency ranges.

specific heat The ratio of the heat capacity of unit mass of a material to the heat capacity of unit mass of water.

spectral hue A hue which is present in the spectral range of white light analysed by a prism or diffraction grating.

spectral quantities A measure of EMR per unit wavelength, as opposed to overall wavelengths. Thus spectral radiance which is radiance per unit wavelength, and so on.

spectral response A general term referring to the amount of light reflected by a surface at different wavelengths, as seen in an image. The spectral response of a surface is controlled principally by its spectral reflectance.

spectroradiometer A device which measures the energy reflected or radiated by materials in narrow EM wavebands.

specular reflection Reflection of EMR from a smooth surface, which behaves like a mirror. A specular reflector has a surface that is smooth on the scale of the wavelength of EMR concerned. If the surface is rough on the scale of the wavelength of the EMR, it will behave as a diffuse reflector.

SPOT Satellite Probatoire pour l'Observation de la Terre, a French satellite carrying two pushbroom imaging systems, one for three wavebands in the visible and VNIR with 20-m resolution, the other producing panchromatic images with 10-m resolution. Each system comprises two devices which are pointable so that off-nadir images are possible, thereby allowing stereoptic viewing. Launched in February 1986.

Stefan–Boltzmann law A radiation law stating that the energy radiated by a blackbody is proportional to the fourth power of its absolute temperature.

stereopsis The ability for objects to be perceived in three dimensions as a result of the parallax differences produced by the eye base.

stereoscope A binocular optical instrument used to view two images with overlapping fields which contain parallax differences, as a means of stimulating stereopsis.

subtractive primary colours The colours cyan, magenta and yellow, the subtraction of which from white light in different proportions allows all colours to be created.

Sun angle When considering the illumination of a surface by EMR from the Sun, the angle between a normal to the surface and the direction of the Sun.

Sun-synchronous orbit A polar orbit where the satellite always crosses the Equator at the same local solar time.

supervised classification A classification technique whereby the human operator identifies training areas on the image that are intended to be representative examples of each surface type.

synthetic-aperture radar (SAR) A radar imaging system in which high resolution in the azimuth direction is achieved by using the Doppler shift of backscattered waves to identify waves from ahead of and behind the platform, thereby simulating a very long antenna.

TDRS Telemetry and Data Relay Satellites, launched by the US Department of Defence into geostationary orbit, primarily for military communications but used for data transfer by Landsat.

texture The frequency of change and arrangement of tones on an image, often used to describe the aggregate appearance of different parts of the surface, but sometimes used for the spacing of drainage elements.

thematic map An image on which are overlaid the results of classification, usually by showing each class in a distinctive colour. The term classified image is synonymous.

Thematic Mapper (TM) An imaging device carried by Landsat-4 and -5, which records scenes in seven wavebands, six in the visible and NIR with a resolution of 30 m, and one in the MIR with a resolution of 120 m.

thermal capacity The ability of a material to store heat.

thermal conductivity A measure of the rate at which heat passes through a material.

thermal emission Emission of EMR from a material due to thermal vibration, as a result of its temperature.

thermal inertia A measure of the response of a material to changes in its temperature. The apparent thermal inertia is calculated from the diurnal change in emitted thermal energy by a material.

thermal infrared (TIR) That part of the spectrum with wavelengths between 3.0 and 100 µm. These are the wavelengths at which thermal emission is greatest for surfaces at normal environmental temperatures. However, hot areas (fires, parts of volcanoes and so on) emit thermally at wavelengths shorter than the thermal infrared.

thermal vibration Vibration of atoms or molecules as a result of their temperature. Because these atoms of molecules contain moving electric charges, this results in thermal emission of EMR.

tie point A point on the ground which is common to two images. Several are used in the co-registration of images.

TIMS Thermal Infrared Multispectral Scanner, an airborne device used by NASA to measure and create images of MIR energies emitted by the surface in six wavebands.

TIROS-N The most widely used series of Sun-synchronous meteorological satellites, carrying the AVHRR visible to thermal infrared imaging system.

tone Each distinguishable shade from black to white on a monochrome image, sometimes called greytone.

training area A sample of the Earth's surface with known properties, the statistics of the imaged data within which are used to determine decision boundaries in classification.

transmittance/transmissivity The ratio of the EM energy passing through a material to that falling on its exposed surface.

transpiration The production and emission of water vapour and oxygen by plants.

tristimulus colour theory A theory of colour relating all hues to the combined effects of three additive primary colours corresponding to the sensitivities of the three types of cone on the retina.

ultraviolet That part of the spectrum with wavelengths between about 0.5 nm and 400 nm. Not useful for most aspects of terrestrial remote sensing, because of scattering in the atmosphere and absorption by ozone.

unsupervised classification A classification technique in which classes are identified by a computer-driven search for clusters in multispectral data space.

variance A measure of the dispersion of the actual values of a variable about its mean. It is the mean of the squares of all the deviations from the mean value of a range of data.

vector format The expression of points, lines and areas on a map by digitized Cartesian coordinates, directions and values.

vegetation index A technique, usually involving ratioing, whereby channels from a multispectral image are combined to show up variations in the amount of vegetation. A simple example is to divide very near-infrared DN by red DN.

vertical exaggeration The extent to which the vertical scale exceeds the horizontal scale in stereoptic viewing of two overlapping images with parallax differences. It is directly proportional to the base height ratio.

very near-infrared (VNIR) The shortest wavelength part of the near-infrared (reflected infrared), with wavelengths between 0.7 and 1.0 µm. Virtually synonymous with photographic infrared.

vibrational transitions A mechanism of spectral absorption of EMR, when the vibration of a chemical bond in a molecule of crystalline lattice changes from one state to another. Vibrations may occur either as stretching or as bending of a bond.

vidicon An imaging device based on a sheet of transparent material whose electrical conductivity increases with the intensity of EMR falling on it. The variation in conductivity across the plate is measured by a sweeping electron beam and converted into a video signal. Now largely replaced by cameras employing arrays of charge-coupled devices (CCDs).

vignetting A gradual change in overall tone of an image from the centre outwards, caused by the imaging device gathering less radiation from the periphery of its field of view than from the centre. Most usually associated with the radially increasing angle between a lens and the Earth's surface, and the corresponding decrease in the light-gathering capacity of the lens.

visible radiation EMR in that part of the electromagnetic spectrum that human eyes respond to. It lies between the ultraviolet and the infrared, with wavelengths from 400 to 700 nm.

271

VISSR   Visible Infrared Spin-Scan Radiometer carried by the GOES satellites.

visual dissonance   The disturbing effect of seeing a familiar object in an unfamiliar setting or in an unexpected colour.

volume scattering   Scattering of EMR, usually radar, in the interior of a material. It may apply to a vegetation canopy or to the subsurface of soil.

wavelength   The mean distance between maxima or minima of a periodic pattern. In the case of EMR, it is the reciprocal of the frequency multiplied by the velocity of light.

Wien's displacement law   A radiation law stating that the peak of energy emitted by a material shifts to shorter wavelengths as absolute temperature increases.

IMAGE INDEX

Numbers given in italic represent colour plates

Locations

Afghanistan 3.31
Africa
    South 5.43
    West 3.3
Algeria 4.37, 7.20
Argentina 4.44, 4.46
Atlantic Ocean 9.1
Australia 4.15, 7.6, *8.18*, *8.20*

Cameroun 4.11
Canada 4.6, 4.17, 4.26, 4.33, 4.47,
    4.53, 5.5–6, 9.5–6
Chile 4.33, 4.40, 4.42, 4.44, 5.2
China *4.38*, 7.7, 7.13

England *3.5*, 3.13, 4.11, 8.10, 8.12,
    8.14–5, 8.17, *8.19*, 9.9, 9.12
Eritrea 3.30, *3.35*, 4.27, 4.32,
    5.4–19, 5.23–8, 5.30–*1*, *5.37*,
    9.4, *9.8*
Ethiopia B.2–5

Global 8.9

Hawaii 4.42

India 4.17, *4.22–3*, 4.33, 4.35, 5.29
Iran 4.30, 4.33, 6.10, 7.12
Irian Jaya 7.8, 7.10

Japan 3.8

Jordan 5.20–2

Kenya 9.11

Libya 7.19

Mars 9.3
Mongolia 7.14
Morocco 4.37, *6.13*

Nigeria 4.15

Oman 4.7, 4.13, 4.16, 4.26, *5.40*

Pakistan 7.11

Red Sea *1.18*

Saudi Arabia 4.29, 4.47
Scotland 4.5, 4.26, 6.9
Somalia 4.10
Sudan 4.14, 4.35, *4.39*, 7.4, 7.17
Syria 7.15

Tibet *4.31*

Uranus 9.2
USA 5.42
    Alaska 8.13, 8.16, 8.21–2
    Appalachia 3.21
    Arizona 3.23, *4.3*, 4.12, 4.41, 4.49,
        7.24

California 4.29, 5.33, 6.7, *6.14*,
    7.17–8
Colorado 6.5, 6.8
Hawaii 4.42
Idaho 4.43
Indiana 4.51
Kansas 4.7
Kentucky 3.29
Mississipi 4.48
Nevada *6.19*
New York 4.48, 4.52
Oklahoma 4.21, 6.6
Pennsylvania 4.8, 7.5, 7.23
Texas 4.37
Utah 4.2, 4.8–9, 4.28, 6.11–2, *7.29*
Washington 4.50
Wisconsin 4.54
Wyoming 4.15, 4.18, *6.20*, 7.25–8

Venezuela 7.22
Venus 9.3

Western Sahara 7.6

Zimbabwe 4.13

Image types

Aerial photographs
    colour
        natural *3.5*
        false *3.5*

273

SUBJECT INDEX

Numbers given in bold represent figures